After Emancipation

Jewish Religious Responses to Modernity

After Emancipation

Jewish Religious Responses to Modernity

David Ellenson

Hebrew Union College Press
Cincinnati

For Jackie

את שאהבה נפשי

the one whom my soul loves

Copyright © 2004 by the Hebrew Union College Press
Hebrew Union College – Jewish Institute of Religion

Library of Congress Cataloging-in-Publication Data

Ellenson, David Harry, 1947–

After emancipation : Jewish religious responses to modernity /
David Ellenson.

p. cm.
Includes index.

ISBN 0-87820-223-4 (alk. paper)

1. Judaism — History — Modern period, 1750-. 2. Jews —
Identity. 3. Jews — Intellectual life. 4. Responsa — 1948 —
History and criticism. I. Title.

BM195.E42 2004
296'.09'03–dc22   2004047372

Printed on acid-free paper in the United States of America
Design and composition by Kelby & Teresa Bowers
Distribution by Wayne State University Press
4809 Woodward Avenue, Detroit, Michigan 48201

Contents

Foreword

In his autobiography, Jacob Katz, the prominent historian of medieval and modern European Jewry, pointed to a paradox: Jewish religious reformers have tended to cling to the formal rules of Jewish law in order to justify religious advance whereas the champions of Orthodoxy have subverted those same rules in order to advance a religious politics intended to preserve the tradition or to rescue it from the danger of Reform.

David Ellenson, who has frequently attested to the influence that the writings of Jacob Katz and his personal experience sitting in Katz's classroom at Columbia exercised upon him, has explored his mentor's paradox in breadth and in depth. A Reform Jew, Ellenson early became an interpreter of modern Orthodoxy. He quickly realized that modern Judaism has to be explored as a whole, not in denominational categories alone. Modernity is not a process that affected only one segment of the Jewish community, but rather, in both similar and different ways, left its impact across the spectrum from Modern Orthodoxy on the right to the most radical Reform in Germany and America on the left. He began his concentrated studies by focusing on Esriel Hildesheimer, the founder of the first modern Orthodox seminary. Hildesheimer was a borderline figure who taught Talmud in the manner of an old fashioned *rav*, but he also wanted to be part of the new world of modern scholarship. Tolerant of religious reformers up to a point, he nonetheless laid down clear boundaries for "Torah-true" Jews, not simply on the basis of Jewish law, but also, as Ellenson was able to point out, by his assessment of what was best for the preservation of traditional Judaism.

In this volume of essays, as well, traditionalists make their appearance — not only those of the nineteenth century, but contemporaries like the modern Orthodox Israeli thinker David Hartman and the foremost American *posek* (decisor of Jewish law), Moshe Feinstein. Ellenson is not a student of Jewish law *per se*. He is less interested in the legal argumentation than in the points where argument intersects with contemporary Jewish reality. Often writing with the non-Orthodox reader in mind, he is especially eager to demonstrate that tolerant currents flow within the responsa literature, instructing questioners how to cope with new realities. Not surprisingly, he has favored the development of Reform responsa. There are not just boundaries that separate, he is saying. There are also bridges, some of them in the Jewish law itself, that connect liberal and traditional Jews.

Although he is a fervent Reform Jew, Ellenson is every bit as much devoted to *klal yisrael*. For him, modern religious Judaism in its broad variety is a single whole. In this volume he seeks to gain a deeper understanding of such diverse figures as the Reformers Samuel Holdheim and Abraham Geiger, the Conservatives Zacharias Frankel and Manuel Joël, and the Orthodox chief rabbis of Israel. What particularly attracts him are liturgical and moral issues. The prayer book has been a source of controversy among modern Jews ever since religious reformers assumed that some of its doctrines conflicted with newly acquired aesthetic or moral values and political allegiances. Yet prayer for Ellenson is essential to the religious life and liturgical change remains a live issue in contemporary Reform and Conservative Judaism. Not surprisingly, prayer receives a great deal of attention in this volume. Similarly, moral questions serve as the subject of a number of essays: for example, equality for women and for minorities as well as bioethical issues.

The essays included here do not propagandize for a particular point of view. David Ellenson has always envisaged his principal role to be that of a scholar and he regards the Hebrew Union College - Jewish Institute of Religion, which he heads, as an institution dedicated to attaining the highest academic levels in the disciplines that it offers. But he is not a passionless scholar. He has a remarkable talent for understanding his subjects from within and explicating points of view that he does not share. Generally, he refrains from subjecting them to detailed critique, looking instead for what Jewish life as a whole can gain from many and diverse sources. Yet it is also clear from his personal life and teaching that Ellenson is an engaged academic, that his studies have consequences for himself, and through him for others. Within the circles of Reform Judaism he is among those who consider observance of Jewish tradition essential even as he is committed to contemporary moral advance. As, in his view, modern Judaism cannot flourish without regular religious practice, so it cannot have a long-term future without the closest connection to the land and state of Israel. This double rootedness of the Jewish people in religious tradition and in its land is for Ellenson the essential foundation for the Jewish future.

This book is directed especially to a broader readership among American Jews that is not likely to have read these essays when they first appeared in scholarly journals and volumes. Some will dip in here and there, perhaps first into Ellenson's autobiographical preface and then into those chapters whose titles seem of special interest. But for the reader who desires to understand more deeply the religious life of modern Jewry in its broad scope and also to gain closer familiarity with the values and concerns of David Ellenson, a study of the volume as a whole will prove the most rewarding.

— Michael A. Meyer

Preface

Emancipation and Enlightenment at the end of the eighteenth century initiated a process of political and social integration of Jews into western culture — a process that transformed the legal status, occupational distribution, cultural habits, and religious beliefs and behaviors of Occidental Jews in revolutionary ways. The essays gathered in this volume, representing the core of my historical research over the last decade, focus on the modern period, the period in which Jews were called upon to redefine and reconceptualize themselves and their traditions as both the Jewish community and individual Jews entered this radically new realm of possibility and challenge.

The responses of Jewish religious leaders to this changed landscape have particularly intrigued me throughout my adult life: it is a subject of profound relevance to modern Jews, whose struggles reveal both their ambivalence and attraction to western culture. Above all, these efforts display the integrity of those who seek meaningful ways to bring their Judaism with them into a new social context. The transforming reality of Emancipation affected all the emerging denominations in this period — from Liberal to Neo-Orthodox — and my essays seek to illuminate the texture of that experience. Before delving further into this multifarious topic, some personal reflections are in order to explain what this research has meant to me as a scholar, as a rabbi, and as a Jew.

My own Jewish journey cannot be understood apart from the region and time in which I was raised. I grew up in Newport News, Virginia, during the 1950s and 1960s, and even now, over thirty years later, the events and attitudes of those days — and how I experienced them as a Jewish boy — continue to inform and shape my way and my work. My grandparents, like millions of others, emigrated from Eastern Europe to the United States around the turn of the century. However, my paternal grandparents, unlike my mother's father and mother, did not move to a major center of Jewish population such as Boston. Instead, they arrived in Baltimore, migrated southward, and settled, along with approximately one hundred other Jewish immigrant families, in Newport News. My father was the youngest of five children, and after his own graduation from the College of William and Mary in 1942, he entered Harvard Law School in 1945, where, at a Friday night Hillel service, he met my mother, a native of Cambridge. Two years later I was born and upon my father's graduation from law school returned with my parents to Newport News. I was six months old.

Newport News, in the 1950s, was no longer a tiny Southern town — though it would be equally unfair to envision it as the metropolitan area Tidewater Virginia has now become. It was, in many ways, a comfortable place to be raised. Approximately 700 Jewish families existed benignly among a population of 250,000 gentiles. There were four synagogues. One, Adath Jeshurun, was Orthodox, with separate seating for men and women. Another labeled itself Orthodox, used an Orthodox *siddur* for prayer, and employed a rabbi who received his ordination from Yeshiva University. However, it had no *meḥitzah* and men and women sat together during services. There was also a Conservative congregation, as well as a Reform temple. In addition, there was a Jewish Community Center, and members of all the congregations knew one another and socialized together. Indeed, my impression was that all Jews in town were affiliated institutionally and belonged to both the JCC and at least one synagogue. I have no idea if this was in fact true. However, my own family's participation in Adath Jeshurun and the active role my mother played as president of the local Federation and as regional vice-president of the Mid-Atlantic Seaboard region of Hadassah undoubtedly shaped this perspective.

Ours was a home where the Sabbath and the holidays were marked with festive meals and observances and where the State of Israel was placed at the center of our consciousness. Indeed, Jewishness was inculcated in the very core of my being from my earliest years. The rabbis of my congregation — Adelman, Bulman, and Horowitz — were significant figures to me, and the Orthodoxy they presented was the only form of religious Judaism I knew. "Torah-true" appeared to me to be synonymous with Judaism, and NCSY conventions each year in the Catskills were events I eagerly anticipated. Diverse liturgical skills and the ability to conduct a variety of Orthodox services comprised the bulk of my Jewish education, and I was, as a boy, an eager student who mastered these many styles of traditional Jewish prayer, a mastery that still remains with me today.

However, ours was not the world of contemporary Jewish Orthodoxy in a metropolitan American area of the North or West. It was the

American South of the 1950s and 1960s. It was a world of gentiles — Southern Baptists and Methodists to be exact — and my family and I eagerly ached to, and did, participate in it. It was a world in which football and basketball, as well as the waters of Hampton Roads and "Negroes," were omnipresent. I loved history and there was the heritage of Virginia and the South itself. George Washington, Thomas Jefferson, Robert E. Lee, and Stonewall Jackson — all of them were figures actively present in my life.

My family participated in the civic life of Newport News. My father and one of his brothers were attorneys, and another uncle was director of Public Works. Politics was a staple part of our family conversation, and my father was strongly opposed to the segregationist policies advocated by Senator Harry Flood Byrd and his followers during those years. Governor Lindsay Almond, who courageously opposed Senator Byrd's policy of "massive resistance" to integration, was a hero in our house.

The South I experienced was far removed from the South of the Ku Klux Klan and the nightmares and fears Northern Jews associate with it. Indeed, I do not recall encountering even one overt incident of antisemitism. Of course, I acknowledge that this failure to remember might constitute a textbook case of repression. However, the truth is, I loved Virginia. Years later, when I read Eli Evans's *The Lonely Days Were Sundays*, I was terribly moved by the lyrical description of how he took dirt from the soil of his native North Carolina and kept it in his pocket in the delivery room when his son Joshua was born in New York City so that Joshua could know his roots. Evans's simple act bespeaks a great deal of my own sensibilities, and his feelings of connection to the South reflect much of my own love for that region — its people and its ways.

Yet, for me as a Jew, there was another side of to the South — and my part it in. In *A Tidewater Morning: Three Tales from Youth*, set around the time of World War II and written by Newport News native William Styron, one of the protagonists, Mr. Dabney, complains about "Franklin D-for-Disaster Roosevelt" and his wife Eleanor. "Eleanor's near as bad as he is," Mr. Dabney observes. "They say she fools around with colored men and Jews." And therein lies the rub. I was a Virginian. At the same time, I was not.

At fifteen, while looking through my grandmother's bookshelves, I ran across Ludwig Lewisohn's autobiography, *Up Stream*. I devoured its pages. Lewisohn, born in Berlin and brought to Charleston, South Carolina as a child, described the sense of indignation, humiliation, and hurt he experienced when, upon completing his doctorate in English at Columbia University in the first years of the twentieth century, he was denied — because of his Jewishness — a faculty position at an Ivy League university. The rage at this injustice and the alienation Lewisohn recounted mirrored part of my own psyche. The book was not just illuminating for me, as Ralph Ellison's *Invisible Man* had been. Nor did it elicit sympathy. It was, instead, an epiphany. I cried as I read its pages. *Up Stream* provided me with a tale of my self, not the Other.

For me, as a Jewish boy in the South, the lonely days were not confined to Sundays. I was in the South and I partook of, and was informed by, its heritage and manners — but as a Jew I was not of it. As I look back upon my childhood and think of my many Jewish friends from that time, I am amazed that many of them do not seem to have experienced it as I did. For them, Virginia is home. For me, it is also a place of intimacy. More profoundly, it is a place of alienation. Part of me felt I never really belonged. It is no wonder, then, in light of all these mixed emotions, that my Jewish journey has taken the direction it has. Certainty has never been mine, and conflicting emotions and a sense of distance from my surroundings has always marked me. The description of such tensions in the lives, thoughts, and institutions of other Jews as they navigate between "Jewish tradition and the larger world" — the stuff of my work — has allowed me to hold up a candle to my own soul, and my decision to live only in areas like Los Angeles, New York, and Jerusalem — with huge Jewish populations — reflects my own desire not to have my children experience the ambivalences and fissures of my own youth.

In 1965, like my father, I entered the College of William and Mary. I was resigned to becoming an attorney and practicing law in Newport News. However, at some point in my junior year, the one decision I had made was that I would not return to my hometown. This meant, for me, that I would not study law. In my senior year, I enrolled in two courses that changed my life — Existentialism, taught by William Cobb, and Contemporary Christian Thought, taught by James C. Livingston. That year I was introduced to Sartre, Nietzsche, Blake, Tillich, Kierkegaard, and others. I found their descriptions of life to be profoundly human. The *angst* of Kierkegaard's diaries and the loneliness that propelled him to seek God made compelling reading for me. I felt more challenged intellectually and emotionally than I had ever been before. I was resolved, upon completing college, to study more. More significantly, I was determined to see whether Jews had said anything that might be of use in exploring the "tear" at the center of my own existence. I had not yet read the essays of Soloveitchik or Heschel, and the rabbis who taught me in my youth always seemed to imply that proper *emunah* (belief) and a life of halakhic observance and *zemirot* (Sabbath and holiday songs and hymns) would mend whatever ills marked the human or my own personal condition. I knew even then that this would not be my way — for I could neither conjure up the type of faith they seemed to demand nor submit myself to the discipline of practice they clearly prescribed.

The next years were spent in a variety of settings and were marked by a number of significant encounters. Foremost among them was my admittance to the graduate program in religious studies at the University of Virginia and my meeting Professor Alan Lettofsky and his wife Jean. Alan directed my studies in Judaica with both erudition and kindness, and the home that he and Jean created was alive with both Jewish tradition and contemporary concerns. At his urging, I enrolled in a graduate seminar taught by David Little on the sociology of religion. It changed my life, for it gave me a vocabulary with which to identify the struggles and social mechanisms upon which I pondered so mightily. Marx, Durkheim, Freud, and most of all, Weber provided me with theories that allowed me to see what I regarded as simple truth — religion is embedded in culture and cannot be understood apart from it. Intellectually, the discipline of sociology of religion was to provide me with the tools to understand my own existence and the existence of my people. My researches and studies in this area were not to be mere academic exercises. They were to become the conduit to my soul.

After completing my M.A. in religious studies at Virginia, I was prepared to leave my native state. I moved to Kibbutz Mishmar Ha-Emek in the Jezreel Valley, where I spent eight wonderful months before entering the Hebrew Union College in Jerusalem for the 1972–1973 academic year. The time in Israel was an exceptional one for me. I felt a wholeness and completion I had never felt before or since — and to this day I will confess that I feel myself to be a "failed Zionist." Only in Israel at that time did I ever approach anything resembling the sense of *shlemut* — not so much "wholeness" as "normalization" — that had desperately eluded me during all my years in Virginia. I am still uncertain why I ever left Israel. I do know that the task of receiving a doctorate from the Hebrew University seemed a daunting one, and that America appeared an easier place in which to study and achieve my academic goals. In any event, I did return to the United States and in the fall of 1973 enrolled at the College-Institute in New York.

Student life in New York was a novel and exhilarating experience for me. I loved my classes at HUC-JIR and could not soak up enough of my teachers' lore. Martin Cohen presented history in a way that made it vital, and if I ever had a kindred spirit, it was Larry Hoffman. His courses in liturgy, medieval Jewish history, and geonic literature — and the sensibility with which he approached each subject — opened new vistas for me and allowed me to see the possibilities for self-discovery and group identity inherent in an approach to Judaism that combined a knowledge of texts and history with the methodology of the social sciences and philosophy. It was he who taught me that while prayer may be a universal phenomenon and reflect a universal impulse, the Jewish prayer book itself is also a systematically constructed and dramatic testimonial of faith and identity composed by a particular community. Hoffman is surely responsible for awakening in me an interest in liturgy as an academic area of investigation.

Eugene Borowitz embodied many of the same academic qualities as Hoffman, and his course in modern Jewish thought, like David Little's in the sociology of religion, provided me with the vocabulary with which to name the struggles and tensions I had felt virtually my entire life. His assertion that modern Jewish thought represents the attempts of diverse Jewish thinkers to calibrate the relationship between "modernity" on the one hand and "tradition" on the other struck me as simple and profound. It has informed my work ever since.

Although I enjoyed and profited immensely from my rabbinical studies at the College-Institute, I remained somewhat uncomfortable with my decision to study for the rabbinate. I therefore took a leave of absence from HUC-JIR during the 1974–1975 academic year and enrolled in the doctoral program in religion at Columbia, which was a wonderful experience for me. I was able to study with scholars like my advisors Gillian Lindt in the sociology of religion and Joseph Blau in modern Judaism, while attending lectures by scholars such as Robert Nisbet on sociological theory and Arthur Hertzberg in modern Jewish intellectual history and Zionist thought. Every course provided me with further insight into my own being and into the world of my people. For me, the study of Judaism had become, and remains, a religious quest, an attempt at self-knowledge and discovery. Hertzberg's courses only reinforced my sense that modern Jewish religion and identity could be understood only within the context of culture and history, and his descriptions and analysis of the period of Emancipation in Europe and its attendant impact upon Jewish religion and identity have shaped the entire trajectory of my academic work.

When Jacob Katz came to Columbia as a visiting professor, I was entranced by the opportunity to study with him. It was Professor Katz and his emphasis on the use of responsa for the writing of Jewish history that inspired me to delve into Jewish legal literature as a rich and virtually untapped resource for understanding the nature of the modern Jewish condition. He pointed out that the responsa literature itself should be conceived as a crossroads where past and present meet in the ongoing history of Jewish legal hermeneutics. Katz also demonstrated how this material could be fruitfully excavated to reveal its dynamic element: namely, how modern champions of Jewish law constantly reinterpreted and reconfigured the Jewish legal tradition in light of their own historical sensibilities and personal judgments to meet the challenges of contemporary settings. He showed me how to write Jewish history from the inside, relying on its own sources and articulations. His influence upon me, as evidenced in the pages of this volume as well as elsewhere in my work, has clearly been immense.

I returned to the College-Institute in 1975–1976, and there I not only continued my studies with the teachers named above, as well as with my teachers at Columbia, but with Fritz Bamberger, who advised my rabbinic thesis and served as the outside examiner for my Columbia dissertation. He was possessed of great knowledge and I learned much from him about modern Jewish intellectual history and the German Jewish experience. By this time my interest had shifted completely to this arena, as it became clear to me that it was in Germany that the models for the Jewish wrestling with acculturation had initially emerged.

Once, in speaking with Dr. Bamberger about my work on Rabbi Esriel Hildesheimer, the subject of my dissertation, he commented that no

German Jew would have ever conceptualized a study of Hildesheimer as I did. By that, he meant that my research constantly focused on the tensions that Hildesheimer must have experienced in trying to construct a Jewish Orthodoxy that could meet the challenges of a changed social, cultural, political, and religious situation in nineteenth-century Germany. Hildesheimer himself would never have seen his efforts as so conflicted and would never have regarded his achievements as so flawed and riddled with contradictions. Only an American, Dr. Bamberger said, could have constructed such a portrait of a German Jew. By this, he did not mean that I was necessarily incorrect. He only wanted to remind me that the perspective I brought to my study of Hildesheimer and other figures in modern Judaism was as much — if not more — a reflection of my own internal conflicts as an American Jew as it was of the thought of Rabbi Hildesheimer or any other figure. As I noted at the outset of this Preface, the questions that I, like every other academic, have repeatedly posed are surely informed and guided by highly personal and subjective elements in my own background.

My studies of the Jewish people — its history, thought, and religion — have linked me to the wisdom and community of generations. Through my work I participate in a conversation that stretches across the millennia. It grants me insights beyond my own time and place, as it takes me back into the past and stretches me into the future. Scholarship, and the roads that have taken me there, have given me both memory and understanding of myself as a modern Jew.

My aim in gathering these essays together is not simply to focus on the diversity and divisions of modern Jewish religious responses in the West and in Israel, but rather to highlight the commonality and adaptability that mark the Jewish condition and Jewish life in the modern situation. The sense of "divided passions" that characterizes the Jewish encounter with modernity, as my friend Paul Mendes-Flohr has so felicitously phrased it, should not be regarded as necessarily negative. I would contend that the Jewish people in the United States and elsewhere in the West as well as in Israel are less "divided" than they are commonly portrayed. Instead, I feel that virtually all Jews in the modern situation stand at different points along the same continuum and that the overwhelming majority of them — of all denominations and viewpoints — have responded positively and in a common vein to the creative possibilities inherent in a world where Jews are able to affirm both their attachment to western culture and their identity as Jews.

This book presents twenty-three essays that are germane to this argument and that reflect the notion that all Jewish religious leaders, after Emancipation, are constantly compelled to reconcile a particular religious tradition with the varied demands of a contemporaneous social and cultural context. With the advent of modernity, Jewish life was transformed in all spheres of social life, and Jewish religious leaders had to mediate between past and present to make Jewish identity a cogent and viable option for Jews in the modern world. These leaders were remarkably successful in achieving this end, and their mediations can be seen in their legal writings and prayer books as well as in the other primary sources explored in these essays.

Part one, "Reflections on Modernity," presents the overarching theme that informs my work in general and this volume in particular. The first essay introduces the ongoing and evolving nature of the Jewish response to the modern enterprise, particularly in the American context. The second essay acknowledges my debt to Jacob Katz and his socio-religious approach to Jewish history. The third, on Max Weber, is the only essay in the book that does not focus on a Jewish thinker. Nevertheless, it highlights the tension that a Jewish insistence on maintaining a distinct identity posed for a modern-day liberal political theorist like Weber. In so doing, this chapter indicates that modern western thought — with its claims to universalism — is paradoxically intolerant of the type of particularity that an ongoing commitment to Jewish — or any other kind of — particularity demands.

Part two, "The Challenge of Emancipation," contains four essays that look at Jewish legal and liturgical writings in nineteenth-century Europe, when Jews were first emerging from the ghetto. It was still a time of great insecurity and uncertainty for them, as political emancipation was promised, granted, revoked, and re-won in the decades following Napoleon's defeat. These essays indicate how Jewish religious leaders of that time labored to demonstrate that the Jewish religion and Jewish culture were worthy of respect by the larger gentile world, and that political emancipation ought to be extended to Jews as citizens of a modern state. Rabbis Samuel Holdheim, Zacharias Frankel, and traditionalists such as Moses Schreiber (the Ḥatam Sofer) and Samson Raphael Hirsch bitterly argued over where to draw the lines for religious innovation. Denominational lines were still quite fluid during this period, and these leaders fought vigorously amongst themselves to preserve what each regarded as Jewish religious integrity. Simultaneously, each strived to demonstrate in pioneering ways that his vision of Jewish religious life was one that was compatible with a modern political and cultural ethos. This section ends with my translation of the *Rabbiner-Seminar Codicil*, a document intended for self-definition and boundary maintenance by the Orthodox of late nineteenth-century Germany.

By the end of the nineteenth century, denominational borders were more firmly established. The essays in Part three, "Denominational Responses," indicate how the leaders of Liberal and Orthodox branches of Judaism in Central Europe constructed novel parameters for their communities through prayer books, legal writings, sermons, and journal articles. In the United States as well, the boundary between Reform and Conservative Judaism emerged at the end of the nineteenth century, and denominational divisions among Reform, Conservative, and Orthodox forms of Jewish religious affiliation were definitively constructed by the 1920s. This is not to suggest that there was no fluidity among the movements. However, denominational commitments and borders were less permeable than before, and the documents of this era attest to the establishment of religious lines that separated the movements even as they all responded affirmatively to a common cultural landscape.

Part four, "Modern Responsa," takes a close look at twentieth-century Jewish legal decisions on a plethora of new issues — the status of women, interfaith relations, modern academic scholarship, recent medical advancements, and the re-establishment of Jewish political autonomy through the creation of the State of Israel. In these responsa, rabbis sought to cull values and principles drawn from precedents found in Jewish law to these novel developments. However, precisely because so many of these challenges were unprecedented, the usual modes of analogical thought generally relied upon to provide solutions to legal dilemmas proved to be insufficient in many of these cases. The *poskim*, rabbis issuing legal opinions, frequently had to draw on models for flexibility and innovation inherent in Jewish legal tradition to deal with these fresh situations and contexts.

The inspired creativity evidenced in these responsa is echoed in the final section of the book, "New Initiatives, New Directions." The review essays in this section analyze a few landmark contemporary works of legal and liturgical creativity by individuals and movements from diverse sectors of the Jewish religious world — the new Israeli-Masorti prayer book *Siddur Va'ani Tefillati,* David Hartman's perspective on covenantal theology and Jewish law, and Marcia Falk's *Book of Blessings.* These last essays indicate that there is a creative and durable Jewish religious impulse that transcends denominational borders and divisions and points towards the future.

This resilience of Judaism in the present-day setting demonstrates that modern Jewish religious leaders from all movements have sought to meet the challenge of allowing an ancient tradition to speak to us in meaningful contemporary cadences. The reality of Jewish cultural and social integration into the larger world did not signal the demise of Judaism. Instead, the modern setting has provided a challenging context where the ongoing creativity and adaptability of Jewish religious leaders of all stripes has been tested and displayed. The essays in this volume aspire to appreciate the vitality of these responses to our times.

As this book enters the world, I would offer a special thank you to Morton Mandel and Lynn Schusterman. Their friendship and generosity have made the publication of this work possible.

I would also express my appreciation to Rabbi Mari Chernow, who first helped me gather and edit these essays. Morton Meyerson and his cousin Susan Schwartz brought me to Bonny Fetterman, and for this I owe them a special debt of gratitude. Bonny went through every one of the pages contained in this book, and helped me articulate my thoughts in an ever clearer fashion. She is an exceptional editor and I was fortunate to have her help. Without her invaluable assistance, this book would not have appeared.

Arnold Eisen and David Myers read every page of the manuscript for the HUC Press and offered many helpful suggestions that I incorporated into the final version of this book. They are brilliant scholars. They are even more wonderful friends.

Michael Meyer offered much support that facilitated the publication of the book, and kindly wrote the Foreword. Barbara Selya did a magnificent job of editing for the HUC Press, Kelby Bowers expertly oversaw the design and typesetting, and Nancy Klein meticulously proofread the galleys. Marca Gay, Pat Gibbons, Cindy Kutas, and Nicole Vandestienne gathered the permissions, and Grace Cohen Grossman and Jean Bloch Rosensaft selected the painting that graces the jacket, which was designed by Nancy Foote. To all of them I say thank you.

I do not know how to thank my family properly — love is always the most difficult emotion to capture. Some time ago, I dedicated to my children a book I had written. On that occasion, I expressed the hope that they would come to embrace the Jewish religious tradition as well as love the State of Israel. Years have passed since that time. I have been blessed to see my children grow and have these hopes fulfilled. They are all vibrant and kind persons as well as committed Jews. Ruth is an exceptional writer, and she has brought Robert into our lives. They have forged a warm and open home and are part of a vital Jewish community. Micah is so outgoing and possesses such unique talents working with young people. He is now a student at the University of Judaism, and I look forward to his future unfolding as a Jewish educator. Hannah and Naomi have blossomed into lovely young women before my eyes. Hannah is so thoughtful and compassionate, connected so strongly to Judaism and the State of Israel. Her concern for Jews and Arabs alike is exemplary, and I am excited to see her take her next steps as she enters Wellesley College this fall. Naomi is effervescent in every way, and I love her sweet voice. Her passion is boundless, and I am grateful for her strong Jewish commitments. And Rafi — *ben zekunai* — is a constant source of joy and entertainment. It is a miracle to behold his spirit. I am aware every day how fortunate I am to have such children.

However, it is to Jackie that I dedicate this book. It is she who is my greatest blessing, and she has made our own home and family possible. She is my compass and my anchor, my best friend and most intimate companion. I hope this dedication is some sign — however incomplete — of my love for her and my appreciation and gratitude for all our journeys. With her to accompany me, I look forward to many more.

Reflections on Modernity

1

Judaism Resurgent?

American Jews and the Evolving Expression of Jewish Values and Jewish Identity

In 1943, at the height of the Holocaust and at a moment of intense agitation for the creation of a Jewish state, Joseph Proskauer, then president of the American Jewish Committee, authored an AJC-sponsored "Statement of Views." Addressed to world leaders who would eventually frame the terms of an armistice and dictate postwar conditions of peace, the document stated: "We urge upon the United Nations and those who shall frame the terms of the peace the relief from the havoc and ruin inflicted by Axis barbarism on *millions of unoffending human beings*, especially Jews." In commenting upon this statement, historian Marc Dollinger has observed, "The AJC's decision to focus on 'human beings' first and list 'Jews' second reflected Proskauer's universalist orientation. American Jews did possess the right to protect their co-religionists, but that campaign must focus on human rights, not Jewish particularism."[1] Or, to phrase it in other terms, the American context did not compel Proskauer to eschew particularism completely. However, it could only be championed comfortably when subsumed within a more universalistic framework and when Jewish concerns could be presented as being completely compatible with the larger humanistic values and affirmations of the broader American culture.

This episode is hardly a singular one, and the primacy Proskauer accorded universalism and the trajectory that marked his statement were hardly idiosyncratic to this particular Jewish leader. Instead, they reflect an ordering of values as well as a sense of Jewish identity that have informed most American Jews throughout U.S. history. Indeed, Irving Howe, one of America's foremost literary critics and Jewish intellectuals, reports a comparable episode that reflects the same American

---

1 Marc Dollinger, *Quest for Inclusion: Jews and Liberalism in Modern America* (Princeton, N.J.: Princeton University Press, 2000), p.95.

Jewish hierarchy of values in his autobiography, *A Margin of Hope*. In it, he recounts a heated public debate he had during the early 1960s with Oscar Handlin, the Brooklyn-born, Harvard-based Jewish historian of the American immigrant experience. At issue was the moral propriety of the Israeli kidnapping of Adolf Eichmann from Argentina to stand trial in Jerusalem. The crimes Eichmann had committed against the Jewish people during the Second World War were by any reckoning immense. According to Howe, however, Handlin unflinchingly condemned the kidnapping as "a violation of international law." Howe, in contrast, defended it "as a necessary moral act by victims of the Holocaust." This debate, held before a predominantly Jewish audience at Brandeis University, produced conflicting emotions among the students, which "it would still be hard to sort out — bruising conflicts between their liberalism and their Jewishness, between what they took to be principle and had to recognize as feeling."[2]

At the conclusion of his narrative, Howe attempts to account for why this debate aroused such "bruising conflicts." In his view, he and the students, no less than Handlin, perceived a tension between their universal heritage of American "liberalism" and the particularistic emotions their "Jewishness" elicited. They, no less than Handlin, seemed to believe that the broad-based ethics of the former tradition apparently demanded that they condemn such an act as "illegal" and "morally unworthy." Only their own "narrow" Jewish patrimony caused them to view the kidnapping as a "necessary" deed. The ambivalence Howe expresses in recalling this event stems from his perception that "principle" alone would surely have compelled them to censure the kidnapping. The fact that Eichmann was brought to trial through such "illegal" means could only be warranted, it seems, through the "particularistic, emotive" demands that "Jewishness" imposed.

The incidents recounted here indicate that for generations of Jews there was surely some degree of discomfort, a perceived incongruity, between "Americanism" and its universal all-embracing values and larger identity, on the one hand, and "Jewishness" and its narrow values and particularistic identity, on the other. Ethnic affirmation was seen

---

2   Irving Howe, *A Margin of Hope: An Intellectual Autobiography* (New York: Harcourt Brace Janovich, 1982), p.188.

as suspect, even base, though its claims were so great that Howe and others could not avoid acting on them.

How different the year 2000 seems — at least from one perspective. In the time that has passed since the Proskauer and Howe episodes recounted here, Jews have gained an access to public positions of power and a proud visibility in American life that were surely unimaginable decades earlier. This novel turn in the public posture of Jews and Judaism can be seen most dramatically in the nomination and campaign of Senator Joseph Lieberman for the office of U.S. Vice President. Although the role of Jews in American public life had increased dramatically since President Woodrow Wilson first appointed Louis D. Brandeis to the Supreme Court in 1916, the nomination of a Jew as a major party candidate for such high elective office was unprecedented. Lieberman's nomination represented an exponential jump toward a maximal acceptance of Jews and a widespread visibility of Jewish values and practices in both the public and private spheres of American society.

Most striking is the fact that Senator Lieberman is a traditional Jew whose public observance of Jewish ritual, as well as public expressions of piety, are considered a significant virtue by a broad array of Americans. His observance of particularistic Jewish laws — for instance, those dealing with kashruth and the Sabbath — exposed Jewish ritual to an audience of millions of Americans. Furthermore, Lieberman did not hesitate to publicly proclaim his devotion to Judaism. As the *New York Times* put it, "Lieberman . . . refers at every campaign stop to his Jewish faith," and he demanded "a role for religion in politics and public discourse."[3]

Many people were not sanguine about this development. Again, in the words of the *New York Times:* "In a remarkable campaign development, Mr. Lieberman is being criticized by some Jewish leaders . . . fearful that his declarations of faith as a devout Jew, and his calls for more religion in public life, are an affront to Americans who are less religious or whose faith comes from a different tradition."[4] Indeed, the Anti-Defamation League has felt compelled to condemn "Lieberman's regular infusions of biblical language and allusions to a heavenly creator" as

3 *The New York Times* (August 28, 2000), p. A14.
4 Ibid. (August 31, 2000), p. A22.

"'inappropriate and even unsettling.'" As both the *New York Times* and the *Los Angeles Times* have observed, such criticism of Lieberman on the part of the ADL stands as one of the greatest "oddities" of recent years, as it has "pitted the nation's oldest battler against anti-Semitism against the first Jew named to a major party presidential ticket."[5]

In contrast, many others — particularly non-Jews — were delighted with Lieberman's injection of religion into the public arena. Richard John Neuhaus, a Catholic priest and the editor of the conservative religious journal *First Things*, has argued that "there is nothing wrong with making policy proposals in frankly moral terms. . . . The only thing strange about what Senator Lieberman is saying is that people think it is strange."[6] According to Richard Land, president of the Southern Baptist Ethics and Religious Liberty Commission, "Just as it took Nixon to go to China, maybe it will require an Orthodox Jew to restore to its rightful place the role of religion in this society."[7] The influential Catholic theologian and social commentator Michael Novak echoed these sentiments in a remarkable op-ed piece in the *New York Times*. In Novak's words: "I love what Senator Lieberman, an Orthodox Jew, is doing to wake this nation up to its deepest identity, rooted in Jewishness."[8]

Such fragments of the twentieth-century American Jewish experience are telling, for they hold up a mirror to the diverse and evolving ways in which Jewish values and identity have been expressed in the United States. They reveal that the public expression of American Jewish identity and American Jewish cultural and religious values must be understood against a larger backdrop of general American social, cultural, and political developments. Indeed, these developments have had far-reaching consequences for the ways in which Jews and Gentiles alike have perceived Jewish identity. By rehearsing and analyzing these changes within American life during the course of the 1900s, this essay will highlight those elements of historical continuity and discontinuity that have marked (and continue to mark) the expression of Jewish values and identity. In this way, the nature and meaning of what has widely been hailed as the resurgence of Jewish values and identity in both the public and

5   *The New York Times* (August 30, 2000), p. A17; and *Los Angeles Times* (August 30, 2000), p. A1.

6   *The New York Times* (August 30, 2000), p. A17.

7   Ibid. (September 3, 2000), "The Nation," p. 5.

8   *The New York Times* (September 4, 2000).

private spheres of American life at the end of the twentieth century can be properly assessed.[9]

The political parameters of the modern West were established upon the basis of individual, not group, rights. In historical terms, dissolution of the medieval world brought with it the demise of corporatism. Civil rights were granted to individual persons within the context of a modern nation-state rather than to corporate semiautonomous ethnic bodies residing within the nation. In an oft-quoted statement, Clermont-Tonnerre, a leader of the French Revolution, articulated this philosophy vis-à-vis the Jew when he proclaimed that "the Jews should be denied everything as a nation, but granted everything as individuals."[10]

In Europe, vestiges of a medieval feudal political order meant that the demise of the Jewish corporate order was not absolute, even with the advent of the nineteenth century. As historian Jacob Katz pointed out in numerous writings, the European Jewish community, though severely reduced in scope and coercive political powers, legally retained some corporate prerogatives and features. However, the United States, conceived as a wholly modern nation free of the medieval past, was different. Jewish communities in America, "where no external forces impinged," were, in contrast to European communities of the 1800s, *completely* voluntary associations, where individual Jews were free "to organize around synagogues with different styles and prayer services [or not], according to their individual choice."[11] America applied

---

9 No one has been more enthusiastic in asserting this position than Charles Silberman. See his book, *A Certain People: American Jews and Their Lives Today* (New York: Summit Books, 1985), for this assessment. The final part of this essay will discuss trends and views that allow for what I consider to be a more balanced appraisal.

10 Quoted in Paul Mendes-Flohr and Jehuda Reinharz, eds., *The Jew in the Modern World* (New York and Oxford: Oxford University Press, 1995), p.115.

11 Jacob Katz, *A House Divided: Orthodoxy and Schism in Nineteenth-Century Central European Jewry*, trans. by Ziporah Brody (Hanover, N.H.: Brandeis University Press, 1998), p.9. For the general treatment Katz accorded this point, see two of his classic works: *Tradition and Crisis: Jewish Society at the End of the Middle Ages* (New York: Free Press of Glencoe, 1961; paperback, New York: Schocken Books, 1971; a newer translation by Bernard Dov Cooperman [New York: New York University Press, 1993] includes the source notes of the Hebrew original) and *Out of the Ghetto: The Social Background of Jewish Emancipation, 1770–1870* (Cambridge, Mass.: Harvard University Press, 1973).

the theory of Clermont-Tonnerre and others in an unqualified way: bestowing full rights on Jews as individuals, it was unwilling to accept the legitimacy of a corporate Jewish community.[12] The Jewish community in America was (and remains) essentially voluntary, and Jews have been viewed as individual citizens of the state devoid of all group political identity.

On a certain level, this created a dilemma for Jews — in some sense, a secular version of the premodern Christian demand for the Jews' conversion. Individuals could fully participate in the larger life of the American polity only if they were willing to divest themselves of particular ethnic traits and group loyalties. Adherence to "universalism" — in effect, Protestant mores and manners — was the price demanded for admission to full participation in American society.

The desire to take on the cultural characteristics, and in large measure, the values of the dominant host society has been typical of Jews of all Western European nations since the onset of emancipation. In Germany, France, and England, this willingness was reflected not only through Jewish participation in the cultural, political, and economic life of host cultures, but also in the way that Jews came to view their religion, and, in turn, themselves. Anxious to divest themselves of ethnic particularism, the Jews of Western Europe consciously came to regard Judaism almost exclusively as a religion and did not see themselves as belonging to a unique ethnic group, i.e., a "Jewish nation." To have done so would have betrayed the very notions of western universalism and liberalism that made the emancipation of the Jews possible in the first place. Thus, the German Jews who immigrated to the United States prior to 1881 brought views of a non-particularistic, universal, and rational religion

---

12 Of course, I recognize that the historical reality was more complex than this overarching observation would indicate. There were surely places in the United States during the Federalist period and beyond where Jews were, in some sense, accorded political treatment as a corporate group and where individual political emancipation was not complete. Morton Borden makes this point quite well in his *Jews, Turks, and Infidels* (Chapel Hill, N.C.: University of North Carolina Press, 1984). These exceptions notwithstanding, the general point made by Jacob Katz still holds: the Jewish community in America has always been essentially voluntary, with Jews being viewed as individual citizens of the state devoid of all corporate political identity. Furthermore, as a result of this modern political order and its liberal trajectory, the key point that emerges is that there was no formal place for Jewish values or identity in the public square.

with them to a country that, it was hoped, was prepared to advance them into positions of prestige and status. Because of both their background and promise of future reward within the American society, they were predisposed to eschew Jewish particularistic values that emphasized group distinctiveness. Hence they created American Reform Judaism, which in the "classical" mold rejected all stress on particularistic Jewish loyalties and practices. Finding expression in documents such as the Pittsburgh Platform of 1885, American Reform purged "Oriental" patterns of worship from the synagogue, devised a liturgy almost wholly universalistic in orientation, abandoned dietary laws, and rapidly conformed to the cultural patterns and mores of the United States.

With the onset of Jewish immigration from Eastern Europe in the late nineteenth and early twentieth centuries, a different type of Jew came to American shores. The experience of East European Jews had been radically different from that of their German-Jewish predecessors, and during the first part of the twentieth century, they both avoided and were purposefully excluded from the American Reform community. These experiences notwithstanding, it is a romantic misconception to claim that East European Jews and their children did not possess the same desire for acculturation that had characterized the German Jews. Indeed, the desire to participate in the life of the larger society has been the most characteristic element of the Jewish response to the American nation.

Commentators such as Arthur Hertzberg and Charles Liebman have explained the East European immigrants' proclivity to acculturate on the basis of their intellectual and cultural characteristics. They have pointed out that these Jews were not carriers of elite Jewish religious values as articulated by the scholarly rabbinic leaders of Eastern Europe. Rather, they were drawn to America by its promise of a brighter future; by and large, they lacked a commitment to those Jewish religious values that could hinder their acculturation. Thus, most of them quickly abandoned observance of the Sabbath and the dietary laws, and their initial failure to construct ritual baths or Jewish day schools indicates their lack of attachment both to the laws of family purity and to traditional Jewish learning.[13] First-generation American Jews and, even more

13 See Charles Liebman, *The Ambivalent American Jew* (Philadelphia: The Jewish Publi-

so, their children, were largely lacking in those inhibitions that might prevent their full involvement in American life. Public expressions of Jewish values and identity that would have reduced their prospects for full participation were discouraged.

To be sure, this orientation exacted certain costs. After all, such public purging of values and identity can be purchased only at the price of a high degree of psychological ambivalence. The author Israel Zangwill mirrored this ambivalence in his 1908 play *The Melting Pot*. Produced on Broadway, the drama gave general currency to a type of thinking that dominated both America's perception of itself and ethnic minority groups' views of the United States for the next sixty years.

The hero of the play, David Quixano, is a Jewish violinist whose parents were killed in a Russian pogrom. He is engaged in writing a great symphony celebrating America when, at a settlement house, he meets and falls in love with Vera — the daughter of a Russian army officer. They decide to marry, but their relationship is almost destroyed when David discovers that Vera's father was the murderer of his parents. Meanwhile, David's symphony is a great success and its triumph revives his faith in the American "melting pot." Determined to cast aside the blood feuds of the past, David rejects his particularistic Jewish heritage and affirms his love for Vera. In the climactic speech of the play, David shouts, "God is making the American . . . he will be the fusion of all races, the coming Superman." Thus the rapturous vision of the play is that of the universalist who rejects selfish and confining particularity.

The Melting Pot advances a vision of ethnicity that is hardly positive. In this context, "ethnic" implies that there is something wrong with the individual or group that is so defined; the religion, character, or speech patterns of the ethnic group is in some way aesthetically amiss, and such characteristics should certainly not be displayed publicly. Most significantly, "ethnicity," by its failure to conform to universal standards of brother- and sisterhood, is also morally wanting. While Zangwill undoubtedly felt some disquietude as an advocate of the "melting pot," there is little doubt that he favored the expansiveness of David Quixano's universalism over the narrowness of particularistic "Old World" loyalties.

---

cation Society, 1973), pp. 42ff.; and Arthur Hertzberg, *The Jews in America* (New York: Simon and Schuster, 1989).

The Melting Pot does more than reflect the conflicts the Jews of those decades experienced in adapting to the demands of a non-Jewish world. It also bespeaks those Jews' intense desire to acculturate, to revel in the freedom the United States promised. The American Jews of these years did so not only by eagerly accepting all the benefits that the American nation was prepared to confer upon them. They also accepted the definition of Judaism as exclusively a religion,[14] and they established systems of religious thought and practice — Reform and Conservative Judaism — that applauded the virtues of democracy and the American way of life. Indeed, an offshoot of Conservative Judaism, Reconstructionism, accorded the status of *sancta* to such American civic festivals as Thanksgiving, Labor Day, and the Fourth of July. Even when a highly particularistic vision of cultural Judaism such as Zionism was affirmed, it was articulated so that Justice Louis D. Brandeis, as well as many rabbis, could confidently proclaim that Zionism and the values of American democracy were one and the same.[15] Finally, committed as well as "deracinated" Jews largely justified and celebrated Jewish particularity by their authorship of apologetic works "proving" Judaism's decisive impact upon this or that value or element of American history and civilization. Such claims to Jewish influence upon the values of the United States, as well as the notion of compatibility between Jewish and American values, undoubtedly contain more than a kernel of truth; vestiges of these attitudes inform the beliefs of countless American Jews to this day.

Yet, even as they rejoiced in this model of adaptation and integration, Jews during these years still socialized almost exclusively among themselves. This outcome was not only the consequence of internal Jewish

14 As Oscar Handlin put it, "Jewish identification remained meaningful in the [only] area of diversity America most clearly recognized — that of religion." For this quotation, see Will Herberg, *Protestant, Catholic, Jew* (Garden City, N.Y.: Anchor Books, 1960), p. 205; throughout the book, Herberg makes this point. Also see Evyatar Friesel, "American Jewry as Bearer of Contemporary Jewish Tasks," *American Jewish History* 78 (1989), p. 492.

15 See Louis D. Brandeis' formulation of the equation between Zionist and American values in Arthur Hertzberg, *The Zionist Ideal: A Historical Analysis and Reader* (New York: Atheneum, 1959), p. 520. On the rabbis, see David Ellenson, "Zion in the Mind of the American Rabbinate during the 1940s," in Robert M. Seltzer and Norman J. Cohen, eds., *The Americanization of the Jews* (New York: New York University Press, 1995), pp. 193–212.

attitudes. External conditions also reinforced a collective distance that kept Jews at a social remove from non-Jews. Simply put, one sociological variable required for large-scale exogamy on the part of any minority group — widespread acceptance of group members as desirable or acceptable marriage partners — was missing. This in turn gave rise to a Jewish social solidarity that promoted group endogamy. In short, prior to the 1960s, intermarriage between Jews and Gentiles was virtually nonexistent. Although America was prepared to advance a model of the melting pot (at least for white ethnics), social reality did not always conform to the vision this model advanced. Hence, a certain sense of unease, though seldom overtly acknowledged, characterized American Jewry during this era. Of course, this is hardly surprising for a predominantly first- and second-generation immigrant community struggling to adapt to the demands and mores of a new country.[16] Less than completely secure, American Jewry was not yet prepared to advocate (nor was American society prepared to accept) a pluralistic cultural model that would have permitted a greater display of public ethnicity.

To the extent that they were observed at all, particularistic Jewish values and rituals were thus confined to the private sphere of life. Indeed, Rabbi Irving (Yitz) Greenberg gives voice to this reality in his account of the Jewish "self-denial and anonymity" of those years. In an interview, Greenberg reports that when he entered Harvard University in the 1950s to study for his doctorate in American history, "everything Jewish was marginal ... when I arrived no one told me, but I just knew you could not wear a *kippah*." While this "bothered me a lot because I was Orthodox," social mores simply did not permit Greenberg to cover his head either in class or at student receptions. In a poignant vein, Greenberg recalls that at such receptions he would "hold a drink in my hand all the time because I would not drink it without covering my head and making a *bracha*."[17] Such confinement of ethnic expres-

16 See Jonathan D. Sarna, "The Cult of Synthesis in American Jewish Culture," *Jewish Social Studies* (new series) 5, nos. 1–2 (Fall/Winter 1998–1999), pp. 52–79.

17 This anecdote appears in Irving Greenberg and Shalom Freedman, *Living in the Image of God — Jewish Teachings to Perfect the World: Conversations with Rabbi Irving Greenberg* (Northvale, N.J.: Jason Aronson Inc., 1998), pp. 6–7. My own father,

sion is hardly unique to the American Jewish community of this period. By constricting Jewish identity and praxis to the private realm, American Jews were displaying a compartmentalization between public behaviors and private manners that also marked members of other racial and cultural minorities who were desirous of acceptance into mainstream American life; indeed, it may be said that the public/private bifurcation was a Protestant American model that became generalized throughout American society.

The 1960s and 1970s changed all this, initiating a trajectory in American Jewish public expression and private commitment that remains in effect until this day. In his influential book *The Rise of the Unmeltable Ethnics* (1972), Michael Novak coined the phrase "the new ethnicity" to describe what he saw as a then-emerging widespread trend in American society. According to Novak, the prevailing cultural image of the ideal American, as established by the WASP, Ivy League educated, upper class of U.S. society, had been substantially discredited among many young Americans as a result of the Vietnam War, urban decay, racial frictions, educational decline, and the gross dishonesty of many public officials.[18] As Novak, writing again on the topic in 1974, put it: "The older image of the truly cultured American is no longer compelling. Many, therefore, are thrown back on their own resources."[19] The times, it seemed, promoted a new and more pluralistic model that would ultimately have a profound impact upon how Jews would understand and express their heritage in public as well as in private.

An explanation for how and why this transformation took place within precincts of the American Jewish community at this time can be found in *The Masks Jews Wear* (1973) by Eugene B. Borowitz, the premier liberal Jewish theologian in the United States. Borowitz, like Novak, noted that significant numbers of Jews (as with members of

---

Samuel Ellenson, a 1948 Harvard Law School graduate, had a similar experience: wearing a *kippah* publicly at the law school, he said, would have been tantamount to declaring, "I do not want to be employed at a law firm."

18   Michael Novak, *The Rise of Unmeltable Ethnics: Politics and Culture in the Seventies* (New York: 1972).

19   Michael Novak, "The New Ethnicity," *The Center Magazine* 7, no. 4 (July/August, 1974), p. 20.

other ethnic groups) were no longer infatuated with the model of the "melting pot." Rather, they prized what he described as a "creative alienation." In his words:

> Today mankind needs people who are creatively alienated. To be satisfied in our situation is either to have bad values or to understand grossly what man can do. . . . Creative alienation implies sufficient withdrawal from our society to judge it critically, but also the will and flexibility to keep finding and trying ways of correcting it. I think Jewishness offers a unique means of gaining and maintaining such creative alienation. This was not its primary role in the lives of our parents and grandparents.[20]

In declaring such a role for Judaism in contemporary America, Borowitz bespoke an ongoing effort involving many Jews throughout the final decades of the twentieth century. As Nathan Glazer observed, such Jews sought to anchor their quest for genuine community and enduring values in a recovery of the resources Judaism was capable of providing without abandoning their concomitant commitment to liberal values.[21]

Of course, this changed posture in American Jewish public and private ethnic expression did not derive solely from trends in the larger American society. Internal rhythms of Jewish history also played a role. The Six-Day War of 1967 prompted countless American Jews (and Jews worldwide) to embrace their Jewish identity. Fearing for the very existence of the Jewish state at the outset of the conflict, they responded to the stunning Israeli victory with both relief and unprecedented pride. As Charles Silberman noted, "The Six-Day War was a watershed between two eras — one in which American Jews had tried to persuade themselves, as well as gentiles, that they were just like everybody else, only more so, and a period in which they acknowledged, even celebrated their distinctiveness."[22]

The nature of the "watershed" of which Silberman spoke and the pride in "distinctiveness" he described can also be seen in an autobi-

20 Eugene Borowitz, *The Masks Jews Wear* (New York. Simon and Schuster, 1973), p.209.
21 See Nathan Glazer, "The Crisis of American Jewry," *Midstream* 16, no.9 (November, 1970), pp.3–11.
22 Silberman, *A Certain People*, p.201.

ographical vignette provided by Harvard Law School professor Alan Dershowitz in *Chutzpah* (1989). In this book, Dershowitz contrasts a number of his own sensibilities regarding matters of Jewish American identity and values with those of the renowned U.S. Supreme Court Justice Felix Frankfurter. In one telling reminiscence, Dershowitz recalls that on his first day as a law student at Yale, "I read a Supreme Court decision [*West Virginia State Board of Education v. Barnette* (1944)] involving a compulsory flag salute during World War II, to which some Jehovah's witnesses objected on religious grounds. The majority agreed with the religious objectors, but Justice Felix Frankfurter dissented . . . on the ground that patriotism during wartime is more important than religious liberty."[23]

Indeed, Frankfurter wrote a dissent in this case that was described by James O. Freedman, the first Jewish President of Dartmouth College, as "one of the most confessional and emotional of Supreme Court opinions." Frankfurter wrote:

> One who belongs to the most vilified and persecuted minority in history is not likely to be insensible to the freedoms guaranteed by our Constitution. Were my purely personal attitude relevant I should wholeheartedly associate myself with the general libertarian views in the Court's opinion . . . But as judges we are neither Jew nor gentile, neither Catholic nor agnostic. We owe equal attachment to the constitution and are equally bound by our judicial obligation whether we derive our citizenship from the earliest or the latest immigrants to these shores.[24]

Frankfurter's dissent in *Barnette* was consistent with the position he had adopted in a similar case three years earlier. In that instance, Chief Justice Hughes had assigned Frankfurter the majority opinion in *Minersville School District v. Gobitis* (1940), a case "upholding the constitutionality of a statute requiring all students, including the children of Jehovah's Witnesses," to salute the flag, an act the Witnesses viewed as

23 Alan M. Dershowitz, *Chutzpah* (Boston: Little, Brown and Company, 1989), p. 48.
24 The Frankfurter opinions cited here can be found in James O. Freedman, "Insiders and Outsiders: Inaugural Lecture of the Center for American Jewish History at Temple University" (November 12, 1990), pp. 8–9.

blasphemous. The Chief Justice had chosen Frankfurter for the task, Hughes recalled, "because of Frankfurter's emotional description, in conference, of the 'role of the public school in instilling love of country' based upon his own experiences as a [Jewish] immigrant child."[25]

Dershowitz, the child of Orthodox Jewish parents raised and educated in an intensely Jewish Brooklyn enclave, comments that he read the 1943 opinion "in astonishment. As a twenty-one-year old student, I simply couldn't identify with it. I didn't feel 'vilified' or 'persecuted,' or even as part of a 'minority.'" Furthermore, the only "insensitivity" Dershowitz observed in these cases was that Frankfurter was "quite 'insensible' to the religious freedoms of the Jehovah's Witnesses."[26]

The gap between Frankfurter's views and those of Dershowitz is emblematic of the transition in attitudes and ethos among American Jewry. Frankfurter, the product of an immigrant Jewish community that internalized the image of a melting pot, could permit no emphasis upon particularism and group distinction. Indeed, he regarded such expressions as ethnocentric and as such, unworthy or even intolerable. Frankfurter felt obliged to insist upon the adoption of "neutral, universal" values in American public life. His vision of Judaism and all other "particularities," like that of countless other Jews of his generation and outlook, was one that allowed no room for the expression of any specific ethnic and religious values and interests.[27]

In contrast, Dershowitz, belonging to a post-Holocaust generation that was no longer dominated numerically by an immigrant population, did not hesitate to affirm his or any other "particularity." For Dershowitz, such affirmation was not only defensible; it was demanded by James Madison's notion, articulated in *The Federalist Papers*, of an "expanding sphere" — a free and open society where values of tolerance and diversity could best be realized. Agreeing with this notion was Norman Podhoretz, the conservative writer and commentator, who viewed as wrong "the conception according to which one [is] supposed to act not as a member of a particular community but as the 'citizen of a human society.'. . ."

25 Ibid.
26 Dershowitz, *Chutzpah*, p.48.
27 See Jerold S. Auerbach, *Rabbis and Lawyers: The Journey from Torah to Constitution* (Bloomington and Indianapolis: Indiana University Press, 1990), p.229 and *passim* for the full development of this argument.

Podhoretz, too, believed that Jews, as well as other ethnic and interest groups, have every right to promote "their own stake in the system."[28] For all the differences that have divided them on a host of political issues, Dershowitz and Podhoretz, in opposition to Frankfurter, represent a shift in how many contemporary American Jews have come to approach the issue of diversity and ethnic expression in a present-day pluralistic American setting. Their security in and understanding of America allowed for a previously unprecedented public expression of Jewish interests and identity in the American context.

By the last decades of the 1900s, a new reality had emerged. More American Jews than ever before had begun to appreciate the wisdom that Judaism could provide, and many of them advanced Jewish interests, agendas, and values in a larger public arena. Silberman's claim that American Jews had now entered an age where they "celebrated their distinctiveness" thus contains more than a kernel of truth. Nevertheless, his claim remains somewhat exaggerated. A more nuanced and judicious assessment of the phenomenon is required for a balanced portrait to emerge. Countless American Jews of this era were also indifferent to their Jewish patrimony and many clearly remain so today as the social and cultural distance that had formerly separated Jew from Gentile in the United States has unquestionably narrowed.[29]

A paradox thus emerges in this analysis of the resurgence of Judaism in contemporary American life, whose roots are to be found in the transformation in the social and cultural status of American Jews. First-generation East European Jewish immigrants and their children socialized almost exclusively among themselves; as late as the 1950s it was extremely rare for Jews — whose roots in Anglo-Saxon culture were so "shallow" — to receive appointments as college professors in top-flight departments of American History and English. Nor could Jews serve as executives or partners in major corporations or elite law firms. Given this situation, the understandable aim of immigrants and their children was to adapt to the manners of the larger American society and in this way earn acceptance into the mainstream. In contrast, their children,

28 Norman Podhoretz, *Breaking Ranks: A Political Memoir* (New York: Harper and Row, 1979), p. 334.
29 For this assessment, see Elihu Bergman, "The American Jewish Population Erosion," *Midstream* 23, no. 8 (October, 1977), p. 9.

third- and fourth-generation American Jews, became less comfortable with the image of a universalistic American melting pot. Instead, they began to proclaim and reclaim their Jewish heritage both publicly and privately. One outcome of this new situation was the steady growth in Jewish day schools during the 1980s and 1990s, and the 2001 National Jewish Population Study indicates that 13 percent of all Jewish college students enroll in Jewish studies courses.[30] Another was the blossoming of college-level Jewish studies programs — currently, there are over a thousand members of the Association for Jewish Studies in the United States; thousands of students are enrolled in college-level Jewish studies courses; and many others attend one-year programs in Israeli institutions of higher learning. While the factors accounting for the growth of Jewish day schools and Jewish studies courses are of course multiple and complex, they indicate that an increasing number of American Jews have come to assert the legitimacy of a Jewish cultural heritage in a multicultural world.

Particularly noteworthy in this regard is the recent case involving five Orthodox Jews who sued Yale University to seek relief from the requirement that first-year students live in a (co-ed) dormitory. However one assesses the merits of their case, these students have exhibited a level of Jewish self-assurance that was virtually inconceivable a mere generation ago.[31] In essence, their argument is that America must uphold its own principles of tolerance and freedom by affirming *their* right to be full participants in American life while at the same time holding to a strict code of Jewish particularistic behavior. In other words,

---

30 For the figures documenting the growth of Jewish Day Schools in the United States, see booklet by Marvin Schick, "A Census of Jewish Day Schools in the United States," (New York: The Avi Chai Foundation, 2000), pp.12ff. See also Jack Wertheimer, "Jewish Education in the United States: Recent Trends and Issues," *American Jewish Year Book* (1999), pp.3–115, in which he relates and analyzes the many factors that account for this increase. Prominent among them are "the attitudinal changes towards matters Jewish among baby-boomers. Many who had a less intensive Jewish education are receptive to giving their children opportunities they themselves did not enjoy" (pp.53–54).

31 For a fuller account of the students' case against Yale, see Samuel G. Freedman, *Jew vs. Jew: The Struggle for the Soul of American Jewry* (New York: Simon and Schuster, 2000), chap.5.

Jewish values are not to be seen as parochial. Rather, the affirmation of Jewish identity implies an advocacy for one of many individual paths through which a universal American spirit can unfold.

Alongside their growing ethnic and religious assertiveness, American Jews today are also far more comfortable in social interactions with non-Jews. In the corporate realm, Jews with names like Shapiro have served as CEOs in corporations such as Du Pont, which in the not so distant past did not have a single Jew on its board of directors. In the educational sector, Ivy League universities that once enforced strict quotas on Jewish students are now headed, in some instances, by a Jewish president.[32] The acceptance and high visibility of Jews in contemporary America is exemplified not only by Joseph Lieberman's vice-presidential candidacy but also by the appointments of Ruth Bader Ginsburg and Stephen Breyer to the U.S. Supreme Court. In contrast to the furor that erupted over President Wilson's decision to elevate Louis D. Brandeis to the High Court in 1916, these two recent appointments were greeted by the general U.S. public with equanimity. Moreover, it is now common for Jews from all parts of the United States, including states with relatively sparse Jewish populations, to be elected to serve in Congress, in state legislatures, and in mayoral offices.[33]

Concurrent with these indications of American Jews' increasing social and professional success is a growing concern with the Jewish continuity in the context of America's open society. The rate of Jewish intermarriage has increased from less than 5 per cent in the 1950s to 31 per

32 The literature on this topic is considerable. Among the most prominent and representative books that deal with the subject of Jews and Higher American Education are Harold S. Wechsler, *The Qualified Student: A History of Selected College Admission in America* (New York: Wiley, 1977); Dan A. Oren, *Joining the Club: A History of Jews at Yale* (New Haven: Yale University Press, 1985); and Paul Ritterband and Harold S. Wechsler, *Jewish Learning in American Universities: The First Century* (Bloomington and Indianapolis: Indiana University Press, 1994).

33 For an analysis of Jewish participation in the United States Congress and American political life, see J. J. Goldberg, *Jewish Power: Inside the American Jewish Establishment* (Reading, Mass.: Addison-Wesley, 1996). In my native region of Tidewater, Virginia — hardly a venue of dense Jewish population — the mayor of Newport News is Joseph Frank; and my cousin, Meyera Ellenson Oberndorf (who attended Stern College of Yeshiva University) is the mayor of Virginia Beach.

cent in 1970 and 52 per cent in 1990. Furthermore, record numbers of
Jews do not affiliate with any sector of the community whatsoever.[34]
American Jewry has thus entered a postmodern situation with antipo-
dean trends: record rates of nonaffiliation and abandonment of Jewish
religion and identity are competing with intense pockets of Jewish commitment and public expression. The pluralism of the modern setting
and the bewildering variety of choices it provides have led many to
forsake Judaism. Simultaneously, other Jews, living within a pluralistic
framework that continues to underscore the importance of individual
choice,[35] have sought out Judaism for the sense of wisdom, security, identity, and community it affords. As has been shown, this was not the function Judaism served for first- and second-generation American Jews.

The twin trends of renewed emphasis on ethnic-religious expression
and pride on the one hand and the ever-growing attenuation of such
attachments, on the other, have been promoted by larger societal trends
that have been identified by sociologist Peter L. Berger. In his influential work *The Heretical Imperative* (1979), Berger points out that the
quintessential feature of modern western culture is *hairesis*, option
or choice.[36] People leave their native towns, women become clergy, and
gays and lesbians "step out of the closet" and have their unions sanctioned by religious denominations. Such examples, among others, characterize the modern world. In Berger's felicitous phrase, modernity is

34 See Bergman, "The American Jewish Population Erosion," for the 5 percent and 31
    percent intermarriage rates; for more recent figures and other statistical information
    relating to the issues of this essay, see Barry A. Kosmin, Sidney Goldstein, Joseph
    Waksberg, Nava Lerer, Ariella Keysar, and Jeff Scheckner, *Highlights of the Council
    of Jewish Federation's 1990 National Jewish Population Survey* (New York, 1991).

35 On the seminal role that individualism and autonomy play in the contemporary
    American psyche and the impact such doctrines have upon the religious expression
    of the American people, see the second edition of Robert N. Bellah, et. al., *Habits
    of the Heart: Individualism and Commitment in American Life* (Berkeley: Univer-
    sity of California Press, 1996). While other significant works have been written
    on this topic, *Habits of the Heart* remains the landmark volume. For an insightful
    treatment of how these themes play themselves out within the Jewish community,
    see Steven M. Cohen and Arnold M. Eisen, *The Jew Within: Self, Community, and
    Commitment in America* (Bloomington, Ind., 2000) and Bethamie Horowitz, "Con-
    nections and Journeys: Shifting Identities Among American Jews," *Contemporary
    Jewry* 19 (1998), p. 87.

36 Peter Berger, *The Heretical Imperative: Contemporary Possibilities of Religious Affir-
    mation* (Garden City, N.Y.: Anchor Books, 1979).

marked by the move from "fate to choice."

As Berger describes it, this movement is liberating. It frees people from the shackles of stultified traditions that define roles and expectations in a narrow and confining way. At the same time, it leaves people feeling bewildered, or, as Berger states in one of his earlier works, "homeless." In *The Homeless Mind*, Berger and his co-authors argue that the modern condition of choice — particularly the displacement that marks the upwardly mobile as they move about in search of career and opportunity — has left many persons without a secure sense of roots.[37] Many have been liberated from "tribal brotherhood," but still more have experienced the anomie and alienation of "universal otherhood."[38] One consequence is the seeking out of fundamentalisms of all sorts in order to cope with anxieties that are engendered by the loss of a stable communal framework.[39] Another is the turn (or return) to religious tradition, which is perceived to offer values that are necessary for the emergence of a "good society."[40]

In Berger's most recent edited collection, *The Desecularization of the World*, he and others argue that the process of secularization (which Berger foresaw as completely triumphant three decades ago) has actually run its course among certain people: modernization, it seems, often strengthens religion.[41] Similarly, Jose Casanova, in his *Public Religions in the Modern World*, notes that many individuals feel "deprived" as a result of the dichotomy between public life and private beliefs. In reaction,

37 Peter L. Berger, Brigette Berger, and Thomas Luckmann address this theme in *The Homeless Mind: Modernization and Consciousness* (New York: Random House, 1973).

38 These phrases were coined by the late Benjamin Nelson, one of the foremost students and observers of societal directions in the modern West, in his *The Idea of Usury: From Tribal Brotherhood to Universal Otherhood* (Chicago: University of Chicago Press, 1969).

39 See Freedman, *Jew vs. Jew*, for a discussion of how this trajectory has marked many in the American Jewish community. For a more general and authoritative scholarly treatment on the topic of the rise of fundamentalism in the modern world, consult the various volumes of the University of Chicago Fundamentalism Project, produced under the editorship of Martin Marty and R. Scott Appleby.

40 In Robert N. Bellah, et. al., *The Good Society* (New York: Vintage Books, 1992), the authors explore this theme in their follow-up study to their *Habits of the Heart*.

41 See Peter L. Berger and Jonathan Sacks, eds., *The Desecularization of the World: Resurgent Religion and World Politics* (Grand Rapids, Mich.: William B. Eerdmans Publishing Co., 1999).

they have become increasingly strident about giving expression to their "full" selves in the larger world — projecting, for instance, their views on issues such as abortion, school vouchers, and school prayer into the political arena.[42]

These particular issues play themselves out in a variety of ways in the American Jewish community.[43] What is clear, though, is that many contemporary Jews, like their Christian counterparts, believe that constitutionally mandated freedom of religion can be maintained without trivializing faith or treating believers with disdain. Thus, a large part of Joseph Lieberman's appeal derived from his well-publicized sense of traditional community as well as his advocacy of time-honored values.[44] Indeed, the sociological tradition to which Peter Berger belongs has long emphasized that human beings (even in the age of the Internet) are social creatures who seek out relationship and community. Moreover, as the sociologist Ferdinand Tönnies commented at the beginning of the twentieth century, "the force of *Gemeinschaft*," that is, small intimate community, "persists even with the period of *Gesellschaft*" — impersonal modern western society.[45] As Sharon Sandomirsky and John Wilson have also pointed out, voluntary affiliation remains as crucial in today's America as it was in the past.[46] Americans remain inveterate joiners, notwithstanding the highly individualistic ethos

42 Jose Casanova, *Public Religion in the Modern World* (Chicago: University of Chicago Press, 1994).

43 For example, in a report on a state of Wisconsin Supreme Court ruling on the issue of school vouchers, *The Jewish Bulletin of Northern California* (June 19, 1998) stated that liberal and traditional camps in the Jewish community split over this issue. Persons such as Marc Stern of the American Jewish Congress and Steve Freeman of the Anti-Defamation League expressed opposition to the Wisconsin court's decision that such vouchers were legal. Others such as Nathan Diament of the Institute for Public Affairs of the Union of Orthodox Jewish Congregations of America and Marshall Berger of the Jewish Policy Center applauded the verdict.

44 See "Al Gore's Leap of Faith," and "The Senator: How Lieberman Walks His Walk," *Time* (August 21, 2000), pp.24–34, for a journalistic presentation and analysis of these points.

45 Cited in David Hackett, "Sociology of Religion and American Religious History," *Journal for the Scientific Study of Religion* 27, no.4, (1988) p.467.

46 Sharon Sandomirsky and John Wilson, "Process of Disaffiliation: Religious Mobility Among Men and Women," *Social Forces* 68, no.4, (June, 1990) p.1211.

that continues to dominate much of American society.

Many people simply do not want to choose between the extremes of a vacuous and ahistorical secularism, on the one hand, and a raging religious fundamentalism, on the other. Rather, they are anxious to perceive a sacred vitality at the core of both their nation and their own private worlds.[47] For these reasons, religion continues to play a crucial role — even in a country like the United States with its constitutional wall between religion and state — in promoting social cohesion as well as group and individual identity.

As Stephen Carter, the Yale University professor of law, has pointed out in *The Culture of Disbelief*, American democracy has always been dependent in part on religion's perceived role as a "mediating structure" between people and the state. Accordingly, many Americans assert that religious faith must continue to be a significant element in American public life at the same time that they insist upon the importance of church/state separation.[48] Here, too, Joseph Lieberman's campaign touched a responsive chord. As Jim Spencer, a middle-American non-Jewish political pundit, stated:

> Joe Lieberman encourages Americans, even politicians and policy makers, to embrace a spiritual life. He tells you what that means to him, not what it should mean to you. The distinction explains why Lieberman might connect with Americans in a way that right-wing Bible thumpers never have and probably never will. While they might sound a tad pious to the cynical, Lieberman's statements about the role of his personal religious beliefs in his life as a U.S. Senator do not presume that Jewish Orthodoxy is the only route to salvation, much less public education. . . . He has not asked to exclude anyone that I am aware of. He has merely asked Americans to think in spiritual terms. Lieberman does not push us

47 See Wade Clark Roof, *A Generation of Seekers: The Spiritual Journeys of the Baby Boom Generation* (San Francisco: HarperSanFrancisco, 1993), for an exposition of this position.

48 This is the essence of the argument put forth in Stephen Carter, *The Culture of Disbelief: How American Law and Politics Trivializes Religious Devotion* (New York: Basic Books, 1993).

toward theocracy, the God-centered government of which so many Christian conservatives dream. He pushes us toward tolerance. He reminds us that, like it or not, spirituality plays a role in the private lives of political leaders. He insists that such considerations are as enviable as they are inevitable. Somewhere, in the recesses of our over-stimulated minds, we know that intuitively.[49]

Religion in general, and Judaism in particular, find acceptance in American society precisely because they provide for a communitarian ethos and a non-relativistic sense of morality in a world where many people are mindful of both the atomizing excesses of individualism and the horrifying consequences engendered by moral relativism. Put somewhat differently, contemporary American expressions of Jewish tradition are viewed by many as bearing an affinity to the positive moral values bequeathed by Enlightenment rationalism to the modern world while at the same time offering a corrective for the fragmentizing effects of that secular tradition. Such Jewish expression, promoted by trends in the larger world, is attractive to many persons both within and beyond the Jewish community.

Nevertheless, any triumphalist conclusion concerning Jewish life and values in contemporary America must be tempered. As Charles Liebman pointed out more than a decade ago, Jewish religious erosion threatens to overshadow the achievements of the committed elite of American Jewry. "What I sense," Liebman wrote, "is an increasingly incoherent pattern of symbols and a random structure of responses that constitute much of American Jewish life."[50] In a world where the political parameters that formerly preserved the premodern Jewish community have been dismantled, Jewish commitments and knowledge have become so attenuated that a diminution of Jewish life in this country is taking place despite an efflorescence of Jewish culture and values.

By and large, modern Judaism has been taken out of the home and placed in public, institutional settings. Although the synagogue and the

49 Jim Spencer, "There is More Than One Way to Get to Heaven," *Daily Press* (Newport News, Va.: September 6, 2000), p. C1.
50 Charles Liebman, "A Grim Outlook," in Steven M. Cohen and Charles S. Liebman, *The Quality of American Jewish Life — Two Views* (New York: American Jewish Committee, 1987), p. 43.

Jewish federation play a critical role in American Jewish life, the public affirmation of Jewishness may well mask the absence of more enduring private commitments. Given the lack of ritual observance on the part of most American Jews, Liebman himself worries about the durability of American Judaism and is pessimistic about its future. He does not dispute the accuracy of observations about the pro-religious achievements of some American Jews. Yet, for him, this reflects no more than "the capacity of a minority to sustain and even strengthen their Jewish commitments despite the tendencies of the majority."[51]

This essay demonstrates the ways in which American attitudes toward ethnic identity and public manifestations of faith have evolved greatly over the past century, with significant implications for the way in which Jewish faith and culture are today expressed. The ideal of the melting pot, dominant at the beginning of the twentieth century, was surely rejected by many beginning in the 1960s, at which time a greater appreciation of ethnic values and identity began to emerge. Yet even as such a groundwork was being laid for a resurgence of Jewish expression, it was being done within the embrace of a larger American culture from which American Jewry was not prepared to retreat. For this reason, the revival of Jewish consciousness that was evinced in the birth of a "new ethnicity" was not identical to the Yiddish culture, ethnic distinctiveness, and associational patterns that had characterized first-generation East European immigrants. By the 1960s, American Jews had overwhelmingly internalized most of the dominant values of their host society, and that society no longer segregated them in any significant way.

All of this must be borne in mind in assessing the renaissance of Jewish life in contemporary America. Jews in the United States are overwhelmingly universalistic, and particularistic affirmations are made in the service of universal moral and spiritual values. For Jews, as well as for members of other U.S. ethnic groups, the question that therefore remains is whether such affirmations will prove strong enough to sustain a broad cultural and communal identity. Jews have been blessed with freedom in America. Such blessing has allowed for the strengthening of Jewish commitment, values, and identity. At the same time, it has proven

51 Ibid. p.51.

to be the solvent in which a distinctive Jewish identity and values often dissolve. This essay has shown that the resiliency of Judaism has been challenged on American shores in a variety of ways, and that the Jewish response to the American crucible has been textured. The story of Jewish resurgence in the United States during the twentieth century is multivalent and complex, and the adaptive capacity of the Jewish people will surely continue to be tested in the future.

2

Jacob Katz on the Origins and Dimensions of Jewish Modernity

The Centrality of the German Experience

The gifts Jacob Katz bestowed upon modern Jewish scholarship were by any standard immense. No one more brilliantly analyzed the course and complexity of modern European Jewish history than he did. In his landmark work *Tradition and Crisis*, Katz fruitfully defined the motifs that were to mark his lifetime of scholarship. In its pages, he also employed the social-scientific methodology he had imbibed during his student years at the University of Frankfurt. With that methodology he illuminated the content and trajectory of the Western European Jewish world as it confronted the ongoing challenges of the modern world. Although he would later supplement that social-scientific methodology with a more conventional narrative approach, Katz remained forever associated with the social-scientific attitudes and concerns that informed his earliest books. This essay will focus on how Katz, through his seminal investigations of the nineteenth-century German Jewish community, defined and investigated the demands that modernity placed upon Judaism and probed the adjustments that Judaism made in response to those demands.

The first section will focus on the sociological methods and concerns Katz employed as the framework for his initial forays into the field of German-Jewish history. This framework was far from incidental to the historical claims he would ultimately make. Indeed, it helped to shape the conclusions at which he would arrive. His decision at that time to eschew the narrative mode of classical historiography in favor of a social-scientific lens permitted him to illuminate with unparalleled clarity what was at stake in the transition of Judaism from the medieval to the modern world. Consequently, an understanding of sociological tradition will help to emphasize the distinctiveness and direction that would always mark his scholarship. The conceptual sophistication he brought with him from the social sciences was instrumental in shaping the questions that would occupy his attention in his later books and essays as well, works that were marked by a narrative method of historical discourse.

Having outlined the disciplinary concerns and concepts that informed Katz's thought, I will then turn to an examination of how he applied these concerns and concepts in the final chapters of his justly acclaimed *Tradition and Crisis*. In those last chapters, he focused on issues of enduring concern to students of Judaism in the modern setting. He provided a summary-analysis of the transition that marked German Judaism as it moved from the world of classical rabbinic traditionalism to the realm of emancipated pluralistic modern Judaism. In these pages, Katz identified certain key issues that were crucial for an understanding of how this transition could be marked, as well as the vectors that would define the complex and uneven course of this transition. Through an examination of *Tradition and Crisis*, as well as several supplementary writings, these issues and vectors will become clear.

The third and concluding section of this essay will investigate how the trajectory plotted by this scholarship found expression in major elements of Katz's later narrative writings on German Judaism. Although a number of these writings will be presented, his widely heralded book *A House Divided: Orthodoxy and Schism in Nineteenth-Century Central Europe*, first published in Hebrew in 1995, will be highlighted. A culminating achievement that goes far beyond its seemingly discrete subject matter, this work displays the concerns and conclusions that a mature Katz brought to this subject of Judaism and the Jewish response to the modern Occident. Here the thematic continuity that occupied his attention for a lifetime will be emphasized, and the precise manner in which he elucidated the Jewish response to the modern world through his work on the German Jewish community will be underscored. In so doing, I hope to emphasize the enduring importance of his work for the scholarly reconstruction of the modern Jewish experience as well as the ongoing vitality his insights provide for understanding the course of Jewish life in the modern West.

Sociological Frameworks and Concerns

In his 1934 doctoral dissertation, "Die Entstehung der Judenassimilation in Deutschland und deren Ideologie" (The Rise of Jewish Assimilation in Germany and its Ideology), Katz already focused on the responses of Jews and Judaism as the people and the religion moved from the confines of a traditional society to the challenges of coping with a neutral one.[1] This motif was to occupy his attention throughout his scholarly career. The task that confronted Katz in addressing this issue was how to define and measure this evolution, and to signify what it meant for the beliefs of Judaism and the structure of Jewish life. The form of history that he ultimately felt to be most suitable to accomplish these goals was what he identified, somewhat idiosyncratically, as social history.[2] Social history, as Katz characterized it decades after his dissertation, "is concerned not with the single occurrence, but with the social reality at a given time. . . . In other words, social history is concerned with describing institutions within the framework of . . . events."[3]

From the very outset of his career, Katz had been profoundly schooled in and influenced by sociologists such as Weil, Mannheim, Weber, and Tönnies. It is thus hardly surprising that he turned, in *Tradition and Crisis*, to the methodology of the ideal-type as well as to the themes and concerns of contemporary sociology. The aim of the ideal-type was to isolate elements of social reality in order to explain their significance and importance. Katz deemed this theoretical construct appropriate for measuring the nature and institutions of Judaism and the Jewish community during the premodern period. He felt it could be employed to characterize the institutional and cultural reality of a nascent Central European Jewish modernity as well. He therefore used the ideal-type to measure the adaptation and persistence that challenged and marked Jewish leaders and organizations as they coped with the onslaught brought on by this transformed setting. Because it was a method designed to focus on institutions, it led him, in *Tradition and Crisis*, to eschew a narrative history and to emphasize how the structures of the Jewish community were altered by its encounter with the modern world.

1 This dissertation is reprinted in Jacob Katz, *Emancipation and Assimilation, Studies in Modern Jewish History* (Westmead, Farnborough: Gregg International, 1972).

2 For a comprehensive treatment of how Katz employed this term, see the analysis of Paula Hyman, "Jacob Katz as Social Historian," in Jay M. Harris, ed., *The Pride of Jacob: Essays on Jacob Katz and His Work* (Cambridge, Mass.: Harvard University Center for Jewish Studies, 2002).

3 Jacob Katz, *Tradition and Crisis: Jewish Society at the End of the Middle Ages* (New

In *Tradition and Crisis*, as well as elsewhere in his writings, Katz offered an overarching and insightful analysis of how modernity had destroyed the traditional parameters that had marked the Jewish community as a public corporation possessing legal authority over all its members. Instead, the modern world, by destroying communal legal bounds, had essentially defined Judaism in religious terms alone. In the process, it reduced Judaism to a largely voluntary association. As a result, Jewish pluralism became unavoidable, and in a country like the United States, voluntarism became virtually absolute.[4] The explanation Katz offered for this phenomenon was straightforward and direct. As the modern state had dismantled the traditional political structure of the community, no one group could any longer impose its definition of proper Jewish practice and belief upon the entire Jewish community. Judaism became a matter of assumed identity for many, and Jewish beliefs and practices became issues of negotiation and re-negotiation. The ideal-type allowed Katz to highlight this change. He was also able to turn to a broad sociological tradition for an analysis of this situation precisely because this tradition centered its discussion of modern western social trends around the theme of community and its political and cultural transformation. From this perspective, it can be said that Katz simply applied the concerns and questions of contemporary sociological discourse to the field of modern European Jewish history.

This view of the transformation in the ideal of community was best captured in the writings of the famed German sociologist Ferdinand Tönnies, who saw the history of the West as marked by a move from the intimate face-to-face personal relationship of the premodern *Gemeinschaft* (community) to the rationally ordered and bureaucratically dominated patterns of an impersonal *Gesellschaft* (society). In this transition from a folk to an urban society, traditional frameworks for community — and the patterns of culture, religion, politics, and social relations that supported them — were challenged and often collapsed.

York: Free Press of Glencoe, 1961; paperback ed., New York: Schocken Books, 1971), p. 5.

4 For Katz's point on this score, see his "Introduction," in Jacob Katz, ed., *Toward Modernity: The European Jewish Model* (New Brunswick, N.J.: Transaction Books, 1987), pp. 1–2. On p. 2, he observes, "Under the impact of rationalization and enlightenment the state relinquished its claim to be directly responsible for the religious

Katz was well versed in these themes and employed the framework provided by this sociological tradition fully and fruitfully to understand and evaluate the impact that these changes had upon the Jewish community. He understood that this transition from *Gemeinschaft* to *Gesellschaft* was a result of the secularization of life that had come to dominate the modern West. As sociologists employ the term, secularization does not signify the disappearance of religion but rather the constriction of religion and the compartmentalization of life. With the distinction between public and private spheres, religion becomes increasingly consigned to the private realm and no longer plays the role it previously did in informing the beliefs and guiding the activities of either individual persons or entire communities. The structures that formerly supported and sustained religious organizations and beliefs are no longer diffused as organic elements throughout all the institutions of a given society. Instead, they are now shifted, as the sociologist Peter Berger has phrased it, "from society as a whole to much smaller groups of confirmatory individuals."[5] In the wake of such a process, traditional religious beliefs and structures sometimes collapse. However, as Katz realized, such beliefs and structures are at other times simply reformulated to accommodate and adapt to a new reality.

In order to explain the situation that characterized the Jewish community and its religion in modern Germany, Katz masterfully applied the sociological paradigm he had learned at Frankfurt to an analysis of the historical conditions of the Jews. Indeed, a great part of Katz's genius was his realization that this model provided a framework for understanding the elements of continuity, as well as change, that marked Jews and Judaism as they entered the modern setting. The social, educational, and religious institutions and patterns that informed Jewish life in the modern West were pluralistic and no longer exclusively Jewish. Consequently, the structures of modern European Jewish life could no longer foster and transmit the same unified notions of value, discipline, and

---

conduct of the population. In the extreme case, *realized first in the United States*, the state's disclaimer *became absolute*, leading to the separation of church and state" (italics mine).

5 Peter L. Berger, Brigette Berger, and Hansfried Kellner, *The Homeless Mind: Modernization and Consciousness* (New York: Random House, 1974), p. 80.

conduct that they had during the Middle Ages. Modern Jewish life was simply too open and diffuse. As a result, it could not reflect the homogeneity of its medieval antecedent.[6] Katz nevertheless insisted that this more open and pluralistic Jewish world could be comprehended, and he employed this notion of the "privatization of religion" to illuminate the process of change that defined modern Judaism as well as the diverse streams and institutions that were to flow from it.

This sociological sensibility and its attendant concerns allowed Katz to identify important themes for indicating how and why pluralism had come to flourish in the modern setting. He now possessed an apparatus for explaining how and why modern Jewish individuals were able to establish and choose discrete collectivities that could serve as mediating agencies for the promotion of particular ideologies and practices. Moreover, his sociological acumen allowed him to delineate the adaptive mechanisms that marked Jews and the Jewish community as they made the transition from the Middle Ages to modernity despite the fact that their identities were now forged from a heterogeneous variety of divergent ideological and religious sources. It provided a framework that could account for how traditional loyalties were simultaneously preserved *and* transformed. As Katz would put it, Judaism and the Jewish people did not simply collapse and expire when they faced the challenges of the modern world. They adjusted and responded to the reality so as to counteract "the anticipation of an abruptly dissolving Jewish community."[7]

The utility of this sociological imagination for an assessment of Judaism in the modern era was self-evident to Katz. Armed with this methodology and cognizant of the themes and concepts identified by the sociological traditions that had informed his thought, Katz was now prepared to write *Tradition and Crisis*.

Tradition and Crisis *and the Pursuits of a Career*

In the final chapters of *Tradition and Crisis*, Katz confronted the inner intellectual processes of the Jews as well as the changes that marked

---

6 For the concise treatment Katz accorded this theme, see *Tradition and Crisis*, pp.184–86.

7 Jacob Katz, *Out of the Ghetto: The Social Background of Jewish Emancipation 1770–1870*

their institutional structures as they began their dialectical encounter with a nascent but insistent modernity. The motifs and concerns he addressed in these pages were to constitute more than mere touch stones in his work on German Judaism. They also defined the scholarly trajectory and agenda of those who would later come to work in this field, for throughout his career Katz would place the history of the German Jewish community and its leadership at the center of modern Jewish historical scholarship. This community and these leaders consistently constituted a vanguard that stood at the cusp of modernity, and they commanded the attention of scholars who would grasp the directions that Judaism would follow as it responded to the challenges imposed by the modern world. Katz asserted that the history of the German community possessed an importance for all modern Jews that extended far beyond its geographical confines.

A summary of the final pages of *Tradition and Crisis* will indicate why this was so. In them, Katz traced the way in which the *Haskalah* (Jewish Enlightenment), not *Ḥasidut* (Hasidism), shattered the institutional and ideological foundations of traditional Jewish society. Although he wrote appreciatively of *Ḥasidut*, he did not consider it decisive for establishing the course upon which Jewish life in Germany and modern Europe was about to embark.

> Our analysis of Hasidism revealed the extent of the transformation that took place in traditional Jewish society during and after the days when that movement flourished. But all these changes applied only to the internal structure of the society — to the mode of organization, the sources of authority, and the criteria of stratification within society itself. In relation to the world outside, no change at all took place.[8]

In contrast, Katz affirmed that the *Haskalah* signaled a revolutionary change in the Jewish world. "The social turning point to which we have alluded is revealed in the emergence of a new type, the *maskil*, who added to his knowledge of Torah a command of foreign languages, general erudition, and an interest in what was happening in the non-Jewish

---

(Cambridge, Mass.: Harvard University Press, 1973), p. 219.

8 *Tradition and Crisis*, p. 245.

world."[9] The type of cultural change this embodied — the creation of a Jew who turned to the non-Jewish world for his intellectual values — was accompanied by other transformations in Jewish life. "After the emergence of the *maskilim*, new ideals pertaining to daily living, the organization and leadership of society, and the methods of education came to be formulated in a programmatic manner."[10] Katz was to devote considerable attention in his later works to a description of how far-reaching these changes in intellectual constructs and organizational frameworks were for the formation of a new type of Jew as well as a new kind of Jewish leader. Indeed, his focus upon cultural warrants and foundations would permit him to emphasize with great subtlety those elements of continuity between past and present that marked nineteenth-century Central European Jewish society. At the same time, this concern permitted him to identify those components of discontinuity that emerged as both Jewish individuals and the Jewish community engaged in the challenges of adjusting to the modern condition.

Of course, in the last years of the eighteenth century, as the larger world moved from the more personal realm of *Gemeinschaft* to the broader dimensions of *Gesellschaft*, it was not entirely clear how this process of adjustment would evolve. As Katz pointed out, a feeling emerged among many "that ultimately the utter eclipse of Jewish society would come about."[11] Nor were such sentiments completely unfounded. Processes of change in the larger world promoted the transformations that were about to take place in the political structure as well as the social boundaries of the community. The activities of the traditional *kehillah* — payment of taxes, liquidation of businesses due to bankruptcy, collection of promissory notes — were transferred to the state, and "direct means of compulsion, i.e., the *herem*," were curtailed. In other words, Jewish political autonomy and the coercive communal legal authority that accompanied it were destroyed with the advent of the modern world. Nevertheless, Katz did not argue that modernity was therefore the absolute solvent in which the Jewish community would dissolve. After all, if complete "withdrawal" from Jewish society were to have occurred, then "not only would the institutions [of that society have broken] down,

9   Ibid. p.246.
10 Ibid.
11 Ibid.
12 Ibid.

but even their reconstruction would be renounced. The individuals in the Jewish society would then be absorbed by the surrounding society and their needs would be met through the institutions operating there. Jewish society... never went to that extreme."[12] Thus, Katz was to focus on the theme of Jewish reformulation, not dissolution, in his historiographic corpus.

As Katz explained, the changes produced by the modern world in no way compelled the individual Jew to abandon Jewish society, though many did ultimately transfer their social-cultural goals "to the context of the surrounding non-Jewish cultural milieu." Echoing themes first discussed in his dissertation, Katz asserted that many Jews began to regard non-Jewish society "as a source of social gratification," and not just "as a framework for economic activity," for a non-Jewish class had emerged, one in "which the difference of religion had lost its circumscribing function."[13] This meant that elite elements in both the Christian world as well as the Jewish community could form a social and cultural order beyond their communities of origin. As Katz phrased it, "The essence of the rationalists' social achievement lay precisely in their creation of a neutral basis above religious difference. . . . From this point on, there was a third sphere — the neutral, human one — to which members of both religions could belong."[14]

To be sure, for some of these Jewish rationalists, the creation of this "neutral sphere" did lead to the abandonment of Judaism. Yet, the emergence of such a realm did not mean that most Jews would follow this path. Indeed, the overwhelming majority continued to adhere in significant measure to Jewish society. Nor did the birth of this world mark the death-knell of Jewish communal structures. Rather, it meant, as Katz was to point out again and again in his *oeuvre*, that a reconfiguration of the structures of Jewish society and the aspirations of Jewish individuals was destined to take place. Indeed, what intrigued Katz was delineating how modernizing Jews such as Mendelssohn and his successors preserved their links to the Jewish community while reformulating both their own values and the institutions of the community during their lengthy acculturation into the politics and norms of a broader German society.

13 Ibid. p. 251.
14 Ibid. p. 255.

Katz repeatedly emphasized that neither Jewish individuals nor the communal institutions of Jewish society atrophied and died with the advent of modernity. Instead, both the Jewish community and Jewish religion were reconfigured and reinvented in light of a changed cultural, social, political, and religious order. Modernity did not simply foster assimilation. It also promoted an integration and adaptation that allowed Jews to create new ways — some more, some less successful — of being Jewish. In this sense, the German *maskilim* were harbingers of what was to come for virtually all western Jews.

After all, as Katz, quoting Gershom Scholem, correctly observed, numerous German Jews in the nineteenth century would discard "the burden of tradition, particularly in its normative halakhic form."[15] Yet, most of them did not leave Judaism, nor would they cast off their identity as Jews. Instead, modernity allowed them to claim "new sources of authority" informed by notions drawn from the surrounding culture that caused them to formulate principles that they claimed constituted sufficient grounds for "a renewal and reconstruction" of Jewish life apart from Jewish law.[16] Thus, the nineteenth century witnessed the birth of diverse Jewish responses to modernity. They ranged from a Reform Judaism that affirmed the Enlightenment axioms of historical evolution and philosophical-scientific-moral progress as the basis for charting a new course for Jewish existence, on the one hand, to a Zionist movement that drew upon the contemporaneous Romantic ideal of *Volksgeist* to promote a renewal of the Jewish national ideal, on the other. Katz paid close attention to the different points on this continuum, and analyzed these and other trends in his academic corpus. In *Tradition and Crisis*, he took careful note of the factors that allowed these changes to emerge so that the Jewish community could reformulate and convert its institutions and cultural-religious patterns to accommodate the parameters fixed by a new era.

The key figure in his analysis was, of course, Moses Mendelssohn, for Mendelssohn established and embodied an ethos and sensibility that fostered and facilitated such transformation. Mendelssohn, Katz

---

15 Jacob Katz, "The Suggested Relationship between Sabbatianism, Haskalah, and Reform," in Katz, *Divine Law in Human Hands: Case Studies in Halakhic Flexibility* (Jerusalem: The Magnes Press, 1998), p.522.

16 Ibid. p.515.

wrote, critiqued Jewish organizations "that continued to operate along traditional lines. . . . In his opinion, all the powers of compulsion which the Jewish organizations had taken into their hands had come about through imitation of the Christian Church."[17] However historically questionable this Mendelssohnian assessment, it led to the position "that . . . only those Jewish organizations that were voluntary associations of individuals whose formation stemmed from the similarity of faith and ritual to which they adhered should be formed."[18] In putting forth this argument, Mendelssohn articulated a rationale that was congenial to the ethos that informed the modern West. It was also a rationale that Samson Raphael Hirsch would adopt and develop a century later in his struggle for Orthodox secession from the general Jewish community. Katz, by identifying it here, was to articulate a concern that would occupy his attention for the next several decades and that would culminate in *A House Divided*.

The alterations in the intellectual warrants that guided the Jewish Enlighteners as well as the transformations that already reduced the political power and social functions of the *kehillah* were signals that Jewish cultural and political life was already in the midst of being overhauled. Indeed, the description and analysis of the ways in which Jews engaged in the process of reconfiguring their institutions and reformulating their culture throughout the subsequent century would remain a matter of constant concern for Katz in his ongoing scholarship. From this perspective, there is a direct line from *Tradition and Crisis* in the 1950s and *Out of the Ghetto* in the 1970s to *A House Divided* in 1995.

In *Tradition and Crisis*, Katz did not confine his analysis of the transformations that marked Jewish life to intellectual and political spheres alone. He also took note of allied educational and religious changes that came to mark the Jewish community at this time. He observed that educational institutions were created along rationalist lines, and he was keenly aware that, in the sphere of religion, a number of Jews began to insist that there could be a "harmonization" between the tradition and the values of the neutral society. Indeed, a number of these people — forerunners of a position that was to characterize modern Orthodox

17 *Tradition and Crisis*, p. 263.
18 Ibid.

Jews — even continued to accept its ritual "yoke in practice."[19] Finally, Katz pointed out that the synagogue was the least shaken and most adaptive of the traditional institutions, though its functions were curtailed. Increasingly, it was devoted to public prayer alone and a western aesthetic increasingly came to inform its external architecture and internal decor as well as the form of ritual that took place there — the melodies and style of prayers.[20] All these modifications in Jewish life would come to inform not only the practices of Liberal German Jews, but also Orthodox Jews such as Samson Raphael Hirsch himself in the next century, albeit that the formal conservatism that guided the Orthodox would not allow them to change the wordings of the prayers themselves. However, given the definition of Judaism as a religion that would come to predominate in the modern setting, as well as the ubiquitous and unrelenting pressures the modern world would exert on Occidental Jews, such reductions in organizational function and changes in cultural expression are hardly surprising.

Writing in *Toward Modernity* almost thirty years after *Tradition and Crisis*, Katz indicated precisely why the themes he had identified in *Tradition and Crisis* occupied his attention throughout his career, and why the German Jewish experience remained so vital a part of his concerns. In arguing for the seminal import of the *maskilim* and the German venue in the shaping of modern Jewish history, Katz wrote about Mendelssohn's role in the process:

> Mendelssohn's contribution [in the shaping of the new trend in Jewish history] became of decisive importance; due to him Jewish aspirations to have access to non-Jewish society were not simply displayed in practice, as in England, but carried out under the cover of intellectual vindication. Jewish modernization in Germany turned articulate. The educational reform was in practice accepted by Austro-Hungarian Jewry out of the hands of the government, but its ideological exposition came from Berlin, from Naftali Herz Wessely.
>
> By virtue of intellectual articulation the German-Jewish social experiment became mobile, and that is why we find its influence

19 Ibid. p.269.
20 Ibid. pp.270–71.

in all the countries where similar experiments became the order of the day. The later stages of modernization, leading up to Reform, *Wissenschaft des Judentums*, and neo-Orthodoxy, came then simply as a continuation of the initial process. They too excelled in seeking literary expression of their tendencies, and due to it they became exemplary, to be emulated by their adherents and shunned and rejected by their adversaries.[21]

In assessing the themes and concerns that marked *Tradition and Crisis*, it is clear that Katz laid the foundation for understanding how Judaism reformulated itself intellectually, culturally, and religiously in light of the impact of the modern world. As Katz saw it, modernity dismantled the political structure of the traditional *kehillah*. At the same time, it promoted new ways for elements in the community to establish structures that would allow for the exercise of influential religious authority. Modernity fostered assimilation. Simultaneously, it allowed for the creation of new ways in which Jewish identity could be expressed. Modernity caused many Jews to abandon a traditional allegiance to *Halakhah* and classical Jewish religious belief. Nevertheless, it permitted the rise of a modern Jewish religious denominationalism that promoted novel ways to live a Jewish religious life. It also led to a nationalist Jewish expression that fostered the Zionist movement, culminating in the creation of the State of Israel. Katz identified all these directions in this early work. His subsequent writings on German Judaism and Jewish communal life would address precisely how these events and movements unfolded over the next century.

Secession and Modernity

The writings of Jacob Katz on the issues delineated above are legion, and a complete discussion and analysis of the attention he accorded all these topics in his many essays and books on Judaism and the Jews in Germany are beyond the scope of this or any single presentation. However, *A House Divided: Orthodoxy and Schism in Nineteenth-Century Central Europe* clearly constitutes his culminating work on a number of

---

21 *Toward Modernity*, pp.11–12.

these themes: it not only brought together in narrative form many of the subjects that he addressed in his earlier work; it also allowed a fully mature Katz to offer a valedictory on a lifetime of scholarship. In it, Katz did more than focus upon the struggle for secession that engaged large elements of the Orthodox Jewish community in Hungary and Germany during the nineteenth century — the ostensible subject of the book. He also allowed his reader to see how this struggle reflected upon the larger issues of political and religious-cultural transformations that marked the Jewish community in its encounter with and response to modernity.[22]

In *Toward Modernity*, Katz had specifically observed that the challenge confronting the scholar in defining Jewish modernity was to determine the criteria whereby "the modern variation of" the Jewish community "could be differentiated from its predecessor, traditional Jewish society." And these criteria, he pointed out, could be summed up as follows: in the earlier society, "the observance of the Jewish tradition could and would be enforced by the organs of the Jewish community. The authority to do so was conferred on the Jewish community by the state, and constituted a part of communal autonomy. There was also a measure of control over the spread of ideas. . . . The post-traditional Jewish community was denied the right to impose its will concerning *thought and action* on the individual."[23]

Hence, in Katz's schematization, modernity arose for the Jewish community when two factors were realized. First, when a limitation was imposed upon the political authority of the community. Then its organizational structures were stripped of virtually all vestiges of legal power, and Jewish institutional authorities could no longer employ coercion to impose their will upon individual Jews. Secondly, when the thought of large numbers of individual Jews no longer derived primarily, if at all, from the intellectual-legal-religious sources of Judaism. In such a setting, Jewish thought expanded beyond the parameters of Jewish tradition, and warrants for legitimating actions were routinely drawn from the surrounding culture. In *A House Divided*, Katz centered his discussion of the Jewish communal schism in nineteenth-century Central

---

22 Jacob Katz, *A House Divided: Orthodoxy and Schism in Nineteenth-Century Central European Jewry*, trans. by Ziporah Brody (Hanover, N.H.: Brandeis University Press, 1998).

23 *Toward Modernity*, p.1 (italics mine).

Europe on these two themes. In so doing, he elevated the significance of his discussion: beyond presenting and analyzing the individual historical events themselves, he demonstrated how the unfolding of this story cast light on the larger issue of how Jews and Judaism responded to the reality of a modern world.

In pointing to this larger theoretical concern, Katz emphasized here, as in past work, that the Jewish responses to the modern condition were multivalent and adaptive. Indeed, the German Jewish community did not disappear, nor did all its members abandon the tradition. In fact, as Katz indicated, one element in this community would ultimately identify itself and be identified by others as Orthodox Jews who "continued to demand the observance of tradition in all its details." It was this group that occupied the great bulk of his attention in *A House Divided*, for these Jews maintained their fidelity to the ritual tradition "despite the changes in the status of the congregations (*kehillot*) and the abrogation by the secular authorities of their power of religious coercion." Furthermore, Katz noted that while Mendelssohn and others in Europe "imagined the Jewish congregations as voluntary frameworks," this vision, he maintained, was in reality "slow to materialize. The inclusion of Jews among the citizens of the state brought about the abrogation of many functions and powers of the *kehillah*, but not of the obligation of membership in it incumbent on all adherents of the Jewish religion. The requirement of membership in a congregation remained in force for most of the nineteenth century."[24] For, as Katz observed, the *kehillah*, "was [still] treated as the organizational framework of a religious community, like one of the Christian churches. Because of this formal classification, the *kehillah* could, with the help of authorities, obligate every Jew in its area of jurisdiction to be a member."[25] Jewish communities in America, "where no external forces impinged," were, in contrast to the German Jewish community of the 1800s, completely voluntary associations, where individual Jews were absolutely free "to organize around synagogues with different styles and prayer services [or not], according to their individual choice." Katz's study of how the German Orthodox reacted to this reality would both embody and illuminate the course of modern Jewish history. The demise of the absolute

24 *A House Divided*, p.7.
25 Ibid. p.9.

power the *kehillah* had enjoyed, as well as the emergence of religious pluralism in the modern situation, proved both challenging and problematic to all Jews. Indeed, in emphasizing this demise and in delineating the diverse ways in which both individual Jews as well as Jewish communal organizations responded and adapted to it, Katz provided the core narrative that has marked the study and teaching of all modern Jewish history. It is Jacob Katz who provided the conceptual framework that has dominated the writing of the modern Jewish experience.

For these reasons, Katz, as he wrote in another essay, turned to modern Orthodox Judaism as *a*, if not *the*, paradigmatic and instructive response to modernity. Orthodox Judaism, like every other stream of modern Judaism, arose in a specific historical context. Like the more liberal branches and movements it ultimately would decry, it did not arise in a vacuum. Orthodox Jews, no less than their non-Orthodox co-religionists, did not live in what Katz — following the insights that modern sociological tradition offered on this topic — labeled a "tradition-bound" society, one where "tradition was a self-understood and uncontested guide to both religious observance and religious thought." Consequently, "The awareness of other Jews' rejection of tradition," Katz averred, "was . . . an essential and universal characteristic of all forms and variations of Orthodoxy." Orthodoxy, he concluded, was therefore a creation of the modern situation itself. It was "a method of confronting deviant trends, and of responding to the very same stimuli which produced these trends."[26]

Those Jews who perceived themselves as the guardians of an unbroken tradition had to confront the novel reality of a German world where the political functions of the community were severely curtailed and where shared religious values could no longer provide the ideological basis for communal unity. After all, Liberal Judaism promulgated principles and practices that many of these Orthodox Jews perceived as destructive to Judaism. The question of how to deal with these other

---

26 *Toward Modernity*, pp. 3–5. For parallels to this insight in modern sociological writing, see Berger, *The Heretical Imperative*, p. 29. There Berger describes the dilemma that the Orthodox of all faiths must confront when dealing with a modern pluralistic situation where empirical reality means that tradition no longer "has the quality of a taken for granted fact." Katz, in *Toward Modernity*, echoes the point made by Berger. Once more, his sociological sensibility is apparent.

Jews in the institutional structures of the community emerged as a focal point of debate and the issue of "organizational affiliation . . . became an important basis of modern Orthodoxy."[27]

As Katz traced the evolution and typology of Orthodox responses on this matter prior to *A House Divided*, he emphasized the centrality of Rabbi Moses Schreiber of Pressburg, also known as the Ḥatam Sofer, or Moses Sofer. In Katz's opinion, the Ḥatam Sofer had articulated the first major Orthodox response that "grasped the full significance of the problem and took a principled, aggressive stance" toward it.[28] In a famous responsum to Rabbi Abraham Eliezer from Trieste on the membership of the Hamburg Reform Temple, the Ḥatam Sofer wrote, "Were their sentence put in our hands, I would separate them from us, forbidding our sons to marry their daughters, so as not to be drawn after them, and their sect would be like that of Zadoq and Boethus, Anan and Saul, they following their ways, and we ours."[29] However, as Katz noted, the Ḥatam Sofer immediately added a disclaimer: "This is only in theory but not in practice, for without the permission of the king . . . my words have no authority." As a result, the Ḥatam Sofer's words, in Katz's phrasing, were "reduced to mere musings." The Ḥatam Sofer understood that the traditional authorities had, "at this stage," already "lost their ability to enforce the observance of the religious commandments. Individuals could violate the Sabbath in public and commit any of the sins proscribed in the Bible, and the leadership of the community, rabbinical and lay alike, had no means to force them to cease their activities or to expel them from the community."[30] The problem that now confronted these men was that "the functioning of the *Halakhah* as a judicial system" became contingent upon the "acceptance of its validity by those involved [in it]," and such acceptance was precisely what the "transgressors" refused to grant.[31]

By the onset of the nineteenth century, the political apparatus that had marked the traditional medieval *kehillah* had been dismantled, and

27 Ibid. p. 8.
28 Katz, "Towards a Biography of the Hatam Sofer," in *Divine Law in Human Hands*, p. 403.
29 *Responsa of the Hatam Sofer* 6:89. This responsum is cited by Katz in "The Controversy over the Temple in Hamburg," in *Divine Law in Human Hands*, p. 225.
30 Ibid.
31 Ibid. p. 228.

whatever vestiges of coercive political authority that remained to the rabbinate were soon destined to disappear. The rabbis were reduced to exercising "influential authority" alone. The genius of the Ḥatam Sofer was that he was the first traditional rabbi to comprehend fully that the world had changed. Katz, in analyzing his statements, was able to assert that rulings of the type issued by the Ḥatam Sofer on such matters did not embody a genuine "halakhic argument." Rather, in a world where the political power formerly enjoyed by the rabbinate had been re-moved, the Ḥatam Sofer was compelled to face the task of "weighing the advantages gained to the cause of religion by [choosing among] var-ious alternative steps." Hence, the Ḥatam Sofer engaged in what Katz labeled "religious policymaking."[32]

In offering this assessment of these responsa, Katz was not dismissing the importance of the stance the Ḥatam Sofer had adopted. Instead, he was displaying an analytic clarity that would better elucidate the significance and meaning of that stance. After all, legal philosophers have routinely indicated that law often functions as what Ronald Dworkin has identified as a "policy." Here the law aims imaginatively to express and preserve the community's highest principles and ideals in the light of the limitations imposed by a contemporary situation. A policy represents a broadly based goal warranted by the overarching spirit that animates the legal tradition, and it becomes legally actionable as a guide that directs the community, or a segment of the community, as its leaders attempt to construct its present and seek to shape its future.[33]

By employing this type of theoretical construct, Katz allowed his reader to understand that the particular events presented regarding one specific historical figure possessed a representative significance for com-prehending the larger story of how Jews and Judaism responded to the modern world. The type of "prudential calculus" involved in "religious policymaking," as advanced in this instance by the Ḥatam Sofer, per-mitted Katz to emphasize the elements of commonality that Schreiber, despite his Hungarian setting, shared with both Mendelssohn, who preceded him, and Samson Raphael Hirsch, who rose to prominence after him. After all, the Mendelssohnian notion of "a voluntary com-

32 Ibid. p. 229.
33 See Ronald Dworkin, "Is Law a System of Rules?" in R. M. Dworkin, ed., *The Philosophy of Law* (Oxford and New York: Oxford University Press, 1977), p. 45.

munity," as well as the "policy of secession" that Hirsch was destined to advance, are highly reminiscent of Schreiber, and they reflect the reality of a Central European Jewish world where secularization had made considerable inroads. The political unity of the Jewish community was splintered, and an attendant compartmentalization of Jewish life resulted, one that would have been impossible in a traditional setting. The description and analysis Katz offered through the utilization of this conceptual category highlighted this reality, for the "old rules" could no longer be applied in a direct manner. Instead, the new age required that "new policies" be formulated to cope with the demands of a changed setting.

At the same time, the focus Katz placed on modernization also allowed him to highlight the lines of distinction that separated these men. By paying careful attention to the intellectual grounds each man put forth to justify his policy on the political nature of the Jewish community in the modern situation, Katz was able to explore the ideological elements that distinguished all of these men from their medieval counterparts. Simultaneously, he provided a subtle description of the intellectual foundations that indicated how these men differed from one another as well.

In *A House Divided*, the reactions of the Orthodox rabbinate in general and Samson Raphael Hirsch in particular to the Reform Braunschweig Rabbinical Conference of 1844 constituted a key chapter in comprehending the course of the Jewish adaptation to modernity. In offering his description and evaluation of this event and these reactions, Katz noted that the overwhelming response of the Orthodox rabbis was a "dogmatic" one that reflected their inability to grasp the nature and enormity of the task the modern world was presenting to them. They put forth a furious attack against the Braunschweig Reformers and asserted rigidly, "Neither we nor anyone else has the authority to nullify even the least of the religious laws." Furthermore, they ascribed only the basest intentions to their opponents, claiming that "the motives of those who rid themselves of the burden of the commandments and customs is only 'the unrestrained pursuit of fame, wealth, and pleasure.'"[34]

Their fury was not difficult to comprehend. After all, the Reform

34 *A House Divided*, p. 234.

Assembly, in the realm of ritual, abolished *Kol Nidrei*,[35] and it discussed
the abolition of *metzitzah* (part of the circumcision ritual). Moreover,
in the realm of personal status, the Assembly addressed the issue of
allowing marriage between Jews and non-Jews of monotheistic faiths.
These matters, combined with a Reform posture that led to the removal
of passages in the traditional prayer book that mentioned the return to
Zion, the rebuilding of the Jerusalem Temple, and the renewal of sacrifices, understandably aroused the ire of the Orthodox. Yet Katz observed
that the arguments put forth by most "Orthodox ideologues" against
these deviations from the tradition reflected "their inability or unwill-
ingness to deal with the intellectual arguments and the rational and
historical critiques which . . . were set forth to justify throwing off the
yoke of the commandments."[36] The polemics these rabbis issued were,
of course, largely irrelevant to those Reform leaders whom they condemned. As Katz indicated, these traditionalists simply did not recognize the changed reality that they now had to face.

To be sure, some rabbis did recognize that a new situation obtained.
Although they remained a minority at the beginning of the decade, Katz
assigned these men, as he had the *maskilim* in the previous century,
great historical significance. For these rabbis recognized, albeit regret-
fully, "that the government [was] no longer willing to serve as an inter-
mediary to force others to observe the tradition as the rabbis [under-
stood] it."[37] By the end of the 1840s, their perception became dominant
in Orthodox circles, and "the idea of collective coercion" had vanished
"from the minds of [even] the most conservative Jew."[38] The Orthodox
no longer sought "to fence in the breaches in the lives of the community"
by appealing to "governmental support."[39] Indeed, this realization was
soon combined with recognition that in Germany, by mid-century,
"the abandonment of a traditional way of life [had become] a common

---

35　Interestingly, Hirsch himself, in response to the same pressures that confronted the
　　Liberals, once abolished the recitation of *Kol Nidrei* early in his career at Oldenberg in
　　1839. See Mordechai Breuer, *Modernity within Tradition: The Social History of Ortho-
　　doxy in Imperial Germany*, trans. Elizabeth Petuchowski (New York: Columbia
　　University Press, 1992), p.32.

36　*A House Divided*, p.34.

37　Ibid. p.240.

38　Ibid.

39　Ibid. p.241.

phenomenon."[40] As Katz had already noted in *Out of the Ghetto*, this placed "conservatives (i.e., Orthodox leaders) in a quandary."[41] Excision of Liberal and secular Jews from the Jewish community was simply not feasible in a situation where the overwhelming majority of Jews had rejected fidelity to the halakhic tradition. Nor, in light of the commitment that the traditionalists had to Jewish law, could they ignore the fact that that same law stipulated that children born of Jewish mothers were marked by Jewish status. Nevertheless, what did emerge from all this, as Katz observed, was that the "[traditional] idea of mutual responsibility [*areivut*]" that one Jew possessed for another did become attenuated as "the bonds of the traditional community" were removed or loosened.[42]

The question confronting the Orthodox remained one of deciding on an appropriate institutional response to this reality. The Ḥatam Sofer had already begun to formulate one response in his reaction to the Hamburg Temple Reformers two decades earlier. Yet, his was a "rejectionist Orthodoxy," one that eschewed the blandishments of modern culture. As Katz pointed out, Moses Sofer believed "that reformulating Jewish tradition in a European idiom meant also exposing it to rationalistic examination. Thus tradition would be brought before the tribunal of reason and called upon to vindicate its truths. It would have to be prepared then to accept the judgment of its investigators, whose method would lead to selective acceptance and rejection."[43]

This approach was not palatable to the German traditionalists, whose chief intellectual feature, like that of the liberals whom they frequently detested, was cultural integration into the surrounding milieu. For this reason, Katz, in *A House Divided*, turned his attention to Samson Raphael Hirsch. Katz identified Hirsch as the central figure in the "neo-Orthodox" response to the modern situation, and he devoted considerable research to exploring the intellectual formulas and organizational solutions Hirsch proposed to meet the challenges of the modern world. He believed that Hirsch, more than any other Orthodox leader of the 1840s, correctly perceived, as the Ḥatam Sofer had two decades earlier

---

40 Ibid. p.254.
41 *Out of the Ghetto*, pp.142–60.
42 *A House Divided*, p.240.
43 *Out of the Ghetto*, p.157.

in reaction to the Hamburg Reformers, the fact that a new reality obtained. Hirsch recognized "that reform was conceived as a reaction, albeit a misguided one, to the disintegration of traditional society." Reform "was not" condemned by Hirsch as "its cause." In offering this assessment of the situation, Hirsch, Katz pointed out, echoed the "ideas . . . expressed by [his teacher] R. [Jacob] Ettlinger." However, "in contrast to his teacher's despair of changing the situation," Hirsch, at this juncture in his career, believed that he had a program "to heal the breach." This program was one of educational adaptation to and cultural affirmation of the contours imposed by this new era. Later known by the slogan *Torah im derekh eretz*,[44] this type of Jewish Orthodoxy, in contrast to the "rejectionist Orthodoxy" advanced by the Ḥatam Sofer and his school, embraced the culture and social mores of the surrounding German society. Hirsch felt influential authority could be exercised by the Orthodox over the total Jewish community only if such adjustments were made by those loyal to the tradition.

In making these observations, Katz alerted his readers to the changes that had taken place in the Jewish world, including its traditional sector, in its encounter with modernity. After all, Hirsch represented "a new type" of Orthodox leader, one who affirmed the cultural worth of the modern world and who looked to intellectual warrants and cultural tropes drawn from figures ranging from Goethe to Kant to justify and bolster the position of the traditionalist camp. The attention Katz had devoted in his earlier works to identifying "new sources of authority," informed by notions taken from non-Jewish culture, as a means of measuring the "renewal and reconstruction" in Jewish life came to guide him here as well. This emphasis upon cultural warrants and intellectual formulations allowed Katz to underscore the critical role Hirsch played in the formation of a new variety of traditional Judaism.

However, Katz was not content to confine his analysis of Hirsch to the cultural realm alone. By continuing his focus upon organizational structures as well, Katz was able to point out how Hirsch's ideological commitments led him to advocate a novel political configuration

---

44 Hirsch popularized this educational philosophy through the saying found in Pirkei Avot 2.2:" Yafeh Talmud torah im derekh erets" (An excellent thing is the study of Torah combined with worldly occupation.) Hirsch interpreted the phrase as signifying modern culture.

for the Jewish community in the modern setting. For Hirsch, like his teacher Ettlinger, soon came to recognize that no program of cultural reconstruction could ultimately succeed in allowing the Orthodox to realize their hegemony over the entire community. Too much had changed. Therefore, as early as 1843, Hirsch, despite the cultural divide that separated him from the Ḥatam Sofer, began to echo Schreiber's thoughts on an organizational solution to this dilemma. Hirsch, as Katz put it, now started to toy seriously with "the idea of schism" as the one way to remedy the ills that confronted Judaism and Jewish people as Jewish traditionalists were compelled to grapple with the transformed reality of the modern era.[45] The solution that occurred to Hirsch, as Katz put it, was "the establishment of separate communities, composed exclusively of those loyal to Torah, which would divorce themselves from the overall organization encompassing all the Jews of a place."[46]

The very contemplation of such a proposal indicated, according to Katz, that Hirsch had already begun by the 1840s to arrive at the conclusion that there was no overarching remedy for the afflictions of widespread non-observance and unbelief that marked modern Central European Jewish life. Only a novel institutional structure could provide relief from the burdens secularization had imposed upon the Jewish world. While the focus here was upon the Orthodox, Katz remained aware that this Orthodox response was of historical significance precisely because it was representative of a broader array of Jewish reactions — traditional and liberal alike — to the conditions imposed by modernity. As a "test case" of the Jewish responses, it reflected how Judaism, including its most traditional sectors, was affected, though not abnegated, by the new realities. The proposed creation of a separatist Orthodox community along the lines of a modern congregational model only testified to the inroads modernization had made in Jewish life, and foreshadowed a growing trend toward a Jewish religious denominationalism that would increasingly come to divide the modern Jewish world. Katz was able to analyze its origins in this episode in modern Jewish history in light of the larger intellectual and political circumstances that modernity had unleashed. Here there is once again

45   Ibid. p.244.
46   Ibid. p.243.

a direct line between the methodology and concerns of social history articulated by Katz in *Tradition and Crisis* and his lifelong project in this area.

Indeed, the historical importance Katz attached to this development is evidenced in the considerable attention he devoted to a description of its content and to an analysis of its meaning. The establishment of a separatist Orthodox community as a way to cope with the challenges of a modern world involved no "mere distancing oneself from an individual who is suspected of one or another transgression." Rather, it required "isolation from a community that has abandoned one of the principles of faith, the subservience to the authority of the Talmud," which alone could serve "as a basis for unity."[47] As a result of Hirsch's efforts, "the idea of separation already began to glimmer in the eyes of the faithful" by the 1840s as a solution to the crisis engendered by the reality of church-state separation.[48]

However, it would take two decades before this policy would fully crystallize. Katz engaged in a meticulous description of the historical factors that promoted this crystallization and crafted a comprehensive analysis of the arguments Hirsch had put forth on this matter during the late 1860s and throughout the 1870s. Katz pointed out that Hirsch had wanted "absolute organizational independence" for the Orthodox by this point in time.[49] In presenting his case for this notion before the gentile authorities of the day, Hirsch acknowledged that the law now granted Orthodox Jews the right to erect separatist congregations apart from the general community. Nevertheless, he complained that despite this privilege, the Orthodox were still compelled to pay taxes to a general *kehillah* that was generally dominated by Reform elements, and he "considered this unfair and a miscarriage of justice."[50] Hirsch claimed that in the premodern world the laity and the rabbinate possessed a shared ideological commitment to Jewish law. For this reason, all Jews obeyed the religious strictures promulgated by the religious leadership of the community. Compulsion, claimed Hirsch, played no

47 Ibid. p.244.
48 Ibid. p.17.
49 Ibid. p.237.
50 Ibid. p.238.

role in promoting such observance. Indeed, Hirsch went beyond the position Mendelssohn had advanced on this issue by denying "the very existence of such coercive measures." As Katz indicated, Hirsch maintained that "the traditional congregation was an institution founded entirely on the will of individuals to observe the *Halakhah;* only a community founded on this principle should be recognized as a legitimate congregation."[51] Of course, as Katz pointed out, this contention was historically unfounded, for, "despite general identification with its values, the leadership did resort to compulsion, the most obvious of which was the ban."[52] Katz concluded from this that Hirsch, in making this claim, had put forth a definition of Judaism that both reduced its traditional parameters and emphasized its religious character in a manner that was in keeping with the ethos of a Protestant-dominated western world that increasingly privatized religious life by removing it from the political arena.

Katz thereby demonstrated that the position Hirsch put forth here was of considerable utility for achieving his political goal of separatist Orthodox congregations. Hirsch had argued that if the Orthodox were compelled by law to continue to pay taxes to the general Jewish *Gemeinde*, it would make it appear as if "Judaism equally grants the right to exist to those who deny religious law and to those who sanctify it."[53] Yet, as Hirsch, writing in 1873 on behalf of a proposed *Austritts-gesetz* ("Law of Secession"), stated, Orthodox Jews "accepted religious customs as the products of revelation, and as Divine Laws," whereas Reform Jews denied this. Consequently, "The differences between the various Christian denominations are no deeper than the differences between Reform Judaism and Orthodox Judaism."[54] Therefore, Hirsch concluded that the State ought to extend the same privilege to Jews that it bestowed upon Christians, and allow Jews, just as it permitted Christians, to leave their religious community if they ceased to identify with its principles.[55] Hirsch thus grounded his argument on behalf of

---

51 *A House Divided*, p. 239.
52 Ibid.
53 Ibid. p. 239.
54 Ibid. p. 242.
55 Ibid.

Orthodox institutional autonomy on a modern warrant embedded in western liberal political theory — the notion of "freedom of conscience." Hirsch, forged as he was by western as well as traditional Jewish culture, may well have actually affirmed this value as worthy in its own right. However, Katz emphasized that what was of special historical note in this episode was that an ideal drawn from the larger culture was assimilated into the consciousness of a modern traditionalist and employed by that figure to serve the cause of tradition in the modern setting. In so doing, Katz illuminated the larger dynamic of how a traditional religion can reach out to a broader intellectual universe and adapt and reformulate itself — its arguments and ideology — so as to cope with the demands of an evolving world.

Of course, here, as elsewhere, Katz was attuned to the subtle dialectics that mark all traditional religious readers, and he did not ignore the role that the religious tradition itself played in the mind of Hirsch as the entire process unfolded. Indeed, Katz offered a minute and characteristically sensitive exposition of the halakhic debate that obtained between Samson Raphael Hirsch and his opponent Seligmann Baer Bamberger, the Würzburger *rav*, over the issue of Orthodox secession from the Frankfurt Jewish community during 1877–1878.[56] Hirsch had maintained that wherever possible, Jewish law demanded Orthodox secession from any Jewish community under non-Orthodox domination. *Contra* Hirsch, Bamberger had argued that Jewish law did not mandate Orthodox secession from a general Jewish communal structure under Liberal control in instances where the community provided financial support for and autonomy to Orthodox institutions. Bamberger based his opposition to secession in part on a legal position that maintained that such Reform Jews did not fall under the Jewish legal rubric of "*mumarim lehakh'is* — principled apostates," but rather under the category of "*mumarim le-tei'avon* — apostates for convenience." The latter category, while serious, did not carry the gravity of the former. By drawing upon these Jewish legal categories and in applying them as he did, Bamberger reasoned that the rebellion these Reform Jews displayed against traditional Judaism resulted from human frailty

---

56 For further discussion of this debate, see chap. 11, "German Jewish Orthodoxy," in the present volume.

and appetite alone. Their rebellion, so construed, did not constitute a dogmatic rejection of classical rabbinic authority. There was no ideological dimension to their non-observance. However incorrect he actually was in applying this typology to the ideology that many of the Reformers in Frankfurt actually championed, the typology itself permitted Bamberger to rule that Jewish law did not proscribe association with such Jews in instances where they supplied for the needs of the Orthodox.

Hirsch responded to this argument by saying, in effect, that this point was completely irrelevant to the case at hand. In fact, Hirsch stated that he in no way prohibited association with Reform Jews as individuals. Indeed, he maintained that in issuing his ruling, he did not speak of Reform Jews at all but was only describing their communities. This distinction was a vital one for Hirsch, for he wrote, "I deliberately use these abstract concepts which refer to the system and not to the people."[57] Indeed, Hirsch engaged here in what legal scholars would label "purposive interpretation" and claimed that the proscriptions found "in earlier sources regarding idolaters, sectarians, and heretics" did not apply to individual persons *per se*, but to "an ideological essence" of heresy. This intellectual construct, as Katz viewed it, meant that Hirsch had no need to apply these sources to "the sectarians and heretics themselves, who no longer exist[ed], but to their spirit, which ha[d] a place of honor in the Reform community."[58] The "burden of the commandments" was now placed on the public, not the individual Jew.[59] In Katz's opinion, "Hirsch's distinction between sectarians and apostates, as opposed to heresy and apostasy, created an unprecedented situation, for which no direct proofs could be found in the sources."[60]

In making this claim, Katz once more revealed his keen sociological-historical awareness and sensitivity. He had learned from his training in history and in the sociology of knowledge that the critical variable involved in an analysis of a legal holding was not determining whether that decision had a precedent. Katz knew that the author of such a ruling frequently had a welter of rules and principles that were capable of providing guidance in a given case. Rather, the point was to focus on

57 Ibid. p.265.
58 Ibid.
59 Ibid. p.275.
60 Ibid. p.271.

the contextual factors that led an author to select one precedent over another, or to indicate what the concerns were that caused that author to reformulate precedents in a novel way. In this instance, Katz emphasized the innovative argument Hirsch used to combine precedents and contemporary language to reconfigure the tradition. Katz was thereby able, through this narration of a discrete historical episode, to underscore the irony inherent in the decision Hirsch rendered on this matter and to highlight the more general process of how religious leaders re-contextualize the past in light of the needs of the present. The Frankfurt rabbi's desire to preserve the Jewish religious tradition drove him to adopt a novel Jewish legal stance unknown to the tradition itself. Through his presentation and analysis of the position advanced by Hirsch, Katz was able to demonstrate the accuracy of the contention he had put forth earlier: that Orthodoxy itself was a creation of the modern world, a self-conscious "method of confronting deviant trends." The consistency of his project and his ability to extract the significant from amidst a mass of details is once more apparent.

Katz's work in *A House Divided* can be seen as the finale of a lifetime of coherent thematic and methodological explorations. In it, he indicated how his lifelong preoccupation with the issue of Jewish continuity and reconfiguration in the face of the challenges imposed by the modern condition played itself out in this instance. In *Tradition and Crisis* and *Out of the Ghetto*, Katz had observed that the early opponents of the *Haskalah* had feared the Jewish Enlighteners' mission of extricating "Jewish society from its cultural isolation by reformulating Jewish teachings in the idiom of the European Enlightenment."[61] They were convinced that such embrace of modern culture would mark the end of Jewish life. Yet, the bulk of the Jewish people remained "linked by deep emotional ties" to their identity as Jews and they insisted on remaining part of the Jewish community.[62] The history Katz offered in *A House Divided* thus confirmed an observation he had made years before. In an article entitled "Judaism and Christianity Against the Backdrop of Modern Secularism," he had written that "history and many other branches of knowledge teach us that the source of religious

---

61   *Out of the Ghetto*, p.157.
62   *A House Divided*, p.266.

commitments lies deeply embedded in the nature of man and that its rational justification is a secondary phenomenon. . . . This is why religion retains much of its power even in the face of [secularism and massive change]."[63]

In *A House Divided*, as in *Out of the Ghetto* and many other essays and books, Katz not only related the way in which neo-traditional German Jewish leaders like Hirsch embraced this cultural change. He also analyzed how the defenders of Jewish tradition, despite such change, refused to allow the Jewish community and its institutions to dissolve. The culture and institutions of the Jewish community did not disintegrate. They were maintained and rebuilt. By emphasizing and illuminating the process and mechanics of this reconstruction, Katz was able to show that such change, "by its very nature, generated the forces that halted and reversed the tide of dissolution" in both the political and cultural realms.[64] The themes of cultural integration and political reorganization that marked his early writings found expression in his later works as well. They have left us with a portrait of the German Jewish response to the modern world that is dynamic and sophisticated. As such, the legacy of Jacob Katz is enduring: he has defined an agenda that later generations of scholars will no doubt explore for years to come.

In his *With My Own Eyes: The Autobiography of an Historian*, Katz observed that Yitzhak Baer had once told him "that the only proof of the validity of a historical method is its ability to describe historical processes in a convincing manner."[65] This essay has attempted to indicate how the historical processes that define the origins and explain the dimensions and directions of Jewish modernity have been convincingly illuminated by Jacob Katz's investigations of the German Jewish experience. His work provides an invaluable intellectual legacy for those of us who follow.

---

63 Jacob Katz, "Judaism and Christianity Against the Backdrop of Modern Secularism," in Katz, *Jewish Emancipation and Self-Emancipation* (Philadelphia: Jewish Publication Society, 1986), p. 47.

64 *Out of the Ghetto*, p. 124.

65 Jacob Katz, *With My Own Eyes: The Autobiography of an Historian* (Hanover, N.H.: Brandeis University Press, 1995), p. 168.

3

Max Weber on Judaism and the Jews

A Reflection on the Position of Jews in the Modern World

Max Weber stands as one of the truly seminal thinkers in the history of western intellectual thought. His interest in understanding how a particular approach to life — which he called "rational" — had become a potent force in history animated and informed his voluminous writings and researches. He was certain that a comprehension of this approach and the ethos that marked it would yield insight into the current nature and future direction of modern society. Weber was further convinced that the teachings of ancient Judaism had played a major role in the development of this ethos, and he therefore devoted a great deal of attention to identifying and exploring the character and significance of classical Jewish teachings and the unique spirit that he believed resided within them. At the same time, he was fascinated, if not disturbed, by the ongoing existence of the Jews, whom he labeled a pariah people, throughout history. Despite what Weber asserted was the Jews' universal significance for the development of Occidental civilization, he found it intriguing that they remained a particularistic — one is tempted to say tribal — body that had endured for centuries in an overwhelmingly non-Jewish world.

In this essay, I aim to explicate and analyze both dimensions of the Weberian project concerning Judaism and the Jews. In so doing, I intend not only to illuminate the role that Weber assigned Judaism in the evolution of the ethos of the modern world. I hope, in addition, to indicate how Weber's writings concerning Judaism and the Jews — taken in their historical context — provide a crucial lens for assessing the character of the modern world and the place assigned Judaism and Jews as a minority religion and minority group within it. This essay thereby aspires to transcend its particular focus in order to comment upon one overarching attitude displayed by significant elements in the modern setting towards Judaism and the Jews.

Weber on Ancient Judaism and the Emergence of the Modern World

As alluded to above, Weber's interest in Judaism was fueled by his judgment that the "rationalization" of life, which came to fruition in the West through the influence of Calvinism and Puritanism, had its roots in ancient Judaism. Weber's own thoughts concerning the scope of and rationale for his work can be seen in his introduction to his famed book *The Protestant Ethic and the Spirit of Capitalism*. Western civilization, in his view, was unique. He contended that "a product of modern European civilization . . . is bound to ask himself to what combination of circumstances the fact should be attributed that in western civilization, and western civilization only, cultural phenomena appear which . . . lie in a line of development having universal value and significance."[1]

The content of Weber's judgment here strikes the contemporary reader as hopelessly Eurocentric. Nevertheless, if one is to comprehend Weber and his work, one must acknowledge that this judgment directed virtually all his writings. The Occident, in his view, had produced a unique culture, one "universal" in its significance. How Europe had produced such a distinct orientation became the focal point for Weber's studies, and his labors in the sociology of religion were guided by his belief that the teachings of the world's religions held the key to understanding why the West had evolved as it had. His characterizations and analyses of the world's religious and belief systems centered around this basic problem — how to explain the distinctive character and different rates of development between eastern and western civilizations. Everything Weber wrote about the world's religions was determined by this interest.

Weber believed that the cause of the West's unique culture lay in the distinctive type of "rationality" and the "progressive rationalization" of life it entailed as the major directional trend of the Occidental world. By this, Weber did not mean that "rationality" was lacking in other civilizations. After all, any mode of conduct that adopts means to arrive at certain ends can be termed "rational." Yet, as Talcott Parsons observed in

---

1　Max Weber, *The Protestant Ethic and the Spirit of Capitalism*, trans. Talcott Parsons (New York, 1958), p.13.

his introduction to the English-language edition of Weber's *Sociology of Religion*, Weber felt that any form of rationality that tended "toward the indulgence of immediate emotional needs and pressures" was unlikely to exert a lasting pressure upon the social order and change it. Such a form of rationality would be confined to a certain set of actions and would be incapable of possessing far-ranging consequences for society.[2]

In Weber's view, western rationality, in contrast to other forms of rationality, developed singular characteristic traits that had long-ranging cultural, social, political, and economic consequences. Its science evolved into a body of knowledge with universal application. While detailed scientific observations had developed in other societies, it was only in the West that science was built upon a mathematical foundation. He also maintained that the Occident was unique in the development of a rational biology, chemistry, and systematic political philosophy. The West was also alone in the formation of a rational jurisprudence, and in no other culture did an equivalent to western bureaucracy form. Moreover, the modern state, with its parliaments and written constitutions regulating political behavior, was, he asserted, a uniquely western phenomenon. Finally, a rational economy in the form of capitalism emerged only in the West.[3]

Weber's discussion of the phenomenon of rationality was hardly uniform or simple. Nevertheless, he frequently pointed to a specific type of rationality, which he identified as "formal," as being uniquely western and served as the foundation for the forms of political and economic organization that dominated the modern world. He contrasted this "formal" type of rationality with a "substantive" one, which, Weber claimed, dominated traditional societies, where norms and directions in the social and political order were defined and articulated solely by traditional institutions and leaders who were not limited by formal procedures and rules. Substantive rationality created a society in which traditional authority as articulated by individual persons dominated. Weber summarized this type of rationality in the following way:

> A system of imperative co-ordination will be called "traditional" if legitimacy is claimed for it on the basis of the sanctity of the order

2 Max Weber, *The Sociology of Religion*, trans. Ephraim Fischoff (Boston, 1963), p. xxxi.
3 *Weber, The Protestant Ethic and the Spirit of Capitalism*, pp. 13–31.

and the attendant powers of control as they have been handed down from the past, "have always existed." The person or persons exercising authority are designated according to traditionally transmitted rules. The object of obedience is the personal authority of the individual, which he enjoys by virtue of his traditional status. The organized group exercising authority is . . . primarily based on relations of traditional authority. . . .[4]

Such authority rests upon the personal relations that obtain between the commander and those commanded. It is not limited by a systematization based upon procedures and rules.

In opposition to traditional-substantive authority lies legal-rational authority, which, according to Weber, stemmed from a formally rational belief system. In such a system, personal relationships become subservient to rationally defined and systematically administered formal procedures and rules. Formal rationality creates a society in which "a system of rules . . . is applied judicially and administratively in accordance with ascertainable principles [and] is valid for all members of the corporate group."[5] Or, in defining legal-rational authority elsewhere, Weber stated:

Submission under legal authority is based upon an impersonal bond to the generally defined and functional "duty of office." The official duty — like the corresponding right to exercise authority: the "jurisdictional competency" — is fixed by rationally established norms, by enactments, decrees, and regulations, in such a manner that the legitimacy of the authority becomes the legality of the general rule, which is purposely thought out, enacted, and announced with formal correctness.[6]

Substantive rationality created an authority based upon persons and personal relationships. Formal rationality — the type that came to

---

4 Max Weber, *The Theory of Social and Economic Organization,* trans A. M. Henderson and Talcott Parsons (New York, 1947), p. 341.
5 Ibid. p. 333.
6 Max Weber, "The Social Psychology of the World Religions," in H. H. Gerth and C. Wright Mills, eds. and trans., *From Max Weber* (New York, 1958), p. 299.

dominate the western world — established authority on the basis of formal procedures and rules. As Arnold Eisen has commented, formal rationality — as Weber saw it — was not calculation alone. It did not simply aim at control of a given situation through action under the conscious control of the actor. Rather, it pointed to action that was purposive, logical, universal, and systematic — all characteristic features of the type of rationality that, Weber asserted, informed the modern Occident.[7]

Due to the influence and dominance of formal rationality in the West, life became demystified and progressively intellectualized. The world came to be governed by explicit, abstract, intellectually determinable rules instead of by sentiment and tradition. As Weber wrote, rationalization "means that there are no mysterious, incalculable forces that come into play, but rather, that one can, in principle, master all things by calculation. This means that the world is disenchanted."[8] The distinctive feature of formal rationality in the West was that it permeated the whole of life and was not confined to a particular sector of human activity. The study of the development of formal rationality in the West was the study of "the disenchantment of the world."

Rationalization reflected humanity's confidence in its own abilities and works. However, Weber was careful to point out that such confidence might not be extended to the individual — that an individual person living in such a society might not possess "an increased and general knowledge of the conditions under which one lives"[9] and might well fail to understand or appreciate the world view that dominated his or her society. Rationalization, for Weber, simply reflected society's ability to exorcise the mysterious. Thus, any society, even the most rational, would contain individuals whose behavior would be characterized as irrational in relation to the *weltanschauung* that dominated the society.

Weber's concern was to explain how the development of this system of formal rationality emerged as the dominant directional ethos of western society. What peculiarity of the premodern West enabled the development of modern economic capitalism and the emergence of

7 Arnold Eisen, "The Meanings and Confusions of Weberian Rationality," *The British Journal of Sociology* 20:1 (March, 1978), pp.58–67.
8 Weber, "Science as a Vocation," in Gerth and Mills, *From Max Weber*, p.139.
9 Ibid.

a form and structure of societal organization that Weber claimed was unique in human history? Weber's *Ancient Judaism* was essentially an attempt to answer that question.

He articulated the explicit nature of his project and the role of Judaism within it in the opening pages of that work. There, he contrasted the orientation Judaism established for the ethos of the West with the direction Asian forms of religiosity created in the Orient:

> Ritually correct conduct, i.e., conduct conforming to caste standards, carried for the Indian pariah castes the premium of ascent by way of rebirth in a caste-structured world thought to be eternal and unchangeable.
>
> The maintenance of the caste status quo involved not only the continued position of the individual within the caste, but also the position of the caste in relation to other castes. This conservatism was prerequisite to salvation, for the world was unchangeable and had no history.
>
> For the Jew the religious premise was the very opposite. . . . The world was conceived as neither eternal nor unchangeable, but rather as having been created. Its present structures were a product of man's activities . . . and of God's reactions to them.
>
> There existed a highly rational religious ethic of social conduct; it was free of magic and all forms of irrational quest for salvation; it was inwardly worlds apart from the paths of salvation offered by Asiatic religions. To a large extent this ethic underlies the contemporary Mid-Eastern and European ethic. World-historical interest in Jewry rests upon this fact.[10]

In setting forth his reasons for investigating ancient Judaism, Weber was interested in determining the causes for what he regarded as the distinctiveness and originality — the tonal direction — of western civilization. His citations of Indian caste-orders and Asian religions were intended as counterexamples to what he viewed as the "rational" religious orientation of Judaism. Weber never claimed that ancient Judaism

---

10 Max Weber, *Ancient Judaism*, trans. H. H. Gerth and Don Martindale (New York, 1952), pp. 3–4.

was free of what he termed irrational elements. Indeed, he stated that "magic continued to exist" in the talmudic era and that magic "never vanished from popular practice."[11] Rather, he simply centered all his interest on a single dimension of ancient Jewish teachings. In so doing, he did not assert that the Jewish people of that era purged all vestiges of the irrational from their midst. He did claim, however, that ancient Judaism developed an ethic that was free of magic as a vital element in its teachings. This ethic was of world-historical importance.

Weber's thesis concerning ancient Judaism can he summarized as follows: The authors of the Bible, by positing belief in a single God who was simultaneously both the purposeful creator of the world and a transcendent agent apart from nature, were able to secularize the cosmos. The prophets, in particular, with their message of moral rationalism, directed worship toward this one sovereign God who was above and beyond the universe. Their teachings not only disenchanted the world by ridding it of other gods; they also led people to focus on the meaning and import of human activity. God was not arbitrary, and the divine could be pleased and the people thereby rewarded through observance of the deity's commandments. In this way, the prophets and the Jewish people of ancient days laid the foundation for the construction of a social ethic of activity within the world that could inform all dimensions of human life. This foundation allowed Judaism to develop ritual and social guidelines for a highly systematic mode of daily conduct based upon a devotion to rationally consistent procedures and rules in the areas of commandment and law. In this way, ancient Judaism contributed to the ethical rationalization of the world and both established a trend and created an ethos that was to have universal consequences for the character and development of the modern world.[12]

Many scholars have maintained that Weber, in offering this portrait of the ethos of ancient Judaism, had little if anything to say of relevance concerning the question and place of the Jews in modern Europe. Representative of these scholars is Guenther Roth, who wrote that although "Weber wanted to explain the distinctiveness of the ethical rationalism of the Judeo-Christian tradition and found the beginnings of western rationalism in the ethical prophecy of ancient Israel," his work on

11   Ibid. pp.394 and 219.
12   Weber develops this point in ibid. pp.213–15.

ancient Judaism had "nothing to do with the position of [European] Jewry in [his] time."[13] This is not to say that scholars such as Roth contend that Weber's scholarship in this area is uncontroversial or undisputed. Indeed, many readily acknowledge that Weber relied heavily upon the biblical scholarship of his era — particularly that of Julius Wellhausen — with all its limitations and cultural biases.[14] Nevertheless, they do assert that Weberian scholarship on Judaism was guided solely by his interest in understanding the origins of a particular ethos, which had lasting consequences for the direction of modern civilization. The next section of this essay, which will analyze and present Weber's views on the Jews as a "pariah people" — will assess the correctness of this observation.

Weberian Methodology and His Characterization of the Jews as a Pariah People

Weber's fascination with Judaism and the Jews did not only emerge from his interest in explaining the origins and development of formal rationality in the West. He was intrigued by their long-term survival as a particularistic body throughout history.[15] As he observed, "The religion of Israel developed into a structure able to resist all disintegrating influences from the outside, and it lived in this form throughout history".[16]

To explain the survival of the Jewish group as a "pariah people" in the history of the West, Weber turned to his methodological researches in the social and cultural sciences and the notion of ideal-type. In writing on the nature of these sciences, Weber asserted that they aimed to "analyze the phenomena of life in terms of their cultural significance." This presupposed, Weber acknowledged, "a value-orientation toward these events. Empirical reality becomes 'culture' to us because and insofar as we relate it to value-ideas. It includes those segments which have

13 Günther Roth, "Responses to Richard Rubenstein's 'Anticipations of the Holocaust in the Political Sociology of Max Weber,'" in Layman Letgers, ed., *Western Society After the Holocaust* (Boulder, Colo., 1983), pp. 187–89.

14 For a full discussion of Weber's sources for his work on ancient Judaism as well as the cultural presuppositions that underlay them, see Jay Holstein, "Max Weber and Biblical Scholarship," *Hebrew Union College Annual* 46 (1975), pp. 159–79.

15 Weber, *Ancient Judaism*, p. 4.

16 Ibid. p. 263.

become significant to us because of this value-relevance."[17] In so far as cultural sciences are concerned with phenomena that are peculiarly human, objects of investigation become relevant only from the specific point of view that the investigator happens to hold. Nevertheless, while Weber was willing to concede that "the guiding point of view" of the investigator was of "great importance for the construction of the conceptual scheme which will be used in the investigation," he still maintained that "in the mode of their use, the investigator is obviously bound by logical norms of . . . thought."[18] Weber, in the final analysis, insisted that the mode of investigation appropriated by researchers in the non-natural and cultural sciences could be as rigorous as those employed by researchers in the natural sciences. His task became one of specifying and defining a concept or theory that could facilitate the construction of an apparatus appropriate to the goal of studying and illuminating social reality. Weber believed that the notion of "ideal-type" allowed this goal to be realized.

The ideal-type achieved this end, Weber stated, precisely because it was intended to resolve and illumine a single problem. Each was framed with a specific problem in view. The ideal-type was not designed to aid in the construction of a grand scheme of scientific theory. Rather, it sought to be used as an instrument, as a "heuristic means of establishing unambiguously the meaning of the subject under investigation."[19] The aim of the ideal-type was constricted and confined to the topic under specific investigation.

> An ideal-type is formed by a one-sided accentuation of one or more points of view and by the synthesis of a great many diffuse, discrete, more or less present and occasionally absent individual phenomena, which are arranged according to those one-sidedly emphasized viewpoints into a unified analytical construct. . . . In its conceptual purity, this mental construct cannot be found empirically anywhere in reality.[20]

17　Max Weber, *The Methodology of the Social Sciences*, trans. and ed. Edward A. Shils and Henry A. Finch (Glencoe, Ill., 1949), pp.77 and 81.
18　Ibid. p.84.
19　Julian Freund, *The Sociology of Max Weber* (New York, 1969), p.61.
20　Weber, *The Methodology of the Social Sciences*, p.90.

Thus the ideal-type was a yardstick for determining what was unique and distinctive about a particular doctrine, situation, or course of events. Its stated purpose was neither to construct a hypothesis nor to describe the totality of an event or process but rather to isolate elements of social reality in order to explain their significance and importance. It was a conceptual tool, one that Weber employed in his stated attempt to ascertain why the Jews had survived as a distinctive minority people in the orbit of numerous civilizations — including the Christian one — for centuries. It was in this sense that it is said that he turned to the concept of the Jews as a "pariah people."

In his *Sociology of Religion*, Weber offered an overarching definition of the features of this ideal-typical construct.

> "Pariah people" denotes a distinctive hereditary social group lacking autonomous political organization and characterized by prohibitions against commensality and intermarriage. . . . Two additional traits of a pariah people are political and social disprivilege and a far-reaching distinctiveness in economic functioning.[21]

In Weber's view, a pariah people was characterized as possessing four distinct features. First, such a people no longer enjoys political hegemony in its native territory. Indeed, it possesses no territory at all. Secondly, a pariah people is limited in the occupations its members are permitted to pursue. Thirdly, it practices endogamy. Finally, a pariah people strives to impose rules that limit social intercourse with persons outside the group and that distinguish sharply between persons who are members of the group and those beyond.

In Weber's view, the ideal-typical concept of pariah people illuminated the situation of the Jews in the Diaspora and their "specific peculiarities" as a guest people among diverse populations.[22]

> The Jews were a pariah people, which means . . . that they were a guest people who were ritually separated, formally or de facto, from their social surroundings. All the essential traits of Jewry's attitude toward the environment can be deduced from this pariah

---

21 Weber, *The Sociology of Religion*, p.109.
22 Weber, *Ancient Judaism*, p.5.

existence, especially its voluntary ghetto, long antedating compulsory internment, and the dualistic nature of its in-group and out-group morality.[23]

To be sure, Weber distinguished between what he identified as the pariah situation of the Jews and that of the pariah castes in India."[24] The Jews developed as a pariah group in a surrounding free of castes. Indeed, the Jewish religious ideology that led to the ritual segregation of the Jews was the antithesis of the Indian religious concept of caste. As pointed out above, it was a rational one that demanded devotion to and performance of the commandments. It was free of the irrational and mystical quests for salvation that marked Indian religiosity. Whereas, for the Indian, the caste order was eternal and immutable, for the Jew, the social structure of the world was a product of human activities and was destined to give way in the future to a God-ordained order in which the Jews would no longer be subjugated to the nations under whose yoke they toiled. In short, the pariah situation of the Jews was worlds apart from that of the Indian situation.[25] Weber, in offering a portrait that distinguished the Jewish situation from that of the pariah castes in India, was attempting to delimit the concept of pariah people as it applied to Jews.

Nevertheless, there is strong evidence that his application of this concept to the Jewish people involved a great deal of ambivalence about Jews. His emphasis on the Jewish belief that they would one day be part of a social order in which they would triumph over their gentile oppressors allowed Weber to claim that Judaism valorized a Nietzschean form of *ressentiment*, the hostility that victims bear towards their oppressors. Indeed, Weber charged that the "moralism of the law" served "as a device for compensating a conscious or unconscious desire for vengeance [against Israel's enemies]." In other words, the Jew's observance of the law and "the virtues enjoined by God are practiced for the sake of the hoped for compensation."[26] These passages have prompted Gary Abraham to note, "Weber works Nietzsche's theory of the

23 Ibid. p.3.
24 Weber, *The Sociology of Religion*, p.108.
25 Weber, *Ancient Judaism*, pp.3–4.
26 Max Weber, *Economy and Society* (New York, 1968), pp.495–96.

functions of religion into his own exposition, absolving Christianity of Nietzsche's charge of serving the interests of *ressentiment*, and bringing the full burden of the Nietzschean charge to bear on Judaism. . . . The purest form of a religious ethic of compensation for the disprivileged, growing out of *ressentiment*, is found in Judaism."[27]

Furthermore, Weber's stress upon the "dualistic nature of [Jewry's] in-group and out-group morality" as a prominent feature of the Jewish group's pariah people status testifies to the early twentieth-century context of Jewish-Christian polemics that regularly produced such portraits. Judaism, in such accounts, had failed to universalize the ethical idealism of the prophets because it had attached this idealism to a single group — the Jews. Christianity, in contrast, extended this idealism to all people and in so doing bestowed an ethos upon the western world that made the legal equality of all persons as individuals possible. Weber's thought was itself informed by and committed to this view.

In a telling passage on the seminal role played by Christianity in the development of a universal western ethic, Weber wrote that the early Church — particularly through the teachings of Paul — had succeeded in breaking through the stultifying tribalisms of Pharisaic Judaism. Weber stated that fraternization and community of worship among all peoples was made possible only because Christianity had shattered the ritual barriers formerly separating Jews and Gentiles. This notion of a community of all persons was established clearly when Paul reproached Peter for his withdrawal from his meal with Gentiles because the Jews had approached and Peter feared their disapprobation (Galatians 2:11–14). In censuring Peter for this behavior, Paul and the early Church established an ethic that broke down ritual barriers and moral distinctions among peoples. Weber regarded this event as one of tremendous import in the development of a modern ethos, for the destruction of such ritual barriers against commensality was an indispensable prerequisite for collective action and solidarity among persons who were not united by kinship ties.[28]

27 Gary A. Abraham, *Max Weber and the Jewish Question* (Urbana and Chicago, 1992), pp. 249–50.

28 Max Weber, *The Sociology of Religion*, pp. 40–41. For the import this Christian ethos played in facilitating the dissolution of narrow clans and allowing for fraternization among diverse peoples, see Weber, *The City*, trans. and ed. Don Martindale and Gerald

Weber has been roundly critiqued by many for his writings on this topic. Ephraim Schmueli has written:

> Weber's analysis disregards most relevant elements in Jewish history and accentuates a one-sided arrangement of the selected elements. The arbitrariness of the selection of the elements in the analysis of the pariah people type may serve as an illustration of the inherent weakness of the whole ideal-type method. It is open . . . to the fallacy of misplaced concreteness through arresting some parts of historical reality.[29]

Others, such as Salo W. Baron and Talcott Parsons, have pointed to the Jewish people's extensive contacts with Christians in periods as disparate as the Middle Ages and the contemporary United States to fault Weber for his insistence that "ritual segregation" marks an essential feature of Jewry's pariah people status throughout history.[30] Still others, such as Schmueli himself, as well as Judah Rosenthal and Freddy Raphael, condemn Weber for what they regard as an insufficiently nuanced treatment of Judaism's attitudes toward the non-Jew.[31] All these critiques are undoubtedly well-taken in their details. What they all point to, however, is that Weber, in employing the concept of "pariah people," appears to have violated his own methodological dicta that the ideal-type was intended neither to be a descriptive statement nor a hypothetical construction of reality. In sum, as Christian Sigrist has maintained, there is a "confusion of definition, description, and hypothesis, and . . . lack of distinction between tautological propositions and statements of fact" in Weber's use of the ideal-type concept of pariah people.[32]

Neuwirth (Glencoe, Ill., 1958), pp.100 and 102–3.

29 Ephraim Schmueli, 'The 'Pariah People' and Its 'Charismatic Leadership'," *Proceedings of the American Academy of Jewish Research* 36 (1968), p.181.

30 For Baron's views, see Salo W. Baron, *A Social and Religious History of the Jews* (New York, 1957), vol.3, p.23 ff. Parson's criticisms are found in his introduction to *The Sociology of Religion*, pp.lxii–lxvi.

31 Schmueli, "Pariah People," p.185 ff.; Judah Rosenthal, "Interest from the Gentile," in *Researches and Sources* (Hebrew) (Chicago, 1966), vol.1., pp.323–53; and Freddy Raphael. "Max Weber et le judaisme antique," in *Archives Europeenes De Sociologie* XI:2 (1970), p.330.

32 Christian Sigrist, "The Problem of 'Pariahs'," Otto Stammer, ed., *Max Weber and Sociology Today* (New York, 1971), p.241.

Weber's conception of the Jews as a pariah people does not appear to have been simply a heuristic device dispassionately employed as an aid in explaining the phenomenon of Jewish group survival in the Diaspora throughout the centuries. Rather, it seems to reflect Weber's own view of the historical status of the Jewish people and their position in diverse societies — including his own. As such, it bespeaks the influences Weber's own cultural setting had upon his own attitudes toward the Jews of Europe. A final comment upon it will not only reveal the ambivalences of Weber's own positions vis-à-vis the Jews and Judaism. It will display the attitudes taken by significant elements in the modern world concerning the place of Jews and Judaism within it.

The Implications of Weber's Work as a Prototypical Response to Jews and Judaism in Modern Society

The writings of Max Weber on Jews and Judaism, despite their methodological sophistication, cannot be seen apart from the historical context in which they were authored. Ancient Judaism was granted an honored place in the intellectual and economic history Weber wrote of the West because it had given birth to an ethic of moral rationalism that would have decisive consequences for the course of modern civilization. However, in the Weberian narrative Judaism attached the truth claims of that moral rationalism too closely to the narrow nationalistic concerns of the Jewish people. Ancient Judaism bound God's will to a specific ethnic group. As a result, the universalism inherent in prophetic teaching could not be unleashed.

In Weber's view, Judaism did not seek a just and egalitarian society; it focused instead upon the fate of Israel and God's vindication of the people Israel in the face of the hostility and indifference of the nations. It was Christianity that allowed the prophetic teachings of moral rationalism to transcend the confines of a single tribe. It was Christianity that made these teachings available to the entire world. In making these claims, Weber reveals himself to be embedded in the cultural and religious context of his day. His views and attitudes toward Jews and Judaism cannot be understood apart from the partisan world of German scholarship and Protestant religiosity that formed him.

However, the views of Max Weber on the topics of Judaism and the Jews represent more than another episode in the history of early twentieth-century Jewish-Christian polemics in Germany: they embody certain attitudes representative of the modern world's attitudes toward Jews and Judaism — attitudes internalized oftentimes not only by non-Jews, but by Jews as well. From the onset of Emancipation and Enlightenment at the end of the eighteenth century in Europe, sectors of European society enthusiastically supported the right of Jews to full participation in the life of the larger world. In the words of Christian Wilhelm von Döhm, the Jews should be "able to fulfill the duties [of all other subjects and] they should be allowed to claim the impartial love and care of the State."[33]

Yet, this "love and care" was to be extended by the state to the Jews, in the famous words of Clermont-Tonnerre, as "individuals," and not as "members of a nation." This distinction has signified, in many instances, what I would term a "secularization of Christian universalism." For the early Church, in the famous words of Paul, proclaimed that all humanity, in light of Christ's redemptive presence in the world, could no longer be regarded particularistically as Jew or Gentile, slave or free, male or female. Instead, "you are all one in Christ Jesus" (Galatians 3:28). In such an ethos, all specific identities are either subsumed under or dissolve into the universal. There is no tolerance for the particular. The modern state, from this perspective, can be said to embody this ethos — albeit in a secularized form. This is why Weber's writings on Judaism and the Jews possess broad significance: they represent more than the attitudes of an individual scholar — no matter how prominent — toward the Jews and Judaism. Indeed, if they were no more than his own attitudes, the Weberian corpus on matters Jewish could be dismissed as merely a curiosity for the antiquarian study of intellectual history.

Instead, these writings are of ongoing importance because they grant insight into one of the dilemmas confronted by Jews in the modern situation. After all, Weber himself was a liberal who desired the Jew to participate fully in the civic and cultural life of Germany. He desired full Jewish integration into the life of Germany's majority culture. The continued Jewish insistence upon particularity — Jewry's "self-segregation" as a "pariah people" — disturbed Weber, who felt that the most appro-

---

33 Presented in Paul Mendes-Flohr and Jehuda Reinharz, eds., *The Jew in the Modern World* (New York, 1995), p.30.

priate Jewish response to the modern setting ought to have been full assimilation into German society. His writings on Judaism and his characterizations of the Jews reflect his impatience with and disapproval of this stance on the part of modern Jewry.[34]

Jews in the modern world, like their ancestors in ancient days and their forbears in the Middle Ages, remained too committed to their community of hereditary origins. Most, even as they acculturated, refused to abandon their identity as Jews. Judaism itself did not atrophy and die despite the onslaught of modernity. This ongoing commitment and vitality disturbed as well as perplexed Weber, and his writings on Judaism and the Jews reflect this ire. Thus they represent more than an attempt to understand the origins of the modern world: they are his comment on the nature of the modern political and cultural order. The work of Max Weber in this area is of enduring relevance not because of the substance of his observations. Rather, it remains of import because it reflects the paradoxes inherent in the liberal ethos that dominates the modern world — an ethos that affirms the worth and dignity of all persons as human beings in a universal sense and yet does not know how to encompass a full affirmation of persons as creatures whose personhood is ultimately embedded and embodied in particularistic cultures, settings, religions, and ways.

34 See Gary Abraham's wonderful study, *Max Weber and the Jewish Question*, pp. 228–98, for a masterful and comprehensive treatment of this point. Abraham's book develops, in a far more comprehensive way, elements of the argument I have presented in this paper.

The Challenge of Emancipation

4

Emancipation and the Directions of Modern Judaism

The Lessons of Melitz Yosher

The impact of Emancipation on Jews living in Western Europe at the beginning of the nineteenth century was decisive and thorough. Its advent created new imperatives and frameworks that influenced and in many ways determined the directions that Judaism would follow in the modern world. Jews assumed a new sense of selfhood in this new political and cultural order, and a new aesthetic as well as new understandings of Judaism subsequently emerged. The resultant patterns of thought and practice led to a set of denominational and aesthetic options that continue to inform Jews in their practice of Judaism even today. This paper seeks to explore the origins of these options and the rise of a changed Jewish religious aesthetic by gazing through the lens provided by *Sefer Melitz Yosher* (Book of Advocacy), a collection of liturgical procedures that were proposed by Aaron Moses Isaac ben Abraham Graanboom in 1808–1809, assembled by his son Israel Graanboom, and subsequently adopted by Amsterdam's Adat Yeshurun congregation.[1]

An exploration and analysis of this work provides a barometer for measuring the impact Emancipation had upon the development and course of modern Judaism. It indicates that Emancipation and the framework it provided for Jewish religious life was significant in informing the aesthetics of Judaism in novel ways, and it also demonstrates that Emancipation hardly led to monolithic and radical Reform. Local context was always a vital factor in determining the particular direction Judaism was to take in that area. Finally, an analysis of this early nineteenth-century document shows that changes in practice and behavior often antedated and took precedence over matters of faith and ideology in determining the various courses that Judaism was to follow in

---

1 ספר מליץ יושר והוא כולל כל המגהגים שתיקן ויסד אדמ״ר אהרן משה יצחק בן כ״ה אברהם זצ״ל [by Israel Graanboom], Amsterdam: Yohanan Levi Rofé and his son Benyamin [5]569 [= 1809], 8°. 16 pages (Roest, p. 424 — press mark Ros. 19 H 20; Zedner, p. 363).

the modern world. Moving beyond the confines of this specific text, conclusions may be drawn concerning the larger issues of the relationship between Emancipation and the development of Judaism in the modern world.

Historical Context
Adat Yeshurun and the Publication of Melitz Yosher

In 1795 the French conquered Holland and removed the House of Orange. The Batavian Republic was soon established and the "new democratic state followed the example of France in promulgating its own 'Declaration of the Rights of Man and Citizen.'"[2] Eighteen months later, on September 2, 1796, the Republic extended full political emancipation to the Jews of Holland. One result was the rise of synagogues in new areas of the city, often in renovated private homes. Adat Yeshurun, one such congregation, was founded in March 1797, dedicating its house of worship on June 23 of that year.[3]

Michael Meyer explains the distinct nature of Adat Yeshurun in the following description of the community's origins.

> Very soon after the French Conquest, the *parnassim* [directors of the traditional Ashkenazic community] found themselves in opposition to a faction whose leadership consisted largely of younger Jewish intellectuals imbued with the ideals of the French Revolution and dissatisfied with the existing community structure. These *maskilim* banded together with a few non-Jews to form a pro-French patriotic society called *Felix Libertate*. When its Jewish members failed in an attempt to bring about changes from within, twenty-one of them created a rival community, Adat Yeshurun, which provided its adherents with their own rabbi, synagogue, slaughtering house for kosher meat, and ritual bath.[4]

2 Michael A. Meyer, *Response to Modernity: A History of the Reform Movement in Judaism* (New York and Oxford, 1988), p.25.

3 Jozeph Michman, "The 'Diskursen' of the New and Old Community in Amsterdam" (Hebrew) in: J. Michman, *Michmanei Yosef Studies on the History and Literature of Dutch Jewry* (Jerusalem, 1994), p.135; and Meyer, *Response to Modernity*, p.26.

4 Meyer, *Response to Modernity*. p.26.

The *parnassim* of the *Alte Kille*, the "old community," were powerless
to prevent this secession from the community because the Batavian
Republic had enacted a public policy of separation between church and
state. The new policy constituted, in Frederique P. Hiegentlich's words,
"an internal [communal] fight against the monopolistic position of the
parnassim." The establishment of Adat Yeshurun "was in the first place a
matter of politics and not religion."[5] While the *Neie Kille*, the "new community," did introduce some minor changes in the ritual ceremony, "they fully
accepted the revelation of the Law by God and the authority of the Talmud."[6]

Jozeph Michman echoes this assessment and asserts that historians
such as Heinrich Graetz, Simon Dubnow, Raphael Mahler, Michael
Meyer, and Jakob Petuchowski have erred in their contention that the
political struggle between the *Alte Kille* and Adat Yeshurun was one
of religion as well as politics. Michman offers a caution on this point:
"It is important to question whether [. . . these] historians are right who
regard Adat Yeshurun as the first 'Reform' community — or at least the
bellwether of the kind of Reform that was to become so widespread in
Germany." He cites Graetz as writing, in his *History of the Jews,* that "the
political divisions also became religious divisions. For the adherents of
the new Adat Yeshurun community started to introduce a kind of Reform." Similarly, Michman demurs from Meyer, who, in Michman's
view, "maintains that the formulation of a singular rite by Adat Yeshurun
was in itself sufficient to qualify it as a forerunner of the Reform, which
in the course of time would take a far more radical course." The issue,
Michman asserts, can only be resolved by determining, "whether the
founders of Adat Yeshurun had religious objectives and whether they
aimed at a reform of religious practices." And Michman's answer, as
we shall see, is an emphatic "No" to each of these questions. The ideals

5   Frederique P. Hiegentlich, "Reflections on the Relationship between the Dutch Has-
    kalah and the German Haskalah" (cited hereinafter as "Reflections") in J. Michman
    and T. Levie, eds., *Dutch Jewish History: Proceedings of the Symposium on the History
    of the Jews in the Netherlands, November 28–December 3, 1982* (Jerusalem, 1984) pp.
    210–11. Michman agrees with Hiegentlich's assessment, and in his recently published
    work *The History of Dutch Jewry During the Emancipation Period 1787–1815* (Amster-
    dam, 1995), p. 69, writes, "It was not differences of opinion about religion that had
    provided the impetus for establishment of the New Community, but the absence
    of a social and political revolution within the Old Community."
6   Hiegentlich, "Reflections," p. 211.

and goals of the *Neie Kille* were, Michman claims, political and social alone, and its members, in his opinion, did all in their power to demonstrate their devotion to the religious inheritance of Israel as embodied in the dicta of Jewish law.[7] This point will soon become the focus of our concern. For the moment, it is sufficient to observe that membership of Adat Yeshurun quickly grew to over one hundred families and that a series of nearly forty polemical Yiddish pamphlets were issued between July 1797 and mid-March 1798. In them, leaders of both Adat Yeshurun and the traditional Ashkenazic community bitterly and often comically attacked one another.[8]

These pamphlets were initiated by the leaders of the *Neie Kille* in order to plead the case of the newly organized community before the masses of Amsterdam Jewry who, on August 1, 1797, were about to participate for the first time in the elections for the National Assembly. The *Neie Kille*'s pamphlets addressed a host of issues that confronted the entire community, and they placed the *Alte Kille* on the defensive in every area except one — that of religion. But in their responses, the attacks of the Chief Rabbi and the *parnassim* of the old established order upon the new community were swift and sharp. They charged that the *Neie Kille* wanted to destroy Judaism and that its members denied the principles on which Judaism is founded and disobeyed the *mitzvot*. The members of Adat Yeshurun were heretics, Karaites, and sectarians, and the Chief Rabbi and the *parnassim* indicted them for the changes — mostly though not exclusively of a decorous nature — that they had introduced into the Jewish religious service. The traditional leadership of the Ashkenazic community excoriated the members of Adat Yeshurun for these alterations and contended that they were forbidden by Jewish law on the basis of the talmudic dictum *minhag yisrael torah hu* — the custom of Israel is Torah.[9] While Michman and Hiegentlich may be

---

7   Jozeph Michman "The Establishment of the Supreme Consistory: A Turning Point in the History of Dutch Jewry" (Hebrew) in J. Michman, ed., *Studies on the History of Dutch Jewry* (Jerusalem, 1988), vol. 5, pp. 184–85; as well as Michman, *The History of Dutch Jewry During the Emancipation Period 1787–1815*, pp. 128–34, for a full statement of Michman's position.

8   See the first ever bilingual edition of a major portion of these pamphlets, *Storm in the Community*, selected, trans. and introd. by Jozeph Michman and Marion Aptroot (Cincinnati, 2002).

correct in their observation that the leaders of Adat Yeshurun never intended to change Judaism or Jewish worship, it appears that the leaders of the *Alte Kille* were threatened by the secession of the upstarts and viewed the changes introduced by the new congregation in a different light. The struggle between the two communities, as these pamphlets testify, had certainly taken on a religious dimension.

The authorities of the traditional Ashkenazic community, fume as they might have over the challenge Adat Yeshurun presented to their authority, were for over a decade essentially powerless to counter the challenge that the new community represented. This changed in 1808, for in that year Louis Bonaparte put an end to the Batavian Republic and ordered the old and new communities to reunite along the lines of the consistory model his brother, the emperor Napoleon, had ordered for the Jews of France that very same year. This caused great consternation among the leadership of Adat Yeshurun. Rabbi Isaac Graanboom, spiritual leader of the *Neie Kille*, had died in 1807 and Adat Yeshurun had already begun to decline in numbers and lose strength when the merger of the two communities was mandated by the French. Adat Yeshurun ceased to exist as an independent community and a united legal community was created.[10] It was against this background that Israel Graanboom, son of Adat Yeshurun's late rabbi, published *Melitz Yosher* in 1808. In writing this pamphlet, Graanboom hoped to explicate and defend the distinctive liturgical practices of the *Neie Kille* against the attacks of the Ashkenazic establishment and, in so doing, justify Adat Yeshurun's independent status.[11]

Melitz Yosher
Contents and Characteristics

An analysis of the contents of *Melitz Yosher* not only reveals the specifics of Adat Yeshurun's ritual. It also reflects the nature of the cleavages that separated Adat Yeshurun from the *Alte Kille* and illuminates the nature of Adat Yeshurun's departure from the letter of Amsterdam's Ashkenazic pattern of worship. More broadly, such analysis grants

9   Michman, "The 'Diskursen' of the New and Old Community in Amsterdam," pp. 135–39.
10   Michman, "The Establishment of the Supreme Consistory," p. 182ff.
11   Ibid. pp. 185–86.

insight into the impact of political emancipation on Jewish religious practice.

A concern with contemporary western aesthetic standards of decorum and order in prayer dominates the pages of *Melitz Yosher*. Throughout the pamphlet, great attention is paid to these issues. At the very outset of the work, the rule is stated that, "Everyday one says one division of the thirty divisions of the Book of Psalms" (2a). This is opposed to the normative Ashkenazic lectionary "in which the entire Book of Psalms is read every week."[12] While acknowledging that this would result in fewer psalms being read, Graanboom did not see this as a fault. On the contrary, "Better a little with devotion than many without — *Tov ta'am be-kavanah me-harbei be-lo kavanah*." Furthermore, this diminution in the number of psalms to be offered during worship allowed those that were recited to be said "quietly and with devotion — *be-naḥat u-ve-kavanah*, and not in confusion (*bilbul*) and haste (*meruah*)" (2a).

This same reasoning was also applied in *Melitz Yosher* to the many penitential prayers (*seliḥot*) written for the High Holidays of Rosh Hashanah and Yom Kippur. Only a few of the many *seliḥot* written for those days were to be included in each service. Furthermore, each *seliḥah* was to be recited verse by verse so that each could be said, as with the psalms, with proper devotion and understanding. Graanboom was careful to point out that this practice was supported by halakhic warrant (2a) and at the end of *Melitz Yosher* noted that this had been a custom advocated years earlier by Chief Rabbi Saul of the larger Amsterdam Jewish community (7b).

Graanboom, in enumerating the liturgical customs of his community, continued by stating that it was the practice of Adat Yeshurun that the mourner's prayer (*Kaddish*) be recited aloud and in unison by the entire congregation. This was in contrast to traditional Ashkenazic practice wherein individuals would recite the mourner's prayer at their own individual pace — which often resulted in a cacophony of voices, an indecorous development that the membership of Adat Yeshurun naturally wanted to avoid. In adopting this practice, Adat Yeshurun was consciously selecting a rite commonly associated with the Sephardim of

---

12 Jakob J. Petuchowski, *Prayerbook Reform in Europe: The Liturgy of European Liberal and Reform Judaism* (New York, 1968), p. 361

Amsterdam. The custom had clear Jewish legal precedent to support it
(2a). At the same time, as Steven Lowenstein has pointed out, the practice of the mourner's prayer being said in unison by all mourners is
found among the *Synagogenordnungen* (synagogue ordinances) adopted
by many Reform congregations in Germany in the early nineteenth
century, for it contributed directly to the decorum of Jewish worship.[13]

The desire for the service of Adat Yeshurun to be a decorous one in
accord with modern western standards can be seen in several ordinances the congregation adopted concerning the role of the cantor (*sha-
liah tzibur*) in leading services. The cantor was instructed to lead worship only while standing on the *bimah*, an elevated prayer platform.
While Graanboom cited talmudic passages from *Sotah* and *Sukkah*
as rabbinic warrants for this practice, he stated that the purpose of this
practice was to add decorum to the service by assuring that the community could hear the words of its prayer leader (2a). In addition, only
the cantor, not the rabbi, was to conclude the reading of the *Shema* (3a).
Similarly, only the cantor, not the mourner, was to recite Psalm 49, traditionally associated with mourning (3a), and only the cantor, not the
community, was to recite the blessing over the *Omer* aloud (5b). The
cantor alone was permitted to recite lamentations (*kinot*) on the 9th
of Av, for this would avoid "confusion and disorder — *irbuv u-vilbul
ha-da'at ve-ha-seder*" in the synagogue (5b). However, concern for order
and decorum affected the cantor as well, and even he was bound by regulations intended to promote greater dignity and formality in public
worship. Thus, the cantor was forbidden to embellish between the designated words of prayer (2b). Again, Granboom cited Jewish legal precedent for many of these strictures, and none appear to be in violation of
Jewish law. Nevertheless, it is once more instructive that each of these
practices foreshadows the many synagogue ordinances adopted by the
Reformers as well as the "cultured orthodox" of Germany in subsequent
decades of the nineteenth century.[14]

Other elements of *Melitz Yosher* embody the community's intense

13 Steven M. Lowenstein, *The Mechanics of Change: Essays in the Social History of
German Jewry* (Atlanta, 1992), p.127.
14 Ibid. p.122 ff.; and Petuchowski, *Prayerbook Reform in Europe*, p.131ff. Petuchowski
presents samples of the *Synagogenordnungen* adopted by Samson Raphael Hirsch's
Frankfurt Religionsgesellschaft as an illustration of the similarities in worship decorum that marked both liberal and orthodox communities in Germany during the

need to create a seemly and polite service. The practice of performing the priestly benediction (*dukhenen*) was confined to the Sabbath and festival morning services, and was to be recited only once. The *Neie Kille* proscribed this rite altogether during *Musaf*, the additional service held on those days, as its recitation at that time was condemned as "a hardship on the community — *tirḥat ha-tzibur*." Furthermore, recital of biblical verses by individual congregants in between each word of the benediction was also banned. Such practice, common in many communities, was clearly seen as a violation of synagogue etiquette by the Adat Yeshurun congregation. Again, Graanboom was careful to cite appropriate passages from rabbinic literature in support of each of these regulations and rulings (3a). Nevertheless, it is once more striking to recall that the rite of *dukhenen* also occupied the attention of a number of reformers later in the century who appear to have been disturbed by a seeming lack of civility that in their opinion accompanied this particular ritual practice.[15]

The concerted efforts exerted by the *Neie Kille* to establish a solemn atmosphere for worship and the desire not to "impose a hardship" on the community figure prominently in many other measures related in the pages of Graanboom's pamphlet. Only seven men were permitted to be called for *aliyot* to the Torah on the Sabbath. To call more, as was traditionally countenanced on that day, would needlessly lengthen the service and would constitute a "hardship to the community" (6a). Additional *aliyot* were also proscribed on Simhat Torah on two related grounds, for this traditional practice injected too much levity into the day and led people into "idle conversation," thereby causing them to ignore the Torah reading as well as the *Musaf* service that followed (6b). The auctioning of Torah honors in the synagogue for specific lectionary readings (*parshiyot*) was forbidden as well. The unseemly quality and offensive nature of such a practice was seen as virtually self-evident (6b).

The liturgical accretions of many generations — *yotzerot, piyyutim, kerovetz* and *zulot* — which had come to occupy a fixed place over the centuries in the liturgies of many Jewish communities were specifically proscribed, as they were seen as both interrupting the proper order of the ser-

---

nineteenth century. For a fuller exposition of this point in relation to German orthodoxy, see chap. 11, "German Jewish Orthodoxy," in this volume.

15 Lowenstein, *The Mechanics of Change*, pp. 120–21 and 130–31.

vice and needlessly lengthening it, thereby leading to "idle conversation — *siḥah betelah*" and "sin — *averah*" (4a–b). Similarly, *Melitz Yosher* forbade the recitation of the Eighteen Benedictions out loud. Indeed, it condemned the recitation as "an erroneous custom — *minhag ta'ut*." Instead, it decreed that the *Shemoneh Esreh* could only be recited silently. Graanboom was once more scrupulous to cite venerable rabbinic precedent in support of the *Neie Kille*'s position. However, it is interesting to read that this departure from accepted Ashkenazic custom was informed by Graanboom's observation that most congregants simply spoke during and paid scant attention to the cantor's repetition of the prayer. He complained, "Only a tiny number actually devote their attention to the prayer of the cantor — *Ki me'at meza'ir she-mekavenim et libam li-tefillat ha-shaliaḥ tzibur*' (6b). *Melitz Yosher* also reports that Adat Yeshurun decreed that its members were not allowed to wear *sargenes* (a white shroud or a *kittel*) on Rosh Hashanah or Yom Kippur. While several reasons are given for this proscription, the most significant here is identical to the reason supplied for the silent recitation of the Eighteen Benedictions cited above. For, Graanboom wrote, "a cessation from and confusion in prayer results from the act of robing and disrobing — *Mi-shum bitul u-vilbul ha-tefillah bi-levishah u-feshitah*" (5a). Again, all of these regulations, while defensible from the standpoint of Jewish law, represented departures from the Ashkenazic customs of the Amsterdam community and each one is paralleled among the Reform *Synagogenordnungen* of the first half of the 1800s.[16]

This quest for decorum in *Melitz Yosher* is highlighted in the regulation that states, "On Sabbath Eve, the whole congregation sings Psalm 29, *Lekha Dodi*, Psalm 92, *Yigdal*, and *Adon Olam* word for word, in one tune, aloud, and musically *Bekol u-vi-ne'imah, milah be-milah, be-niggun eḥad*." On the Sabbath and festivals, the entire service, from *Pesukei de-Zimrah* (Verses of Song) through the second of the Eighteen Benedictions (*Teḥiyat ha-Meitim*) was to be recited in a like manner, as were other parts of the service. Furthermore, when *Hallel* (Psalms of Praise) was recited on festivals, the cantor alone was to lead, and the community, when it did sing certain designated passages of this prayer, was instructed, as it was on the Eve of the Sabbath, to do so "in unison, aloud, and musically." In conclusion, Graanboom cited several rabbinic passages

16 Ibid. pp. 120–31.

to indicate that Jewish tradition in effect supported and contained an
aesthetic totally compatible with a modern western sense of decorum
and order (2b).

His sensitivity on this point may well have stemmed from a pejorative image of the synagogue as a place of raucous and cacophonous
behavior in the minds of Dutch and German gentiles. Joachim Heinrich
Campe, in his famous 1808 *Wörterbuch*, noted under *Die Judenschule*,
that common German usage employed this term to mark a place (*Orte*)
or a society (*Gesellschaft*) which is "noisy and confusing *laermend und
verwirrt*." Similarly, under *Jodenkerk* (Jewish church), the Dutch *Woordenboek der Nederlandsche Taal* indicates that this word is used to refer
to a situation "where everyone is screaming, or speaking, simultaneously."
Indeed, F. A. Stoett notes that the negative Dutch expression, *'t Is hier een
Jodenkerk* (It's like a Jewish church here), is "what people say when everyone is shouting." Stoett further observes that this phrase emerged from
a gentile perception that cacophonous behavior dominated the aesthetic of Jewish worship.[17] *Melitz Yosher* clearly wished to substitute a
western and Sephardic aesthetic of worship decorum for the traditional
Ashkenazic *davenen* for, it would seem, two related reasons. The first
was that those persons who formed and attended Adat Yeshurun were
themselves members of an upwardly aspiring bourgeoisie who had internalized a more decorous form of worship than *davenen* as appropriate
for their own experience of divine worship. On another level, this new
aesthetic was apparently to counter the negative stereotypes and images of indecorous Jewish behavior, as cited above, commonly associated with Ashkenazic ritual prayer practices.

17 For Joachim Heinrich Campe's definition, see his *Wörterbuch der deutschen Sprache*
(Braunschweig 1808) s.v. *Die Judenschule*. I thank Prof. Paul Mendes-Flohr for
bringing this reference to my attention. The *Woordenboek der Nederlandsche Taal*,
vol. 7 (1926), column 314, s.v. Jodenkerk writes: *Dit zegt men wanneer ergens allen
door eikaar schreeuwen, te gelijk spreken*. It further notes the presence in Dutch of
a number of expressions, including the one cited in the article, that employ this
word in the pejorative manner related in the essay. Stoett's commentary on the
phrase, *'t Is hier een Jodenkerk*, appears in F. A. Stoett, *Nederlandsche Spreekwoorden,
Spreekwijzen, Uitdrukkingen en Gezegden* (W. J. Thieme and Cie, Zutphen 1923) p. 398,
no. 1028. I would like to thank two graduate students, Leon Mock of Bar-Ilan University and Shanti Suzanne van Dam of the University of Amsterdam, for translating
these passages from Dutch to English for me.

Graanboom seems not to have thought that this new worship aesthetic would be easy to achieve even within the confines of a synagogue like Adat Yeshurun, which was committed to instituting such a change. A midrash that reflects this is one Graanboom took from *Bereshit Rabbah* 54:4. It states that Moses was "most weary — *kamah yegi'ot yage'a*" when he taught the Levites to sing. Graanboom, commenting upon the passage, queried, "And why was Moses weary?" Because Moses was compelled to teach them to "harmonize — *le-shorer be-kol u-ve-niggun eḥad, u-vi-ne'imah*" (2b)! The goal of a properly decorous and spiritually appropriate service, which Graanboom sought, apparently did not obviate his sense of humor.

Michman, in assessing the character of *Melitz Yosher*, acknowledges that an intense desire to assure proper decorum during prayer was a hallmark of the *Neie Kille*'s concerns, and concedes that this was a dominant characteristic of early Reform. Yet, he contends that the changes that Adat Yeshurun introduced into the services of its community were not the result of any Reform religious tendency on the part of either the members or the leaders of the *Neie Kille*: they were the product of a desire among the young, upwardly-mobile Ashkenazim of Adat Yeshurun to emulate Sephardic practice. After all, Sephardic influence upon Ashkenazim in the Amsterdam community had been pronounced from the time that Ashkenazim first arrived there in 1619. The Sephardim had long informed every dimension of Ashkenazic culture and the Sephardim, not the Ashkenazim, had always set the tone for the Amsterdam Jewish community. Indeed, the Ashkenazim of Amsterdam had always felt inferior to the Sephardim and they experienced a keen sense of status deprivation when compared to their Sephardic brethren.[18]

It is no wonder, in light of this Sephardi dominance, that Michman, in measuring the nature of the liturgy produced by Adat Yeshurun, concludes,

> The inspiration and legitimacy [for these new patterns of worship] came from [Amsterdam's indigenous] Portuguese Jewish Community. . . . The liturgy of Adat Yeshurun was the product of specific

18 J. Michman, "The Relationship between Sephardim and Ashkenazim in Amsterdam," in *Michmanei Yosef*, pp. 28–39.

circumstances, a newly established congregation not bound to old customs. The *Neie Kille* therefore felt free to fashion a service that received its inspiration from Sephardic models. [Adat Yeshurun was not] unfaithful to the *Halakhah* on even a single point.[19]

The analysis of *Melitz Yosher* offered above marks Michman's views as highly plausible. Many of its regulations support his notion that the *Neie Kille* and its liturgy were inspired by a Sephardic *tendenz*. In the *Hallel*, Adat Yeshurun elected to use *"ligmor* — to conclude," a Sephardi wording, in place of *"likro* — to read" in the blessing recited prior to the Psalms of Praise (3a). Similarly, Adat Yeshurun adopted the Sephardic customs of reciting *Hallel* in the synagogue on the first two nights of Passover with a blessing (3b–4a) as well as inserting the *Aleinu* between the afternoon (*Minḥah*) and evening (*Maʾariv*) services (2b). In addition, the practice of lifting and unfurling the Torah scroll before the congregation prior to the chanting of the weekly Torah portion — a Sephardic custom — was adopted by Adat Yeshurun (8a). Graanboom was careful, in these instances as in others, to provide rabbinic justification for these changes from the received Ashkenazic liturgy of the *Alte Kille*.

The major regulation Michman points to in *Melitz Yosher* as evidence that Adat Yeshurun did not embody a reform religious impulse, but was rather informed by the Sephardic model and piety in general, was the *Neie Kille*'s decision to abrogate the long-standing Ashkenazic ban against the consumption of legumes during Passover. Indeed, Graanboom specifically cited the Sephardim as the source for his community's decision to allow such grains. He argued that their consumption was permitted from a strictly legal point of view (*min ha-din*) since their prohibition was an erroneous custom (*minhag taʾut*) and imposed economic hardship on the poor (5a). To Michman, this decision — based as it was upon accepted Sephardic custom — simply reflects the ongoing influence of Sephardim upon Ashkenazim in Amsterdam and in this way testifies to the traditional religious character of the Adat Yeshurun community.[20] However, Michman's view does not exhaust the possible

---

19 J. Michman, "The Establishment of the Supreme Consistory," in *Studies on the History of Dutch Jewry*, pp. 186–88.

20 Ibid. p. 187.

interpretations one could offer of this regulation and the significance it holds for an understanding of *Melitz Yosher.*

As early as 1793, the issue of the consumption of legumes during Passover had become an ideological dividing point between traditionalists and *maskilim* in the European Jewish world. In that year, Saul Berlin, a rabbi turned *maskil*, published his pseudo-epigraphic volume of responsa, *Besamim Rosh*, which he ascribed, for the most part, to the great medieval Rabbi Asher ben Yehiel.[21] In responsum number 348, he attacked, on two grounds, the prohibition against legumes on Passover and argued for its abolition. In the first place, Berlin stated, falsely I might add, that it was a custom of the Karaites not to eat legumes during Passover. Secondly, he claimed that this prohibition imposed economic hardship on the poor, precisely the same argument that was made in *Melitz Yosher.* This custom was seen by Berlin as symbolic of an unenlightened medieval Judaism, which had to be transcended if Judaism was to enter the modern world. Hiegentlich and Dan Michman have pointed out that German *Haskalah* was far from unknown in Dutch circles in the late 1700s.[22] It may well be that a Dutch Jew like Graanboom had direct knowledge of Saul Berlin's writings. That remains in the realm of conjecture and possibility.

What is certain is that in the next half century the prohibition against legumes during Passover was elevated into an issue of the greatest symbolic importance for the modernization of Judaism. Indeed, proponents of permission to ease or rescind the traditional Ashkenazic restriction against the consumption of legumes during Passover were also enthusiastic advocates of liturgical change and the entry of Jews into the modern world. The Westphalian Consistory of Israelites, for example, issued a proclamation in 1810 that permitted soldiers to eat legumes during Passover.[23] During that same year, the Consistory also

---

21 Meyer, *Response to Modernity*, p.19.

22 Hiegentlich, "Reflections," pp.207–18; and Dan Michman, "David Friedrichsfeld" (Hebrew) in *Studies on the History of Dutch Jewry* (1981), pp.151–99.

23 Marc J. Rosenstein, "Legumes on Passover," *CCAR Journal* (Spring 1975), p.35. Rosenstein provides a fascinating and thorough discussion of the course of the debate over this custom among nineteenth-century Ashkenazic authorities and demonstrates the all-embracing symbolic significance it came to have in discussions of Jewish modernization.

issued a "Proclamation concerning the Improvements of the Worship Service in the Synagogues of the Kingdom of Westphalia," which decreed a number of reforms in Jewish liturgical practice identical to those enumerated in *Melitz Yosher*.[24] This suggests that what transpired in the Adat Yeshurun community can be seen against a backdrop other than Amsterdam. Thus, I would maintain, *Melitz Yosher* and the changes it enumerated concerning its community's form of worship ought not to be viewed simply as yet another example of Sephardic domination over and influence upon Ashkenazim in Amsterdam. Other motives must clearly be explored to fully explain the regulations adopted by Adat Yeshurun.

All this does not mean the members of Adat Yeshurun were Reform. Furthermore, their liturgy was defensible in every one of its strictures from a Jewish legal perspective, and the influence of Sephardic liturgical practices on its rite is undeniable. However, all of their changes, combined with the emphasis *Melitz Yosher* placed on an aesthetic of order and decorum, indicates that *Melitz Yosher* may also be viewed in another way — as part of a nascent trend towards modernization that was beginning to take place in the Jewish world of Western and Central Europe as a result of Emancipation. *Melitz Yosher* both reflects that trend and takes on added significance as a harbinger of what was to come in modern Jewish religious life. It both illuminates and provides insight into the kind of impact Emancipation had on the religious condition of western Jewry.

Melitz Yosher
Its Wider Significance

The paradigmatic import and significance of *Melitz Yosher* for an understanding of the characteristic manner in which Emancipation had a direct influence on the development of modern Judaism can be assessed in several ways. One way is to acknowledge that the directives displayed in its pages were not unique to Amsterdam. The restrictions placed on the recitation of the medieval martyrology, *Av ha-Raḥamim,* in the liturgy of Adat Yeshurun offers one testimony of this reformist trend (4b), as does the aversion to and removal of customs and prayers that were

24 For a listing of representative samples of the Consistory's ordinances, see Petuchowski, *Prayerbook Reform in Europe*, pp.106–10.

deemed "uninformed" (5a – the shroud) or "superstitious" (8a – prayers on the High Holidays that depicted angels as intermediaries between God and humanity). Most significantly, the community demanded that the rabbi deliver a sermon designed for moral edification and spiritual uplift, "*middot u-maʾalot tovot*," each Sabbath. This regulation also specifically instructed the worshippers to sit attentively during the rabbi's sermon and forbade them from interrupting and contradicting the rabbi by engaging in any talmudic casuistry (*pilpul*) while the rabbi delivered his speech (3b). Once more, a western aesthetic derived from the larger culture took precedence over the practice and custom of the Ashkenazic Jewish past.

This stipulation, perhaps more than any other, reveals the innovative spirit of the *Neie Kille*. After all, sermons were not customarily delivered in traditional Ashkenazic European Jewish communities in the course of the service. Furthermore, when they were – on the Sabbaths prior to Yom Kippur and Passover – they were limited to halakhic topics. The delivery of a homiletic sermon offered in a "modern spirit" became a hallmark of all nineteenth-century European Jewish congregations – liberal and orthodox alike – informed by the dual process of political emancipation and general cultural enlightenment. Indeed, as late as 1865, Hungarian orthodox rabbis, meeting in conference in Mihalowitz and anxious to resist such changes to Judaism, proscribed entry into any synagogue that adopted this custom.[25] The introduction of the sermon, like the eating of legumes during Passover, can therefore be seen as more than an innocuous halakhically-warranted innovation of the Adat Yeshurun community. It reveals the direct impact of

---

25 On the significance of this type of sermon in the development of modern Judaism, see Alexander Altmann, "The New Style of Preaching in Nineteenth-Century German Jewry" in Altmann, ed., *Studies in Nineteenth-Century Jewish Intellectual History* (Cambridge, Mass., 1964), pp. 65–116. For the key role the modern sermon played in early Reform, see Meyer, *Response to Modernity*, p. 48. I describe the adoption of this practice among the "cultured orthodox" of Germany in my *Rabbi Esriel Hildesheimer and the Creation of a Modern Jewish Orthodoxy* (Tuscaloosa, Ala., 1990) pp. 3, 47, 71, and 118. For a description of the attack against this innovation by members of the Hungarian orthodox rabbinate, and particularly the Mihalowitz Conference, see M. Silber, "The Emergence of Ultra-Orthodoxy" in Jack Wertheimer, ed., *The Uses of Tradition: Jewish Continuity in the Modern Era* (New York and Cambridge, 1992), pp. 23–84.

Emancipation on the *Neie Kille*, an impact that would soon come to be felt among all Western and Central European Jewish communities — liberal and orthodox alike — that fell under the sway of Enlightenment and Emancipation during the nineteenth century. This change, like others mentioned here, does not mean that Adat Yeshurun was Reform. However, it reflects the birth of a new orientation toward Jewish religion unleashed by Emancipation and its attendant ideologies.

Furthermore, even if it is true that the influence of the Spanish-Portuguese model on the rite of Adat Yeshurun was pronounced, it is equally correct to observe that Adat Yeshurun was not unique among "modern synagogue communities" in the Sephardic influences it displayed. As Eric L. Friedland has pointed out, the influence of Sephardic liturgical and poetic-religious texts as well as Sephardic modes of worship on post-Emancipation generations of Jews was profound. In the Hamburg Temple of 1819, the adoption of "certain Sephardic practices such as the elevation of the unfurled Torah scroll before the reading of the weekly lesson" reflects this influence, as does the substitution of Sephardic *piyyutim* for the customary Ashkenazic ones in the famous 1819 Hamburg *Gebetbuch*. Such usages were clearly adopted from the Sephardic-Portuguese *minhag* and were present in Adat Yeshurun and Hamburg, as well as other communities. In addition, scholars such as Leopold Dukes, Michael Sachs, and Leopold Zunz wrote magisterial books "spotlighting the matchless lyricism of the Jewish religious poets from Islamic Spain,"[26] whose works made their way into a number of the liturgies produced by rabbis of the nineteenth century. These books and liturgies reveal the Ashkenazi effort to mine the Sephardic tradition, an effort initiated precisely because there was in part what Friedland has labeled "a growing aversion to what were perceived as lengthy, unintelligible" elements of the Ashkenazic tradition.[27]

While it is undoubtedly true that the appropriation of Sephardic litur-

---

26 Eric L. Friedland, "Sephardic Influences on the American Jewish Liturgy," in *Shofar* 11:1 (Fall, 1992), pp. 13–15 and in his *Were Our Mouths Filled With Song: Studies in Liberal Jewish Liturgy* (Cincinnati, 1998). In 1842, Dukes published *Zur Erkenntniss der neuhebraeischen religiosen Poesie*, while Sachs's *Die religiose Poesie der Juden in Spanien* appeared in 1845. Zunz's *Die synagogale Poesie des Mittelalters* was written in 1855.

27 Ibid. pp. 13–14.

gical customs and texts by the Ashkenazim of Adat Yeshurun was not a novel development in the Amsterdam Jewish community, the fact that these forms found parallel expression in numerous modernizing Ashkenazic European communities indicates how vital they were for emancipated Jews possessed of contemporary western aesthetic sensibilities and aspirations who were searching for authentic and alternative models of Jewish religion and practice. Friedland sums up well the attraction the Sephardic religious legacy had for emancipated Jewry when he writes,

> The fact that medieval Spanish Jewry in the Islamic milieu was as much at home in secular society as in the world of Jewish faith and culture offered post-Emancipation Jews a pattern worth emulating. [The Sephardic *minhag* struck...] a responsive chord [in] the modern era.... The expansiveness of the Sephardic sensibility provided Ashkenazim ... with a sense of release, an alternative, and a legitimation. The newfound appreciation for the aesthetic and decorous form in poetic word and liturgical execution among Jews not long out of the ghetto ... met with fortification from those who had cultivated that appreciation and skill ages ago.[28]

The changed ethos and aesthetic sensibilities *Melitz Yosher* displays were neither accompanied nor supported by any type of elaborate new reform ideology or theology of the type that was to emerge several decades later in Germany. Indeed, the argumentation in Graanboom's work was quite traditional. Graanboom displayed great care to defend the statutes and practices of his community in terms taken from the tradition itself. He took exception to the talmudic notions, "that custom uproots law" and "that the custom of the people Israel is tantamount to Torah," which were advanced by the *Alte Kille* in the *Diskursen*,[29] and went to great lengths to delimit their application. Indeed, on the basis of the Talmud, Graanboom argued that in the event of "an erroneous custom

28 Ibid. pp. 20–21. For a parallel assessment of the impact of the Sephardic paradigm upon modern Jewry in the West, see Ismar Schorsch "The Myth of Sephardic Supremacy" in Schorsch's *From Text to Context: The Turn to History in Modern Judaism* (Hanover, 1994), pp. 71–92.

29 J. Michman, "The 'Diskursen' of the Old and New Community in Amsterdam," p. 138.

— *minhag ta'ut*," the custom must not be observed. Moreover, he asserted that if the social reality that originally led to the creation of a custom had been altered, then it was "permissible to change the custom in the light of the needs of the day" (7a). This had long been the practice among the Sages of Israel. In fact, committed Jews were obligated to reject customs that were themselves "contrary to the law and that which was upright — *neged ha-din ve-ha-yosher*." A community that did this was not guilty of violating the biblical injunction, "*Lo titgodedu* — do not split into camps" (7b–8a).

Once more, there is nothing novel about any of these final defenses with which *Melitz Yosher* concluded. Graanboom's defense had ample rabbinic precedent and it was argued in terms familiar to those immersed in the tenets and literature of classical rabbinic Judaism. From this perspective, the dispute between the *Neie Kille* and the *Alte Kille* does not appear unique among the arguments and disputes that have marked and divided countless Jewish communities committed to rabbinic tradition throughout history. Yet, this dispute was undoubtedly something more. As Michael Meyer, in speaking of *Melitz Yosher* and the Adat Yeshurun community, has observed:

> It is correct [to note] that the proclivity [that the members of Adat Yeshurun displayed] towards the world of the Enlightenment [taken in concert with the granting of] civic equality which had been bestowed upon the Jews of Holland in the year prior to the establishment of the synagogue, influenced the men of the new community. However, this influence did not give rise to [any formal new] expression [of Jewish religious ideology].[30]

Meyer's observations indicate that *Melitz Yosher* hardly constituted an assault on Jewish tradition. Precedent was honored and fidelity to the canon of tradition was maintained. Nevertheless, it was a document crucially influenced and informed by the spirit of the time and the reality of an eagerly sought political emancipation. Elements in the tradition

---

30 Michael Meyer, "Changes in the Relationship of Liberal Judaism to Halakhah (Law) and Minhag (Custom)" (Hebrew) in *Proceedings of the Eleventh World Congress of Jewish Studies — Division C, Vol. 1: Rabbinic and Talmudic Literature* (Jerusalem, 1994), p. 244.

that bore an affinity to the ethos and aesthetics of modern culture were elevated and chosen over those elements that were deemed antagonistic or out of step with the ethos and aesthetics of modern times. As it happened, most of the elements deemed positive in the tradition were selected from the Sephardic legacy, for the reasons reviewed above. Adat Yeshurun and Amsterdam Jewry, as indicated, were not unique in this way, but rather paradigmatic of the direction many in the western Jewish world were about to take. In this sense, all of the regulations in *Melitz Yosher* reflect a selection and affirmation of those elements within the classical tradition of Judaism that were not only consonant with a modern western aesthetic of order, decorum and dignity, but also promoted it. From the perspective of the sociology of knowledge, the regulations of *Melitz Yosher* display what Max Weber would have labeled an "elective affinity" to the sensibilities and ethos of a contemporary world — a world thrust not only upon the Jewish community of Amsterdam, but upon Jewish communities throughout the Occident, by the reality of political emancipation and secular enlightenment. The Jews of Adat Yeshurun, through the establishment of their own *minhagim*, sought a practical expression of Jewish ritual and practice compatible both with the larger culture in which they lived and with their recently acquired political status. They chose those elements within Jewish tradition that permitted them to achieve that goal.

Concluding Thoughts

The task of the intellectual historian is to focus as much on "the context of an idea as on its text."[31] In this essay, I have attempted to do just that. *Melitz Yosher* and the community of Adat Yeshurun were clearly not Reform with a capital "R." No novel ideology warranted its regulations nor was any change endorsed that did not have some support in Jewish tradition. *Melitz Yosher* shows that religious change need not be radical. It can be rooted in tradition. In this manner, the document reflects one of the various ways in which Judaism responded to the modern world. Simultaneously, the document was creative, not simply exegetical. It does not (nor could any document) reflect a mode of reading Jewish texts apart

---

31 This wording is taken from Paul Mendes-Flohr, *Divided Passions: Jewish Intellectuals and the Experience of Modernity* (Detroit, 1991), p. 60.

from the socio-cultural reality in which it was immersed. It allowed for the construction of a novel ritual world different from that of the dominant community from which it seceded. And it foreshadowed, as this paper has shown, liturgical changes that were to become common among European Jews confronting the same structural reality of political emancipation that these Dutch Jews had in the first years of the 1800s.

To paraphrase Jerome Bruner, human beings possess the "capacity to turn around on the past in the light of the present. Neither the past nor the present stays fixed in the light of this reflexivity. The 'immense repository' of our past may be rendered saliently in different ways." The specific way particular human beings choose to render this past "salient" at a given moment indicates that human beings are not simply "creatures of history" bound to the past. Human beings caught up in community "are autonomous agents as well. [A community] stands both as the guardian of permanence and as a barometer responding to the local cultural weather."[32]

In creating a specific ritual for its own community, *Melitz Yosher* displays both features. This pamphlet not only adopted and confirmed elements of traditional Sephardic ritual as an expression of fidelity to Jewish tradition. It also purposefully created one that was in harmony with the aspirations of a bourgeois congregation anxious to forge a Judaism that would be appropriate for the mores of contemporary European civil society. Bruner's insight provides an apt way of comprehending the meanings of *Melitz Yosher* and the Jewish religious world it sought both to conserve and conceptualize anew.

The socio-political reality of Emancipation shattered the mold in which the world of Ashkenazic European Jewry had previously been cast. The members of Adat Yeshurun and the Jews of Holland wanted full and equal integration into the cultural and political world of their surrounding environs. In seeking this, they were not unusual. This quest for acculturation without a concomitant abandonment of Jewish identity has been the hallmark of virtually all religious Jews in the West during the past two centuries. *Melitz Yosher* is both representative of and ahead of its time. As such, it has a significance beyond the Amsterdam Jewish world that created it.

32 These observations are taken from Jerome Bruner, *Acts of Meaning* (Cambridge and London, 1990), pp.109–10.

Paul Mendes-Flohr has observed that Jewish intellectuals in the modern world have been identified as "cognitive insiders." By this, he means that Jewish intellectuals in the modern world have largely been shaped by the dominant non-Jewish majority culture in which they have lived. Their understanding of "the *Lebenswelt* of the society" which has shaped them is profound and accurate. Simultaneously, these persons have been alienated as intellectuals from many of the norms and values of the bourgeois societies in which they have lived. "Cognitive insiders" forged by and familiar with the larger culture, they remain what Mendes-Flohr labels "axionormative outsiders," persons alien to and distant from the "axiological system" of "religious, moral, political, or economic ideal[s]" that direct the societies in which they live.[33] This status permits them to actively criticize and redirect the society and culture of which they are a part. It also frequently marks them as "social outsiders" from the larger gentile world.

This stance, Mendes-Flohr suggests, does more than characterize the Jewish intellectual in the modern world. It also represents one option that Jews have adopted in confronting the "divided passions" brought on by the dual demands imposed upon those torn between contemporary non-Jewish culture and Jewish tradition. These Jews have sought "an alternative axionormative universe in the form of either escapism or rebellion." In this way, they have attempted to overcome the "status inconsistency" and "social frustration" brought on by their alienation from the broad axionormative consensus that marks their societies. Other Occidental Jews — in nineteenth-century Germany and beyond — have tried to deal with this problem in ways that distinguish them from the intellectual. These Jews have simply "live[d] with it" and accepted the role of "social outsider" imposed upon them by their Jewishness in a non-Jewish world. And others have opted for "the baptismal font, hoping that baptism" would allow them to achieve "respectable social status." These Jews have consciously sought to abandon their Jewishness in the hope that full integration into a larger society, deemed superior to a Jewish patrimony, can be attained.[34]

If Mendes-Flohr's typology is correct, I would add that the members of Adat Yeshurun appear to reflect a fourth type of Jewish response to

---

33 Mendes-Flohr, *Divided Passions,* pp. 32 and 28.
34 Ibid. p. 44.

the conditions imposed on Jews by the realities of political emancipation and cultural enlightenment in the modern era. Adat Yeshurun's Jews aspired to be "social insiders" to the demands and currents of the gentile world on both "axionormative" and "cognitive" levels. In this way, their stance provides a precedent for understanding the response of many Jews in the modern world to the reality of political emancipation and cultural integration. These Jews contend that fidelity to Jewish tradition, religion, and identity in a suitable western form need not demand either total assimilation or profound alienation. Nor will these Jews "live with" and accept the notion that their Jewishness condemns them to being "social outsiders." For these Jews, a complete compatibility between Jewish and western values and aesthetics is perceived as attainable.

Melitz Yosher was composed by this latter type of Jew. It indicates that even when a document is written in Hebrew and informed by classical rabbinic tradition, it can self-consciously be designed to reflect an ethos totally in harmony with the culture and manners of the larger world. At the same time, Graanboom, in championing such an ethos, reflected the desire to be a full participant — not an outsider or a critic — in the larger world brought to the Jew by Emancipation. For him, as well as for the members of Adat Yeshurun and countless other Jews during the last two centuries, this engendered no conscious conflict between Judaism and civil society. The two were seen as harmonious, and the next decades of the nineteenth century were to witness the creation of a variety of Judaisms — liberal as well as orthodox — that would embody the same stance.

Melitz Yosher is therefore a paradigmatic document for comprehending another type of Jewish response to the modern world beyond those delineated by Mendes-Flohr. It allows us to understand how many religious Jews responded both initially and in everyday life to the structural challenges presented to the Jewish condition by the reality of the modern political and cultural order. It was a response that was to be followed, as well as challenged, by others in the decades ahead.

5

A Disputed Precedent

*The Prague Organ in Nineteenth-Century
Central European Legal Literature and Polemics*

When the Hamburg Reform temple was dedicated on October 18, 1818, the employment of an organ during worship was among the central innovations the Reformers proposed in order to enhance the aesthetics of the contemporary Jewish service. This innovation, as well as other changes the Reform temple had introduced, aroused the fierce opposition of the Orthodox. In 1819, a pamphlet issued by the Orthodox Rabbinic Court of Hamburg under the title *Eileh Divrei ha-Brit* (These are the Words of the Covenant) collected twenty-two opinions signed by forty rabbis asserting that the "work of the 'innovators' stood outside the pale of Judaism."[1] The authors of this pamphlet were particularly anxious to respond to and counter claims supporting Reform innovations that had been made two years earlier in Berlin. These warrants on behalf of Reform had been collected in Dessau in 1818 by Eliezer Liebermann, a teacher and itinerant preacher, and issued in two volumes, *Nogah ha-Tzedek* (The Radiance of Justice) and *Or Nogah* (Radiant Light).[2] The Orthodox rabbis of *Eileh Divrei ha-Brit* were aware that the arguments contained in these Reform pamphlets drew upon classical rabbinic sources and practices that could "mislead" the unsuspecting into believing that the employment of instrumental music, among other things, was justified in religious devotions. In this way, the two Reform volumes came to play a central role in the struggle over Reform in Hamburg in 1818 to 1819.

Rabbi David Zvi Hoffmann, professor of Talmud and Codes, and since 1899 head of the *Rabbiner-Seminar für das orthodoxe Judentum* in Berlin

---

1 *Eileh Divrei ha-Brit*, Altona 1819, repr. Farnborough 1969 (in Hebrew); see Michael A. Meyer, *Response to Modernity. A History of the Reform Movement in Judaism* (New York and Oxford, 1988), p. 58.

2 Ibid. pp. 50–51; Eliezer Liebermann, *Nogah ha-Tzedek,* Dessau 1818 (in Hebrew); idem. *Or Nogah,* Dessau 1818 (in Hebrew).

(Rabbinical Seminary for Orthodox Judaism), testified almost eighty years later to the significance this event and these writings held for the history of modern Jewish religious denominationalism. It was there, "in the city of Hamburg," he wrote, that "the evil [of Reform] first burst forth." Despite the protests of the Hamburg rabbinate, "the destroyers" insisted on unleashing their "destructive innovations" on Judaism and the Jewish public. Chief among these innovations was the organ.[3] Debate over the employment of an organ in Jewish worship remained the single most significant marker of the boundary between Liberal and Orthodox Judaism in Germany throughout the nineteenth century.[4] Disputes over its use abound in Central European legal literature of this age.[5] Its importance was such, Hoffmann observed, that a codicil was "issued to each student of our seminary here in Berlin along with his certificate of ordination stipulating that the organ was forbidden." If a student, in later years, elected to serve a community that employed the organ either on the Sabbath or during the week, then, the codicil stated, the ordination certificate that had been issued to the student was to be considered "completely cancelled, null and void."[6] The full text of the codicil, translated into English, appears below on 187–89.

In view of the importance assigned to the issue, it is particularly noteworthy that both sides in this controversy pointed to the precedent of an organ that had allegedly been played during worship in the Maisel Synagogue in Prague. At the onset of the struggle between the Reform and Orthodox factions in early nineteenth-century Germany, the Reformers, Hoffmann noted, had in *Or Nogah* and *Nogah ha-Tzedek* drawn legal justification for this practice from "the organ that existed in the Holy Community of Prague."[7]

---

3 David Zvi Hoffmann, *Melammed Le-Ho'il, Oraḥ Ḥayim*, No. 16. At the end of this responsum, Hoffmann reveals its date to be 1897.

4 See David Ellenson, *Tradition in Transition: Orthodoxy, Halakhah and the Boundaries of Modern Jewish Identity* (Lanham, Md., 1989), pp. 34–46.

5 For a bibliography of much of this literature, see the article by Abraham Berliner, "Literargeschichtliche Belege über die christliche Orgel im jüdischen Gottesdienste," in Berliner, ed., *Zur Lehr' und zur Wehr. Über und gegen die kirchliche Orgel im jüdischen Gottesdienste* (Berlin, 1904).

6 Hoffmann, *Melammed Le-Ho'il, Oraḥ Ḥayim*, no. 16. See also Berliner's discussion of this codicil, loc. cit., p. 58.

7 Hoffmann, *Melammed Le-Ho'il, Oraḥ Ḥayim*, no. 16.

Testimony to the employment of this organ can be found in a 1679 Prague *siddur*,[8] where, prior to the recitation of the hymn *Lekha Dodi* in the service welcoming the Sabbath, the following instruction is found: "A pleasant song by Rabbi Solomon Singer, played in the Maisel Synagogue of the Holy Community of Prague, on the organ (*ugav*) and lyre prior to *Lekha Dodi*." The Reformers cited this custom as a legitimate precedent for their employment of the organ. In contrast, the Orthodox proclaimed it inapposite as a justification. Thus a description and analysis of the dispute that initially raged about the Prague organ, as well as the ongoing debate this precedent evoked in Orthodox legal literature during the middle and again at the end of the century, comprises an interesting and overlooked chapter in the history of Reform-Orthodox disputations of the nineteenth century.

The Reform Position

Rabbi Aaron Chorin of Arad, Hungary, writing in *Nogah ha-Tzedek*, pointed out that most Jewish legal authorities forbade the use of the organ in Jewish worship on the grounds that it violated the biblical

---

8   This *siddur* is contained as an appendix in Shabbatai Bass, *Siftei Yeshenim* (Amsterdam, 1680) (Hebrew). The use of an organ in the liturgical and ceremonial life of the Prague Jewish community prior to the nineteenth century is attested to and described in other sources as well. Johann Jakob Schudt, *Jüdische Merckwurdigkeiten,* 4 vols., (Frankfurt a. Main – Leipzig 1714–1718), makes several references to the employment of the organ in the synagogue life of Prague. For example, in vol. 1, p. 218, Schudt writes "that the Jews in Prague in the Old-New Synagogue have an organ which, however, they use in the religious service only when on Friday evenings they sing the welcoming song for the Sabbath." On that same page Schudt adds that the organ that accompanied this service welcoming the Sabbath was also played by a Jew. See also vol. 4, p. 366. Dr. Alexander Putik of the Jewish Museum in Prague, in a personal letter dated 6th May 1994, asserts that "in the baroque period," as these sources indicate, there is reference to the organ in both "the Old-New and Mayzl Synagogues" and he does not preclude the possibility that the organ was also used in the liturgical rites of other contemporaneous Prague synagogues. He adds, "I assume that both [the organs employed at the Old-New and Mayzl Synagogues] were portable." Dr. Putik makes this assumption because there appears to be no place designated for the permanent placement of an organ in either of these synagogues and as a 1716 copperplate engraving reveals, portable organs were played in public processions marking the arrival of rulers and coronations. Furthermore,

injunction "Thou shalt not walk in their ways." This reasoning, Chorin contended, was applicable only if the particular practice current in gentile usage fell under a category labeled "ways of the Amorites." Inasmuch as such a custom was either idolatrous in and of itself, or facilitated or contributed to idolatry, it was strictly forbidden. A Jew could not "walk in such ways." If, on the other hand, a gentile practice enhanced the glory of God, then it did not belong in this category. The organ, in Chorin's view, was an instance of the latter type of custom, one designed to enhance the honor and respect due to God, and not an example of the former, which would foster idolatry. Consequently, the custom of employing a musical instrument during worship was not one that Jews were forbidden to adopt or imitate. Indeed, they could and should adopt it. Chorin supported this position by observing that Christians, after all, were by halakhic consensus not idolaters. They, like Jews, "recognize the Creator and His attributes" (*middot*). Hence the organ, admittedly employed by Christians during their worship, could not be considered an instrument of idolatry or the use of an organ during prayer an "imitation of the Amorites." Rather, it is a "sweet practice," and its pleasant tones aim at and promote "the uplifting of the soul" (*hitorerut ha-nefesh*). The Polish rabbi and talmudic scholar Moses Isserles (1510/20–1572), Chorin suggests, had recognized this: in *Oraḥ Ḥayim*, 560:3, Isserles wrote that musical accompaniment was permitted for the sake of observing a commandment. Since the act of public prayer was such a commandment, it was permissible to employ the organ during worship. Chorin further argued, in a point particularly germane to our concerns, that actual Jewish custom and usage legitimated this understanding of Jewish law. "Even today," Chorin observed, "holy communities are accustomed to employing musical instruments when singing *Lekha Dodi* at the reception of the Sabbath." The practice of the Jewish people during worship indicated that Jewish law countenanced musical accompaniment as a valid element in the choreography of public prayer.[9]

Chorin, to be sure, did not mention the Prague precedent explicitly,

---

a circular which illuminates a 1741 copperplate engraving depicting a celebratory procession of Prague Jews at a similar occasion makes reference to a *Positiv* oder *Orgel = Fliegel*," a portable organ. It is printed in Milada Vilimkova, *The Prague Ghetto* (Prague, 1993), p. 48.

9 Liebermann, *Nogah ha-Tzedek*, p. 21.

though he no doubt had it in mind. It was left to Eliezer Liebermann, in his *Or Nogah*, to refer to it directly. After producing extensive classical textual sources and arguments calling for the employment of music during prayer, Liebermann added the following observation:

> I have also not forgotten that which several elders related to me at the time I was in Prague. They remember the organ that was in the *Altneuschul*. There, on every Sabbath, Rosh Hodesh, and holiday eve they would play it, and even today they receive the Sabbath in the *Altschul* with musical instruments. The music continues for a half hour into the night, and those who perform it are Jews.

Liebermann's account of the Prague rite, as we shall see, would not go undisputed. Be that as it may, he concluded that there was no Jewish legal prohibition against employing the organ or any other musical instrument during worship. "On the contrary," Liebermann concluded, "the honor of God [demands that we] laud him with song and praise, in joy and mirth, with every musical instrument."[10] Liebermann's argument obviously paralleled that of Chorin. The actual practice of the Prague community validated a particular understanding of Jewish law on the question of whether musical instruments could be used during prayer. It testified to the manner in which observant Jews had comprehended and applied the law, and it provided a powerful precedent for the Reformers in their quest to warrant the employment of the organ in Hamburg and elsewhere. In view of the halakhic dictum "The custom of the people of Israel is Torah," the case of Prague was too significant for the Orthodox to ignore. Their attempt to grapple with this precedent, and to dispute its Reform interpretation and application, was immediate and strong.

The Response of Contemporaneous Orthodoxy

Rabbi Hirtz Scheur of Mainz, at the outset of *Eileh Divrei ha-Brit*, underscored that the issue of the organ was critical for establishing Orthodox boundaries against the incursion of Reform practices.

10   Liebermann, *Or Nogah*, part 1, p.17.

Although he conceded that there was some traditional legal justification for permitting the organ to be employed in a synagogue service, as well as for joyous occasions such as weddings or the celebration of the king's birthday, "in our generation," he wrote, "where the lawless among our people have publicly increased . . . and where many publicly profane the Sabbath, we have no right at all to permit such a thing." Instead, the rabbis of this generation should be as stringent in condemning the use of the organ as the authorities in the generation of Elisha ben Avuyah had been when they stoned him for riding his horse on the Sabbath. Rabbi Scheur implored his colleagues, "on account of the needs of the hour," to be unyielding in their opposition to musical instruments in the synagogue. There was no matter of "lawlessness" more pressing than this, Scheur concluded, "against which you must erect a barrier."

In the course of his argument, Scheur explicitly addressed the challenge presented to his position by the precedent of the organ in Prague. He noted that there were nine synagogues in that city, and observed that in the largest of them, "the Sabbath has been ushered in with song and musical instrument." However, unlike Liebermann, Scheur would not concede that the organ was played there "for a half hour into the night." Instead, he maintained, it was employed only "up to *bo'i be-shalom* [i.e. in a hymn sung before the Sabbath actually begins] and it never occurred to anyone to do so [employ a musical instrument] on the Sabbath or a holiday." Scheur argued, in effect, that Liebermann had misrepresented the facts. The Prague organ had not been used, and therefore it could not be employed as a precedent to justify the use of a musical instrument as an accompaniment to prayers on the Sabbath or holidays. Scheur also reiterated his earlier observation that the organ was employed in only one synagogue in Prague. Its absence in the other eight synagogues indicated that the single precedent of the one synagogue hardly constituted what the law would consider "custom and usage." Scheur, in this way, hoped to emphasize how limited the use of the organ had been in Prague. The isolated case of a single organ did not constitute a precedent. Even if it did, he intended to limit its scope and application and, in light of the Reformers' emphasis upon the importance of the organ, to argue against its contemporary use altogether.[11]

---

11 Scheur's position is stated in Letter 2 of *Eileh Divrei ha-Brit.*

Scheur's arguments, as well as an explicit assault against the Reformers' attempts to employ the precedent of Prague as a warrant for their use of the organ, are echoed in a letter sent to the Hamburg Rabbinical Court by the members of the Orthodox Rabbinical Court in Prague. Rabbis Eleazar Fleckeles, Samuel Segal Landau, and Leib Melish began their letter to the Hamburg rabbis by asserting that what was happening in the Hamburg temple "sickens and pains the heart of the listener. Woe to the generation where such a thing has occurred." The Hamburg Reformers were for them persons of no religion, neither Jews nor gentiles. Particularly disturbing to the Prague rabbis was the use the Reformers had made of the Prague rite in justifying their employment of the organ. Immediately after their introductory words of lament, they turned to the Reformers' claims and addressed the issue directly. The honor of Prague was clearly at stake! "It is an absolute prohibition" (*issur gamur*), they wrote, to play any type of musical instrument on the Sabbath or holidays. Although they acknowledged that there were "those in our community who play instruments to welcome the Sabbath, . . . the custom here is that the musicians must put their instruments away a half hour before the *Barekhu*" [i.e., the prayer that marks the onset of the Sabbath itself]. Consequently, what was "printed in that invalid book (*sefer pasul*) in Dessau" should be recognized for the lie it is. "Called *Nogah ha-Tzedek*, it is evil darkness[12] and should not be relied on at all. Everything in it is a devilish lie (*taḥbulot shaker*) [designed] to blind the eyes of the Jews and lead them astray." The Prague organ was irrelevant as a precedent for the playing of the organ in a synagogue on either holidays or the Sabbath. The Reformers had misinformed and misled the public in their citation of it.[13]

Rabbi Moses Sofer (Schreiber) of Pressburg, the Ḥatam Sofer, also dealt directly with the Prague precedent in his arguments against the employment of the organ during prayer, and he expanded the parameters of the ban that Rabbi Scheur and the members of the Prague Rabbinic Court had issued. Like the others, Rabbi Sofer had read *Nogah ha-Tzedek*, whose authors he called the "wicked of the earth" (*rish'ei aretz*). The organ itself, even in antiquity, "was placed in the temples of

---

12 "Evil darkness" is probably a response to the term *Nogah ha-Tzedek* (literally meaning, "Illumination of Righteousness").

13 *Eileh Divrei ha-Brit*, Letter 5.

ancient idol worship, and it was not used for any other purpose." It was therefore the only musical instrument prohibited in the ancient Temple — banned on account of Leviticus 18:3, "Thou shalt not walk in their ways." Sofer's use of this biblical commandment in his argument compelled him to confront the precedent of the Prague organ in a way in which his colleagues in *Eileh Divrei ha-Brit* had not. For the latter, it was sufficient to refute the claim that the organ was used on either the Sabbath or holidays. To demonstrate that the Prague precedent was not valid, these men simply had to argue that Liebermann was incorrect in *Or Nogah* when he reported that the organ had been used in the Prague synagogue after the Sabbath had already begun. Sofer, in contrast, went much further. The prohibition against the organ was a *din torah*, a law derived from the Torah itself, and, in his view, had been enacted prior to the destruction of the Temple. The law was, and continued to be, designed to separate the Jewish people from the idolatrous ways of the pagans.

Sofer's understanding of this issue placed him on the horns of a dilemma. The Jews of the Prague synagogue were traditionally observant, as was the ritual conducted within its walls. If this was so, then how could one understand the claim that the organ had been employed for so long in even this one Orthodox synagogue? Sofer needed to explain, in light of his claim that the ban against the use of the organ stemmed from the days of the Temple itself, how it was that the traditional Prague community had come to employ the organ even in a circumscribed way. Furthermore, he had to demonstrate why even this limited precedent did not justify use of the organ in a synagogue at times other than the Sabbath or holidays. At the outset, Sofer stated:

> Our fathers told us that in earlier days there was an organ in the *Altneuschul* in Prague and this is cited in the book "A-ve-n" ["Wickedness," an acronym for *Or Nogah*]. However, [the author] testified falsely that a Jew plays there on the Sabbath eve until a half hour into the night, God deliver us . . . We have reliable testimony that they ceased their playing in Prague before the recitation of Psalm 92 [well before the Sabbath actually begins].

Sofer, like the other authors, disputed the claims advanced by the Reformers concerning the use of the organ during worship in Prague.

Liebermann had "testified falsely" and reliable testimony contravened the assertion that the organ was used to accompany prayers on the Sabbath. The Prague precedent, in this reading, had absolutely no bearing on the question of whether instruments could be employed in prayer on the Sabbath or holidays. Since the instance of Prague did not even address, much less justify, that practice, the Reformers were therefore wrong to cite it. Up to this juncture, the Ḥatam Sofer's position simply echoed that of his colleagues. Yet his claim that the organ was banned on the basis of Leviticus 18:3, even during the time that the Temple stood, caused him to expand his arguments beyond those of his contemporaries. "It is true," Sofer conceded, "that in Prague they did employ the organ in song [in the *Altneuschul*] . . . but not in any of the other synagogues in this great city of God." His observation once more parallels that of Scheur. However, he immediately went on to assert: "In addition, even here, when it broke, they did not repair it" — a fact that was of supreme importance to Sofer. He construed this decision as an acknowledgment on the part of the Prague Jews that the entire custom was based on an error (*ta'ut*). They had mistakenly assumed that the organ (*ugav*) had been played in the Temple. Consequently, they were not aware of the prohibition against it and believed its use to be legitimate and countenanced by Jewish law. When they realized that this practice constituted an erroneous custom (*minhag ta'ut*), they ceased employing the organ altogether.

The Ḥatam Sofer clearly felt he had succeeded in doing more than narrowing the potential conclusions to be drawn from the Prague precedent. The Prague congregation's decision to discontinue its previous custom bore witness to their acceptance of his understanding of the rule. It reflected a universal Orthodox recognition of the correctness of his position and refuted Reform claims to the contrary. This, in effect, allowed Sofer to contend that the precedent was in fact no precedent at all! He had, to his own satisfaction, demonstrated that the Prague organ could not be cited as a precedent for employing an organ in a synagogue even during weekdays.[14]

A variant of the Ḥatam Sofer's position concerning Prague also "appears in Rabbi Abraham Levy Löwenstamm of Emden's *Tzeror ha-Ḥayim* (Bundle of Life), which was published in Amsterdam in 1820. Michael Meyer has identified this work as, "the most extensive polemic against religious reform" published at that time.[15] Löwenstamm labeled the first responsum in his collection *Kol ha-Shir* (Sound of the Song) and devoted it to the issue of the organ. On the title page he declared, "In this [responsum] it is explained that it is forbidden to pray in a synagogue accompanied by the musical instrument called an organ (*Orgel*)." On the first page of his ruling, Löwenstamm quoted the by now familiar passage from Liebermann that asserted that the organ was played in Prague by Jews on the Sabbath itself. He concluded his citation of this precedent with the query, "May one depend upon these words to permit the organ or not?" Not surprisingly, Löwenstamm, in response to his own question, proceeded to marshal, quite apart from the precedent of Prague, an impressive array of classical rabbinic sources to refute the Reformers' reading of the sources and to support his own contention that it was not permissible to play an organ at any time in a synagogue. Like Sofer, he based his ruling on the basis of Leviticus 18:3. When he came to the case of Prague itself, Löwenstamm acknowledged, as had his other colleagues, "that there was an organ in Prague in earlier times." Unlike Sofer, however, he did not argue that the organ had been banned from the time of the Temple itself. Instead, he hypothesized:

> . . . perhaps the synagogue [in Prague] was constructed with this organ at a time when this custom [of playing the organ] was not part of their [Christian or pagan] worship. In truth, according to what we have heard, this synagogue has been standing since the time of the Second Temple. Consequently, [the organ] was installed legally (*nitkanah be-heter*). The prohibition against imitating the ways of the Gentiles did not apply in this instance, and was therefore not moved from its place. However, when it broke, they did not repair it or erect another, because at the time of its destruction, the Gentiles already employed this musical instrument, i.e. the organ, in their houses of worship for the specific purpose of idol worship. [Hence] it is forbidden.[16]

Both Löwenstamm and Sofer banned the organ altogether as "an imitation of the gentiles." The differences in their dating of the prohibition

15 Meyer, *Response to Modernity*, p.59.
16 Abraham Levy Löwenstamm, *Tzeror ha-Hayim* (Amsterdam 1820), p.6b.

of organs during Jewish worship should not obscure this fundamental point of legal agreement between them. Indeed, the genuine distinction marking Löwenstamm's treatment of the Prague precedent is his seeming lack of concern with the fact that an organ was played at all in Prague. Unlike his other Orthodox colleagues, including the Ḥatam Sofer, Löwenstamm did not, at this juncture, even bother to brand Liebermann's report about the playing of the organ in the Prague synagogue after the beginning of the Sabbath as a lie. It was sufficient for him to assert that any playing of the organ constituted "an imitation of the gentiles." The historical conditions that obtained at the moment of the synagogue's construction accounted for the previous practice. An awareness of these conditions indicated why the practice did not comprise a precedent for the playing of the organ in either the present era or the future. In short, the Prague precedent, for Löwenstamm as for Sofer, was no precedent at all. The decision to neither repair nor replace the organ once it was broken indicated that all traditional Jewry recognized the reason for, and universality of, the prohibition. The organ could not be employed in a Jewish house of worship on either a holiday or a weekday. The custom of Prague, in the end, supported this ruling.

Mid-Century Discussions

The struggle over the organ in the responsa literature of the nineteenth century did not end with *Eileh Divrei ha-Brit* or with *Tzeror ha-Ḥayim*. Many prominent nineteenth-century Central European rabbinical authorities — including Esriel Hildesheimer and Samson Raphael Hirsch among the Orthodox, and Ludwig Philippson and Abraham Geiger among the Reformers — addressed the issue in their legal writings.[17] However, these writings, in their discussion of the matter, focused exclusively on the literary precedents in the Jewish legal tradition. They did not mention the precedent of the Prague organ.

17   For Hildesheimer, see the *Responsa of Rabbi Esriel, Yoreh Deah,* no.187; and Novellae to *Yoreh Deah,* p.362. Hirsch's views are contained in his *Shemesh Marpei, Orah Hayim,* no. 2, section 3. Geiger's views, issued on 30th October 1861, were published under the title, "Gutachten uber die rituale Statthaftigkeit der Orgel bei dem synagogalen Gottesdienste," and can be found in his *Nachgelassene Schriften,* ed. by Ludwig Geiger, 5 vols., Berlin 1875–1878, vol.1, pp.283–95. Philippson's opinion was

A major exception was Rabbi Zvi Hirsch Chajes of Zolkiew. In his *Minḥat Kenaʾot* (An Offering of Zealotry) (1845), in the course of his arguments against the Reformers, he cited the case of Prague. In arguing against the organ, he reiterated the positions enumerated by his Orthodox colleagues two decades earlier. He repeated Liebermann's claim that "there was an organ in the *Altneuschul* in an earlier period." However, like Löwenstamm, he contended that "perhaps they established this [practice] before the gentiles were accustomed to doing this in their houses of worship." He therefore concluded that this precedent was inapposite for the same reason cited by Löwenstamm, and forbade the organ on the same biblical grounds that his senior colleagues had put forth in their fight against Reform in 1819.[18]

In the 1860s another dispute over the organ erupted in Berlin. Reform members of the community urged that an organ be installed in a synagogue then being constructed in Oranienburgerstrasse in the Prussian capital. The governing board of the community sought out rabbinic opinions on the matter.[19] Among them, two, written by Michael Sachs of Berlin and David Oppenheim of Nagy-Becskerek, cited disputes over an organ in Prague in their responsa. Sachs, a traditionalist sympathetic to the Positive-Historical Judaism of Zacharias Frankel, had served in Prague during the early part of his career. He asserted that an organ had been played there "in the so-called *Neuer Tempel.*" However, it had not been used on the Sabbath or holidays. While the bulk of his responsum was primarily devoted to aesthetic objections to the employment of an organ, Sachs, in his discussion of the Prague case, was careful to note that there were "ritual-legal limits" (*ritualgesetzliche Grenzen*) that even the Reformers in the Prague community had been careful to observe. Hence, the employment of the organ, even in this one liberal Prague synagogue,[20] was confined to weddings, services for

---

published as the leading article in his *Allgemeine Zeitung des Judenthums,* no. 48 (17 November 1861).

18   *Minḥat Kenaʾot,* in *Kol Kitvei Maharatz Ḥayot,* vol. 2, p. 990. For more on Zvi Hirsch Chajes, see chap. 7, "Traditional Reactions to Modern Jewish Reform," in the present volume.

19   Berliner, "Literargeschichtliche Belege," p. 48.

20   Vilimkova, *The Prague Ghetto,* pp. 107–10, has a general discussion of the history of this synagogue building. She notes that the synagogue, known both as "The Temple"

the New Month and half-holidays (*Halbfeiertage*), and the service welcoming the Sabbath.[21] As for Oppenheim, he branded the type of claims put forward in *Or Nogah* concerning the organ in Prague as belonging to "the realm of fantasy" (*das Reich der Phantasie*). The organ was not played on the Sabbath or holidays. In reality, it was only the hymn *Lekha Dodi* that was regularly accompanied by instrumental music, and this was done in accordance with Jewish law, so that the entry of the Sabbath bride could be appropriately marked and celebrated.[22] Sachs and Oppenheim, like Scheur and others forty years earlier, were not concerned with banning the organ altogether as a violation of Leviticus 18:3. They only sought to ban its use on Sabbaths and holidays. As their goals were more limited than those of Sofer and others, they were content to demonstrate that Prague could not be employed as a precedent to justify the usage of an organ on those days. Their arguments allowed them to assert, like earlier opponents of the organ, that the case of the Prague organ — whether found in a traditional or a Reform synagogue — constituted no precedent whatsoever.

Final Echoes

Although the "Prague precedent" remained dormant for the next thirty-five years, it resurfaced during the last decade of the nineteenth century. The problem presented by the use of an organ during worship continued to plague German Orthodox rabbis operating within the context of *Einheitsgemeinden* (the unified communities of Orthodox and Liberal Jews) In the latter part of that decade, an Orthodox rabbi serving

---

and "The Old Shul," was completely demolished in 1867 and subsequently rebuilt as "The Spanish Synagogue." In 1837 it became "the first synagogue in Prague to introduce the reformed rite." As it "allowed for the use of music . . . an organ was installed." Meyer, *Response to Modernity*, p.154, comments that Sachs officiated at this synagogue at the inaugural service in April 1837, and that he "presided over a service that included German sermons, a few German prayers and songs, a choir and organ accompaniment, though in the Prague tradition the instrument was not played on the Sabbath itself."

21 Sachs's responsum, dated 13th November 1861, is found under the title, "Gutachten des Dr. Michael Sachs gegen die Orgel," in Berliner, ed., *Zur Lehr' und zur Wehr*, p.21.

22 David Oppenheim, "Die Synagoge und die Musik. Eine antiquarisch-historische Studie," p.37.

in such a community approached Rabbi David Zvi Hoffmann with a dilemma. The questioner, a former student of the *Rabbiner-Seminar*, reported that his congregation had installed an organ against his wishes. He clearly would not countenance its use on the Sabbath or holidays. However, the problem, as this rabbi saw it, was whether he could remain in the congregation even if the use of the organ was limited to weekday occasions such as weddings. He worried that if he did leave the community as a result of this reform, the rabbi selected as his replacement would undoubtedly not only permit the organ on weekdays, but would introduce and embrace other reforms as well. The rabbi wanted to know, in light of all this, what Jewish law required of him.[23]

Hoffmann's response was lengthy and reflected his command of the issue. At the outset, he noted that this question had been a focal point of contention between Orthodoxy and Reform in the struggle that had ensued between both sides between 1817 and 1821. Among many other points, Hoffmann observed that those who defended the use of the organ did so, in large measure, on the basis of the precedent provided by the organ in Prague. There was no doubt, Hoffmann conceded, that the organ had indeed been employed in Prague as a musical accompaniment to worship in the service immediately prior to the onset of the Sabbath. Inasmuch as Hoffmann, like the Ḥatam Sofer, wanted to ban the instrument altogether on the basis of Leviticus 18:3, he had to address this precedent and abrogate the seeming justification it offered for this practice for the same reason as several of his Orthodox predecessors seventy years earlier.

In his discussion of the precedent, Hoffmann initially noted that the organ, as his Orthodox colleague in Hamburg had pointed out to him, had actually been employed in Prague's Maisel Synagogue, and not the *Altneuschul* as Rabbi Sofer and other respondents in *Eileh Divrei ha-Brit* had incorrectly asserted.[24] The observation of his Hamburg contemporary was corroborated, Hoffmann reported, by Jakob Wagner, "an expert in Hebrew literature," as well as by his student (and later son-in-law) Alexander Marx. Marx had shown Hoffmann a copy of Shabbatai Bass's *Siftei Yeshenim* which included, as reported above, the 1679 Prague *siddur* with Rabbi Singer's poem prior to *Lekha Dodi*. The content of

---

23 See Berliner, "Literargeschichtliche Belege," pp. 58–59.
24 See n. 8 above.

the poem, Hoffmann felt, contained the key to understanding why this traditional synagogue in Prague had employed the organ in its service welcoming the Sabbath. The relevant lines in the poem compared the Sabbath and its reception by the community of Israel to the union between a bride and groom. Rabbi Singer's composition, preceded by the instruction that the song should be accompanied by an organ and a lyre, clearly drew upon Jewish mystical themes. The lines stated,

> The Sabbath bride with the groom, in splendour and greatness; if we observe the two of them according to proper rite, law and custom, we will immediately merit redemption; and God will send a redeemer, in joy he will surely come. This is the day that God has made, the joy of his heart; we will rejoice and be glad in it.

Rabbi Hoffmann therefore reasoned "that because they [were accustomed] and permitted the organ to be played to honor a bride and groom, they also permitted it [to be played] to honor the union of the Sabbath Queen and Israel, for they are to be likened to a bride and groom."

Hoffmann was compelled to concede that the employment of the organ was historically part of the accepted "custom and usage" of the Maisel Synagogue. As the Ḥatam Sofer had maintained, the members of that congregation had mistakenly believed that the organ was among the musical instruments that had been sanctioned for use in the ancient Temple. Furthermore, as Rabbi Löwenstamm had argued, the organ was not associated with gentile worship at the time the Maisel Synagogue was constructed. Indeed, Hoffmann stated, "it is well known that in earlier times the organ was not so commonly employed in their [the Christians] houses of worship." In a later era, when it became more common, the practice, as both Sofer and Löwenstamm had testified, was "abolished" by the congregation. "As they later abrogated the practice," Hoffmann concluded, "the end proves its beginning. They erred [in employing the organ altogether]." As a "postscript" to this section of his responsum, Hoffmann, like Scheur in *Eileh Divrei ha-Brit*, added that even in past centuries the Maisel Synagogue was alone among all the congregations in Prague in employing the organ. It was the practice of a single congregation and ran counter to accepted custom in every other synagogue among the people of Israel "until the time when the hand of the destroyers grew." The organ in the Maisel Synagogue could not be deemed a sufficient warrant for Jewish custom and practice. The precedent of the Prague organ, for Hoffmann, as for his Orthodox predecessors two generations earlier, was in the end no precedent at all. Hoffmann, in effect, distilled the arguments of these rabbis and reasserted the correctness of their stance seven decades later. Like Sofer, he labeled the use of the organ as both "an imitation of the Gentiles" and "an imitation of the heretics" and, on the basis of Leviticus 18:3, forbade its employment in the synagogue.[25]

Precisely because he viewed this issue as critical to Orthodox identity in Germany, Hoffmann was not content to express a lone opinion on the matter. He wrote to several Orthodox colleagues asking them to respond to his writing on the subject — undoubtedly wanting to enlist their support. Among the replies was that of Rabbi Marcus Horovitz of Frankfurt am Main, who had been a close friend of Hoffmann from student days. In addressing the issue of the precedent created by the organ in Prague, Horovitz began by asserting that because their teacher Rabbi Esriel Hildesheimer had already ruled negatively on the matter, he would not disagree. However, he felt compelled to dissent from the notion that the organ was forbidden on account of Leviticus 18:3, basing this dissension, in part, on the precedent of the Prague organ. Horovitz wrote: "On weekdays, it is clear that they [played the organ] in the holy congregation of Prague with the sanction of the greatest authorities of earlier times. And who will come after them and contend that it is forbidden on account of Leviticus 18:3." The rabbis, not the Bible, had prohibited the use of the organ on Sabbath and holidays and for the "faithful," those committed to Orthodox Judaism, this was sufficient reason. Horovitz did not countenance the use of the organ in the synagogue, and his responsum makes clear his unalterable opposition, at least as far as far as Sabbaths and holidays were concerned. However, the precedent of the Prague organ caused him to disagree with the reasoning his friend and colleague Hoffmann offered for the ban. Prague, in Rabbi Horovitz's opinion, demonstrated that Leviticus 18:3 could not be cited as a justification for the prohibition.[26]

Horovitz's opinion closed this nineteenth-century chapter in the ongoing struggle over the use of the organ in Central European com-

25 Hoffmann, *Melammed Le-Ho'il, Orah Ḥayim*, no.16.
26 Marcus Horovitz, *Matte Levi, Orah Ḥayim*, no.6.

munal worship. He ultimately came to assume the same position that the Prague Rabbinic Court and Rabbi Scheur had put forth on this issue in *Eileh Divrei ha-Brit*, and which Rabbis Sachs and Oppenheim had advanced later in the century. Rabbi Hoffmann, in contrast, took the same stance that Sofer and Löwenstamm had adopted. The disagreement between these two Orthodox colleagues provided a fitting closure to the debate the precedent of the Prague organ had engendered in nineteenth-century Jewish legal writings.

Conclusion and Final Considerations

The dispute over the Prague organ at the beginning of the nineteenth century between warring Reform and Orthodox camps reflects a community engaged in the nascent stages of denominational struggles. Liebermann and Chorin, no less than Sofer or Löwenstamm, were enmeshed in tradition. They were, therefore, committed to debating the issue of the organ within the framework of a traditional Jewish legal system that ascribed an authoritative role to the legal convention of precedent. Consequently, the precedent provided by Prague was crucial to them, and their attention to it reflects a Reform Judaism that saw itself as part of the historical community of rabbinic Judaism. Concomitantly, the lack of interdenominational debate over this precedent in Central Europe by the end of the nineteenth century reflects a Reform Judaism that no longer defined itself in legal categories and employed other arguments to defend and justify Reform practices. The evolution and direction of Reform Judaism in the course of that century are foreshadowed in the legal literature of 1818 and its use of the precedent of the Prague organ. The absence of such literature by the 1890s reveals that Reform Judaism ultimately came to abjure law as a defining characteristic of the movement — and marks its departure from the classical legal canon of rabbinic civilization. This study of the Prague organ in nineteenth-century Jewish legal literature thus helps to illuminate the course of Reform Judaism during that century. It was a Reform, as Gerald Blidstein has observed, that was no longer tied to "the authority of precedent" to sanction its actions.[27]

Conversely, the Orthodox reliance upon precedent as a source for

---

27 Gerald Blidstein, "Early Reform and Its Approach," in *Tradition* 11, no. 3, (1970), p. 85.

Jewish law compelled them to respond to Reform claims concerning the Prague organ as soon as they were put forth. The continuing debate Prague engendered at the end of the century between Hoffmann and Horovitz testified not only to the vital and authoritative role that precedent occupied for both these men, but to the continuing commitment they both held as Orthodox rabbis to this legal invention. Indeed, the continuing vitality of precedent in Jewish law in general, as well as the relevance of the Prague precedent in particular, are evidenced in the continued citation of the Prague organ in twentieth-century rabbinic discussions of the issue.[28] Should the issue arise in the future, others may undoubtedly have occasion to employ it.

Accepted custom and usage, in Jewish law as in other legal systems, remains a principal source of law. However, as has been demonstrated here, precedent can seldom be applied in a direct and uncontroversial way. Different rabbis, whether in identical or in distinct denominational camps, depending upon their own goals and convictions, understand and affirm the validity of a precedent in disparate ways. This study of the precedent of the Prague organ and the dispute surrounding it in the nineteenth century indicates that precedent gives rise to judicial disagreement. The unresolved nature of that debate as well as the conflict over the meaning of the precedent only underscores the role that judicial interpretation plays in the legal process. An analysis of the dispute over the Prague organ thus provides insights into the character and evolution of Jewish religious denominationalism in Central Europe during that period. It also casts light on the commitments of these movements and illuminates something of the character and directions of Jewish law in the modern period.

---

28 See for example, Rabbi Jehiel Jacob Weinberg, *Seridei Eish, Oraḥ Ḥayim*, No. 12; and Rabbi Aharon Epstein's 1933 volume of responsa, *Kapei Aharon, Oraḥ Ḥayim*, No. 20:1.

6

Samuel Holdheim and Zacharias Frankel on the Legal Character of Jewish Marriage

An Overlooked Debate in Nineteenth-Century Liberal Judaism

Samuel Holdheim (1806–1860) was the preeminent spokesman for radical Reform during the nineteenth century. He assessed the *Halakhah* as a transitory element within Judaism and abjured law as an enduring dimension of the Jewish religion. Nevertheless, in his most famous work, *Über die Autonomie der Rabbinen und das Princip der jüdischen Ehe* (On the Autonomy of the Rabbis and the Principles of Jewish Marriage) (1843)[1] he offered a serious and insightful analysis of *kinyan* (the legal act of acquisition) as it related to *dinei kiddushin* (laws of marriage) in Jewish law. The reasoning he employed in this analysis can be seen as supplying a base for comprehending the stance he adopted at the Brunswick Rabbinical Conference of 1844 regarding the question of Jewish-Christian intermarriage.

In contrast to Holdheim, Rabbi Zacharias Frankel (1801–1875) was the champion of the traditional wing of Liberal Judaism in nineteenth-century Germany. Committed to the centrality of *Halakhah* in Jewish life, Frankel became a great scholar of *Wissenschaft des Judentums* (the Scientific Study of Judaism) and, in 1854, was appointed head of the Breslau Jewish Theological Seminary. Disturbed by the stance Holdheim adopted in his 1843 work, Frankel felt constrained to respond to the halakhic analysis Holdheim had put forth. This essay will delineate Holdheim's arguments on these matters as well as Frankel's critique. By placing this debate within its historical context, we will see how the diverse positions of these two men on the subject of marriage and

---

1 Samuel Holdheim, *Über die Autonomie der Rabbinen und das Princip der jüdischen Ehe* (Shwerin, 1843); (hereinafter cited as *Die Autonomie der Rabbinen*).

Jewish law sheds light on the history of an incipient Jewish religious denominationalism.

Holdheim's Analysis of Kinyan *in Relation to* Dinei Kiddushin

Holdheim's halakhic analysis of *dinei kiddushin* focused on the nature of *kinyan* in Jewish matrimonial law. In offering his analysis, Holdheim set for himself the task of determining whether *kinyan* as it related to marriage was distinct from the mechanism of *kinyan* in other cases of acquisition.[2] In the first half of *Die Autonomie der Rabbinen*, Holdheim noted that Jewish law used the term *kinyan* to refer to a variety of acts in which a person voluntarily obtains legal rights — both proprietary and contractual. *Kinyan*, for example, was the legal mechanism whereby one could acquire legal right to ownerless (*hefker*) or neglected (*yei'ush*) property. It was also the means through which one acquired ownership over property through sale or gift, and it referred as well to contractual or personal rights one party held in relation to another, such as servitude (*shi'bud*) or debt. Holdheim noted that for *kinyan* to be legally valid and binding in Jewish law, in every instance the person or party who obtained legal rights had to affirm the acquisition by his or her own free will. Secondly, in cases where a previous person or party held legal rights, he or she had to consent freely to the transmission of those rights. If these conditions were met, then *kinyan* could be effectuated. This was true of every mode of *kinyan* in Jewish law. As the act of *kinyan* was a standard part of virtually every act of acquisition in Jewish law, Holdheim argued that *kinyan* was a civil act.[3]

In light of these observations concerning the overarching nature of *kinyan*, Holdheim went on to address the question of whether *kinyan* in connection with the institution of Jewish marriage also constituted a civil act. In other words, did the act of marriage transform the character

---

2   For the *locus classicus* of his discussion on the nature of marriage as a civil act in Jewish matrimonial law, see Samuel Holdheim, *Die Autonomie der Rabbinen* (Schwerin, 1847), pp.137–65.

3   Holdheim delineates the different modes of acquisition in Jewish law in ibid. pp.85 ff. For an excellent English language treatment of the details and complexities of *kinyan* in Jewish law, see *Encyclopedia Judaica*, s.v.,"Acquisition."

of *kinyan* in such a way that the *kinyan* of marriage could be regarded as so qualitatively distinct from *kinyan* in other cases of legal acquisition that it no longer constituted a civil act? He ultimately concluded that it did not accomplish this transformation. Jewish law regarded the act of *kinyan* in relationship to marriage as a civil act, just as in any other instance of acquisition. As long as all the conditions of the acquisition were known to all involved in the transaction, *kinyan* was established and a state of *kiddushin* (marriage) obtained between the husband and his wife. Though the sentiments of love and trust may well have existed between the man and woman, in his view they were of no legal relevance in establishing a state of *kiddushin* between them as husband and wife. Even if these sentiments were lacking, the *kiddushin* between them was valid and binding as long as the parties involved gave their consent and the husband gave his bride a coin worth at least a *perutah*.[4]

Holdheim buttressed his logical but admittedly novel contention by comparing Jewish legal sources that dealt with the process of acquisition in the case of slaves and real estate with the stipulations put forth concerning the act of *kinyan* in regard to marriage. In the instance of slaves and real estate, the Talmud asserted that legal title could be acquired in one of three ways: money, contract, and usucaption (*kesef, shtar, veḥazakah*).[5] Holdheim pointed out that a husband acquired a wife in a parallel fashion. As the Talmud states in *Kiddushin* 2a, "A woman is

---

4 Holdheim, *Die Autonomie der Rabbinen*, pp.139ff. See *Mishnah Kiddushin* 1:1.

5 Holdheim, *Die Autonomie der Rabbinen*, pp.137ff. and p.86. On p.86, Holdheim cites the famous passage in *Kiddushin* 26a that lists these three modes of acquisition and on the previous page in his footnote lists the various types of *kinyan* that exist in Jewish law along with their Roman equivalents. For the mishnaic sources that prescribe the same modes of acquisition for a wife as for Cannanite slaves and real property, see *Mishnah Kiddushin* 1:1, 3, and 5. Judith Romney Wegner, a modern scholar, offers the following commentary upon these sources in her outstanding book *Chattel or Person? The Status of Women in the Mishnah* (New York and Oxford, 1988), p.42. Wegner writes, "The procedure for acquiring a wife (set forth in tractate *Kiddushin*) treats marriage as a formal sale and purchase of a woman's sexual function — a commercial transaction in which a man pays for his bride's virginity just as for any other object of value." For a comprehensive English-language treatment of the many sources involved in the Jewish laws of matrimony and divorce, see Elliot N. Dorff and Arthur Rosett, *A Living Tree: The Roots and Growth of Jewish Law* (Albany, N.Y., 1988), pp.442–545.

acquired in three ways: money, contract, and intercourse."[6] The first two modes of acquisition — money and contract — provided the normative means whereby title was established in Jewish law, and Holdheim stated that these modes were absolutely identical whether the object of acquisition was a wife or anything else.

Interestingly, Holdheim observed that the third way — *bi'ah*, here meaning consensual intercourse — seemingly distinguished the act of *kinyan* in marriage from (and perhaps even elevated it above) the act of acquisition in other types of property transactions. He even conceded that the foundation of this mode of acquisition was the love and trust that existed between the couple. Furthermore, he acknowledged that in Jewish marriage law the bride and groom had each freely pledged to sanctify their union. Nevertheless, he contended that neither these sentiments nor the sanctity involved in the couple's union distinguished *kinyan* in marriage from *kinyan* in regard to other contractual arrangements between two parties. Interestingly, he compared *bi'ah* as a mode of *kinyan* in marriage to the act of *akhilat ha-peirot* (the eating of fruits) as a means for establishing ownership in the case of a field. Just as *bi'ah* constituted an act sufficient to establish ownership, so *akhilat ha-peirot* was an act sufficient to establish *ḥazakah* (*usucapio*). *Bi'ah*, from this point of view, was formally no different a mechanism. Just as possession or investment of labor could give rise to title in the domain of the ordinary civil law of property, so too could intercourse give rise to possession in the case of a wife. *Bi'ah*, in Jewish law like *kesef* and *shtar*, was a civil mode of acquisition.[7]

Holdheim further bolstered his argument by citing two other Jewish

---

6 Holdheim, *Die Autonomie der Rabbinen*, p.138.

7 Ibid. pp. 86 and 137ff. Of course, as my friend and colleague Nomi Stolzenberg has pointed out to me, Holdheim's analogy here is quite problematic from a logical standpoint. For *ḥazakah* in relation to an ownerless field displays no contractual features. Absolute title to the field is established by possession of the property for an uninterrupted and specified period of time (three years — on this point see *Mishnah Baba Batra* 3:1). There is no contractual element here, nor are there two persons involved as there would be in the case of marriage. As stated in the body of the paper itself, *bi'ah* must be consensual if *kinyan* is to be established. It is impossible to imagine how one could speak of a field in these terms. In light of this point, it is significant that in *Baba Batra* 48b there is a discussion in which the betrothal of a woman is compared to the acquisition of a field, the sale of which is valid even if

precedents: proscribed activities on Sabbath and holidays and *dina de-malkhuta dina* (the law of the land is the law). He first pointed out that Jewish law would not permit any type of *kinyan* to take place on either the Sabbath or the holidays. As these were designated as days of rest in *Halakhah*, many forms of work and all civil transactions were proscribed on them. Yet Holdheim noted that certain actions, which would normally have been forbidden as violations of the interdiction against proscribed forms of labor on these days of rest, were permitted if these actions were defined as religious ones. Hence, Jewish law ruled that *milah* (ritual circumcision) and *avodah* (Temple worship), *as religious acts*, superseded the Sabbath.[8] Since marriage, though possessed of religious import and meaning, did not, Holdheim took this as a

---

the sale occurs under coercion. However, the rabbis ultimately reject this position. Consent remains a vital component of the marriage process. I am aware of only two exceptions to this requirement. The first is where a father designates the betrothal of his minor daughter without her consent. *Bi'ah* is not at all involved here. The second exception concerns the case of levirate marriage. In *Mishnah Yebamot* 6:1, it is written that a state of marriage is established between the *yabam* (the brother of the deceased husband) and the *yabamah* (the widow) when intercourse takes place between them even when the intercourse is unintentional (mistaken identity) or involuntary by either party. Here *bi'ah* is involved, but it is the only place in Jewish law where a marriage is established by non-consensual intercourse. In sum, there are two instances in Jewish law where a woman may be married despite her lack of consent. In the case of a male, there is only one.

One more point of distinction is to be made concerning the analogy Holdheim drew between the *kinyan* of a wife and the *kinyan* of an ownerless field. In the case of a wife, *bi'ah* establishes the absolute right of the man to the woman only in an instance where the woman is unmarried. A married woman who willingly has intercourse with a man other than her husband is simply an adulteress. The consensual intercourse in which she has engaged with a man other than her husband does not effectuate *kinyan* in such a circumstance. Ḥazakah is distinct from *bi'ah* then on the grounds that the former establishes absolute, not relative, title. Even if the original owner of the property should return to claim title after three years, that person could not do so. However, *bi'ah*, in contrast to *ḥazakah*, can be said to establish only a presumptive right. Even if the woman has honestly assumed that her first husband was dead, if the first husband is alive and there has been no divorce, then *bi'ah* could not establish *kinyan* between the "adulteress woman" and the man other than her presumably dead husband with whom she engaged in consensual intercourse.

8 Holdheim, *Die Autonomie der Rabbinen*, pp.107–8.

clear indication that marriage and the act of *kinyan* associated with it remained an act of civil law — *ein civilrechtlicher Act.*[9]

Holdheim immediately expanded and elaborated upon the line of reasoning used to support this conclusion. His argument can be summarized as follows: inasmuch as the Talmud forbade *kinyan* of any type to take place on the Sabbath or Jewish holidays, the talmudic prohibition that specified that a marriage ceremony could not be held on these days of rest demonstrated that *kiddushin* and the act of *kinyan* associated with it were not defined primarily as religious acts. If Jewish law had regarded marriage as a religious and not a civil act, then *kiddushin* — like *milah* and *avodah* — would have superseded the Sabbath and *kinyan* could have taken place. In Holdheim's opinion, the failure of Jewish law to do so constituted a warrant for the position that the *kinyan* of marriage was not distinct in this way from the civil character with which *kinyan* was invested in other transactions. Thus Judaism regarded marriage as a civil-legal transaction, not a religious-moral act. Holdheim supplemented this argument by pointing out that the autonomy accorded the husband in biblical law to divorce the wife he had acquired through *kinyan* was identical to the right of any owner of any object to dispose of that object at will;[10] *kinyan* in Jewish matrimonial law was a civil, not a religious, deed.

Holdheim's analysis led him to conclude that marriage properly fell under the category of civil law, *dinei mamanot*, and not Jewish religious law, *dinei issura*. After all, *kinyan* in marriage constituted no less a commercial transaction than would *kinyan* in any other business matter. Holdheim was thus able to contend that just as Jewish law — through the principle of *dina de-malkhuta dina* — accorded state law sovereignty over Jewish law in civil matters, so too should state law have dominion over Jewish law in relation to marriage. In short, marriage came within the jurisdiction of the state, and civil law in this area superseded Jewish law. As Holdheim put it,

> That which is of an absolutely religious character and of a purely religious content in Mosaic legislation and in the later historical development of Judaism . . . and which refers to the relationship

9 Ibid. p.159.
10 Ibid. p.138.

of man to God . . . has been commanded by God to the Jew for
eternity. But whatever has reference to interhuman relationships of
a political, legal, and civil character . . . must be totally deprived
of its applicability everywhere and forever when Jews enter into
relationships with other states.[11]

The Response of Zacharias Frankel

Holdheim's position met with swift and critical response. Samson
Raphael Hirsch immediately published *Zweite Mitteilungen aus einem
Briefwechsel über die neueste jüdische Literatur* (A Second Set of Information on the Exchange of Letters Regarding the Most Recent Literature)
and fulminated against Holdheim's abdication of rabbinic authority
in Jewish matrimonial law. Hirsch contended that the application of
dina de-malkhuta dina to this area was unnecessary and unwarranted.[12]

Another polemical work issued by Orthodox rabbis thundered,

> I ask you, Holdheim! Tell me, where has your heart gone? And if,
> according to your word, you would say, "All who are sanctified in
> marriage are sanctified according to the authority of the rabbis," —
> "according to the authority of the rabbis" we have heard! "According
> to the authority of heretics and non-believers like you," we have
> not heard! . . .
>   "According to the law of Moses and Israel," we have heard in con-
> nection with *kiddushin*. We have never heard, "According to the
> law of the king and the customs of the nations."[13]

Other Orthodox leaders joined in the chorus against Holdheim as well.[14]

---

11 Ibid. pp. 49ff. The translation is taken from Jakob J. Petuchowski, "Abraham Geiger
  and Samuel Holdheim," *Leo Baeck Institute Year Book,* XXII (1977), p. 143.

12 S. Holdheim, ed., *Zweite Mittheilung aus einem Briefwechsel über die neueste jüdische Literatur: Ein Fragment von S. R. Hirsch* (Schwerin, 1844).

13 Pinchas Heilpern, ed., *Teshuvot be-anshei aven — Holdheim v-rei'av* (Frankfurt, 1846), p. 71.

14 Zvi Hirsch Chajes, Jacob Ettlinger, and others joined the chorus of protest against
  Holdheim and his followers. An account of the ire Holdheim aroused can be found
  in chap. 7, "Traditional Reactions to Modern Jewish Reform," in the present volume.

It was left to Zacharias Frankel, however, to produce the chief legal arguments against Holdheim's assessment of *kinyan* in relationship to *dinei kiddushin* (the laws of marriage).

Frankel had initially attacked Holdheim's position immediately after the publication of *Die Autonomie der Rabbinen*, and, again, shortly after the Brunswick Rabbinical Conference of 1844.[15] In his initial responses to Holdheim's work, Frankel was full of invective; he accused Holdheim of being a traitor to the Jewish religion.[16] Nevertheless, it was in an article Frankel published fifteen years later, *Grundlinien des Mosaisch-talmudischen Eherechts* (Outlines of Mosaic-Talmudic Marriage Law), that he explicitly advanced a strong argument against the interpretation of Jewish law Holdheim had put forth.[17] Although Frankel did not mention Holdheim explicitly, his essay put forth a case for refutation of the claims Holdheim had made in *Die Autonomie der Rabbinen* and provided a more elaborate response to them.

Frankel agreed that the means whereby *kinyan* was established in regard to *kiddushin* — *Geld oder Geldeswerth, Urkunde, oder Beischlaf* (*kesef, shtar, u-bi'ah*) were parallel to those modes whereby *kinyan* was effectuated in other civil matters.[18] The *kinyan* of marriage, however, diverged from the *kinyan* of objects immediately after the act of *kiddushin* was performed: the love and trust that obtained between the couple transformed the *kinyan* of marriage from a matter of acquisition into a matter of holiness and ethics.[19] Frankel pointed out that in Judaism the institution of marriage had developed in accordance with the principles of morality (*der Sittlichkeit*) and the act of acquisition (*Handlung*) itself had to be accompanied by the words, "*Du seiest mir geheiligt* — You are sanctified unto me."[20] Furthermore, the holiness accorded

---

15 Holdheim's response to Frankel's initial critique can be found in S. Holdheim, *Das Religioese und Politische im Judentum, mit besonderer Beziehung auf gemischte Ehen* (Schwerin, 1845).

16 For Frankel's critique of Holdheim at this juncture, see Frankel's several articles on this issue in his *Zeitschrift für die religioesen Interessen des Judenthums*, Heft 5–8, 1844.

17 Z. Frankel, "*Grundlinien des mosaisch-talmudischen Eherechts*," in *Jahresbericht des jüdisch-theologischen Seminar* (Breslau, January 27, 1860), pp. i–xvii.

18 Ibid. pp. xi and xxv.

19 Ibid. p. xliii.

20 Ibid. p. xxv.

marriage in Jewish tradition led the rabbis to frown upon intercourse as a proper mode for establishing *kiddushin*. Indeed, Frankel cited a passage in the *Mishneh Torah* of Maimonides, *Hilkhot Issurei Bi'ah* 21:14 ("Any man who sanctifies his wife by means of intercourse . . . lashes are applied to him.") — to support the view that the rabbis condemned *bi'ah* as "*Unsittlichkeit* — immoral."[21]

Holdheim, too, had stated that *kiddushin* involved an understanding that love and trust existed between the couple. He had argued, however, that these factors of sentiment were not legally actionable; they neither effectuated nor annulled the *kinyan*.

Frankel considered this position incorrect. The recitation of the words, "You are sanctified to me," indicated that marriage was marked by more than a legal (*rechtlicher*) act. It had a religious (*religiöser*) dimension,[22] and this dimension meant that the *kinyan* of marriage could not be equated with *kinyan* in other transactions; it was *sui generis*.

Frankel further supported this contention on two other grounds. He noted that in the case of marriage, an act of infidelity on the wife's part required the husband to issue a *get* (a divorce) to her. The authority of the husband to do with his wife what he might wish in such an event was abrogated; by the same token, he had no license to forgive her. Jewish law provided no other option. Divorce was unavoidable. From this, Frankel concluded that *kiddushin* and the act of *kinyan* associated with it could not be equated with other instances of *kinyan*: the wife was a person in her own right; she was not simply an inanimate piece of property over whom the husband could exercise total domination. If marriage was simply a civil act and if his wife was simply akin to a piece of property, then the husband could retain or dispose of his wife according to his will. The institution of marriage, however, was viewed from a religious-moral, not simply a legal, perspective; thus the act of *kinyan* that established it had to be regarded as unique and therefore distinct from every other type of *kinyan*. The adulterous act

21 Ibid. p.xxvi. Frankel also cited the talmudic passage (*Kiddushin* 12b) upon which Maimonides based his ruling. In that passage, Rav, a third century rabbinic authority, sought to discourage betrothal through intercourse by imposing lashes upon men who betrothed women in this way.

22 Ibid. p.xxxi.

of the wife was a "moral abomination — *sittlicher Abscheu*." It violated both culture and modesty and represented a rupture in the moral order of society.[23]

In categorizing the laws of marriage as matters of religion, Frankel believed that he undermined Holdheim's position on the matter. Marriage was not simply a civil affair. Judaism could not surrender its right to regulate marriage through an unwarranted application of *dina de-malkhuta dina* as Holdheim had proposed.

Frankel continued his case against Holdheim's stance by pointing out that a husband could not in every instance do with his wife as his heart desired. Indeed, the wife retained the right not to have intercourse with her husband if she so chose. Moreover, if she found her husband repulsive, then Jewish law held that the rabbinic court had the power to compel him to issue her a divorce. Citing Maimonides, *Hilkhot Ishut* 14:8, Frankel held that the wife was not a "*Kriegsgefangene* — a captive."[24] Once more, he held that in Jewish law, she was a person possessed of rights, not an object subject to the caprice and whim of her husband.

The husband's control over his wife in the Jewish marriage relationship was circumscribed in other ways as well. Frankel observed that in other ancient cultures the husband could terminate his relationship with his wife at any time; she was identical to any other object he owned. He had no need to issue his wife a divorce should he desire to rid himself of her. This situation did not obtain in Judaism. If the husband wished to terminate their relationship, he had to issue his wife a *get* and recite the words that allowed her to remarry.[25]

For Frankel, the phrase, "*Harei at mekudeshet li — Du seiest mir geheiligt*," uttered by the husband when he betrothed his wife under the *ḥuppah*, elevated the act of marriage in Jewish religious law as well as the act of *kinyan* which accompanied it to a level of holiness. The external acts associated with the process of marriage within Judaism might appear identical to those acts that accompany civil transactions, but *kedushah*

---

23   Ibid. p. xliv.
24   Ibid. p. xlviii.
25   Ibid. p. xi ff. See especially pp. xliv–xlv and xlvii–xlviii. Of course, one could look at the institution of divorce in Judaism from another perspective as well. For one could maintain that the divorce simply renders the women "unowned." In this way, the institution of divorce might be said to make the woman more rather than less akin to other forms of property.

(holiness) was an integral part of the relationship established between the bride and groom at the Jewish wedding ceremony. It transformed the mechanism of *kinyan* with regard to marriage from a civil to a religious act. Marriage, from the perspective of Judaism, was a religious affair. Frankel, unlike Holdheim, refused to reduce it to a civil matter.

In assessing Frankel's critique of the position Holdheim advanced, one must bear in mind that Frankel's essay was intended as more than a narrow, albeit interesting, disagreement with Holdheim about the character of *kinyan* in Jewish marriage law. Rather, Frankel's assault on Holdheim betrays a different perception about the character of Judaism in the modern world. To understand precisely what was at stake in this halakhic debate as well as to ferret out the meaning of this last statement, we need to place this entire argument within the historical context of the mid-1800s.

The Historical Context for Holdheim's Position and Frankel's Response

The argument advanced by Holdheim in *Die Autonomie der Rabbinen* was prompted by the continuing political struggle for Jewish emancipation that marked the Germany of his day. Holdheim's immediate target was Bruno Bauer. A Protestant theologian, Bauer published his "Judenfrage" ("Jewish Question") in 1842 in the *Deutsche Jahrbücher* and reissued it as a pamphlet in 1843.[26] In it, he argued that the Jew, by his very nature, could not be emancipated. "As long as he is a Jew," he wrote, "his Jewishness must be stronger in him than his humanity, and keep him apart from non-Jews. He declares by this segregation that this, his Jewishness, is his true, highest nature, which has to have precedence over his humanity."[27] For this reason, "the Jews as such cannot amalgamate with the nations and cast their lot with them."[28] They must "always remain a foreign element."[29]

Bauer, in effect, argued that the "Jewish Question" in the modern political order could not be resolved because the Jew, by his very nature, placed fidelity to religion over allegiance to a state characterized by a

26 Bruno Bauer, "The Jewish Problem," trans. by Helen Lederer (Cincinnati,1957).
27 Ibid. p.22.
28 Ibid. p.47.
29 Ibid. p.55.

putatively neutral public sphere. Emancipation could be granted the Jew in the modern political order only when he was prepared to surrender the imperatives of his religion — when he was willing, for example, "to go to the Chamber of Deputies on the Sabbath and participate in public discussions."[30] In short, the condition modernity established as a prerequisite for Jewish emancipation and Jewish participation in the modern political order was for the Jewish people to agree voluntarily to surrender their particularity — their language, the initiatory rite of circumcision for their sons, and their observance of the dietary and Sabbath laws. Only then could the Jew become a full member of the nation. Until that time, the nature of Judaism made full citizenship an impossibility for the Jew.[31]

Bauer pressed this point by devoting an entire section of his pamphlet to an analysis of the transactions of the Paris Sanhedrin.[32] He dismissed as a lie the distinction the delegates to the Sanhedrin had made between the political and the religious obligations Judaism imposed upon its adherents, and he observed that many of the major addresses the delegates delivered to the Assembly were offered in Hebrew and only afterwards translated into French. This was emblematic of the primacy the Jews accorded their own nation. Bauer wrote,

> It would be fine if the Jew openly declared, "I want — since I wish to remain a Jew — to keep only that much of the Law which seems to be a purely religious element. Everything else which I recognize as anti-social I shall weed out and sacrifice." But instead he pretends to himself, and wants to make others believe that in this distinction between political and religious commands he remains in accord with the Law, that the Law itself establishes this distinction . . . . Judaism cannot be helped, the Jews cannot be reconciled with the world, by the lie.[33]

Dina de-malkhuta dina was at best an illusory remedy to the dilemma of the Jew. The nationalist component in Judaism could not be eliminated.

---

30 Ibid. p.67.
31 Ibid. pp.110ff.
32 Ibid. pp.114ff.
33 Ibid. p.122.

The Jew *qua* Jew could not be made fit for participation in the modern political order.

Bauer's argument garnered a great deal of attention. Indeed, Karl Marx himself issued a response to it. He criticized Bauer for failing to take the implications of his argument to their logical conclusion. Marx charged that Bauer, in singling out the particularity of Judasim as he had, neglected the particularity of the State itself and the role assigned to religion in it. He argued that present-day Jews and Christians could be free only when society was emancipated from religion altogether. The essential "species-being" of humanity demanded nothing less. There could be no distinction between political and private spheres. People could not be regarded as communal beings in the arena of politics while acting as private individuals in the realm of civil society.[34]

Holdheim disagreed, and his *Die Autonomie der Rabbinen* was no less a response to Bauer than was the work of Marx. Holdheim's book can be seen as an expression of classical nineteenth-century liberal political theory. It attempted to distinguish between public and private spheres and sought to carve out a position for particularistic religious commitments in the private realm. Indeed, Holdheim advanced the position that religion continued to possess a legitimate right to exist in the setting of the modern nation-state. It simply had to demonstrate that it could be confined to the private sphere and would not interfere with the individual citizen's performance of duties for the modern nation-state in the public realm. Bauer, Holdheim contended, was wrong not to recognize that Judaism allowed for these civic responsibilities no less than Christianity in the setting of the modern nation-state. A Jewish soldier, for example, was no less obligated to serve in the military on the Sabbath than was his Christian counterpart to serve on Sunday. Nor would a Jewish bureaucrat neglect his duties as a citizen on the Sabbath. Indeed, the dictum of *dina de-malkhuta dina* provided a religious sanction for these acts. It directed the Jew's actions in the political realm and made the Jew fit for life as a citizen in the modern political setting.[35]

In short, the Jew's obligation to observe the laws of the state sprang from meaningful religious warrants contained in Judaism itself. Moreover, the doctrines of Judaism directed the Jews to an appropriate role

34 Karl Marx, *On the Jewish Question*, trans. by Helen Lederer (Cincinnati, 1958).
35 Holdheim, *Die Autonomie der Rabbinen*, pp. 96ff. See especially p. 100.

in the emancipated world of nineteenth-century Germany.

Holdheim's argument concerning the nature of marriage in Judaism as well as his analysis of *kinyan* in relation to *dinei kiddushin* were intended to further complement his brief on behalf of the suitability of Judaism in the present-day political order. His position was informed in large measure by instrumental considerations and was designed to advance the cause of Jewish political emancipation by demonstrating that Judaism recognized and affirmed a distinction between the domain of politics and the realm of religion. His stance on this matter comported with the distinction he drew between the transitory national-ritual-legal dimensions of Judaism and the eternal ethical-religious sentiments he claimed informed its core.[36]

In asserting that Judaism did distinguish between civil and religious spheres, Holdheim was arguing that Jews, without abandoning their religion, were therefore fit for citizenship in the modern order. Meeting Bauer's challenge, he was prepared to "weed out and sacrifice" the "antisocial" elements in Judaism that were incompatible with that order. The distinction drawn in Judaism between religious and political commands was not, as Bauer had charged, an illusory principle. It was a vital component of the teachings and ethos of Judaism, and thus they were not incompatible with the contours of a contemporary secular order that attempted to confine religion to a private sphere. Holdheim's position on the nature of *kinyan* in Jewish matrimonial law was designed to support this stance. It is not surprising, then, that one year later, at the famed Brunswick Rabbinical Conference, he led the proponents of a measure that stated,

> Members of monotheistic religions in general are not forbidden to marry if the parents are permitted by the law of the state to bring up children from such wedlock in the Jewish religion.[37]

36 In making this argument, Holdheim was taking a stance in direct opposition to Bauer, who had branded the distinction made between political and religious commandments in Judaism "a lie." See n.31 above. On the distinction Holdheim drew between the "perishable" ritual and national elements within Judaism, and the "eternally valid" religious teachings that comprised the essence of the Jewish religion, see David Philipson, *The Reform Movement in Judaism* (New York, 1967), pp.252–53.

37 Gunther Plaut, *The Rise of Reform Judaism* (New York, 1963), p.222.

Indeed, his advocacy of this measure in 1844 was totally consistent with the posture he adopted in his *Die Autonomie der Rabbinen* in 1843. His actions on behalf of this resolution reflect more than an alleged comment upon and affirmation of sentiments expressed by the rabbis of the Paris Sanhedrin in 1807.[38] They bespeak a heartfelt longing for Jewish political emancipation and the articulation of a posture designed to accomplish this goal. Holdheim's views on *kinyan* in connection with *dinei kiddushin*, as well as the open stance he took in regard to intermarriage, are paradigmatic of the efforts made by some Jews to be deemed worthy of enfranchisement in the modern state.

Nothing in Frankel's writings indicates that he was not an advocate of classical liberal political theory: he also wanted the Jew to be a full participant in modern society, But unlike Holdheim, Frankel did not believe that for such enfranchisement to take place, it was necessary to assign marriage to the public sphere as opposed to the private realm. Indeed, given Frankel's own views, not only was Holdheim's application of the principle of *dina de-malkhuta dina* to the area of Jewish laws of marriage unprecedented from an halakhic standpoint, but it also marked Holdheim, in Frankel's eyes, as an opportunist who would destroy the religious integrity of Judaism for "a mess of pottage." Frankel not only disagreed with Holdheim's characterization of Jewish marriage as an exclusively civil act, but he could not, in effect, understand why Jewish participation in the modern political order was dependent upon the assignment of Jewish marriage to the civil realm. Further research may shed light on the historical factors that caused Holdheim to disagree. For our purposes, it is enough to observe that the setting of the 1840s and the struggles for Jewish political emancipation that this decade witnessed provide a context for understanding some of the factors that motivated the positions adopted by both Holdheim and Frankel in their debate over the civil and religious nature of Jewish matrimonial law. Their stances surely illuminate the divisions that distinguished the Positive-Historical and radical Reform wings of German Liberal Judaism at this juncture.

38 Ibid. p. 220.

7

Traditional Reactions
to Modern Jewish Reform

The Paradigm of German Orthodoxy

Rabbi Leo Baeck, in his famous essay "Does Traditional Judaism Possess Dogmas?" pointed out that "whether Judaism, in its form of belief, is a religion without dogmas is a question that has often been raised."[1] At the outset of this article, Baeck recalled that Moses Mendelssohn, in *Jerusalem*, had maintained that "the Israelites have a divine legislation: commandments, statutes, rules of life . . . but no dogmas." However, Baeck noted that a number of Jewish scholars disagreed with Mendelssohn's assertion and claimed that Judaism had a number of theological assertions and dogmas that provided the foundation for Jewish faith. Rabbi David Einhorn, for example, stated that "freedom from dogma is so little known to historical Judaism that the Talmud includes him who denies the divine revelation of even a single letter of the Torah in the category of *minim* [sectarians or heretics]." Einhorn's colleague Rabbi Samuel Holdheim asserted that Judaism promulgated "eternal religious truths," and Leopold Löw of Hungary contended that the liturgies of the synagogue "protest loudly and solemnly against the doctrine of the nonexistence of dogmas."[2]

Baeck himself, in approaching the subject, sided with Mendelssohn. In support of this position, he cited the stance of Abraham Geiger, who, echoing Mendelssohn, asserted, "Judaism has no dogmas, that is . . . articles of faith . . . the denial or doubt of which would place him who negates them outside the fold of the ecclesiastical community."[3] Offering a definition of dogma as "a doctrine backed up by authoritative power," Baeck concluded that, in so far as "the exact formulation of creedal concepts" was unknown in classical rabbinic literature and that inasmuch

---

1 Leo Baeck, "Does Traditional Judaism Possess Dogmas?" in *Studies in Jewish Thought: An Anthology of German-Jewish Scholarship*, ed. by Alfred Jospe (Detroit: Wayne State University Press, 1981), p.41.

2 Ibid. pp.43–44.

3 Ibid. pp.41 and 44.

as "the existence of an ecclesiastical authority empowered to formulate decrees" had been absent among Jews for over two millennia, "Judaism . . . has no dogmas."[4] He dismissed the contrary claims of Einhorn and Holdheim, proponents of what Baeck labeled "uncompromising Reform Judaism," as attempts to construct a "formulated credo" that would "secure a foundation for the religious community."[5] These men, Baeck continued, "wanted to transform . . . Judaism into a Jewish *Konfession*, which could have its place alongside the Christian denominations. And, therefore, they wanted to formulate Jewish articles of faith which . . . would distinguish their Jewish denomination from the others."[6]

Whether Baeck or his opponents are correct is beyond the scope of this chapter. However, Baeck's last observation, that men such as Einhorn were driven "to formulate Jewish articles of faith" in order to distinguish Reform Judaism from other Jewish denominations, provides an appropriate starting point, for it cautions the observer to pay attention to the roles that religious dogma, as well as religious practice, have occupied in struggles that have divided Jewish denominations in the modern world. Traditionalist reactions to Reform, no less than classical Reform responses to Orthodoxy, hinged not only upon disputes over religious behaviors but upon disagreements over faith as well. The Orthodox, like many Reformers, were often moved by the conditions of the modern world to establish a "formulated credo" that would draw boundaries over against the Reformers and, in this way, "secure a [distinct] foundation for the [Orthodox] religious community" in the world of nineteenth-century Jewish religious denominationalism.

This chapter, in delineating the indictment Orthodoxy hurled against Reform in nineteenth-century Germany, will pay attention to both poles of the indictment. Orthodox charges against Reform did not only include attacks on what were seen as unwarranted departures from traditional Jewish customs and practices; they also attacked what were regarded as unforgivable deviations from traditional Jewish religious ideology and belief. As Germany was the crucible in which both Reform and Orthodox Judaism were formed in the first half of the

4   Ibid. pp. 46–50.
5   Ibid. p. 42.
6   Ibid. p. 50.

nineteenth century, a description and analysis of Central European Orthodox polemics against Reform in that time and place will do more than illuminate the contours of the traditionalist case against Reform in Germany during the 1800s. They will demonstrate that the Orthodox case against Reform in our contemporary world, on the levels of both practice and belief, had already been well established in Germany long before the onset of the twentieth century — and that present-day traditionalist criticisms of liberal varieties of Judaism simply echo positions that were advanced by Central European Jewish leaders over a century earlier.

Eileh Divrei ha-Brit
The Initial Orthodox Response to Reform

With the rise of the Reform movement in Germany at the beginning of the nineteenth century, the ire of the traditional rabbinate was aroused. The Orthodox were particularly infuriated by innovations in prayer and ritual that the Reformers introduced in Hamburg during the second decade of the 1800s. As noted in chapter five, Rabbi David Zvi Hoffmann (1843–1921), head of the Orthodox Rabbinical Seminary in Berlin at the beginning of the twentieth century, later observed, "[It was there] in the city of Hamburg [between 1817 and 1819] that the evil [of Reform] first burst forth."[7]

The transgressions of the Hamburg Reformers were many in the eyes of the Orthodox, and the traditional European rabbinate found the Reformers' care to legitimate their changes in Jewish ritual and custom on the basis of warrants drawn from halakhic precedent outrageously galling. As we saw in our discussion of the Prague organ issue, in 1818, Eliezer Lieberman, a teacher and itinerant preacher, collected and issued two volumes of responsa — *Nogah ha-Tzedek* (The Radiance of Justice) and *Or Nogah* (Radiant Light) — that provided Jewish legal justification for the innovations in liturgy and synagogue practice that Reformers in Berlin had made two years earlier. The subsequent reforms in Hamburg bestowed additional import upon these volumes, and the Orthodox were unable to ignore them. Their reaction found expression in the 1819 work published by the Orthodox Rabbinic Court of Ham-

---

7 David Zvi Hoffmann, *Melammed Leho'il, Orah Hayim* (New York, 1954), pp. 11–13.

burg under the title *Eileh Divrei ha-Brit* (These are the Words of the Covenant), a pamphlet containing twenty-two opinions signed by forty Orthodox rabbis.[8] Rabbis Eleazar Fleckeles, Samuel Segal Landau, and Leib Melish — members of the Orthodox Rabbinical Court in Prague — began their letter to the Hamburg rabbis by asserting that what was transpiring in Hamburg, "sickens and pains the heart of the listener. Woe to the generation where such a thing has occurred." Moreover, these Prague rabbis went beyond excoriating the Reformers for their departures from the realm of traditional Jewish practice. They asserted that these deviations constituted, in effect, a rebellion against the authority of tradition itself and that consequently, the Hamburg Reformers were persons of no religion, neither Jew nor Gentile.[9] In making such a charge, the Prague rabbis were implicitly issuing a theological claim against the Reformers. Reform changes in the realm of practice were accompanied by and signaled a concomitant abandonment of traditional Jewish faith. The nature of this initial Orthodox argument against Reform, in a nascent though not yet fully developed fashion, indicted Reform for failing to acknowledge the proper parameters and foundations of the Jewish faith. It was an argument that was to be more explicitly put forth by others, including Rabbi Moses Schreiber of Pressburg, the Ḥatam Sofer, who was destined to become the most influential architect of the Orthodox polemic against Reform.

In *Eileh Divrei ha-Brit*, as well as elsewhere in his writings, the Ḥatam Sofer fully crystallized the nature of this twofold Orthodox complaint against Reform, and his Orthodox contemporaries, as well as later generations of Orthodox leaders, echoed the structure and sentiments of his position. He savagely attacked the Reformers for the innovations they had introduced into Jewish worship: their omission of prayers calling for the coming of the messiah, the return of the Jewish people to the land of Israel, and the re-establishment of the Temple service as conducted in ancient days all drew his ire. In addition, Schreiber insisted that Jewish prayer be conducted only in Hebrew, and he objected strenuously to the introduction of musical instruments into the synagogue. On the level of practice; his complaints against Reform were many.[10]

---

8 For excerpts from *Eileh Divrei ha–Brit* and a discussion of the disputed use of the organ in Reform synagogues, see chap.5, "A Disputed Precedent," in the present volume.

9 *Eileh Divrei ha-Brit* (Jerusalem, 1980), p.17.

10 *Eileh Divrei ha-Brit*, pp.6–11 and 30–45. Schreiber's attacks against Reform on the

He condemned their deeds as "pernicious." However, Schreiber did not stop there. He, like the Prague rabbis, attacked the Reformers as persons of no religion. Moreover, he explicitly linked this position to the fact that the Reformers denied the validity of the Oral Law. They were "heretics — *apikorsim*,"[11] who merited censure not simply for their failure to preserve Jewish traditions and practices, but for their denial of classical Jewish religious doctrine. Belief in the eternality and divinity of the Oral Law established the foundation for the Ḥatam Sofer's denominational identity, and it provided him with an Archimedean point from which he could attack Reform.

Schreiber's positions are echoed in the writings of other colleagues in *Eileh Divrei ha-Brit*. Representative of them are Mordechai Benet, rabbi of Nikolsburg, and Akiba Eger, rabbi of Posen and Schreiber's father-in-law. Eger maintained that the fundamental Jewish belief in the divinity of the commandments — upon which Jewish observance depended — could be preserved only by a "faith in the [revealed nature] of the Written and Oral Law" and in the authority of the traditional rabbinate to interpret it. To neglect even a single dictum of the rabbis as prescribed in the Oral Law would result in the downfall of the entire Torah. Reform Jews who did not affirm a belief that all of the Torah was revealed "from the mouth of the Almighty to Moses" and passed on in a legitimate chain of tradition were guilty of denying the basic foundation of Jewish faith. The Reformers, who denied such beliefs, should be understood, like the Sadducees and Karaites before them, as sectarians who had separated themselves from the community of Israel.[12] It was the Reformers' rejection of theological doctrine, and not just their deviations from what these Orthodox rabbis considered to be authentic Jewish practice, that formed the essential basis for the Orthodox rejection and condemnation of Reform. It is small wonder that the Ḥatam Sofer, on another occasion, wrote of the Reformers:

> Our daughters should not be given to their sons, and their sons to our daughters. Their community is like the community of the

---

level of practice in *Eileh Divrei ha-Brit* are paralleled in his legal writings as well. See, for example, M. Schreiber, *She'elot u-Teshuvot he-Ḥatam Sofer* (Jerusalem, 1972), 6:84.

11 *Eileh Divrei ha-Brit*, p. 9.

12 Ibid. p. 12.

Sadducees and the Boethusians, the Karaites and the Christians. They to theirs and we to ours. And if they were subject to our jurisdiction, my view would be to push them beyond the boundaries [of our community].[13]

The Reformers, in these rabbis' opinions, were not simply "sinners." They were, in a fundamental sense, a separate sect apart from the community of Israel. Contemporary political conditions did not allow these rabbis to excommunicate them. However, these conditions did not prevent them from viewing and condemning Reform as embodying a religious ideology distinct from their own. *Eileh Divrei ha-Brit* indicates the emerging contours and content of the Orthodox polemic. It reveals that Orthodox dissatisfaction with Reform rested upon issues not only of practice but of belief as well. Owing in part to the efforts of the rabbis who mounted their attack against Reform in that work, Reform remained an isolated Hamburg phenomenon for nearly two decades. Ultimately, however, through the criticisms Reform leaders leveled at traditional Jewish religious practice and belief — and in view of emancipatory aspirations for equality and opportunity that were then prevalent among masses of Jews and in society at large, Reform could no longer be confined to Hamburg. It had begun to take root throughout Germany.

Incorporating the legacy of early leaders of nineteenth-century Central European Orthodoxy, the next generation of Orthodox leaders dealt with this reality and evolved a more complete policy in respect to Reform. An analysis of how they did so will be the focus of the next section.

The 1840s and the Maturation of the Orthodox Response

As Steven Lowenstein has observed, "The 1840s were the crucial decade for the creation of a Jewish religious Reform Movement in Germany."[14] While the Hamburg Temple, as we have seen, gave rise to great controversy, it was not until the late 1830s that a significant number of secularly

---

13　Schreiber, *She'elot u-Teshuvot he-Ḥatam Sofer* 6:89.
14　Steven Lowenstein, *The Mechanics of Change: Essays in the Social History of German Jewry* (Atlanta: Scholars Press, 1992), p. 85.

trained and Reform-oriented rabbis began to introduce innovations into a number of German communities. In 1841 the first Reform prayer book since the 1819 Hamburg Temple prayer book was issued, and in 1843 the radical Frankfurt Society of Friends of Reform, the "*Reformverein*" — organized by Theodor Creizenach and M. A. Stern — was formed. This Society rejected the ritual of circumcision for Jewish boys, advocated moving the Jewish Sabbath to Sunday, and opposed the authority of talmudic law in Jewish life. Though virtually all German Jews opposed the radicalism of the Society's proposals, the Society did "push the more moderate Reform rabbinical leadership to call the First [of what were to be three] Rabbinical Conference[s] in Braunschweig [Frankfurt, and Breslau in 1844, 1845, and 1846]."[15] While Reform may not have come to dominate completely the communal-religious life of German Jewry by the end of the 1840s, its ever-escalating influence was apparent.

The leadership of the German Orthodox community was aware of the precariousness of its own position, and Orthodoxy's responses to Reform at this time were sharp and multifaceted. These attacks both drew upon and more fully crystallized the parameters of the Orthodox polemic against Reform found in *Eileh Divrei ha-Brit*. A number addressed the Hamburg Temple Reform prayer book, which was reissued in 1841. Isaac Bernays, Orthodox rabbi of Hamburg, asserted that it was forbidden to pray from this work and said that people who did so had not fulfilled their obligations concerning prayer.[16]

His colleague in Altona, Jacob Ettlinger, issued a circular on the first night of Hanukkah, December 8, 1841, stating that the Reformers, in offering this revised edition of the original 1818 prayer book, had solicited opinions from rabbis outside of Hamburg in support of their own. In so doing, the Reformers had transformed the struggle over Reform in Hamburg from a local debate to one that involved profound religious principles and had implications for Jews throughout Germany. As "spiritual leader" of the Jewish people, Ettlinger felt compelled, as a mat-

---

15 Ibid. pp. 85–86. For a detailed account of Reform's growth in Germany at this time, see Michael Meyer, *Response to Modernity: A History of the Reform Movement in Judaism* (New York: Oxford University Press, 1988), pp. 100–142, as well as Robert Liberles, *Religious Conflict in Social Context: The Resurgence of Religious Orthodoxy in Frankfurt am Main* (Westport, Conn.: Greenwood, 1985), pp. 23–86.

16 *Theologische Gutachten über das Gebetbuch nach dem Gebrauche des Neuen Israelitischen Tempelvereins in Hamburg* (Hamburg, 1842), p. 15.

ter of conscience, to respond to the Reformers' claims and to offer his opinion on the prayer book in support of Bernays. Citing the views of those rabbis whose opinions had been collected in *Eileh Divrei ha-Brit*, Ettinger reiterated their contentions that Jewish communal prayer should be conducted only in Hebrew and that it was forbidden to change either the order or contents of the traditional services. Beyond this, Ettlinger was profoundly disturbed, as his predecessors had been two decades earlier, that the Hamburg Temple prayer book rejected the classical Jewish belief in a personal messiah who would bring about redemption for the Jewish people and all of humanity. For all these reasons, Ettlinger, like Bernays, proscribed the employment of this prayer book and concluded, "It is forbidden for any Jew to pray from this book."[17]

The radical Frankfurt *Reformverein* also elicited passionate Orthodox commentary. Rabbi Ettlinger's comments about the *Reformverein* are representative of Orthodox responses to the group's stances and activities. On August 20, 1843, Ettlinger described the group as a "calamity" and not only attacked their denial of traditional Jewish messianic doctrine but also their insistence that the commandment of circumcision was given only to Abraham, that it was not transmitted by Moses to the Jewish people, and consequently, that it was no longer incumbent upon Jews to have their sons circumcised on the eighth day of their young lives as a sign of the covenant that obtains between God and the people Israel.[18]

Rabbi Zvi Hirsch Chajes of Zolkiew, one of the foremost rabbinic scholars of the nineteenth century, elaborated on this development in a blistering polemic, *Minhat Kenaot* (An Offering of Zealotry), which he issued in 1845 and to which he added an excursus in 1849. Like Ettlinger, Chajes was shocked that these Reformers advocated abandoning this central Judaic rite of passage. Past generations of Jews had willingly chosen martyrdom and death rather than not perform it on their sons. How could one attached to the Jewish people even consider such a possibility?[19] Chajes, like Ettlinger, noted that the Frankfurt Reformers defended their position on the grounds that the commandment was given to Abraham alone. When their critics pointed out to them that in

17 J. Ettlinger, *Binyan Tziyon ha-Shaleim* (Jerusalem, 1989), p.157.
18 Ibid. p.73.
19 Zvi Hirsch Chajes, *Minhat Kenaot* (Jerusalem, 1958), vol.2, pp.1003–4.

Leviticus 12:3 the commandment was also issued to Moses, Stern and Creizenach, as leaders of the Frankfurt *Reformverein*, claimed that the Leviticus passage was a later addition to the biblical text. Chajes indignantly observed that faithful Jews had nothing in common with these people: "In their disgusting opinion, the Torah is not eternal." These Reformers, as "*kofrim* [heretics]," denied the fundamental religious beliefs upon which traditional Judaism rested. Their abrogation of the commandment of circumcision resulted from and reflected their rejection of traditional Jewish dogma.[20]

As in Chajes, this linkage of faith and practice, and the causal relationship that obtained between them, is further evidenced in the remainder of Ettlinger's attack upon the Frankfurt *Reformverein*. Ettlinger observed that these Reformers, by rejecting the doctrine of biblical inerrancy, had not only gone beyond the parameters of Jewish faith; they had attacked the foundations of Christianity as well. Like Chajes, Ettlinger asserted that any Jew who concurred with their religious views was, "without a doubt, a *kofer be-ikkar* — one who denied the most fundamental tenet of Jewish faith." Indeed, echoing the rabbis of *Eileh Divrei ha-Brit*, Ettlinger concluded that "from a universal-religious perspective," it could well be maintained that these Reformers were persons "of no faith and no religion." The Torah, for these people, was simply a product of ancient Near Eastern civilization. The notion of a supernatural revelation at Sinai was, in effect, denied by the Reformers, which, in Ettlinger's opinion, reduced Judaism to a product of "human understanding" and invention. The Reformers should therefore be regarded as "a wolf of prey that seeks to destroy the holy sheep of the flock of Israel." They should be watched carefully and it was incumbent upon Orthodox Jewish leaders to protect and warn the people against their deceptions, denials, and lies.[21]

This obligation was felt keenly by a whole host of Orthodox leaders as a result of the three Reform rabbinical conferences that were held between 1844 and 1846 in three German cities. Since Reform, at this point, had begun to make significant inroads in the German Jewish community, the Orthodox rabbinate responded immediately to the 1844 conference in Braunschweig, as they had a quarter century earlier, by issu-

---

20 Ibid. 2:1004.
21 Ettlinger, *Binyan Tziyon ha-Shaleim*, p.74.

ing spirited broadsides against the Reformers. The need for a concerted Orthodox response against the conference engendered more than one collective critique. Rabbis Zvi Hirsch Lehren and Abraham Prins gathered together attacks from over forty Orthodox rabbis (including Samson Raphael Hirsch) against the work of the conference.[22] Rabbi Ettlinger shared their convictions and, in a spirited response, charged that the conference participants unjustifiably claimed for themselves the title of "rabbi." Their words disgraced the Talmud and threatened authentic Jewish tradition; the Reformers' decision to publicize their resolutions compelled the Orthodox to respond so as "to awaken those who slumber"; the people needed to be warned of "the approaching danger" that Reform represented.

In addition, Ettlinger circulated a petition protesting the conference among the Orthodox rabbis of Central Europe. In introducing his protest to his correspondents, he expressed the hope that "the ambitions of Reform and the destructiveness [of their] party would not vanquish our holy Torah." God, Ettlinger was sure, would protect the contemporary faithful of Israel from the Reformers as God had protected the past faithful of Israel from the Sadducees and the Karaites. Nevertheless, God needed the Orthodox to act so that the Torah and its ways would be defended. One hundred and sixteen Orthodox rabbis from Germany and surrounding countries responded to Ettlinger's appeal and signed his petition, which both protested the actions of the Reformers and called upon the traditionalists to remain strong in their faith. Among those who signed or supported the resolution were Samson Raphael Hirsch and the Ktav Sofer, Rabbi Abraham Samuel Benjamin Wolf, son of the Hatam Sofer as well as his father's successor as head of the Pressburg yeshiva.[23]

Individual rabbis responded as well. The work of Maharam Schick, Rabbi Moses Schick of Hungary, the outstanding student of the Hatam Sofer, is representative of these individual traditionalist critiques. Schick, like other Orthodox champions of the day, offered the oft-repeated claim that the Reformers should be seen as "Karaites." Like Ettlinger, he derisively noted that the members of the Braunschweig conference referred

22 Michael Meyer, *Response to Modernity*, pp.134–35, and Samson Raphael Hirsch, *Shemesh Marpei* (New York, 1992), p.188.
23 Ettlinger, *Binyan Tziyon ha-Shaleim*, pp.148–56.

to themselves as "rabbis." "At night," Schick scoffed, "they went to bed with nothing and in the morning they opened their eyes and were rabbis." Rehearsing a standard litany of Orthodox charges against the Reformers, Schick contended that the Braunschweig Reformers had attacked the divinity of the Written Torah as well as the Oral Law, blasphemed God, and denied the coming of the messiah. Schick angrily asserted, "I am ready at any time to smash and break the molars of the sinners to the limits of my strength."[24] Other Orthodox rabbis also questioned the Reformers' integrity and knowledge, asserting that they were motivated primarily by the opportunity for material gain.[25] The sentiments as well as the substance of these attacks were akin to the tone and content of the Schick responsum.

Yet others engaged the Reformers in point by point arguments. In looking at them, one appreciates the genuine divisions of belief and practice that distinguished Orthodoxy from Reform. Chajes' *Minḥat Kenaʾot*, cited previously, stands out among such works as one of the most extensive Orthodox reactions elicited by the conferences. It bespeaks the specific nature of Orthodoxy's quarrels with Reform as well as the magnitude of the case Orthodoxy had developed against Reform by this time.

In *Minḥat Kenaʾot*, Chajes labeled the Reformers as *madiḥim* (those who lead others astray) and *mumarim* (open opponents of Jewish law), terms, as Jakob Petuchowski has observed, reserved for apostates in medieval rabbinic literature.[26] These "legislators of sin" haughtily transgressed the commandments and caused the community to violate the tradition. Chajes, in his brief against Reform, initially turned his attention to the Hamburg Temple Reformers of 1818. By employing the vernacular as a vehicle for prayer, these men abandoned centuries of traditional Jewish practice. They changed the formula of the traditional *Shemoneh Esreh* by omitting prayers that called for the resurrection of the dead, the rebuilding of the Temple, and the restoration of the Davidic dynasty.[27]

Besides these liturgical changes and the *Reformverein*'s rejection of

---

24 M. Schick, *She'elot u-Teshuvot Maharam Schick, Yoreh Deah*, no. 331.

25 Jacob Katz, *Ha-Halakhah ba-Meitzar* (Jerusalem: Magnes Press, 1992), pp. 43–72.

26 Jakob Petuchowski, "The *Mumar* — A Study in Rabbinic Psychology," *Hebrew Union College Annual* 30 (1959), pp. 179–91.

27 Chajes, *Minḥat Kenaʾot*, 2:981–5.

the commandment of circumcision, contemporary Reformers, Chajes pointed out, employed the organ on the Sabbath. In addition, they no longer read the entire lectionary on the Sabbath but opted for a triennial Torah reading in which only one-third of the assigned lectionary was read. In matters of personal status, too, the Reformers totally abandoned traditional Jewish standards. In violation of traditional Jewish law, the Reformers would allow an *agunah* to remarry without receiving a Jewish divorce[28] and they would permit a *kohen*, a man of priestly descent, to marry a divorcee. The Reformers also rejected the traditional stricture regarding levirate marriage and the practice of *halitzah* associated with it.[29]

In the course of this indictment against the deviations the Reformers had introduced into Jewish religious practice, Chajes went on to single out the activities of the most radical Reform rabbi in Germany, Rabbi Samuel Holdheim of Berlin, for special censure. Holdheim, Chajes charged, opposed, as the members of the Frankfurt *Reformverein* had, all traditional Jewish laws of marriage and divorce as well as the ritual of circumcision as a required rite for entering baby boys into the covenant. Holdheim also advocated that Sabbath services be moved from Saturday to Sunday in his *Genossenschaft für Reform im Judenthum*, the separatist Berlin Reform congregation that he headed. Finally, Holdheim would neither allow the *shofar* to be blown on Rosh Hashanah nor would he countenance the recitation of the traditional *Musaf* (additional morning) or *Minḥah* (afternoon) services on Yom Kippur. Indeed, he had these

---

28 An *agunah* is literally "a chained woman." It refers to a woman whose marriage has been terminated *de facto* (for instance her husband is missing in war or has abandoned her for another reason), but not *de jure*. As husbands alone possess the right to initiate divorce in Jewish law, the *agunah* is prohibited from remarrying because she is still technically married to her previous husband.

29 Chajes, *Minḥat Kena'ot*, 2:997–99 and 1004. When a woman's husband dies without male offspring, Jewish law requires woman to marry her husband's brother in the hope that this union will produce a surrogate son and heir to the dead brother, so that the dead brother's name "may not be blotted out in Israel" (Deuteronomy 25:6). Should the living brother reject his deceased brother's widow and opt not to fulfill his levirate duty, he is able to do so through the ritual of *ḥalitzah*, "unshoeing," whereby he releases the levirate widow from her automatic marital tie to him. His sister-in-law is then free to remarry or not at will.

services removed from the prayer book of the community. Chajes noted that even Abraham Geiger and Ludwig Philippson, the two other great rabbinic leaders of Reform in Germany, were more moderate than Holdheim. Philippson, Chajes observed, had attacked the Frankfurt Reformers for their stance on the matter of circumcision and both Philippson and Geiger had opposed Holdheim's plan to move the Sabbath from Saturday to Sunday. Chajes was thus able to distinguish among contemporary Reform leaders, and he did not lump the views and practices of a Philippson or a Geiger together with the stances of a Holdheim. Nevertheless, neither Philippson nor Geiger, despite their greater moderation, was able to avoid Chajes' ire. Neither of them, Chajes observed, was careful to observe the details of Jewish law and Geiger, Chajes charged, permitted traveling, writing, and smoking on the Sabbath despite the traditional halakhic proscriptions forbidding these activities. Differences among these Reformers were therefore insignificant. All had traversed the boundary of acceptable Jewish practice.[30]

Chajes was particularly agitated by the debates concerning the issue of mixed marriage that took place at the Braunschweig conference of 1844. While the assembled rabbis rejected a motion that stated that "marriages between Jews and Christians, in fact, marriages with monotheists in general, are not forbidden," they did agree to the following resolution: "Members of monotheistic religions in general are not forbidden to marry if the parents are permitted by the law of the state to bring up children from such wedlock in the Jewish religion."[31] To Chajes, such a resolution was a serious and unforgivable breach of Jewish tradition. His fury over this interpretation of Jewish custom and practice knew virtually no bounds.[32]

30 Ibid. 2:999–1003 and 1006–8.
31 Gunther Plaut, *The Rise of Reform Judaism* (New York: World Union for Progressive Judaism, 1963), p.222. Also see Meyer, *Response to Modernity*, 1988, pp.134–35.
32 Chajes, *Minḥat Kena'ot*, 2:996–7 and 1008–9. Indeed, Chajes' outrage on this point was paralleled by the anger other Orthodox rabbis expressed on this particular issue. Rabbi Samson Raphael Hirsch, whose response to the conference was written at the end of 1844 during the festival of Hanukkah, compared the efforts of the Orthodox to save Jewish faith in contemporary Germany to those exerted by the Maccabees twenty centuries before. Both were determined to save Jewish faith from those who would cause the teachings of God to be forgotten and transgressed among the people Israel. Hirsch singled out the Reformers' stance on intermarriage between Jews and monotheistic gentiles as a particularly glaring example of the Reformers'

Most importantly, Chajes, as has been pointed out earlier, recognized that the Reformers' abandonment of traditional Jewish law and practices in so many areas resulted from their rejection of the classical rabbinic beliefs upon which authentic Judaism rested. He charged that the Reformers did not accept the doctrine of *"Torah min ha-shamayim u-nitzḥiteha,"* "the divinity and eternality of Jewish law." Instead, the Reformers maintained that the commandments of Judaism were embedded in culture and reflected the various times and places in which they were promulgated. They saw Jewish laws and practices, like woman's fashions, as going in and out of style. Like fashion-conscious women, they were all too anxious to discard the old in favor of the new.[33]

The Reformers of the 1840s claimed that Ezra himself wrote elements of the Torah; and they contended that the Torah was not complete during the time of the First Temple. In making these claims and by accepting as true the assertions of biblical criticism, in Chajes' view they revealed themselves to be more outrageous in their heresy than comparable sectarian groups in the Jewish past. After all, the Sadducees accepted the divinity of the Written Law, and the Karaites, despite their rejection of the authority of the rabbis and the Oral Law, were punctilious in their observance of the Written Law and unshakable in their belief that it was divinely revealed. The Reformers, alone among all the sectarian groups in Jewish history, denied the very foundation upon which Judaism had rested for millennia.[34] There was a causal link, in Chajes' opinion, between the Reformers' rejection of classical Jewish belief and their failure to observe and maintain traditional Jewish standards of practice. It is small wonder, in light of all this, that Chajes queried, "What do we [Orthodox Jews] have in common with these people? . . . How are these people able to call themselves by the name of Israel?" They were heretics (*kofrim*) who, through their denial of traditional rabbinic doctrine, had abandoned the fundamental dogmas that served as the foundation of Jewish faith. In so doing, they placed themselves beyond the parameters of the faithful within the Jewish community.[35] Indeed, for Chajes and many of his colleagues, as for Reformers such as Einhorn and Holdheim, religious

---

distortions of Jewish faith and practice. This sermon is contained in Hirsch, *Shemesh Marpei*, pp.188–90.

33   Chajes, *Minḥat Kena'ot*, 2:978–81 and 985.
34   Ibid. 2:979 and 985–86.
35   Ibid. 2:1004 and 1008.

dogma had come to occupy a central role in their assessment and presentation of Judaism.

The need to defend the integrity of traditional Jewish belief from the heresies of the Braunschweig Reformers compelled the Orthodox to confront the critical historical claims that undergirded Reform as well. The realm of modern academic scholarship, which the Reformers employed to defend their positions, could not be ignored, and the scholarship and commentaries of non-Orthodox Jews were increasingly subject to Orthodox onslaught at this time. Typical is the following remark found in the mishnaic commentary (*Tiferet Yisrael*) of Rabbi Israel Lipschutz of Danzig, a signator to Ettlinger's circular protesting against the Braunschweig conference. Published in Danzig in 1845, one year after the Braunschweig conference, the *Tiferet Yisrael*'s commentary (upon the mishnaic order *Nezikin*) ridiculed an element of Ludwig Philippson's comments upon the Bible as "words of double stupidity — *divrei burut kaful.*"[36]

Meir Leibish Malbim, who was then serving as a rabbi in the Prussian town of Kempen, went far beyond even such detailed strictures as Lipschutz's. In the Preface to his Commentary on Leviticus, entitled *Ha-Torah ve-ha-Mitzvah*, Malbim composed a conscious Orthodox intellectual response to the challenges the Braunschweig Reformers presented to traditional Jewish belief and dogma. Addressing the events of the 1844 conference, Malbim furiously asserted that "the Torah of God was crying bitterly, . . . as its friends had betrayed her." The Reformers, in gathering together and passing their resolutions, had "denied God." These "shepherds" of Israel had betrayed the community and devoured "the sheep under their care." As a result of these events, Malbim concluded that it was necessary for him to "construct a reinforced wall for both the Written and the Oral Law, [a wall] with locks and bolts surrounding its doors so that [the wall itself] cannot be breached." The Reformers, "an evil congregation," had equated the Written Torah with the myths of previous civilizations, and they had viewed the wisdom of the Bible as parallel to the wisdom of other religions. The Oral Law, in their eyes, was reduced to the fanciful imaginations of the ancient rabbis. Indeed, the Reformers held the rabbis of the tannaitic and amoraic periods in contempt

36 I. Lipschutz, *Tiferet Yisrael, Baba Metzia* (New York: 1953), p.60a.

and arrogantly believed that the authors of the Talmud and ancient rabbinic midrash had no knowledge of either linguistic principles or grammar. The Reformers perceived the classical explanations of biblical passages these ancient rabbinic authorities offered as twisted, ignorant, and superstitious. Malbim felt constrained to respond to these charges. The intellectual integrity of traditional Judaism was at stake.[37]

Malbim constructed his response by insisting that the words of the ancient rabbis conformed to accepted "linguistic principles as well as to the laws of rhetoric and logic." *Ḥazal* (the ancient rabbis) "had in their hands vast treasures and storehouses full of wisdom and knowledge, overarching principles and fixed rules concerning grammar linguistics, and knowledge." While the majority of these rules and principles had been lost by those who followed these earliest sages, Malbim claimed to have rediscovered them. His task, as he saw it, was restorative — to recover the pristine meaning of the text. This could be done, Malbim insisted, only through rabbinic commentary. As he asserted, "I have [in this work] shown and explained clearly that the exegesis of the ancient rabbis (*ha-drash*) in fact literally embodies the actual meaning (*ha-pshat*) [of the biblical text] and [the grammatical principles and usages employed by the ancient rabbis to establish such meaning] are fixed and stamped in the depths and principles of the Hebrew language."[38] Malbim detailed these principles and usages in an introduction to the Commentary. The introduction, entitled *Ayelet ha-Shaḥar* (Morning Star), self-consciously defended the truth of Jewish tradition and law by enumerating 613 such principles and usages!

Malbim's novel defense of the Tradition — that *drash* embodied the plain meaning of the Bible and that classical rabbinic tradition had developed 613 grammatical and logical principles and usages to achieve such plain meaning — was obviously artificial and contrived. Nevertheless, in making these assertions, Malbim felt that he had composed a successful intellectual response to the heresies of the Reformers, "[those] Karaites who deny the traditions of *Ḥazal*." His argument and exposition defend the notion that the Written and Oral Laws were two parts of a seamless whole. Rabbinic exegesis, far from being fanciful, was

37 M. L. Malbim, *Ha-Torah ve-ha-Mitzvah* (Jerusalem, 1969), p. 3.
38 Ibid. p. 1.

coherent and consistent. Rabbinic interpretations, based as they were on rules of grammar and usage, were the keys to unlocking the meaning of God's revelations as they appeared in Scripture. The Reform attack upon the Oral Law was misguided and ignorant, for it failed to understand the logic inherent in rabbinic tradition. The Oral Law and rabbinic exegesis were essential if the meanings of God's revelation were to be made manifest in the contemporary world.

Malbim's defense of Jewish oral tradition, however, ignored the challenges Reform had presented to the authority of Scripture itself. He clearly felt that an intellectual defense of the Oral Law was sufficient to repel the claims of the Reformers. Indeed, his contention that the Oral tradition displayed an internal coherence informed by a fidelity to rules and principles of logic and grammar was propelled and informed by the intellectual context of his day. His was an argument consciously designed to respond to the challenges presented by Reform Judaism in the 1840s. Malbim's conclusion, that *drash* alone could provide for the plain meaning of a biblical text, was driven by the need to defend the traditional Jewish belief in the sanctity of the Oral Law from its Reform detractors.

In short, Malbim's arguments indicate that an Orthodox defense of Jewish tradition was not confined to the realm of practice. That defense also addressed issues of religious belief. Orthodox polemics against Reform affirmed the classical rabbinic dogma that asserted that a twofold revelation — both Written and Oral — was vouchsafed Israel by God at Sinai. As Samson Raphael Hirsch phrased it, Orthodox Jews believed that "the law, both Written and Oral, was closed with Moses at Sinai."[39] To deny this, as Rabbi Ettlinger put it, "was to deny God."[40] For these Orthodox leaders, dogma had come to occupy the same central role in defining Judaism as it had for Reformers such as Einhorn and Holdheim.

The Development of an Orthodox Attitude and Policies Final Parameters

In the pages of *Der Zionswächter*, a prominent journal of traditionalist thought edited by Rabbi Ettlinger, a number of Orthodox Jews offered their opinions as to what they felt a proper Orthodox policy toward

39 Hirsch, *Horeb*, trans. by I. Grunfeld (New York and London: Soncino, 1962), p. 20.
40 Ettlinger, *Binyan Tziyon ha-Shaleim*, p. 146.

Reform ought to be. One writer, typical of many others, claimed that the Reformers ought to be excluded from the Jewish community altogether. Echoing the sentiments of the Ḥatam Sofer, this author contended that it was permitted neither to eat in their homes nor to marry their daughters. "No common religious bond exists between us," he wrote. "They must be viewed as any other religious confession."[41] Rabbi Mattathias Levian of Halberstadt issued a responsum enunciating the implications of this approach in 1847. Levian, responding to the first manifestations of Reform in his bailiwick, condemned as "apostates (*mumarim*) to the entire Torah" eight Jewish citizens of the community who had requested permission from secular city officials to leave the Orthodox-controlled Jewish community. Levian suspected that these men intended to convert to Christianity. However, even if they did not formally do so, they were, by virtue of their rejection of the Oral Law and traditional rabbinic authority, "akin to gentiles." They were not to be married in a Jewish wedding ceremony, be counted as Jews for purposes of a prayer quorum, or receive a Jewish burial. In addition, they were not to be called to a public reading of the Torah nor were they to be permitted to recite the mourner's prayer on behalf of deceased relatives.[42] Levian's responsum gave practical expression to the words of Rabbi Solomon Eger of Posen who, at the same time, wrote to Ettlinger urging him to heed a decree issued by the rabbis of Posen to ban the Reformers from the community. The Orthodox were obligated, Eger wrote, "to separate them from Israel for they are not in any way to be considered as belonging to the people Israel."[43] Ettlinger, despite the vociferous attacks he had issued against Reform, was not prepared to honor Eger's request. To have done so would have reduced Judaism to a confession of faith alone — and Ettlinger, like most other Orthodox leaders, refused to do this. Historian Jacob Katz has explained why this is so. "As Orthodoxy adhered to Jewish tradition and especially to the *Halakhah* (religious law), it could hardly dismiss one of the law's basic principles: that being Jewish was a question of descent rather than of conviction."[44] A person born of a Jewish

---

41　*Der Zionswächter* (1846), p.50.

42　Hildesheimer, E., *She'elot u-Teshuvot Rabbi Esriel* (Tel Aviv: Chaim Gittler, 1969 and 1972), *Oraḥ Ḥayim*, vol.1, no.7.

43　*Iggerot Soferim*, ed. by S. Sofer, (Tel Aviv, 1970), vol.1, p.84.

44　Jacob Katz, *Out of the Ghetto* (Cambridge, Mass.: Harvard University Press, 1973), p.210.

mother, irrespective of actions or beliefs, remained a Jew. The Orthodox were thus presented with a quandary. On the one hand, Orthodox polemics consistently and vehemently denounced the Reformers for their deviations from traditional Jewish thought and practice. On the other hand, the strictures of Jewish law proclaimed them Jews. The challenge remaining for the Orthodox was to articulate a policy concerning the Reformers that would take account of all these considerations.

One of the earliest proponents of what was to become the dominant Orthodox attitude toward Reform was the university-educated Rabbi Esriel Hildesheimer, holder of a doctorate from Halle and an ordinand of Rabbi Ettlinger. Hildesheimer was destined, in 1874, to establish and head the Orthodox Rabbinical Seminary of Berlin. An exposition of his position concerning Reform will reveal the parameters and complexity of the Orthodox reaction to Reform. In 1847 Hildesheimer, like his senior colleague Levian, served the Halberstadt community. However, unlike Levian, Hildesheimer acknowledged that a decision to reject the traditional basis of Jewish faith need not be accompanied by a desire to convert to Christianity. The Reformers' desire to secede was not tantamount to an effort "to destroy God's covenant with Israel at Sinai"; they were not "apostates to the entire Torah." Rather, they were persons "who separated themselves from the ways of the community," a lesser, albeit serious, offense. This caused Hildesheimer, like his senior colleague Levian, to issue several proscriptions against the Reformers. However, like his teacher Ettlinger, Hildesheimer insisted that these men remained Jews.[45]

Hildesheimer's decision on this occasion does not mean that he ignored the significance of either dogma or practice in his approach to Reform. Nor does it indicate that he granted Reform any religious legitimacy. Indeed, an episode regarding an ordinand of the Breslau Jewish Theological Seminary reveals that neither he nor his colleague Samson Raphael Hirsch was prepared, on grounds of religious dogma and practice, to accord any religious legitimacy to the Positive-Historical School, much less the Reform trend in German Liberal Judaism. On October 20, 1879, Hildesheimer wrote the following to Wilhelm Karl Von Rothschild:

---

45 Hildesheimer, *She'elot u-Teshuvot Rabbi Esriel, Oraḥ Ḥayim,* vol. 1, no. 7.

I do not know whether you are aware that three-quarters of a year ago some members of a community in Russia turned to Samson Raphael Hirsch and myself with the question as to whether one can put one's mind to rest with the appointment of a graduate of the Breslau [Jewish Theological] Seminary to the post of community rabbi. . . . Our judgment of course was negative.[46]

In reporting this decision, Hildesheimer was accurately reflecting the position of Hirsch, who, in addressing this matter on May 5, 1879, had asserted that no Orthodox community could feel secure with a religious leader trained in Breslau.[47] The opposition of Hildesheimer and Hirsch to religious reform was intractable. An explication of their views will indicate why this was so and will illuminate the attitude and policy positions Orthodoxy ultimately came to hold concerning religious reform.

When, early in 1879, a group of men from the community of Trier asked Hildesheimer whether it was permissible for the community to select a graduate of Breslau as its rabbi, Hildesheimer's reply was an emphatic no. Hildesheimer delineated the reasons for this decision in a correspondence he carried on with Theodor Kroner, the ordinand of the Breslau Seminary who had applied for the post of community rabbi in Trier. Kroner considered himself a knowledgeable and observant Jew and rabbi, and he was upset with Hildesheimer's negative recommendation to the community. Hildesheimer responded by assuring Kroner that he bore him no personal animus. Rather, his opposition to Kroner's appointment was a principled one. The graduates of the Breslau Seminary could not be recognized as legitimate rabbis, Hildesheimer maintained, because both its students and faculty were not wholly committed "to the words of the Sages and their customs." Breslau graduates did not prohibit the purchase of milk produced under gentile supervision. Furthermore, their failure to forbid the buying of gentile wine constituted a major violation of Jewish law. Finally, these men allowed their wives to appear in public without a head covering. This was an extremely serious trespass of Jewish religious practice, and Hildesheimer insisted

46 Mordechai Eliav, ed., *Rabbiner Esriel Hildesheimer Briefe* (Jerusalem: Verlag Rubin Mass, 1965), Letter 46. (Hereinafter cited as *Hildesheimer Briefe.*)

47 Hirsch, *Shemesh Marpei*, p.206.

that no man could be considered a fit candidate for the rabbinate if he permitted such behavior. Hildesheimer thus initially posed his objections to the more religiously conservative Positive-Historical trend in German Liberal Judaism on the grounds of religious practice.[48]

However, Hildesheimer did not stop with these practical objections to the Positive-Historical School. Instead, he added that "there are important differences of [religious] opinion between us." These differences focused on matters of doctrine. In highlighting the significance these doctrinal differences held for distinguishing between Orthodox and non-Orthodox varieties of Judaism, Hildesheimer was not alone. Indeed, Hirsch shared Hildesheimer's views. Hirsch, years earlier, had assailed the religious views of both Zacharias Frankel and Heinrich Graetz, the leaders of the Positive-Historical school. Frankel served as head of the Breslau Seminary while Graetz, the most famous Jewish historian of his era, was the Seminary's most prominent faculty member. The research of both men, in Hirsch's opinion, denied the divinity and eternality of the Oral Law and emphasized, in its stead, the human and developmental nature of Jewish law. In 1860 and 1861, Hirsch, in his journal *Jeschurun*, published a series of articles by Rabbi Gottlieb Fischer attacking Frankel for his famous work *Darkhei ha-Mishnah* (The Ways of the Mishnah). This book, Fischer charged, maintained that elements of the Oral Law had evolved in history. Frankel had contended that talmudic laws subsumed under the category *halakhah le-Moshe mi-Sinai*, were not, as a literal translation would understand it, laws given orally by God to Moses at Sinai. Instead, these laws were of such great antiquity that it was *as if* they had been revealed to Moses. As Fischer and Hirsch understood it, Frankel had written that the authors of these laws were unknown and they were not given by God to Moses at Mount Sinai at all. Rather, they were the enactments of later generations. While Frankel cited a traditional rabbinic warrant — Rosh on *Hilkhot Mikva'ot* — to indicate that his stance on this phrase did not deviate from that adopted by classical rabbinic tradition, Frankel's understanding of the Rosh, in the view of both Hirsch and Fischer, was incorrect. Fischer and Hirsch, who believed in the divinity and the immutability of the Oral Tradition, therefore

---

48   Azriel Hildesheimer, ed., "Ha-rav Azriel Hildesheimer al Zechariah Frankel u-veit ha-midrash be-Breslau," *Ha-Ma'ayan* (1953), 1:69 and 71.

accused Frankel of "*kefirah gemurah* — absolute heresy."[49]

Hirsch, several years earlier, attacked Graetz in a similar vein. Graetz, in the fourth volume of his *History of the Jews*, which dealt with the talmudic period of Jewish history, had presented the rabbis of the Talmud — the *tanna'im* and *amora'im* — as the creators, not the bearers, of Jewish tradition. This meant that Graetz, no less that Frankel, advanced a religiously unauthentic portrait of Judaism that was subversive of traditional Jewish dogma.[50] Doctrine was elevated to a position of such supreme importance by Hirsch that, in 1861, he wrote that it was unimportant whether a man such as Frankel was personally observant if his observance was unaccompanied by correct belief. Affirmation of the principle of *Torah min ha-Shamayim* — that the Oral Law as well as the Written Law was revealed from the mouth of the Almighty to Moses at Sinai — was a prerequisite for an authentic Judaism.[51]

Hildesheimer, who shared Hirsch's doctrinal views, therefore asserted that, before any Breslau graduate could be confirmed as a legitimate rabbi, the ordinand would have to repudiate the views of his teacher Frankel and declare that he believed that the phrase *halakhah le-Moshe mi-Sinai* referred directly and literally to Moses' receipt of certain laws while he was on Mount Sinai. Second, such a rabbi would also have to indicate his belief in the holiness and divinity of both the Written and the Oral Law. Finally, the graduate would have to acknowledge publicly the erroneous conclusions of historical investigation about the development of the Oral Law as put forth by Frankel and, by extension, Graetz. Only if all these conditions were fulfilled did Hildesheimer indicate that he might accept such a person as a rabbi.

However, he gave no assurances that he would do so even in the unlikely event that all these criteria were met.[52] Jewish tradition, for the Orthodox, was clear. Judaism rested upon the notion, as Hirsch phrased it, "that the Written Law and the Oral Law were equal, as both were revealed to us from the mouth of the Holy One, Blessed be He."[53]

49 Hirsch, *Shemesh Marpei*, p. 205 and idem, *The Collected Writings* (New York: Feldheim, 1988), vol. 5, pp. 229–30.
50 Hirsch, *The Collected Writings*, 5:3–201.
51 Hirsch, *Jeschurun* (Periodical) (1861), pp. 297–98.
52 Hildesheimer, "Ha-rav Azriel Hildesheimer al Zechariah Frankel," 1:71.
53 Hirsch, *Shemesh Marpei*, p. 206.

Liberal Jews — whether Reform or Positive-Historical — had, through their insistence that Jewish law was the product of historical development, rejected classical rabbinic doctrine and, in so doing, had gone beyond the pale of authentic Judaism. The case against the Reformers had been made. The issue that remained for the Orthodox was crucial. In light of this posture, what should be the nature of the Orthodox community's policy towards these Reformers? Here the Orthodox were divided among themselves.

One group, as seen above, wanted to deny the "Jewishness" of the Reformers altogether. However, this was impossible. Jewish law clearly defined these people, born as they were of Jewish mothers, as Jews, regardless of their departures from the realms of traditional observance and authentic belief. Nevertheless, Orthodox Jews sympathetic to the direction indicated by this school of thought advanced a policy of separation from and non-cooperation with Reform Judaism as the policy best suited to the defense of traditional Judaism in the modern world. As Jacob Katz has worded it, "The only guarantee for pure Orthodoxy" lay in a refusal "to cooperate with those not absolutely traditional and observant."[54] Orthodox rabbis such as Maharam Schick therefore routinely forbade Orthodox Jews to enter into Liberal synagogues. Nor would a rabbi like Schick permit his community to intermarry with non-Orthodox Jews.[55] Indeed, Schick became a driving force among the Orthodox at the Hungarian Jewish Congress of 1868–1869 and was instrumental in constructing a policy that called for the creation of separate and distinct Orthodox and Liberal Jewish communities in Hungary. In this way the Orthodox could maintain legally sanctioned autonomy and separation and assure the integrity of an Orthodox way of life. The constraints that a non-Orthodox Jewish population might impose as well as the temptations they might present could be avoided by this policy of strict separation. As Schick wrote, "The people who were a singular nation on earth have been divided, and now we are in two camps — one camp which clings to God's Torah . . . and a second which . . . in its haughtiness says that it is progressive when, in reality, it is regressive."[56]

54 Jacob Katz, "Religion as a Uniting and Dividing Force in Jewish History," in *The Role of Religion in Modern Jewish History*, ed. by Jacob Katz (Cambridge, Mass.: Association for Jewish Studies, 1975), pp. 11–12.

55 Schick, *She'elot u-Teshuvot Maharam Schick, Oraḥ Ḥayim*, no. 304.

56 Ibid. no. 309; see also David Ellenson, *Between Tradition and Culture: The Dialectics*

In Germany it was Samson Raphael Hirsch who was the chief architect of this policy of separatism vis-à-vis the Reform. In 1876, owing principally to the efforts of Hirsch, a bill was passed by the Prussian Parliament that modified the Prussian Jew Law of 1847. That law raised each Jewish community to the status of a "public body" and required each Jew "to become a member of the community in his place of domicile."[57] While the 1847 law guaranteed the legal unity of each Jewish community in Germany, it also prevented Orthodox Jews from seceding from a community dominated by Reformers. As far as Hirsch was concerned, such a law imposed an unwarranted constraint upon Orthodox Jews and denied them what should have been their legitimate right to exercise their freedom of conscience. Compulsion, Hirsch wrote, could not bring shared religious duty into existence. Only a sense of common religious purpose could do that. Hirsch concluded,

> The divergence between the religious beliefs of Reform and Orthodoxy is so profound that when an individual publicly secedes he is only giving formal expression to convictions which had long since matured and become perfectly clear to himself. All the institutions and establishments in the care of a community are religious in nature, and they are . . . intimately bound up with religious law [and belief].[58]

Hirsch, no less than Reformers like Einhorn or Holdheim, viewed Judaism in religious-dogmatic terms.

Hildesheimer supported Hirsch in this struggle for Orthodox separatism from Reform in Germany. Like Hirsch, Hildesheimer argued that a Jew's decision to participate in the life of a Jewish community ought to be a matter of conscience, not compulsion, and he declared that this entire matter was one "between man and God," not between an individual and the state.[59] The efforts of Hirsch and Hildesheimer were rewarded.

---

of Modern Jewish Religion and Identity (Atlanta: Scholars Press, 1994). pp. 51–53.

57 Quoted in Salo W. Baron, "Freedom and Constraint in the Jewish Community" in *Essays and Studies in Memory of Linda R. Miller*, ed. by I. Davidson (New York: Jewish Theological Seminary, 1938), p. 12.

58 Quoted in H. Schwab, *The History of Orthodox Jewry in Germany* (London: Mitre, 1950), pp. 68–9.

59 Eliav, *Hildesheimer Briefe*, Letter 29.

When the bill was passed on July 28, 1876, it stated, "Every Jew is entitled, without severing his religious affiliation, to secede, on account of his religious scruples, from the particular community to which he belongs by virtue of a law, custom, or administrative regulation."[60] Orthodox secession from the general Jewish community was now made possible and a policy of strict separatism could be effectuated by the Orthodox Jews of Germany who viewed this course of action as desirable.

Hirsch himself did more than see Orthodox separation from the religious institutions of a Reform-dominated community as desirable. Such separatism, as he viewed it, was mandated by Jewish law.[61] Furthermore, Hirsch believed that Orthodox Jews should not interact with non-Orthodox Jewish organizations at all, not even when they were of a charitable or communal non-religious nature. For example, Hirsch proscribed Orthodox participation in the *Alliance Israelite Universelle*, a Paris-based international Jewish charitable and educational organization, and chided his colleague Hildesheimer for doing so on several occasions. Hirsch, in a letter to Hildesheimer, stated that non-Orthodox Jews, including graduates of the Breslau Seminary, were active members of the group and he noted that Adolphe Crémieux, the Paris head of the Alliance, was not only non-Orthodox but he had permitted his wife to have their children baptized! As a result, Hirsch wrote, "I have absolutely no connection with the Alliance. . . . I fail to see how a man imbued with proper Jewish thought can attach himself to a group founded for the sake of a Jewish task when its founder and administration are completely removed from genuine religious Judaism." He concluded by stating that this was not the way of the pious men of old who dwelt in Jerusalem and separated themselves absolutely from the rest of the community for the sake of preserving Judaism. A total separatist, Hirsch contended that Orthodox Jews in nineteenth-century Germany needed to follow their example.[62]

The consistency of the Hirsch position can be further viewed in an episode involving Hirsch's son-in-law Solomon Breuer in the 1890s.

60 Quoted in Baron, "Freedom and Constraint in the Jewish Community," p.15.
61 Hirsch, *Shemesh Marpei, Yoreh De'ah*, no.46 and *Shemesh Marpei*, pp.202–4.
62 Hirsch, *Shemesh Marpei,*, pp.201–2.

Breuer had succeeded Hirsch as the rabbi of the Orthodox separatist community in Frankfurt and was very upset that a number of Orthodox rabbis had joined with non-Orthodox rabbinic colleagues in signing a petition protesting antisemitic attacks upon the Talmud. These Liberal rabbis were, in Breuer's opinion, *posh'im* (sinners). To cooperate with them in any way implied, in Breuer's view, tacit recognition of their visions of Judaism. He therefore not only refused to join in general communal protests against antisemitic attacks but condemned those Orthodox colleagues who did so.[63]

The absolutist posture adopted by Hirsch on the question of Orthodox separatism is most fully revealed in an episode involving Heinrich Graetz. In 1872, Graetz, along with two companions, went to Israel and toured the entire land. Upon their return, they reported that there were a number of Jewish orphans there and that Christian missionaries were luring these youngsters into the Christian fold by offering them physical sustenance in Christian homes and educational opportunities in Christian schools. These men, including Graetz, recommended that an orphanage under Jewish auspices be established to remedy the situation. Hirsch and a number of other Orthodox leaders in Europe objected to this recommendation for several reasons. Chief among them, as Hirsch put it, was that "the idea to establish an orphanage in Israel both to rescue the orphans from the hands of the missionaries and to raise the level of culture is the idea of Graetz."[64] Hirsch's commitment to a policy of Orthodox separatism, based as it was on a strict allegiance to the dogma of *Torah min ha-Shamayim*, was so uncompromising that even in a matter such as this no cooperation with those deemed religiously heretical could be countenanced. Hirsch, Schick, and other Orthodox rabbis of this school recognized that such persons were Jewish. However, segregation from such Liberal Jews was a necessity if traditional Judaism was to maintain itself in the modern world. All joint activity with them had to be proscribed.

Other Orthodox leaders advanced a different position. While members

63 David Ellenson, *Rabbi Esriel Hildesheimer and the Creation of a Modern Jewish Orthodoxy* (Tuscaloosa, Ala.: University of Alabama Press, 1990), pp.102–3.

64 Azriel Hildesheimer, ed., "Ḥiluf mikhtavim bein ha-rav Azriel Hildesheimer u-vein ha-rav Shimshon Raphael Hirsch al inyanei eretz yisra'el," *Ha-Ma'ayan* (1954), 2:45.

of this other group were no less concerned than Hirsch with *Recht-gläubigkeit* (correct belief), they did not feel that such concern demanded a policy of absolute separation on all matters from non-Orthodox Jews. Hildesheimer himself actually became the foremost proponent of this position. While he supported Hirsch in the 1876 struggle over Orthodox secession from the general Jewish community in Germany, Hildesheimer was anxious that Orthodox Jews not avail themselves of this right except in instances where Orthodox institutions and religious principles were compromised. Indeed, he wrote that "it is not only not forbidden" to strive for communal unity between Reform and Orthodox Jews in situations where the integrity of the Orthodox position could be assured, but to do so was, in fact, "a noble deed."[65] Hildesheimer's students often served as communal Orthodox rabbis in non-separatist Orthodox congregations and his own policy positions allowed for a clear distinction between religious and communal activities. While Hildesheimer proscribed Orthodox cooperation with Liberal Jews and Liberal Judaism in the religious domain, he simultaneously felt obligated to work together with non-Orthodox Jews on matters of charitable and communal concern. As Hildesheimer wrote, "I am of the . . . opinion that . . . one is obligated to act in concert with [Liberal Jews] as far as the conscience permits."[66]

The substance of the policy position advanced by Hildesheimer can be seen in contrasting his actions in several episodes to those of Hirsch. Hildesheimer, in contrast to Hirsch, enthusiastically supported the work of the *Alliance Israélite Universelle*. The charitable enterprises of the Alliance caused him to remark, "I feel myself obligated to promote the unity of various Jewish communities throughout the world [through the work of this group]." Crémieux, in Hildesheimer's opinion, was not a fit representative of religious Judaism. However, neither the active participation of Breslau Seminary graduates in the Alliance nor Crémieux's irreligiosity could obscure the positive functions the Alliance performed. It would be a grave mistake, Hildesheimer concluded, for Orthodox Judaism to adopt a separatist stance in regard to such organizations.[67]

Hildesheimer, in contrast to Hirsch and his circle, felt that concern for the religious purity of Judaism should not take priority over the threat

---

65   Eliav, *Hildesheimer Briefe*, Letter 12.
66   Ibid. Letter 94.
67   Hildesheimer, "Ḥiluf mikhtavim," 2:48–50.

posed by antisemitism. In the face of this threat, Hildesheimer felt it was obvious that Jewishness was a matter of fate, not choice. Consequently, he actively supported defense efforts organized by non-Orthodox elements of the Jewish community and participated actively in their endeavors.[68] The attitude Hildesheimer adopted in 1872 toward the orphanage in Israel that Graetz and his party proposed brings into sharp focus the distinctive nature of the policy position Hildesheimer and his followers adopted towards Reform. Hildesheimer asserted that no one had condemned Graetz as a "religious heretic" more than he. However, he was convinced that Graetz's report concerning the plight of Jewish orphans in Israel was accurate and felt that it ought to be relied upon to coordinate the active response of the European rabbinate. Hildesheimer therefore complained to Hirsch, "A grave situation has arisen . . . among circles who do not wish to distinguish between the heresies of Graetz and his reports concerning established facts in our times. There are great dangers bound up with this approach." To abstain from vital work that would enhance the lives of Jewish people throughout the world for these reasons was tantamount to "throwing the baby out with the bath water."[69] As Hildesheimer phrased it elsewhere, "The truth is the truth even if it be on the side of our opponents."[70]

As an Orthodox Jew, Hildesheimer was no more disposed than Schick or Hirsch to countenance any interpretation of Judaism that was not based upon the principle of *Torah min ha-Shamayim*. Like his other Orthodox colleagues, he was determined not to grant any legitimacy to Jewish religious liberalism and he advocated complete separation from religious institutions and organizations tainted by Reform. However, this did not lead him to adopt a policy of complete separation from non-Orthodox Jews and non-Orthodox Judaism. Hildesheimer felt that the Orthodox were obligated to work in conjunction with their fellow Jews on matters of shared communal concern, even when the institutions that addressed these concerns were not only populated by Liberal Jews but were, in addition, under non-Orthodox auspices. His was a position that allowed for a moderation on this issue that Schick, Hirsch, and their supporters could not abide.

68 Ellenson, *Rabbi Esriel Hildesheimer,* pp. 101–2.
69 Hildesheimer, "Ḥiluf mikhtavim," 2:44 and 51.
70 Eliav, *Hildesheimer Briefe*, Letter 22.

Conclusion

As this chapter has demonstrated, Orthodox polemics against Reform in Germany displayed a remarkable consistency throughout the nineteenth century. From the rabbis of *Eileh Divrei ha-Brit* at the beginning of the 1800s through rabbis such as Chajes, Ettlinger, Hirsch, Schick, and Hildesheimer in mid-century, Orthodox opposition to Liberal Judaism addressed and vehemently denounced Reform departures from traditional Jewish practice and the perceived deviance of Liberal ideologues in matters of doctrine and belief as well.

Every Orthodox leader surveyed in this chapter focused upon matters of dogma as much as practice in voicing their reaction to Reform. Indeed, for these Orthodox leaders, dogma was elevated to a position of such supreme importance that the Positive-Historical Judaism of a Frankel was attacked as strongly as the Reform of a Holdheim. The position of these Orthodox spokesmen appears to negate Baeck's contention that Judaism possesses no "formulated credo." Or, to be more exact, this chapter indicates that the same conditions that led certain Reform leaders "to formulate Jewish articles of faith which . . . would distinguish their Jewish denomination from the others" prompted these Orthodox rabbis as well. This focus upon dogma pushed Orthodox leaders such as Malbim and Hirsch to formulate intellectual positions defending traditional rabbinic doctrine. Simultaneously, this emphasis allowed the Orthodox to distinguish themselves from every variety of Liberal Judaism and provided them with a warrant for their refusal to cede even a modicum of legitimacy to religious Reform. This posture has remained the foundation for Orthodoxy's principled objection to religious Reform up to the present day.[71]

Orthodox reaction to the religious illegitimacy of Reform was unanimous. However, disagreement did arise among the champions of Orthodoxy as to whether there were any areas where Orthodox and Liberal Jews and Judaism could engage in joint endeavors. Here, two distinct Orthodox policy positions were put forth. According to one group, the integrity of Orthodoxy demanded complete separation from the Reform.

---

71 David Ellenson, "The Integrity of Reform Within *Kelal Yisrael*," *The Yearbook of the Central Conference of American Rabbis* (1986), pp.23–26

To associate with the non-Orthodox in any way was seen as tantamount to granting Reform an absolutely unacceptable degree of religious legitimacy. The purity of Orthodoxy could be assured only through a policy of total non-association with Reform. Other Orthodox leaders disagreed. In the opinion of these men, Orthodox cooperation with the non-Orthodox in areas of common communal and charitable concern did not imply any act of Orthodox religious recognition of Reform. Instead, these persons simply regarded Orthodox participation in certain projects as desirable and advantageous to the Orthodox and Jewish cause. In advancing these distinctive attitudes, these Central European Orthodox rabbis adumbrated two distinct policy positions vis-à-vis Liberal Jews and Judaism that continue to be operative within the world of contemporary Orthodoxy.[72] This chapter, in presenting the reaction of nineteenth-century German Orthodoxy to Reform, has illuminated a vital period in modern Jewish intellectual and religious history that remains instructive for an understanding of Orthodoxy and its attitudes toward liberal varieties of Judaism in the present.

---

72 Nahum Bulman, "A Healing Sun," *The Jewish Observer* (February, 1993), pp. 20–21.

8

The Rabbiner-Seminar Codicil
An Instrument of Boundary Maintenance

On October 22, 1873, the *Rabbiner-Seminar für das Orthodoxe Judentum* opened its doors in Berlin under the leadership of Rabbi Esriel Hildesheimer. From the outset, the seminary intended, as its name indicated, to "increase the power of Orthodox Judaism internally and raise its esteem externally."[1] It saw itself as a rival to both the Jewish Theological Seminary in Breslau and the *Hochschule für die Wissenschaft des Judentums* as a source of rabbis for the Jewish community in Germany and central Europe. Within a decade after its inauguration, the hope of its founder was realized and the position of the *Rabbiner-Seminar* as the German Jewish community's leading institution of higher Orthodox education was secure. Its graduates quickly obtained rabbinical posts and by 1888 Hildesheimer could proudly "complain" that he could not fulfill all the requests for rabbis that he received.[2]

In 1883, with its status as an Orthodox institution assured, the *Rabbiner-Seminar für das Orthodoxe Judentum* changed its name to *Das Rabbiner-Seminar zu Berlin*, omitting all explicit references to itself as Orthodox. One scholar, M. A. Shulvass, asserts that "Orthodox" was dropped from its name because the boundaries between Liberal and Orthodox Judaism in Germany had by that time been firmly set and their struggle relaxed to one of "peaceful coexistence."[3] There was no longer a need to proclaim differences publicly, as these distinctions were now sufficiently acknowledged and recognized both within the general Jewish community in Germany and among the protagonists themselves. In addition, it may well be that Hildesheimer was implicitly

---

1 This quotation is found in *Das Rabbiner-Seminar zu Berlin: Bericht über die ersten fünfundzwanzig Jahres seines Bestehens* (1873–1898) (Berlin, 1898), pp. 7–8.

2 Mordechai Eliav, ed., *Rabbiner Esriel Hildesheimer Briefe* (Jerusalem: Verlag Rubin Mass, 1965), Letter 84.

3 M. A. Shulvass, "The Rabbiner-Seminar of Berlin" (Hebrew), in *Institutions of Higher Learning in Europe: Their Development and Destruction* (Hebrew), ed. Samuel Mirsky (New York: Ogen, 1956), p. 695.

asserting that his school represented more than a mere branch of Judaism. It was, rather, the legitimate bearer of Jewish tradition on German soil. Indeed, the decision to avoid denominational labels in their names parallels decisions made at both the *Hochschule* and the Breslau Seminary, thereby implying that each spoke for the whole of religious Judaism. In either event, Hildesheimer was determined that graduates of his seminary not work in exclusively Orthodox institutions, but that they relate to the broader Jewish community as well.[4]

Graduates of the *Rabbiner-Seminar*, in accord with the philosophy of its founder, generally chose not to serve as Orthodox rabbis within separatist Orthodox institutions. Most elected posts as Orthodox rabbis within the structure of *Einheitsgemeinden*, the unified communal organizations that dominated the German-Jewish institutional scene in each city. The decision to serve in such settings was not without its problems for ordinees of the *Rabbiner-Seminar*. In many of these communities, the advocates of reform were eager to introduce the organ and other forms of liturgical innovations into worship services.

While the pressure upon these Orthodox rabbis to acquiesce in such instances was often considerable, these changes were defined by the leadership of the Orthodox community as major violations of Jewish law, and therefore absolutely unacceptable from an Orthodox standpoint. The *Rabbiner-Seminar* identified these changes — particularly the organ — as boundary points that no Orthodox rabbi, regardless of the pressure exerted upon him in his particular community, could countenance.

Indeed, as we have seen in chapter five, the organ itself became the single most significant point of boundary demarcation between Liberal and Orthodox Judaism in Germany throughout the nineteenth century and the early 1900s.[5] Noting the importance of this issue, Rabbi David Zvi Hoffmann (1843–1921), rector of the *Rabbiner-Seminar*, observed in a responsum written in 1897, that a codicil was "issued to each student of our seminary here in Berlin along with his certificate of ordination stipulating that the organ was forbidden on account of the biblical

4   For Hildesheimer's attitudes in this respect, see my "Modern Orthodoxy and the Problem of Religious Pluralism: The Case of Rabbi Esriel Hildesheimer," *Tradition* 17 (1979), pp. 74–89.

5   For further discussion of the significance of the organ issue, see chap. 5, "A Disputed Precedent," in the present volume.

injunction, 'You shall not walk in their ways' (Leviticus 18:3)." If a student, in later years, elected to serve a community that employed the organ either on the Sabbath or during the week, then the ordination certificate would be rendered "completely cancelled, null and void — *be-teilin u-mevutalin, la-sharirin ve-la-kayamin*."[6]

The writings of Professor Abraham Berliner, the famed historian and Hoffmann's colleague on the faculty of the *Rabbiner-Seminar*, provide another source testifying to the significance of organ use as a boundary issue for the Orthodox elite in Germany. In his *Zur Lehr' und zur Wehr: über und gegen die kirchliche Orgel im jüdischen Gottesdienste* (To Teach and Defend: About and Against the Church Organ in Jewish Worship), Berliner, like Hoffmann, asserted that a *"schriftlichen Mahnung (hoda'ah ne'emanah),"* a written admonition in Hebrew, was given to every graduate of the *Rabbiner-Seminar* at the time of his ordination. The admonition, as Hoffmann had earlier indicated, forbade the ordinee from presiding as a rabbi over a community where the organ had been introduced. If the graduate failed to obey this codicil, then his ordination was to be rescinded. Of the 120 students who had been ordained by the *Rabbiner-Seminar* by 1904, only five, according to Berliner, had violated this dictum.[7]

Professor Lou Silberman has graciously provided me with the actual text of the codicil and allowed me to publish it for the first time in English translation; (the full text appears below). It is signed by Rabbi Hoffmann as Director of the *Rabbiner-Seminar* and by Dr. Joseph Wohlgemuth as head of the faculty and as instructor in applied Jewish law.[8] Silberman's teacher at the Hebrew Union College, Professor Jacob

6 David Zvi Hoffmann, *Melammed le-Ho'il, Oraḥ Ḥayim*, no. 16. The actual formula from the codicil is taken from the text provided me by Professor Lou Silberman. The translation is printed in this article.

7 See Abraham Berliner, "*Literar-geschichtliche Belege über die christliche Orgel im jüdischen Gottesdienste*," in his edited volume, *Zur Lehr' und zur Wehr: ueber und gegen die kirchliche Orgel im jüdischen Gottesdienste* (Berlin: Nathansen und Lamm, 1904), p. 58.

8 For a brief description of Wohlgemuth's role in the Rabbiner-Seminar, see Moshe Auerbach, "Rabbi Yechiel Yaakov Weinberg as a Member of the Berlin Rabbiner-Seminar Faculty" (Hebrew), in *Y. Y. Weinberg Memorial Volume* (Hebrew), ed. A. Hildesheimer and K. Cahana (Jerusalem: Feldheim, 1969), p. 360. In addition, Juda Ari Wohlgemuth, in his article, "Joseph Wohlgemuth," in *Guardians of Our Heritage*, ed. by Leo Jung (New York: Bloch, 1958), p. 546, writes, "There was one more discipline

Lauterbach, was an ordinee of the *Rabbiner-Seminar* and he bequeathed his own copy of the *hoda'ah ne'emanah* to his student, Professor Silberman. It is my hope that this introduction to and translation of the Codicil will provide a contribution to the history of modern Jewish religious denominationalism and that it will grant insight into the struggles that marked these nascent religious movements at the end of the nineteenth century.

Hoda'ah Ne'emanah
An Admonition of Faithfulness

On the day of your departure from our seminary, at the moment when your teachers will take their leave from you — at this time your ears should heed these words as we say, "This is the way in which you should walk. Do not swerve from it either right or left."

You are the man upon whom will be thrust [the responsibility] for one of our holy communities. You are charged [with the duty] of establishing the yoke of the written Torah and the Tradition [upon it], according to the foundations and principles which our holy Sages taught, and which has been told to you and which you have heard times without number from the mouths of those who taught you for your benefit[9] and who guided you in the way of God.

You, taught of God — do you not know, have you not heard that the communities have multiplied that have cast off the yoke of Torah and commandments, and that rebellious elders have arisen within them who do not heed the voice of their teachers. They have begun to imitate the practices of adherents of other faiths by introducing musical instruments into the house of God, playing it even on the holy Sabbath, thereby publicly profaning God's Sabbath in the community among the people.

[in addition to philosophy of religion and homiletics] which Joseph Wohlgemuth taught in the seminary: *Hora'ah*, which means the ability to decide matters of Jewish law, covering the laws of *kashrut*, with all their infinite details, and many issues of marriage and divorce, as well as problems in civil law."

9   The phrase here in the Hebrew is "*melammedecha le-ho'il.*" It is taken from Isaiah 48:17 — "I am the Lord Thy God, who teacheth thee for thy profit." It is precisely the same phrase that Hoffmann selected for the name of his responsa collection, *Melammed le-Ho'il.*

Nor should the fact escape you that this very, very great and serious sin has yet become the root that bears gall and wormwood (Deuteronomy 29:17). For one sin brings other sins and great abominations in its wake. Not long after the introduction of the organ, the voice of women's choirs singing was heard in the temple of God, and the order of prayers that we received from our fathers was breached time and again. The basis of the service of the heart was destroyed through addition and deletion, through changes and alterations, which testify and bear witness that the destroyers[10] denied and mocked the promises God made through His prophets to return His divine, indwelling presence to Zion and [to restore] the order of sacrificial worship in Jerusalem at the end of days.

And now you, son who is so dear to us, if the people of a community who have acted wantonly in committing one of these sins, should call you to be their rabbi and teacher, do not consent to listen to them until they have lifted and removed every stumbling block from the house of prayer in which they intend for you to pray and preach. For you should not approach the threshold of such a synagogue wherein they have acted insolently with a haughty hand against the precepts of our religion.

If, however, you already occupy a rabbinical post in the Jewish community, and persons arise there who lead the inhabitants of the city astray by introducing one of these sinful imitations mentioned above to your house of prayer, do not stand idly by and [accept their innovations]. Rather, cast this rabbinical position off your shoulder. Leave your office and place your hope in God. Throw your burden upon Him.

And behold, on this day you have been authorized to teach and judge in Israel; on this day you have been ordained by the authority of the Sages; on this day you have received your rabbinical diploma. This was done to you at our hands because we are certain that you will observe, as you well know, the aforementioned directives. For your spirit is faithful to God and His Torah, and we fully expect you to always walk uprightly and act with righteousness as you have until now. And if, God forbid, another spirit should overcome you and you should cast our warning aside, then understand the [consequences that lie] ahead of you. Know and be well aware that [in such an instance] all the words

---

10 The word *meharsim,* meaning "destroyers," is used for Liberal Jews.

of authorization, permission, and ordination that [have been bestowed upon you], whether in the certificate of rabbinical ordination (*hatarat hora'ah*) or the rabbinical diploma (*te'udat ha-rabanut*) which is in your hands,[11] are completely cancelled, null and void.

Nevertheless, our deepest hope is that the commandments of the Torah will always be on your heart and that you will walk in the way of the good and follow the paths of the righteous. For then you will succeed and grow in wisdom.

---

11 The Rabbiner-Seminar actually issued two distinct rabbinical certificates to its ordinees. Those who displayed superior mastery of Jewish law and who were authorized to issue halakhic rulings themselves received the traditional *hatarat hora'ah*. The majority of students were granted a rabbinical diploma (*te'udat ha-rabanut*) which authorized the bearer to serve as a rabbi and religious teacher. It was akin to the certificate issued by the Jewish Institute of Religion to its graduates prior to its merger with Hebrew Union College or by the Jewish Theological Seminary from its inception until today. For a fuller discussion of this point, see my *Rabbi Esriel Hildesheimer and the Creation of a Modern Jewish Orthodoxy* (Tuscaloosa, Ala.: University of Alabama Press, 1990), p.159.

Denominational Responses

9

The *Israelitische Gebetbücher* of Abraham Geiger and Manuel Joël

A Study in Nineteenth-Century German-Jewish Communal Liturgy and Religion

The nineteenth century was a time of great liturgical ferment in the life of the German-Jewish community.[1] Reform Judaism bounded onto the stage of history in the 1810s as a movement of liturgical change, but Hebrew prayer book creativity, as evidenced in the production of a constant stream of new *siddurim*, continued unabated among all the religious streams in Germany throughout the 1800s. These prayer books played a central role in the religious developments and conflicts of the nineteenth-century German-Jewish community, and the theological nuances and sensibilities of the leaders in these denominational struggles were reflected in the prayer books they produced. The *siddurim* of this time and place are therefore ideal barometers for measuring the moods and attitudes of the variegated religious streams of Judaism in Germany in modern times. In this essay, the Hebrew liturgical creativity of two authors — Abraham Geiger and Manuel Joël — will be analyzed so that the nature and course of those streams can be measured.[2]

Abraham Geiger has of course long been recognized as the outstanding Reform figure of his day, and he first wrote his *Israelitisches Gebetbuch*

---

1 This paper was originally delivered at the Jewish Theological Seminary on November 11, 1997, at a conference entitled, "Voices of Ashkenaz: An International Conference on the Music and Culture of German and Central European Jewry," presented by the Jewish Theological Seminary and Hebrew Union College-Jewish Institute of Religion in cooperation with the Leo Baeck Institute and the Elaine Kaufman Cultural Center.

2 Jakob Petuchowski, in his seminal *Prayerbook Reform in Europe* (New York, 1968), has been the foremost scholar to point all this out. Robert Liberles has followed Petuchowski and in "The So-Called Quiet Years of German-Jewry 1849–1869: A Reconsideration," *Leo Baeck Institute Year Book* XLI (1996), p.72, emphasized the importance of these works as sources for the construction of modern Jewish religious history.

in 1854 while serving as *Rabbiner der israelitischen Gemeinde zu Breslau,* rabbi of the Breslau Jewish community. Joël, in contrast, has long been associated with the Positive-Historical wing of *Liberales Judentum* in Germany, and he served in the Religious Philosophy Faculty at the Breslau Rabbinical Seminary. Joël succeeded Geiger as *Rabbiner der israelitischen Gemeinde zu Breslau* in 1863, and his *Israelitisches Gebetbuch* was composed in 1872. By analyzing the contents of the *siddurim* of these two men within the nineteenth-century context that fostered and informed them, this paper will illuminate the nature of German Liberal Judaism. The sensibilities that united the Reform and Positive-Historical wings of nineteenth-century *Liberales Judentum* will be made manifest, as will the differences between these religious trends. In this way, this chapter — through the lens provided by the prayer book — will contribute towards a fuller understanding of nineteenth-century German-Jewish religious denominationalism.[3]

3   In this paper, I travel further down the path of prayer book research initiated by Petuchowski. I also consciously take up the suggestions offered by both Michael Meyer and Robert Liberles concerning the need for more historical research into the Positive-Historical trend in nineteenth-century Germany. In his article 'Recent Historiography on the Jewish Religion,' *Leo Baeck Institute Year Book* XXXV (1990), pp. 10–11, Meyer stated: "While the field of recent German-Jewish Orthodoxy has been well ploughed in recent scholarship, that of Positive-Historical Judaism has lain almost fallow." He therefore called for new research on those he termed "middle of the road figures," persons such as "Michael Sachs in Berlin, Isaac Noah Mannheimer in Vienna, and Manuel Joël in Breslau." Robert Liberles, in "The So-Called Quiet Years of German Jewry," pp. 71ff., has repeated this call and has asserted: "Until recently, German Jewry was strongly associated with the Reformers in its midst. . . . But over the past two decades, several writers . . . have contributed to a richer and more varied perspective on German-Jewish life by focusing on its more traditional sectors. It is to be hoped that this perspective will be broadened to include studies of Positive-Historical Judaism." Therefore, this study purposefully centers upon the Joël *siddur,* in conjunction with that of Geiger, so that a fuller understanding of Positive-Historical Judaism in particular, as well as the contours of German-Jewish religious denominationalism in general, can emerge. Since the article by Meyer was written, Franz D. Lucas and Heike Frank have published their book *Michael Sachs: Der konservative Mittelweg* (Tübingen, 1992). On p. 6, they explicitly note the suggestions made by Meyer. In addition, my essay "The Mannheimer Prayerbooks and Central European Communal Liturgies," in David Ellenson, *Between Tradition and Culture: The Dialectics of Modern Jewish Religion and Identity* (Atlanta, 1994), pp. 59–78, devotes itself to an element of Mannheimer and his work. This essay will treat the third figure specifically mentioned by Meyer and identified by Liberles

The Legacy of Hamburg

In analyzing the character and content of Geiger's and Joël's *Gebetbücher*, it is essential to note that their liturgical work did not arise in a vacuum. They did not have to confront the task of composing a communal *Gebetbuch de novo*. Indeed, Joël's *Israelitisches Gebetbuch* was based upon the 1854 *Israelitisches Gebetbuch* written by Geiger. Geiger, in turn, was highly cognizant of attempts made by his German predecessors earlier in the century to reformulate Jewish liturgy in keeping with the attitudes and conditions of a novel era. By the time he wrote his 1854 *Israelitisches Gebetbuch*, which bore the Hebrew title *Seder Tefillah Dvar Yom be-Yomo* (Order of Prayer Day by Day), Geiger had already published a number of articles and opinions expressing his views on the subject of Jewish prayer. Indeed, he had been an active participant in the acrimonious debates that had surrounded the Hamburg *Gebetbuch* of 1841, and an analysis of his words on that occasion, as well as an understanding of the prayer book upon which he was commenting, are crucial if we are to grasp Geiger's own attitudes towards Jewish liturgy.

The Hamburg Temple prayer book of 1841, entitled *Gebetbuch für die öffentliche und häusliche Andacht der Israeliten, nach dem Gebrauche des Neuen Israelitischen Tempels in Hamburg* (Prayer Book for the Public and Private Worship of the Israelites, according to the Rite of the New Israelite Temple in Hamburg), was a revision and expansion of the famous 1819 *Gebetbuch* published by the Hamburg Temple. Limited to services for the Sabbath and Festivals, the 1819 prayer book was influenced by the Berlin 1817 *siddur* of *Die Deutsche Synagoge oder Ordnung des Gottesdienstes für die Sabbath- und Festtage des ganzen Jahres, zum Gebrauche der Gemeinden, die sich deutscher Gebete bedienen* (The German Synagogue or Order of Service for the Sabbath and Festivals of the Entire Year, for the Use of Communities that Use German Prayers), edited by Eduard Kiey and C. S. Günsburg. The 1819 Hamburg rite was dedicated to Israel Jacobson and has been identified by Michael Meyer as "the first comprehensive Reform liturgy."[4] This 1819 liturgy expressed the concerns and aspirations of a nascent Reform Movement, the postures and rituals of which were not fully formed. Much of it was composed

---

as central to an understanding of Positive-Historical Judaism — Manuel Joël.

4 Michael Meyer, *Response to Modernity: A History of the Reform Movement in Judaism* (New York and Oxford, 1988), p. 56.

in Hebrew, and the order and structure of the traditional service were retained in their entirety. Indeed, its editors, Meyer Israel Bresselau and Seckel Isaac Frankel, were anxious to affirm their ties to Jewish tradition and did not want to foster division within the community. They did not intend a radical reform.

At the same time, Bresselau and Frankel were informed by the rational ideology of the Enlightenment, and they were excited by the opportunity that Emancipation afforded Jews for full participation in gentile society. They were anxious to author a prayer book the manifest content of which would be consistent with the spirit and aesthetic of this new age. The 1819 *Gebetbuch* therefore opened from left to right and contained prayers composed in the vernacular. There was also a pronounced tendency to favor Sephardic formulae over the Ashkenazic liturgy that had guided German Jews in prayer for years. As Ismar Schorsch explains, "As construed by Ashkenazic intellectuals, the Sephardic image facilitated a religious posture marked by cultural openness, philosophic thinking, and an appreciation for the aesthetic."[5] Thus, only Sephardic *piyyutim* were included in the Hamburg rite. The Sephardic *Le-Moshe Tzivita* was substituted for the Ashkenazic *Tikanta Shabbat* in the Sabbath *Musaf* service, while *Menuḥah Nekhonah* replaced the *El Malei Raḥamim* as contained in the *Hazkarat Neshamot* memorial prayer of the Polish rite that had been favored in northern Germany during the previous century.

Other dimensions of the manifest content of the received Ashkenazic liturgical rite of the previous century were also deemed problematic by the Hamburg Reformers, and elements of that rite were rejected or reformulated in keeping with what the editors of the Hamburg *Gebetbuch* perceived as the modern ethos. Prayers concerned with the restoration of the sacrificial cult and those expressing a desire for a physical return to Jerusalem and Zion were among those regarded as particularly troublesome, as were prayers that affirmed a belief in a personal messiah and in angelology, as well as those that articulated what the editors regarded as offensive attitudes towards gentiles. Bresselau and Frankel saw these prayers as inappropriate for Jews living in the modern

5 Ismar Schorsch, "The Myth of Sephardic Supremacy," in Schorsch, *From Text to Context: The Turn to History in Modern Judaism* (Hanover, N.H., 1994), p. 71.

era and in their *siddur* addressed the issues these prayers raised. A representative survey of some of these prayers will indicate how they handled these issues, as well as illuminate the character of the prayer book they composed.[6]

The Hamburg liturgists expressed their distance from those prayers that expressed a hope for the reinstitution of the sacrificial cult by amending the text for the *Shabbat Musaf* service, with its call for a restoration of sacrificial worship, to read, "May it therefore be Your will, O Lord our God and God of our fathers, to accept in mercy and with favor the expression of our lips in place of our obligatory sacrifices." Similarly, in the *Musaf* service for the Pilgrimage Festivals, the same phrase was placed in the *Mipnei Ḥata'einu* prayer. The phrase "And bring near our dispersed from among the nations" and the line that asserts "And gather us to Zion, Your city, in joy" were completely removed from this prayer.

These last changes express an antipathy towards more than the Temple with its mode of sacrificial worship. They reflect an opposition to a call for Jewish national restoration as well, and this hostility is contained in other places in the Hamburg *Gebetbuch*. Indeed, the entire traditional content of the *Kedushah* for the Sabbath *Shaḥarit* service was deleted, and the *Kedushah* for *Musaf* was substituted in its stead — so that the paragraph which begins with the words, "From Your place, our King, You will appear," and asks, "When will You reign in Zion," and asserts in response, "May You be exalted and sanctified within Jerusalem, Your city," could be removed. Hence, the sentence beginning with the words, "O, may You cause a new light to shine upon Zion" is also deleted from the 1819 Hamburg *Gebetbuch*, as is the line from the prayer prior to the recitation of the *Shema* that reads, "And bring us forth in peace from the four corners of the earth, and cause us to walk upright into our land." Instead, this line is replaced by the words, "Bring blessing and peace upon us" in accordance with the Spanish-Portuguese rite, though the Hamburg prayer does not contain the words, "And break the yoke

---

6   For these points as well a complete account of the posture these men adopted in their approach to their prayer book, see Seckel I. Frankel, *Schutzschrift des zu Hamburg erschienenen Israelitischen Gebetbuchs* (Hamburg, 1819).

of the gentiles from upon us," as does the Sephardic ritual.[7] The conditions of oppression that had prompted this prayer no longer existed in Germany, in the opinion of Bresselau and Frankel. As a result, its sentiments seemed inappropriate and, in keeping with this view, they omitted the line from the High Holy Day liturgy that read, "Our Father, our King, avenge the blood of Your servants that has been shed" as well as the sentence from the Sabbath morning *Tefillah* that states of the Sabbath, "You did not give it, O Lord our God, to the nations of the earth, nor did You make it the inheritance, our King, of the worshipers of graven idols. And in its rest the uncircumcised shall not abide."

At the same time, the Hamburg Temple *Gebetbuch*, in view of the sensibilities of its authors, displayed in certain respects a surprising fidelity to tradition.[8] While the authors possessed a definite antipathy towards angelology and the notion of a personal messiah, the weight of centuries of tradition and their own determination to compose a liturgy that could appeal to a broad spectrum of the community caused them to retain the Hebrew of traditional prayers that incorporated these themes. Hence, the *Kedushat de-Yotzer*, a staple of the morning service replete with references to angelology, was retained in its entirety and *"go'el"* (redeemer) was maintained in the first benediction of the

---

7   Indeed, in making this change, as well as the previous two, which have been mentioned, the authors of the 1819 Hamburg *Gebetbuch* employed elements of other accepted Jewish liturgies as precedents for the legitimization of their ritual. In the case of the *Kedushah*, they had the precedent of Yom Kippur, where the *Kedushah* service on that day in both *Shaharit* and *Musaf* was based on the *Musaf Kedushah,* while many prayer books, as far back as the *siddur* of Saadia Gaon in the tenth century, had omitted the line *"Or Ḥadash."* The fact that the Hamburg Reformers drew upon traditional Jewish practices as warrants for their changes is historically noteworthy, and indicates how deeply embedded they remained in the rabbinic tradition. At the same time, this should not obscure the fact that they drew upon these warrants rather selectively, and that they selected them so as to forge a new Jewish communal identity over and against the traditional rabbinic establishment and because these precedents allowed them to compose a liturgy whose manifest content was more in keeping with their own beliefs than that of the traditional Ashkenazic rite that was their immediate patrimony.

8   Baruch Mevorach, "The Belief in the Messiah in Early Reform Polemics," in *Zion* (1969) [Hebrew], pp. 189–218, has noted this with regard to the doctrine of the messiah, and has explained why this was so with regard to this particular notion, in this thorough and insightful piece.

Amidah. In so doing, Bresselau and Frankel signaled that their intention was twofold: to reformulate the old order of prayer while bearing in mind diverse contemporary sensibilities to avoid the creation of a sectarian prayer book. However, in instances such as these, where they retained the Hebrew prayer intact despite the problems they felt with its manifest content, they employed translation as a vehicle to mute or transform the meaning of the Hebrew. Thus, the word "Creatures" in the *Kedushat de-Yotzer* was translated as "*Lichtgestalten*" (figures of light). The manifest content of the entire prayer was thereby changed. The words of the liturgy no longer referred to heavenly creatures in a mystical sense; instead, they were transformed — at least in German translation — into metaphors for the powers of nature. In the same vein, while "*goʾel*" was maintained in the Hebrew, the 1819 Hamburg *Gebetbuch* translated it not as "*Erlöser*" (redeemer) but as "*Erlösung*" (redemption). This tactic — retaining the Hebrew while employing translation to obviate meanings that were perceived as objectionable — was to become a hallmark of countless numbers of subsequent Liberal liturgies.

The appreciation for, as well as ambivalence towards, tradition that such an approach displays was evidenced by the 1819 Hamburg Temple prayer book in other ways as well. Despite the hostility the authors of the *Gebetbuch* had for those prayers that called for the restoration of the sacrificial cult and the return of the Jewish people to Zion, the 1819 liturgy maintained the prerogatives classically assigned the *kehunah*, the priesthood, in Jewish liturgy. A *kohen*, a man of priestly descent, was assigned the first *aliyah* to the Torah in the Hamburg rite and the ritual of *dukhenen*, where the priests ascend the *bimah* (prayer platform) to bless the people on Holy Days, was retained. In addition, the passage in the *Shemoneh Esreh* that reads, "Restore the sacrificial worship to Your sanctuary, and accept Israel's fire offerings and their prayer with love and favor" was retained in its entirety and translated into German. Similarly, the traditional *ḥatimah* of this benediction, "Who restores His divine presence to Zion," was also included, and phrases beseeching God to restore the Temple "and rebuild it soon and magnify its glory" were included in the Festival *Musaf* service.

Of course, from the standpoint of the Orthodox, none of this spared the Hamburg Temple prayer book condemnation. The 1819 *Gebetbuch* elicited a storm of protest and the collection of Orthodox rabbinic responsa entitled *Eileh Divrei ha-Brit* (discussed above in chapter seven) savagely attacked the prayer book for its deviations from received Jewish liturgical tradition.[9] Yet, from the viewpoint of Reform Judaism, the 1819 Hamburg Temple Prayer Book constituted a balanced first attempt to compose a liturgy that would calibrate between the push of tradition and the pull of the present. The 1841 *Gebetbuch* constituted a second attempt in this vein.

While the first Hamburg *siddur* was limited to services for the Sabbath and Festivals, the 1841 edition added a daily service as well as a Sabbath afternoon service (*Minḥah*). Though it continued many of the practices and embodied many of the same sensibilities and concerns that had marked the 1819 *Gebetbuch*, this latter liturgy represented on the one hand, as Petuchowski phrased it, "a return to Tradition, and, on the other, an espousal of a more 'radical' Reform point of view."[10] For example, *Pesukei de-Zimrah* (the Verses of Song), which had virtually disappeared in the first Hamburg prayer book, were restored, in Hebrew, in the 1841 edition. In addition, the phrase "O, may You cause a new light to shine upon Zion . . ." was reinserted in the 1841 liturgy; however, it was set in small type, placed in parentheses, and left untranslated. Similarly, the sentence "Restore the sacrificial worship to Your sanctuary, and accept Israel's fire-offerings and their prayer with love and favor" was set in small type and placed in parentheses in the Hebrew text of that prayer. In addition, this Hebrew text did not appear in German translation in the 1841 prayer book. Thus, a prayer that was omitted in the earlier edition was restored half-heartedly in the later one, while a prayer found in the first edition was inserted parenthetically and untranslated in the second.

The 1841 *Gebetbuch* also attempted to be more thoroughgoing in its elimination of passages referring to the centrality of Zion and to the physical restoration of the Jews to Palestine than had its predecessor. Thus, in the rendition of the *ḥatimah* for the *Hashkiveinu* prayer on the eve of the Sabbath, the 1841 *siddur* completely omitted the traditional conclusion "Blessed be You, O God, who spreads the tabernacle of peace

9 For a description of the Orthodox responses as collected in *Eileh Divrei ha-Brit* to the 1819 Hamburg Reform rite, see my comments in chap. 7, "Traditional Reactions to Modern Jewish Reform," in the present volume.

10 Petuchowski, *Prayerbook Reform in Europe*, p. 54.

over us, over Your people Israel, and over Jerusalem" and substituted in its place, "*Gelobt seiest du, Gott, der du dein Volk Israel ewiglich beschuetzest*" (Blessed are You, O God, who protects Your people Israel forever). In addition, the ḥatimah of the first of the last three benedictions in the *Amidah*, "who restores His divine presence to Zion," was replaced by the words "whom alone we serve in reverence." A note at the end of the 1841 edition of the Hamburg *Gebetbuch* cited a remark by Rashi upon *Berakhot* 11a to justify this ḥatimah from the standpoint of Jewish tradition. Indeed, the production of such warrants from Jewish literature to legitimate the changes they introduced in their order of prayer was characteristic of the approach taken by the authors of these *siddurim* in both 1819 and 1841.[11] However, the authors of this prayer book undoubtedly selected this conclusion to the prayer because its manifest content was more in accord with their religious sentiments than the one that featured Zion. The precedent undoubtedly would not have been selected had this not been so.

The universalistic and anti-nationalistic proclivities and views of the 1841 prayer book are also evidenced in the intermediate benedictions its authors composed for the daily *Shemoneh Esreh*. Written in German, the manifest content of these Hamburg blessings departed radically from that of the traditional Ashkenazic rite. An analysis of two of them will suffice to illustrate the religious viewpoint that marked them. The eleventh benediction, *Kibbutz Galuyot* (The Ingathering of Exiles), which calls upon God to bring freedom to the people Israel and asks that all the Jews of the Diaspora be returned to the Land of Israel, was altered to assert that the banner of freedom will be lifted up "for all who sigh in their servitude" and asked that God gather up not the "dispersed," but the "disowned" among the people Israel. In a similar universalistic vein, the next benediction, *Jerusalem*, abandoned its hope that God would rebuild Jerusalem and establish His divine dwelling, as well as the Davidic throne, there. Instead, the Hamburg edition of this blessing inserted the words of Isaiah 2:3, "For from Zion shall go forth Torah, and the word of God from Jerusalem" to obviate the particularistic thrust of the traditional prayer and to emphasize in its stead the universal mission of Jewish teaching.

11   See n.7.

In its composition of these intermediate blessings, the 1841 *Gebetbuch* continued the thrust evidenced in its predecessor of removing or muting passages that referred to the elimination and downfall of Israel's enemies. Thus, the benediction *Malshinim* (Slanderers), asking that God's wrath be visited upon those who have slandered the Jewish people and those who are the enemies of God, was simply omitted. Similarly, in the Torah service, the 1841 prayer book reaffirmed an alteration initiated in the 1819 *Gebetbuch* and eliminated the passage from Numbers 10:35, "Arise, o God, and let Your foes be scattered, and let those who hate You flee from You." However, it went even further in this direction than the 1819 service had, as can be seen from an analysis of the 1841 edition of the *Ezrat Avoteinu* prayer. In this prayer, one traditional passage reads, "From Egypt You redeemed us, Lord our God, and from the house of bondage You liberated us. All their first-born You slew, but Your first-born You redeemed. You split the Red Sea, and You drowned the evil sinners. The beloved You brought across, and the water covered their foes, not one of them was left." While the authors of the 1819 Hamburg prayer book kept these lines intact, the editors of the 1841 Hamburg *siddur*, cognizant of the hostility these lines displayed towards the enemies of Israel, felt these sentences to be inappropriate for the universalistic orientation that marked their community. The later prayer book therefore muted the tone of this passage and deleted the phrases "All their first-born You slew, but Your first-born You redeemed" and "The water covered their foes, not one of them was left." In short, the Hamburg Temple prayer book of 1841, while distinct in certain respects from the preceding liturgy, continued the basic thrust and sentiments of the earlier *siddur*.

While the Hamburg Temple *Gebetbücher* were the works of an independent Reform congregation, the authors of these *siddurim* did not see themselves as promoting a radical disjunction with the past. They remained active members of the Hamburg Jewish community, and they were eager, as we have seen, to demonstrate their compliance with Jewish law. As Petuchowski has commented,

> The farthest thing from their mind was the formation of a new Jewish sect . . . The Judaism to which they wanted to bring liturgical reform was a Judaism based on Bible, Talmud, and Codes; and it was

by an appeal to these accepted bases of Jewish life that they sought to justify their place *within* Judaism[12]

Nevertheless, the changes the Hamburg Temple Reform liturgists introduced into the traditional order of prayer elicited the wrath of the Orthodox in 1841, just as they had in 1819. Isaac Bernays, Orthodox rabbi of Hamburg, attacked this new Reform effort, and issued a *moda'ah*, a public pronouncement, declaring "that a Jew could no more recite his obligatory prayers from this new edition than the earlier prohibited old one," and he cast aspersions on the motivations of its editors, using terms such as "frivolous" and "mischievous" to describe their work."[13] The Reformers decided to respond to Bernays, and in 1842 published a series of rabbinic responsa, *Theologische Gutachten* (Theological Legal Opinions), to defend the Jewish character of their *siddur*. Among the respondents was Abraham Geiger, and it is to an analysis of his liturgical writings, both theoretical and applied, that we now turn.

Geiger and Jewish Liturgy
Theoretical Views and Applications

In the *Theologische Gutachten*, Geiger offered a brief explanation of his own views on Jewish prayer in general and on the Hamburg *Gebetbuch* in particular. In this document Geiger defended the Hamburg Reformers from the onslaught of Bernays and said of the 1841 Hamburg *Gebetbuch*:

> I can assert with full conviction that the ordering of the prayers does not contradict the laws of the Talmud and the rabbis as long as the essential prayers, *Shema* and its blessings, expressing the acceptance of the yoke of the kingdom of Heaven and the remembrance of the Exodus from Egypt, and the *Amidah* are contained therein.

As the Hamburg rite contained all these elements, Geiger concluded

---

12 Petuchowski, *Prayerbook Reform in Europe,* pp. 33 and 98. The precise quotation is found on p. 98.

13 Meyer, *Response to Modernity,* p. 117.

that the public condemnation of the Hamburg prayer book by Bernays was completely unfounded from the standpoint of the Jewish laws of public prayer.[14]

However, during that same year, in another forum, Geiger displayed a rather critical attitude toward the liturgy of the Hamburg Temple, accusing it of displaying unwarranted inconsistencies in its application of Reform principles. He wrote in the *Allgemeine Zeitung des Judenthums:*

> I see no excuse for the fact that, in a period of 23 years, the leaders of the Temple have achieved nothing beyond a second edition of their prayer book which reflects the same lack of decisiveness as the first one did. Despite their avowed Liberal position . . . they have done almost nothing for the proper advancement of those ideas of which . . . the reforms in divine services are merely an outgrowth . . . The fact of the matter is that they are still beating about the bush today; they still refuse to speak out openly, and still persist in seeking to make the difference appear minute. . . . All that these gentleman can make of these things is just a number of paltry changes in a few isolated words.[15]

Geiger offered a much fuller explication of his attitudes on the topic in another work published that same year. Entitled *Der Hamburger Tempelstreit. Eine Zeitfrager* (The Temple Dispute in Hamburg: A Contemporary issue), the document contained more than eighty pages. In it, Geiger wrote a rather lengthy prologue describing the history of the development of Jewish prayer. In so doing, he indicated that Jewish worship had always been rather fluid and flexible, and that the reforms he would like to have seen introduced into the modern prayer book possessed historical warrant.

After he had completed this preliminary historical survey, Geiger turned directly to the topic of the Hamburg Temple *Gebetbücher*

---

14 *Theologische Gutachten über das Gebetbuch nach dem Gebrauche des Neuen Israelitischen Tempelvereins in Hamburg* (Hamburg, 1842), pp. 63ff.

15 *Allgemeine Zeitung des Judenthums* XXIII:29, pp. 345ff., as cited and translated in Max Wiener, *Abraham Geiger and Liberal Judaism: The Challenge of the Nineteenth Century* (Philadelphia, 1962), pp. 93–94.

themselves. He made note of all the reforms these prayer books were meant to address, and lauded the spirit of change that motivated their authors. However, he objected strenuously to the lack of consistency these prayer books displayed in the application of Reform principles and compiled a litany of charges that indicted these works for their failure to fulfill the Liberal liturgical promise their vision championed. A rehearsal of several of these charges will illustrate the nature of the critique Geiger offered. For example, both prayer books were inconsistent in the manifest content of the liturgy they presented. Each denied any desire for the restoration of the priesthood and sacrificial cult. Yet, at the same time, they failed to excise the rite of *dukhenen* in *Birkat Kohanim* (the Priestly Blessing), thereby maintaining a priestly prerogative. Similarly, these prayer books did not eliminate — despite their avowed goal of doing so — all passages dealing with the sacrifices themselves, and there were remnants of such prayers in various places in both *siddurim*. Geiger also felt that the Hamburg *Gebetbuch* of 1841 represented, in many places, a retreat from the advances embodied in the earlier liturgy. The restoration of the passage "May You cause a new light to shine upon Zion" was deemed unfortunate, since it reflected a Jewish national hope, and while Geiger approved the removal of the ḥatimah "who restores His divine presence to Zion," he questioned the retention of the passage immediately preceding: "May our eyes behold Your return to Zion in compassion." Furthermore, the editors' effort to remove passages denigrating other peoples was surely praiseworthy. Nevertheless, they completely failed to articulate positively the great principle that prompted their removal — the universal mission assigned Israel by God. He asserted:

> The doctrine of the election of Israel echoed in the prayer book should have made room for the idea of the mission of Israel, her acceptance of the belief in the one God, and her task to preserve this belief and to bear this mission throughout history until that time when all mankind will be united in the acceptance of this belief.[16]

16 For all the information contained in these paragraphs, see Abraham Geiger, *Der Hamburger Tempelstreit. Eine Zeitfrage* (Breslau, 1842). For this particular quotation, see p. 47.

In short, the Hamburg Temple *Gebetbücher* were inconsistent in their incomplete attempts to compose a liturgy that embodied the integrity of Liberal Jewish belief.

While the Hamburg Temple prayer books were noble first steps in this direction, more work needed to be done, and Geiger, in subsequent years, accepted the challenge of composing a Liberal Jewish liturgy, as well as the task of articulating the principles that such a liturgy had to embody. Foremost among these principles was the notion of Jewish mission, the belief that "the true Israelite testifies gladly to Israel's high vocation to carry the faith in the One and Holy God in all its purity to the world." This meant that "outgrown attitudes" that still appeared in Jewish prayer had to be eliminated, and a systematic reform of the prayer book had to be undertaken.[17]

In the preface to his 1854 prayer book, Geiger defined the particular features of this modern liturgy:

> The lamentation about the lost national independence of Israel, the plea for the gathering of the dispersed in Palestine and the restoration of the cult and priests — all that is relegated to the background. Jerusalem and Zion are places whence instruction went forth, and to which holy memories are attached. But, on the whole, they are to be celebrated more as a spiritual idea, as the nursery of the Kingdom of God than as a certain geographical locale connected with a special divine providence for all times. Likewise, the hopeful look into the future is directed to the messianic kingdom as a time of the universal reign of the idea of God, of a strengthening of piety and righteousness among all men, but not as a time for the elevation of the People of Israel.[18]

In addition, Geiger wrote that the *siddur* should preserve its traditional character so that its links to Jewish history could be maintained. Thus, he favored the retention of Hebrew as the primary language of Jewish public

---

17 See Abraham Geiger, "Suggested Changes," in Gunther Plaut, ed., *The Rise of Reform Judaism* (New York, 1963), pp.156ff.

18 The preface to the 1854 Geiger prayer book appears in English translation in Petuchowski, *Prayerbook Reform in Europe*, pp.150–52. The translation is found on those pages.

prayer. However, he was also cognizant that most Jews in his day either did not know Hebrew at all, or "do not know it sufficiently to find edification in Hebrew prayer." Consequently, rather than a German translation of the Hebrew text, the German part should constitute "a completely new reworking of the Hebrew prayers in the German language."[19]

Fifteen years later, in 1869, Geiger published a *Denkschrift* in which he articulated in great detail the principles that had guided and would continue to direct him in the construction of his liturgy. As in 1854, he asserted that the prayer book "should continue to express in a precise form its connection with the whole history of Judaism. Consequently, . . . the worship service remains in Hebrew. The traditional Hebrew expression . . . is, on the whole, to remain untouched." However, Geiger once again insisted that the Hebrew text not be translated literally. Rather, "the Hebrew text must be accompanied by a *German adaptation*" in keeping with contemporary sensibilities. In addition, Geiger declared that "religious *concepts* that have a temporal validity, but which have been displaced by a *progressively purer conception*, must not be retained in a one-sided and sharp accentuation." This meant that the Hebrew text, in certain instances, must be recast. Indeed, he went on to specify precisely what he intended by this.[20]

Geiger asserted that anthropomorphic descriptions of the deity as commonly found in the *piyyutim* had to be removed from the prayer book, and that references to angelology were to be eliminated. The belief in immortality was not to emphasize the notion of physical resurrection, but was to include "the concept of spiritual continuity."[21] Finally, the universal mission of Israel as "the bearer and herald" of the doctrine "of truth and light" to all humankind had to find expression in the *siddur* and the "*national* aspect" of Jewish tradition "must recede into the background." As a result, any prayers that expressed a separation between

19　Ibid. p.151.

20　The Geiger *Denkschrift* is found in English translation in Petuchowski, *Prayerbook Reform in Europe*, pp.165–67.

21　As Jakob Petuchowski has pointed out in his "Modern Misunderstandings of an Ancient Benediction," in J.J. Petuchowski and Ezra Fleischer, eds., *Studies in Aggadah, Targum, and Jewish Liturgy in Memory of Joseph Heinemann* (Jerusalem, 1981), pp.45–46, European Liberal Jews were comfortable with and therefore stressed the "idea of immortality . . . at the expense of the belief in Resurrection." Geiger affirmed this belief in this part of his prayer book.

Israel and the other peoples were to be eliminated, as were "any side glances at '*other peoples*' that possessed the 'appearance of *overbearance*.'" The hope for the unification of all mankind dictated that a modern Liberal liturgy must purge all prayers of a national and superstitious character from the prayer book. Thus, prayers that asked for the restoration of a Jewish state in Palestine, the building of a Temple in Jerusalem, and the return of the sacrificial cult, as well as those that expressed the hope for the ingathering of the dispersed, were to be eliminated. In short, Geiger intended that a Reform *Gebetbuch* be cut from whole-cloth and he insisted that an authentic Liberal liturgy both display a complete adherence to principles and avoid the inconsistencies evidenced in the Hamburg prayer books. This was of the utmost importance and concern to him, and Geiger repeated *verbatim* the principles for the composition of a Liberal liturgy he had articulated the previous year in the preface to his 1870 *Gebetbuch*.[22]

For a period of three decades, Geiger displayed consistency in his theoretical approach to Jewish prayer. An analysis of the *Gebetbücher* he himself produced indicates that he did create an unmistakably Liberal liturgy. However, an examination of his works also demonstrates that, like the Hamburg *Gebetbuch* authors of whom he had been so critical, Geiger did not apply the principles and notions he established for the writing of a Jewish prayer book with absolute consistency. The same ambivalence that marked the liturgy of Hamburg characterized the prayer books of Geiger, especially the 1854 version upon which Manuel Joël based his own *siddur*.

In keeping with those principles, Geiger consistently eliminated those passages from his prayer books that called for the restoration of the sacrificial cult. While, in his 1854 *siddur*, he retained the passage in the Sabbath *Musaf* service that began with the words, *Tikanta Shabbat*, Geiger changed its wording so as to purge all those references to sacrifices contained in the traditional version of the prayer. Similarly, the 1854 prayer book removed such elements from the *Mipnei Ḥataʾeinu* prayer for the Festival *Musaf* service. Yet, in light of his own ideological pronouncements, Geiger felt a problem still remained, and in his 1870 *Gebetbuch*, Geiger did not simply reformulate the manifest content of these two paragraphs in the Sabbath and Festival *Musaf* services, but

22 Petuchowski, *Prayerbook Reform in Europe*, pp.165–70.

removed these two paragraphs altogether. In addition, he completely omitted the line "Restore the sacrificial worship to Your sanctuary, and accept Israel's fire-offerings and their prayer with love and favor" from the first of the final three benedictions of the *Amidah*. In so doing, he displayed a greater degree of consistency on this issue than did the Hamburg Temple prayer books. Other areas in the Geiger liturgy display this principled Reform approach to Jewish prayer.

In accord with his writings on the topic, Geiger, like the Hamburg Reformers, attempted to remove those passages that alluded to the centrality of Zion and that asked for Jewish national restoration in Palestine. While he retained the traditional formulae for the Sabbath *Shaḥarit Kedushah*, Geiger resolved the problem of the paragraph beginning with the words "From Your place, our King, You will appear" by removing those phrases from the prayer — "When will you reign in Zion" and "May You be exalted and sanctified in Jerusalem" — that he regarded as offensive. In a comparable vein, he, like the Hamburg Temple prayer book authors, removed the famous passage "And bring us in peace from the four corners of the earth, and cause us to walk upright into our land" altogether, and, like them, he did not include lines such as "And bring near our dispersed from among the nations" in his Festival liturgy. In the Torah service, Geiger retained the famous Hebrew proclamation of Isaiah 2:3: "For from Zion shall go forth Torah, and the word of God from Jerusalem" but rendered "*teitzei*" (shall go forth) in German in the past tense, as "*ist ausgegangen*" (went forth). All this accords with Geiger's notion that Zion was the place "whence instruction went forth, and to which holy memories are attached." However, Israel surely was not the "geographical locale connected with a special divine providence for all times."

As a result, Geiger also altered a number of the middle benedictions in the *Shemoneh Esreh* that embodied a nationalist ethos. For example, in the tenth and eleventh blessings of his 1854 daily *Amidah*, Geiger radically altered the traditional Hebrew text so as to eliminate the nationalistic hopes that these blessings classically expressed. In *Kibbutz Galuyot* (The Ingathering of the Exiles), Geiger offered the Hebrew prayer, "Sound the great *shofar* for our freedom and save, O Lord, Your people, the remnant of Israel, in the four corners of the earth. Praised are You, O Lord, who saves the remnant of Israel," — in lieu of asking God to restore the Jewish people to Zion. The opening line of *Birkat Mishpat*

(Justice), which traditionally states, "Restore our judges as before and our counselors as at the beginning," was changed to read "Restore us to the joy of Your salvation and may a noble spirit sustain us." Geiger also amended the fourteenth benediction, *Jerusalem*, and omitted the classical phrase, "And rebuild it speedily in our day," so that it no longer called for the holy city to be reconstructed.

Geiger was committed to innovations in the received Ashkenazic rite of German Jewry in other areas as well. Like his Hamburg counterparts, he attempted to rid his *siddurim* of passages that expressed seemingly derogatory attitudes towards gentiles. Thus, in the 1854 *Gebetbuch*, he substituted the phrase "Who has made me to serve him" in place of "*who* has not made me a gentile." In addition, Geiger purged, as had the Hamburg *Gebetbücher*, the passage that asked that God avenge "the blood of Your servants that has been shed," as well as the prayer concerning the Sabbath that began "You did not give it, O Lord our God, to the nations of the earth, nor did You make it the inheritance, our King, of the worshipers of graven idols. And in its rest the uncircumcised shall not abide. . . ." Furthermore, in the *Aleinu*, he removed the words "who has not made us like the peoples of the lands, and has not given us a position like the families of the earth, since he did not let our portion be like theirs, nor our lot like that of the multitude" and substituted in its place "who has been revealed to our fathers, and who informed them of His will. He established His covenant with them, and bestowed upon us His Torah as an inheritance." Finally, in his 1854 *siddur* he altered the wording of *Birkat ha-Minim* (The Benediction Concerning Heretics) in the *Shemoneh Esreh* to read "slander" (*malshinut*), instead of "slanderers" (*malshinim*), and he removed the phrase "May all your enemies be cut down speedily" and reworded "May You speedily uproot, smash, cast down, and humble the wanton sinners" to state simply, "May You humble wantonness speedily." In 1870, Geiger reworded the prayer more positively to read, "And may those who stray return unto You." In so doing, Geiger sought to give positive expression to the hope that all humanity would one day be united in truth and integrity.

The universalistic thrust of the 1854 Geiger prayer book is evident in other passages as well. In the *Birkhot ha-Shahar* (Morning Blessings), Geiger reworked the blessing that concludes "who bestows beneficent kindnesses to His people Israel" to read "who bestows beneficent kindnesses upon His creatures." Indeed, this trend towards the inclusion of all humanity, and the rejection of Jewish particularity, is apparent throughout the prayer book. Geiger constantly omitted the phrase "From among all peoples" in his *siddurim*, including the *Kiddush* for Sabbaths and Festivals and the Torah blessings. To have included such a phrase would have displayed, in his view, a "side glance at *'other peoples,'* . . . an overbearance." He therefore altered the *Havdalah* benediction recited at the end of the Sabbath, omitting the words "between Israel and the nations," so that the prayer no longer proclaimed, as did the received rite, that God distinguished Israel from the nations.

This trend towards universalism found expression in other places in his *Gebetbücher*. In both the *Sim Shalom* and *Shalom Rav* prayers for peace, the final benedictions of the morning and afternoon *Shemoneh Esreh*, Geiger retained the particularistic Hebrew texts of the prayers, texts that asked that God bestow peace upon Israel. However, in German translation, Geiger added the phrase "*unter den Völkern*" (among the peoples) so that the wish could be expressed that God bestow peace upon all humanity. Likewise, in the prayer for the New Month, Geiger preserved the traditional Hebrew that reads "May the Holy One, Blessed be He, renew this month upon us and upon all His people, the Household of Israel," but refused to translate the words "and upon all His people, the Household of Israel." Instead, he simply asserted "*uns*" (us). His conviction that the modern *siddur* had to purge itself of a noxious particularity and to articulate, in its stead, the ideal of Jewish mission found additional expression in his German phrase, "who has chosen Israel for His teaching" (*der Israel zu seiner Lehre erkoren*), which he offered for the Hebrew statement, "Who has chosen His people Israel in love." As inheritors of the covenant, the Jews are reminded by the prayer book that their task as Israel is to proclaim God's teachings to humankind.

As so many of these citations demonstrate, Geiger, like the Hamburg Reformers he had criticized, frequently maintained the Hebrew prayers of the traditional *siddur* even when he had difficulties with their manifest content. On other occasions, he, like the Reformers of Hamburg, employed translation as the vehicle whereby the ideals of Reform Judaism could find expression. Several last examples will illuminate how he did this. Like the Hamburg *Gebetbücher*, the 1854 Geiger prayer book retained the word "*go'el*" (redeemer) in the Hebrew, though it offered, "*Erlösung*" (redemption), not "*Erlöser*" (redeemer), in German. Similarly,

Geiger, like the Hamburg Temple Reformers whom he chastised, preserved the references to angelology contained in the Hebrew text of the *Kedushat de-Yotzer* located in the 1854 *Gebetbuch*, while at the same time offering a vernacular prayer that praised God as the creator of the natural world. In so doing, he obviated the literal meaning of the words. Geiger also retained those Hebrew phrases in the *Amidah* that spoke of "resurrection of the dead" (*tehiyat ha-meitim*) but did not translate them literally. Thus, the *hatimah* of the second benediction of the *Amidah*, "who resurrects the dead" (*mehayei ha-meitim*) was translated as, "who dispenses life here and beyond" (*der Leben spendet hier und dort*).

The Geiger *Gebetbücher* displayed far-reaching Reform. Yet, like the authors of the Hamburg *Gebetbücher*, Geiger was not absolute in his application of Reform principles — particularly in the 1854 edition of his liturgy, where he included the Hebrew passages "May You cause a new light to shine upon Zion" and "May our eyes behold Your return to Zion in compassion." In addition, Geiger also printed the *hatimah* "who restores His divine presence to Zion" in his 1854 *siddur*, though the formula "whom alone we serve in reverence" was substituted in the 1870 prayer book. Echoes of the approach adopted by the Reform editors in Hamburg can be heard here as well. Furthermore, Geiger, despite his own strictures, retained the *Musaf* service itself in both his prayer books. In this way, he displayed a sensibility akin to that of the Hamburg Reformers. Like them, Geiger also maintained the rite of *dukhenen* in both his *siddurim*, thereby continuing, despite his own protests, elements of the priestly prerogatives. In addition, in his 1854 *Gebetbuch*, Geiger, in keeping with Jewish tradition, stipulated that a Levite was to be the second man called to the reading of the Torah. Indeed, the structure and order of the actual services he composed demonstrates how traditional his practical approach was to Jewish public prayer. There are daily morning, afternoon, and evening services, including *Tahanun*, as well as Sabbath and Rosh Hodesh services. Prayers for Purim and Hanukkah, as well as evening and morning services for Tisha b'Av are included. The services for the three pilgrimage festivals, in addition to the already-mentioned *Musaf* services for these days, contain the texts of the Torah readings for each holiday, both first and second days. In addition, there is a service for Simhat Torah, prayers for *Tal* (Dew) and *Geshem* (Rain) on Passover and Shemini Atzeret, and *Hoshanot*.

The Geiger prayer books, especially the 1854 liturgy, were no more consistent in their application of Reform principles than were the *Gebetbücher* of the Hamburg Temple that Geiger had so vociferously denounced. The 1854 *Gebetbuch* displayed the same departures from a principled Reform, as Geiger himself defined it, that the Hamburg Temple *Gebetbücher* had. In light of his strong views, it seems that Geiger failed to construct a comprehensive Reform liturgy that embodied a total fidelity to the ideals of Reform.

The spirit of compromise that marked the prayer book creations of Geiger, as well as of the Hamburg Reformers who had preceded him, was the result of several factors. One was the view of Jewish communal unity that informed the authors of these Reform liturgies. They had internalized an approach to Judaism that led them to seek attachment to the Jewish past, and their *siddurim* reflect the views of men who saw themselves as part of historical Jewish tradition. They aspired to be members of the larger Jewish community, and they rejected a sectarian posture. As Petuchowski has noted, "Geiger . . . twice refused to heed the call to the pulpit of the Berlin Reform Congregation," a separatist congregation that was "as radical in its Reform as Hamburg tended to be moderate." Instead, Geiger, "the liturgical practitioner, . . . set out to lead whole Jewish communities, and not merely 'denominational' Reform groups."[23]

Again, this does not mean that either the *Gebetbücher* of Hamburg or those of Geiger did not attempt to reform elements in the traditional service that their authors regarded as atavistic. These prayer books were written to reflect a redefinition of Jewishness in keeping with the position and ideals that marked the Jewish community in nineteenth-century Germany. As this analysis reveals, Geiger did compose a Reform *siddur*. On the level of manifest content, his *Gebetbücher* embodied significant departures from the Ashkenazic liturgical tradition that he had received. Nevertheless, his was a reform of evolution, not revolution. From the perspective of the Orthodox right, his *siddurim*, like those of Hamburg, were seen as radical departures from the received Ashkenazic rite. At the same time, a radical Reform left could condemn them as inconsistent and piecemeal.

---

23   Jakob J. Petuchowski, "Abraham Geiger: The Reform Jewish Liturgist," in Petuchowski, ed., *New Perspectives on Abraham Geiger* (Cincinnati, 1975), pp. 48–49

The existence of the *Einheitsgemeinde*, the unified Jewish political-communal structure that obtained in Germany during the 1800s, also had a conserving effect upon these Liberal liturgists. Rabbis like Geiger served venerable communities that were embedded in tradition, and they had to take into consideration the sentiments and feelings, as well as the religious commitments, of many. In short, the prayer books of Geiger, as well as those of the Hamburg Temple, reveal a Jewish world caught between tradition and modernity. Manuel Joël also participated in this arena. His specific resolution of the problem will reflect how a more conservative Liberal Jew — one who identified with Positive-Historical Judaism as formulated by Zacharias Frankel — struggled with this dilemma.

The Response of Manuel Joël
The Liturgy of a Positive-Historical Jew

As Petuchowski has explained, "While Geiger sat in Frankfurt, preparing the new edition of his prayer book, his old congregation in Breslau had entrusted his successor there, Manuel Joël, with the task of revising Geiger's 1854 prayer book in a more traditionalist direction." As Joël himself testified in his introduction to his *Israelitisches Gebetbuch*, "The erection of a community synagogue, one which, for the first time was built to be representative of the community as a whole," occasioned the "need" for this new liturgy to be written. While Geiger was not altogether sanguine about this development, Joël, in his introduction to his *Israelitisches Gebetbuch*, wrote: "After Dr. Geiger had given the desired approval to the board of the Breslau community, the further discussion of the principles governing the new prayer book was begun, and, after their determination, the undersigned rabbi was entrusted with the editorial work." In composing his *siddur* for the entire community, Joël had to pay attention to those persons in the community who, as he noted, had preserved the traditional Ashkenazic liturgy "unchanged" in their synagogues. At the same time, he was careful to honor, both because of his own internalization of certain values and norms as well as the prestige Geiger still commanded in the Breslau community, the model the Geiger prayer book provided. Indeed, Joël expressed the hope that, "the many parts of it which have proved themselves through years of experience would be preserved for us."[24] The Joël prayer book thus cannot be understood, nor can his own distinctive stance be illuminated, without reference to Geiger and the 1854 Breslau *Gebetbuch* that Geiger authored. Michael Meyer has summed it up well when he writes, "[T]he lay leadership . . . charged Geiger's successor in Breslau, Manuel Joël, to come up with an acceptable compromise between the traditional prayer book and Geiger's. Joël . . . agreed to use Geiger's first edition as the basis, *retaining the fundamental ideological tendency with which he sympathized*. But he modified it somewhat in a traditional direction.[25]

Joël was undoubtedly more conservative than Geiger. In 1869, he described himself at a rabbinic synod as a person who was "rather inclined to retain than to destroy."[26] Yet, his sentiments and inclinations were not altogether different from those of Geiger. Indeed, as Meyer observed, Joël agreed to use the 1854 edition of the Geiger *Israelitisches Gebetbuch* precisely because he identified with its fundamental ideological tendency. Joël was a man who applauded the importance that modernity had placed upon the dignity of the individual. In antiquity, Joël observed, "the individual had no rights vis-à-vis the community. Our time is great because we emphasize individual more than communal tendencies." Yet, in a tone reminiscent of Zacharias Frankel, he maintained: "True greatness comes from the community." In constructing a prayer book, Joël said, "On the one hand, we must express the freedom of the individual, but, on the other, especially as far as ritual is concerned, the individual must give expression not merely to that which moves him, but also to that which affects Israel and the total community."[27] In the effort to maintain a common worship service for all Jews, the autonomy of the individual, in the opinion of Joël, was not absolute. It had to be curbed, and a spirit of compromise had to prevail. Joël, like Geiger, sought to calibrate the proper response to this dilemma.

In the preface to his 1872 liturgy, Joël outlined the points that guided his response. Addressing himself to the Hebrew section of his liturgy, Joël, as a Positive-Historical Jew informed by the historicism that marked this trend in German Judaism, contended that "even the

---

24 Petuchowski, *Prayerbook Reform in Europe*, pp.171–72.
25 Meyer, *Response to Modernity*, p.187 (italics mine).
26 As quoted in Plaut, *The Rise of Reform Judaism*, p.181.
27 Ibid.

conservatives do not close their minds to the recognition that the removal of numerous prayers is not only religiously *permitted*, but religiously *commanded*." The historical development of Jewish tradition — including the liturgical one — was too apparent to be denied. At the same time, restoration, not just innovation, must mark the Jewish public prayer book. Joël was concerned that, "through an unjustified and far too pedestrian evaluation, some prayers which undoubtedly have retained their ability to edify to this day were reckoned among the doubtful prayers." Prayer book reform must therefore proceed cautiously.[28]

Joël insisted that two prayers were of fundamental importance — "The Confession of Faith (*Shema*) with its Blessings" and "The so-called *Tephillah* proper." With regard to the latter, Joël observed that the formulae of the middle blessings in the *Amidah*, blessings dealing with the restoration of Zion and Jerusalem as well as the reinstitution of the sacrificial cult, were those that gave rise to controversy in the present-day community. Therefore, he suggested, as was already the custom in German Liberal prayer, that these benedictions should not be recited aloud, but only prayed silently. In this way, "there could be no objection to the retention of the old formulation by the side of the reformed one, which latter corresponds more to our views — provided, of course, that the new formulation does not bear the stamp of arbitrariness, but likewise demonstrates the retention of that which is fundamental." In other words, Joël proposed to solve the dilemma of communal worship in a pluralistic setting where different members of the community held different attitudes and sensibilities towards prayer by including several versions of the text in the *siddur*. As Petuchowski accurately describes it, Joël printed a "reformed" text of the controversial passages "in large print, and the German translation would refer to that 'reformed' version. But also, in small print and without translation, Joël would restore the traditional text, for the benefit of those congregants who were uncompromisingly attached to it."[29] In addition, Joël declared, "For congregational purposes, I regarded as correct and appropriate the method of Geiger, i.e., to substitute a free paraphrase for a literal translation." In

---

28 The citations and arguments in this paragraph are found in Petuchowski, *Prayerbook Reform in Europe*, p.173.

29 Ibid. p.171.

so doing, Joël claimed that he strove for fidelity to the Hebrew text and its spirit. Nevertheless, Joël confessed, "What appears to be faithful to one looks like being too free to another."[30] The task of navigating between the Scylla of tradition and the Charybdis of modernity was a formidable one. An analysis of the elements of his prayer book reveals how Joël sought to accomplish this goal.

Like Geiger and the Hamburg Reformers, Joël often displayed a penchant in his liturgy for the Sephardic rite. For example, he retained the formula of *Menuḥah Nekhonah* that Geiger had introduced into the Breslau rite for the Memorial service. Joël also sought to purge the prayer book of those passages that presented gentiles in a derogatory fashion, as well as those phrases and sentences that needlessly distinguished between Israel and the nations — all of which he found inappropriate and offensive to the spirit of the modern age. He substituted the phrase "who has made me an Israelite" for the traditional "who has not made me a gentile." Similarly, he removed the passage in the Sabbath *Shaharit* service that asserted that the "uncircumcised" could not enjoy Sabbath rest, and declared simply and positively, "And You have given it, O God, to Your people Israel." While he retained the controversial passages in the Hebrew text of the *Ezrat Avoteinu* that referred to the drowning of the Egyptians at the Red Sea, Joël, like Geiger in 1854, left them untranslated. Joël's wording for *Birkat ha-Minim* was somewhat different from Geiger's. However, his prayer conveyed the same meaning and he, again following Geiger, substituted "slander" (*malshinut*) for "slanderers" (*malshinim*) in the first word of the prayer. Joël elected to preserve the 1854 Hebrew text Geiger had produced for the *Aleinu* and, though his German translation of the prayer differed from that offered by Geiger, it conveyed a comparable meaning and emphasized that God had bestowed upon Israel "a holy teaching as an inheritance." The universal mission assigned Israel to disseminate this teaching meant that "noxious passages" that distinguished Israel from the nations — like that found in the *Havdalah* ceremony — had to be removed from the prayer book, and the Joël *Gebetbuch*, like that of Geiger, did so.

Joël followed the model Geiger had established in other ways as well.

30 Ibid. p.175.

He removed the passage prior to the recitation of the *Shema* that asked God to restore the people of Israel to its land, and he offered an alternative to the traditional *Kibbutz Galuyot* benediction in the *Amidah*. Instead of asking God "to gather us together from the four corners of the Earth," Joël composed a prayer that expressed the hope that "the voice of freedom and salvation would be heard in our tents." Joël's *siddur* asked that the "offspring of righteousness" and not "the offspring of David Your servant" flourish, and it provided an alternative for the benediction that asserted, "Restore our judges as at first. . . ." with the words "Justify us with Your judgments and guide us with Your counsel." In his prayer for Jerusalem, Joël praised God, "who remembers Jerusalem and its ruins."

Joël's imitation of Geiger is also apparent in other prayers he composed. Like Geiger in 1854, Joël left the traditional Hebrew text of the first two blessings of *the Amidah* undisturbed. However, like Geiger, he used translation as a vehicle to obviate meanings he found disturbing. Thus, he retained the Hebrew word *go'el* (redeemer) but translated it as *Erlösung* (redemption). Furthermore, his German translation offered a spiritual understanding of *tehiyat ha-meitim;* Joël refused to affirm the notion of bodily resurrection contained in the Hebrew. Finally, like Geiger, Joël retained the angelology of *Kedushat de-Yotzer* in Hebrew, but provided a German translation that neglected those elements of angelology and instead exclusively affirmed God as the creator and master of the universe.

In keeping with German Jewish liturgical tradition, Joël rewrote the middle benediction of the Sabbath *Musaf* service. Instead of asking God to restore the sacrificial cult, Joël wrote, "May it be pleasing before You, O Lord our God, that You prepare our hearts to observe Your Sabbaths, and may You bring blessing upon our land and contentment within our borders, so that our hearts will be open to Your service. And may the expression of our lips instead of the additional sacrifice of this Sabbath that our ancestors offered before You be pleasant unto You." In these brief lines, Joël displayed significant departures from the ideological content of the traditional liturgy. The sacrificial cult was reduced to an historical memory, and the prayer now focused on Germany, not *Eretz Yisrael*, as the focus of Jewish hopes and prayers.

Despite all the innovation present in the Joël prayer book, his *siddur* also displayed some departures from a rigid Liberal tradition. For example, Joël, despite his apparent distaste for the priestly cult, retained, as Geiger had, the rite of *dukhenen* in his service. He restored the phrase, "When will You reign in Zion," to the *Kedushah* of the Sabbath *Shaḥarit* service, though he continued to omit the phrase, "May You be exalted and sanctified in Jerusalem Your city." Unlike Geiger, Joël retained the phrase, "from among all peoples," throughout his prayer book, and while, as we have seen, he emphasized the notion of Jewish mission, he was more comfortable with Jewish particularity than was Geiger. His German translation of the lines "And may You cause our eyes to behold Your return to Zion . . ." and "who restores His divine presence to Zion," was faithful to the Hebrew and, in the final benedictions of the *Amidah* in both morning and evening services, Joël felt free to emphasize in German translation, in a way that Geiger had not, that God had extended the teachings of peace to Israel — though, to be sure, the mission of Israel to spread those teachings to humanity is as apparent in the German rendition of the Joël prayer as it was in the Geiger prayer book.

The spirit that marked the Joël prayer book is perhaps best captured in an analysis of Joël's treatment of the line, "Cause a new light to shine upon Zion . . . ," Joël, as had Geiger in 1854, retained this line in the Hebrew text of his liturgy. However, unlike Geiger, he restored this prayer fully by translating it into German as well, rendering it in the words "*So lass, o Gott, em neues Licht auch Zion leuchten.*" Nevertheless, Joël then felt constrained to add the phrase "*und dieses Licht auch uns den Weg erhellen*" (and this light will also illumine the way for us). The particularity of the prayer was thereby muted, and the spirituality of the universal mission assigned Israel thereby highlighted. The Joël *Gebetbuch*, like the Geiger *siddurim*, was very much a product of the spirit that infused German *liberales Judentum*.

Concluding Considerations

An analysis of the manifest content of the Geiger and Joël prayer books, as well as those of the Hamburg rites that preceded them, has revealed that a broad consensus of feeling and belief marked the leaders of German Liberal Judaism during the nineteenth century. Themes and innovations present in one *Gebetbuch* found expression in the others as well. This does not mean that these prayer books were identical. However, an assessment of these works unmistakably yields the conclusion that a common Central European context informed these authors, and that similar sensibilities characterized the framers of these liturgies.

The *siddurim* of Geiger and Joël explain, in part, why separate Liberal Jewish religious denominations, akin to Reform and Conservative branches of Judaism in the United States, did not emerge in Germany at this time. Simply put, the traditionalist ideological consensus and cultural proclivities that marked Joël and Geiger were simply too great to justify the creation of separate religious movements. The attitudes and principles, as well as applications, evidenced in the *Gebetbücher* of these men do not distinguish them sufficiently to speak of distinct Reform and Positive-Historical denominations. The differences that do distinguish these *siddurim* are, at best, ones of degree, not kind. Joël, like Geiger, embodied the ethos of *Liberales Judentum*. His Positive-Historical Judaism, as displayed in his *Gebetbuch*, represented a trend, not a distinct denomination, within German Liberal Judaism.

Of course, an analysis of other prayer books produced by other rabbis associated with the Positive-Historical trend in German Jewish religious life might well produce a different portrait of German religious denominationalism in general and Positive-Historical Judaism in particular. For example, *Das Gebetbuch der Israeliten*, published by Rabbi Michael Sachs of Berlin in 1855, represented a different sensibility and approach to Judaism and liturgy than was evidenced in the Joël *siddur*. Sachs was a preeminent spokesman for Positive-Historical Judaism in nineteenth-century Germany, and Joël had been his pupil and remained among his closest colleagues and friends in the years thereafter.[31] However, the Sachs *Gebetbuch*, unlike that of Joël, maintained the traditional Ashkenazic liturgy of German Jewry in its entirety. Indeed, the traditional nature of the Sachs *siddur* aroused the ire of Reform col-

---

31 Rivka Horowitz includes Sachs among those contemporaries of Zacharias Frankel whose views were representative of the Positive-Historical School. See her book *Zacharias Frankel and the Beginnings of Positive-Historical Judaism* (Hebrew) (Jerusalem, 1984), pp. 185–94. For an account of the relationship between Sachs and Joël, see Lucas and Frank, *Michael Sachs*, pp. 98 and 118.

leagues, and Sachs's studies in liturgy as well as the translation he offered in his prayer book exerted a profound influence on Orthodox as well as Liberal circles in Germany.[32]

The Sachs *Gebetbuch* possessed an aesthetic appearance, and provided a graceful German translation that marked its author as an individual embedded in and informed by contemporary Central European culture. Nevertheless, Sachs consistently maintained the Hebrew text and his translation always rendered the Hebrew faithfully. Occasionally, passages concerning sacrifices at the beginning and end of various services were left untranslated, as were several other prayers such as *Yekum Purkan*, which asked divine blessing upon the heads of the Babylonian Jewish community. However, these details could be found in other Orthodox liturgies of the day as well. Indeed, the only places where there was even a hint of apology on the part of Sachs for the traditional *siddur* were in two translations he provided concerning gentiles. In one, Sachs rendered "*She-lo asani nokhri*" (who has not made me a gentile) with the gentler phrase "*der mich nicht gemacht zum Nichtisraeliten*" (who has not made me a non-Israelite). In a parallel vein, Sachs offered *Fremde* (the strangers) as the translation for *areilim* (the uncircumcised) in the Sabbath morning service.

The Sachs *Gebetbuch*, unlike that of Geiger or Joël, was thoroughly traditional. It was not part of the Liberal approach to prayer book reform that marked both the Reform and Positive-Historical trends in German *Liberales Judentum* during the nineteenth century. It provides a powerful and instructive counter-model to the *siddurim* of Geiger and Joël and indicates that nineteenth-century Positive-Historical Judaism in Germany was not confined to a liberal expression. It had its conservative wing as well. The situation that obtained in German Positive-Historical Judaism foreshadowed developments that were to emerge in American Conservative Judaism — the heir to German Positive-Historical Judaism — in the twentieth century, where traditional

---

32 See Lucas and Frank, *Michael Sachs*, pp.115–16, for a description of the conflict and criticism the Sachs liturgy engendered among Reform circles of his day. For a discussion of the role that Sachs occupied in the formation of the modern German Orthodox service, see E.D. Goldschmidt, "Studies on German-Jewish Liturgy by German-Jewish Scholars," in *Leo Baeck Institute Year Book* II (1957), pp.122–23.

and liberal wings of that movement have struggled for hegemony. Contemporary American Jewish intra-denominational differences thus have their parallels in the German situation of the nineteenth century.

This study, by allowing the Joël and Geiger *Gebetbücher* to provide foci for analysis, has contributed to an understanding of the nature and evolution of Jewish religious denominationalism in both nineteenth-century Germany and the modern era. At the same time, it points in the direction of further research. For while the Geiger and Joël *siddurim* testify to the state of nineteenth-century German *Liberales Judentum* and demonstrate that there was a Positive-Historical wing fully ensconced within its precincts, additional investigation into the *siddurim* of figures like Sachs will eventually provide a fuller understanding of the nature of German Liberal Judaism in general and its Positive-Historical wing in particular.

10

The Prayers for Rain in the *Siddurim* of Abraham Geiger and Isaac Mayer Wise

An Exploration into the Relationship Between Reform Jewish Thought and Liturgical Practice

As is well known to students and practitioners of classical Jewish prayer, there are two seasonal insertions in the daily liturgy of the traditional *Amidah* that express a Jewish acknowledgment of God's mastery over nature as well as a specific request for rain. The first of these insertions is found in the second benediction of the *Shemoneh Esreh*. In this blessing, labeled *Gevurot*, all traditional *minhagim*, Sephardic and Ashkenazic, add the phrase, "*Mashiv ha-ruaḥ u-morid ha-gashem* — who causes the wind to blow and the rain to fall," during the fall and winter months, after the words, "*Ata rav le-hoshi'a* — You are abundantly strong to save." The traditional Sephardic rite also inserts the words, "*Morid ha-tal* — who causes the dew to fall," at this point in the service during the summer season. In addition, a prayer for precipitation, "*ve-tein tal u-matar li-vrakha* — and grant us dew and rain for blessing," is also placed in the ninth blessing, *Birkat ha-Shanim* — Benediction of the Years, of the *Amidah* during the winter months. In this prayer, God is asked to bestow abundance upon the earth.

This essay will focus upon how the two preeminent leaders of Reform Judaism during the nineteenth century — Abraham Geiger of Germany and Isaac Mayer Wise of the United States — dealt with these prayers for rain in their own *siddurim*. Through an analysis of these seldom-discussed passages[1] and their treatment in these classical expressions

---

1   For example, none of the leading English-language scholarly works on the history of Reform Jewish liturgy — Jakob J. Petuchowski *Prayerbook Reform in Europe* (New York: The World Union for Progressive Judaism, 1968); Lawrence A. Hoffman, *Beyond the Text* (Bloomington, Ind.: Indiana University Press, 1987) and Eric L. Friedland, *Were our Mouths Filled With Song: Studies in Liberal Jewish Liturgy* (Cincinnati: Hebrew Union College Press, 1997) — deal with these particular insertions, though

of Reform liturgy, we will see how the approaches taken by Geiger and Wise towards these insertions reveal an important dimension of nineteenth-century Reform Jewish thought. In order to comprehend the distinctive nature of their perspectives on these prayers, the initial section of this essay will discuss the relevant talmudic and later rabbinic sources that legislate and describe the rationales for these insertions in the traditional Jewish order of prayer, for it was to this tradition that Geiger and Wise reacted. Finally, through a selective sampling of representative twentieth-century non-Orthodox prayer books on these insertions, the course of modern Jewish Liberal ideology beyond Geiger and Wise as well as something of the variegated directions of contemporary Liberal Jewish religious practice will be illuminated.

Classical Rabbinic Precedent and Legislation

Our talmudic discussion of these prayers for rain begins with a consideration of the first insertion, "who causes the wind to blow and the rain fall," referred to in *Mishnah Ta'anit* 1:1 as "*Gevurot Geshamim* — The Power of Rains." In accord with the dictates of *Mishnah Berakhot* 4:5 and *Ta'anit* 2a, this line is recited in the *Gevurot* benediction of the *Amidah*, and it is defined technically in Hebrew as a *hazkarah*, a "remembrance" (*Ta'anit* 4a–b). That is, the rabbis understood this insertion not as a prayer for rain, but as a statement of the power of God over nature. Indeed, for this reason, Rabbi Eliezer stated that this line should be made a permanent part of the liturgy, asserting, "And just as one makes mention of 'the Revival of the Dead' (*Tehiyat ha-Meitim*) all the year round although it will only take place in its proper time, so too should mention be made of the Power of Rain all the year round although it only comes in its due season" (*Ta'anit* 2b). Nevertheless, the *din* (Jewish law) was not fixed in accord with Rabbi Eliezer, and *Ta'anit* 4a actually fixed the exact time for the recitation of this prayer, decreeing that it would be prayed from *Musaf* on Shemini Atzeret until the onset of Passover. The rationale, as stated in *Mishnah Ta'anit* 1:2, is that "one does not pray for rain except near the time of rain," and these dates, from mid-fall to early spring, correspond to the rainy season in Palestine. Hence, the liturgical insertion of *Gevurot Geshamim* is attached to the time of antici-

---

Friedland does make mention of them in a sentence at the bottom of p.240.

pated rainfall in *Eretz Yisrael*. Furthermore, the recitation of the phrase "Who causes the dew to fall" during the summer months, was similarly attached to climatic conditions in the Land of Israel, and mention is not made of this specific insertion in the Babylonian Talmud, but in the Jerusalem Talmud alone (T. Y. *Ta'anit* 1:1). Indeed, the Babylonian Sages, in *Ta'anit* 3a ruled, "The Sages did not make it obligatory to refer to dew and wind," and as Ismar Elbogen has observed, this latter insertion was "unknown in Babylonia."[2] While, as mentioned above, the inclusion of *"Morid ha-tal"* during the summer months became a standard part of several Sephardic rites, mention of dew at this point in the service never became part of the Ashkenazic order of prayer.[3]

As with *Gevurot Geshamim*, the Talmud fixed a place in Jewish liturgy for the recitation of the insertion "And grant us dew and rain for blessing." Indeed, both *Berakhot* 5:2 and *Ta'anit* 2a held that this line should be included in the ninth benediction, *Birkat ha-Shanim*, of the *Amidah*. However, unlike *Gevurot Geshamim*, this line was not understood as a *hazkarah*, but as a *she'elah*, a petitionary insertion asking for the rain to fall (*Ta'anit* 4a–b). In establishing the time for the recitation of this prayer, the Talmud, in *Ta'anit* 10a, records the following statements by Rabban Gamliel and Rabbi Ḥananiah. The former authority ruled that it should first be recited on Marḥeshvan 7, fifteen days after Sukkot, while Ḥananiah fixed its recitation "in the *Golah* (i.e., Babylonia) from the sixtieth day of the autumn equinox — *U-va-golah ad shishim yom ba-tekufah.*" As Arnold A. Lasker and Daniel J. Lasker have noted in their perceptive and comprehensive article on this topic, crops had already been gathered in *Eretz Yisrael* by the seventh of Marḥeshvan. Hence, the recitation of this prayer during mid-fall in October, as prescribed by Rabban Gamliel, was to correspond to the anticipated and hoped-for rainy season in Palestine. However, as the Laskers observe, "Babylonia neither receives nor needs rain until well in November."[4] Therefore, the ruling of Rabbi Ḥananiah, which serves as the foundation for the insertion of *Tal u-Matar* in the ninth benediction of the *Amidah* in the late

2 Ismar Elbogen. *Jewish Liturgy: A Comprehensive History,* trans. by Raymond P. Schendlin (Philadelphia: Jewish Publication Society,1993). p.39.

3 Ibid.

4 Arnold A. Lasker and Daniel J. Lasker, "The Jewish Prayer for Rain in Babylonia." *Journal for the Study of Judaism* 15 (1984), p.136.

fall (corresponding to December 4 or 5 today), was based upon a solar calculation attuned to the need for precipitation in Babylonia in late fall and throughout the winter.

Two different liturgical customs concerning these prayers therefore arose during talmudic times. One was attached to *Eretz Yisrael* and the rainy season there, in keeping with the rabbinic principle that one recites the prayers for rain at the appropriate time of year. Eventually, this meant that in the Palestinian rite the recitation of these prayers would commence with the *Musaf* service on Shemini Atzeret and would continue until the onset of Passover, in accord with the talmudic dictum, "*Eretz Yisrael, she'elah ve-hazkarah ha-da miltah hi* — In the Land of Israel, 'praying' and 'remembrance' are one and the same thing" (*Ta'anit* 4a). Indeed, this remains the custom in Israel today.[5]

In Babylonia, as the Laskers put it, "the case was different."[6] The Jews of Babylonia did agree to insert "the remembrance *hazkarah*" for rain in the second benediction of the *Amidah* beginning with Shemini Atzeret so as to express their solidarity with the Jews of *Eretz Yisrael*. However, in light of the different climatic and agricultural conditions that prevailed in Babylonia, they delayed "praying" for precipitation until late fall in keeping with the by-now familiar talmudic principle that one only prays for rain in its season. In so doing, they maintained the position that "*she'elah la-hud, hazkarah la-hud* — 'praying' is one thing, 'remembrance' another" (*Ta'anit* 4b).

Rashi, in a commentary upon *Ta'anit* 10b, asserted, "All our customs follow Babylonia." Jews in Europe thus adopted the Babylonian custom in their liturgy of inserting *Tal u-Matar* in the *Birkat ha-Shanim* benediction of the *Amidah* beginning on December 4 or 5. However, as Lasker and Lasker have commented, "The widely-held belief that through the insertion of this blessing, Jews in the Diaspora pray for rain to fall in Israel is fallacious."[7] Indeed, several prominent modern commentators have maintained that this insertion is connected to the Land of Israel.[8]

5　See any contemporary standard Israeli Orthodox prayer book, e.g., *Siddur Rinat Yisrael*.

6　Lasker and Lasker, "The Jewish Prayer for Rain in Babylonia," p.141.

7　Arnold A. Lasker and Daniel J. Lasker. "The Jewish Prayer for Rain in the Post-Talmudic Diaspora," *AJS Review* 9 (1984), p.146.

8　No less a distinguished and learned authority than Rabbi Isaac Klein writes in *A Guide to Jewish Religious Practice* (New York: Jewish Theological Seminary, 1979),

However, as has been shown, the inclusion of this prayer is linked to the *Golah*, i.e., the time of anticipated precipitation in Babylonia.

On the basis of the reasoning that supported this Babylonian precedent — that the recitation of *Tal u-Matar* correspond to the rainy season in a particular country — no less prominent a rabbinic authority than the European *rishon*, Rabbi Asher ben Yeḥiel (Rosh), urged the Jews of Germany in a 1313 responsum to look to local climatic conditions, and not Babylonian custom, as the decisive factor in determining when this prayer was to be recited. Rejecting the notion of Babylonian hegemony over Jewish prayer practice advanced by Rashi, Rosh felt that the prerogatives of the German Jewish community on this matter were no less than those of the venerable Babylonian settlement. In light of weather conditions in Germany, he stated that the Jews of Germany were entitled to insert this line between the seventh of Marheshvan and Shavuot. While his ruling was rejected by the European Jewish community, it was, as the Laskers have put it, "based on the logic of the situation rather than on accumulated custom."[9]

Having provided this background summary of classical rabbinic literature concerning the nature and content of *Gevurot Geshamim* and *Tal u-Matar* we are now able to analyze the treatment of these insertions in the *siddurim* of Abraham Geiger and Isaac Mayer Wise. Both these men and, as we shall see, other Jewish Liberal liturgists as well, in effect adopted and extended the line of reasoning put forth by the Rosh in regard to these prayers. It is to their prayer books that we now turn.

Gevurot Geshamim *and* Tal u-Matar *in Geiger and Wise*

Both Geiger and Wise were convinced that "outgrown attitudes" which still appeared in Jewish prayer had to be eliminated, and a systematic

---

p. 34 of *Tal u-Matar*: "This blessing expresses the concern of the inhabitants of the Holy Land for adequate rainfall during the rainy season." Similarly, the "Commentary" upon this insertion in *Kol Haneshamah* (Wyncote, Pa: Reconstructionist Press, 1996), p. 111, states of *Tal u-Matar*: "According to the rabbis, the rainy season in Israel starts on December 4th, which is about sixty days after the fall equinox." As we have seen, the December 4th date corresponds to the onset of the rainy season in Babylonia, not *Eretz Yisrael*.

9   This information drawn from the responsum of the Rosh, as well as the quotation

reform of the prayer book had to be undertaken.[10] In the preface to his 1854 prayer book, *Seder Tefillah Dvar Yom be-Yomo. Israelitisches Gebet-buch für den öffentliche Gottesdienst im ganzen Jahre* (Order of Daily Service. Israelite Prayerbook for the Public Worship of the Entire Year), Geiger defined the particular features of his modern liturgy. He stated, "Jerusalem and Zion are places whence instruction went forth, and to which holy memories are attached. But, on the whole, they are to be cel-ebrated more as a spiritual idea, as the nursery of the Kingdom of God than as a certain geographical locale connected with a special divine providence for all times."[11]

Fifteen years later, in 1869, Geiger published a *Denkschrift* in which he reiterated the ideological-theological strictures that would guide the construction of his liturgy on this matter. He stated that the uni-versal character of Judaism had to find expression in the *siddur*, and the "national aspect" of Jewish tradition "must recede into the back-ground." The hope for the "unification of all mankind" dictated that a modern Liberal liturgy must purge all prayers of a national character from the prayer book. In short, Geiger wanted all prayers that empha-sized the centrality of *Eretz Yisrael* in anything other than a spiritual manner to be deleted from the prayer book.[12]

In view of these sentiments, it is fascinating to observe that Geiger, in the 1854 edition of *Dvar Yom be-Yomo*, retained the traditional inser-tions of *Gevurot Geshamim* and *Tal u-Matar* in the Hebrew text of his prayer book and stated, in instructions printed in the *siddur*, that these lines should be recited at the times established in the traditional Ashke-nazic rite. This meant that *Gevurot Geshamim* was to be recited begin-ning from the *Musaf* service on Shemini Atzeret "until the first day of Passover — *bis zum ersten tagen Pessach*," while *Tal u-Matar* was to be said "*Im Winter bis zum 1 Tage Pessach*, in winter until the first day Passover."

---

itself, are taken from Lasker and Lasker, "The Jewish Prayer for Rain in the Post-Talmudic Diaspora," pp.153 and 156.

10   See Abraham Geiger, "Suggested Changes," in Gunther Plaut, ed., *The Rise of Reform Judaism* (New York: World Union for Progressive Judaism, 1963), pp.156ff. For a summary of Wise's position on this point, see Eric Friedland, "Isaac Mayer Wise and *Minhag Amerika*," in *Were Our Mouths Filled with Song*, pp.50–54.

11   The preface to the 1854 Geiger prayer book appears in English translation in Petuchowski, *Prayerbook Reform in Europe*. pp.150–52.

12   For a translation of the *Denkschrift* as well as the quotations found in this paragraph, see ibid. pp.165–67.

The 1854 Hebrew text of the Geiger prayer book displayed an absolute fidelity to Ashkenazic liturgical tradition concerning the content and timing for both of these insertions. On the other hand, the German translation of *Gevurot Geshamim* omitted this phrase altogether while the German rendering of *Tal u-Matar* neither translated the Hebrew literally nor did it link the phrase to a particular time of year. Instead, the German of the Geiger *siddur* asked that God allow the earth to offer its "rich yield — *reichen Ertrag*" so that "our year — *unser Jahr*" would be blessed. The particularity of *Gevurot Geshamim* and *Tal u-Matar* — their attachments to the Land of Israel and the Babylonian Diaspora — could be tolerated in the Hebrew. The vernacular demanded a more universalistic rendering confirming the majesty of God over nature and abundance beyond those particular venues.

The "inconsistency" the 1854 Geiger liturgy displayed regarding the Hebrew and German texts of these insertions can be explained in several ways. Foremost among them was the view of Jewish communal unity that informed its author. Geiger aspired to be a leader of the larger Jewish community, and he rejected a Reform sectarian posture. As Jakob Petuchowski has noted, "Geiger . . . twice refused to heed the call to the pulpit of the [radical separatist] Berlin Reform Congregation." Instead, "Geiger, the liturgical practitioner . . . set out to lead whole Jewish communities, and not really 'denominational' Reform groups."[13] As we noted in chapter nine, Geiger advanced a Reform of evolution, not revolution. Electing to serve a venerable community that was embedded in tradition, he took into consideration the sentiments and feelings, as well as religious commitments, of many. The existence of the *kehillah* — the unified Jewish political-communal structure that obtained in Germany during the 1800s — had a conserving effect upon him. It led to a liturgical "compromise" between German and Hebrew texts described in these instances.

This does not mean that Geiger hesitated to reform elements in the traditional service that he regarded as atavistic. As we have seen, the 1854 *Gebetbuch* of Geiger could not abide the geographical particularity inherent in *Gevurot Geshamim* and *Tal u-Matar* and the German translation was written to reflect a redefinition of Jewishness in keeping

13   Jakob J. Petuchowski, "Abraham Geiger, The Reform Jewish Liturgist," in Petuchowski, ed., *New Perspectives on Abraham Geiger* (Cincinnati: Hebrew Union College Press, 1975), pp. 48–49.

with his own Reform position and ideals. However, Geiger ultimately could not tolerate what he himself saw as the "inconsistency" of this position.[14] He therefore amended the Hebrew text of these insertions in his 1870 edition of *Dvar Yom be-Yomo* in keeping with the sentiments expressed in his 1854 translation. Rather than making the insertions of *Gevurot Geshamim* and *Tal u-Matar* seasonal, he made them permanent parts of his liturgy. While the German translation of the second and ninth benedictions of the *Amidah* remained identical in both the 1854 and 1870 editions of the Geiger prayer book, *Gevurot Geshamim* and *Tal u-Matar* were now fixed, not seasonal, parts of the Geiger Hebrew liturgy. The Geiger prayer book was now consistent. God was praised and petitioned in both Hebrew and German as the master of nature throughout the world, and prayers for rain and abundance were no longer limited to seasonal conditions in *Eretz Yisrael* and Babylonia.

Given the nature of his Reform ideological commitments, these evolutions in the Hebrew text of the Geiger prayer books are hardly surprising. After all, neither insertion was connected to a "spiritual idea." The first was connected to *Eretz Yisrael*, while the second was attached to a very specific "geographic locale" — i.e., Babylon. As stated above, the manner in which the 1854 edition of *Dvar Yom be-Yomo* dealt with these passages already reflected the decision of its author to place the "national aspect" of Jewish tradition "into the background." By making these additions established parts of his 1870 liturgy, Geiger was only giving practical Hebrew liturgical expression to a more universalistic ideology that had long since crystallized.

By advancing this position and granting it liturgical expression, Geiger was in effect both confirming and extending the theoretical and practical postures put forth on these prayers by the Rosh. Like Rabbenu Asher, Geiger rejected the hegemony of Babylonian liturgical custom. However, by making *Gevurot Geshamim* and *Tal u-Matar* permanent parts of his liturgy, Geiger departed from the Rosh and extended his logic. After all, Rabbenu Asher did not dissent from the talmudic reasoning that connected the time for these prayers to local climatic conditions. Indeed, he confirmed that logic by defending the prerogative of the

14 For a fuller exposition of Geiger's views on liturgical consistency, see chap. 9, "The *Israelitische Gebetbücher* of Abraham Geiger and Manuel Joël," in the present volume.

German community to establish the period for the recitation of these prayers in accord with the rainy season in Germany, not Babylonia.

Through the insertion of these lines as fixed elements in his 1870 liturgy, Geiger also advanced a prayer posture that tied these prayers to climatic conditions. However, he refused to limit these conditions to a single country or season. To have done so would have confirmed a geocentric vision of Judaism that he absolutely rejected. By reciting *Gevurot Geshamim* and *Tal u-Matar* during the entire year, Geiger emphasized a vision of divine providence beyond the confines of a single nation or season. As precipitation took place in different places throughout the world at different times, Geiger ultimately decreed that these prayers for rain had to be recited on a daily basis throughout the year. The traditional times set for their recital, as well as the geographical venues to which such times were attached, were too particularistic, and not sufficiently expansive to suit the theological vision Geiger advanced. While the German translation of his 1854 *Gebetbuch* reflected this stance, the permanent insertion of these Hebrew texts in the 1870 edition of his liturgy allowed for its full expression. The 1870 edition of *Dvar Yom be-Yomo* thereby displayed a theologically consistent vision that was absent from the 1854 prayer book. The orientation that marked these insertions was an expression of the universalism that marked Geiger and his thought.[15]

Such an orientation also characterized the treatment Isaac Mayer Wise accorded these passages in his *Minhag America*. Like Geiger, Wise

---

15   In offering this interpretation of Geiger's decision to include *Gevurot Geshamim* and *Tal u-Matar* as permanent parts of his liturgy, I depart from the explanation offered by Jacob Levinger, *Entziklopeidya Haivrit* 10, s.v., "Abraham Geiger." Levinger maintains that Geiger did connect these insertions to Germany, reasoning that since it rains in Germany in summer as well as winter, the *hazkarah* and *she'elah* should be recited on a year-round basis. While there may be some foundation to this view, it provides only a one-dimensional explanation for this practice. Given the universalistic sentiments that Geiger expressed throughout his writings, my explanation for these insertions accords with the overall thrust of his thought. It also accounts for the practices of other Reform liturgists on this matter, and allows us to see the response Geiger put forth on these questions as part of a larger Liberal Jewish liturgical response to the realities of a modern situation.

believed that Reform Judaism could not be disconnected from "the historical development of Judaism."[16] As a result, his inclination was to proceed cautiously with liturgical reform. In the writing of the *Minhag America*, Wise declared that prayer book changes should not be made unilaterally by a single individual, nor should the form of the service be changed.[17] At the same time, he asserted, "It was out of the questions to retain the old prayers unchanged. . . . The return to Palestine, the restorat-ion of the Davidic dynasty, of the sacrificial cult, and the accompanying priestly caste, were neither articles of faith nor commandments of Judaism."[18]

Informed by the same attitudes that marked Geiger, Wise possessed a strong communal-historical sensibility that precluded liturgical radicalism. Simultaneously, he insisted, as had Geiger, on the right possessed by contemporary liturgists to adapt and change the traditional liturgy in light of present-day beliefs and concerns. This led Wise, as it had Geiger, to preserve *Gevurot Geshamim* and *Tal u-Matar* in his prayer book while, at the same time, inserting them in a manner that purged them of their particularity.

In *Gevurot Geshamim*, Wise added the phrase, "*Morid ha-tal, mashiv ha-ruaḥ u-morid ha-gashem*," which he translated as, "The dew falls, the winds blow, and the rain descends, to sustain life with grace,"[19] as a permanent part of the *Gevurot* benediction. He thereby combined Sephardic and Ashkenazic customs so that *Gevurot Geshamim* could be maintained in the *Minhag America* in a manner that obviated its connection to *Eretz Yisrael*. Similarly, Wise established "*Ve-tein tal u-Matar li-vrakha al pnei ha-adamah* — give dew and rain for blessing on the face of the earth" as a fixed element in *Birkat ha-Shanim*. As with *Gevurot Geshamim*, Wise fixed the words of *Tal u-Matar* as a constant element in his liturgy so that the prayer would no longer be linked to a specific geographic venue. In this way, he retained *Gevurot Geshamim* and *Tal u-Matar* in his

---

16 *The Israelite*, 11 (May 9, 1856), p.356, as cited in Jakob J. Petuchowski, "Abraham Geiger and Samuel Holdheim: Their Differences in Germany and Repercussions in America," *Leo Baeck Institute Year Book*, XXII (1977). p.152.

17 Quoted in James G. Heller, *Isaac M. Wise: His Life, Work and Thought* (New York: Union of American Hebrew Congregations, 1965), p.302.

18 Isaac M. Wise, *Reminiscences* (New York: Reprint of the 1901 Edition by Arno Press, 1973), p.50.

19 The phrase "to sustain life with grace" has been added to the original Hebrew.

siddur. At the same time, he removed both prayers for precipitation from their particularistic associations with the rainy seasons in *Eretz Yisrael* and Babylonia. God was now explicitly praised and petitioned as the master of nature throughout the world. Divine concern and providence were neither seasonal nor local. The same ideology that had guided Geiger concerning *Gevurot Geshamim* and *Tal u-Matar* and that found full expression in the 1870 edition of *Dvar Yom be-Yomo* informed Wise as well, prompting an identical approach and an almost identical treatment of these prayers in *Minhag America.* In the final section of this paper, the distinctive nature as well as the influence of the Geiger-Wise approach to Reform Judaism will be measured by an analysis of how subsequent Liberal Jewish liturgies have dealt with these passages.

Gevurot Geshamim *and* Tal u-Matar *in Representative Twentieth-Century Liberal Liturgies*

The universalistic sentiments that played such a dominant role in the approach Geiger and Wise adopted towards *Gevurot Geshamim* and *Tal u-Matar* have also been evidenced in the treatment other modern Liberal liturgies have accorded these prayers. However, not all have attempted to resolve the problems inherent in balancing the universal and the particular in these instances as did Geiger and Wise. Indeed, even during the nineteenth century, David Einhorn, in his *Olath Tamid*, displayed none of the concern for tradition that marked Geiger and Wise in their liturgical efforts regarding the *Gevurot Geshamim* insertion. Thus, in the *Gevurot* benediction of the *Amidah*, Einhorn resolved the universal-particular tensions attached to these insertions by simply omitting *Gevurot Geshamim* altogether.

Despite the critical roles Geiger and Wise played in the rise and growth of Reform Judaism, most Reform liturgies have adopted the model established by Einhorn on this point. Thus, the major liturgical works of twentieth-century American Reform Judaism — *The Union Prayerbook* and *Gates of Prayer* — removed *Gevurot Geshamim* from their order of prayer, and two major prayer books adopted for use by British non-Orthodox Judaism in this century — *Forms of Prayer for Jewish Worship* by the Assembly of Rabbis of Reform Synagogues of Great Britain and *Service of the Heart*, published by the Union of Liberal and Progressive Synagogues of Great Britain — have likewise dropped this insertion from their *siddurim*. Indeed, even the classical Reconstructionist prayer books of Mordecai Kaplan followed the Einhorn model and failed to include *Gevurot Geshamim* in their texts.

A much smaller number of Liberal liturgies have patterned themselves after the Geiger-Wise model in the case of *Gevurot Geshamim*. The most prominent such work in English-speaking lands is the 1995 prayer book of the Union of Liberal and Progressive Synagogues of Great Britain, *Siddur Lev Chadash*. In this prayer book, the phrase "*Mashiv ha-ruaḥ u-morid ha-gashem, mazriʿaḥ ha-shemesh u-morid ha-tal*," translated as "You cause the wind to blow, the rain to fall, *the sun to shine*, and the dew to descend," is inserted as a permanent element in the *Gevurot* blessing. Here the example set by Geiger and Wise has been adopted, and even expanded to include year-long praise for God as the source for the power and warmth of the sun as well as other natural phenomena![20]

As for *Tal u-Matar* in the *Birkat ha-Shanim* benediction, virtually none have adopted the solution that Geiger and Wise advanced. Reform liturgies that have included this blessing — e.g., *Gates of Prayer, Service of the Heart, Forms of Prayer for Jewish Worship*, and *Siddur Lev Chadash* — have simply purged *Tal u-Matar* from their services and have instead fixed, "*Ve-tein brakha al pnei ha-adamah* — Bestow your blessing on the earth," as the permanent formula for this benediction.

It is apparent that few Liberal prayer book authors have felt the constraints Geiger and Wise did to include these insertions in their prayer books. In the case of *Gevurot Geshamim*, these persons may have simply felt that the insertion was not only highly particularistic-nationalistic, but extraneous to the benediction as well. In the *Birkat ha-Shanim* blessing, the specific petition for dew and rain may also have been viewed in the same way. After all, the purpose of benediction was to beseech God for abundance from the earth. Requests for dew and rain were no more than the means to achieve this end, and omitting them from the *siddur* removed the nettlesome problem of particularism while preserving the basic thrust of the prayer.

20 Another European Liberal liturgy that adopted this approach was the 1964 Dutch *Sidoer Tov L'hodot — Gebeden voor Sjabbat en Feestdagen ten gebruike in de Liberaal-Joodse Gemeenten in Nederland*, published in Amsterdam. There the phrase, "*Mashiv ha-ruaḥ u-morid ha-tal ve-ha-geshem* — who causes the wind to blow and the dew and rain to fall," is inserted as a permanent element in the *Gevurot* benediction.

Regardless of the model Reform liturgists have employed to deal within these insertions, one point is clear. Geiger, Wise, Einhorn, and most subsequent Liberal Jewish liturgists have all sought to purge Reform liturgy of its nationalistic-particularistic dimensions at these junctures in the service. Both the Geiger-Wise and Einhorn models display a Reform Judaism anxious to express itself in universal terms. Consequently, in both approaches, the universal is granted hegemony over the particular.

In light of this trend, it is vital to note that *Ha-Avodah Shebalev*, the prayer book of the Israeli Reform Movement, has adopted an orientation towards these prayers that distinguishes it from the Diaspora Jewish prayer books discussed above. In this Israeli *siddur*, traditional Jewish practice concerning *Gevurot Geshamim* and *Tal u-Matar* has been restored. In the *Gevurot* benediction, the *hazkarah* for wind and rain is inserted during the winter, while the insertion for dew, evoking Sephardic tradition, is added during the summer. Similarly, *Tal u-Matar* is included as a seasonal petition attached to the rainy season in *Eretz Yisrael* in the *Birkat ha-Shanim* blessing. *Ha-Avodah Shebalev* affirms these prayers as expressions of the attachment the Jewish people have to their Land and their classical heritage. The authors of this *siddur* did not, in these instances, subordinate the particularistic heritage of the Jewish people to the ideological demands imposed by a classical Reform theology created in the Diaspora.

That a prayer book composed in Israel should adopt this stance towards these passages is hardly unanticipated. Far more noteworthy is that the latest expression of Liberal Jewish liturgy on American soil, the 1996 Reconstructionist *Kol Haneshamah*, has taken a similar position. In this prayer book, "*Mashiv ha-ruah u-morid ha-gashem* — You cause the wind to blow and the rain to fall," is now recited in the *Gevurot* benediction during the winter, while "*Morid ha-tal* — You send down the dew" is recited during the summer. Similarly, in *Birkat ha-Shanim*, *Tal u-Matar* is inserted from December 4 until Passover. In so doing, the authors of this *siddur* have consciously affirmed the centrality the reborn Jewish state has for contemporary Jews.[21] Like Geiger and Wise, they have attempted to balance a myriad of Jewish concerns in their approach to these passages.

---

21 *Kol Haneshamah*, p.11.

Whether other Liberal liturgies in the Diaspora will in the future follow the approach of *Kol Haneshamah* regarding these insertions is uncertain. After all, the treatment Geiger and Wise accorded *Gevurot Geshamim* and *Tal u-Matar*, as well as the approach most subsequent Liberal editions of the *siddur* have taken towards these insertions, has demonstrated how strong the universalistic thrust is that characterizes Liberal Judaism. Despite the reality of Israel reborn, this universalistic orientation will likely prevent other Liberal Jewish liturgies in the Diaspora from following this Reconstructionist precedent.[22] While the particular practice adopted by *Kol Haneshamah* to these passages embodies an affirmation of Jewish particularism that is distant from the solution offered by Geiger and Wise, the struggle between past and present that marks this Reconstructionist liturgy surely echoes the nature of the approach that informed *Dvar Yom be-Yomo* and *Minhag America*.

As Jakob Petuchowski has stated, "*Mutatis mutandis*, Geiger's evolutionary concept of Reform, of a Reform growing *organically* out of the previous stage of religious development, was championed in America by Isaac Mayer Wise."[23] Theirs was a particular Reform Jewish sensibility. Cognizant of tradition, Geiger and Wise did not shrink from contemporaneous demands to forge a Reform Judaism they deemed faithful to the past while appropriate for the present. The treatment they accorded *Gevurot Geshamim* and *Tal u-Matar* in their *siddurim* is a single detail that reflects the nature of their larger Jewish project. Their model of how to calibrate the demands of the past against the claims of the present provides a rich legacy for the people Israel even today.

---

22 However, my assumption, based on present-day American and British Liberal prayer books, is not necessarily correct, for there is counterevidence to this trend. For example, the newest prayer book published by the Liberal Jewish Community of the Netherlands in 1996, *Sidoer Tov Lehodot — Ochtenddienst voor Sjabbat en weekdageb*, reverses the formula adopted by its 1964 predecessor liturgy as mentioned in n. 20 above. Instead, traditional Ashkenazic liturgical practice is adopted in regard to both *Gevurot Geshamim* and *Tal u-Matar*. There is no doubt that the authors of this *siddur* have done so in order to express the centrality that the State of Israel possesses for contemporary Dutch Jewry. Here, the same trend affirmed in *Kol Haneshamah* manifests itself in a contemporary European Liberal liturgy.

23 Petuchowski, "Geiger and Holdheim," p. 151.

11

German Jewish Orthodoxy

Tradition in the Context of Culture

The study of German Jewish history of the last two hundred years has primarily centered around a description of Jewish religious and cultural reform. Jewish defense organizations and the rise of a small but significant Zionist movement have also garnered considerable academic attention. With the exception of some work on Rabbi Samson Raphael Hirsch, the Orthodox have not been a major focus of these investigations: Orthodox Judaism has largely been perceived as irrelevant to this tale of how Jewish tradition confronted the challenge of living in a radically changed milieu. Since the focus of Jewish academic concerns has been the response of Jewish tradition to the challenges of a modern world, it has been tacitly assumed that Orthodoxy has succeeded in sealing itself off hermetically from the effects of a contemporary setting. The accepted view is that a study of Orthodoxy would thus have little or no bearing on this tale of oscillation between an undifferentiated medieval past and the excitement and dynamism, the pluralism, of a modern Jewish present.

This, of course, is understandable. After all, the Orthodox, as adherents of Jewish tradition, viewed themselves as part of an eternal reality. The German Orthodox Jew, like all religious traditionalists, believed that Judaism endured in an eternal present. Tradition may evoke precedent, but it does not have, for the adherent, a history. Tradition may relate to context, but it nevertheless exists, for the believer, in an enduring moment. This is why, as Peter Berger has observed, it requires neither defense nor explanation from its followers. The tradition itself, to its practitioners, provides the internalized contours within which reality is experienced. Life in accord with its beliefs and prescriptions is perceived as the only proper way in which an authentic religious existence can be attained. The "very nature of tradition," writes Berger, is to "be taken for granted."[1] This "taken-for-grantedness" is what allowed Rabbi Samson

---

1 Peter Berger, *The Heretical Imperative* (New York: Anchor Books, 1979), p.30.

Raphael Hirsch of Frankfurt to view himself, in contrast to the Reformers, as defender of an eternal, unchanging tradition that measured the contemporary world against the yardstick of an immutable law. It also permitted Hermann Schwab, the chronicler and apologete of Orthodox Judaism in Germany, to assert, "German-Jewish Orthodoxy was Sinai Judaism."[2]

Recent years have witnessed the emergence of a critical and reflective attitude among academics toward this German Jewish Orthodox self-assessment. There has been a new appreciation that German Orthodoxy, like other Jewish movements and trends in that land, was shaped in great measure by the external German environment. In addition, scholars have recognized that an understanding of the German Orthodox responses to a modern world — where no external signs of dress or appearance distinguished Orthodox Jews from their non-Orthodox coreligionists — is vital if a full portrait of modern Judaism and its struggles with the reformulation of tradition is to be complete. Studies of Samson Raphael Hirsch and his community by Noah Rosenbloom and Robert Liberles, Marc Shapiro's study of Jehiel Jacob Weinberg, and the comprehensive thematic study of German Orthodoxy by Mordecai Breuer clearly bear witness to this inclusionary trend in modern Jewish historiography.[3]

Undergirding these studies is the proposition that a religious tradition stands in conjunction with, not separate from, the world in which it exists. While adherents of a tradition may constantly proclaim their religion's changelessness, the interpreter of a tradition affirms the axiom, as Heraclitus observed millennia ago, that change, even within the realm of tradition, is constant. The task of the student of German Orthodox Judaism is thus to make sense of a particular world of ethnicity

2   Hermann Schwab, *The History of Orthodox Jewry in Germany* (London: Mitre, 1950), p.11.

3   Noah H. Rosenbloom, *Tradition in an Age of Reform* (Philadelphia: Jewish Publication Society, 1976); Robert Liberles, *Religious Conflict in Social Context: The Resurgence of Orthodox Judaism in Frankfurt am Main* (Westport, Conn.: Greenwood, 1985). Breuer's magisterial and comprehensive study of German Orthodoxy is entitled *Jüdische Orthodoxie im Deutschen Reich, 1871–1918* (Frankfurt a.M.: Jüdischer Verlag bei Athenaum, 1986). Also see Marc B. Shapiro, *Between the Yeshiva World and Modern Orthodoxy: The Life and Works of Rabbi Jehiel Jacob Weinberg, 1884–1966* (London and Portland: Valentine Mitchell and Co. Ltd., 1999).

and belief. It is to ask about the specific matrix in which German Orthodoxy had its being, and to comprehend the shape and meaning of Orthodox Judaism in Germany by describing the dialectical interplay between Jewish tradition, on the one hand, and the social and cultural world that was Germany on the other.

Foremost among the concepts social scientists have employed to describe such interplay is the notion of modernization. Modernization is, of course, a multifaceted and complex phenomenon. Yet secularization is among its primary elements. By employing this term, sociologists do not mean that religion or religious tradition disappears when it confronts the process of modernization. Rather, secularization signifies that religion comes to inform and direct fewer activities in the lives of both individuals and communities. Nontraditional, nonreligious warrants and motivations come to fill the vacuum that the disappearance of the religious in various spheres has left. If the attitude of the premodern traditionalist is captured in the words of the Psalmist, "I have placed the Eternal before me always," the paraphrase uttered even by the religious traditionalist in a secularized world is, "I place the Eternal before me, but not all the time." Such a concept provides a fruitful paradigm for comprehending the nature of Jewish Orthodoxy within the context of German culture and for grasping the dynamic that characterized its approach to and reformulation of tradition.

Secularization and the Struggle Over Secession

The German Orthodox, unlike Jewish traditionalists elsewhere, accepted with equanimity the diminution of traditional Jewish influence and guidance in vast areas of life. With Emancipation and citizenship, the dismantling of the *kehillah* — the self-governing political structure of the medieval Jewish community — constituted a development that the German Orthodox applauded. As Ismar Schorsch has observed, Samson Raphael Hirsch, the leading ideologue of modern German Orthodoxy, "dropped all demands for judicial autonomy and continuance of Jewish civil law."[4] Simply put, the German Orthodox recognized that Jewish tradition now had to confront a political reality where the *Ḥoshen Mish-*

---

4 Ismar Schorsch, *Jewish Reactions to German Anti-Semitism* (Philadelphia: Jewish Publication Society, 1972), p.10.

pat, the traditional Jewish code of civil law, had fallen into desuetude. Acknowledgment of this acceptance is seen not only in the position of Hirsch, but in the fact that no course on Jewish civil law was included in the curriculum of the Orthodox Berlin Rabbinical Seminary. The German Orthodox simply surrendered to the facticity of this development and became enthusiastic proponents of Jewish political emancipation. Like their Reform counterparts, they applauded and eagerly embraced the political character of the modern world.

Secularization and its effects, however, were not confined to the political arena. They evidenced themselves in the areas of dress, language, education, and religious custom as well. One sees this most clearly if elements of German Orthodoxy are contrasted with the notion of traditional Orthodoxy put forth by their Orthodox peers in Hungary. Rabbi Moses Schreiber, the Ḥatam Sofer, leader of Hungarian traditionalism whose legacy continued to inform sectors of Hungarian Orthodoxy throughout the 1800s, discouraged Jewish usage of the vernacular and asked that Jews maintain distinctive garb that would separate them from non-Jews. Schreiber conferred the status of religious obligation upon such items. He, quite clearly, desired to resist those secularizing trends in the modern world that defined such areas in areligious terms. For Schreiber, dress and language were as much matters of religious concern as observance of the dietary and marriage laws.[5] It was otherwise for the German Orthodox. Matters of dress and language were seen essentially as matters of custom and manners. They were, in the strictest sense, religiously neutral. Judaism, in their opinion, simply did not demand that Jews distinguish themselves from their gentile neighbors in these ways. Thus, Hirsch, Hildesheimer, and other German Orthodox leaders dressed in contemporary western garb and mastered and championed the vernacular in their speech and writings, developments that aroused the ire of their traditionalist brethren in Hungary.[6]

This tendency can also be seen in the area of religious customs. The

5 See Jacob Katz, "Contributions toward a Biography of the Ḥatam Sofer" (in Hebrew), in *Studies in Mysticism and Religion Presented to Gershom G. Scholem*, ed. by E.E. Urbach *et al.* (Jerusalem: Magnes Press, 1967), pp. 115–61, for a summary of Schreiber's positions on these matters.
6 See the translation of Hungarian Rabbi Akiva Y. Schlesinger's polemic, for example, against Esriel Hildesheimer in Alexander Guttmann, *The Struggle Over Reform in*

Hungarian Orthodox, gathered in Mihalowitz in 1865, banned entry into synagogues where sermons were preached in the vernacular, where unaccompanied all-male a capella choirs participated in services, where weddings took place within them, where the architecture could be confused with that of a church, and where Jewish religious officiants wore clerical robes like clergymen in non-Jewish religious traditions. The German Orthodox, informed as they were by nineteenth-century standards of German aesthetics and ritual, introduced all these reforms into their synagogue buildings and worship services.[7] Guidelines were often drawn up for German Orthodox synagogues forbidding indecorous or uncivil behavior, even on Purim. Clearly, nineteenth-century German standards of behavior, not Jewish tradition, informed the practice of German Orthodox traditionalism on all these matters.[8]

Most significant for this analysis, the German Orthodox often justified these innovations in the synagogue life of German Judaism on the grounds that such innovations were religiously neutral. That is, the *Halakhah* (Jewish law), in their view, often took no direct stance on some of these matters. Thus, Esriel Hildesheimer, in responding to these directives issued by the Hungarian Orthodox, said that the architectural style of a synagogue was essentially insignificant to Judaism. Instead what mattered was that a "genuine Jewish spirit" reside in the hearts of those who worshiped within such a building.[9] Jewish tradition simply was not paramount in informing matters such as ritual dress and synagogue architecture, nor in several of the other items listed above. The impact of secularization — meaning that religion comes to inform fewer spheres of life — can thus be seen even in the liturgical life and practice of the German Orthodox community.

Secularization theory also helps cast light on one of the famous

---

Rabbinic Literature (New York and Jerusalem: World Union for Progressive Judaism, 1977), pp. 289–91. See also the memoir of Hildesheimer's daughter, Esther Calvary, in her "Kindheitserinnerungen," *Bulletin des Leo Baeck Instituts* VIII (1959), pp. 187–92.

7   These prohibitions arc listed in Esriel Hildesheimer, "Ein Beitrag zur Bedeutung von *Chukot Ha-Goyim*" in *Rabbiner Dr. I. Hildesheimer, Gesammelte Aufsatze*, ed. by M. Hildesheimer (Frankfurt: Kauffmann, 1923), pp. 24–26.

8   See Jakob Petuchowski, *Prayerbook Reform in Europe* (New York: World Union for Progressive Judaism, 1968), 123ff, for some representative examples of these Orthodox ordinances.

9   Hildesheimer, "Beitrag," p. 19.

episodes in the history of nineteenth-century German Orthodox history, the struggle over the *Austrittsgesetz* (Law of Secession) in 1876. This law ultimately permitted German Orthodox Jews to secede legally, if they so wished, from the *Einheitsgemeinde* — the unified Jewish community, to which all Jews were formerly required by Prussian law to belong and pay taxes — in the cities and towns where they lived. Hirsch was the principal architect of this bill and it allowed him to realize his long-cherished dream of a Separatist Orthodox congregation unencumbered by the constraints that a predominantly Reform community might impose. As Hirsch saw it, Orthodox Jews had to establish Orthodox institutions such as synagogues, ritual baths, schools, and ritual slaughtering as private societies at their own expense, while still being forced to pay taxes to the state-sponsored *Gemeinde*.[10] With the passage of the *Austrittsgesetz*, Hirsch immediately cut all ties to the *Gemeinde*, the existing "city congregation," and urged the membership of his congregation, the *Israelitische Religionsgesellschaft* (IRG), to do the same.

Even after the *Einheitsgemeinde*, alarmed over a potential loss of membership and over the divisions that secession would cause, agreed to grant the Orthodox all the institutions they needed, Hirsch ruled that Jewish law forbade any affiliation with the general Jewish community. In September 1876, he announced his intention to secede from the *Einheitsgemeinde* and instructed all the members of the IRG to follow his example. A number of them did so, but a majority elected to disregard their rabbi on this matter. They continued to remain with the general Jewish community while simultaneously paying dues to the IRG. Rabbi Moshe Mainz, a prominent talmudist and a member of a venerable Frankfurt family renowned for its piety and learning, gave sanction to the actions of these people. He opposed Hirsch's ruling on halakhic grounds and stated that so long as the *Einheitsgemeinde* established institutions and provided for the religious needs of Orthodox Jews, then secession was unwarranted. Hirsch was greatly disturbed by Mainz's ruling and by the resolve of so many of his own congregants to maintain membership in both the *Religionsgesellschaft* and the general community.[11]

10 On these points, see Paul Ansberg, *Die Jüdischen Gemeinde in Hessen* (Frankfurt, 1971), pp. 22ff.

11 See Saemy Japhet, "The Secession from the Frankfurt Jewish Community under Samson Raphael Hirsch," *Historica Judaica* 10 (1948), pp. 99–122.

Several of Hirsch's supporters then approached Rabbi Seligmann Baer Bamberger (1807–1878), the Würzburger *rav* and a preeminent talmudist, expecting that he would provide valuable support for Rabbi Hirsch's position. After all, just several years earlier, in 1872, Bamberger had signed an opinion (*Gutachten*), in response to a request by Solomon Spitzer of Vienna, stating that an Orthodox Jew was obligated by Jewish law to resign from a community that had introduced and embraced certain religious reforms.[12] Furthermore, as late as February 1, 1877, Bamberger, in response to a direct query from supporters of Hirsch, had supported Hirsch's position regarding secession.[13] This time, however, much to their chagrin, Bamberger, after consulting with Mainz and others in the Frankfurt community, refused to give his blessing to the stance of Hirsch and his supporters. Bamberger held that secession from the general Jewish community by Orthodox Jews was not legally necessitated in the case of Frankfurt. In this instance, where the officers of the Frankfurt *Gemeinde* had agreed to Orthodox stipulations about the religious administration of the community, secession was unnecessary from the standpoint of Jewish law.[14]

Hirsch was outraged by Bamberger's position, and the conflict between the two men intensified. Indeed, Hirsch was so angry that when Bamberger died in 1878, he refused to attend his funeral. Hirsch's ire must be understood as more than just personal pique. After all, their controversy had erupted into a public debate of significant proportions, and at issue were sincerely held and vastly different understandings of

---

12 The opinion is reprinted in Samson Raphael Hirsch, *Gesammelte Schriften,* 6 vols. (Frankfurt, 1906–1920), 4:359ff.

13 See the excellent discussion of Bamberger's overall stance on the matter of secession, as well as details concerning the Bamberger-Hirsch controversy, in Robert Liberles, *Religious Conflict in Social Context: The Resurgence of Orthodox Judaism in Frankfurt am Main, 1838–1877.*

14 For Bamberger's opinion, see Hirsch *Gesammelte Schriften,* 4:539–67. The entire correspondence between Hirsch and Bamberger on this matter can be found there. For a full description and analysis of their debate, see Leo Trepp, "Segregation or Unity in Diversity: The Controversy Between Samson Raphael Hirsch and Selig Baer Bamberger and Its Significance," in *Bits of Honey: Essays for Samson H. Levey,* ed. by Stanley Chyet and David Ellenson (Atlanta: Scholars Press, 1993). For a much briefer analysis and summary, see my *Rabbi Esriel Hildesheimer and The Creation of a Modern Jewish Orthodoxy* (Tuscaloosa, Ala.: University of Alabama Press, 1990), pp. 86–92.

religious principles. Thus the struggle over secession in Frankfurt elicited responses from leading Orthodox figures both in Germany and in Hungary.

From the perspective of secularization theory, one can assert that for a rabbi like Bamberger, one of the principal reasons for opposition to passage of the law was a traditionalist commitment to the notion of a unified Jewish community, a commitment that could not be shaken even by the rise and dominance of Reform in most German Jewish communities by the third quarter of the nineteenth century.

Unlike Bamberger, Hirsch and Esriel Hildesheimer (who together led the battle for secession) spoke a pure German. They had received educations not only in yeshivas, but in modern German universities. They were undoubtedly more sensitive, on many levels, to the challenges Reform posed for Orthodoxy than was Bamberger. Their stance may well have been more prudential, given the realities of the situation. The same impulse toward Jewish communal unity, an impulse informed by the tradition that had previously led Hirsch and Hildesheimer in the 1840s to fight Reform efforts in several communities to secede from the larger community, continued to inform Bamberger here. However, by 1876 the reality of a secularized world led Hirsch and Hildesheimer to support separatism as a viable Orthodox position. Secularization and its consequences caused them to surrender any aspiration for a unified community. It inclined them to formulate the mandate of Jewish tradition on this issue in a way that was distinct from Bamberger's and that departed from the way that tradition had been understood in Germany during the premodern era. The process of secularization indicates that religious tradition could no longer hope to inform all sectors of a modern Jewish community, and a perceptive modern Orthodox leadership understood this reality. Consolidation of the traditionalist segment of the community, not outreach to the nonobservant, dominated their program for late nineteenth-century German Jewish life. The impact of secularization, and Hirsch's and Hildesheimer's awareness of that impact, indicate why this was so. It illuminates this conflict between Bamberger and Hirsch over the mandates of Jewish law regarding secession and yields considerable insight into the development of Jewish Orthodoxy's attitude toward the non-Orthodox sectors of the community in the modern period.[15]

This episode also reveals something significant about the nature of tradition itself. Tradition, it is clear, is constantly involved in a process of reformulation. It both contracts and expands in response to a new setting. It does not remain static. The position of Hirsch and Hildesheimer — the champions of Jewish tradition in this German setting — on the matter of secession reveals that tradition neither continues undisturbed nor totally evaporates as it moves on in time and place. Instead, like a river, it flows through set banks and meanders through new channels.

Acculturation and the Defense of Traditional Institutions, Practices, and Beliefs

Cultural integration, as all scholars have observed, was the hallmark of German Jewry. The Orthodox, as much as the liberals, were thoroughly acculturated, and they, like their liberal colleagues, had internalized the Germanic notion of *Bildung* (culture) and the educational ideals and sensibilities that were a part of it. Orthodox leaders themselves employed these notions to guide the tradition through the shoals of this new era. One interesting example of such accommodation by tradition to its nineteenth-century German context can be seen in a responsum issued by Esriel Hildesheimer. As rabbi of Congregation *Adass Jisroel* in Berlin, Hildesheimer had to confront the reality that many of the congregation's children attended *Gymnasium* on the Sabbath and consequently were unable to attend Saturday morning services. Hildesheimer feared that if these children did not hear the traditional Sabbath morning Torah reading, the Torah would be "forgotten in Israel." He therefore issued the unprecedented decree that a Torah reading with the traditional seven Torah readers be held on Saturday afternoon when the students had returned from school. After the Torah reading,

15 For a fuller account of this episode and the use of sociological theory to illuminate it, see David Ellenson, "Church-Sect Theory, Religious Authority, and Modern Jewish Orthodoxy,", in *Approaches to the Study of Modern Judaism*, ed. by Marc Raphael (Chico, Calif.: Scholars Press, 1983), pp. 63–83.

the *Musaf* service was to be chanted, followed by the prescribed *Minḥah* service. He made no attempt to justify this measure from a Jewish legal point of view other than to label it as an "emergency measure."[16] A generation later, Hildesheimer's successor, David Zvi Hoffmann, admitted that this practice was of dubious Jewish legality. However, in defending his own decision to continue this custom into the twentieth century, Hoffmann quickly cited the verse employed by rabbis throughout the centuries to legitimate extraordinary measures taken in times of stress: "It is time to serve the Lord, make void thy Law" (*Mishnah Berakhot* 9:5).[17]

The evolution of tradition as a constant in human history can also been seen in the use German Orthodox leaders made of philosophy in their efforts to conceptualize and defend Jewish tradition in this changed setting. The matters of sacrificial references and prayers for restoration of the Temple cult were a point of controversy and great debate in nineteenth-century German Jewry. The Reformers, for the most part, labeled such references as atavisms from an ancient past and removed petitions for the return of the sacrificial cult from their liturgy. While a rabbi such as David Zvi Hoffmann recognized that no less authoritative a Jewish figure than Maimonides had explained the sacrificial cult in a similar way as a primitive mode of worship, he and other Orthodox leaders realized that Maimonides, whatever his misgivings, retained such passages in his prayer service.[18] As champions and defenders of an eternal tradition, the Orthodox, like Maimonides before them, would not countenance removal of these passages from the liturgy of the synagogue. Sacrifices and the Temple cult were simply too integral a part of Jewish tradition and messianic hopes.

Yet for these acculturated leaders of German Orthodoxy, the idea of literally slaughtering animals as a mode of worshiping God appeared repugnant. Moreover, for them, no less than for the Reformers, the expiatory function often attributed to sacrificial worship in both the Bible and Christian exegesis not only ran counter to many Jewish interpretations of selected scriptural passages, but, perhaps even more significantly, conflicted with a Kantian notion that a moral act is an autono-

---

16   Esriel Hildesheimer, *The Responsa of Rabbi Esriel, Orah Hayim* (Tel Aviv: C. Gittler, 1969), p.123.

17   Ibid.

18   Hoffmann quotes Maimonides, *Moreh Nevuhim* 3:32, in David Hoffmann, *Das Buch Leviticus*, 2 vols. (Berlin: Poppelauer, 1905), 1:79.

mous one done at the behest of the individual's own moral will and for which the individual must be prepared to shoulder full ethical responsibility. The contention that an individual's sin could be forgiven through the death of an animal was one that did not appeal to these German bourgeoisie.

The paradigmatic Orthodox response to this dilemma is contained in the writings of Samson Raphael Hirsch. While Hirsch's attention to this subject is voluminous, the key point that emerges from an examination of his interpretations on this matter is that the sacrifices and prayers for their return must be understood on a metaphoric and symbolic, not a literal, level. Symbols, Hirsch wrote, testify to the human ability to "express ideas by physically perceptible signs."[19] They are as natural a means of human communication as the written or spoken word. Symbols, and their contemporary exposition, permit the eternal truth and validity of Jewish laws that might otherwise be branded as outmoded to be affirmed. Indeed, there were those who wished to assert, stated Hirsch, that "if a divine law has only symbolic value," then the act itself "can be discarded like an empty shell."[20]

Such a conclusion, Hirsch felt, was totally unwarranted. Inasmuch as the ideas "which permeate the symbols are eternal," then the symbols possess "a meaning which raises them high above all changes of time amid place.[21] Those who view the sacrificial cult and prayers for the restoration of Temple worship in Jerusalem as literary references to a primitive Jewish past that would better be banished miss the point of their mention. "Must we," asks Hirsch, "see an object or phenomenon simply in terms of its apparently literal meaning or is it possible that the object or phenomenon before us is a symbol?" If the object can be interpreted as such, then removal of the symbol would be tantamount to abrogating the "eternal ideas" that permeate them.[22] This is the mistake the Reformers made in their zeal to either remove such passages from the liturgy or consign them to the past.

Hirsch continued his defense of the sacrificial cult, as men such as Nahmanides and Mendelssohn had done before, by elucidating their symbolic significance. His commentary on Leviticus 16:21ff. illustrates

19 Hirsch, *Gesammelte Schriften,* 3:214.
20 Ibid. p.229.
21 Ibid.
22 Ibid. p.220.

the nature of his approach and tells us a great deal about how German Orthodoxy reformulated tradition. These verses, which speak of the he-goat upon whose head the High Priest casts all the sins of the people Israel, are not understood as describing an act of expiation. Instead, the passage is understood allegorically as referring to human rebellion against God's will. "Placed at the threshold of the Sanctuary of His Torah, . . .," writes Hirsch, "we fight shy of giving up our selfish living for our own leisure, and, repulsed by and afraid of the demands of God's laws of morality, we hold ourselves stubbornly against Him as a *sa'ir hai*, a 'live he-goat.'"[23] However, the Jewish people have the capacity to acknowledge their sins and errors and to vow that these will not be repeated. The goat that is sent out of the camp is "the embodiment of that mistaken way of life which misuses the divine gift of free decision by giving oneself up to be mastered by one's senses, and which turns that which was given to us to devote to moral freedom, to devotion, into moral lack of freedom."[24] The hurtling down of the goat is no offering sent down to appease a demon of the wild, nor is the goat's destruction a substitute "scapegoat" for the sins of the people.[25]

Instead, Hirsch explains in his commentary on Leviticus 16:10: "But the he-goat upon which the lot 'Azazel's' fell is to remain standing alive before God, to effect atonement on it, and to let it go as 'Azazel's' into the wilderness," that each of us is the "he-goat" of this passage. Each human being is blessed by God with freedom, and thus with the moral power to resist temptation and do God's will, or else to acquiesce to such temptations and rebel against God and God's "holy Laws of morality." "This surrender to the power of sensuality, in contrast to attachment to God and obedience to His moral law, is described by the term *le-azazel*. The most straightforward, natural interpretation of the word *azazel* would be to explain it as *oz azal*, the kind of headstrong 'goat-like' obstinacy which is *azal*, which has no future and which, precisely by imagining itself to be *oz* (strong), digs its own grave."[26] Hirsch, in keeping with rabbinic exegesis of these passages in Leviticus, not only avoids interpreting the function of the *sa'ir* as an expiatory one; rather, through his

23 Samson Raphael Hirsch, *Leviticus* (Frankfurt a.M.: Kaufmann, 1873), p. 390.
24 Ibid. p. 397.
25 Ibid. p. 392.
26 From Hirsch, *Leviticus*, p. 375. Quoted in *T'rumath Tzvi: The Pentateuch with a Translation by Samson Raphael Hirsch and Excerpts from the Hirsch Commentary,*

symbolic and metaphoric exegesis, he demonstrates that these passages, with their mention of *azazel*, bear no "superstitious" content. Through his emphasis on the human ability to decide between good and evil, obedience and rebellion, Hirsch supplies a Kantian understanding of these passages in keeping with nineteenth-century German moral sensibilities.

Hirsch emphasized that God's Law is a universal law, a "moral law." By allegorizing these passages and interpreting them symbolically, he was able to transform them into a parable that affirmed humanity's free will and ability to recognize and perform the moral law. Indeed, it is only when humanity turns in sincere contrition to God and earnestly resolves not to sin that God, in a spirit of divine graciousness, will receive humanity's atonement and offer forgiveness of humanity's sins. There is nothing in these passages, as interpreted by Hirsch, that would offend a Kantian notion of ethics. All individuals bear full responsibility for their actions. One's own turning to the good, not the death of an animal, effects reconciliation with God and God's Law of morality. The expiatory function of the animal's death is denied. The supremacy of a modern notion of morality, and the insistence that Judaism possesses an ethic fully in keeping with such a notion, is maintained. Hirsch is thus able to provide, in a world where the tradition was under attack, an Orthodox understanding of atonement and refute those who would literally read such passages in a way that would cast aspersions upon the tradition and the maturity of its ethic.

Hirsch's exegesis and symbolic approach to the issue of sacrifice indicates that the German Orthodox, like Jews in the world of medieval Islam, employed philosophy as the medium to explain and defend Judaism to Jew and gentile alike. Philosophy, not history, became a weapon to wield on behalf of Orthodoxy in a world hostile to tradition. The role assigned philosophy as a defender of tradition can be seen in all its specificity in the debate Orthodoxy carried on with the Positive-Historical School over the issue of divine revelation. Hirsch was intent on employing dogma as a means of distinguishing Orthodox views of tradition in a time and place where the community's structure had been transformed and where a traditionally-oriented Positive-Historical trend appeared at the Breslau Seminary. He thus wrote, "The

ed. by Ephraim Oratz and trans. by Gertrude Hirschler (New York: Judaica Press, 1986), p. 437.

Law, both Written and Oral, was closed with Moses at Sinai.[27]

This belief, which denied the possibility that the Law had developed in time, touched off a major controversy between the Orthodox and Positive-Historical camps in Germany between 1859 and 1861. Zacharias Frankel, father of Positive-Historical Judaism and head of the Jewish Theological Seminary in Breslau, had maintained in his *Darkhei ha-Mishnah* that elements of the Oral Law had evolved in history. Particularly galling to the Orthodox was Frankel's contention that talmudic laws subsumed under the category *Halakhah le-Moshe mi-Sinai* were not, as a literal translation would understand it, laws given orally by God to Moses at Sinai. Instead, they were of such great antiquity and so firmly established that it was *as if* they had been revealed to Moses. Frankel in effect was asserting that these laws were the enactments of later generations,[28] and he had a traditional rabbinic warrant for this position.[29] Nevertheless, the need to defend Jewish tradition against the encroachments of this perceived threat to the Law caused Hirsch and others to claim that Frankel had misused this rabbinic precedent.[30] The need to protect the tradition as they understood it led these Orthodox defenders to elevate the dogma of an unchanging law to a position of supreme importance in their struggle to preserve traditional Judaism in the German context. It legitimated their own view that Frankel's position – that elements of Jewish law had developed in time, in history – posed a grave danger to the normative traditional belief that the Law was eternal and beyond the ravages of time. In a series of articles published by Hirsch in *Jeschurun*, he and Rabbi Gottlieb Fischer accused Frankel of *kefirah*, heresy.[31]

Interestingly, Hermann Cohen, who was then a young student at the Theological Seminary in Breslau, wrote privately to Hirsch after these articles appeared. Cohen described his teacher Frankel as an observant Jew who conducted himself in all respects in a strict rabbinical

---

27 Samson Raphael Hirsch, *Horeb*, 2 vol. (London: Soncino, 1962), 1:20.

28 Zacharias Frankel, *Darkhei ha-Mishnah* (Leipzig: Hunger, 1859), p.20.

29 Frankel quotes here from the Rosh, *Hilkhot Mikva'ot*, to support his nonliteral understanding of the phrase. I am grateful to Professors David Kraemer and Eliezer Diamond of the Jewish Theological Seminary of America for bringing this to my attention.

30 Hirsch, *Gesammelte Schriften*, 6:340.

31 Ibid. pp.339–41.

manner, "standing in the synagogue with the prayer shawl over his head, singing *zemirot* (hymns) . . . on holiday evenings, and also on occasion in his talmudic lectures zealously commenting: 'A God-fearing person must here be stringent.'" Hirsch printed part of this letter in the pages of *Jeschurun* along with his own reply. Frankel's level of practice, Hirsch charged, was unimportant if it was not accompanied by proper internal beliefs. In fact, affirmation of the divine origins of the Oral Law was as much a *sine qua non* of an authentic Orthodox Judaism as belief in the Mosaic revelation of the Written Law.[32] A philosophical system that could explain and defend this notion became of paramount importance to the Orthodox in their relationship to contemporary German culture and thought. It was this need that may well hold the key to comprehending how and why the Orthodox leadership of German Judaism at the turn of the century appropriated the teaching of Kant in the way that it did. Because Kant focused on both the nature of obligation and the ideal of a noumenal, nonphenomenologial realm, he was eventually seen, in a way that Hegel was not, as particularly amicable to the doctrines of Jewish Orthodoxy. While a Kantian strain was seen above in Hirsch's interpretation of Leviticus, this entire tendency reaches its zenith in the writings of Hirsch's grandson, Isaac Breuer, in the first half of the twentieth century. Breuer, one of the leading members and founders of Agudat Yisrael, wrote:

> It is my deep conviction that the God and King of Israel sends enlightened men among the nations from time to time, called and destined to play a part in Jewish "Meta-History.". . . And when the hour . . . broke . . . in which Israel . . . had to protect herself against the pressures of the outside world . . . , God caused to rise among the nations the exceptional man Kant, who, on the basis of the Socratic and Cartesian skepticism, brought about that "Copernican Turn," whereby the whole of man's reasoning was set in steel limits within which alone perception is legitimized. Blessed be God, who in His wisdom created Kant! Every real Jew who seriously and honestly studies the "Critique of Pure Reason" is bound to pronounce his "Amen" on it.[33]

32 *Jeschurun* 7 (1861), p.297f.
33 Quoted in Salomon Ehrmann, "Isaac Breuer," in *Guardians of Our Heritage*, ed. by Leo Jung (New York: Bloch, 1958), p.624f.

Kant, for Breuer, became a weapon to protect Judaism and an Orthodox view of revelation from the presumptions "of the *Kundschafter* (adventurers) of our times."

It did so, as Zvi Kurzweil has explained, in the following way. Breuer employed Kant's well-known distinction between the phenomenal and noumenal worlds to demonstrate that human knowledge was limited to the realm of appearances exclusively. Humans were unable to penetrate into the world of the noumena — the world-in-itself, to use Kant's term. The latter remained unknown to human intelligence and hidden from human perception.[34]

Breuer made use of this distinction to defend the notion that what the Torah records is literally the word of God, as well as to affirm the inerrancy of scripture against attacks launched by biblical critics. In his *Der neue Kusari: Ein Weg zum Judentum*, he criticized both literary and philological attempts to cast doubt upon the accuracy of the Masoretic text of the Bible and maintained the historical veracity of certain biblical narratives. Drawing upon the Kantian distinction between phenomena and noumena, Breuer claimed that Torah was something noumenal, a miraculous appearance of the "metahistorical" in time.[35] Biblical critics and the Higher Criticism failed to grasp this supernal character of the Torah.[36] Academic inquiry into Scripture, he concedes, might have validity in the sphere of phenomena. However, it is irrelevant to the noumenal reality of Torah. Scripture, written in Hebrew and endowed with holiness, is both phenomena and noumena, creation and nature. Thus, the contents of Scripture, to human understanding, are phenomena. Yet this by no means exhausts the meaning of Scripture. The significance of this defense of Torah is articulated by Breuer when he writes, "Philologists, using their methods, view [the Bible] as merely something that has evolved . . . and relate it to a specific language group. Its role as the mouthpiece and the Word of God . . . remains totally concealed from them."[37] In sum, the Torah as *Erscheinung* (appearance) must not be

---

34   See Zvi Kurzweil, *The Modern Impulse of Traditional Judaism* (Hoboken, NJ: Ktav, 1985), p. 36.

35   Isaac Breuer, *Der neue Kusari: Ein Weg zum Judentum* (Frankfurt: Rabbiner-Hirsch-Gesellschaft, 1934), p. 341f.

36   Ibid. pp. 326–29.

37   Ibid. p. 393.

mistaken for the Torah as the *Ding an sich* (thing-in-itself).[38]

Critical methods of inquiry are unable to penetrate the deepest layers and ultimate meaning of the noumenal content of the Bible. Instead, it is only the guiding interpretation of the Oral Law, itself divine in origin, that can rescue us from this dilemma and allow us to unlock the secret, or more precisely, the hidden and true meaning of Scripture. As Kurzweil has pointed out, when the Bible narrates human situations, "The Torah speaks in human language." However, when the Torah makes statements of a metaphysical nature, that is, pertaining to acts of creation, revelation, and redemption, we can never be sure of grasping their ultimate meaning. As a result, the Oral Law, as well as Kabbalah, must be studied assiduously so as to uncover the noumenal character of Scripture. It was this appropriation of Kant's distinction between the phenomenal and noumenal worlds that provided the epistemological basis for Breuer's immersion, as Gershom Scholem noted over fifty years ago, into the realm of Kabbalah.[39] Kant's philosophy enabled Breuer to answer the challenges of biblical criticism and the notion of an evolving Jewish law to his own satisfaction.

Breuer was thus able to describe Judaism, as did his grandfather S. R. Hirsch, as a *Gesetzesreligion*, a religion of law. Law was defined by these Orthodox defenders of tradition as constituting the essence of Judaism. However, the law of Torah is not, as Kant characterized it, a heteronomous one. Instead, it is a *Naturrecht*, a "Law of nature," and there is a natural harmony between the law of Torah and the Jewish people. This relationship between God, Torah, and the Jewish people is thus one that points in the direction of autonomy rather than heteronomy. As Breuer phrased it, "The way of Judaism . . . starts out with the heteronomy of God's Law and . . . leads to an autonomy . . . which embodies God's will completely in the will of self."[40] Kant himself correctly perceived, wrote Breuer, "that the world as conceived conforms to law. . . ." Kant's one deficiency, according to Breuer, was that he was unable to identify this law, the content of this law, because he lacked revelation.

38 Ibid. p.328.

39 See Kurzweil, *Modern Impulse,* 37. Scholem's essay on Breuer appears in English translation as "The Politics of Mysticism: Isaac Breuer's *New Kuzari,*" in *The Messianic Idea in Judaism,* ed. by Gershom Scholem (New York: Schocken, 1971), pp.325–34.

40 Quoted in Ehrmann, "Isaac Breuer," p.627.

Since he had no share in the revelation of the correct deed, he abandoned the deed as such in despair and only retained freedom — as a motive. From freedom — to Law: he could not tread this path of Judaism since he had not stood before Mount Sinai. So he had to be content with filling up the gap, where the law should have been, with the idea of the law. If they are to be free, men must act as if their action were demanded by a law which is binding upon everyone. Your action is correct if you can wish all men act in the way in which you are now acting. And you possess freedom of action if you act in the way you do solely because you wish that everyone would act in precisely the same way.[41]

Breuer can thus be said to outdo Kant in his own application of Kantian principles to an understanding of Judaism and Torah. As an acculturated German, Breuer had internalized Kant: he understood his world in light of Kantian teachings. However, he also had a need to defend and explain Judaism in contemporary cultural and philosophical terms. Kant gave him the language to do so. Thus, he was able to write, in words reminiscent of Hermann Cohen, "In Judaism law and ethics are in essence absolutely identical. Our highest goal is to fulfill God's royal law out of love for the Torah. The path leads . . . from man in the multiplicity of his phenomena to man-in-himself; from the Torah of the spoken word to the Torah of the written word — to Torah-in-itself."[42] The words of *Pirkei Avot*, 2:4, "Make God's will your own," thus bespeaks the moral task incumbent upon every Jew.

In summary, it is clear that German Orthodox Jewish thinkers were as anxious as their liberal colleagues to articulate a philosophy of Judaism in modern philosophical terms. The manner in which they employed Kant to defend their notion of the place of Law in Judaism is representative of how they did this. Other philosophers, such as Schopenhauer, Hegel, or Schleiermacher, may have played equally critical roles in other areas of their thought. Furthermore, in utilizing these non-Jewish philosophers as the medium to explicate and defend Jewish tradition in a changed world, they were certainly mirroring a path

41 Isaac Breuer, *Concepts of Judaism,* ed. by Jacob S. Levinger (Jerusalem: Israel Universities Press, 1974), p.277.
42 Ibid. p.280.

trodden by Jewish philosophers in the Middle Ages. This should not obscure the specificity of their response, however. They were themselves acculturated members of German society who had internalized the values and teachings of *Bildung* and who were addressing their works to a comparably acculturated audience. Because of this background, there was nothing alien or artificial to them about explaining and defending Judaism in contemporary philosophical language. In so doing, the tradition was both defended and reformulated in a novel way.

Epilogue

German Orthodox Judaism, like all historical phenomena, was unique in its individuality. Yet, like other Jews in the modern world, the German Orthodox constructed a meaningful traditional Jewish life and faith in the face of a transformed environment. They did not allow Jewish tradition or Jewish identity to atrophy and die when confronted by modern culture.

An anecdote related by Rabbi Nehemiah Anton Nobel, who served as *orthodoxer Geimeinderabbiner* in Frankfurt from 1910 to 1922, illustrates something of German Orthodoxy's synthesis of the contemporary and the traditional. Recalling his own student days at the *Rabbiner-Seminar*, Nobel wrote that he was asked to deliver an address at the founding ceremony of *Dibbuk Ḥaverim*, the seminary's student association, in 1894. At the conclusion of his talk, he offered a student toast, a "*Salamander*" in honor of his teacher Rabbi Hildesheimer and the other members of the Orthodox rabbinical school's faculty. According to Alexander Altmann, who remembers similar toasts offered during his student days at the *Rabbiner-Seminar* in the 1920s, the German, Teutonic student custom of the *Salamander* "consisted in everybody standing up, circling their beer glasses on the table, and draining them to the last dreg."[43]

As graphic testimony to the acculturated nature of German Orthodoxy, this episode bears witness to the symbiotic nature of German Orthodoxy itself and the sensibilities of those, like Hildesheimer and Nobel, who shaped it. Nothing in this scene would have struck

43 Quoted in Alexander Altmann, "The German Rabbi: 1910–1939," *Leo Baeck Institute Yearbook* XIX (1974), p. 47.

Hildesheimer, Hirsch, or any other German Orthodox Jew as dissonant with tradition. After all, these were people who sang Heine to their children along with traditional *zemirot* on Sabbaths and holidays.[44] As such, the toast represents the successful synthesis they had achieved between Jewish tradition and German culture. However, it also suggests that such synthesis succeeds when it is experienced as effective from the inside. That is, Hildesheimer, his colleagues, and his students had so completely internalized the values of the surrounding German-Jewish atmosphere that nothing struck them as discordant about this event.

However, an enigma remains. It seems that the German Orthodox were able to achieve this successful synthesis precisely because they did not too closely examine or reflect on their efforts in this episode or any of the other phenomena described in this paper. This is why Schwab, in all candor, could assert, "German-Jewish Orthodoxy was Sinai Judaism." The German Orthodox, like countless other Jews in the modern world, thus resolved the problem of modernity not through "logic," but through "creation." This study indicates that Orthodox Jews in Germany, like their liberal Jewish p eers, adapted the tradition to its German context. They, like other German Jews, possessed a "hyphenated identity," a reformulation of Jewish tradition that works not because it is logical but because one lives it. The synthesis inheres in the doing. Thus, the German Orthodox, like other western Jews, were able to create a modern Orthodox traditionalism that worked. This may be why, in the end, these people hold up a mirror to other modern Jews who are engaged in the same process of constructing and living within a tradition in a modern, pluralistic world. All Jews who affirm their identity and religion in today's world are ultimately engaged in the same task. All Jews who struggle with the Tradition in the modern West employ, as the German Orthodox did, a new language to awaken and defend an ancient faith and tradition.[45]

---

44 See Calvary, "Kindheitserinnerungen," pp.187–92.

45 On Nobel's tombstone, the epitaph reads, "He awakened an ancient faith through a new language."

12

Gemeindeorthodoxie in Weimar Germany

The Approaches of Nehemiah Anton Nobel and Isak Unna

Historians and sociologists of the twentieth century have frequently filtered their discussion and analysis of social and political trends in the modern Occident through the lens provided by the theme of community and its decline. They have asserted that European life at the end of the Middle Ages was marked by an organic sense of community that provided individuals with institutional and cultural patterns, forms, activities, and values that allowed for group solidarity and identification. The premodern community has been depicted as a haven from the existential fears of solitude and individual isolation that are increasingly said to characterize and dominate human life in the modern period.

This view of the transformation in the ideal of community in the West has perhaps best been captured in the writings of the famed sociologist Ferdinand Tönnies. Tönnies saw the history of the West as marked by a move from the intimate face-to-face personal relationships of the premodern *Gemeinschaft* (community) to the relationally ordered and bureaucratically dominated patterns of an impersonal *Gesellschaft* (society). In this transition from a folk to an urban society, traditional frameworks for community — and the patterns of culture, religion, social relations, and politics that supported them — were challenged and often collapsed.

Sociological thinkers have contributed a great deal to the creation of a theoretical framework for understanding this change. Many social theorists have observed that the transition from *Gemeinschaft* to *Gesellschaft* brought in its wake a distinction between public and private spheres. The institutional consequences for religion have included its consignment to the private realm and the subsequent creation of a society in which the structures that have formerly supported and sustained religious organizations and beliefs shifted "from society as a whole to much smaller groups of confirmatory individuals." This "privatization of religion" has permitted pluralism to flourish in the modern setting, for individuals have been able to choose voluntarily those collectivities that promote specific ideologies and that provide highly significant relationships and emotional resources for mediating between the individual and the larger "multi-relational reality 'outside.'"[1]

Peter Berger's writings on this point provide the foundation for illuminating a typology of communal visions that held sway among the German Orthodox during the period of Weimar (1919–1933). Berger reminds us that with the advent of the modern political setting, the traditional *kehillah* (community) and its institutions were altered and in significant ways often dismantled as the Jewish community passed from the corporate political structure provided by the world of medieval European feudalism into the congregational patterns of association that mark religious life in the modern West. Of course, such a transition from the medieval to the modern world was uneven in the nineteenth-century German setting. The traditional *kehillah* still retained some of its classical prerogatives, and all Jews were required by law to pay taxes to support the institutions of the community. This requirement was eased somewhat with the 1876 Law of Secession. Nevertheless, the question of how to create a political structure appropriate to the institutional needs of the Jewish community in this passage from medievalism to modernity was a challenge taken up by all segments of the German-Jewish religious world in the modern setting. This essay will be devoted to the way in which two leaders within one camp of the Weimar Orthodox community — Rabbis Nehemiah Anton Nobel and Isak Unna — responded to this challenge in light of diverse religious sensibilities and distinct communal attitudes.

In assessing the stances of these two men, it is essential that we place them in proper historical context. German Jewish Orthodoxy found itself embroiled in a struggle between those elements that sought to secede from the Jewish polity as a whole and those who did not.[2] Many Ortho-

---

1   Peter Berger, Brigette Berger, and Hansfried Kellner, *The Homeless Mind: Modernization and Consciousness* (New York, 1973), pp. 80, 186.

2   See chap. 11, "Germany Jewish Orthodoxy," in the present volume for a more extensive discussion of this struggle. [X-ref.]

dox Jews no longer affirmed the traditional notion that a sufficient ground for the creation and maintenance of a unified Jewish community was provided by the fact that Jews constituted what was widely regarded as an *Abstammungsgemeinschaft*, a common community of descent. Nor, more importantly, did these Jews assert that all Jews were part of a *Schicksalsgemeinschaft*, a community of shared destiny. Instead, these Orthodox Jews — like many of their Reform peers in the nineteenth century — viewed Judaism in terms that were almost exclusively based on religious dogma. They held that only a sense of common religious purpose and vision could foster community.

Other Orthodox German Jews dissented from this position and clung to the notion that the modern Jewish community demanded institutional expression in the traditional structure of an *Einheitsgemeinde*, a united community. Yet, even here the reasons put forth to justify such a position were radically different from the attitudes held by communal leaders in the past. This essay will explore two such positions by examining selected writings of two prominent exponents of *Gemeindeorthodoxie* (an Orthodoxy whose institutions were supported by and considered part of the general Jewish community) during the Weimar period — Nehemiah Anton Nobel of Frankfurt am Main (1871–1922) and Isak Unna of Mannheim (1872–1948).

Nobel, though born in Nagymend, Hungary, was raised in Halberstadt, where his father served as *Klausrabbiner* (rabbi of an endowed study house). He attended the rabbinical seminary of Esriel Hildesheimer in Berlin during the 1890s and was ultimately selected as *orthodoxer Gemeinderabbiner* in Frankfurt. In accepting this post, Nobel positioned himself as heir to a legacy of *Gemeindeorthodoxie* bequeathed to him by his predecessor, Rabbi Marcus Horowitz. Unna was born in Würzburg; he was the grandson of Seligmann Baer Bamberger, the Würzburger *rav* and great German talmudist who refused to support Hirsch's notion that Orthodox Jews were duty-bound, in all instances, to secede from *Einheitsgemeinden*. As a young man, Unna journeyed to Frankfurt, where he studied with Marcus Horowitz. Like Nobel, Unna was ordained at the Berlin rabbinical seminary, and he too argued for a united Jewish communal structure that would include both Orthodox and non-Orthodox Jews. Indeed, Unna constructed rather elaborate statements on the structure and framework of the *Jüdische Gemeinde* during the modern era. Yet, his arguments on behalf of Jewish communal unity were distinct from those of Nobel and represent an alternative vision of community among the Orthodox of this time and place. Seen against the backdrop of a larger Occidental context, the presentation and analysis of their approaches to the issue of community will provide insight into the two dominant visions of *Gemeindeorthodoxie* that reigned during the Weimar period.

Nobel
Vision and Ideals

Gemeindeorthodoxie in early Weimar found its most charismatic spokesman in the person of Nobel. Ordained at the rabbinical seminary in 1895, Nobel possessed a stellar reputation as a talmudist. Indeed, Mordecai Breuer has identified him as a "star pupil of [Esriel] Hildesheimer."[3] However, Nobel's academic talents were not limited to the realm of rabbinic literature. He also journeyed to Marburg in 1900 and there studied philosophy under Hermann Cohen. So accomplished did he become in that field that Alexander Altmann was able to describe him years later "as the only true philosopher amongst German-Jewish Orthodoxy."[4] Others have shared this assessment.[5]

For our purposes, what is most significant is that Nobel maintained "a long-lasting and close friendship" with Cohen until his teacher's death in 1918, despite the considerable religious differences in their views of Judaism. Nor were his relationships and encounters with Liberal and secular Jews limited to Cohen. As we shall see, Nobel had many such associations.[6] Moreover, his ability to sustain such encounters with non-Orthodox Jews reflects more than the openness and warmth of his personality. It indicates that he saw non-Orthodox Jews as persons of

---

3 Mordechai Breuer, *Modernity within Tradition: The Social History of Orthodox Jewry in Imperial Germany* (New York, 1992), p. 246.

4 Alexander Altmann, "Theology in Twentieth-Century Germany," *Leo Baeck Institute Yearbook* I (1956), p. 211.

5 Rachel Heuberger, "Orthodoxy versus Reform: The Case of Rabbi Nehemiah Anton Nobel of Frankfurt a. Main," *Leo Baeck Institute Yearbook* XXVII (1992), p. 47.

6 Ibid.

integrity and knowledge, and it provides the evidence of his judgment that such persons — whatever his condemnation of and dissent from their religious positions — were his brethren and as such part of his community. This conviction was characteristic of Nobel throughout his life. It informed his myriad activities within the Jewish community, and it guided his writings on the nature of that community both before and after Weimar.

None of this should obscure the fundamental Orthodox postures Nobel affirmed. Indeed, his religious Orthodoxy led him to offer a sharp critique of Reform and its theological postulates. He was particularly agitated by *Die Richtlinien*, guidelines of a program for Liberal Judaism issued by sixty-one German rabbis for adoption as a statement of principles and beliefs by a conference of the Union for Liberal Judaism held in Posen in 1912. His response to this statement is paradigmatic of attacks he made on Liberal Judaism throughout his career. Nobel was disturbed by the claim put forth in the guidelines that Jewish law was subject to historical processes and, as such, could be amended or abrogated in light of academic research or the needs of the time. The Liberals claimed that "every generation adopted the faith of the fathers through its own particular religious concepts and expressed it in its own particular forms." *Die Richtlinien* continued:

> Liberal Judaism therefore recognizes the validity of evolution, which gave Judaism in every age the right and duty to abandon certain historically conditioned beliefs and forms, or to develop them, or to create new ones, while safeguarding its own essential content. This duty speaks with special urgency to our time. Through the entrance of Jews into the . . . community of this age . . . many traditional concepts, institutions and customs have evaporated and disappeared and thereby lost both content and significance.

Some ordinances, the Liberal rabbis contended, remained obligatory for modern Jews, while others could simply be abandoned. For example, in addressing the issue of the Sabbath, these rabbis held that whatever "disturbs [the] solemnity [of the Sabbath] must be avoided and, conversely, whatever does not disturb it cannot be considered as prohibited." Liberal Judaism, the rabbis concluded, "recognizes as worthwhile only that which for the individual has the power to elicit pious sentiment, to advance moral action, and to recall religious truths and experiences vividly."[7]

It was this emphasis on the law as historically conditioned and subject to the will of the individual that so disturbed Nobel's Orthodox sensibilities. He acknowledged the purity and sincerity of the Liberal rabbis' intentions. Nevertheless, he condemned the sentiments contained in *Die Richtlinien* as springing from the soil of a "Protestant communal consciousness." They constituted a "war against the *Halakhah*," against the system of "statutes and judgments" that lay at the heart of authentic Judaism.[8] For Judaism, as Nobel had asserted in an article in *Die Jüdische Presse* years before, "could never have become a universal religion had it confined itself to a system of abstract thought."[9] The *Halakhah* permitted the moral values of Judaism to become manifest in life.

Unlike the Liberals and individuals in the Jewish past such as Paul of Tarsus, the prophets themselves — whom the Liberals loved to cite in support of their antinomian posture — never, Nobel claimed, opposed the Law. They only opposed its rote performance by those who observed it in a "superficial and external manner." Like the German Liberals, Nobel asserted that there could be no authentic "religion without morality." However, the Liberals in *Die Richtlinien* failed to realize that the Law was eternal and that genuine Jewish observance of the Law did not result from heteronomous coercion but from an internal state of freedom that permitted the Jew to accept God's commandments autonomously. Law and ethics were not opposed in Judaism. On the contrary, they were complementary. The Law, as Nobel put it, did not impose an onerous "yoke" upon the freedom of the Jew. Instead, the faithful Jew observed the Law with joy and celebration.[10] Its observance was not a mark of bondage; it was the essence of Judaism. It was not transitory but eternal,

7 As translated in W. Gunther Plaut, *The Growth of Reform Judaism* (New York, 1965), pp. 69–71

8 Nehemiah Anton Nobel, *Hagut ve-Halakhah* [Meditations and Halakhah] (Jerusalem, 1969), pp. 66–70, 89.

9 Quoted in Eugen Eliahu Mayer, "Nehemia Anton Nobel," in *Guardians of Our Heritage*, ed. by Leo Jung (New York, 1958), p. 567.

10 Nobel, *Hagut ve-Halakhah*, p. 90.

and the Liberals, in striking at the Law as they did in *Die Richtlinien*, threatened "the existence of Judaism itself."[11]

In view of the sharp rebuke Nobel aimed at the Liberals in response to *Die Richtlinien*, it is significant that he refused to join in the attacks his Orthodox colleagues immediately mounted at the Liberals upon its publication. The *Vereinigung der traditionell-gesetzes-treuen Rabbiner Deutschlands* (Union of Traditional and Torah-Faithful Rabbis of Germany), of which Nobel was a member, "laid emphasis on the problems that would occur in the future in the joint work of *Einheitsgemeinde*." Religious instruction offered by Liberal "rabbis and based on the 'Guidelines' would constitute 'a danger for Jewish youth.'"[12] When one hundred eleven of his Orthodox colleagues in the *Vereinigung* signed a circular condemning the Guidelines, Nobel, in the words of Mordechai Breuer, "went so far in his tolerance that he did not sign the protest,"[13] despite, as we have seen, his disdain for its content. By his refusal to participate, Nobel signaled his determination to maintain a united Jewish community in spite of religious differences that might divide its members. For him, the community could not be reduced to a congregation of "confirmatory individuals." His allegiance to communal Orthodoxy and to the traditional structure of an *Einheitsgemeinde* could not be shaken, even in the face of Liberal impieties.

Nobel supplied a rationale for his posture early in his career. On April 30, 1897, in a letter to the *Synagogengemeinde Köln*, he offered his view of rabbinical office:

> I hold that a rabbi can fulfill his task successfully only if he stands above all parties within and outside his community. He himself must have a firm and unflinching standpoint — one not given to appeals — on all the religious issues of his time. For myself, this standpoint is that offered by Judaism in its historical tradition. This

11 Ibid. For my treatment of these writings in a different context, see David Ellenson, *Between Tradition and Culture: The Dialectics of Modern Jewish Religion and Identity* (Altanta, 1994), pp.19–21. For Rachel Heuberger's presentation of these sources, see her article, "Orthodoxy versus Reform," pp.52–55.

12 Heuberger, "Orthodoxy versus Reform," p.53.

13 Breuer, *Modernity within Tradition*, p.246.

alone seems to me to guarantee the proper development toward a sound future. But, I consider it my duty to examine every religious trend within Judaism, to meet it with objective arguments only, and to treat the representatives of opposition movements and viewpoints with the kind of respect we owe to ardent opponents. I want to lay greater stress in my public activities on that which unites different trends than on those causes which separate them. . . . This is my ideal of the rabbi as I see it, and to strive for its realization is my life's task.[14]

Nobel remained faithful to this vision of the rabbinical office and the institutional expression of a united community it entailed throughout his career. His communal activities and attitudes gave practical expression to these commitments. Preeminent among these activities was Nobel's active participation in the *Allgemeiner deutscher Rabbinerverband* (General German Rabbinical Association). Indeed, Nobel was elected president of the organization in 1921, the first Orthodox rabbi to serve in that capacity. Organized by Orthodox and Liberal rabbis, this rabbinical union affirmed a unique sense of solidarity among all Jews despite doctrinal differences that might separate them in the religious realm. Nobel was also constantly involved in serious outreach to non-Orthodox students and intellectuals, and he engaged actively with them even if they did not affirm his own stance of religious Orthodoxy. His power and charm as a preacher and lecturer were legendary, and he attracted hundreds of listeners — Orthodox and non-Orthodox alike — to the lectures he delivered each year at the Frankfurt *Lehrhaus* that Franz Rosenzweig had established during the early years of Weimar.[15] At the same time, he established a circle of young Jewish intellectuals —

14 Nobel, *Hagut ve-Halakhah*, p.138. This text, so crucial for elucidating Nobel's attitudes toward the Jewish community and the role of Orthodoxy in it, is also cited and translated in Mayer, "Nehemia Anton Nobel," p.576; and Heuberger "Orthodoxy versus Reform," p.51

15 See Michael Brenner, *The Renaissance of Jewish Culture in Weimar Germany* (New Haven, 1996), p.84; Breuer, *Modernity within Tradition*, pp.152–53; and Ernst Simon, "N. A. Nobel as Preacher," in Hebrew translation in Nobel, *Hagut ve-Halakhah*, pp.29–38.

including not only Rosenzweig but also Ernst Simon, Erich Fromm, and Nahum N. Glatzer among others — "whose impact rejudaicized broad circles outside Orthodoxy."[16]

Nobel was also an active Zionist, and despite his attachment to Mizrachi, accorded nonreligious Zionists such as Chaim Weizmann the same respect and concern he displayed toward non-Orthodox Jews in the communities of Germany. At the Twelfth Zionist Congress held in Karlsbad in 1921, Nobel sought, as he did elsewhere, to emphasize the commonalities shared by secular and religious Zionists.[17] In taking this stance, Nobel displayed fidelity to the principles he had articulated and the actions he had taken in connection with the whole of the Jewish community throughout his life. Nevertheless, the uniqueness of his stance in the Orthodox world is summed up well by Mordechai Breuer when he writes, "N. A. Nobel stood virtually alone in the [German] Orthodox rabbinate as an advocate of association with the Zionist movement and as a co-founder of Mizrachi."[18]

Nobel was a charismatic and scholarly individual whose insistence on *Gemeindeorthodoxie* was fueled, in Leo Baeck's words, by his "lively feeling for Jewish community wholeness (*Gesamtheit*)."[19] Rachel Heuberger sums up Nobel's position well when she observes, "His belief, that there existed a Jewish entity and a Jewish solidarity resulting from it, was fundamental. The feeling of obligation to *Klal Yisrael* . . . made him a strict adversary of separatist community politics."[20] In this way, Nobel stood in absolute opposition to views in support of Orthodox separatism expressed by both Samson Raphael Hirsch and his own teacher, Esriel Hildesheimer, when the Law of Secession was passed in the 1870s. Hirsch, the chief architect of the policy of secessionist Orthodoxy, had written, "The divergence between the religious beliefs of Reform and Orthodoxy is so profound that when an individual publicly secedes

---

16 Heuberger, "Orthodoxy versus Reform," pp. 48–49.

17 For Nobel's attitudes and activities as a Zionist, see the brief description of this dimension of his life by Yeshayahu Aviad, "Rabbi N. A. Nobel," in Nobel, *Hagut ve-Halakhah*, pp. 29–38.

18 Breuer, *Modernity within Tradition*, p. 370.

19 Cited in Heuberger, "Orthodoxy versus Reform," p. 57.

20 Ibid.

he is only giving formal expression to convictions which had long since matured and become perfectly clear to himself." Separatist Orthodox congregations were mandated, Hirsch maintained, for "all the institutions and establishments in the care of a community are religious in nature, and they are . . . intimately bound up with the religious law." Hildesheimer, though he did not insist as Hirsch did on a policy of Orthodox institutional separation from Liberal Judaism in every community, did support Hirsch's position on the passage of the *Austrittsgesetz*. In a letter to the Prussian Diet, Hildesheimer wrote, "The gulf between the adherents of traditional Judaism and its religious opponents is at least as deep and wide as in any other religious faith and, in fact, is larger than in most."[21] Nobel, in contrast, wrote, "Both trends [Liberal and Orthodox] have enough in common, so that the consciousness of belonging together and forming one entity can develop its social, polit-ical, and religious creative strength. The majority of German Jews take the Solomonic view that the maternal love of conviction proves itself in its love to the whole."[22]

Nobel's policy of *Gemeindeorthodoxie* emanated from an open and broad personality that fostered an attitude of tolerance and respect, even for those with whom he disagreed on religious grounds. However, that personality emerged from and was informed by a principled commitment to the classical rabbinic teaching that God is exalted when all Israel is united in a single fellowship and that Jews should not needlessly divide themselves into factions. Drawing upon Leviticus 19:1, "Speak unto *all* the congregation of Israel,"[23] Nobel was able to assert that the proper task of the Jewish leader was to serve all the people — observant and non-observant alike — for all were part of the Jewish community. "Party slogans," as Eugen E. Mayer has pointed out, were alien to Nobel. As "a protagonist of '*Klal Yisrael*,'" Nobel believed, "in Solomon Schechter's felicitous phrase, [in] catholic Judaism."[24] This conviction

---

21 These citations from the work of Hirsch and Hildesheimer are taken from David Ellenson, *Rabbi Esriel Hildesheimer and the Creation of a Modern Jewish Orthodoxy* (Tuscaloosa, Ala.: 1990), p.87.

22 Cited in Heuberger, "Orthodoxy versus Reform," p.57.

23 See Mayer, "Nehemia Anton Nobel," p.578, for a discussion of the content and style of Nobel's sermons as well as the citation of this particular biblical passage.

24 Ibid. p.570.

caused him to conclude that the religious imperatives of Judaism frowned upon an institutionalized Orthodoxy apart from the *Einheits-gemeinde*. In advocating such a policy, Nobel resisted significant trends in the modern world that combined to splinter and transform the Jewish community from its status as a unified medieval legal corporation to a quasi-voluntary association or group of associations of individuals in twentieth-century Germany. Nobel, unlike the advocates of *Trennungs-orthodoxie* (an Orthodoxy whose institutions were completely apart from and not supported by the general Jewish community), refused to see Judaism solely as a religious confession. He did not regard mem-bership in the *Einheitsgemeinden* of modern Germany as a matter of voluntary consent. The traditional Jewish communal ethos he had inter-nalized led him to view all Jews — regardless of the religious orienta-tions they advocated — as members of one body. The concept of *Klal Yisrael* demanded institutional expression in *Einheitsgemeinden*.

Unna
Principles and Pragmatism

Nobel was not alone among the Orthodox in adopting this position. As Donald Niewyk has observed about the Jewish world of Weimar, "In most urban centers unified Jewish communities governed all the local congregations, from the most conservative to the most liberal."[25] For some of the proponents of *Gemeindeorthodoxie*, the attacks on com-munal Orthodoxy that emanated from the separatist Orthodox circles of Samson Raphael Hirsch and his ideological descendants demanded a Jewish legal response. An examination of the halakhic arguments advanced by Rabbi Isak Unna on behalf of communal Orthodoxy will display the nature of this response and present a more complete spec-trum of the views advanced by the Orthodox advocates of this policy during Weimar.

Unna's legal writings on behalf of *Gemeindeorthodoxie* must be seen against the backdrop of internal events and divisions within the ranks of German Orthodoxy in particular and European Orthodoxy in gen-eral. In 1885, Samson Raphael Hirsch established the *Freie Vereinigung*

---

25 Donald L. Niewyk, *The Jews in Weimar Germany* (Baton Rouge, 1980), p. 122.

für die Interessen des orthodoxen Judentums (Free Union for the Interests of Orthodox Judaism) as an institutional vehicle for the promotion of Orthodoxy. Many of its members were supporters of *Trennungsorthodoxie*. Solomon Breuer, the son-in-law of Hirsch as well as his successor in 1888 as rabbi of the *Israelitische Religionsgesellschaft*, along with his son, Isaac Breuer, a Frankfurt attorney, and Jakob Rosenheim, another prominent member of the Frankfurt *Austrittsgemeinde* (a separatist congregation), were all active members of this union, and they were the chief proponents of the notion that Orthodox Jews in Germany were obligated to be members — where possible — of separatist Orthodox congregations.

When, on March 28, 1912, an international assembly of Orthodox Jews took place in Kattowitz for the express purpose of uniting Orthodox Jews from East and West institutionally under the banner of *Agudat Yisrael*, Solomon Breuer attempted to extend the Hirschian principle of separatism to this international body. He supported the position that Orthodox Jews who were not connected to the *Austrittsgemeinde* that existed in their place of dwelling not be allowed to hold office in the international group. Breuer's position met with severe opposition and was not adopted at the Kattowitz conference. However, in Vienna in 1923 a Great Assembly (*Kenesiyah ha-Gedolah*) of the Agudah was convened. There the Agudah — at the initiative of Breuer and his group as well as some Hungarian colleagues — did adopt an article that imposed an ideological test for determining membership. While the article did not deal specifically with the matter of separatism, Breuer's opponents on this issue seized the opportunity to establish an alternative Orthodox organization that would not be identified with *Trennungsorthodoxie*. Hence, on December 26, 1923, *Achduth-Vereinigung gesetzestreuer Juden Deutschlands* (Union of Torah-Faithful Jews in Germany) was formed. Rabbi Unna, who was a member of Agudat Yisrael and who had participated in the 1923 Assembly in Vienna, was among its founders and was its first leader.[26]

26 This information on the background of Unna's statements in defense of *Gemeindeorthoxie* is taken from Moshe Unna, "Isak Unna: The Man in His Generation," in Isak Unna, *For the Sake of Unity and Uniqueness* (in Hebrew) (Jerusalem, 1975), pp. 64ff. On the debate between Hirsch and Bamberger over the question of *Austritt*, see Leo Trepp, "Segregation or Unity in Diversity," in *Bits of Honey: Essays for Samson H. Levey*, ed. by Stanley Chyet and David Ellenson (Atlanta, 1993), pp. 289–310.

Rabbi Unna's speech at the founding assembly of *Achduth*, "Der Gedanke der Arewuth in seiner praktischen Bedeutung" (The practical meaning of the idea of "mutual responsibility"), was directed toward an Orthodox audience. It both surveyed the struggle between separatist and communal Orthodoxy in Germany during the previous half century and offered a Jewish legal defense of *Gemeindeorthodoxie*.[27] Unna began by pointing out that from the moment Reform became a force in German Jewish life during the first half of the nineteenth century, an Orthodox minority came to be subject to scorn and derision by a dominant Reform majority in virtually every community in Germany.[28] The Reformers consistently and deliberately refused to respond to Orthodox requests for communal support of Orthodox institutions, and this fostered a desire among the Orthodox to be freed from the shackles and intolerance of Reform-dominated communities. The mechanism for achieving this aim was secession, and when the *Austrittsgesetz* was passed on July 28, 1876, the Orthodox minority had the means it needed to compel the Reform-dominated *Gemeinden* to accede to their requests lest the community be destroyed. As a result, the Liberals, in virtually every Jewish community in Germany, surrendered to Orthodox demands. Despite this, Hirsch ruled that secession was a religious obligation thrust upon every Orthodox Jew regardless of the newfound willingness of the *Einheitsgemeinde* to finance Orthodox Jewish religious institutions and needs. Seligmann Baer Bamberger disagreed with Hirsch and asserted that if the administration of a unified community was both willing to support Orthodox institutions and prepared to

27 Isak Unna, "Der Gedanke der Arewuth in seiner praktischen Bedeutung," *Jüdisches Wochenblatt* 1 (March 13, 1924), pp. 4–5.

28 In making this claim, Unna was repeating a story concerning the plight of German Orthodoxy during this period that was commonly told in German Orthodox circles. As Robert Liberles has written in his insightful study *Religious Conflict in Social Context: The Resurgence of Orthodox Judaism in Frankfurt am Main, 1838–1877* (Westport, Conn.: 1985), pp. 19–20, "This picture . . . [was] put forth by the German Orthodox themselves. . . ." He argues that "this view derived from a hagiography greatly influenced by the writings and teachings of Samson Raphael Hirsch [himself]." Thus, whatever its historical accuracy, this perspective on the past and the ill-treatment accorded Orthodoxy by a dominant Reform majority from the period beginning in the 1820s until the passage of the Law of Secession in 1876 was one commonly held in German Orthodox circles even during the 1900s. Unna, in this particular statement, was simply echoing this view.

have these institutions be supervised by Orthodox Jews, then there was no obligation for Orthodox Jews to secede.[29]

In a polemical thrust clearly directed at Breuer and Breuer's desire to apply Hirsch's 1876 demand to Orthodox Jews in 1923, Unna pointed out that secession was never a practical possibility — even in Hirsch's day — for most Orthodox Jews in Germany. Their numbers in most communities were simply too small to maintain separatist Orthodox institutions. What was true in Hirsch's time was all the more true later. Nevertheless, Hirsch, and later Breuer, as well as many in their camp, persisted in claiming that authentic Judaism demanded Orthodox secession from the *Einheitsgemeinde* in every instance. This caused division among the Orthodox, with the supporters of *Austritt* going so far as to seek separation from the proponents of *Gemeindeorthodoxie*. Unna thundered against the application of this position and condemned the Hirschian ideology that warranted it as "sectarian dogma-tism" (*Parteidogma*).[30]

Unna then went on to the heart of his argument. He maintained that the halakhic principle of *areivut* had been unjustifiably ignored by the separatists in their rulings and actions on this matter, and he contended that this notion had to be assigned decisive weight in guiding Orthodox policy on the question of secession from the *Einheitsgemeinde*. This principle, based on *Sanhedrin* 27b, held that "all Israel is responsible for one another." In assessing its significance, Unna stated, "I emphasize at the start that what we have before us [in this principle] is no mere sermonic flourish [*keine homiltische Floskel*] concerning the solidarity of all Jews. Rather, it is a halakhic principle of decisive practical importance."[31]

Unna continued by offering an exegesis of Deuteronomy 29 from the weekly Torah portion *Nitzavim* to support his assertion that the principle of *areivut* should be applied by the Orthodox to the challenges posed by the existence of Reform throughout Germany. The biblical chapter begins with an admonition concerning the sins of individuals and goes on to warn of the punishments that will befall the entire people should such individuals sin. Why should the community suffer because of the transgressions of isolated individuals? The explanation

29 Unna,"Der Gedanke der Arewuth in seiner praktischen Bedeutung," p. 4.
30 Ibid.
31 Ibid.

is to be found in the principle of *areivut*. For the concluding verse of the Torah portion (Deuteronomy 29:29), which states that "The secret things belong unto the Lord our God, but those things which are revealed belong unto us and our children forever," indicates that when the community is capable of preventing the public sins of an individual and does not, then it is culpable for the sins of that single person. "The reciprocal responsibility that *Klal Yisrael* possesses for one another is here established."[32]

Unna further cited Rabbi Isaac Elchanan Spektor of Kovno, Eastern Europe's greatest halakhic authority, to buttress his case concerning the import and dimensions of this principle. Unna wrote of Rabbi Spektor:

> He has demonstrated from a survey of the sources themselves that the sin of the individual is the sin of *Klal Yisrael* and therefore attached to every single person among the people Israel in accord with the notion of reciprocal responsibility. And this principle . . . obligates us to become involved in every instance where we are capable of preventing transgression . . . In so doing we not only attempt to act for the benefit of the sinner himself, we also grant merit to ourselves and *Klal Yisrael*. This *areivut*, this solidarity, includes the people of Israel in all its branches, even those who have abandoned their faith. . . . The law of *areivut* excludes only those who have actually apostasized to another religion.[33]

Unna maintained that Spektor's position was conclusive for Orthodox Jews on this matter. The law of *areivut* extended to Liberal Jews. Consequently, the Orthodox were halakhically bound to maintain relations with them in *Einheitsgemeinden* so long as these Liberal Jews — regardless of their motives — allowed for Orthodox institutions under Orthodox control in their communities. These people — albeit "sinners" whose disbelief and nonobservance could only be abhorred by those faithful to the Law — remained part of *Klal Yisrael*. By participating in the *Einheitsgemeinde*, the Orthodox Jew increased the opportunities for engagement with these people. In so doing, the Orthodox Jew

32 Ibid.
33 Ibid. p.5.

could both promote Orthodox concepts and organizations to a larger public and engage more directly in war against Reform. Furthermore, through Orthodox supervision of communal institutions, the proponents of *Gemeindeorthodoxie* were better positioned than their colleagues in the camp of *Trennungsorthodoxie* to prevent non-Orthodox Jews from sinning through their insistence that communal institutions comport to the dictates of *Halakhah*. In this way, the supporters of *Gemeindeorthodoxie* displayed a greater fidelity to the requirements of *areivut* and Jewish law than did the advocates of separatism.

Unna also dismissed two other criticisms that the advocates of *Trennungsorthodoxie* commonly hurled at the proponents of *Gemeindeorthodoxie*: first, that the participation of Orthodox Jews in an *Einheitsgemeinde* granted recognition and religious legitimacy to Liberal Judaism. Unna cited the example of Shimon ben Shetach in support of his position. In seeming violation of the Law, Shimon ben Shetach had once entered the Sanhedrin, in which Sadducees participated. However, he did so in order to combat the Sadducees and to purify the Sanhedrin. Unna saw the position of the communal Orthodox as identical to that of Shimon ben Shetach. The talmudic sage's actions admitted of only one conclusion. Unna wrote, "We will be able to work for the authority of Torah and combat those erroneous tendencies connected to Judaism only if we are found in the midst of the community." Unna also refuted the second criticism: Orthodox participation in the *Einheitsgemeinde* would violate the rabbinic prohibition against abetting sinners (*she-lo lesayei'a ovrei aveirah*). Such a prohibition, he maintained, only applied in instances where the sinner could perform the sin only with the direct aid of the abettor. This condition did not obtain in the communities of Germany where the Orthodox by and large constituted a small minority. Indeed, it could only apply in a community where the Orthodox had complete control. Interestingly, Unna added parenthetically that if such were to be the case, then the Orthodox, in full conscience, "could not permit Reform institutions" (*Reformeinrichtungen*).[34]

Unna's essay indicates that his policy of *Gemeindeorthodoxie* was not without textures and ambivalence. It was informed in large measure by a sense of commitment and obligation to the religious well-being of the entire community of Israel. After all, as Unna observed at the conclu-

34 Ibid.

sion of his article, "Israel cannot be redeemed until it is united in a single fellowship."[35] Nevertheless, the main thrust of the essay indicates that his advocacy of *Gemeindeorthodoxie* sprang primarily from pragmatic considerations. The exigencies of the day, not a principled commitment to the unity of the Jewish people, demanded tolerance of Liberal Judaism and participation in the *Einheitsgemeinde*. It was a tactic that best advanced the interests of Orthodox Judaism in the contemporary situation.

Unna's approach to *Gemeindeorthodoxie* clearly distinguished him from Nobel. He was informed with a different sensibility than Nobel, and he did not accord even a modicum of integrity to the religious positions advanced by Liberal Jews. A fuller picture of the distinctive posture Unna adopted is apparent when we turn to another essay, "Das Trennungsprinzip und die Zusammenarbeit der Gesetzestreuen" (The principle of secession and the cooperation of the Orthodox), which Unna wrote in 1924.[36] Here, as in his speech before the founding assembly of Achduth, Unna addressed himself principally to his Orthodox coreligionists — supporters and critics alike. At the outset he distinguished between *edah* and *kahal*, two terms for community in Jewish tradition. The former term signified unity of religious purpose, while the latter referred to the entirety of the people in a civil sense. In the period of the Second Temple, no distinction was made between these two dimensions of community, and "the civil and religious community was one" (*die bürgerliche und die religiöse Gemeinde [war] eins*). All residents of the city (*bnei ha-ir*) were by definition members of the community and every member of the community was responsible, according to the Mishnah (*Nedarim* 5:5), for providing for public needs. In Babylonia, the notion reigned that the civil and religious community were congruent and that all members of the community (*Gemeindemitglieder*) were also partners (*Gesellschafter [shutafin]*) in the institutions and property of the community. This situation persisted through the Middle Ages, and the Jews of this period constituted "a state within a state."[37]

With the advent of the modern era, the unity of the civil and religious dimensions of the Jewish community was shattered. The Jewish

35 Ibid.
36 Isak Unna, "Das Trennungsprinzip und die Zusammenarbeit der Gesetzestreuen," *Jeschurun* 13, no 7/8 (1924), pp. 403–18.
37 Ibid. pp. 404–6.

community was reduced to a religious *Gemeinschaft* in civil law. The community no longer constituted a "state within a state." It ceded its civil authority to the state and was now legally assigned the status of a *Privatkirchengesellschaft*, a private religious or church association. As such, its members were no longer *Gesellschafter* (*shutafin* or legal partners) from a Jewish legal point of view.[38]

This point was crucial to Unna. The *Einheitsgemeinde* of the contemporary era was legally distinct from the Jewish community of premodern Jewish history. Its members were no longer *shutafin*. Consequently, the supporters of *Gemeindeorthodoxie* were not halakhically responsible — as all premodern Jews would have been in the period when the Jewish community constituted "a state within a state" — for every appropriation the *Einheitsgemeinde* made.

While this was a necessary argument for the defense of *Gemeindeorthodoxie*, Unna does not seem to have regarded it as sufficient to respond to the attacks of the *Trennungsorthodoxen*. He admitted that *Gemeindeorthodoxie* was disturbed by the *Einheitsgemeinde*'s establishment of non-Orthodox religious and educational institutions despite the lack of Jewish legal responsibility the Orthodox members of the *Gemeinde* had for such institutions. *Gemeindeorthodoxie* had been made possible, in Unna's opinion, only because each *Einheitsgemeinde* in Germany had agreed that tax money paid to the community by Orthodox Jews would be used solely for social, not religious or cultural, purposes. Hirsch believed that such a distinction was specious.[39] He contended that Orthodox Jews who maintained membership in the community were — protestations to the contrary notwithstanding — in actuality supporting Liberal religious and educational programs. Unna disagreed and stated that this conclusion was unfounded. He pointed out that if one could not pay taxes to the *Einheitsgemeinde* on the grounds that money was being designated for institutions and programs that were suspect or forbidden in the eyes of Jewish law, then each Jew would have to stop paying taxes to the government of Germany itself. After all, the German government appropriated tax dollars for the support of non-Jewish religions that, in the eyes of Jewish law,

38 Ibid. pp. 406–9.
39 Ibid. For Hirsch's position in his own words, see Samson Raphael Hirsch, *The Collected Writings* (New York, 1990), vol. 6, pp. 193–97.

may well have promoted *avodah zarah*, idolatry. In addition, it was unquestionably true that the government financed educational institutions that taught biblical criticism, a topic whose content was surely forbidden by the *Halakhah*. Yet, no Orthodox Jew would refuse to pay taxes for those reasons. Even the suggestion of such a thing was ridiculous! Therefore, the *Gemeindeorthodoxen* were justified in designating tax funds for one purpose in the united community while refusing to apply them for another.[40]

Unna also supplemented the argument he had made in his earlier address concerning the issue of "*siyu'a yedei ovrei aveirah*" (abetting sinners). He repeated his previous claim that the Orthodox were in the minority in every community in Germany. Consequently, Reform Jews did not need the aid of Orthodox Jews. Rather, the Orthodox needed the aid of the Reformers to maintain Orthodox institutions.[41] In an astonishingly candid vein, Unna even pointed out that the *Gemeindeorthodoxen* were in fact diminishing the support for Reform institutions by participating in *Einheitsgemeinden*. After all, money spent by the Reform majority that would have been used for the support of Reform institutions was now being appropriated for the support of Orthodox ones. Orthodox participation in an *Einheitsgemeinde* certainly did not constitute a violation of the rabbinic dictum of "*hahzakat yedei ovrei aveirah*" (strengthening the hands of sinners). Indeed, wrote Unna, "It is well known that we do not affirm their deeds. We emphasize repeatedly our opposition to them. We do not enter their synagogues, nor do we join in their prayers or religious ceremonies. We remain with them in one community only because they maintain those institutions that we need in accord with traditional forms."[42] *Gemeindeorthodoxie* aided Orthodoxy while weakening Reform.[43]

40 Ibid. pp. 412–13, 410.
41 Ibid. p. 410.
42 Ibid. p. 413.
43 In taking this stance, Unna foreshadowed an argument that was to be made decades later in the United States by Rabbi Moshe Feinstein. In one responsum, Rabbi Feinstein was asked whether it was permissible for Orthodox Jews to contribute funds to Jewish Federations inasmuch as such funds were generally administered by non-Orthodox Jews and portions of the funds were appropriated to the religious institutions of *kofrim* (heretics), Reform and Conservative Jews. Rabbi Feinstein was disposed not to allow Orthodox Jews to contribute to these charities. How-

Unna conceded, as he had in his speech to *Achduth*, that secession from the unified community had been necessary for the nineteenth-century Orthodox. The stringent stance on this matter taken at that time by the great scholars of Hungary constituted "an emergency measure" (*le-migdar milta*) designed to check the lawlessness of early Reform. Nevertheless, this policy was not in the best interests of contemporary Orthodoxy. An Orthodox Jew would certainly have preferred to be in a community with like-minded Orthodox individuals. However, given the minority status of Orthodox Jews in Germany, such an option was impossible to attain — for economic reasons. To insist upon *Austritt* was to "impose a decree upon the community that the majority could not abide" (*gezeirah she-ein rov ha-tzibur yekholin la'amod bah*).[44]

Unna concluded his essay on a note of Orthodox triumphalism. Fifty years earlier, many had seen secession as the only way to preserve Orthodoxy. However, in the atmosphere of Weimar, such a policy was no longer necessary. Liberal Jews were no longer as strident in their anti-nomianism as they had been, and many Reform rabbis even embraced, in a reversal of the position advocated by their nineteenth-century predecessors, the cause of Jewish nationalism from a religious perspective. Still other non-Orthodox Jews acknowledged, despite their nonobservance, the failure of Reform. Third and fourth generation descendants of Reform Jews no longer felt as their ancestors did, and Unna heralded the fact that many in the younger generation sought to return to traditional Judaism. The goals and interests of Orthodoxy could best be served by participation in *Einheitsgemeinden* and by a rejection of the policy position put forth by *Trannungsorthodoxie*.[45]

Unna, like Nobel, supported *Gemeindeorthodoxie*. However, the tenor of his arguments could hardly have been more distinct. Unna

---

ever, he indicated that it was permissible for Orthodox Jews to do so if the moneys designated by the charity for Orthodox institutions exceeded the contributions made by Orthodox Jews. In this way, Orthodoxy and its institutions would be strengthened and Reform and Conservative Judaism and their institutions would be diminished. See Feinstein's *Iggerot Moshe, Yoreh De'ah*, no. 149. The last paragraph on pp. 289–99 speaks directly to this point.

44   Unna, "Das Trennungsprinzip und die Zusammenarbeit der Gesetzestreuen," pp. 413–15.

45   Ibid. pp. 416–17.

displayed neither the tolerance nor the respect for the concept of the *Einheitsgemeinde* that Nobel did. Indeed, his Jewish sensibilities seem rather distinct from those of Nobel. His *Gemeindeorthodoxie* did not embrace a "lively feeling of Jewish community wholeness." It was instead informed by a sense of pragmatism and opportunism. His vision of the community was directed at his opponents in the Orthodox camp, and it was they whom he addressed in offering his defense of *Gemeindeorthodoxie*.

Conclusion

The manifold changes that marked the modern West as it moved from the *Gemeinschaft* to *Gesellschaft* were accompanied and informed by the process that sociologists have labeled secularization. As sociologists employ the term, secularization does not signify the disappearance of religion. Rather, it points toward the constriction of religion and the compartmentalization of life. A distinction between the public and private spheres arises and religion becomes increasingly consigned to a private realm. Religion no longer plays the role it previously did in informing the beliefs and guiding the activities of either persons or entire communities. In the wake of such a process, traditional beliefs sometimes collapse. At other times, such beliefs are altered to accommodate and adapt to a novel reality. In either case, they are surely challenged. Noble and Unna, like other Jewish religious leaders of their time and place, were compelled to construct an institutionalized framework for the *jüdische Gemeinde* in a world where the political realities of the modern era had transformed Jews into citizens of the German state. The intimacies as well as the communal structures that had characterized the traditional *jüdische Gemeinschaft* had become severely attenuated, if not, in many instances, completely obliterated.

As Orthodox Jews, Nobel and Unna had sworn fidelity to Jewish religious tradition. Nevertheless, theirs was a world where political, cultural, social, and religious changes had long since dismantled the structure and nature of the premodern Jewish community. Nobel and Unna were both fully cognizant of this reality, and both attempted to provide a vision of community for the Jews of Weimar that would maintain proper faith with the past while adapting Judaism to the communal needs of the present. For both men, this meant that their conceptions of community had to be rooted in Jewish tradition. Yet, as we have seen, each man understood the dictates and applications of that tradition in distinct ways.

While both Nobel and Unna supported a policy of *Gemeindeorthodoxie*, Nobel supported a vision of and framework for community informed by the primacy of kinship. The Jewish people constituted a single entity, and the group solidarity that characterized the Jewish people was absolute. As the teachings of Judaism demanded an institutional pattern of community in keeping with this holistic vision, Nobel held that the only form of community that would appropriately embody these teachings was the *Einheitsgemeinde*. The changes that the modern world introduced into the Jewish situation could not alter Nobel's belief that the concept of *Klal Yisrael* demanded institutional expression in a united community.

A different vision informed the stance of Isak Unna. Like the proponents of *Austrittsorthodoxie*, Unna embraced a vision of *Gemeinde* attuned to the dictates of a modern setting that differentiated between religious and communal spheres. He, like his opponents in the separatist camp, viewed Judaism essentially, though not exclusively, as a religious confession.[46] His approach to community arose from a recognition that the religious and ethnic components of Jewish identity and status had been torn asunder by the realities of the modern world. His *Gemeindeorthodoxie* ultimately distinguished between religious dogma and ethnic solidarity and accorded the former primacy over the latter. Considerations of prudence — the practical benefits that would accrue to the Orthodox through their participation in the political structure of the *Einheitsgemeinde* — were the factors that led Unna to embrace *Gemeindeorthodoxie*. His commitment to this policy was instrumental.

---

46 Unna's support of Zionism, as well as the approbation he offered those Liberal rabbis who embraced the cause of Zionism, indicates that Unna did not reduce Judaism to a religious confession alone. However, it is important to bear in mind that his own advocacy of the Zionist cause arose from what he deemed a religious imperative. The Zionism of Unna was completely removed from the secular nationalism of Herzl and his followers.

The writings of Nobel and Unna on the issue of community indicate that both men were wedded to the imperatives of Jewish law and teachings as well as to the application of those imperatives in a contemporary communal setting. At the same time, their writings testify to the power of adaptation and the manner in which even religious traditionalists advance visions of community in response to the dictates of an age. Their views illuminate the pluralism that characterized the Orthodox camp in Germany during Weimar. Study of their views illuminates some of the dynamics that have informed the development and evolution of Judaism in the modern age.

13

The Curriculum of the Jewish Theological Seminary in Historical and Comparative Perspective

A Prism on the Emergence of American Jewish Religious Denominationalism

In a sermon delivered at Congregation Chizzuk Emunah in Baltimore during the winter of 1886, Sabato Morais, founder of the Jewish Theological Seminary of America, made the following pledge to his audience:

> A seminary of sacred learning will be set up. . . . I acknowledge that as far as it lies in *my* power, the proposed seminary shall be hallowed to one predominating purpose — to the upholding of the principles by which my ancestors lived and for which many have died. From that nursery of learning shall issue forth men whose utterances will kindle enthusiasm for the literature of Holy Writ, but whose every-day conduct will mirror forth a sincere devotion to the *tenets* of Holy Writ.[1]

For Morais and his colleagues the tasks involved in the establishment of the Seminary over the next decade were manifold. The goals these men set for themselves were surely daunting. A building had to be constructed, a faculty secured, an endowment raised, students enrolled, a library stocked, and a curriculum established. This last item — the history and evolution of the curriculum — is our subject.

In offering such a study, we are mindful that curricular specialists employ the term "curriculum" to denote "all of the experiences . . .

---

1 *American Hebrew,* February 19, 1886, p.19.

[a student] has under the aegis of [an educational institution]." Indeed, the educational theorist Elliot Eisner divides these experiences into two categories — a written course of study that identifies the central subjects, themes, and goals that are part of an instructional program and all the other activities associated with an educational institution from which a student learns both inside and outside of the classroom. In this paper, our focus will be on the former category: what Eisner has identified as the "explicit curriculum" of an educational institution — the formal content and announced educational goals that a school, university, or seminary consciously and specifically defines.[2]

Our goal in this essay is therefore circumscribed. It is to present and analyze the historical context and educational aims that guided and informed the leaders of the Seminary from its inception to the present as evidenced in written records such as speeches, newspaper reports and articles, and catalogs. In so doing, we are mindful that the implicit dimensions of seminary training — the "hidden curriculum" that informs the ethos of an institution and that is not transmitted formally but through the overarching social and educational culture of a school and in the personal interactions between students and teachers that transpire in the classroom — may well be neglected in this study. We hope that, by focusing on the "explicit curriculum" of the Seminary, we will nevertheless display the ongoing as well as innovative vision of the rabbinate advanced by the leadership of the Conservative movement. We also trust that this display and discussion of the constant yet evolving nature of the Seminary's curricular deliberations will shed some light on the nature and evolution of Judaism itself in twentieth-century North America.

European Models

The educational and religious philosophy of the Jewish Theological Seminary of America (JTS) and the initial curriculum for the training of rabbis established by its founders to reflect that philosophy did not arise in a vacuum. The leaders of the Seminary — and those of the Hebrew Union College, for that matter — did not have to confront the task of

---

2   Elliot W. Eisner, *The Educational Imagination: On the Design and Evaluation of School Programs* (New York: Macmillan, 1994), pp. 26–27.

imagining a modern rabbinical seminary and its curriculum *de novo*. Instead, the outlook and curriculum that marked and defined the Seminary as a distinct institution were rooted in large part on the model of rabbinical training provided by the modern European rabbinical seminary. Zacharias Frankel and his Breslau Jewish Theological Seminary in particular were of seminal import for the men who created JTS. The name alone of the fledgling American rabbinical college testifies to the central role the Breslau Seminary played as a model for the founders of the American institution. A review of the sources and personalities associated with the creation and initial years of the Seminary makes these points abundantly clear.

Morais himself, as the first President of both the Seminary and its advisory board, was a native of Italy. His vision for the new American seminary was in large measure informed by Western and Central European Jewish educational models and sensibilities as he, along with his colleagues, undertook the task of forging the new institution. It is therefore hardly surprising that, in his first report as President to the Board of Trustees of the Seminary, he wrote, "What the seminaries at Breslau and Berlin, in Germany, at Buda-Pesth, in Hungary, at Rome, in Italy, are to Europe, this Jewish Theological Seminary should be to America. It [is] indeed time that New York should be in possession of such a place of Jewish learning."[3]

Morais's hopes in this regard were shared by virtually every person involved in the creation of the Seminary. Members of the original JTS faculty and its Advisory Board of Ministers such as Alexander Kohut, Frederick de Sola Mendes, and Bernard Drachman were themselves graduates of the Jewish Theological Seminary of Breslau. Others, such as Aaron Wise and Marcus Jastrow, were also trained in Europe, and they too were shaped and informed by the ethos of the European seminary. They, like their Breslau colleagues, identified with the notion of a Positive-Historical Judaism that Zacharias Frankel, as head of the Breslau Seminary, had articulated, and they were particularly receptive to the educational patterns Frankel had established in his institution. The curriculum structured by these men in the early years of JTS will — as we shall see — bear witness to this.

---

3 *Proceedings of the First Biennial Convention of the Jewish Theological Seminary Association*, 1888, p.10.

In the curricula of all the European seminaries, the study of Talmud and codes occupied a central role. The yearbooks of all three of the major seminaries that served German Jewry — the Orthodox *Rabbiner-Seminar*, the Positive-Historical Jewish Theological Seminary of Breslau, and the Liberal *Hochschule* established by Abraham Geiger in 1872 — indicate that the greatest bulk of the curriculum in these institutions was assigned to the study of rabbinical literature and codes and that the titles of subjects taught in this area were similar in each school. Particular attention was paid to Jewish laws of marriage and divorce. At the Breslau Seminary, this area was considered to be of such import that Frankel himself taught the talmudic tractates related to this theme. The laws of *Ḥoshen Mishpat*, the section of the *Shulhan Arukh* that deals with Jewish civil law, were totally ignored in the curricula of all three institutions. In focusing the course content on the study of rabbinical literature as they did, these schools reflected the reality of a world where Jewish civil autonomy had disappeared.[4]

Other areas of study also received considerable attention in the seven-year course of study at the Breslau Seminary. Students were expected to master the following subjects: Holy Scriptures and their exegesis, Hebrew language and grammar, historical and methodological introduction to Mishnah and Talmud, history of the Jews together with a history of Jewish literature, religious philosophy and ethics according to Jewish sources, midrash, ritual practice, pedagogy, and homiletics. The modern European seminary was surely different from traditional Jewish centers of learning. It was not a yeshiva. Instead, it was designed to train and educate rabbis for a contemporary western cultural setting. The expansion of the curriculum beyond exclusive emphasis on the study of traditional rabbinic texts (the classical "four ells of *Halakhah*") and the modern academic categories employed to transmit Jewish knowledge to the students surely reflect this mission.[5]

In addition, students at the Breslau seminary, like their counterparts at the *Rabbiner-Seminar* and the *Hochschule*, were required to complete a doctorate at a secular university as a prerequisite for ordination at all

---

4 For an English language summary of these reports, see David Ellenson, *Rabbi Esriel Hildesheimer and the Creation of a Modern Jewish Orthodoxy* (Tuscaloosa, Ala.: University of Alabama Press, 1990), pp.158ff.

5 Ibid.

the German seminaries.[6] Faculty and students alike at these institutions were imbued with ideals imparted by western culture and were absolutely committed to a belief in the centrality of *Wissenschaft des Judentums*, which in turn — they believed — would lead to a proper understanding of Judaism. As Frankel himself wrote, "Without the academic study of Judaism, Judaism could not exist [in the present day]."[7]

Hebrew Union College and American Realities

As we have seen, the cultural ideals and models that guided the founders of the Jewish Theological Seminary of America were strongly western. Nonetheless, these men, like Frankel and the Positive-Historical school in Europe, were quite traditional in religious orientation and observance. It was precisely this distinctive orientation that led to the creation of JTS, for the religious directions that informed Morais and his colleagues were decidedly different from the sensibilities and practices that were then beginning to mark the course of American Reform. Indeed, JTS arguably arose as an "opposition Seminary" to the Hebrew Union College.[8]

HUC, it should be remembered, initially claimed that it would not be a sectarian or denominationally distinct Reform institution. As Isaac Mayer Wise himself declared in 1879,

> [Hebrew Union College] shall be an orthodox Jewish academy.... The Masoretic text of the Bible with the fundamental principle of God, revelation, Providence, immortality, righteousness, justice, truth, and freedom, is the rock of foundation, and our post biblical literature contains the material upon which and with which our structure of education is to be erected under the help of God.[9]

While Wise aimed to create rabbis who were "American with heart and soul,"[10] he had, in the words of the *American Israelite*, "no *isms* or *schisms* to impose." Instead, as his journal described it, he will

6 Ibid. p.160.
7 Ibid.
8 The phrase, "opposition Seminary," is taken from a speech delivered by Alexander Kohut. See *American Hebrew*, January 7, 1887, p.8.
9 *American Israelite*, September 1879, p.2.
10 *American Israelite*, July 21, 1871, p.8.

earnestly and steadily endeavour with the aid of a competent and distinguished Faculty, to open the treasures of Israel's literature to . . . reformer and orthodox, in justice to all and offence to none. . . . The Hebrew Union College . . . [intends to offer] an enlightened religious and moral training in temples grand and gorgeous as well as in the orthodox synagogue, to see Judaism in its glory and to hear it expounded intelligently.[11]

In offering this vision of the College, Wise clearly showed that his aim in these early years was to create a seminary that could provide rabbis for all American Israel. His true sentiments, however, were undoubtedly not those of an Orthodox Jew. After all, in his address on the occasion of the opening of HUC, Wise stated, "Where the old Talmud appears to us contrary to the spirit of Thorah, we reject its teaching." Nevertheless, he also praised the Talmud and claimed that the rabbinical students would be obligated to acquaint themselves with "the Jochanans, Gamaliels, Jehudas or Rabbina and Ashi," all great figures in rabbinical literature. Indeed, "Kuenen, Wellhausen, Renan, Ewald, or Smith," all modern biblical critics, were "no more reliable authorities" than these rabbinical sages. The Hebrew Union College, in its training of rabbis, would embody

historical Judaism . . . the rock upon which the temple of Israel proudly stands and has stood these three thousand years and more. . . . There is no Judaism without Thorah and revelation. The college was established to teach the literature of Israel; to train, educate, and license rabbis for real Judaism.[12]

These words indicate that at this time Wise was greatly concerned to reassure traditionalists in the American Jewish community that his Cincinnati school would educate rabbis who had mastered the gamut of traditional Jewish literature and who could therefore serve them as well. Of course, he also sought to train an American Jewish clergy thoroughly conversant and comfortable with contemporary forms of academic scholarship. No less than that of the men who would establish

11 *American Israelite*, September 3, 1875, p. 4.
12 David Philipson and Louis Grossman, ed., *Selected Writings of Isaac Mayer Wise*, (New York: Arno Press, reprint, 1969), pp. 395–96.

the Jewish Theological Seminary several years later, his outlook was informed by the model of the European rabbinical seminary. The curriculum he designed reflected these commitments and attitudes.

In a pamphlet entitled "Propositions," submitted on July 11, 1878 to a "Commission appointed by the Council of the Union of American Hebrew Congregations [UAHC]," Wise defined the "Subjects, Aims, and Methods of Instruction" that were to mark the curriculum of the Hebrew Union College. Section I stated,

> The principal subjects of the College shall be the Bible, with its Commentaries and Paraphrases, the Talmud and its Commentaries, the Jewish philosophical literature, all in their respective original tongues, the Theology, Ethics and History of the Hebrews, together with the various disciplines of Hermeneutics, Exegetics, Homiletics, Criticism, and Semitic philology.

These goals were to be accomplished in two ways — through the reading of "original sources" on the basis of "scientific principles" as well as through "systematical lectures." Wise asserted that no more "than two-sevenths of the whole school time shall be devoted to the lectures." Indeed, the overwhelming bulk of instructional time — "ten out of the fourteen hours of weekly instruction" — given to the students in Judaica was "devoted to the study of original sources."[13]

Lest it appear that fourteen hours a week of instructional time in Judaica was meager, it should be noted that the first students at the College were required to do more than study Jewish subjects. Many were teenage boys, and the College was committed to the modern seminary model of producing rabbis who were well educated in secular subjects. It therefore granted students time during these years to devote to those studies so that they might thereby qualify for and earn a bachelor's de-

13 Isaac M. Wise, "Propositions Submitted to the Gentlemen of the Commission Appointed by the Council of the Union of American Hebrew Congregations at Milwaukee, July 11, 1878," pp. 5–6, 11. In addition, see "Report of the President of the Hebrew Union College to the President and Members of the Board of Governors of Hebrew Union College," *Proceedings of the Union of American Hebrew Congregations* (1873–1879), vol. 1, p. 336, for a confirmation of the daily time allotted to the study of texts.

gree. Only then could they stand as candidates for ordination. To this end, HUC established a Preparatory Department that had as one of its aims the grounding of the student in the linguistic, historical, philosophical, and textual foundations necessary for advanced rabbinical studies. During his years in the Preparatory Department, the student was not only expected to earn a Bachelor of Hebrew Letters degree (*atzilei bnei yisrael*), but to earn a secular degree from a university as well. Only then could he qualify for admission to the Collegiate Department, where he would engage in advanced studies and qualify for ordination as a rabbi. Thus students were required to "give good evidence of their ability to pass ... the examination for admission into such institutions as Columbia College (New York); the University of Pennsylvania (Philadelphia), or the McMicken University (Cincinnati)."[14] By 1894, the College was able to state simply in its first catalog that each ordinand "must be a graduate of the University, with the degree of at least B.A. or B.L."[15]

While this first rabbinical seminary on American soil did not require an earned doctoral degree from its students to qualify for ordination as its German counterparts had, the demand that each student possess a university diploma bespeaks a comparable sensitivity to the academic ethos of the larger world. Further evidence of the Hebrew Union College's commitment to the inclusion of *Wissenschaft* in its curriculum is displayed in several other statements issued by Wise and the College. For example, in 1877 Wise contended that while familiarity with the researches of Frankel, Geiger, Graetz, Luzzatto, and Zunz, among others, was not sufficient to qualify one as a rabbi, he left little doubt that these "excellent works" were an invaluable part of a modern rabbinical education.[16] In addition, the catalogs of the College explicitly stated that the "main object" of the "four years' course" in the Collegiate Department was "to enable the student to read and expound *scientifically* the original sources of Judaism and its History."[17] Finally, the internalization of a

14 *Proceedings of the Union of American Hebrew Congregations,* vol.1, pp.98, 704. By the 1890s the curriculum in the Collegiate Department had developed into a set four-year program. See the section entitled, "Course of Studies in the Collegiate Department," in *Program of the Hebrew Union College,* 1894–1895, pp.17–19.

15 Ibid. p.20.

16 *Proceedings of the Union of American Hebrew Congregations* (July 1877), vol.1, p.342

modern academic ethos on the part of the Hebrew Union College and its manifestation in the curriculum is evidenced in the requirement that each student had to write "an original thesis proving research and originality" in order to graduate as a rabbi.[18]

In his "Propositions" of 1878, Wise explicitly delineated what he expected the students of the Preparatory Department to attain during their four years of study: "competency in Jewish history; Hebrew, Chaldaic and Syriac grammar; in reading fluently the rabbinical Hebrew as used in the commentaries; and in the translation of any passage or passages from the originals of the Bible, the Mishnah in *Mo'ed* and *Nezikin*, and the Talmud from any one of the one hundred and fifty pages read in the department."[19] As Michael Meyer has observed,

> The curriculum devised for the Preparatory Department was remarkably, even absurdly ambitious. At the end of four years — and before beginning the Collegiate Department — a student was to have mastered Hebrew and Aramaic grammar, read in the original most of the Bible and large selections from rabbinical literature, including portions from both the Babylonian and the Palestinian Talmuds, and familiarized himself with the entire span of Jewish history.[20]

Nevertheless, as later catalogs indicate, Wise appears to have maintained these standards. Hence, in a catalog of the 1890s, under the rubric, "Standard of Admission to Collegiate Department," it states,

> Thorough knowledge of Hebrew and Aramaic grammars (Luzzatto's), and Hebrew translation from English or Aramaic; *prima vista* translation of the Biblical books and . . . readiness to read Rashi passages. In Mishna is required the knowledge of *Aboth* and at least two other *Mesachtoth*; in Talmud, *prima vista* reading of at least fifty

17 *Program of the Hebrew Union College*, 1894–1895, p.16. (Emphasis mine.)
18 Ibid. p.20.
19 Wise, "Propositions," p.15.
20 Michael Meyer, "A Centennial History of the Hebrew Union College," in *Hebrew Union College-Jewish Institute of Religion at One Hundred*, ed. by Samuel E. Karff (Cincinnati: Hebrew Union College Press, 1975), p.20.

pages in one or more *Mesachtoth* previously prepared; also the best parts of *Sepher Hamadda* in the code of Maimonides, and history from Zerubabel to Rabbi Jochanan ben Saccai.[21]

Particularly noteworthy in view of the antinomian course upon which the Reform Movement was about to embark was the stress Wise placed on rabbinical literature and codes in the curriculum of the College during these early years. In the manner of the German rabbinical seminaries, no time was devoted to a study of Jewish civil law as contained in *Ḥoshen Mishpat*. However, considerable attention was given to mishnaic and talmudic tractates that were deemed to be of "ethical and historical value" such as *Aboth*, *Sanhedrin*, and *Sotah* as well as to tractates, legal codes, and responsa that dealt with matters of current concern to segments of the American rabbinate and laity such as dietary laws, personal status, and the holidays. Hence, the talmudic tractates of *Gittin*, *Kiddushin*, *Ḥullin*, *Yebamoth*, *Yoma*, and *Megillah* were studied as were large portions of *Berakhot*. In addition, courses were given on select chapters of *Eben ha-Ezer* and in *Yoreh De'ah*, *Hilkhot Tzedakah*, *Milah*, *Gerim*, *Bikkur Ḥolim*, and *Abeloth* as well as in *Oraḥ Ḥayim*, *Hilkhot Ḥanukkah*, *Purim*, and *Pesaḥ*.[22] The appearance of these texts in the curriculum of the College seems to reflect the influence of a European seminary model upon the embryonic Cincinnati institution: such study constituted the central element in the curricula of each the major rabbinical schools of Germany and Central Europe. Further, the significant role assigned such texts in the curriculum of the Hebrew Union College at this juncture in history indicates that the College regarded itself as embedded in classical Jewish tradition, and that it still aspired to address traditional as well as liberal segments of the American Jewish community.

The course of studies in the advanced rabbinical track at the Hebrew Union College was of course not limited to classical rabbinical texts. In the Collegiate Department, the history of Judaism from the tannaitic period through Mendelssohn and the emergence of American Juda-

21 *Program of the Hebrew Union College*, 1894–1895, p.14.
22 Wise, "Propositions," pp.11–13; *Proceedings of the Union of American Hebrew Congregations* July 1877, and July 1878), vol.1, pp.341 and 450; and *Proceedings of the Union of American Hebrew Congregations* (July 1890), vol.3, p.2625.

ism was covered, and readings in medieval philosophy focusing upon Albo, Saadia, and Maimonides were required. The Tanakh was studied along with classical rabbinical commentaries, *targumim*, and contemporary critical scholarship. The study of languages such as Syriac and Arabic was included in the curriculum, and homiletics as well as lectures on pastoral theology were given to the students in the realm of practical rabbinics.[23]

By 1899, Wise could look back with pride upon his achievements as the architect of the Hebrew Union College and its curriculum. In his address that year to the ordinands of the College, he stated that the College had as its object the perpetuation of "the covenant and the Thorah," the establishment of "the continuity of Judaism on this continent under the new light of a new world, a new civilization of freedom, equality, justice, and humanity, the morning dawn of the future of the human family." His curriculum was designed to facilitate that goal's attainment — to educate rabbis who could expound the "sacred lore of Israel" to an American audience."[24] Others shared his vision for the creation of an American rabbinate. However, they were certain the Hebrew Union College was not the appropriate institution for the attainment of that goal, and so they created the Jewish Theological Seminary of America.

The Jewish Theological Seminary of America Vision and Curriculum

In the view of Sabato Morais and his colleagues, HUC had betrayed the ideal it purported to espouse of a united American Judaism by serving non-kosher food at a banquet honoring its first class of ordinands in 1883. Marcus Jastrow, the ordination speaker on that occasion, and many other persons both lay and rabbinic, were incensed by the sectarian division they felt Hebrew Union College had introduced into the life of the American Jewish community through the violation of this classical pillar of Jewish observance. Furthermore, this action contributed to the view that an alternative seminary — one more devoted to classical Jewish patterns of observance — was a necessity for American Jewry.

---

23 *Catalogue of the Hebrew Union College*, 1896–1897, pp.16–20.
24 *Proceedings of the Union of American Hebrew Congregations* (June 1899), pp.4102–3.

This led Morais to assert in December 1884:

> To save the religion for which Mattathias staked his existence and
> of which Chanukah is a glorious exponent, a seminary of learning,
> where *all* the ordinances of the Pentateuch, compatible with our
> state of dispersion, will be taught and enforced, must be set up in
> obedience to the demands of an enlightened 'Orthodoxy.'[25]

Throughout 1885 Morais continued to call for the creation of a new
seminary. The adoption of the Pittsburgh Platform by the Reform rabbinate in November of that year only reinforced his resolve. Furthermore, the theological vision articulated in the Pittsburgh Platform of
Judaism as a universal religion totally in accord with the dictates of reason and absolutely hostile to the ritual and national elements traditionally associated with the Jewish religion estranged many others from
support of HUC and caused them to rally around Morais and his proposal. A declaration in the pages of the *American Israelite* by Marcus
Kohner, honorary secretary to the Trustees of Temple Ahavath Chesed
in New York, is typical of the critical sentiments shared by many on the
perceived direction of the Hebrew Union College:

> At the convention of rabbis, held at Pittsburgh, several resolutions
> were adopted, and still others proposed, of which the Trustees of
> Congregation Ahavath Chesed are not in accord. I am instructed
> by said Trustees to state that if these articles, as adopted and pro-
> posed, are to be the instructions at the Hebrew Union College,
> that they, as a member of [the Union of American Hebrew Con-
> gregations], find themselves morally bound to protest against such
> teachings.[26]

The Pittsburgh Platform, following as it did so shortly after the infamous
Cincinnati ordination banquet of 1883, caused Morais to state that his
goal in the establishment of the Jewish Theological Seminary of America
was to forswear the impieties of Wise's "blatant 'American Judaism'" and

---

25 *American Hebrew,* December 19, 1884, p. 84.
26 *American Israelite,* December 18, 1885, p. 6.

preserve in its stead "the pure Judaism of Moses and all the righteous in Israel."[27] Alexander Kohut gave eloquent expression to the difference in philosophy that was to distinguish the new seminary from its older sibling in Cincinnati. Kohut contended, "In the new seminary, a different spirit will prevail, different impulses will pervade its teachings and animate its teachers. This spirit shall be that of *Conservative* Judaism, the *conserving* Jewish impulse which will create in the pupils of the Seminary the tendency to recognize the dual nature of Judaism and the Law; which unites theory and practice, identifies body and soul, realizes the importance of both matter and spirit, and acknowledges the necessity of observing the Law as well as studying it."[28] Only the establishment of the Jewish Theological Seminary of America could produce a class of rabbis capable of rescuing American Judaism from the compromising and destructive tendencies inherent in Cincinnati and Reform.

Morais, like Wise, had a distinct vision of Judaism, and he was determined to fashion an institution for the training of rabbis who would be able to disseminate that vision so as to give life to Jewish tradition in the United States. Like Wise, Morais shared an enthusiasm for the ideals of America. As he himself phrased it, "Heartfelt is, indeed, our devotion to the constitution of the country that has leveled inequality and clothed Israelites with all the franchises of free men." His aim was therefore to create rabbis sympathetic "with the spirit of our American institutions, . . . imbued with . . . firm and intelligent . . . patriotism."[29]

Morais was also completely committed to offering Jewish instruction in accord with a modern scientific spirit. He maintained, "The entire work of the institution must be conducted in accordance with collegiate methods now prevalent." He was also "gratified" by the association the Seminary had in its first few years established with Columbia College, for it confirmed the high level of academic instruction the Seminary offered.[30] By 1896, only a decade after its founding, he proudly claimed, "We can train scholarly rabbis here in America as well as in Europe."[31]

Yet Morais, unlike Wise, was not interested, as one admirer put it, in

27 *American Hebrew* 34, no.7, p.100.
28 *American Hebrew*, January 7, 1887, p.8.
29 *American Hebrew* 34, no.7, p.99; and *Proceedings of the Second Biennial Convention of the Jewish Theological Seminary Association*, 1890, p.7.
30 *Proceedings of the Fourth Biennial Convention of the Jewish Theological Seminary Association*, 1894, p.17.

creating "an *American* Judaism." Rather, he was concerned about preserving "*Judaism* in America."[32] Morais and men such as Jastrow and de Sola Mendes were committed to what they defined as historical Judaism. They were quite disturbed by what they considered to be Hebrew Union College's ever increasing drift in the direction of Reform during the latter decades of the nineteenth century. Their opposition to this direction not only gave birth to JTS and the Conservative movement in this country. It also caused them to assert that "fidelity and devotion to Jewish law" was a prerequisite for the rabbinical office.[33] Indeed, even admission to the institution required "adherence to a mode of life consonant with Jewish laws."[34] Thus, they explicitly drew a boundary between the Seminary and the Hebrew Union College.

Morais also offered a description of the ideal course of instruction at the Seminary:

> The traditions of the fathers are therefore coeval with the written statutes of the five holy books … It follows then that the Bible constitutes the primary object of our pupils' tuition; Mishnah and Talmud are studied by them as an indispensable corollary. Those branches of sacred literature with kindred ones, systematically imparted without pre-judgment by men whose characters we believe to be unassailable, must inspire the scholars with love for their religion and reverence for the ancients who honestly handed it down.[35]

Or, as he observed elsewhere concerning the subject content of his nascent seminary, "The word of the Bible in its original purity shall command profound attention; its purport, when obscure, shall be sought at the hands of commentators, trustworthy by reason of their thorough

31 *Proceedings of the Fifth Biennial Convention of the Jewish Theological Seminary Association,* 1896, p. 17.

32 *Proceedings of the Sixth Biennial Convention of the Jewish Theological Seminary Association,* 1898, p. 12.

33 *Proceedings of the First Biennial Convention of the Jewish Theological Seminary Association,* 1888, p. 9.

34 See, for example, *Proceedings of the Third Biennial Convention of the Jewish Theological Seminary Association,* 1892, p. 39.

35 *American Hebrew* 34, no 7, p. 99.

acquaintance with the construction, the genius, the spirit of Holy Writ." In a tone that foreshadowed his successor Solomon Schechter's enmity towards the discipline of Higher Biblical Criticism, Morais continued,

> Ewald shall not supersede our Kimchi and Nachmanides, nor shall Luzzatto be set aside to make room for Gesenius. Like the word of the Bible, so shall its history also be studied in the original, not in Kuenen, Wellhausen, or Robertson Smith; not in the works of Gentiles or Jews that deny Moses the authorship of the Pentateuch, make our patriarchs sheer myths, our priests tyrannical egotists, our Ezra a pretender, our progenitors unmitigated dupes.

For Morais, as for many Jews of this era, biblical criticism was a not-so-covert form of antisemitism. It would have no role at the Seminary.[36]

Given the commitment Morais displayed towards Jewish observance, it is fascinating to observe the role to be assigned rabbinical studies in his curriculum.

> It is very far from my thoughts to belittle Talmudism. . . . [However], it shall be the boast of that institute hereafter that the attendants are unsurpassing Scripturalists . . . though they may not rank foremost among skilled Talmudists. The latter have, at times, degenerated into hair-splitting disputants — *pilpulists.*

It is the Bible, he asserted, which is "the book without which post-biblical literature lacks the foundation stone; it is simply — a castle in the air.[37]

In offering such thoughts, Morais undoubtedly reflected the influence that the bibliocentrism of occidental culture had upon him as well as his own impatience with those modes of "talmudic sophistry" that dominated certain Eastern European *yeshivot.* This latter mode of talmudic methodology would certainly find no home at JTS. On the other hand, these statements of Morais simultaneously betray the lack of influence he may have exerted over the design of the actual Seminary

36 *American Hebrew,* February 19, 1886, p.19. Also see Morais's statement concerning the "insidious" nature of such criticism *in American Hebrew,* January 7, 1887, pp.4–5

37 *American Hebrew,* February 19, 1886, p.19.

curriculum itself. While nothing was taught at JTS in opposition to Morais's sentiments, an investigation of the Seminary's curriculum for its rabbinical students even during these early years indicates that the study of rabbinical literature, not Bible, constituted the heart of instruction at the New York institution.

The JTS rabbinical curriculum must therefore be approached and analyzed in the fullness of a multi-layered context. The curriculum was a patrimony from the seminaries of Central Europe and Germany. At the same time, the ethos of the institution was constructed in light of the sentiments of its founders and in opposition to the specific reality of American Reform Judaism and the Hebrew Union College.

JTS offered a Preparatory Department akin to that at HUC and established for precisely the same reasons. Rabbinical students were required to earn a bachelor's degree and be well versed in secular subjects. And the Seminary itself assumed responsibility for providing such instruction so that candidates suitably qualified for entering the Rabbinical School of JTS could be produced. Indeed, in many of his reports to the association, President Morais describes the valiant efforts of his young charges to acquire both the secular and Jewish education necessary to qualify them for admission to the rabbinical program. In the Preparatory Department the student was instructed in Hebrew and biblical Aramaic grammar, Bible with Rashi and Targum, Mishnah, and Jewish history through the tannaitic period. Its curriculum, though not identical with, closely paralleled the curriculum offered in the Preparatory Department of the Hebrew Union College.[38]

The most striking feature of the course of instruction offered at the Seminary and described in the various *Proceedings* of the 1890s is the seminal though hardly surprising role that the Breslau Seminary played in shaping the contours of its curriculum. The course of study for ordination at JTS was set for seven years in what were labeled "Junior Department" and "Senior Department." The program stressed not only Talmud and codes, but Bible, Jewish history, philosophy, midrash, homiletics and pedagogy, *hazzanut*, and lectures on biblical archaeology. As Bernard Drachman observed, the program at JTS was practically identical to that

---

38 *Proceedings of the Second Biennial Convention of the Jewish Theological Seminary Association,* 1890, pp. 52–54.

offered at the Breslau Seminary.[39] It should also be apparent that it bore strong affinities to the curriculum of the Hebrew Union College as well.

A closer look at the subjects of instruction only confirms this latter point. In Jewish philosophy at both institutions, Albo, Maimonides, and Saadia were stressed. Approximately three-quarters of instructional time were devoted to talmudic texts and related rabbinical literature. *Gittin, Ḥulin, Kiddushin, Yoreh Deʾah, Eben ha-Ezer,* and *Oraḥ Ḥayim* constituted the major talmudic and rabbinical legal texts and codes that were read by the students. And at both institutions, the courses in history as well as Bible also possessed similar titles.[40]

None of this disconfirms the point that the curriculum of JTS was modeled after that of Breslau. Rather what it does display is how deeply embedded the men who established both HUC and the Seminary were in the ethos of the German seminary and how desirous they were of patterning their institutions after the model such seminaries provided. This, more than any other factor, appears to have informed the curricula they initially established. In their minds, the route to legitimization as a serious and worthy institution of higher Jewish learning necessitated the creation of a curriculum and ethos modeled after the European seminary.

The issue here is not whether JTS or HUC, at this juncture in history, was the academic equal of the *Hochschule* or the Breslau Seminary. Men such as Morais or Wise, to put it mildly, were surely not the scholarly peers of Frankel or Geiger. Rather, what is crucial is that each of these men aspired to create institutions patterned after the seminaries founded by Frankel and Geiger. One only has to read a representative statement uttered by Morais in 1890 to recognize how deeply he and his colleagues in both New York and Cincinnati had internalized the European values and models. Morais happily noted that academic lectures on topics such as "Biblical Archaeology" and "The History of Hebrew Grammar" as well as "The Talith and the Pallium" and "The Siloam Inscription and the Moabite Stone" had been delivered at JTS;

39 Bernard Drachman, *The Unfailing Light* (New York: The Rabbinical Council of America, 1948), pp. 99–109.

40 See any curriculum from the *Proceedings of* the 1890s for the course content of the instructional program offered by the Seminary during these years.

and he proudly observed that the *Allgemeine Zeitung des Judenthums* "devoted considerable space to an appreciative article in regard to the course of lectures delivered [at the Seminary] last summer, in which it said, 'We can with gratification observe from this that in the New World too, Jewish learning is making its way.'"[41] While the student at JTS was expected to display a level of Jewish ritual observance distinct from that of his student colleague at the Hebrew Union College, an investigation and analysis of the catalogs, reports, and articles concerning these two institutions of rabbinical training reveal no genuinely discernible differences in their curricula during this era. With the advent of the 1900s and the appointment of Kaufmann Kohler as president of the Hebrew Union College, such differences would begin to appear, but under Wise and Morais, the legacy of Europe remained paramount in guiding each institution.

The Impact of Solomon Schechter

On April 1, 1902, Solomon Schechter — arguably the preeminent scholar of Judaica during his era in the English-speaking world — assumed his duties as president of JTS. During the thirteen years he occupied this position, Schechter succeeded in placing his stamp on the character and curriculum of the institution that he headed and through that stamp managed to influence the course of American Judaism and rabbinical training far beyond his time. Schechter was determined that the Seminary would be a fertile training ground for rabbis who would be devoted to the promotion and dissemination of the Law to all Israel. Judaism, he stated to the ordination class of 1910, was principally committed to

> [the] binding authority of law and the absolute sovereignty and grace of law. . . . Ethics are good, but laws and commandments bidden and commanded by God are better; and all such phrases as idealism, spirituality, and religiosity will avail us nothing as long as you omit to urge the great principle that the Holy One of Israel,

41 *Proceedings of the Second Biennial Convention of the Jewish Theological Seminary Association*, 1890, p.10.

"in His Holiness, gave law unto His people. . . ." To urge this upon your community in all its force and all its significance seems to me the mission of the Rabbi in the present generation.[42]

Furthermore, the rabbi was "not only responsible to his congregation, but to the whole of Israel for [the] preservation and perpetuation of To-rah.[43] Indeed, he asserted, "The Directors of this institution, by term-ing it the Jewish Theological Seminary of *America*," have distinctly shown their [understanding of the historical nature of Judaism and their] intention of avoiding sectarianism. . . . The Seminary to be really great will have to be catholic [i.e., broad and universal] and of a uniting nature."[44]

To succeed at this, the Seminary had to remain faithful to its original mandate — "the promotion of Jewish learning and the training for the Jewish ministry."[45] The legitimacy and authority of the rabbinate depended upon the ability of the Seminary to inculcate a knowledge and appreciation of the Jewish past and its literature in its graduates. It was imperative to anchor the rabbi in this way, for otherwise he could only champion a Judaism that would "turn out to be a mere caprice of the mob, or a whim of fashion, or the hobby of some willful individual, sure to disappear when viewed *sub specie aeternitatis*." No "instruction suited to the needs of such an isolated and detached present [will] ever embody any features of greatness."[46]

Authentic Judaism required rabbis and teachers whose roots were firmly planted in the historical soil of traditional Jewish scholarship. A rabbi bereft of such learning was a "nude soul." For, as Schechter was to maintain in 1908, "No man in authority is greater than the source whence his authority is derived. The authority of the Rabbi is derived from the Torah; he is its servant."[47] The ongoing passion and commitment Schechter displayed to the ideal of a learned rabbinate was evident, when, in 1912, he thundered, "Judaism need not be advertised. Judaism

42 Solomon Schechter, *Seminary Addresses and Other Papers* (New York: Burning Bush Press, 1960) pp.133–34.

43 Ibid. p.126.

44 Ibid. pp.48, 50.

45 Ibid. p.14.

46 Ibid. pp.45, 46.

47 Ibid. pp.21, 125.

needs to be taught."[48] Learning, Schechter maintained, was "the only safeguard against . . . sham cherubs. Piety without learning is apt . . . to degenerate into mere ranting, making religion a caricature of itself."[49]

To be sure, Schechter was not entirely impervious to the practical demands of the rabbinate. "The Rabbi," he acknowledged, "is expected to 'do things.' Upon this we are all agreed."[50] The rabbi was required to be a model for others. His home was to be "strictly Jewish," and he was obligated to "faithfully and manfully maintain [a] loyalty to Torah." Furthermore, the rabbi needed to perform "social work included under the name of *Gemilath Chasadim*" (performance of kind deeds), for in Judaism this formed "a part of Israel's great *Imitatio Dei*."[51] As Schechter put it,

> Mercifulness and loving kindness are, according to our Sages, among the criteria distinguishing the people of Israel. You . . . know the regular Jewish expression, *Yisrael raḥmanim b'nei raḥmanim*, "Israel are a compassionate people, the descendants of a compassionate people." You have also heard of the Jewish heart. Do not fail to cultivate these sentiments and to keep them alive among your congregants.[52]

At times, this meant that the rabbi was called upon to be "an organizer, a social agitator, an expert on all topics of the day."[53] Yet, all of these latter functions were secondary. The task of the rabbi was "to think things" from a Jewish perspective. The rabbi could do this only if he was "a sound Hebrew scholar."[54]

Consequently, in his 1902 inaugural address, Schechter assigned top priority to the creation of a curriculum and the recruitment of a faculty that would enable the prospective rabbi to receive "such training as to enable him to say: '*Judæici nihil a me alienum pluto* — I regard nothing Jewish as foreign to me.' He should know everything Jewish — Bible, Talmud, Midrash, Liturgy, Jewish ethics and Jewish philosophy; Jewish

48 Ibid. p.227.
49 Ibid. p.131.
50 Ibid. p.198.
51 Ibid. pp.129, 23, 30.
52 Ibid. p.204.
53 Ibid. p.200.
54 Ibid. pp.198, 200.

history and Jewish mysticism; and even Jewish folklore. None of these subjects . . . should be . . . strange to him."[55]

Such training, Schechter insisted, would be rigorous. He hoped to produce a rabbi who would be capable of engaging from "time to time . . . in some scientific work, publishing occasionally a learned article on some historical topic, or even editing some ancient Hebrew text."[56] For, as Schechter put it, "The crown and climax of all learning is research." It alone could facilitate the search for "truth."[57] It was his hope that the "spiritual destinies" of Israel "in this country" would "be presided over by men of the stamp of Dr. Kohut and Dr. Jastrow, who left us the greatest Rabbinical Dictionaries . . . or Dr. Szold, who bequeathed to us one of the most lucid commentaries on the Book of Job."[58] To produce such men, Schechter required that his students obtain

> a thorough and accurate knowledge of Jewish literature . . . The duty of accuracy, even in the most minute details of a subject, cannot be shirked. . . . I know that the acquiring of details is a very tiresome and wearisome affair, and may well be described in the language of the old Rabbis: "The part of wisdom learned under wrath." But, unfortunately, there is no 'snapshot' process for acquiring learning. It has its methods and its laws, as ancient as time itself, and these none can evade or escape.[59]

With this challenge in mind, Schechter stated:

> We — my colleagues and I — [have] tried to draw up the curriculum of studies for the classes, in such a way as to include in it almost every branch of Jewish literature . . . [We must] attempt to bring the student on terms of acquaintance at least with all those manifestations of Jewish life and Jewish thought which may prove useful to them as future ministers, and suggestive and stimulating to them as prospective scholars.[60]

55 Ibid. p.19.
56 Ibid. p.200..
57 Ibid. p.16.
58 Ibid. p.199.
59 Ibid. p.14.

For Solomon Schechter, knowledge and careful scholarship were the *sine qua non* that established the grounds for exercising legitimate rabbinical leadership. The education and ordination of such rabbis now became the focus of his life's work.

To aid him, Schechter assembled some of the greatest scholarly luminaries of his day and appointed them to the faculty of the Seminary. Foremost among them was Louis Ginzberg, whom Schechter immediately appointed as professor of Talmud in 1902. Over the course of the next several years he recruited Israel Friedlaender as professor of Bible and Alexander Marx to serve both as professor of history and as chief librarian. Joseph Mayor Asher, who had studied with Schechter in England, was appointed professor of homiletics. Upon his death in 1910, Mordecai Kaplan assumed that position. In addition, Israel Davidson was appointed to a faculty position as instructor in Hebrew and Rabbinics in 1905. In little more than a decade, Davidson was made a full professor.[61]

In appointing such scholarly giants, Schechter underscored the academic seriousness of the institution he had come to head. Each of these men was a distinguished scholar, and the academic reputation of the Seminary soared with the addition of these men to the faculty. In his memoirs, Bernard Drachman attests to the transformation these men wrought in the atmosphere of the Seminary. As Drachman observed, "A new and, from a certain point of view, more brilliant period began [with the ascension of Schechter to the presidency]."[62] Schechter was determined to carve out the highest academic reputation for the Seminary. There would be no room under his administration for faculty members who could not make the most significant contributions to their chosen field of scholarship. This meant men such as Drachman

---

60 Ibid. p.20.

61 On these appointments, see the catalogs of the Jewish Theological Seminary — variously entitled "Register," "Announcement," or "Circular of Information"-for the years of Schechter's presidency. In addition, consult Israel Davidson, "The Academic Aspect and Growth of the Rabbinical Department-The Seminary Proper," in *The Jewish Theological Seminary of America-Semi-Centennial Volume*, ed. by Cyrus Adler (New York: The Jewish Theological Seminary of America, 1939), pp.79ff. Finally, see Drachman, *The Unfailing Light*, pp.253–54.

62 Drachman, *The Unfailing Light*, p.253.

and Joshua Joffe — stalwarts of JTS during the 1890s — had to be content with comparatively minor roles as instructors under Schechter.

A brief analysis of Drachman's career at the Seminary during the first decade of the twentieth century reflects the changes wrought in the atmosphere of JTS as well as Schechter's determination to appoint only men of the greatest scholarly competence to the faculty. Drachman felt that he had been "the logical candidate for the successorship to Dr. Morais. The least to which I was logically entitled," he continued, "was a professorship in some major subject."[63] Indeed, Drachman's hopes do not appear to have been unreasonable. After all, he had served as dean of the faculty from 1889 "until the reorganization of the Seminary in 1901 under the presidency of Dr. Solomon Schechter."[64] However, Drachman was compelled to recognize that his "just claims were apparently not even considered. I was offered the position of instructor in Hebrew and acting reader of rabbinical codes." He accepted this obvious demotion because he "hoped . . . that with unremitting devo-tion to the duties of my appointed task I would be able to win the approval of the new powers that be."[65]

Such hopes were not fulfilled. Drachman devoted himself to scholarship and in 1908 produced a work on "an abstruse Talmudic discussion or controversy between two of the greatest and most renowned Talmudic authorities of the Middle Ages, Rabbi Abraham ben David of Posquieres in France and Rabbi Zerahiah ben Isaac Ha-Levi, originally of Gerona in Spain, and afterwards a resident of Lunel in France." When Drachman presented Schechter with a copy of the book, he anticipated a warm and complimentary reception. To his dismay, "the learned head of the Seminary accepted my book most ungraciously, hardly said a word in acknowledgment thereof, and was unmistakably displeased." One year later, in 1909, Drachman "received an official letter from the board of directors of the Jewish Theological Seminary. It contained a notification that my appointment to the teaching staff was terminated and that my services would no longer be required."[66] While some have suggested that it was Drachman's commitment to Jewish Orthodoxy

63 Ibid. p.254.
64 Ibid. p.184.
65 Ibid. p.254.

that found disfavor in the eyes of Schechter,[67] such an explanation seems highly implausible. If Schechter had sought to transform the Seminary into a denominationally distinct Conservative institution by purging all Orthodox persons from positions on the faculty, he would hardly have appointed — as he did — men such as Alexander Marx, a fully Orthodox Jew who was the son-in-law of the famed Orthodox savant Rabbi David Zvi Hoffmann of Berlin; or Orthodox Rabbi Moses Hyamson, formerly *dayyan* of the Beth Din in London, to the Chair in Codes in 1915.[68] Instead, the whole incident with Drachman and the ultimate decision to remove him from the faculty altogether reflects Schechter's judgment that Drachman was not a first-rate scholar. Indeed, if one compares the academic attainments of Drachman with the other men Schechter appointed to the faculty, one can hardly avoid this conclusion. Schechter was absolutely committed to having only men of the highest scholarly capability and achievement instruct his students as they proceeded through their course of study.

To make sure that candidates qualified for the privilege of being taught by these men, formal standards of admission were established. Students were required to "be members of the Jewish faith [and] of good moral character." They were also "expected to observe the Jewish Sabbath and to conform to the Jewish dietary laws." Piety and character were necessary ingredients for a student's admission into rabbinical candidacy. However, they were not sufficient.[69]

Schechter further demanded that each successful candidate for admission to the Rabbinical Department "should have received from a university or college in good standing the Degree of Bachelor of Arts." The Seminary was poised to become a post-baccalaureate institution. The days of devoting instructional time to the teaching of high school students had long passed. Furthermore, students were expected to pass a battery of entrance examinations on a variety of subjects prior to their admission to the rabbinical course of study. The successful candidate was al-

---

66 Ibid. pp.258–60

67 Ibid. p.261.

68 Israel Davidson, "The Academic Aspect and Growth of the Rabbinical Department," p.82.

69 *The Jewish Theological Seminary of America — Circular of Information* 1903–1904, pp.5–6.

ready to know the "elementary grammar of the Hebrew language" and was expected to display an ability to translate and interpret "the whole of the Pentateuch" at sight. Mastery of the Book of Genesis, along with "Targum Onkelos and the commentary of Rashi and Rashi characters," was required, as was familiarity with portions of the Books of Judges, Isaiah, Psalms, and Daniel. Beyond erudition in the Bible, the fledgling candidate had to display his facility in rabbinical literature as well. He was required to pass an examination in the mishnaic order *Seder Mo'ed*, and he was further expected to be familiar with the "first perek of Tractate *Berakhot*, pages 1–13." Finally, the successful candidate had to demonstrate a "general acquaintance" with Jewish liturgy and history. In formalizing these requirements for admission. Schechter was determined that the course of instruction in the rabbinical program at JTS be conducted on an advanced level.[70]

The curriculum in the Rabbinical School, as Schechter himself phrased it, "tried . . . to include . . . almost every branch of Jewish literature."[71] At the outset of the Schechter era, the course of instruction fell into six categories — Bible, the Babylonian and Jerusalem Talmud, Jewish history and the history of Jewish literature, theology and catechism, homiletics (including elocution and pastoral work), and *hazzanut*. The course of study was to extend "over a period of four years" and involved "lectures and instruction." The student — at the completion of four years of study — was required to "pass a satisfactory examination and write a thesis approved by the Faculty" in order to "be entitled to the Degree of Rabbi."[72] These last requirements underscore and highlight the vision Schechter held of the rabbinate as a learned academic modern profession.

The actual course content of the JTS curriculum at the beginning of Schechter's administration continued to center around the study of rabbinical literature as it had under Morais. Senior students were enrolled weekly in twenty-five hours of classroom instruction. Seven hours were devoted to the study of Talmud — four hours to Tractate *Hullin*, one hour each to *Shabbat* and *Gittin*, and one hour to Tractate *Shekalim*

70 Ibid.
71 Schechter, *Seminary Addresses*, p.20. In keeping with the "rationalistic outlook" of the era, texts in Jewish mysticism-Schechter's sentiments notwithstanding-were of course not included in the curriculum.
72 *The Jewish Theological Seminary of America — Circular of Information*, 1903–1904, p.6.

in the Jerusalem Talmud. In addition, students engaged in the study of the *Shulḥan Arukh* for four hours each week — two hours in *Yoreh Deʾah*, and one each in *Eben ha-Ezer* and *Oraḥ Ḥayim*. *Ḥoshen Mishpat* remained totally ignored. Midrash occupied another hour of classroom instruction each week, as did Judeo-Aramaic grammar, history of Jewish literature, Jewish history, theology, and Hebrew grammar. There was a weekly one-hour lecture devoted to theology and two more hours were spent on philosophy. In the fall semester, Cyrus Adler delivered a one-hour lecture on the Jewish calendar, and in the spring Schechter taught the students liturgy during the same time period. Bible — in the form of Leviticus, Psalms, and Jeremiah and their traditional rabbinic commentaries — was confined to three hours a week, and one hour a week was devoted to the "practical rabbinate" under the title of homiletics.[73]

Several observations are apposite at this point. First, the content of the curriculum reveals that at this juncture in the history of the Seminary virtually no time was spent on practical training for the rabbinate. As David M. Ackerman has observed,

> Homiletics included all the "practical" training deemed necessary for the Jewish ministry. By 1912 this area filled three hours a week of class time, up from one hour in 1902, reflecting an increased awareness on the seminary's part of the need for training in such areas as education and "ministering to the sick and dying," all in "preparation for the practical part of the minister's vocation."[74]

During the course of the decade, Schechter may have been forced to concede that more than one hour each week had to be spent on issues of the practical rabbinate if his ordinands were to be prepared to fulfill their vocational tasks. Nevertheless, the small amount of time spent on such topics bespeaks his belief that a mastery of classical Jewish literature — not attention devoted to practical matters — was the prerequisite that would qualify an individual student for the title of rabbi. In this sense, the content of the curriculum was totally consonant with the sentiment Schechter had expressed years earlier when he wrote, "No man

73 Ibid. p.10.
74 David M. Ackerman, "A Not Too Distant Mirror: The Seminary Rabbinical School Curriculum," *Conservative Judaism* (Summer, 1992): p.51.

in authority is greater than the source whence his authority is derived. The authority of the Rabbi is derived from the Torah."

The heart of the JTS course of instruction during the Schechter era centered upon Talmud and related literature. The study of Talmud and codes alone comprised almost half the instructional hours. Furthermore, many of the other courses, such as theology liturgy, midrash, history of Jewish literature, and even Bible, focused on classical rabbinical sources as well. Hence, the advanced Seminary student of this era — as had his student predecessor a decade earlier — devoted at least three-quarters of his week to what could be labeled classical rabbinic literature. In addition, the courses in philosophy and Jewish history were devoted to reading the works of Saadia, Halevi, and Maimonides in Hebrew. All of this testifies to the text-centered nature of the Schechter curriculum and the Schechter ideal of a rabbi as one grounded in classical Jewish sources.

The role occupied by Bible in the curriculum also merits special commentary. From its inception, the Seminary — all its pious claims to the import of critical scholarship notwithstanding — held that the Bible was off-limits to critical inquiry. Kohut had stated, "To us the Pentateuch is a *noli me tangere!* Hands off! We disclaim all honor of handling the sharp knife which cuts the Bible into a thousand pieces."[75] Schechter shared this view and, in a famous and oft-quoted phrase, equated "Higher Criticism" with "Higher Anti-Semitism." In a passionate passage, he wrote, "The Bible is our sole *raison d'être*, and it is just this which the Higher Anti-Semitism is seeking to destroy, denying all our claims to the past, and leaving it without hope for the future. . . . The Bible is our patent of nobility granted to us by the Almighty God, and if we disown the Bible, leaving it to the tender mercies of a Wellhausen, Stade and Duhm, and other beautiful souls working away at diminishing 'the nimbus of the Chosen People,' the world will disown us."[76] Decades were to pass before the Seminary would embrace a critical approach to the teaching of Bible. During this era, and for years to follow, JTS would be content in its curriculum to avoid critical questions concerning the Bible and its authorship. Instead, as the explicit curriculum demonstrates, the hours of instruction devoted to Bible would be limited altogether, just as they

75 Ibid. p. 49.
76 Schechter, *Seminary Addresses*, pp. 37–38.

had been during the Morais era. Furthermore, the instruction that was offered in Bible would be conducted — at least during these years — in accord with classical rabbinical commentary.

The Adler Years

Schechter's successor, Cyrus Adler, became president in 1915 and remained in office until his death in 1940. An analysis of the catalogs published during the Adler era reveals that the curriculum during these years remained substantially unchanged. While the scope of instruction by 1917 had expanded to include midrashim, codes, and liturgy as separate subject areas,[77] this only gave formal expression to a curriculum that already was being taught.

The alterations that did emerge during the Adler years were relatively minor in terms of their impact upon the overall curriculum of the Seminary Senior Rabbinical Department. In 1919, a new subject area — Jewish Communal Studies — was developed. The inclusion of this field "no doubt reflected," as Ackerman has put it, "Mordecai Kaplan's influence, as it indicated a shifting view of the rabbi's role. . . . While still training scholars, teachers, and preachers, the Seminary recognized a need for the performance of 'social work' and various other communal functions by American rabbis."[78] Fourteen years later (in 1933) Simon Greenberg was added to the faculty as lecturer in education.[79] However, as we shall see, such courses for the "practical ministry" never occupied more than a tiny fraction of the student's weekly schedule. Indeed, it would be a mistake to view the inclusion of these areas as reflecting any type of significant transformation in course content of the curriculum. In a representative *Register* from this period, the area of Jewish Communal Studies is described as being comprised of a single course, entitled "Problems of the Rabbinate," and one hour per week of actual class time was allotted to it. It consisted "of lectures on Jewish education, Jewish philanthropy, industrial problems, correctional work and recreational institutions."[80]

The only other significant change that occurred in the emphasis of the curriculum also took place in 1933. As Israel Davidson has observed:

---

77 The Jewish Theological Seminary of America — Register, 1917–18, pp. 10–11.
78 Ackerman, "A Not Too Distant Mirror," p. 53.
79 Davidson, "The Academic Aspect and Growth of the Rabbinical Department," p. 84.

On June 9, 1933, the Faculty recommended that the curriculum of the Seminary be changed, so as to concentrate on the lectures in the first two years and to enable the student to take specialized work in the Seminar courses during the third and fourth years. . . . In the third and fourth years students were [also] required to select at least one seminar chosen from among the following subjects: Bible, History and Literature, Talmud, Liturgy and Medieval Poetry, Modern Hebrew Literature, Codes, History of Religion, and Theology.[81]

The thesis requirement had been abandoned as a prerequisite for ordination in 1928. As a result, Ackerman has speculated that this system of lectures and seminars "was intended to replace the old thesis requirement . . . as a means of achieving scholarly expertise in a particular field."[82] In sum, these changes in no way attenuated the commitment of the Seminary to the ideal of *Wissenschaft*. Indeed, they only reinforced the vision of the rabbi as scholar.

Otherwise, the actual hours and content of instruction throughout the 1920s remained remarkably similar to what had obtained in the curriculum during the years of the Schechter administration. Requirements for admission by and large remained the same. Students had to observe "the Sabbath and holidays" as well as "the dietary laws." They were also required to earn the "bachelor's degree from a college or university in good standing" in order to gain admission "into the . . . upper classes" and were subjected to a battery of examinations in Bible, Hebrew grammar, and Talmud. In 1920–1921, the course of study was set at seven years, and student classes were "designated as Freshman A and B, Sophomore A and B, Junior A and B, and Senior." Students who did well on their entrance examinations were allowed to be admitted to the upper classes. In this way, the Seminary took cognizance of the diverse levels of Judaica backgrounds and textual competencies that increasingly marked the members of the student body.[83]

An examination of the actual twenty-three to twenty-six hours devoted each week to formal classroom instruction throughout the 1920s and

80 The Jewish Theological Seminary of America — Register, 1923–1934, pp. 11, 15.

81 Davidson, "The Academic Aspect and Growth of the Rabbinical Department," p. 84.

82 Ackerman, "A Not Too Distant Mirror," p. 53.

1930s reveals that Bible continued to be studied for two to three hours per week. Again, critical study of the biblical text was eschewed in favor of rabbinical commentaries. In addition, students were required to read additional chapters of the Bible over their summer vacation and were tested upon their mastery of the text "in the Autumn soon after the beginning of the term."[84] Four to five hours were devoted to talmudic tractates such as *Yoma, Kiddushin, Sanhedrin, Ḥullin, Shabbat, Gittin,* and *Pesaḥim.* Texts from the *Shulḥan Arukh* (with the continued exception of *Ḥoshen Mishpat*) were studied two hours weekly by students in the four upper classes while one to two hours weekly were spent upon Hebrew grammar and composition. Medieval Hebrew texts were studied one hour weekly, and lecture courses on the Bible and Talmud, with titles such as "Monuments and the Bible," "Biblical Archaeology," "History of the Halakhah," and "Outlines of Rabbinic Jurisprudence" comprised two hours of the weekly curriculum. One hour of medieval philosophy was required, and one hour of weekly course work was devoted in the last three years to the study of liturgy. Midrash and "Lectures on the Religious Functions of the Rabbi" received an hour each of instructional time, and three hours of lecture focused upon "Post-Biblical History" and "Literature" — each year of the latter course being devoted to texts from a different period of the Jewish past. "Courses in the Practical Ministry" were confined formally in the 1920s to two hours per week — one hour listed under the rubric, "Problems of the Rabbinate — Special Lectures," and another to *hazzanut.* In the 1930s, an additional hour under this category was devoted to "Education" and one more to "Public Speaking." Finally, all students were required to spend additional time on the study of Talmud. The more advanced students were "required to read privately . . . 30 folios" of Talmud each year while only "15 folios" were demanded of the

83 The Jewish Theological Seminary of America — Register, 1923–1924, pp. 15–16. Catalogs for diverse years such as 1927–1928 and 1936–1937 reflect virtually the same requirements for admission. The similarity — if not identity — of these requirements bespeaks a continuity in the vision of the rabbinate held by the Seminary during the first half part of century. In fact, with allowance being made for the fact that the Seminary came to recognize that more students with little or no facility in classical Judaica desired to be admitted to the Rabbinical School at the end of the century, these requirements for admission have basically remained in force until the present day. As such, they reflect the constancy of the Seminary ideal of the rabbi as one who possesses textual competency.

84 The Jewish Theological Seminary of America — Register, 1927–1928, pp. 12–13.

less advanced students. In sum, the curriculum throughout the Adler administration remained overwhelmingly devoted, as it had under Schechter, to the study of texts and historical scholarship.[85]

The fidelity displayed in the curriculum to the rabbinical vision articulated by Schechter during the period of 1915 to 1940 can be explained in several ways. First, throughout these twenty-five years Adler himself was involved in a whole host of activities. In fact, throughout his incumbency as President of the Seminary, Adler did not even establish his principal residency in New York. Instead, his home remained in Philadelphia, and he divided his time between Philadelphia and New York.[86] Consequently, he actually had relatively little time to devote to curricular matters at the Seminary. Moreover, his admiration for Schechter was unbounded. Adler had not only been instrumental in persuading Schechter to come to the Seminary in 1902; he had also agreed to serve as chair of the Board of Directors during the Schechter administration. When Schechter died, Adler delivered the eulogy at the funeral and said of Schechter, "Through his teachings and the inspiration of his character, he has raised up a following not only of his immediate disciples, but among the larger number that he influenced, who in their humble way will carry on his traditions of character and learning. The hope of Israel will live through him."[87] All this reveals that Adler not only lacked the time to alter the curriculum of the Seminary in a significant manner but also had little inclination to do so. He shared Schechter's vision of Judaism and the rabbinate and, with the exception of a few minor changes, was content to allow the content and scope of the curriculum as developed by Schechter to remain undisturbed during his tenure as president.

The distinctive nature of that curriculum and the vision of the rabbinate it embodied can be highlighted when we compare it briefly to the curricula of the Rabbi Isaac Elchanan Theological Seminary of Yeshiva Univer-

---

85 All of these curricular details can be found in the Jewish Theological Seminary of America Register for the years 1923–24, 1927–28, and 1936–37.

86 Cyrus Adler, *I Have Considered the Days* (Philadelphia: Jewish Publication Society, 1941), p. 291. This autobiographical memoir describes in great detail the myriad activities in which Adler was involved throughout his variegated and multi-faceted career.

87 Ira Robinson, ed., *Cyrus Adler: Selected Letters* (Philadelphia: Jewish Publication Society, 1985), vol. 1, p. 298.

sity and Hebrew Union College during the first decades of the 1900s. As Aaron Rothkoff has indicated, during the 1920s many members of the American Jewish community "did not understand wherein . . . Yeshiva differed from the Jewish Theological Seminary." After all, "many persons active in the administration and faculty of the Jewish Theological Seminary during this period were Orthodox or close to Orthodox in their theology and practice." Indeed, this was a period in American Jewish history when a man such as Adler could still be invited to address a convention of the Orthodox *Agudat ha-Rabbanim* on the subject of Sabbath observance. As a result, laypersons such as Louis Marshall from the board of the Seminary and Judge Otto Rosalsky of Yeshiva "felt there was no need for the community to support two major rabbinical seminaries if their religious viewpoints were so similar" and they even went so far as to advocate a merger of the two institutions during the last half of the 1920s.[88]

Rabbi Bernard Revel, president of Yeshiva, was adamantly opposed to a merger, and he took up the cudgels against such a proposal in a mimeographed article entitled "Seminary and Yeshiva" which he circulated to the entire membership of Yeshiva's Board of Directors. In it, Revel pointed to curriculum as the distinguishing characteristic between the two institutions. He claimed that the students at Yeshiva — whether native or foreign born — had uniformly intensive backgrounds in the study of talmudic texts and commentaries and could study Talmud at Yeshiva on a highly advanced level. Students at the Seminary generally did not possess such backgrounds; thus the level of talmudic study at JTS could not match that of Yeshiva. Moreover, Revel noted, students at Yeshiva spent ten months of the year studying twenty-three hours of Talmud weekly. This was in contrast to the eight hours weekly devoted to Talmud and codes for eight months each year at the Seminary. "This difference in time," Revel wrote, "must show in the nature of the material presented for study, in the method pursued, and in the students' achievements." Revel conceded that the Seminary gave its students extensive training in Jewish history and literature. However, as an Orthodox rabbi, his vision of the rabbinate compelled him to assert that such study was irrelevant to qualifying an individual for rab-

88   Aaron Rothkoff, *Bernard Revel: Builder of American Jewish Orthodoxy* (Philadelphia: Jewish Publication Society, 1972), pp. 99–103.

binical ordination. Instead, Revel held that the curriculum in a rabbinical school should focus almost exclusively on intensive talmudic study.
Mastery of this literature alone could qualify the student for the title of
rabbi. The level of talmudic instruction and the time allotted to it at Yeshiva reflected his vision. The content and structure of the curriculum
at the Seminary reflected another.[89]

If the Seminary curriculum of this period could be perceived by the
president of Yeshiva University as insufficiently devoted to the study of
Talmud and overly directed towards *Wissenschaft* and academic scholarship, a different type of perception emerges if we contrast the Schechter
curriculum to that of Hebrew Union College during these years. As
noted earlier, there were no discernible differences in the curricula of
the two institutions at the end of the era of Morais and Wise. With the
selection of Kaufmann Kohler as president of HUC in 1903, however,
significant distinctions in the rabbinical courses of instruction began to
appear. This is not to say that there were not vital points of agreement
between them as to the manner in which the modern rabbi should be
trained and educated. After all, Kohler and Schechter possessed similar backgrounds: both were European born and had an absolute command over both rabbinical literature and modern scholarship. The two
worked together on a number of academic projects – notably *The Jewish Encyclopedia* – and were close personal friends. In an address he
delivered at the dedication of the new building at the Jewish Theological
Seminary on April 26, 1903, Kohler, in a tone reminiscent of Schechter,
spoke both of the indispensable role that contemporary scholarship
played in legitimating the claim of the rabbi to authority and of the obligation of the modern rabbinical school to impart such knowledge to
its students. "Pulpit oratory evokes tears or smiles, assent or dissent; *it
is the seat of learning vested with authority which endows the man in
the pulpit with the knowledge and skill to substantiate every righteous
claim*."[90] Or, as Kohler once more contended thirteen years later, "In
order to be a true leader, ... the modern rabbi must take his stand on
high, keeping ever abreast of ideas, the philosophical and scientific ...
problems of the age in order to be a safe and trusted guide to the erring

89 Ibid. pp.108–10.
90 Typescript taken from the American Jewish Archives of "An Address Delivered by
    Kaufmann Kohler at the Dedication of the New Building of the Jewish Theological
    Seminary of America, April 26, 1903." (Emphasis mine.)

and struggling. . . . We need more leaders who go back to the fountains of Jewish lore and know how to strike the dry rock to make it flow with living waters of knowledge."[91]

In order to achieve this goal, Kohler, like Schechter, appointed masters of *Wissenschaft* to the faculty of HUC. During his tenure, great scholars such as Jacob Lauterbach, David Neumark, and Julian Morgenstern were added to the teaching staff. In fact, it was the aim of Kohler, as it had been of both Morais and Schechter, to create a seminary for "American Israel" that could "well boast that its work for the Jewish faith and Jewish learning" would "outdo that of European Jewry."[92] Nevertheless, the shared commitment Kohler and Schechter displayed toward the mastery of modern scholarship as a prerequisite for the rabbinical office should not mask the considerable differences in attitude between them. Nor, as alluded to above, were these differences confined to the theoretical realm. They were to find concrete expression in the content of the curriculum each man initiated.

Kohler, unlike Schechter, possessed what can charitably be described as a noticeable disdain for the Talmud. In 1904, he wrote, "There is no justification whatsoever for . . . the most precious time of the student" to be "spent upon Halakic discussions." He spoke disparagingly of the "hair-splitting dialectics of the Talmud" as well as "the stagnant form of the Halakah and the inane discussions that fill so many pages of the Babylonian Gemarah." Kohler therefore contended, "A Jewish Theological School concentrating its efforts upon the Halakah resembles a medieval fortress which looks formidable to the beholder but can not hold out against the implements of modern warfare."[93] This did not mean that the Talmud and classical legal codes of the rabbinical tradition were of no import to Kohler. However, as he asserted, "The teaching of the Talmud and Codes becomes profitable for us, who are no longer bound to the Shulḥan Arukh, only when such practical questions as

91 Kaufmann Kohler, "The Staff of Priesthood and the Staff of Leadership," in *A Living Faith: Selected Sermons and Addresses from the Literary Remains of Kaufmann Kohler*, ed. by Samuel S. Cohon (Cincinnati: Hebrew Union College Press, 1948), pp. 148–49.

92 Kaufmann Kohler, "The Hebrew Union College of Yesterday and a Great Desideratum in its Curriculum Today," in *Studies, Addresses, and Personal Papers* (New York: Alumni Association of Hebrew Union College, 1931), pp. 555–57.

93 Kaufmann Kohler, "The Four Ells of the Halakah and the Requirements of a Modern Jewish Theological School," *Hebrew Union College Annual*, 1904, pp. 9–10, 17.

the marriage and divorce laws, the funeral and mourning rites, or the Sabbath and Festivals are discussed, so as to be brought into relation to modern life."[94]

Kohler further distinguished himself from Schechter in his attitude toward biblical criticism and its place in the curriculum of a rabbinical school. Kohler held that it was "only in keeping with this narrow Halakistic view that Higher Criticism" could be deemed "dangerous or alien to the scope of Rabbinic theology. The entire history and literature of Judaism remains a book with seven seals to him who shuts his eyes to the disclosures of . . . modern Bible research." In what must be seen as a barb directed at Schechter, Kohler continued:

> Such brilliant phraseology as is the label "Higher Anti-Semitism" given to Higher Criticism may captivate many — *baaḥizat enayyim* — by its seeming truth, but it cannot stand the test of scrutiny. . . . We cannot escape the conclusions of Higher Criticism. . . . What geology did for us in laying bare the different strata of the earth telling of the various epochs of creation, Higher Criticism does in disclosing the various stages of growth of the truth of divine revelation.[95]

Furthermore, Kohler felt the Hebrew Union College, "with its outspoken Reform principle,"[96] could express its view of Judaism as one of "progress, of growth and transformation" only through the medium of "critical and historical research."[97] Biblical criticism was not to be eschewed in the curriculum of HUC during the Kohler administration. Instead, it was to become a handmaiden for the legitimization of Reform in what was now to be a distinctly Reform rabbinical seminary.

The curriculum taught within the walls of the College during the era of Kaufmann Kohler increasingly conformed to Kohler's vision of Reform Judaism. It was a vision that conceived of Judaism in religious-

94 Kohler, "The Hebrew Union College of Yesterday and a Great Desideratum in its Curriculum Today," p. 558.

95 Kohler, "The Four Ells of the Halakah and the Requirements of a Modern Jewish Theological School," pp. 10, 12–13.

96 Kohler, "The College and the Seminary."

97 Kaufmann Kohler, "What the Hebrew Union College Stands For," in *Studies, Addresses, and Personal Papers*, p. 443.

spiritual categories alone and condemned Zionism as "ignorance and irreligion." Kohler told students that they had two choices — to serve "a Jewish nationalism without God, or a Judaism inseparably linked to its universal God, its Torah, and its world-mission."[98] As Michael Meyer has observed, modern Hebrew literature and Zionism would find no place in the curriculum of HUC during the Kohler years. Talmud and classical rabbinical literature would recede in importance, and the Bible — particularly the books of the Prophets — would be assigned the central place in the HUC course of study.[99] An analysis of the catalogs published during these years bears out the accuracy of Meyer's observation.

By 1903, the year before Kohler was appointed as president, the ideal of a rabbinical student mastering 150 folios of Talmud prior to his entry to the five-year Collegiate Department of HUC had long since been abandoned. Nevertheless, five to six of the fifteen weekly class hours were assigned to Mishnah, Talmud, and codes. Courses examined the tractates of *Gittin, Yebamot, Kiddushin, Ketubot,* and *Shabbat* during the five-year course of study in the Collegiate Department along with the codes relevant to these talmudic sources. Bible was confined to two to four hours a week. In addition, one- to two-credit courses in philosophy, history, grammar, modern Hebrew, and Arabic were given. Systematic theology and ethics were also taught — as they were at JTS — to students in their final year; and there was a thesis requirement. Courses in the practical rabbinate were essentially confined to homiletics in the third and fourth year and pastoral theology in the fifth.[100]

Kohler immediately sought to expand and change the course of study. In 1904, he drew up a proposed curriculum for the College, which eliminated modern Hebrew. Furthermore, in the Preparatory Department, no Talmud at all was required. In the five-year Collegiate Department, Mishnah, Talmud, and *Halakhah* were assigned six hours in the first two years and four credits in years three and four. In the fifth year, no Talmud was taught, though Kohler did propose that graduating students study the "History of Talmudism, Karaism, and Cabbalah" two hours weekly. A course on the "History of the Sadducees, Pharisees, and Essenes" was proposed for the fourth year. In suggesting

98   Ibid. pp. 441–42.
99   Meyer, "A Centennial History of the Hebrew Union College," pp. 59–60.
100   *Hebrew Union College Catalog and Fragrant,* 1903, pp. 20–24.

these latter two courses, Kohler emulated the curriculum initiated by Abraham Geiger at the Berlin *Hochschule*, for there Geiger had included courses on the history of Jewish sectarianism as well as of those groups in Jewish history that did not acknowledge the authority of the Talmud.[101] Interestingly, in light of the paramount role they were later to assume in the curriculum, Bible and commentaries were offered only three hours weekly in the first three years, and an additional hour was proposed for years four and five. Other courses in history, philosophy, grammar, midrash, aggadah, liturgy, apocalyptic and pseudepigraphic literature, Apocrypha, comparative religion, New Testament and Koran, systematic theology, and Jewish ethical literature were offered at various points during the student's matriculation in the Collegiate Department. All these academic courses were to be supplemented by practical courses on pedagogy, Sabbath School work, homiletics, and elocution. These latter courses were generally restricted to two hours each week, though in the final year they were expanded to five of the twenty weekly course load hours in which each senior student was required to matriculate.[102]

The HUC 1906 catalog indicates that Kohler was not able to realize his ideal curriculum immediately. Of the 138 units prescribed for graduation over the five-year course of study in the collegiate classes, thirty units fell under the rubric of Talmud, though only ten to twelve were actually assigned to talmudic text. The other eighteen to twenty required units were taken from Mishnah and codes. An equal weight of thirty credits was assigned to the study of Bible, reflecting the increasing importance attached to this subject area in the curriculum. Midrashic literature was defined as a separate subject area and was elevated to fourteen required units of study. The student took four units each year in philosophy and history, and in the third year a two-unit course in liturgy was required. Theology, homiletics, ethics, and pedagogy were assigned students during their last three years of study. Electives in all these areas, as well as Hebrew and cognate languages, music, sociology, and elocution were also provided to complete the curriculum.

101   Ellenson, *Rabbi Esriel Hildesheimer and the Creation of a Modern Jewish Orthodoxy* (Tuscaloosa, University of Alabama Press, 1990), p.160.
102   Kohler's proposed curriculum is found in Kohler, "The Four Ells of the Halakah and the Requirements of a Modern Jewish Theological School," pp.21–25.

These course allotments are indicative of the shifts that were beginning to take place in the curriculum of HUC. Several subject areas had been added to the course of instruction extant during the Wise era. Most significantly, more weight was now assigned to Bible and midrash, while Talmud and halakhic literature — still occupying a significant place in the HUC curriculum — started to diminish in prominence.[103] This trend, seen in nascent form in 1906, was fully manifest by 1921–1922, the last year of Kohler's presidency.

Courses in a wide variety of subject areas such as philosophy, history, and midrash were still included in the 1921–1922 curriculum. In addition, Kohler demanded that each student enroll in a course entitled "The History of Judaism and its Sects." Courses designed to prepare students for the practical rabbinate still constituted a relatively small part of the entire curriculum, but this area was expanded. For example, six of the fifteen class hours during the senior year were devoted to issues related to the practical rabbinate — homiletics, practical theology, ethics and pedagogy, and applied sociology. A commitment to *Wissenschaft* remained paramount, and HUC continued to stipulate a written thesis based on original research as a requirement for ordination. Most important, Kohler constructed a curriculum that centered upon the study of Bible. Classical rabbinical texts — particularly Talmud — continued to receive less and less attention. The 1921–1922 catalog indicates that five to seven hours of instruction were devoted each week to Bible—particularly the prophetic books — for students during their first four years in the Collegiate Department. Talmud, in contrast, was not even taught during the first year of the advanced program. Instead, first-year students studied Mishnah two hours each week. They were exposed to Talmud for three hours in the second year and two hours weekly in the third. Students in the junior and senior years were enrolled in "Topics from Hullin and Codes" for two units both semesters during the former year and in "Topics from Kiddushin, Gittin, Yebamot, and Codes" for the same amount of credit during the latter one. In sum, the student who completed his rabbinical training during the last year of Kohler's tenure as president took a minimum of twenty-seven units of Bible, but only eleven units of Mishnah, Talmud, and codes by the time he completed his course of study. The curriculum of HUC at the end of the Kohler

103 *Catalog of the Hebrew Union College*, 1906, pp. 59–75.

Administration displayed little fidelity to the course of instruction of the Wise era.[104]

Kohler's aim was to produce a Reform rabbi prepared to serve a denominationally distinct movement. The era of Wise, when Hebrew Union College strove to educate rabbis who could serve traditional as well as liberal Jewish American congregations, had passed. Orthodox Judaism was obviously of no concern to Kohler. Nor did this transformation in the curriculum of HUC disturb Julian Morgenstern, Kohler's successor to the presidency (in 1923). An eminent biblical scholar, Morgenstern shared the curricular vision and Jewish outlook of Kohler. This is not to say that their views were identical; nor does it mean that there were no curricular changes at HUC during the Morgenstern years. The appointment of a man like Samuel S. Cohon to the faculty during the 1920s assured modern Hebrew and Zionism a voice in the life of the College that was absent during the Kohler administration. Nevertheless, Morgenstern basically perpetuated the curriculum he had inherited from Kohler. It principally focused upon Bible and paid considerable attention to history and literature, philosophy, and midrash. Courses in theology and ethics persisted, and a minimum of eleven of the seventy-three total credits required for ordination were devoted to concerns of the practical rabbinate. The Talmud, in contrast, was relegated to a minor place in the curriculum. A student could complete his course of study with only eight credits in Talmud, a subject area that included Mishnah and codes. The College no longer strove to imbue its graduates with a high degree of proficiency in classical rabbinical texts. Kohler's curricular vision would govern the Hebrew Union College for most of the twentieth century.[105]

This analysis of the rabbinical school curricula at both Yeshiva University and Hebrew Union College during the first decades of the twentieth century highlights the distinctive nature of rabbinical training offered by the Jewish Theological Seminary. On the one hand, the

104 Catalog of the Hebrew Union College, 1921–1922, pp. 15–23.
105 See, for example, the Catalogue of the Hebrew Union College (1923–1924), pp. 45–51, for a representative presentation of the curriculum at HUC during the Morgenstern years. Indeed, a decade later, the Catalogue of the Hebrew Union College, 1932–1933, pp. 61–71, displays the same emphases.

Seminary clearly rejected the educational model of YU. The insularity of the traditional yeshiva curriculum perpetuated what the Seminary saw as a limited and parochial vision of the inner life and creative dynamics of the people Israel. Conversely, the content of the HUC curriculum as it evolved under Kohler was equally unacceptable — albeit for different reasons — to men such as Schechter and his colleagues. The limited requirements of HUC in the area of talmudic literature and the elevated role assigned to Bible in the curriculum of the Reform seminary reflected what the men at JTS regarded as a truncated understanding of Judaism, despite the importance both Schechter and Kohler ascribed to critical study and modern scholarship.

The curriculum established in each of these three schools embodied three distinctive approaches to Judaism. The days when matters of observance alone divided the Seminary in New York from the College in Cincinnati were over. Diverse curricula now clearly differentiated these schools from one another — and by extension these differences reflected alternative visions of Judaism that remained definitive for both Conservative and Reform Judaism throughout the succeeding century.

Modern Responsa

14

Women and the Study of Torah

A Responsum by
Rabbi Zalman Sorotzkin of Jerusalem

Patriarchal cultures have regularly assigned separate spheres of influence to men and women. In general, such cultures have reserved the public arena for men, and designated the domestic realm as the proper area for the activity of women. Jewish civilization, as Susan Grossman and Rivka Haut have pointed out, has been no exception to this pattern.[1] As a result of this role-assignment, the realm of Torah study within traditional Judaism has throughout history remained the near-exclusive province of men. Undoubtedly, students of gender would link this phenomenon to the implications that such study possesses for the exercise of public positions of power and authority. In classical Jewish religious civilization, one unlettered in the law could hardly hope to exercise control in communal affairs. Indeed, the source of Jewish religious authority has traditionally been grounded in a mastery of classical Jewish legal texts. Assignment of women to the domestic sphere has therefore naturally placed a concomitant limitation on the access granted women to the study of traditional Jewish legal-literary texts, for allowing women such access would have facilitated expression of a female public voice.

In light of these gender-role considerations, it is hardly a surprise that the ideal position allocated women in the field of Torah study has not been that of active participants in the educational process, but rather that of domestic facilitators for their husbands and sons. The following passage from the Babylonian Talmud, *Berakhot* 17a justifies and reflects these notions and attitudes regarding gender roles and status:

> Whereby do women earn merit? By making their sons go to synagogue to learn Scripture and their husbands to the House of Study

1 Susan Grossman and Rivka Haut, *Daughters of the King: Women and the Synagogue* (Philadelphia: Jewish Publication Society, 1992), pp.xxii–xxv. Also see chap.15, "Gender, Halakhah and Women's Suffrage," in the present volume.

to learn Mishnah, and waiting for their husbands until they return from the House of Study.

Consequently, the statement of Ben Azzai in *Sotah* 20a, "A man is obligated to teach his daughter Torah," was not cited in traditional Jewish society as providing a warrant for establishing schools for the Jewish education of girls. More often, the attitude expressed by Rabbi Eliezer (*Sotah* 21b) — "Anyone who teaches his daughter Torah, it is as if he taught her *tiflut* (licentiousness)" — was more often quoted as a compelling rationale for denying women access to Torah study.[2]

Despite this attitude, there have been women of great Jewish learning possessed of religious authority throughout Jewish history.[3] Furthermore, as the notion of gender equality has spread throughout the modern world, the opportunity as well as the necessity for women to participate actively in the realm of advanced text study has grown considerably even in traditional Jewish circles. Historians such as Paula Hyman and Deborah Weissman have provided ample documentation of and explanation for this phenomenon, and there are today an unprecedented number of women involved in serious Jewish textual study.[4] A number of Jewish legal authorities have applauded these developments. Others have opposed them.[5] In this essay, we present a responsum by Rabbi

2   For the meaning of these *Sotah* passages in their original context, see Judith Hauptman, *Rereading the Rabbis: A Woman's Voice* (Boulder, Colo.: Westview Press, 1998), pp. 22–23 and 43; and Judith Romney Wegner, *Chattel or Person? The Status of Women in the Mishnah* (New York and Oxford: Oxford University Press, 1988), p. 161.

3   The historical literature on this topic is voluminous in both English and Hebrew. One of the most important historical surveys of this issue is Judith R. Baskin, ed., *Jewish Women in Historical Perspective* (Detroit: Wayne State University Press, 1991). For a fine presentation and analysis of the halakhic literature on this subject, see David Golinkin, "Women as Halakhic Authorities," *Responsa of the Va'ad Halakhah of the Rabbinical Assembly of Israel* (1992), vol. 4, pp. 107–17.

4   See Paula Hyman, *Gender and Assimilation in Modern Jewish History: The Roles and Representation of Women* (Seattle: University of Washington Press, 1995); and Deborah Weissman, "Education of Jewish Women," *Encyclopedia Judaica Yearbook* (1986–1987). Again, the literature on this subject is quite extensive. In citing Hyman and Weissman, we do not mean to neglect others who have written on it. Instead, we cite them as two of the most prominent representative scholars who have addressed this matter.

5   For a representative and instructive bibliography of the halakhic sources — ancient

Zalman Sorotzkin (1881–1966) on this issue: it reflects how and why the classical attitudes of rabbinic civilization were challenged, and arguably altered, as a result of the Jewish encounter with modernity.

The Sorotzkin Responsum in Orthodox Writings on Women and Torah Study

While the Sorotzkin responsum is hardly the only modern responsum concerning the question of women and Torah study, this text bears careful analysis for several reasons. First, it confronts the issue in a way that is representative of the approach taken by a number of modern *poskim* on this and related matters.[6] Sorotzkin's viewpoint was not an isolated one. His stance both echoed attitudes that had already been put forth by several earlier rabbis on this issue and foreshadowed a position that would be adopted and expanded upon by other halakhic authorities later in the century. These trends will be considered more fully below.

Secondly, the Sorotzkin responsum can be said to possess something akin to "canonical status" in subsequent Orthodox writings and rulings on the topic. In *The Jewish Woman in Rabbinic Literature*, Menachem M. Brayer cites Sorotzkin as "a leading rabbinic authority" on this matter, as does Avraham Weiss in his *Women at Prayer*.[7] Elyakim Ellinson, in his widely circulated and highly influential *Bein ha-Ishah le-Yotzrah*, notes that Sorotzkin is a vital link in the chain of great twentieth-century rabbinic authorities who wrote on this issue. Of course, Ellinson correctly observes that the Sorotzkin position was already foreshadowed in an earlier statement composed by the towering Eastern European rabbinic authority Rabbi Israel Meir Ha-Kohen (1838–1933), better

---

and modern, positive and negative — on this issue, see David Golinkin, "Responsa Regarding the Ordination of Women as Rabbis," *Responsa of the Va'ad Halakhah of the Rabbinical Assembly of Israel* (1994) (Hebrew), vol. 5, pp. 65–66.

6 Ibid. pp. 46–48, where Rabbi Golinkin provides a full list of these authorities and their writings on the topic.

7 See Menachem M. Brayer, *The Jewish Woman in Rabbinic Literature: A Psychohistorical Perspective* (Hoboken, N.J.: Ktav, 1986), vol. 2, p. 127; and Avraham Weiss, *Women at Prayer: A Halakhic Analysis of Women's Prayer Groups* (Hoboken, N.J.: Ktav, 1990), p. 62.

known as the Ḥafetz Ḥayim. In 1918, the Ḥafetz Ḥayim had stated that the study of traditional ethical-pietistic literature on the part of girls was an absolute necessity in light of the secular reality that marked the modern era. Indeed, if girls were not instructed in such teachings, he feared that they would inevitably go astray and leave the fold of religious Judaism. Therefore, he ruled that girls and women should be encouraged to study ethical treatises such as *Pirkei Avot* and *Sefer Menorat ha-Maʾor*. As Ellinson notes, the Ḥafetz Ḥayim confined instruction for women in rabbinic literature to these two works.[8]

In contrast, Ellinson points out that Sorotzkin, who argued in the same vein as the Ḥafetz Ḥayim, nevertheless composed a more expansive argument that extended the scope of the ruling. He held that women could also study halakhic selections from the Mishnah and sections in legal codes, such as the *Mishneh Torah* and the *Shulḥan Arukh*, that possessed practical significance for women.[9]

Moshe Meiselman has also identified this Sorotzkin responsum as a seminal one: it established a trajectory that has guided the evolution of Jewish law on this issue within the Orthodox Jewish world to the present day. As we shall see, the specific content as well as rhetorical power of the Sorotzkin ruling has allowed Meiselman to characterize it as "an ingenious *tour de force*." Consequently, the "overwhelming majority of modern [rabbinic] authority" follow the "line of reasoning" Sorotzkin put forth. Indeed, "the existence of schools of higher Jewish learning for women among all factions of contemporary Orthodoxy is ample proof of this fact."[10]

This judgment is borne out by the fact that leading Orthodox *poskim* such as Gedalia Felder in his *Yesodei Yeshurun* (1954), David Neumark in his *Eshel Avraham* (1954), and Benzion Firer in *Noam* all echo

---

8 *Menorat ha-Maor* is a fifteenth-century manual of ethical instruction written by Rabbi Isaac Abuham the Sefaradi. Widely popular in traditional Jewish circles, some sections in it were composed specifically for women.

9 Elyakim Ellinson, *The Woman and the Commandments, Between the Woman and Her Creator, Halakhic Sources Explained* (Hebrew) (Jerusalem: World Zionist Organization, 1984), vol. 1, pp. 159–60.

10 Moshe Meiselman, *Jewish Woman in Jewish Law* (New York: Ktav and Yeshiva University Press, 1978), p. 40.

Sorotzkin's reasoning in their writings on the subject.[11] Moreover, the preeminent contemporary Jerusalem rabbi, Eliezer Waldenberg, in a 1967 ruling contained in his famed *Tzitz Eliezer* (9:3), accorded the Sorotzkin *teshuvah* a special place as a decisive precedent for his own decision to permit women to engage in the study of the Written and the Oral Torah.

While this list of Orthodox authorities who have looked to the Sorotzkin responsum for guidance on this question is hardly exhaustive, it is sufficient to indicate that this opinion has enjoyed authoritative status in the Orthodox world. Indeed, because of its widespread dissemination in Orthodox precincts, the Sorotzkin responsum grants clear insight into how a significant percentage of the modern Orthodox rabbinate has defined gender roles. In explicating this responsum, we will indicate how a particular view of gender was of crucial importance in this case and by extension in parallel ones. At the same time, we will argue in the conclusion that the reasoning Sorotzkin as well as his colleagues adopted entailed more implications for change than they imagined. In fact, we are still living with the transformations his attitudes both reflected and helped to inaugurate in terms of the Jewish response to the modern world.

In this case, Sorotzkin acknowledged and felt constrained to respond to the religious crisis brought on by secularization. His recognition of the pervasiveness of Jewish ignorance and non-observance in the modern situation directly guided his determination. An analysis of the responsum on this matter therefore provides significant insight into the overarching mechanisms operative in the processes of Jewish law. We hope to indicate that the way in which an individual rabbi perceives social conditions and societal realities often plays a decisive role in informing his ruling. For all these reasons, the Sorotzkin responsum merits special scrutiny. We now turn to a presentation of the historical context in which it was situated as well to an analysis of the actual arguments Sorotzkin put forth.

11   See ibid. p.181, for a citation and brief mention of these sources. On the Firer piece in *Noam* 3, see Ellinson, *Between the Woman and Her Creator*, p.161; here Ellinson notes the parallel between the argument Sorotzkin advanced and the position Firer adopted.

Rabbi Sorotzkin's Biography and the Historical Context of the Responsum

Zalman Sorotzkin, born in Russia and trained in the great Lithuanian *yeshivot* of Slobodka and Volozhin, labored in the field of education throughout his career. He reorganized and administered the famed yeshiva of Telz during the first decade of the 1900s and went on to hold a number of prominent posts in various places in Lithuania over the next thirty years. He worked closely with Ḥayim Ozer Grodzinski, rabbi of Vilna, to reorganize the yeshiva system there in the late 1930s. Soon after the outbreak of World War II, Sorotzkin moved to *Eretz Yisrael*, where he eventually came to serve as head of the *Mo'etzet Gedolei ha-Torah* (Council of Torah Sages) of the *Agudat Yisrael* movement. His works include a commentary on the Pentateuch and published collections of sermons and responsa.[12]

Most importantly for our purposes, Sorotzkin devoted the bulk of his efforts after his arrival in Israel to the educational sphere. When the State of Israel was born in 1948, he was appointed director of the *Ḥinukh Atzma'i* (Independent Education) network of schools. Sponsored by *Agudat Yisrael*, this school system had initially been established during the period of the British Mandate in Palestine. Rabbi Avraham Yeshayahu Karelitz (the Ḥazon Ish, 1879–1953) of Bnei Brak, whose influence on the life and institutions of religious Jewry in *Eretz Yisrael* is legendary,[13] had been instrumental from the time of his *aliyah* in 1934 in establishing religious schools for both boys and girls under the auspices of *Agudat Yisrael*. After the establishment of the State in 1948, he recognized that this network of schools required governmental support in order to survive and grow. He successfully negotiated an arrangement whereby the government recognized the schools and agreed to provide over eighty percent of their budget, but they remained

---

12 *Encyclopedia Judaica,* s.v.,"Sorotzkin, Zalman Ben-Zion."

13 For two fascinating articles that bespeak the power and influence that Karelitz exerted on the Orthodox *haredi* community of *Eretz Yisrael* during his lifetime, see Lawrence Kaplan,"The Ḥazon Ish: Ḥaredi Critic of Traditional Orthodoxy"; and Menachem Friedman,"The Lost Kiddush Cup: Changes in Ashkenazic-Haredi Culture — A Tradition in Crisis," in Jack Wertheimer, ed., *The Uses of Tradition: Jewish Continuity in the Modern Era* (New York and Cambridge, Mass.: Jewish Theological Seminary of America and Harvard University Press, 1992), pp.145–90.

officially independent of the state system. Thus Orthodox control of the schools and their curricula could not be influenced by non-Orthodox interests and sensibilities in any way.[14] These historical considerations are crucial for appreciating why Sorotzkin was approached in 1941 on the question of Torah study for girls and women and of how his responsum was received in Orthodox circles. Indeed, Sorotzkin's appointment as head of Ḥinukh Atzma'i bespeaks the high esteem the Ḥazon Ish had for him as well as the preeminence he enjoyed as a rabbi-educator in the Israeli Orthodox Jewish community.

As part of its portfolio, *Ḥinukh Atzma'i* oversaw all the Beis Yaakov girls' schools in Israel. Designed to provide proper religious education for Jewish girls, the first Beis Yaakov school had been established in 1918 in Cracow by Sarah Schenirer with the blessing of recognized rabbinical authorities. No less a rabbinic personage than the Ḥafetz Ḥayim publicly expressed the need for these schools, and biblical and rabbinic texts — particularly those of an ethical nature, to an exclusion, as we have seen, of the Talmud — were taught within its walls. These schools soon expanded and spread throughout Europe.[15]

The first ultra-Orthodox school for girls in Israel had been established in Jerusalem in 1921. Ten to fifteen girls attended, and an older girl offered instruction.[16] This school was regarded with great suspicion by many elements in the *haredi* world of the Old City, as even the slightest degree of formal textual instruction in *sifrei kodesh* (holy books) for girls was viewed as a radical innovation within such ultra-Orthodox precincts. Consequently, the growth of schools for Orthodox girls in Israel was negligible during the 1920s. However, with the onset of a religious *aliyah* from Europe after Hitler rose to power in 1933, a number of Orthodox educators from Poland arrived in Israel and initiated the

14 For a description of the role the Ḥazon Ish played in establishing religious schools in *Eretz Yisrael* after his immigration there in the 1930s, as well as the position he occupied in securing Israeli governmental support for these schools, see Aharon Sorski, *A History of Torah Education in the Modern Era* (Hebrew) (B'nai B'rak: Or ha-Hayim, 1967), pp. 263–71.

15 For a brief general English language history of these schools, see Deborah Weissman, "Beis Yaakov: A Historical Model for Jewish Feminists," in Elizabeth Koltun, ed., *The Jewish Woman: New Perspectives* (New York: Schocken, 1976), pp. 139–48.

16 On this school, which was later renamed "Old Beth Yacov," see Raphael Schneller, "Continuity and Change in Ultra-Orthodox Education," *The Jewish Journal of Sociology* 22:1 (June, 1980), p. 40.

first Beis Yaakov schools. Among them was Rabbi Meir Sharansky, who founded the first Beis Yaakov school in Tel Aviv in 1934. The school had a humble beginning, with seven girls enrolled in two grades, but overcame all obstacles and ultimately became the model for other Beis Yaakov schools in the new settlement. Sharansky regarded the training of teachers for these elementary schools as absolutely essential, and two years later, in 1936, the first Beis Yaakov Teachers' Seminary was established in Tel Aviv, with women who had been pupils of Sarah Schenirer in Europe serving as instructors. Another advanced seminary in Jerusalem followed this one shortly thereafter.[17]

These schools represented great advances for the cause of female Jewish religious education in *Eretz Yisrael*. Nevertheless, their Orthodox proponents had to approach their creation with the utmost delicacy precisely because their groundbreaking character so aroused the ire of indigenous Orthodox rabbinic elements in the old *yishuv*, the Jewish community that had antedated the Zionist waves of settlement. Indeed, even when those *haredi* elements responded to contemporaneous pressures and created institutions such as *Bnos Yerushalayim* for the education of girls, the notion of formal Jewish education for women remained so radical that the school would not allow its pupils to study the *Ḥumash* (Pentateuch) in Hebrew. That they prohibited study of the Oral Law for women in such a school goes without saying. Moreover, the establishment of the co-educational Ḥoreb school in Jerusalem in 1935 by German Orthodox immigrants, on the basis of the *Torah im derekh eretz* philosophy that had informed Orthodox Judaism in Germany for the previous century, occasioned an immense outcry on the part of the Jerusalem rabbinate.[18]

Nevertheless, the commitment of Sharansky and others in his camp to providing formal religious instruction in Jewish texts — including

---

17 All of these details are taken from Sorski, *A History of Torah Education*, pp. 261–72 and 455ff. In addition, there is a fascinating Hebrew pamphlet written by Meir Sharansky, "A History of Beis Yaakov in *Eretz Yisrael*," in *The Twenty-Fifth Anniversary Volume of the Beis Yaakov Seminary in Tel Aviv* (1961), that relates many of these details as told through the eyes of a participant-founder.

18 All of the information found in this paragraph is taken from Sorski, *A History of Torah Education*, pp. 458ff.

perhaps the Oral Law — for Jewish woman remained absolute, and they searched for halakhic approval on the part of recognized Orthodox leadership to legitimate their efforts. It was in this spirit and in light of this context that Sharansky approached Sorotzkin in 1941, and asked him to issue a *psak* on the matter of Torah education for women. Sorotzkin's response, first published in 1941 and included in his *Moznayim La-Mishpat* (Scales of Justice) (1942) will be the subject of analysis in the remainder of this paper.

Rabbi Sorotzkin's Response

When Rabbi Sharansky asked Sorotzkin whether, "according to the spirit of the Torah," all girls should be eligible for instruction in the Written Torah, he was not posing a theoretical question. He wanted the approval of a recognized rabbinic authority in *Eretz Yisrael* for a practice that was already extant in Beis Yaakov schools in Israel as well as abroad. When he desired, further, to know whether it was permissible to teach select girls of singular academic talents the Oral Law, he was actually asking Sorotzkin for guidance in establishing the curricula for his schools and undoubtedly betraying a hope that such permission would be granted.

In his response of May 11, 1941, Sorotzkin declared at the very outset that there was no doubt, especially in our generation, that all girls should receive instruction in the Written Law. Sorotzkin pointed out that the Taz, Rabbi David ben Samuel Halevi (1586–1667), in his commentary on the *Shulḥan Arukh* (*Yoreh De'ah* 246:6), had already ruled that it was permissible for women to study the Written Law.[19] It would be unthinkable, Sorotzkin argued, not to affirm and continue the practice indicated by this three-hundred-year-old precedent. Later on in his responsum, Sorotzkin would indicate precisely why this was so.

However, at this point, Sorotzkin stated that the issue of whether women were permitted to study the Oral Law was distinct from the question of whether women could study the Written Law. Furthermore,

---

19 In Deuteronomy 31:12, it is explicitly stated that women participate in the commandment of *hakhel*, the assembly the Jewish people held every seven years to hear the Torah. The Taz relied upon this passage in issuing his ruling on the matter.

he claimed that the former matter was not pressing, since girls were not presently taught Talmud in Beis Yaakov schools. Nevertheless, as Sharansky had inquired, Sorotzkin chose to address this question – at least theoretically. On the one hand, Sorotzkin stated, Jewish law seemingly prohibited women from engaging in an intensive dialectical study of Talmud. He noted that R. Eliezer's statement in *Sotah* 21b ("Anyone who teaches his daughter Torah, it is as if he taught her *tiflut*,") was traditionally interpreted as meaning that women were forbidden to study the Oral Law. In addition, *Yoreh De'ah* 246:6, clearly defined most women as too "feeble-minded" to engage in talmudic study.[20] On the other hand, Sorotzkin immediately qualified this proscription, stating that it was not absolute. Citing an earlier address he had delivered on the topic (*Ha-De'ah ve-ha-Dibbur* 1:3 and 17), Sorotzkin, quoting the Taz on *Yoreh De'ah* 246:6, held that it was "permitted women to *hear* lessons in the Oral Law." Indeed, God had commanded the Torah to the entire people Israel, men and women. How, then, would it be possible for a Jewish woman to fulfill the strictures of the Law, including the Oral Law, if she did not know what it contained? Consequently, it was not only *permitted* women to know the teachings of the Oral Law; it was *necessary* that they be informed of its contents. While this may not have been his intent, Sorotzkin constructed an argument holding out the possibility that women could even study Talmud. As we have noted, others were to expand upon the permission he granted.

Sorotzkin acknowledged that many traditionalists completely opposed the notion that girls should receive a formal Jewish education. He wrote, "The education of daughters in the spirit of the Torah through the study of Torah arouses concern and fear in the hearts of pious Jews." Yet, he claimed, this was so "only because of its novelty. They have not seen their fathers acting thus." In other words, the innovative nature of the practice – the fact that it did not constitute "accepted custom and usage" among the people Israel – was seen as sufficient reason to oppose it. However, Sorotzkin dismissed such objections, claiming that they did not stem from the Torah itself.

20   The position of the *Shulhan Arukh* here is based on BT *Kiddushin* 80b, "Women are light-minded." For a treatment of this passage within its own context, see Hauptman, *Rereading the Rabbis*, pp. 37–38. Meiselman deals with this saying in *Jewish Woman in Jewish Law*, p. 41.

Expanding upon the statement he had made at the outset of the responsum, Sorotzkin asserted that the need to provide women with a formal Jewish education was absolutely mandated by the conditions that marked the modern world. In earlier generations, Jewish homes were marked by fidelity to the *Shulḥan Arukh* and its strictures. The Torah was absorbed experientially. "Therefore," Sorotzkin wrote, "there was no need to teach Jewish girls Torah formally from the book." These statements indicate that Sorotzkin affirmed a traditional construction of gender roles. In an "ideal world," where observance was an integral part of Jewish life and where Jewish knowledge was transmitted through mimesis both at home and in the street, there would be no need to offer formal Jewish education to girls. However, in the modern situation, most homes either neglected or were unaware of the Torah, its statutes and commandments. One could no longer depend upon the Jewish home to transmit Jewish life. Therefore, concluded Sorotzkin, "A Jewish girl who comes from these homes to study in a religious school, is akin to a gentile girl who comes to convert. It is an absolute necessity to teach her Torah formally, so that she will know the way in which she should walk and the deeds that she should perform — so that she will be a Jew."

Textual Supports

Sorotzkin was not content to let his case rest on these pragmatic grounds. As a *posek* issuing a halakhic ruling, he wanted to reference legal sources that would support his position. He found a textual precedent in *Sanhedrin* 94b where the talmudic narrative reports that King Hezekiah, ruler of Israel during a period of oppression by the Assyrian king Sennacherib, succeeded in leading Israel to cast off the yoke of oppression. He did so by planting "a sword by the door of the schoolhouse, proclaiming: 'All who will not study Torah will be pierced by the sword.'" His efforts led all the Jews to engage in Torah study. As the Talmud relates, "Search was made from Dan unto Beer Sheba, and no ignoramus (*am ha-aretz*) was found, from Gabbath unto Antipris, and no boy or girl, man or woman was found who was not thoroughly conversant in the laws of purity and impurity (*taharah* and *tumah*)." Furthermore, Sorotzkin — basing himself upon the commentary of the

Maharsha, Samuel Eliezer Edels (1555–1631), on this passage — claimed that the expertise of those women and girls was not confined to matters of *taharah* and *tumah* alone. Instead, these women were also experts in matters of *heter* and *issur*, areas of Jewish law that were normally off-limits to women.

In light of the prohibition that normally obtained, Sorotzkin asked rhetorically, "How is it they were permitted to study these areas of Torah?" His response was straightforward. He simply asserted, "The hour demanded it." After all, King Ahaz, Hezekiah's father, "had caused the sacrificial service to cease, and sealed the Torah" (*Sanhedrin* 103b). By seizing synagogues and study houses, Ahaz had attempted to deny Jewish men and women access to the lifeline that preserved the Jewish people then and now — the study of Torah. This was tantamount to spiritual genocide, for the *Shekhinah*, the Divine Presence rests upon Israel only by virtue of knowledge of Torah (*Genesis Rabbah* 42:2). On account of Ahaz, "Torah was almost completely forgotten among them." His son Hezekiah knew that drastic steps were necessary to rectify the situation. He reversed his father's ways and strengthened the bond between Israel and God through his insistence that all Israel — men and women — study Torah (*Sanhedrin* 94b).

For Sorotzkin, the situation that obtained in the era of Ahaz was identical to that of his own "inverted generation." He complained that this was a time in which "faithless teachers" easily planted disbelief in the minds and hearts of innocent students. "We hope for God and for the fulfillment of His divine promise," he wrote, that the Torah will not be forgotten from the seed of Israel. "In this hour, where the secularists (*hofshim*) perform the deeds of Ahaz, we must walk in the footsteps of Hezekiah — to strengthen the bond between Israel and their Father in Heaven by means of Torah study, whether for men or women, boys or girls." Only the knowledge of Torah could overcome the bitterness of Exile. Only Jewish learning, for males and females, could assure the preservation of Jewish life and faith.

Sorotzkin buttressed his position by citing a midrash to Genesis 12:8.: "From there [Abraham] moved on ... and pitched *his tent.*" In *Genesis Rabbah* 39:15, Rabbi Hanina pointing out that the word vocalized as "*ahalo* — his tent," concludes with the letter *hey*, so that it is actually written as, "*ahalah* — *her* tent." This discrepancy between how the word was spoken and how it was written, he explains, indicates that Abraham pitched not one, but two, tents. As the midrash states, "After having pitched Sarah's tent (*ahalah*), Abraham pitched his own (*ahalo*)." According to Sorotzkin, Abraham erected these "two tents" for two separate academies to be established — one for women and one for men. Sarah taught the women in the first tent, while Abraham instructed the men in the second.

Sorotzkin considered the order in which Abraham planted these tents as instructive for his own generation. After all, "any pious individual, wise and discerning, should be astonished by this arrangement. Why did Abraham erect her tent prior to his?" Indeed, if one were to ask any man, "Which section of a synagogue ought to be constructed initially, that of the men or that of the women," all would answer, without hesitation, "the men's section." Men, after all, were required to pray three times a day, while many women did not engage in formal prayer at all, or, if they did elect to pray, did so publicly only on Sabbaths and holidays.[21] On account of this, many synagogues did even not bother to create a section for women.

Sorotzkin then offered an analogy between the issue of a section for women in the synagogue and the matter of their education. If one were to ask, which should be built first, "a school for boys, or a Beis Yaakov school for girls," all would prioritize the establishment of a school for boys. This would accord with the talmudic dicta, "We are obligated to teach Torah to a son, but not to a daughter" (*Kiddushin* 29b),[22] and, "One who teaches his daughter Torah, it is as if he taught her *tiflut* (*Sotah* 20a)." Indeed, it was only in the face of considerable pressure that the formal Torah education of women had been allowed at all. Therefore, it would be unthinkable that educational institutions for girls would precede the establishment of schools for boys. And yet, "our father Abra-

---

21 To be sure, Sorotzkin noted that while it was true that many women did not choose to engage in formal public prayer, they were nevertheless obligated to do so according to Maimonides, *Mishneh Torah: Hilkhot Tefillah* 1:1–3.

22 For a fine exposition of this passage, see Rachel Biale, *Women and Jewish Law* (New York: Schocken, 1984), pp. 31ff. Also note the commentary upon it offered by Wegner, *Chattel or Person?* p. 242.

ham came and reversed the order. He first established a house of prayer and study for women, and only then did he create one for men." Furthermore, Scripture made this point twice — *Ahalo/ah* appears a second time in Genesis 13:3 — to indicate that when "an era such as his own should arise," Abraham "commanded his sons after him" to follow this example forever.[23]

As a further warrant for this position, Sorotzkin turned to Exodus 19:3. He pointed out that when God revealed the Torah through Moses to the people Israel at Sinai, the verse read, "Thus you should say to the house of Jacob, and tell the children of Israel." The rabbis, commenting upon these words, wrote, "'Thus you should say to the house of Jacob' — this refers to the women. 'And tell the children of Israel' — this refers to the men" (*Exodus Rabbah* 28:2). Sorotzkin challenged, "Is this not an explicit caution (*azharah*) to you that the education of women in matters of faith and religion should take precedence over the education of men?" Sorotzkin was now satisfied that he had marshaled sufficient textual precedents to support the position he was advancing in this responsum.

Notions of Gender

Sorotzkin then turned to the issue of gender. He observed that two major attributes defined and distinguished humanity. The first was that of intellect, or, as he put it, "a brain that permits one to acquire wisdom." Sorotzkin contended that, in a majority of cases, men displayed greater aptitude in this area than women did. As a result, males were dominant in fields such as Torah, philosophy, and mathematics. Indeed, women did not generally receive instruction in either philosophy or mathematics, nor were they taught the advanced study of Torah, as the intellectual demands such disciplines imposed were beyond the intellectual talents that marked most women. Sorotzkin based this view upon a statement found in the *Shulḥan Arukh, Yoreh Deah* 246:6, that describes women as "intellectually limited" (*aniyut daatan*).[24] Thus, in his view, the failure of women to become great Torah scholars did not stem from

23 See Genesis 13:3, where "*ahalo/ah*" appears for a second time.
24 See above, n.20.

a cultural construct that forbade them access to classical Jewish legal texts. Rather, the cultural arrangements that denied women the opportunity to study these texts simply emerged from and reflected the nature of reality itself.

On the other hand, Sorotzkin claimed, again on the basis of rabbinic sources, that women were gifted in another way. Human beings were marked by more than intellect. Their souls were distinguished by an affective element, "*ha-regesh she-ba-lev ve-ha-binah ha-teluyah bo* — the feeling in the heart and the understanding that depends upon it." In this area, the woman was more advanced than the man, "for the feelings of a woman are much more developed than the feelings of a man." Therefore, the ancient rabbis wrote, "Women are tender-hearted" (*Megillah* 14b), and, "The Holy One gave an additional measure of understanding (*binah yeteirah*) to women" (*Niddah* 45b). As a result, women were responsible for their oaths at twelve, while men were not held accountable until they reached the age of thirteen; nature, they wrote, graced women with an intuition that permitted them to "recognize their Creator, the One before Whom they swear an oath," at an earlier point in their lives than men.[25]

From all this, Sorotzkin concluded that there were natural factors that led men and women to display their talents in distinct arenas. The acute analytic skills that marked men made them better suited than women for talmudic dialectics and logic. However, the emotional sensibilities that characterized women made them better suited than men "to recognize the One who spoke and created the world, as well as to believe in Him with a simple faith (*emunah peshutah*), for faith depends upon the heart and its sentiments." The natural world offers testimony as to "its Creator, as it is said, 'The heavens tell of God's glory'" (Psalm 19). Women, whose instincts and character caused them to appreciate, more fully than men, the wonders of the natural world that God had created, were therefore better suited than men to recognize the Creator. They were naturally inclined to recognize that God oversees the world with "His Divine Providence." Taking a highly traditional view, Sorotzkin believed that God had assigned distinct roles and talents to each gender.

25 For the talmudic discussion of this point, see BT *Niddah* 45b.

A Novel Turn in the Argument

Throughout this last section of his responsum, there is not a hint that Sorotzkin entertained any modernist notion of gender equality. Indeed, he championed an idea of separate spheres for men and women by pointing out that males and females possessed distinct talents in very different areas. Yet, he now subtly employed this position to formulate a novel argument that would allow women to study the texts of Jewish tradition at an advanced level. In so doing, he not only reaffirmed the position he had put forth at the outset of his responsum; he adopted a stance that allowed for innovation in Jewish life, only by paradoxically defending the tradition and its notions of appropriate gender roles. Indeed, as a traditionalist whose ideology insisted that Judaism was changeless, he was compelled to affirm the status quo. Belonging to a religious camp that was averse to innovation, Sorotzkin had to speak of a changeless *masoret* (tradition) even as he acted to adapt the institutions of his community to the challenges of the moment. He was about to ally himself — perhaps unwittingly — with forces that could and ultimately would alter Jewish life, for the entrance of women into the educational arena had the potential to transform the regulation of gender roles.

Sorotzkin stated that at the present time, when faith was weak and the saving "remnants (*seridim*)" of the Jewish people searched for ways to attract their fellow Jews to a proper devotion to God, those faithful remnants were compelled to favor the "heart" over the "brain." Jewish leaders had to concern themselves initially with the education of girls and women. Sorotzkin reasoned that if "wise and sensitive women" were taught "knowledge and fear of God," they would be the first "to cause the King to return — *lehashiv et ha-melekh*." Were not women better suited than men to believe in God with a faith that emerged from the depths of the heart? Were they not more likely to recognize the reality of God than men who, whatever their intentions, were condemned by nature to be marked by the guile and guided by the criticism that stems from the side of cold logic? Such women would influence their husbands and their children, "warming the heart of man in the light of faith."

In every age where faith was weak and where rebellion against God and the divine will was commonplace, the leaders of the Jewish people had recognized that the education of girls had to take precedence over the education of boys. Abraham had established "the tent of Sarah" prior to "his own tent," for he lived during the time of Nimrod, and he recognized that Nimrod had employed his power "to cause the entire world to rebel against the Holy One, blessed be He" (Rashi on Genesis 10:8). By prioritizing the education of women for his own rebellious generation, Abraham intended to set an example for later Jewish leaders. For all who lived in faithless times, "faith could be rooted in their hearts" only through the education of women.

This was as true during the time of Moses as it was during the era of Abraham. Sorotzkin contended that even at the moment the Torah was revealed by God to Israel at Sinai, "faith was weak among the Jewish people." Hence, God commanded Moses to follow the precedent set by Abraham, and Moses, like Abraham, attended first to the educational needs of the "house of Jacob." Only later did he address the "house of Israel." In the present era, dominated by an "inverted generation" and marked by widespread non-observance and lack of faith, the Jewish people was required to follow the pattern established by Abraham and Moses.

Sorotzkin expressed astonishment that so many pious contemporary Jews (*haredim*) did not affirm this model. Many neglected the formal Jewish education of their daughters, failing to grasp how essential it was that their daughters be taught "that the beginning of wisdom is fear of the Lord." Sorotzkin observed that many fathers were properly scrupulous (*makpidim*) about the education of their sons and zealously saw to it that their boys were educated in *yeshivot* where they "could take refuge in the shadow of *tzaddikim*." Yet, they cavalierly sent their daughters to non-Jewish schools, or to schools that were under non-religious Jewish sponsorship where the girls were "educated in a spirit foreign to the Torah and taught "to profane the religion of Moses and Israel and all that is holy to us." Naturally, they became ensnared in a web of secularism that led to non-observance and religious disrespect. Such girls grew up to despise the faith of their husbands and to lead their families to lives of Jewish "non-observance and licentiousness (*holelut ve-hefkeirut*)." Sorotzkin could not fathom why these fathers failed to see this causal chain. A refusal to provide formal Jewish education for girls condemned Judaism to oblivion in the lives of countless Jews, males as well as females.

"In our time," Sorotzkin wrote, "all of life is secular, lacking all values and content in general, and Jewish values and content in particular." One is confronted everywhere with a culture that is "completely alien and foreign to the spirit of Judaism." In an inversion of Rabbi Eliezer's dictum, he charged that any father who neglected "to teach his daughter the proper knowledge of God and authentic Jewish values and content," was guilty of teaching her *tiflut*, "on account of the influence of the larger world." Immorality, in the current context, surely did not stem from learning Torah; on the contrary, it resulted from an ignorance of Torah. The licentiousness of the street and the influences it exerted upon the Jewish people could only be contained by the power of Torah education. The prohibition against formally instructing women in the sources of Jewish tradition could not possibly be applied in the present era. Indeed, education of females was now mandatory. It was the only surety that could guarantee the Jewish future in light of an ascendant secular Jewish society in *Eretz Yisrael*.

In concluding his responsum, Sorotzkin acknowledged that those who, guided by the spirit of Torah and authentic Jewish religious faith and practice, opposed the establishment of schools for girls, did so on the grounds that pious Jews should continue to walk "in the footsteps of their forefathers." After all, our ancestors had raised girls who were faithful "to their people and their religion" without the benefit of such schools. Therefore, they reasoned, "we should be like them." To such people, Sorotzkin responded, "The latest generations are not like the earlier ones." The earlier generations were "like angels," and faith was then strong among the Jewish people. Observance and piety marked the Jewish people as a community, and individuals in those days were completely committed to a life of Torah. It was impossible in that epoch for "a destroyer — (*mashḥit*)" to enter into homes "to smite — (*lingof*)" the children. In those epochs, "The king's daughter [was] all glorious within." (Psalms 45:14). Jewish maidens (*bnot yisrael*) did not go out into the streets and schools did not attempt "to uproot Jewish faith from the heart of the youth." Instead, they aimed "to magnify and glorify it." However, "we — in the later generations — are like persons who sit in darkness and the light of God does not shine upon us." Therefore, "we have no right," Sorotzkin decisively asserted, "to distance our daughters from the *heder* (the classroom), for anyone who does not receive instruction in "*talmud torah* (the study of Torah) in this age, whether man or woman, it is as if they were separated from eternal life."

Sorotzkin completed his responsum with the following declaration:

I assert that it is not only permitted to teach Torah and fear of heaven to girls in our present generation. Rather there is an absolute obligation to do so, as we have explained. It is a great commandment (*mitzvah rabbah*) to establish schools for girls and to plant pure faith and the knowledge of Torah and commandments in their hearts, and the reward for "converting" the women in our generation is very great. For through the merit of the righteous women our ancestors were redeemed from Egypt.

Final Reflections

In issuing this ruling, Sorotzkin displayed a type of reasoning that most feminists can hardly applaud. Nowhere in his responsum does he approach anything akin to an ethos of gender equality, nor does he in anyway affirm the intellectual abilities of women. Instead, like other rabbis who countenanced Jewish education for women, Sorotzkin advanced purely pragmatic considerations to justify the formal Jewish education of young women and girls. As wives and mothers, these girls would one day play a key role in instilling authentic Jewish consciousness in their families. The need to educate young Jewish women formally in selected Jewish texts and traditions was thereby justified in instrumental terms. The knowledge and attitudes they would imbibe through such learning would one day more properly allow them to fulfill their traditional obligations as wives and mothers. Sorotzkin retained a negative view of the modern world and the culture that informed it, a view that — as this analysis has shown — ironically served as a vital element in his decision to advocate formal Jewish education for women. As we have seen, his responsum displays the traditional views of gender that informed him and his rabbinic colleagues.

While an analysis of this responsum reveals its limitations from a modern feminist perspective, it ought not diminish an appreciation for its significance. It remains vital in several ways. First, the Sorotzkin ruling unquestionably granted women the access to the study of the

Written Torah that many authorities in past generations had denied them; moreover, it established a theoretical rationale that ultimately was employed by others as a warrant for allowing women full engagement with Oral Law. For those committed to the rabbinic tradition, such a precedent is hardly trivial. The responsum represents an important departure from the past, and those who would advocate equal access to Torah for women in our day should see it as constituting a rabbinic precedent that contributes to the justification and legitimization of such access. Indeed, in the Beis Yaakov schools that Sorotzkin oversaw as head of *Hinukh Atzma'i* in the 1940s and 1950s, twelve out of thirty-two weekly hours of instruction were devoted to study of Jewish texts. The curriculum even allowed for instruction in halakhic rulings — through such study did not involve detailed analysis of the Talmud. The ruling thus had immediate though limited practical effects.[26]

The Sorotzkin responsum indicates that even as men marked by his views affirm the enduring worth and value of Jewish tradition, they may simultaneously re-form it. By adopting the position he did, Sorotzkin allowed for a reshaping of Judaism and its institutions. In a larger hermeneutical sense, this text demonstrates that the *posek* possesses the capacity to reflect upon and reformulate the past in light of the present. Neither the past nor the present remains fixed in light of the reflexivity that marks the interpretive project. The immense repository of the past can be rendered saliently in diverse ways, and the specific way in which Sorotzkin understood that past in this instance indicates that while he served as a guardian of permanence, the unchanging *masoret*, he also responded to contemporaneous cultural and social conditions.

The Sorotzkin ruling, whatever the intent that informed it, had political implications and unanticipated consequences. In a traditional Jewish world, the will of God had been and continues to be seen as being expressed in these Jewish legal texts. The refusal to allow women access to these sources has meant that women have been unable to attain the public status and authority that such study has conferred upon men,[27] making it impossible for them to exercise public political power in traditional Jewish religious society. This classical posture consigned

---

26   Sorski, *A History of Torah Education*, p.272.
27   Paula Hyman makes this point in *Gender and Assimilation*, p.54.

women to the domestic realm alone. The decision to grant them even a limited opening to study these texts thus had revolutionary implications, beyond anything Sorotzkin probably imagined. Responsa such as Sorotzkin's both reflected and facilitated a reality wherein women have increasingly aspired to assume positions of public power and prestige that were formerly off-limits to them.

The trajectory of the Sorotzkin responsum indicates that the Agudah sage allied himself with a posture concerning the necessity of Jewish education for women that would become more pronounced in ensuing years. The establishment of numerous contemporary Orthodox institutions where Talmud is regularly taught to women reveals how much matters in this area have changed in many Orthodox precincts since the time that Sorotzkin wrote his responsum. To be sure, such Talmud study has primarily been located in modern Orthodox or National Religious Party quarters and not in the *Agudah* community in which Sorotzkin himself was situated. Nevertheless, the vector that marked Sorotzkin's decision entailed consequences and extensions that he could hardly have anticipated. The argument he constructed reinforced a Jewish legal foundation that has permitted women to overturn a barrier that had precluded their contact with the classical literary legacy of Judaism. His decision constitutes a novel chapter in the ongoing story of the Jewish people, one that has witnessed an unprecedented transformation in gender roles. It is a story of change that is still unfolding.

15

Gender, Halakhah, and Women's Suffrage

Responsa of the First Three Chief Rabbis on the Public Role of Women in the Jewish State

As discussed in the previous chapter, a modern notion of gender equality is foreign to classical rabbinic Judaism. The ancient Sages, like patriarchs in other cultures, assigned men and women distinct gender roles. In their view, Psalm 45:14, where it was written, "*Kol kevodah bat melekh penimah* – the King's daughter is all glorious within,*"* consigned women to the domestic realm. Susan Grossman and Rivka Haut, in commenting upon this passage, have observed that it serves as the halakhic warrant for the position that a woman can play no role in public life.

> This verse has been cited as proof that, according to tradition, women have divinely ordained roles that preclude any public activity. Rabbis throughout the ages, including our own, have cited this beautiful image to justify excluding women from public life, . . . and stressing that women's sole legitimate sphere of activity is *within* the home.[1]

During the past century, many Jews have expressed opposition to this traditional gender ideal and the socially constructed behavior patterns it has established for each sex. Among them were the non-religious Zionist *ḥalutzim* who migrated to *Eretz Yisrael* at the turn of the century. These people were adamant in their conviction that traditional notions of gender roles were at least in theory, outmoded. They believed that men and women should be equal participants in society, and they insisted that the role of women in the public life of the *yishuv* (the Jewish

---

1 Susan Grossman and Rivka Haut, eds., *Daughters of the King: Women and the Synagogue* (Philadelphia: Jewish Publication Society, 1992), pp. xxii–xxiii.

settlement in pre-state Israel) had to be broadened.[2]

For the Orthodox of *Eretz Yisrael*, it was another matter. Many religious members of the old *yishuv* promoted traditional gender-role notions and were determined to resist and protest any changes proposed. As late as 1946, this determination could be witnessed in the pages of *Ha-Tzofeh*, the organ of the Orthodox National Religious Party. During that year, Golda Meir replaced Moshe Sharet as head of the Political Department of the Jewish Agency. Commenting upon her ascension to this post, *Ha-Tzofeh*, on August 28, 1946, did not hesitate to employ Psalm 45:14 as a basis for opposition to her appointment.

While the paper acknowledged that Meir was, without question, "understanding, industrious, ethical, a distinguished woman," she was, "all that notwithstanding — a woman!" This fact led *Ha-Tzofeh* to express the intractability of their position:

> It is hard to become accustomed to the fact that this people, which, for generations, has been guided by the formula, 'The king's daughter is all glorious *within*,' whose Torah has imposed commandments on the man and not the woman, [and which has denied women] the right to serve as judges, in administration, and as witnesses, which has established for her an honored place *within the tent —* that a woman stands at the head of the political department of this people. . . . It is impossible to appoint her [to such a post]. This is a law like the laws of nature. This is eternal Jewish law. There are boundaries and borders, and each sex needs to know its limits. . . .[3]

As this source indicates, all Orthodox Jews had to acknowledge the realities of the modern setting and were compelled at least to grapple with

2   The gap between a theoretical commitment to gender equality on the part of the Zionist settlers who established the State and the reality of an Israeli society that never realized this commitment, has been well-documented. In the voluminous literature on this topic, three books stand out. They are Deborah Bernstein, *The Struggle for Equality: Urban Women Workers in Pre-state Israeli Society* (New York: Praeger, 1987); Lesley Hazelton, *Israeli Women: The Reality Behind the Myths* (New York: Simon & Schuster, 1977); and Natalie Rein, *Daughters of Rachel: Women in Israel* (Harmondsworth, England: Penguin Books, 1979).

3   *Ha-Tzofeh* (August 28, 1946).

the ideal of gender equality. While one faction remained determined to resist any concession to this notion, another group pragmatically conceded that an Orthodox accommodation was inevitable. Finally, some Orthodox Jews had themselves internalized this western ethos and held that Jewish law ought to embrace the position that both men and women can be full participants in the public life of society. *Eretz Yisrael* quickly became an arena wherein conflict ensued among these camps of Orthodox Jews.

This paper will present and analyze selected responsa of three leading twentieth-century Orthodox Israeli decisors — Rabbis Isaac Halevi Herzog (1888–1959), Abraham Isaac Ha-Kohen Kook (1865–1935), and Ben-Zion Meir Ḥai Ouziel (1880–1953) — on the matter of women's suffrage and the related issue of women's participation in the public political life of Israeli society. In so doing, it will indicate how *Eretz Yisrael* served as a venue for Jewish legal struggles with issues of gender and how those struggles produced diverse halakhic responses when Jewish law had to grapple with the demands of governance in a modern Jewish nation. After all, each of these men occupied the post of Chief Rabbi in *Eretz Yisrael*. Kook was the first ever to hold the position and served from 1921 until his death in 1935. Herzog was elected as his successor in 1936 and assumed the post of Chief Ashkenazic Rabbi in 1937, remaining in office for over two decades. Ouziel, the son of the *av bet din* of the Sephardic rabbinic court of Jerusalem, was elected as the first Chief Sephardic Rabbi in 1939 and served until his death in 1953. After outlining the historical and social contexts that prompted these writings, we will show how the rulings of these men on issues of women in the political order reflect the gamut of positions advanced by Orthodox Jews on these matters in the modern era.

Initially, we will consider the writings of Rav Kook, whose thoughts were penned in 1920, when the issue of women's suffrage was still a matter of great debate in the *yishuv*. Following that analysis, we will take up the writings of Ouziel. Although his opinions on this subject, as well as on the attendant issue of women's suitability for public office, were written at the time that the State of Israel was established, Ouziel employed the debates of the 1920s as the grounds for his discussion. Finally, Herzog, like his Sephardic peer, also wrote on this matter as the fledgling Jewish State emerged in 1947–1948. Aware of the ferocious debates that had wracked the *yishuv* during the 1920s and knowing that the nascent Israeli government was about to enact laws that would govern elections for the Knesset, Herzog felt it imperative that he articulate the attitude of Jewish law on the question of female voting and eligibility for public office. Both Ouziel and Herzog, as officers of the state, considered themselves obligated to express the halakhic position on matters of gender. In this sense, the rulings they issued are part of a larger project that occupied all of these men as they confronted the challenge of adapting *Halakhah* to the demands of a modern nation.

In considering these writings, we as Liberal Jews not only uncover documents of history. We also measure our own attitudes towards gender over against the writings of these Orthodox authorities and clarify the principles that operate within our community. In so doing, we witness the vitality of the halakhic system and gain some understanding of the resources it might provide us as we strive to create an authentic Judaism capable of meeting the demands of the modern world.

Historical Background of the Responsa

After World War I, an Occidental trend emerged that extended the right of suffrage to women. In 1918, Germany and Poland decided to grant women this right, as did England. Czechoslovakia followed suit in 1919, and the United States in 1920.[4] The pre-state *yishuv* in *Eretz Yisrael* was destined to be part of this trend.

In 1917, the British Mandatory Government in Palestine decided to create the Jewish Assembly (*Knesset Yisrael*) as the institutional structure that would govern the affairs of the Jewish community, and an Elected Assembly (*Asseifat ha-Nivḥarim*) was to be chosen. On December 28, 1917, the committee charged with responsibility for the first Elected Assembly decided that its members should be chosen through direct elections based on proportional representation. The electorate was to be composed of all Jews in the *yishuv* who did not explicitly deny membership in the organized Jewish community, and the committee main-

---

4   Shulamit Aloni, *Nashim kiv'nei adam* (Jerusalem: Keter, 1976), p. 21.

tained that suffrage should be granted to all men and women above the age of twenty.[5]

This last recommendation was vehemently opposed by ultra-Orthodox elements in the *yishuv ha-yashan*, the "old" *yishuv*, which saw this advancement in the rights of women as an attack upon their efforts to preserve a traditional way of life in *Eretz Yisrael*. In contrast, the Zionists of the *yishuv he-ḥadash*, the "new" *yishuv*, saw this proposal as an indispensable foundation for the creation of a modern nation. Over the next two years, stormy arguments ensued and although one representative of the ultra-Orthodox party in 1918 conceded that a compromise wherein women could vote might be acceptable, the Orthodox community could never countenance the notion that women could also be elected to office. Progressive forces within the *yishuv he-ḥadash*, however, would brook no compromise on this matter, and they prevailed in their insistence that full rights be granted women to vote and to serve in office. This led to a movement among *ḥaredi* elements in Jerusalem that called for non-participation in any election that would allow female participation. At this point, the more moderate Orthodox Mizrachi party dissented from the stance of the *ḥaredim* and elections — in which women would participate as the full equals of men — were ultimately set for April 19, 1920. The ultra-Orthodox, fearing that their non-participation would be against their self-interest, ultimately chose to vote, though they did insist on special polling places where women could not appear.[6]

Even after the elections for the *Asseifat ha-Nivḥarim* in 1920, however, the *ḥaredi* factions in the *yishuv* refused to give up on this issue, and the debate over women's suffrage did not abate. The right-wing Agudah minority anxiously strove to rescind the women's rights, though their efforts were to no avail, as the overwhelming secular majority of the community opposed any surrender on this point. The Mizrachi sought to effect a compromise, and they called for a public referendum on the matter. When the Agudah issued a ban of *ḥerem* upon participation

5 The primary source for this information is drawn from Moshe Atias, *Kenesset yisrael be-eretz yisrael: yesodah ve-irgunah* (Jerusalem, 1944), pp. 11ff. In addition, valuable material on this matter is contained in Dan Horowitz and Moshe Lissak, *Origins of the Israeli Polity: Palestine Under the Mandate* (Chicago and London: University of Chicago Press, 1978), pp. 21ff.

6 All this information can be found in Atias, *Kenesset yisrael b'eretz yisrael*, pp. 14–21.

in the referendum, the Mizrachi ceased its efforts, as its leadership felt nothing could be done to pacify the *ḥaredi* elements within the *yishuv*. At this point, the Agudah withdrew from the larger community and adopted a sectarian posture, while Mizrachi joined the communal polity that was to govern the Jewish inhabitants of the land. On December 6, 1925, votes were cast for the second Elected Assembly, and the debate over women's suffrage came to an end. It is against this background that we are now able to turn the writings of Kook, Ouziel, and Herzog on these issues.[7]

The Stance of Rav Kook — Unequivocal Rejection

On May 28, 1920, a scant month after elections for the *Asseifat ha-Nivḥarim* had been held, a letter penned by Kook was printed in *Ha-Ivri*, an organ of Mizrachi, on the question of whether women should be allowed to vote in elections for public office. In light of what was universally perceived as his positive attitude towards the Zionist enterprise, the modernist Orthodox members of Mizrachi fully expected Rav Kook to take a lenient position and issue a strong ruling that would favor the addition of women to the electorate.[8] To their great astonishment, however, Kook unequivocally condemned such inclusion as a complete break with Jewish tradition and law.[9]

7 Atias, ibid. pp. 21–28. In addition, see S. Zalman Abramov, *Perpetual Dilemma: Jewish Religion in the Jewish State* (London: Associated University Presses, 1976), pp. 108–9; as well as Menachem Friedman, *Society and Religion: The Non-Zionist Orthodox in Eretz-Israel 1918–1936* (Hebrew), chapters 5 and 6.

8 See Friedman, *Society and Religion*, pp. 158–69, for a discussion of the relationship that obtained between Kook and the Mizrachi on this matter.

9 *Ha-Ivri* 20 (May 28, 1920), pp. 11–13. Rav Kook's writings on this and other halakhic topics have been treated in Michael Nehorai, "Remarks on the Rabbinic Rulings of Rav Kook," *Tarbitz* 59 (1990), pp. 481–505. In addition, Zvi Zohar has analyzed the Kook responsum, as well as the Ouziel responsum dealt with in this paper, in his insightful piece, "Traditional Flexibility and Modern Strictness: Two Halakhic Positions on Woman's Suffrage," in Harvey Goldberg, ed., *Sephardi and Middle Eastern Jewries* (Bloomington: Indiana University Press in association with the Jewish Theological Seminary of America, 1996), pp. 119–33. Nehorai, in his essay, focuses principally on the Jewish legal issues involved in the Kook responsum, while Zohar concentrates on the political-social implications of these writings. While we speak of these issues as well in our paper, we provide a gender-focus that distinguishes our paper from theirs — even in the treatment of these two figures.

At the very outset of his piece, Kook maintained that the entire weight of the tradition was opposed to such an innovation. He wrote, "The one voice that we hear from the Torah, the Prophets, and the Writings, from both *Halakhah* and *Aggadah*, asserts that the national spirit is entirely opposed to this modern innovation." It is the last part of this statement, his invocation of the "national spirit" of the Jewish people, that is most crucial for an understanding of why he ruled that suffrage should not be extended to women. For, in looking at his position on this issue, Kook did not put forth specific legal arguments, i.e., citations of Jewish legal precedents, against such extension. Instead, he composed a "meta-legal" argument that centered on what he perceived as the nature of the Jewish people and on the need for *am yisrael* to construct a state that would be true to its authentic character and indigenous religious-national principles. Indeed, Kook argued that the Jewish people possessed a unique national value system and he maintained that the imposition of this innovation would run counter to the Jewish national character.

Kook continued by stating that the "national spirit" of the Jewish people was more refined than that of other modern nations, and he maintained that the family unit animated this spirit. Indeed, the Jewish family served as the vortex of the nation. Furthermore, within the family, the wife was at the center. It was she who held the family together and, as wife and mother, the attendant responsibility she possessed for the welfare and purity of the Jewish nation knew no bounds. Allowing women to vote could thus only have negative consequences, and Kook cited two reasons for this belief. First, the wife might well bow to the will of her husband and vote as he instructed. If this were the case, it would constitute an "obsequiousness — *hanufah*" on her part that would compromise her "internal freedom — *hufshah ha-penimit*." On the other hand, should she differ with her husband, the tranquillity of the home would be shattered and domestic discord would result. Either behavior would be inappropriate for a Jewish woman and the subsequent rent in the life of the family would only undermine the people, bringing shame to *am yisrael* in the eyes of the nations.

Kook therefore called upon his "modern brothers" in the *yishuv* to "act beyond the letter of the law and surrender their novel demand." The extension of suffrage to women should not be forced upon the Jewish nation, as it was completely alien to its national spirit. Kook recognized that the modern advocates of this position "claim that morality demands that what they call equal rights for women — their participation in the public realm in accord with the modern spirit — is a fine and acceptable thing." However, this is "not as it is with us." Instead, the Jewish spirit regards this innovation as a "repulsive thing — *davar ka'ur*," and could not accept it. Every nation has the right to construct a state in keeping with its own character, to weigh that which is "good and bad, beautiful and repulsive, in accord with its own values." In refusing to acknowledge this change in gender roles for women as legitimate, Kook contended that he was only asking that the Jewish people be allowed "to build our nation according to our own values."

In looking at Kook's argument, it is noteworthy that he did not cite a single halakhic precedent to support his position. After all, female participation in the public life of liberal civil society may well be said to have no exact precedent in the Jewish past. It is thus not surprising that Rav Kook was compelled to define what he regarded as the overarching ethos of Jewish tradition to guide his ruling on this matter. And there is no question that this decision was, in the final analysis, consistent with his *weltanschauung*. Throughout his writings, Kook was able to support the Zionist movement precisely because he regarded the Zionist endeavor as part of a divine plan that would allow the Jewish people to achieve their spiritual destiny. As such, he could support the Zionists and regard their work as "holy," even if they themselves did not recognize it as such. As Kook wrote in his posthumously-published book, *Orot* (1942):

Many of the adherents of the present national revival maintain that they are secularists. If Jewish secular nationalism were really imaginable, then we would, indeed, be in danger of falling so low as to be beyond redemption. But Jewish secular nationalism is a form of self-delusion: the spirit of Israel is so closely linked to the spirit of God that a Jewish nationalist, no matter how secularist his intention may be, must, despite himself, affirm the divine. An individual can sever the tie that binds him to life eternal, but the House of Israel as a whole cannot. All of its most cherished possessions — its land, language, history, and *customs* — are vessels of the spirit of the Lord.[10]

In this instance, Kook was convinced that this transformation in gender custom and role on the national soil of the Jewish homeland would undermine the Jewish soul. Consequently, he felt compelled to oppose those secular Zionists who favored granting suffrage to women. In his view it was they, not the *haredim*, who were required to compromise on this issue "for the greater good." Kook's view of gender roles was absolute. He would brook no change. Ouziel, as we shall see, was of a different halakhic opinion.

The Position of Rabbi Ouziel — Complete Approval

In 1948, at the time the State of Israel was founded, Ouziel decided to publish a responsum on the topic, "Concerning the Participation of Women in Elections for Public Institutions."[11] While he asserted that he wrote this opinion during the 1920s, when the issues discussed in the responsum had not yet "been resolved," he did not publish it at that time. Rather, he elected to do so two decades later, he claimed, "so that the greatness of Torah could be magnified."

While there is no reason to doubt his sincerity on this point, it is equally true that the moment he did decide to grant public expression to his views was decisive in Zionist history. The Jewish State had just been declared, and though the issue of female participation in the public life of the nascent nation no longer elicited the furor it had twenty years earlier among all sectors of the Orthodox world, debates over the proper role of women in the public life of *Medinat Yisrael* nevertheless persisted in Orthodox precincts.[12] As Sephardi Chief Rabbi, Ouziel's *psak* in this responsum had practical importance for informing the

---

10 Abraham Isaac Kook, "Lights for Rebirth," in Arthur Hertzberg, ed., *The Zionist Idea* (New York: Harper Torchbooks, 1959), p. 430. (Italics mine.)

11 *Mishpetei Uziel, Ḥoshen Mishpat*, no. 6.

12 Indeed, the last responsum we will consider in this paper, issued by Rabbi Isaac Halevi Herzog, *Teḥukah le-yisrael al pi ha-torah* I (Jerusalem: Mossad Harav Kook), pp. 95ff., indicates that this issue was still a controversial one among some Ortho-

attitudes that marked many traditional Jews as they considered the roles that women would play in the Jewish nation as both voters and office-holders. Furthermore, as the "public face" of Orthodox Judaism in Israel, his writings commanded the attention of the secular populace, and his views informed their attitudes toward Jewish religious traditionalism and its ability to adapt to the demands of a modern world. Ouziel understood all this, and his publication of the responsum at this moment should be regarded as a crucial policy statement on his part concerning the place of women in the public sphere.

In approaching this matter, Ouziel noted that the 1920s had been marked by the daily publication of circulars, pamphlets, warnings, and newspapers articles that opposed women's participation in elections for the *Asseifat ha-Nivharim*. He observed that some rabbis asserted that the Torah itself prohibited extending suffrage to women, whereas others argued that the prohibition would serve as a hedge to guard morality and modesty. Still other authorities insisted that this prohibition would preserve peace in the family. All of these men relied upon the slogan popularized a century earlier by the Ḥatam Sofer (1768–1839), "All innovation is forbidden by the Torah itself." In this responsum, Ouziel intended to respond to all these viewpoints, contending that the issue itself was divided into two parts: (1) May women vote? and (2) May women be permitted to be elected to office?

At the outset of his discussion, Ouziel asserted that there was no clear halakhic foundation that would prohibit women from voting. Indeed, elsewhere in his responsum, Ouziel did note that one rabbi had opposed extending the vote to women on the halakhic ground that women constituted neither an *edah* (community) nor a *kahal* (congregation). In response to this position, Ouziel wrote, "Let us assume that they do not constitute a 'congregation' or a 'community.' . . . Nevertheless, are they not creatures created in God's image and possessed of intelligence!" Logic itself therefore rejected the idea that women should be denied this basic human right (*zekhut ishit zot*). After all, through these elections, officials were granted power and authority to levy taxes and order public affairs. Women, no less than men, accepted the rule

---

dox Jews. As a result, Ouziel's decision to publish his decision at this time was more than an intellectual exercise. It addressed what was still a vital public matter.

of those elected and obeyed their directives. In light of this, he felt it was wrong to thrust these decisions upon them on the one hand and deny them the right to vote on the other. Simple justice demanded that women be granted this right.

Ouziel then responded *seriatim* to the objections raised by those who would deny extending the vote to women. First, he noted that some opponents claimed that women were intellectually incapable of casting ballots. These opponents cited two talmudic passages to buttress their position. The first passage, found in two places (*Shabbat* 33b and *Kiddushin* 80b), stated, "Women are feeble-minded," and a second (*Yoma* 66b), "A woman's wisdom is only in the home," confined women to the domestic realm. Ouziel dismissed both citations as mere rhetoric. Indeed, if one wanted to cite talmudic precedent to discover a warrant for how women ought to be regarded, he stated that *Niddah* 45b — "God gave extra understanding to women" — more accurately described the ability and talent that characterized them. Educated women in the modern era, like those in the past, were fully as able as men. Their business skills, as well as their talents for organization and administration, demonstrated this truth. Moreover, even if some women did lack intellectual ability, so did many men. If lack of intellectual acuity was to be put forth as a criterion for excluding women from voting, then Ouziel bitingly asserted, "Let us also exclude from the electorate those men who are feeble-minded, of whom there has never been a lack in the land."

Ouziel then went on to consider the arguments of those who charged that sexual misconduct would result from the sexes mingling at polling places. He immediately dismissed such fears as absurd. After all, people go to the ballot box for the express purpose of casting a vote. If extending suffrage for women could be denied on the grounds that this might lead to sexual licentiousness, then no semblance of normal life could remain unregulated. Such logic would require that men and women be forbidden from walking together in the street and would not countenance the joint presence of a man and woman in a store. Furthermore, men and women would also be prohibited from speaking with one another on business matters, as this would lead to proximity that, in turn, could surely foster sexual impropriety. Yet, no reasonable person, Ouziel maintained, would entertain such notions.

Ouziel also condemned the notion that domestic tranquillity would be shattered if women were given the right to vote. Indeed, he viewed such a claim as ridiculous. He pointed out that the Talmud (*Baba Metzia* 12b) compared women to adult sons who were still dependent on their fathers. Ouziel therefore approvingly cited the words of the Malki Ba-Kodesh, Rabbi Ḥayim Hirschenson: "If this is so, then we would also deprive sons and daughters still living at home and dependent upon their father the right to vote," as a warrant for his own views on the matter of women's suffrage. Just as no one dared suggest that suffrage not be extended to adult dependent males on the grounds that their rejection of their fathers' position might create domestic discord, so no one should suggest that voting rights be denied women on that basis. After all, differences of opinion on such matters cannot be suppressed and the strength of family bonds would surely prove more enduring than whatever ire might result from familial disagreements on political issues.

On the other hand, Ouziel, at the end of the entire responsum, took note of Rav Kook's position, and noted that some critics maintained that the vote should be denied women because it might lead to obsequious behavior on their part. That is, a wife might fear expressing her own will, and might simply vote for the party or candidate that her husband favored. However, Ouziel was not distraught at such a prospect. Instead, he contended, if this were the case, it should simply be viewed as a "gift of instruction and love" that the husband shared with his wife. Indeed, said Ouziel, "Who would not desire such an act, one wherein the wife would display such esteem for her husband that she would defer to him in this way?" In fact, this outcome might constitute the strongest possible argument for extending suffrage to women, for this would allow the wife to display her love for her husband in an active way, thereby increasing domestic peace among the Jewish people!

In concluding the first half of his responsum, Ouziel turned to *Hagigah* 16b as a warrant for his position. There, the Talmud relates that Rabbi Yose permitted women to lay their hands on a "peace-sacrifice" if they so desired. As the Talmud states, "Once we had a calf that was a peace sacrifice, and we brought it to the Women's Court, and women laid hands on it — not that the laying on of hands had to be done by the women, but in order to gratify them." One commentator, in explaiing this passage, noted, "So that they should feel that they have a share, like men, in the sacrificial rites of their offering." Inasmuch as this was their offering, the women, like the men, were called upon to participate actively in the ritual. This precedent was relevant here, claimed Ouziel. Women, he reasoned, should participate in elections just as men would, for their interests in this matter, like the interests of the women called upon to participate in the "peace-offering," were involved. In the case of voting, where there was no ground for prohibition, failure to grant them this right would constitute "an insult and an oppression – *elbon ve-honaʾah*." Jewish law and equity demanded that suffrage be extended to women.

Having disposed of the question of whether voting rights should be granted women, Ouziel now turned to the second issue: Can women serve in public office? Here he noted that some halakhic precedents seemingly opposed granting women this privilege. In *Sifrei Deuteronomy* 157, the midrash, citing Deuteronomy 17:15, "Thou shalt in any wise set a king over thee," commented, "a king, but not a queen," and Maimonides, on this basis, ruled in *Hilkhot Melakhim* 1:5 that there was a prohibition against a woman serving in public office.

Ouziel took these sources seriously, and addressed them directly. In analyzing them, he observed that there was actually no prohibition in either Mishnah or Gemara that prohibited women from holding public office. Furthermore, the Bible itself contradicted the sense of these rulings, for the story of the prophetess Deborah in Judges 4 surely indicated that Judaism allowed women to serve as public officials. The Sages themselves, in commenting upon Judges 4:4, noted that Deborah officiated as a judge and that the Children of Israel "were compelled to obey her legal judgments." This precedent proved that the statement contained in *Sifrei Deuteronomy* 157 did not prohibit women from all public service.

Ouziel indicated that the scope of the rulings in both *Sifrei* and the Rambam was circumscribed and he maintained that each ruling applied only to appointments made by the Sanhedrin. In cases where the Sanhedrin was involved, women were indeed ineligible for office. In other instances, however, women are able to serve. Indeed, this was the case with Deborah, for she was not appointed by the Sanhedrin. Moreover, Ouziel wrote that the people were not simply forced to accept her rule. Rather, basing himself upon the classical talmudic commentary of Rabbenu Nissim on a passage in *Shavuot*, he asserted that the Children of Israel willingly accepted Deborah as their leader. In a modern state, wherein the polity, through direct elections, expresses "its opinion, its agreement, and its faith in those elected," present-day women can therefore surely serve in office. Should women be the choice of the electorate, they have the right to wield public authority and power, for their election would demonstrate that present-day *am yisrael* accepts them, just as *bnei yisrael* received Deborah in the hoary past. *Halakhah* is clear — "From [the standpoint] of the *din*, [we] are also able to elect women."

In concluding his responsum, Ouziel noted that the same objection concerning licentiousness lodged against extending suffrage to women might be applied to the question of their serving in office as well. Indeed, "from an ethical standpoint, as a hedge to modesty, perhaps there is a prohibition concerning this," he wrote. Yet, he dismissed this objection on this point just as he had rejected it when applied to the question of whether women should be allowed to vote. As Ouziel commented, "Since we have learned that the Torah did not prohibit [women occupying public office] except by appointment of [the Sanhedrin], there is no justification for prohibiting [such occupation] on account of licentiousness, for if there was any justification for such prohibition on account of licentiousness, then the Torah would not have permitted [Deborah to serve as a judge]."

Echoing the position he had taken earlier, Ouziel observed that men and women had business transactions together every day. They constantly engaged one another in such negotiations, and there was no hint of untoward conduct in them. The rabbinic statement, "Do not speak overly much with women," (*Pirkei Avot* 1:5) applied only to idle talk. Matters of public import, however, were not included in this prohibition. Indeed, to even think such thoughts of Jewish men and women engaged in public affairs was insulting, and Ouziel claimed that the people Israel were holy and should not be suspected of improper sexual conduct. He concluded this argument by asserting that *Sukkah* 51b, where the Sages ruled that men should sit downstairs while women should sit upstairs in the Temple courtyard during the time of the Sukkot water libation festival, did not apply to the current case, for the talmudic ruling dealt with a large gathering during a time of rejoicing when it was likely that the "evil inclination" might dominate. In the *Asseifat ha-Nivḥarim*, however, such misconduct was inconceivable. Behavior of this type "among the people Israel" in an Elected Assembly "could never be." He therefore concluded that just as women possessed a "meaningful obligation" to vote, so all women — elected as they would be with the approval and consent of the public — were eligible for political office. Traditional gender roles that confined women to the domestic realm while rendering them ineligible for participation in the political order had no Jewish legal basis and Ouziel considered them inapplicable in the modern Jewish state.

The Approach of Rabbi Herzog — Equivocating Acceptance

Herzog wrote his response to these issues at the time of the creation of the Jewish State. The Israeli government was preparing to enact legislation that would define the process and procedures whereby the Knesset would be selected. At the very outset of his work, Herzog stated that he supported a position that would permit women to vote as well as to be elected. He derived a Jewish legal precedent for this stance from the work of Rabbi David Zvi Hoffmann (1843–1921) of Berlin, who had ruled in a 1919 responsum that Jewish law allowed for the extension of suffrage to women. Although Hoffmann had not addressed the question of whether Jewish law permitted the election of women to public office, Herzog simply cited Hoffmann's ruling and indicated that he countenanced a public policy position that favored the admission of women into the body politic both as voters and as office-holders.[13] At the same time, he stated that he had grave personal reservations about these developments and that as an individual he was displeased that traditional gender roles had been so transformed in the present era that the extension of these rights to women in the mod-

---

13 Hoffmann's responsum on this matter was originally published in two parts as "*Ein Gutachten*," in *Jeschurun* VI (1919), pp. 262–66 and 515–22. It has been republished in Hebrew translation in *Ha-kibbutz be-halakhah: Asseifat ma'amarim* (*Kevutzat sha'alavim*: 5744), pp. 286–90. It is interesting to note that Herzog did not actually have the Hoffmann responsum before him. Rather, he simply knew its holding and cited it as a warrant for his own position. This is unusual, as an halakhic decisor generally wants to examine the argument of the authority that he has quoted. Herzog's use of the Hoffmann decision in this way testifies to the high regard Herzog had for Hoffmann.

ern nation-state was unavoidable. His subsequent exposition of the stance that he adopted on these questions is interesting and noteworthy precisely because it reflects the complex and ambiguous welter of pragmatic and legal considerations that informed his own thinking on these issues.

In the first part of his responsum, Herzog took into account a number of pragmatic points that informed the decision he was about to render. Indeed, these considerations and the political realities of his day caused him to assert that Jewish law was sufficiently flexible to meet the challenges of an era where radical innovations had taken place in the roles assigned men and women. Indeed, he noted that it was committed to a notion of gender equality in this area and that the United Nations would demand that suffrage be extended to women as a precondition for recognition of Israel as a nation. Although he himself was personally opposed to granting women the vote, the necessity that the State of Israel be created overrode all other considerations, including this one.

Since the extension of suffrage to women was simultaneously unthinkable and unavoidable in the contemporary setting, Herzog was completely opposed to any Orthodox attempt to boycott the election as a mark of protest against this innovation. Indeed, he wrote, "The rabbis will dissuade no one[14] from going to the ballot box," and an Orthodox refusal to cast ballots on this account would therefore constitute "an internal disaster" for the religious community, as "Orthodox Judaism would lose all its strength and influence" in the emerging State. He therefore bluntly concluded, "The matter does not depend upon my opinion, or the opinion of the rabbis at all." The classical model of a community responding to rabbinical rulings had no force in the modern world. To pretend that it did would only further weaken Orthodox interests. Indeed, he observed that a "great deal had already been lost" by the failure of the *ḥaredi* community to participate during the 1920s in the elections for the *Asseifat ha-Nivḥarim*. Present-day Orthodox Jews ought not to repeat their mistake. Instead, they should follow the example of Simeon ben Shetah, who participated in a Sanhedrin dominated by Sadducees so that Pharasaic interests could be championed.[15]

14 That is, no non-Orthodox Jew.
15 See *Megillah Ta'anit* 10.

Having delineated these pragmatic considerations, Herzog now shifted his discourse to a discussion of the classical sources. Like Ouziel, he argued that there was no precedent that would clearly prohibit women from participating either passively (voting) or actively (serving in office) in the modern democratic order. Although those opposed to female officeholders routinely cited *Hilkhot Melakhim* 1:5 as a warrant for their position, Herzog, like Ouziel, argued in this instance that this law did not constitute a precedent. The Maimonidean ruling applied only in a case where a woman would occupy her position, as a king would, for life, and where she could transmit her post as a birthright, again as a king would, to her sons. Yet, these conditions clearly did not obtain to a seat in the Knesset, as these posts had fixed terms of three, perhaps five, years, and were the result of election, not hereditary right. Hence, the *Mishneh Torah* passage did not constitute a prohibition against women serving in public office in *Medinat Yisrael*.

Furthermore, Herzog noted that despite this ruling that prohibited a woman from serving as sovereign, there was in fact a precedent in the Talmud that contravened the prohibition. After all, the Sages had countenanced the rule of Salome as Queen over Israel without even a hint of protest. Herzog said this was so because the Sages knew that she was faithful to the Oral Law and upheld it. Not a single halakhic source, therefore, raised an objection to her rule. This indicated that in an instance such as this, where "the perpetuation of the faith — *kiyum ha-dat*" depended upon the queenship of a woman, the rule, as found in the *Sifrei* and the *Mishneh Torah*, could be set aside for the sake of the greater good. In adopting this stance, Herzog was implicitly invoking a utilitarian calculus that had an halakhic source. In *Berakhot* 9:5, the Tannaim, in a wordplay on Psalm 119:126, "It is time to work (*et la'asot*) for the Lord: they have made void Your Torah," reread the verse as, "They have made void Your Torah because it is a time to work for the Lord," which they employed as a warrant for uprooting a single commandment during a time of emergency so that the Law as a whole could be saved. Consequently, the Sages, as Herzog pointed out, suspended the prohibition that forbade the writing of the Oral Law and they permitted its written composition so that the Torah would not be forgotten in Israel. The writing of the Oral Law was, of course, considered a defining act in rabbinic history. The Sages had assented to this suspension, for the alternative would have been the consignment of the Tradition to death. Herzog drew upon this precedent precisely because it granted him tremendous flexibility to dislodge a single tradition while staunchly defending the Tradition as a whole. As a result of these considerations, Herzog concluded that the present-day Orthodox community, even if it felt that Jewish law prohibited women from participating in public life either as voters or as officeholders, had no right to boycott elections for the Knesset. By exercising their franchise and casting ballots, the Orthodox today, like their ancestors who displayed their commitments in the past, could affirm "the Torah in its entirety," for through the political power they would wield, they would "prevent the destruction of the faith in the Jewish state."

Having put forth this argument, Herzog completed this segment of his responsum by stating that one need not actually depend upon this extraordinary warrant to sanction Orthodox involvement in a modern political process where women would participate as equals. After all, there was no explicit halakhic prohibition that forbade women from voting. Nor, in light of the historical-legal precedent of Salome the Queen, was there a cause for maintaining that women could not hold office. Jewish law allowed for an interpretation that permitted women to participate as the equals of men in the present-day political order, and there was no doubt that such an interpretation, for all the reasons advanced above, was in the best interests of Orthodox Jews in the newly-established State of Israel.

Herzog then considered the opinion that Rabbi Salomon Spitzer of Hamburg had written on this matter. Spitzer forbade both the extension of suffrage to women and the right of women to hold public office on the grounds that each innovation violated the dictum contained in Leviticus 19:2, "You should not walk in their ways." Spitzer maintained that such practices constituted an imitation of gentile ways, and he condemned female participation in the political process as unseemly for a Jewish woman. Indeed, he feared that these innovations would lead to sexual misconduct.

Herzog dismissed this objection as groundless and pointed out that men and women already mingled together constantly both in the courts and in the marketplace. Like Ouziel, Herzog argued that if one defined such conduct as immodest, then no semblance of normal life would be "left any human being." The appearance of women at the polls was no different than their presence in any other arena of public life. Nor would the existence of female members in the Knesset lead to sexual transgression. The members of Knesset were engaged in their work and had no time for these sorts of thoughts to get in the way of their work!

Herzog then went on to examine the nature of the prohibition concerning *ḥukkat ha-goy* (imitation of the gentiles), based on Leviticus 19:2. Spitzer had quoted Mordechai Benet, who, in the famed anti-Reform 1819 Orthodox polemic, *Eileh Divrei ha-Brit* (These are the Words of the Covenant), had stated that *any* custom or law that originated among the gentiles — not only an idolatrous one — was forbidden on the basis of Leviticus 19:2. Spitzer therefore reasoned that as the extension of suffrage to women fell under this category, it was forbidden. Herzog countered by condemning such reasoning as faulty. Indeed, if this logic were to hold, then the State of Israel could not have an army, as other nations before Israel had established a military. He therefore stated, "It is as clear as the noonday sun that the prohibition of Leviticus 19:2, 'You shall not walk in their ways,' is a fence that the Torah erected as an obstacle to idolatry [only]." The role of women in the modern political order possessed no relationship to idolatry. It was simply the custom of civilized nations. As such, the concept of *ḥukkat ha-goy* did not apply here.

As a postscript to this point, Herzog observed that the extension of these political rights to women could not be defined as an imitation of gentile practices even in a general sense. After all, until modern times no one ever extended suffrage to women. Universal suffrage was a modern phenomenon, and women were only granted these political privileges now because of the social reality that marked the present era. While these practices, he wrote, were "never observed among the people Israel, neither were they observed among the nations." These innovations "stemmed from a sociological change in the status of women [in western society]," and this resulted in the demand that the right of suffrage as well as the right to be elected be extended to women. Herzog maintained that Jewish law now, as in the past, possessed the flexibility and resources to countenance changed gender roles in a way that Jewish law could deem acceptable, and he cited medieval rabbinic precedent as a warrant for this assertion.

Herzog pointed out, for example, that the role of women in the realm of commerce had been altered during the Middle Ages and that the rabbis of that era had little trouble in interpreting Jewish law so as to cope with a transformed setting where women played a visible role in the economic marketplace. The modern political phenomena of women casting ballots and holding office surely posed no greater challenge to present-day halakhic authorities than those business developments had presented to medieval decisors. Medieval rabbis did not view these changes as threatening the foundations of Jewish law. Instead, these authorities recognized that these changed gender roles could be incorporated within "the four ells of *Halakhah*," and they accommodated the changes brought on by their era by plumbing the range of resources Jewish law provided them.[16] Modern rabbis should do no less. They should follow the example set by their medieval predecessors and recognize that although social-political reality in these areas compelled Jewish law to respond, such responses could be positive, for these changes posed no danger to the authority of the halakhic system. Instead, Herzog observed that the expansion of roles played by women in these areas "removed a discrimination that had led to the denial of their rights as human beings," and that there was "no prohibition at all" against these changes from a halakhic perspective.

Herzog concluded his responsum by employing the legal convention of "accepted custom and usage" to support his stance. He noted that the pious Sephardic community of London had extended women the right to vote more than one hundred years earlier.

> The members of this *Kehillah* were observers of the Torah . . . and all of their actions were done by the authority of Sages. I do not claim that we should do so in our *kehillot*. Nevertheless, from this it is apparent that there is no absolute prohibition [against extending the right of suffrage to women].

Given the *weltanschauung* that marked Herzog as an Orthodox rabbi and as the holder of a doctorate in literature from the University of

---

16 Herzog cited the commentaries of the *Ba'er Heitev* and *Pithei Teshuvah* on *Even ha-Ezer* 80 as examples of rabbinic authorities who had dealt with these novel developments in their interpretations of Jewish law.

Liverpool, the precedent supplied by the London Sephardic community was particularly crucial. After all, the London Sephardic *kehillah* was simultaneously western and observant. It constituted an apt model for the nascent Jewish state, and Herzog was clearly delighted that there was such precedent in the modern Jewish world for countenancing gender-role innovation.[17]

Conclusion

In comparing the stance that Kook adopted concerning these issues with those advanced by Ouziel and Herzog, we see that Rav Kook viewed traditional gender roles as inviolable. Social reality might extend female gender roles into the public sphere. Women's assigned realm, however, remained a domestic one, and all change was to be resisted. Indeed, Kook seems to have believed that transformations in this arena threatened the very framework of traditional Judaism.

Ouziel and Herzog adopted a different perspective. Both men rejected the classical legal category of kingship as the appropriate one for approaching these matters. While each conceded that these innovations were driven by the unprecedented phenomenon of parliamentary democracy and universal suffrage, they believed that this reality no more challenged the viability of Jewish law in the twentieth century than the presence of women in the business world had challenged Jewish law during the Middle Ages. As such, the question of whether the *Halakhah* could permit women to vote and stand for public office in the modern setting could be dealt with as the expansion of women into the economic sphere had been handled in a previous time. For these men, these changes in the political realm were not revolutionary events. They were simply additional considerations that had to inform the rabbinic leaders of the community as they chartered a future course for Judaism and the Jewish people. Their view of gender was surely more elastic than was that of Kook.

These responsa constitute interesting data for the analysis of the attitudes Jewish law permits concerning gender, but they reveal — in a normative sense — something more as well. In looking at the responsa

17 On this change in the life of the London Sephardic community, see Albert M. Hyamson, *The Sephardim of England: A History of the Spanish and Portuguese Community, 1492–1951* (London: Methuen, 1951), p.380.

of Ouziel and Herzog, there is much we applaud. Their writings reflect an ethical vision that "both men and women should be equal and full social participants."[18] It is a liberal vision that informs western culture. At the same time, we contend that our Jewish heritage contains this truth as well. Genesis 1:27 teaches us that women as well as men are created in the divine image. Precisely because women share a common humanity with men, they cannot be denied the basic right of full and equal participation in the modern political process.

Yet, Ouziel and Herzog compartmentalized this teaching of equality, and they sought to limit its application to the political realm. They were willing to extend the gender role assigned women in politics, but they would not, elsewhere in their writings, expand that role in the public realm of Jewish religious life. Neither rabbi drew what we would consider the logical conclusion that might have been derived from their teaching. If the humanity that marked women meant that they could not be denied their political rights as full and equal participants in the political domain, then that same humanity ought to have led those rabbis to conclude that women be granted full and equal expression in the religious realm as well. Indeed, Reform, Reconstructionist, and Conservative Judaism have internalized this egalitarian vision and, as a result of the ethos that marks it, have celebrated female entry into the public religious life of the Jewish people.

In looking at. Kook's responsum, we see the classical rabbinic separation of women in sharper focus. Women are identified with the domestic realm; men are actors in the political sphere. We would reject this assignation of roles for men and women. At the same time, we acknowledge that Kook was correct when he warned that the entry of women into the public domain of politics could not be confined there, and that the ethos that sparked this innovation was destined to have revolutionary implications for Judaism as well. Rather than decrying these implications, however, we welcome them as a fulfillment of the moral challenges that face all Jews.

As Rachel Adler has indicated in her path-breaking book *Engendering Judaism: An Inclusive Theology and Ethics*, Judaism confronts an "ethical task" as it begins "to reflect and address the questions, understandings,

---

18 This wording is taken from Rachel Adler, *Engendering Judaism: An Inclusive Theology and Ethics* (Philadelphia: Jewish Publication Society, 1998), p.xiv.

and obligations of both Jewish women and Jewish men. It is not yet fully attentive to the impact of gender and sexuality either on the classical texts or on *the lived experiences* of the people Israel."[19]

Our study has demonstrated that Jewish legal literature has approached "gender categories and distinctions" in diverse ways. Yet, despite our awareness of those categories and distinctions, this study, like others, does not tell us "what sorts of changes we ought to make in the future." That will unfold over time. We are confident, however, that changes inspired by these sensitivities will be "negotiated in conversations where participants invoke and reexamine the values and priorities enunciated in Jewish tradition in light of the current needs, injuries, or aspirations demanding to be addressed."[20] As such, their outcomes need not be feared. Instead, they should be celebrated, as Jewish women, along with Jewish men, seek to realize the messianic promise of truth and joy that lies at the heart of Jewish faith.

19 Ibid.
20 Ibid. pp. xiv–xv.

16

Parallel Worlds

Wissenschaft and Psak in the Seridei Eish

In his remarkably insightful memoir-essay, "Confluent Myths," Arnold Band, scholar of Hebrew and comparative literature, wrote what he has described as an element of his "intellectual biography."[1] He observed that as a Boston-area Jewish child of the 1930s and 1940s, he was involved in "two educational systems," that of the public elementary school and Boston Latin School for Boys as well as Harvard University, on the one hand, and the Boston Hebrew College, on the other. Each of these universes had its own "elitist myth." The former promoted a Jeffersonian ideal of the individual as paramount and contended that it was the duty of the state to provide a pathway that would allow all students, including Jewish children of immigrant parents, to realize their own ambitions and aspirations. The latter emphasized "the primacy of the group over the individual" and promoted the more collectivist hope for "Jewish national cultural revival" as expressed in an attachment to Hebrew language and a vaguely defined Zionism. One world was Gentile and Christian. The other was fiercely Jewish.[2] These worlds, and the myths they embodied, were, as Band described them "confluent and fused in the imagination of each person."[3] In those days, little time was devoted to an analysis of what these two disparate myths actually implied. Nor was the cognitive distance between them explored.

In this autobiographical vignette, Band has demonstrated his awareness of the modern condition and the manner in which it has enveloped contemporary persons in the Occident — Jews especially. Peter Berger has given precise expression to what this means in sociological terms. In his influential work *The Heretical Imperative*, he has pointed out

---

1 Arnold J. Band, "Confluent Myths," in Haim Marantz, ed., *Judaism and Education: Essays in Honor of Walter I. Ackerman* (Beer-Sheva: Ben Gurion University Press, 1998), pp. 1–19. The term "intellectual biography" is taken from p. 1.

2 Ibid. While this paragraph draws freely from the entire essay, see especially pp. 4–6 and 16–19 for the primary expression of the themes herein summarized.

3 Ibid. p. 17.

that *hairesis*, understood as option or choice, has become the defining characteristic of the modern Occident. Persons are no longer born and socialized into a single community as if by fate. Rather, identity becomes a matter of negotiation for each person. Each individual must choose among competing modes and models of values and culture as he or she undertakes the arduous task of constructing a life that is ordered and coherent in the context of a pluralistic and divided world.[4] As the anthropologist Mary Douglas has observed, "For the Bushman, Dinka, and many primitive cultures, the field of symbolic action is one." In contrast, modern persons in the West are quite conscious that they "operate in many different fields of symbolic action."[5]

In the modern setting, identity cannot be constructed in isolation from a distant "other." Band, as the Boston boyhood he has described indicates, instinctively understood this. His autobiographical fragment testifies to his realization that social, religious, and cultural identity is not simply an established fact. It is produced and reproduced within a matrix of complex social, cultural, political, religious, and economic traditions and realities. Identity is embedded in the many circles that constitute and inform a life, and these circles, rather than being fully harmonious, often promote a dissonance that must be overcome if a person seeks to achieve synthesis, or perhaps ignored if the person seeks to attain comfort.

This means, as W. E. B. Dubois once phrased it, that modern people are marked by what he labeled a "double consciousness." This phrase refers to the sense that modern persons possess — particularly persons who are members of minority cultural, religious, and racial groups — of "always looking at one's self through the eyes of others."[6] The "self" is realized and established in confrontation with "other inhabitants" — persons and cultural systems — of a world that is both broad and diverse.

While Band adumbrated this position in his 1998 "Confluent Myths," he had already, three decades before, pointed to the tensions such "double consciousness" frequently produced. In his 1966 article "Jewish Studies in American Liberal Arts Colleges and Universities," Band focused

4 Peter Berger, *The Heretical Imperative* (Garden City, N.Y.: Anchor Books, 1979).
5 Mary Douglas, *Purity and Danger* (London: Routledge and Kegan Paul, 1966), pp. 68–69.
6 W. E. B. Dubois, *The Souls of Black Folks in Three Negro Classics* (New York: Avon Books, 1965), pp. 215 and 218.

attention on the stress that living in multiple cultural worlds could produce for university scholars in the field of Jewish studies. He indicated that for over a century — since the rise of *Wissenschaft des Judentums* in nineteenth-century Germany — academicians in the field had been trained to study and explicate Judaism "as a historical phenomenon." Such an approach stood in direct contrast to one that many had imbibed in their childhood study of Judaism, an approach that had taught them, as Band has phrased it, that Judaism was "a truth to be propagated."[7] Those Jewish scholars who came within the ambit of the university were instructed to substitute "scientific study, based on the principle of historical evolution, for tradition as the foundation for Judaism." This substitution, as Band has observed, "exacted a high price for those Jews who sought it, and often ended in the loss of specific cultural identity." In other cases, it simply released "tensions" that remained either unexamined or "unresolved."[8]

Band's two articles, taken in tandem, indicate that he has done more than present the cultural dilemmas that the present-day Occident has posed to all committed Jews. He has also focused on the specific challenges confronting Jewish academicians devoted to the study of Judaism as they engage in the arduous and complex task of constructing their own identities as modern Jews while remaining faithful to their vocation as critical scholars.

Orthodox Jews who entered the academy experienced the challenges involved in these tasks with a special intensity. Among these Jews, no one has confronted the challenge of straddling two worlds more directly than Eastern European-born, yeshiva-educated Rabbi Jeḥiel Jakob Weinberg (1884–1966). The famed author of a responsa collection entitled *Seridei Eish* (Remnants of Fire), Weinberg was forged in the crucible of two disparate worlds. In *Seridei Eish* 2:92, he addressed a matter where these two worlds met. In responding to the question as to whether Jewish law permitted a Jew to lecture on the topic of Jewish law (*mishpat ivri*) in a secular university, Weinberg demonstrated how he had internalized the sometimes discordant values of each one. The reflections Band has offered in his articles on this topic, as well as

---

7 Arnold J. Band, "Jewish Studies in American Liberal-Arts Colleges and Universities," *American Jewish Year Book* 67 (1966), p.12.

8 Ibid. p.5.

the seminal role he has played in fostering the growth of Jewish studies in this country and throughout the world, makes this responsum a particularly apposite text to analyze in his honor.

After presenting a brief portrait of Rabbi Weinberg that will situate this text within the context of his life and times, this article will present a synopsis of some of the major legal elements he drew upon in explaining the decision he rendered on this matter. We will also take a close look at the section of the responsum that touches upon the domain of *psak* (Jewish legal ruling) and the realm of *Wissenschaft* (academic study). This section of the text demonstrates how completely Weinberg had internalized both these areas within his own person. At the same time, these lines indicate how disparate the ethos that informs these worlds can be and thus how difficult it may be to attain a complete synthesis between Jewish tradition and western culture. As such, the text not only sheds light upon a specific challenge that confronted Rabbi Weinberg. It points to the larger dilemma posed to all committed modern Jews as they struggle with the task of constructing a meaningful and authentic Jewish identity within the parameters of pluralistic and at times discordant cultural worlds.

Jeḥiel Jacob Weinberg – Background and Context

Rabbi Weinberg is considered one of the leading Jewish jurists of the twentieth century.[9] The last head of the Berlin Orthodox Rabbinical Seminary before its destruction by the Nazis in 1939, Weinberg survived the Holocaust by escaping to Switzerland. He lived in Montreux, Switzerland, for the next two decades, until his death in 1966. Educated originally in the rabbinical yeshivot of Lithuania, Weinberg was also trained in the canons of the academy at a modern German university. Throughout his life, he remained absolutely committed to an Orthodox Judaism that proclaimed the authority and truth of the tradition. This he learned from his childhood and during his adolescent years as a student in Slobodka at the Kenesset Yisrael yeshiva headed by Rabbi Na-

9 The biographical details that follow regarding Rabbi Weinberg are taken from Marc B. Shapiro, *Between the Yeshiva World and Modern Orthodoxy: The Life and Works of Rabbi Jeḥiel Jacob Weinberg, 1884–1966* (London: The Littmann Library of Jewish Civilization, 1999).

than Zvi Finkel (1847–1927), where he was deeply steeped in a broad variety of classical rabbinic texts. In 1914, after having served as rabbi of the Lithuanian town of Pilwishki for over seven years, Weinberg journeyed to Berlin for medical treatment. While the outbreak of World War I initially prevented his return to Russia, Weinberg apparently found the intellectual and cultural life of the German capital to his liking, and he elected to stay there even when the opportunity to return to Pilwishki presented itself in 1916. As his biographer Marc Shapiro has phrased it, "Despite all his nostalgia for the east, he was now under the spell of the west."[10]

Indeed, several years later, Weinberg, like a number of other Eastern European Jews who had received traditional training in Talmud,[11] chose to expose himself to the rigors of modern academic study. In 1920, after a semester at the University of Berlin, he moved to Giessen, where he enrolled at the university under the tutelage of "the great Semitic and masoretic scholar Paul Kahle (1875–1965), a pious Christian and a vigilant defender of Jewish literature against anti-Semitic attacks."[12] There, Weinberg also studied Old Testament with Professor Hans Schmidt and philosophy under Ernst von Astor. During the summer of 1923, he completed examinations for his doctorate and wrote a dissertation on the *Peshitta*, the Syriac translation of the Bible. In addition, Weinberg taught courses at Giessen on a variety of subjects — Bible, Mishnah, and Talmud — for both beginning and advanced university students. His feet were now firmly planted in the soil of two worlds, the traditional realm of the Lithuanian yeshiva and the western universe of modern academic discourse. Both were now parts of his patrimony. How he was to calibrate an allegiance to each of them was to be a major focus of his life.

The Responsum — Legal Considerations and Ruling

At the very outset of his academic career at Giessen, Weinberg had to confront the problem addressed by the text analyzed in this essay. The

10 Ibid. p.65.
11 For a description of this phenomenon, see Hillel Goldberg, *Between Berlin and Slobodka: Jewish Transition Figures from Eastern Europe* (Hoboken, N.J.: Ktav, 1989).
12 Shapiro, *Between the Yeshiva World and Modern Orthodoxy*, p.65.

halakhic tradition clearly contained texts that forbade Jews to teach Torah to non-Jews. Two major talmudic warrants for this negative posture are commonly adduced. One is found in *Ḥagigah* 13a, where the Talmud states, "R. Ammi further said, 'The teachings of Torah are not to be transmitted to an idolater,' for it is said, 'He has not dealt so with any nation. And, as for His ordinances, they have not known them' (Psalms 147:20)." *Sanhedrin* 59a constitutes a second *locus classicus* for this prohibition. There the Talmud asserts, "R. Yoḥanan said, 'A heathen who studies the Torah deserves death,' for it is written, 'Moses commanded us a law for an inheritance' (Deuteronomy 33:4). It is our inheritance, not theirs."

Weinberg, aware of these proscriptions, had to resolve for himself the question as to whether Jewish law provided an alternative path whereby these prohibitions could be circumvented or muted. Otherwise, as a pious Jew committed above all to Jewish law and its strictures, his participation in the enterprise of *Wissenschaft des Judentums* would have been severely limited. Indeed, if these rulings remained uncontested, it would have been impossible for him to offer lectures on the topic of Jewish law before what must have been a predominantly gentile audience in a secular university. Therefore, in the responsum under consideration in this paper, Weinberg states that he initially addressed this issue in an unpublished opinion while serving as a lecturer in Jewish Studies at Giessen in 1923. His conclusion at that time, as Shapiro has pointed out, was "that teaching gentiles Torah solely for academic purposes is not proscribed."[13]

Weinberg further notes in the responsum before us that he had affirmed this stance earlier in another written responsum. In *Seridei Eish* 2:92, he adds that he wrote an additional responsum on this subject "several years earlier," at a time when Rabbi Teitz, a highly prominent Orthodox rabbi in Elizabeth, New Jersey, wrote an article on this matter in the rabbinic journal *Ha-Pardes*.[14] The responsum addressed to Rabbi Teitz is not contained in the four volumes of *Seridei Eish;* it does appear,

13 Ibid. p. 85.
14 The Teitz responsum dealt specifically with the issue of radio broadcasts. Rabbi Teitz offered a regular lesson on Talmud over the radio air waves. As gentiles would presumably be among the listeners to these programs, the matter of the proscription against teaching Torah to gentiles arose.

however, in his posthumously-published collected writings,[15] where it is dated as having been composed in 5714 (1953–54). Thus, the Weinberg responsum under consideration in this essay must have been written several years after 1955, during the last decade of his life.

In *Seridei Eish* 2:92, Weinberg reveals the legal reasoning that allowed him to arrive at this position. He states that in his first considerations on the subject in 1923 he relied upon Maimonides, *Hilkhot Melakhim* 10:9, for his ruling. There, Maimonides writes,

> A heathen who busies himself with the study of the Law deserves death. He should occupy himself with the [study] of the seven [Noahide] commandments only. So too, a heathen who keeps a day of rest, even if it be on a weekday, if he has set it apart as his Sabbath, is deserving of death. It is needless to state that he merits death if he makes a new festival for himself. The general principle is this — none is permitted to introduce innovations into religion or devise new commandments. The heathen has the choice between becoming a true proselyte by accepting all the commandments, or adhering to his own religion, neither adding to it nor subtracting anything from it.

Weinberg, in interpreting this halakhic passage, averred that the prohibition against a Jew teaching Torah to a gentile served a boundary maintenance function. Indeed, he claimed that Maimonides affirmed these strictures against gentiles on the grounds that they created a barrier (*meḥitzah*) that would separate Jew from gentile. Consequently, Maimonides was careful to point out that these prohibitions applied only in those instances where the motivation that prompted the gentile to observe the Sabbath or study Torah stemmed, in the words of Rabbi Weinberg, from "religious intent — *kavanah datit.*" Only then would the line dividing Jew from gentile be in danger of being blurred.

In the case of Sabbath rest, Weinberg explained that Maimonides

15 Marc B. Shapiro, *Collected Writings of Rabbi Yeḥiel Yaakov Weinberg* (Scranton: University of Scranton, 1998) (Hebrew), #15, vol. 1, pp. 26–30. Here Weinberg indicates that the Teitz article on this matter appeared in *Ha-Pardes* 14 (5714). In addition, it should be noted that Weinberg, *Seridei Eish* 2:90, wrote yet another responsum that touches upon this question. However, he does not allude to that ruling in 2:92.

would therefore not have held gentiles culpable if their rest on the Sabbath day was prompted solely for the sake of "rest itself — *menuḥah*." Nor would he have found gentiles "guilty" if they ceased to work on the Sabbath on account of "laziness — *atzlut*." After all, in these instances, they had no desire to erase distinctions between Jews and gentiles. Motivated by fatique or "laziness," they did not intend to claim the Jewish religious heritage as their own. As the actions of these gentiles were not prompted by religious motives and threatened no religious borders, Jewish law — in such instances — did not proscribe their act of Sabbath rest.

That which obtained in regard to the gentile and Sabbath observance pertained as well to the matter of the gentile and Torah study. Just as motive was determinative in the former case, so it was of seminal import as regards the latter question. Consequently, in this first part of the responsum, Weinberg concluded that gentiles could not be held liable if the rationale that prompted them to engage in such study was that of intellectual curiosity, not religious intent. Thus the Maimonidean proscriptions in the *Mishneh Torah* were not absolute. The matter of intent circumscribed the ruling.

Of course, Weinberg was aware that this exegesis hardly exhausted the Maimonidean corpus on this issue, for he immediately pointed to a responsum Maimonides had written on the issue that seemingly indicated that Maimonidean opposition to a gentile being taught Torah by a Jew — regardless of the gentile's intent — was uncompromising. As Weinberg stated,

> Concerning that which Maimonides wrote there in his responsum number 364, "And if the hand of Israel is dominant over them, he should be prevented from studying Torah until he is converted." This prohibition is not based upon the legal category, "You should not place a stumbling block before the blind" (Leviticus 19:14).[16]

---

16 This prohibition stems from the commentary of the *Tosafot*, early medieval rabbinical authorities, on *Ḥagigah* 13a, where the issue of "placing a stumbling block before the blind" is raised. Yet the *Tosafot*, basing themselves upon passages in *Sanhedrin* 59a and *Avodah Zarah* 6b, ultimately indicate that the rationale of not "placing a stumbling block before the blind" for the prohibition does not necessarily apply to the question of Torah being taught to a gentile. Weinberg obviously followed their reasoning here, focusing instead on the discussion in *Sanhedrin* 59a concerning "stealing an inheritance" or "violating a betrothed maiden."

Instead, if Israel is politically dominant, we need to prevent the gentile from transgressing the prohibition against "stealing an inheritance" or "violating a betrothed maiden."

In taking this stance, Maimonides based himself upon the passage contained in *Sanhedrin* 59a, where the Sages commented upon the statement made by Rabbi Yoḥanan, "A gentile who studies the Torah deserves death, for it is written, 'Moses commanded us a law for an inheritance (*morashah*)' (Deuteronomy 33:4)"; they stated, "On the reading *morashah* (an inheritance), he steals it; on the reading *meʾorasah* (betrothed), he is guilty as one who violates a betrothed maiden, and is stoned." The talmudic reading here in *Sanhedrin* 59a is based upon a passage in *Pesaḥim* 49b, where two opinions on the reading of Deuteronomy 33:4 are recorded on the basis of a word play on the unpointed Hebrew text. One view is that the key word in the passage should be read as, "Moses commanded us a law for an inheritance (*morashah*)." An alternate reading is, "Moses commanded us a law for a betrothal (*meʾorasah*)." In the former instance, the prohibition that forbids a gentile from studying Torah falls under the category of theft. In the latter case, the prohibition results from the stricture against adultery. On either reading, the teaching of Torah to a non-Jew is forbidden: as the Torah is the heritage of Israel alone. Maimonides appears to hold that this result is legally actionable, i.e., Torah must not be taught to a non-Jew, in every instance where "Israel is dominant."

Yet, as Weinberg quickly pointed out, historical circumstances blunted the force of this ruling because Israel was seldom dominant. Indeed, the Diaspora condition of Jewish life as well as geopolitical realities in the contemporaneous international community meant that Israel virtually never enjoyed absolute hegemony in the world. As a result, the prohibition was seldom legally in force. Consequently, wrote Weinberg, "There is no prohibition against a Jew writing words of Torah in a foreign language for fear lest a gentile come and read them. Indeed, if this were the case, it would also be forbidden us to write books in Hebrew, for a significant number of gentiles study the Hebrew language and master it."

As his last comment reveals, Weinberg was quite conscious of present-day realities. In fact, he cited the *Besamim Rosh* of Rabbi Saul Berlin, who confirmed his observation that Jewish learning had spread among gen-

tiles. This authority had asserted that no Jew who taught a gentile Torah in this era was culpable, for, as "in our day, study [of Torah] has become disseminated among them."[17] The spread of *jüdische Wissenschaft*
meant that a goodly number of gentiles in the modern setting were capable of reading the primary texts of Jewish tradition in the original. As
it was impossible under such conditions for Jews to prevent non-Jews
from engaging in the act of Jewish learning, Weinberg concluded, not
even Maimonides would have held that present-day Jews were under
an obligation to refuse such learning to gentiles. In the modern situation, a Jew who taught Torah to a gentile was hardly guilty of transmitting the heritage of Israel to non-Jews. Israel surely did not enjoy absolute dominion in the world, and Judaism itself was certainly not sealed
off hermetically from the larger world.

Furthermore, the Tradition also provided precedents that ran counter
to the proscriptions discussed above. Indeed, these warrants indicated
that Jews could share Torah study with gentiles. To be sure, some of
these lenient rulings were essentially motivated by prudence. For example, Weinberg noted that *Megillah* 9b was such a text. There it stated
that the Sages rendered a particular passage as they did in their Greek
translation of the Bible because of their "fear of the government."[18] Consequently, at the end of his responsum in *Seridei Eish* 2:92, Weinberg
cited "fear" as a factor for allowing Torah to be taught to non-Jews, for
failure to do so might lead to an increase in anti-Jewish sentiment
among gentiles.

However, there were other warrants for teaching Torah to non-Jews
that could hardly be described as emerging from such pragmatic interests. After all, *Megillah* 9b also approvingly quoted Rabbi Yoḥanan as
citing Genesis 9:27 as a proof text for sharing words of Torah with gentiles, as Weinberg pointed out: "Rabbi Yoḥanan said, "As Scripture states,
'God enlarge Japeth, and he shall dwell in the tents of Shem'" (Genesis
9:27)." Genesis 10:2 stated that Javan, the father of the Greek nation, was

---

17 While Weinberg does not cite the precise source here, it is found in *Besamim Rosh*:
327. I would thank Marc Shapiro for locating this reference for me.

18 Weinberg wrote, "And the Sages of Israel who translated the Torah into Greek did so
'on account of fear of the government,' as it says in *Megillah* 9b that they feared to
'write "the hare" (*arnevet*) in the Torah (Leviticus 11:6) because the name of Ptolemy's
wife was Arnevet' (hare)."

reckoned among the sons of Japeth. Shem, of course, was regarded as the progenitor of the Jewish people. Therefore, Rabbi Yoḥanan interpreted this verse as a call for Jews to recognize that God desired that the children of Shem, i.e., the Jewish people, share the gift of Torah with the children of Javan, i.e., non-Jews. Furthermore, Onkelos rendered the Torah in the vernacular, i.e., Aramaic, thereby making the words of Scripture accessible to many, and, in *Sotah* 35b, the medieval commentators on the Talmud noted that "the Torah was translated into seventy tongues," i.e., all the languages of humanity. Consequently, there was no question that knowledge of the Written Torah could freely be shared with gentiles. Otherwise, there would have been no precedents in Jewish tradition that would have countenanced the rendering of Torah into every tongue. Nor would a whole host of later rabbinical authorities have explicitly ruled "that it was permitted to teach non-Jews the Written Law."

Weinberg also argued that this permission was not confined to the Written Law alone. Indeed, it embraced elements of the Oral Torah as well. After all, *Baba Kama* 38a reported that there were two gentile Roman commissioners who desired to learn dimensions of the Oral Law, and the Sages agreed to teach them. While the medieval commentators on this text observed that this might be regarded as forbidden, these *Tosafists* acknowledged that these gentiles were allowed to study laws of damages (*hilkhot nezikin*), as the Noahide Covenant obligated gentiles as well as Jews to observe these statutes.[19] Moreover, Rashi, commenting upon *Baba Metzia* 119a, noted that the "King of Persia was an expert in these laws." From these standpoints, Jewish law could be construed as permitting non-Jews to study the Oral Law, as well as the Written Law.

19   On the basis of the Noah story in Genesis 9, the rabbis of the Talmud, in *Sanhedrin* 56a, posited that God enjoys a universal relationship with all humanity as well as the Jewish people. This relationship, known in Jewish tradition as the Noahide Covenant, caused the rabbis to assert that God issued seven commandments through Noah to all humankind. These commandments were later viewed as constituting the minimal moral demands that God made, and makes, upon all non-Jews. One was positive, to establish courts of justice for society. The other six were negative, and they included prohibitions against eating flesh from a living animal, adultery, murder, robbery, blasphemy, and idolatry. Laws of damages governing civil society were seen as an integral part of these commandments. Hence, their observance was enjoined upon gentiles and Jews.

These arguments, along with others that Weinberg marshaled throughout his responsum, allowed him to maintain that the setting of the modern university was surely an appropriate venue for Jews to instruct non-Jews in the study of Jewish law. Indeed, citing the Netziv, Rabbi Naftali Zvi Judah Berlin (1817–1893), head of the famed Volozhin yeshiva, on *Hagigah*, Weinberg maintained that the talmudic proscription, "A gentile who studies Torah deserves death," applied only when Jewish law was taught the gentile "in depth — *derekh ha-iyun*." As Weinberg summarized the matter, "It seems absolutely incontrovertible that the prohibition applies only to fixed times for Torah study in holy books and in deep dialectical discussions concerning Torah." Hence, while a prohibition did exist, its application was so limited that there was no question that it was permissible to inform gentiles "of the wisdom of Torah via lecture and narrative." A Jew could lecture on Jewish law (*mishpat ivri*) at a secular university.

Wissenschaft and Psak — A Significant Digression

In the course of his discussion on this matter, Weinberg provided an aside that directly addresses the issues raised at the outset of this essay by Band, for it displays the two diverse worlds of Jewish legal tradition and modern critical scholarship that Weinberg inhabited. In this section of his responsum, Rabbi Weinberg directly commented on the passage contained in *Sanhedrin* 59a that forbade non-Jews from either observing the Sabbath or engaging in the study of Torah. It was on the basis of this passage that Maimonides and other medieval rabbinic authorities had issued their proscriptions that banned gentiles from such activities. However, as Weinberg here pointed out, the actual meaning of this *Sanhedrin* text in its original context had been informed and illuminated by modern critical scholarship on the topic. Indeed, this scholarship was unavailable to premodern Jewish jurists like Maimonides. These authorities had interpreted the meaning of the *Sanhedrin* text upon which they had based their rulings in the absence of such knowledge. Had this knowledge been available, it may well have altogether altered the content of the law as it had been codified and applied in numerous precedential holdings by countless rabbis.

Furthermore, Weinberg not only made reference to this scholarship.

He also reflected, as will be shown, on the legal weight such scholarship should be assigned in Jewish jurisprudence. The passage in Weinberg's responsum reads as follows:

> And I will not hesitate to inform you what I found more than thirty years ago in a book written by a certain scholar [*ḥakham eḥad*]. He stated that the passages found in Sanhedrin concerning a gentile who observed the Sabbath and who engaged in Torah study were directed against the sect of earliest Christians who released themselves from the obligation of *brit milah*, but observed the Sabbath and also engaged in Torah study. They would join with the people Israel on the Sabbath and on holidays, and listen to their words. Afterwards, they would go and slander the Jews before the gentile authority. And he brought forth proof for this from what was said in *Deuteronomy Rabbah* 1:18, "And R. Yosi ben Ḥanina said, 'A gentile who observes the Sabbath, but does not accept the obligation of *milah* upon himself, deserves death. Why? For he was not commanded concerning it.'" Despite this, Maimonides and other *rishonim* understood the words according to their plain meaning and believed that they applied to every gentile. And we have no right to change the rulings of the *rishonim*, even on the basis of reasoned assumptions.

Throughout his responsum, Weinberg, as is the wont of every respondent, was most careful to name every authority he mentioned. Of course, the views of all the authorities he cited were sanctioned by venerable rabbinic precedent. Each stood as a recognized link in the *shalshelet ha-kabbalah*, the chain of Jewish legal tradition revered by Orthodox *poskim* for generations. By quoting these men, Weinberg indicated that he was mindful that there was a "rule of recognition" that demanded that he cite each authority by name. Indeed, such citation served to legitimate his decision on this matter.

As a rabbinical jurist, Weinberg saw himself above all as firmly ensconced within this Jewish legal tradition. For the decision he would render in this responsum to be an authoritative one, he was required to justify it explicitly through the precedents provided by later rabbinic tradition. Though trained in modern critical scholarship, he was, in this text, writing as a rabbi, not an academic. The distinction is not insignificant.

As David Weiss Halivni has observed, "The roles of historian and jurist must be differentiated. The historian seeks to register and unravel the objective data of history by searching for the origins of society and culture."[20] Through an investigation of pertinent sources, he seeks to determine what that data actually signified in its original temporal context. In contrast, the jurist operates within a framework where facts are "harnessed and manipulated" in light of an ongoing process of legal hermeneutics.[21] The meaning of the data is not necessarily established by recourse to what it may actually have meant in the original setting. Rather, the meaning is determined by the way that subsequent literature in the legal tradition has defined it. Indeed, the well-known Jewish legal principle, "*Hilkhata ke-vatra'ei* — the law follows the latest authorities," captures the point that Halivni is here making. Consequently, he concludes, "A jurist must work from within the parameters of a tradition of precedents and a system of regulations."[22] Indeed, this "requirement of adhering to systemic rules of authority and hierarchy... constitute restraints" upon the jurist.[23] What is decisive for the historian may be of no consequence to the jurist.

To be sure, Weinberg did see himself as part of the academic world. As Shapiro puts it, "Weinberg was never totally removed from modern Jewish scholarship, and it was important to him that his views should find favour in the academic community."[24] Indeed, he even co-authored an article in the academically acclaimed *Hebrew Union College Annual*, an extraordinary act for a man of his background and position.[25] The quest of the critical scholar was thus hardly alien to him, and he frequently maintained that when textual variants could uncover the true meaning of a rabbinic text, they had to be discussed. Indeed, on more than

---

20 David Weiss Halivni, *Peshat and Derash: Plain and Applied Meaning in Rabbinic Exegesis* (New York and Oxford: Oxford University Press, 1991), p.99.

21 Ibid. p.98.

22 Ibid. p.171.

23 Ibid. p.169.

24 Shapiro, *Between the Yeshiva World and Modern Orthodoxy*, p.201.

25 See his monograph, "The Mishna Text in Babylonia: Fragments from the Geniza," *Hebrew Union College Annual* 10 (1935), pp.185–222, which he co-authored with his teacher, Paul Kahle.

one occasion he engaged in textual emendations of classical texts on the basis of such sources.[26]

However, his willingness to "grant legitimacy" to such academic explanations in the realm of Jewish law was severely circumscribed. Indeed, it was indulged only so "long as practical *halakhah* was not thereby affected."[27] In his responsa, Weinberg functioned not as an academician, but as a *posek*. As such, he was compelled to pay attention, as Shapiro phrases it, to "well-established principles which must not be abandoned." Foremost among them is the notion "that it is forbidden to issue halakhic rulings which have no sound basis in earlier rabbinic authorities."[28]

As stated above, Weinberg was consistent in attempting to acknowledge every legitimate legal authority cited in his responsa. His failure to do so in this instance of the "*ḥakham eḥad*" leads to the inevitable conclusion, as Shapiro has put it, that "Weinberg is here referring to an academic scholar,"[29] not an established Jewish legal authority. Otherwise, Weinberg would have identified him. In light of the canons established by Orthodox Jewish jurisprudence for arriving at *psak*, the academic scholarship of this *ḥakham*, while interesting, could be assigned no legal importance. This scholar and his work, however respected, were not part of the *shalshelet ha-kabbalah*, the legitimate chain of Jewish legal tradition mentioned above.

While the identity of the *ḥakham* cited in *Seridei Eish* 2:92 remains something of a mystery, it appears that it might be Louis Ginzberg (1873–1953), for significant elements of the scholarship quoted by Weinberg are found in his work. Ginzberg served for decades as professor of Talmud at the Conservative Jewish Theological Seminary in New York, and was arguably the world's foremost academic scholar of rabbinic literature during his lifetime. His work was routinely consulted by academics in this area, and Weinberg was quite familiar with the corpus of his scholarship. Indeed, in another responsum published in *Seridei Eish* 3:49, Weinberg referred to Ginzberg not only by name,

26 Shapiro, *Between the Yeshiva World and Orthodoxy*, pp.193ff.
27 Ibid. p.202.
28 Ibid. p.195.
29 Personal communication from Shapiro to the author on January 6, 2000.

but with the honorific, "Rabbi L. Ginzberg of blessed memory." In that responsum, Weinberg indicated that research Ginzberg had conducted on the Cairo Geniza clarified a problem in Jewish law concerning the ritual of *ḥalitzah*.[30] Weinberg was delighted because Ginzberg had published a previously unknown responsum contained in the Geniza that a medieval Babylonian rabbinical authority had issued on the matter. Weinberg wrote of this research, "I rejoiced in it in the way that one would if one discovered a great treasure. For this research confirms the explanation of the Noda be-Yehudah on the matter. Indeed, the Noda be-Yehudah had the merit of taking a stance on this matter that comported to the position advanced by the earlier Babylonian authority. *And their words are words of Tradition (kabbalah)*."[31]

The Noda be-Yehudah, Rabbi Yehezkel Landau of Prague (1713–1793), has long been recognized as one of the preeminent jurists in Jewish legal history. Ginzberg's research in this instance had uncovered a traditional text written by an earlier authority in the chain of Jewish case law that confirmed the stance Rabbi Landau had put forth on the issue. Weinberg did not hesitate to cite Ginzberg in this instance. In fact, he was obviously pleased to cite the scholarship Ginzberg had authored, despite his association with a non-Orthodox seminary. It would appear he did so here for two reasons. In the first place, Ginzberg had not offered any type of historical commentary or theory on the medieval responsum that he printed. Instead, his research in this case had simply disseminated to a wider audience a traditional legal text hidden away for centuries in the attic of a Cairo synagogue. Secondly, the content of that responsum supported the position a great *posek* had advanced on the matter two centuries prior to Weinberg. As such, the text published by Ginzberg not only presented the writing of a medieval Jewish

30 When a woman's husband dies without male offspring, Jewish law requires the woman to marry her husband's brother in the hope that this union will produce a surrogate son and heir to the dead brother so that the dead brother's name "may not be blotted out in Israel" (Deuteronomy 25:6). Should the living brother reject his deceased brother's widow and opt not to fulfill his levirate duty, he is able to do so through the ritual of *ḥalitzah*, "unshoeing," whereby he releases the levirate widow from her automatic marital tie to him. His sister-in-law is then to remarry or not at will.

31 See *Seridei Eish* 3:49, especially p.179. (The emphasis here is mine.) See also the comments of Shapiro on Weinberg and Ginzberg, *Between the Yeshiva World and Modern Orthodoxy*, p.205.

authority, but also reinforced a vital stream in the ongoing tradition of Jewish law as well. His scholarship, in this instance, therefore did not contradict the received legal tradition. On the contrary, it had a "sound basis in earlier rabbinic authority." As such, Weinberg felt there was no constraint, despite Ginzberg's institutional affiliation, against employing it.

In the case before Weinberg in *Seridei Eish* 2:92, the issue was different. In the first place, it may be that the anonymous *hakham* was not Ginzberg, but another scholar. Indeed, I will indicate why this may be so below. Yet, there is the strong possibility that the scholar in question was in fact Ginzberg. After all, Weinberg, in the text before us, stated that he had read the scholarship of the anonymous *hakham* over three decades earlier. This is precisely the period when Ginzberg's *Ginzei Schechter* — published in Hebrew in 1928 under the aegis of the Jewish Theological Seminary — had appeared.

In an essay there, Ginzberg stated that the statements found in *Sanhedrin* 58b and 59a proscribing gentiles from either observing the Sabbath or engaging in Torah study on pain of death were not aimed at all gentiles.[32] In fact, he claimed that the Sanhedrin texts had to be read in light of the wording found in *Deuteronomy Rabbah* 1:18, where a parallel and more complete version of the Sanhedrin passages was found. As Ginzberg wrote, "From this midrash we learn ... that the Sages feared that those righteous gentiles (*hasidei umot ha-olam*) who had accepted the yoke of the Sabbath, but not the entire Torah, would be led to 'heresy — *minut*,' i.e., to the faith of the Christians (*le-munat ha-notzrim*). Therefore, the Sages protested their observing the Sabbath while they were yet uncircumcised."[33]

The passages located in *Sanhedrin* 58b–59a are, as Ginzberg put it, "there abbreviated — *she-sham ne'emar be-kitzur*."[34] Instead of reading, "A gentile who observes the Sabbath deserves death," the *Sanhedrin* 58b text should have added the phrase, as the midrash did, "but does not accept the obligation of *milah* upon himself," after "the Sabbath." Similarly,

32 Louis Ginzberg, "The Y'lamdenu Sermons in Midrash Deuteronomy Rabbah," (Hebrew) in Louis Ginzberg, ed., *Ginzei Schechter* (Jerusalem: Jewish Theological Seminary of America, 5688–1928), vol. 1, pp. 495–96. I would like to thank Marc Bregman for helping me locate this source.

33 Ibid. p. 496.

34 Ibid. p. 495.

in *Sanhedrin* 59a, the same wording should have been entered after "Torah study." The proscriptions they contain did serve a boundary maintenance function — just as Weinberg had stated Maimonides maintained. However, the boundary they established did not include all non-Jews. Instead, they were specifically limited to the early Christians. Assuming that Ginzberg was correct, the implication would be that the rulings of Maimonides and other *rishonim* proscribing gentile study of Jewish texts were based on a non-contextual and therefore faulty understanding of the Sanhedrin passage!

Indeed, later academic scholarship on this passage in the Talmud supports Ginzberg's insight. Lee Levine points out that there was a fierce rivalry that marked Jewish-Christian relations in Palestine at the time these texts were written. Each religion was anxious to make proselytes. As a result, writes Levine, "This competition for converts created antagonisms which were compounded by the exclusive claim of each side to legitimacy in religious matters." Consequently, the text in *Deuteronomy Rabbah* 1:18, where Yose ben Ḥaninah contends that a gentile who observes the Sabbath, but refuses circumcision, is deserving of death, must be understood as emerging from this crucible of Jewish-Christian competition.[35] Furthermore, Ephraim Urbach, in his magisterial study *The Sages*, explains "A gentile who studies the Torah is deserving of death," in *Sanhedrin* 59a, as follows: "The exposition of the verse supports the assumption that the claim of the Christians, who sought to make the Torah their heritage, led to this sharp repudiation."[36]

To be sure, this does not prove conclusively that Ginzberg was the *ḥakham* Weinberg was quoting in his responsum. After all, Weinberg pointed out that this anonymous scholar had also claimed that those gentiles of this period who observed the Sabbath and engaged in Torah study "would go and slander the Jews before the gentile authority." This contention is absent in Ginzberg. Hence, it may be that Weinberg had a scholar other than Ginzberg in mind. However, if this was so, then it appears obvious that this other scholar either relied upon Ginzberg for his insight or that he simply had arrived independently at an iden-

35   Lee Levine, *Caesera under Roman Rule* (Leiden: E.J. Brill, 1975), pp. 82 and 207.
36   Ephraim E. Urbach, *The Sages: Their Concepts and Beliefs* (Jerusalem: Magnes Press, 1975), p. 550.

tical position. On the other hand, it may be that Weinberg, depending here upon his memory, accurately recalled Ginzberg's suggested emendations of the Sanhedrin passages but collapsed details he had derived from other sources into this citation. Indeed, standard scholarly sources of this era routinely maintained that passages such as those in *Ḥagigah* 13a and *Sanhedrin* 59b that proscribe teaching Torah to gentiles stemmed from the fear that these gentiles, including gentile Christians and semi-proselytes, would employ such knowledge "against the Jews" before public authorities.[37] Hence, it is entirely possible that Weinberg did indeed project these elements from his storehouse of knowledge onto the Ginzberg writing.

Whether the *ḥakham* in question is Ginzberg or another scholar, there is no doubt, as stated above, that Weinberg has here cited an academic-critical scholar, not a rabbinic authority. His failure to provide a precise identification of the work and its author indicates this. Of course, if he is referring to a gentile scholar, his reluctance to supply the name and title of the work in a traditional responsum is readily comprehensible. The appearance of such humanistic scholarship by a gentile scholar in an Orthodox Jewish legal text would be virtually unthinkable in the traditional religious precincts Weinberg inhabited. Indeed, were it not that Weinberg cited Ginzberg elsewhere, I would add that it would be equally improbable for an academic-critical piece of historical scholarship by a famed scholar at a Conservative seminary to find a place in such a work as well.[38]

However, as we have seen, Weinberg did refer to Ginzberg by name in *Seridei Eish* 3:49, and even identified him by an honorific generally reserved only for Orthodox rabbis. In part, this reflects the rarefied status Ginzberg enjoyed in the realm of Jewish learning as well as the unusually broad scholarship that Weinberg commanded. Yet, a substantive distinction must be drawn between the two types of scholarship

---

37 For example, see the 1907 *Jewish Encyclopedia*, s.v., "Gentile," and the bibliography contained there.

38 In this regard, it should be noted that Shapiro writes in *Between the Yeshiva World and Modern Orthodoxy*, p. 205: "Ginzberg also accepted some of the tenets of the Higher Biblical Criticism . . . It is doubtful whether Weinberg was aware of this." Indeed, had Weinberg been cognizant of this, it is interesting to speculate as to whether this would have led him to ignore Ginzberg and his scholarship altogether.

mentioned in these two responsa, and this distinction may well account for the different treatment that Weinberg displayed towards such scholarship in each of them. In the previous responsum, as mentioned above, the critical scholarship of Ginzberg simply provided a text written by a medieval rabbinic authority that had previously been unpublished. Furthermore, the text itself constituted a source for Jewish legal tradition and advanced a viewpoint that no less a personage than the Noda be-Yehudah had advocated. In the case of *Seridei Eish* 3:49, the academic scholarship of Ginzberg informed and corroborated a stance sanctioned by venerable Jewish legal tradition.

In *Seridei Eish* 2:92, the scholarship moves in another direction altogether. Here, a critical-historical point is made, and an academic hypothesis concerning context and meaning is put forth. In addition, the entire theory put forth in this instance runs completely counter to the legal tradition as codified by Maimonides and other early medieval legal authorities. There is simply no basis for this understanding in the legal sources of the Jewish tradition. As a result, whether the scholar cited by Weinberg is Ginzberg or another, the point made by the scholarship itself, from the viewpoint of a traditional Jewish jurist issuing a *psak*, would be problematic. It would be pertinent in a text such as the Weinberg responsum only if the type of scholarship it embodied was regarded as an independent legitimate source for determining the law. Otherwise, it could not be deemed admissible, as it had no basis in earlier rabbinic legal writings. Consequently, Weinberg's failure to provide the exact citation for this *ḥakham* indicates that he was not simply uncomfortable with identifying the author of this hypothesis because the author was either a gentile or a non-Orthodox Jew. Rather, his refusal to identify this author undoubtedly stems from his recognition as a Jewish jurist that such critical-historical scholarship, while intriguing, had no place in the realm of *psak*.

Of course, a different conclusion might be reached after analyzing all this data. It may be that Weinberg, in assessing this scholarship, regarded its argument as no more than highly plausible. Indeed, he asserted that this theory concerning the real meaning of the Sanhedrin passages only reflected a "reasoned assumption — *hashʿarah meḥukhamah*." It was hardly incontrovertible. Therefore, it may be that while Weinberg considered it probable that "Maimonides and other *rishonim*" did not correctly understand the texts upon which they established their rulings, he would not change those rulings on the basis of such conjecture alone — however likely. Such unconfirmed scholarship could not trump a millennium of Jewish law. As he wrote, "We have no right to change the rulings of the *rishonim*, even on the basis of reasoned assumptions." Thus, it may be that one could argue that his two worlds — the domain of the critical scholar and the realm of the Jewish jurist — were completely compatible. If the academic results put forth by the *ḥakham* had been absolutely certain, not just "a reasoned assumption," perhaps Weinberg would have altered the holdings of earlier legitimate authorities. However, this position, while possible, is quite unlikely. For, as explained above, in the realm of Orthodox *psak*, historical-critical scholarship of the type manifest here is seldom, if ever, assigned any weight.

Moreover, the pronouncements that many of the major spokesmen of the Conservative Movement have put forth on the relationship that obtain between *psak* and historical-critical scholarship highlight the distinctiveness of the posture that marks the universe of Orthodox jurisprudence on this matter. Conservative Judaism has long been recognized as the ideological offspring of and heir to the Positive-Historical School of Judaism advanced by Zacharias Frankel (1801–1875), one of the foremost practicioners of *jüdische Wissenschaft* in the nineteenth century. Frankel actively engaged in critical scholarship and was comfortable with the notion that Jewish law had evolved organically in history. Indeed, Orthodox rabbis such as Samson Raphael Hirsch (1808–1888) of Frankfurt savagely attacked Frankel for these views.[39]

Nevertheless, the Conservative Movement and its halakhic authorities insisted upon affirming the approach of Frankel to the realm of Jewish law despite such Orthodox criticism. Indeed, the Jerusalem-based contemporary Israeli Conservative rabbinical authority David Golinkin, in a trenchant analysis of a major responsum issued by Ginzberg, has pointed out that the Ginzberg responsum pays great atten-tion to history and bears "the indelible imprint of *Ḥokhmat Yisrael.*"[40]

---

39 For an understanding of Frankel's approach to Jewish law, as well as the condemnation it elicited from Orthodox peers in Germany such as Hirsch and others, see chap. 7, "Traditional Reactions to Modern Jewish Reform," in this volume.

40 See David Golinkin, "The Influence of Seminary Professors on Halakha in the Conservative Movement: 1902–68," in Jack Wertheimer, ed., *Tradition Renewed: A History of the Jewish Theological Seminary* (New York: Jewish Theological Seminary of

As a result, it is hardly surprising that Golinkin himself has maintained that a major guideline that informs Conservative Movement jurisprudence is its inclusion of "critical-historical" scholarship as an integral element in the halakhic process. He asserts that there is a conscious attempt in the *psak halakhah* of Conservative Judaism to elicit testimony from experts in fields such as archaeology or history in legal matters where such academic expertise may be relevant to the holding that will emerge. Such critical scholarship, for Rabbi Golinkin, is a formal part of the halakhic process, and it must be employed in arriving at the determination of the law in instances where its findings are relevant.[41]

Joel Roth, Professor of Talmud at the Jewish Theological Seminary, echoes this view and gives full voice to this position in his influential work *The Halakhic Process: A Systemic Analysis.*

> The goal of the critical study of rabbinic texts is to discover the *peshat* of each statement, comment, and question in a passage, and then to establish the *peshat* of the entire passage. *If the end product of such an analysis results in an interpretation different from the interpretation of the passage offered by the classical commentators or from that codified by the codifiers, its legal status is the same as that of another interpretation or a variant reading, and carries with it all the options that we have seen new interpretations and variant readings provide a posek.* . . . Sages in all ages have accepted reliable new data from any source if it permitted them to better understand the texts to which they devoted their lives.[42]

In staking out this position, Golinkin and Roth insist that this posture is fully consonant with the legal practices of rabbis from the talmudic era on into the Middle Ages. Indeed, Golinkin contends that preeminent modern halakhic exemplars such as the Vilna Gaon and his circle also employed such guidelines in reaching their own judgments con-

---

America, 1997), vol. 2, p. 479. Golinkin provides a detailed discussion of Ginzberg as a *posek* on pp. 461–67 of this article.

41 David Golinkin, "Introduction," *Responsa of the Va'ad Halacha of the Rabbinical Assembly of Israel* 3, pp. 1–2.

42 Joel Roth, *The Halakhic Process: A Systemic Analysis* (New York: Jewish Theological Seminary, 1986), pp. 373–74. (Emphasis mine.)

cerning the law.[43] And Roth, in an extensive discussion of extra-legal sources and their impact on Jewish legal rulings, demonstrates convincingly that sociological, economic, medical, scientific, ethical, and psychological findings and sensibilities have all, at times, brought about a reformulation of Jewish law on the part of recognized authorities. Jewish law, he states, has often employed such sources to meet the challenges of new problems.[44]

Nevertheless, Roth himself, in discussing the import of history for the determination of Jewish law, admits that its results may well be "legally irrelevant." Thus, his contention — that "the end product" of such historical-critical analysis would possess "legal" significance if it arrived at a conclusion other than that offered by the classical codes and decisions of Jewish law — must be qualified. Critical scholarship does not function in any formal sense as an independent variable that can direct the law. It does not necessarily, if ever, provide additional options for the *posek* in arriving at a ruling. Thus, as Roth himself writes, "Only statements that are systemically acceptable as legal sources have a claim to normativeness. The validity of the arguments of any legal system is internal to that system, not external to it."[45] In making this last point, Roth replicates the observations made above by Halivni. His own analysis reveals that the realm of the jurist is frequently distinct from the domain of the historian. What is of central interest for the latter may be of no concern to the former.

Concluding Reflections

The section of the Weinberg responsum that has been featured in this paper demonstrates the point that Weinberg the jurist dwelt in a realm distinct from that of Weinberg the modern academic scholar. His text indicates that one of the hallmarks of the Orthodox world in which he lived was the limitation it placed on the relevance of critical scholarship for the process of Jewish jurisprudence. To be sure, the mention of the unidentified *ḥakham* in the Weinberg text is more than intriguing, for the citation of such critical scholarship in this genre of Jewish

---

43   Golinkin, "Introduction," p. 2.
44   See Roth, *The Halakhic Process*, pp. 231–304.
45   Ibid. p. 117.

jurisprudence is itself quite rare. It demonstrates that Weinberg was no ordinary respondent. He was clearly informed by the academic world of the modern university. At the same time, his failure to name the *ḥakham* remains striking, though, in light of this discussion, quite understandable. It indicates his discomfort with this type of citation in a responsum, as well as his recognition that reference to critical scholarship of this type was assigned no valence in the realm of traditional Jewish jurisprudence that he inhabited.

If this was so, the issue that remains is one of explaining why Weinberg mentioned this scholarship at all in this genre of Jewish legal literature. While the question cannot be resolved with absolute certainty, Halivni does provide a theory that may provide insight into the matter. In his *Peshat and Derash*, Halivni contends that there is a "double-verity theory" that sometimes operates in the world of rabbinic Judaism. He writes, "To be sure, nowhere do the rabbis explicitly state, let alone, explicitly justify, the double-verity theory." Moreover, to say that there is such a theory "does not mean that it is unanimous, that every rabbi accepted it."[46] Yet, some rabbis have and do, and they assert that there is often more than one "truth" contained in a text. Furthermore, Jewish religious tradition sanctions the discovery of these multiple truths. As Halivni defines and explains:

> [This double-verity theory] accredits critical textual scholarship both of the Bible and Talmud as a bona fide religious activity, the practitioner of which fulfills the commandment to study Torah (by critical study, I mean here interpreting an authoritative text in a manner different from the interpretation which is endorsed by an earlier authority or upon which a practical law is based). [However], its verity belongs to the realm of intellect, not to the realm of practice. To practice according to critical norms is strictly forbidden, but to study critically as a religious activity... is nevertheless a legitimate historical aspect of religious learning.[47]

As Halivni has here put forth, Jewish legal tradition could view the Weinberg reference to critical scholarship in this responsum as per-

46 Halivni, *Peshat and Derash*, p. 112.
47 Ibid. p. 104.

fectly in accord with the canons of Jewish jurisprudence. His description contends that at least one branch of traditional Jewish legal research would countenance such citation as an acceptable intellectual activity that can take place in Jewish legal discussions. However, this branch simply would not extend the license granted this research into the realm of *psak* itself. In the domain of intellectual speculation, such research is completely acceptable. From this standpoint, Weinberg, in pointing to the hypothesis of the *ḥakham*, did nothing to violate the norms of the traditional rabbinic world that had formed him. His act comported to the standards established by normative elements in this society. The intellectual arrangements that marked Weinberg and that permitted him simultaneously to be an active participant in the world of *jüdische Wissenschaft* as well as the domain of classical Jewish legal decision-making can thus be viewed as a reflection of the world view Halivni has described. From this perspective, it would seem that the citation of critical scholarship by Weinberg in his *Seridei Eish* 2:92 was completely normative. His act in this instance conformed to the canons and norms of traditional Jewish legal investigation as evidenced in one stream of Jewish law. This explanation is certainly plausible, and it may well explain the mind-set that characterized Weinberg.

However, the writings of Band on the notion of confluent worlds provide another angle from which to view the entire matter. The two worlds that Weinberg inhabited may be more distinct than a "double-verity theory" would suggest, and that the ethos that informs each of them may be in greater tension than a "double-verity theory" would imply. Indeed, Weinberg may well have been able to resolve this tension only by leaving it unexamined.

In each of these worlds, there are always modes of behavior and investigation that are designated as normative and appropriate. After all, there are directives that regulate the construction and flow of norms within the major institutional spheres of all traditions. These guidelines often specify with great precision the process whereby norms are legitimately determined. When individual persons conduct themselves in accord with a process established by a particular tradition, it constitutes an act of solidarity that confirms their membership in the group that has promulgated these standards.

In the case discussed in this paper, it was seen that Conservative *poskim*, as members of a denomination that ideologically embraces the ethos of modern critical-historical scholarship, were able to affirm the notion that such scholarship be assigned normative weight in arriving at a Jewish legal decision. For them, the ethos of the academy and the values of rabbinic tradition, as they perceive them, converge. Indeed, their self-conscious and stated acceptance of the position that the realm of modern historical scholarship has the right to inform and guide the rulings of Jewish law not only bespeaks their judgment that there is a lack of tension between these two worlds; it confirms their identity as Conservative Jews.

For Orthodox rabbis like Weinberg, the matter was different. The decision he made to cite critical-historical scholarship in his respon-sum demonstrates that he was socialized into the world of modern ac-ademic research, and that he was both familiar and comfortable with it. At the same time, his rejection of that scholarship as a source for the norms of his community reflects a distinct Orthodox understanding of what a traditional rabbinic order demands. The values and beliefs that had nurtured him as a child and that had shaped his identity as an ado-lescent and as a young adult asserted that there were specified rules that had to be followed for the determination of Jewish law. As Weinberg understood them, these rules did not permit insights derived from the fruits of modern historical research to enter into the arena of *psak* unless sanctioned by classical rabbinic precedent. Indeed, his resolve not to grant the information provided by the anonymous *ḥakham* a norma-tive voice in the realm of *psak* can be regarded as a sign that his alle-giance to the rules established by the rabbinic order that had first formed him was accorded primacy in his life. As such, his decision reflects his own self-perception as an Orthodox Jew and constitutes an important act of self-definition as an Orthodox decisor.

His life-situation caused Weinberg, like all moderns, to choose between various roles. It placed Weinberg in an ambiguous situation in which his identity as an Orthodox Jew was potentially endangered, for the scholarship of the university had the power to shatter the existing social-cultural rabbinic order that bound him. By rejecting the nor-mative claims the *ḥakham* could place upon him, Weinberg confirmed his own social location as part of the Orthodox world and his own status as an Orthodox *posek*.

In looking at the Weinberg responsum from this perspective, it seems that Weinberg could no more completely avoid compartmentalization than a young Arnold Band could when he was growing up in the parallel worlds of Dorchester and Brookline, on the one hand, and Boston and Cambridge, on the other. Band has permitted us to see that an Orthodox authority like Rabbi Weinberg was no more immune from wrestling with the struggle presented by diverse cultural settings than any other modern Jew.

The challenge of constructing an authentic Jewish identity within the modern situation does not arise only *in extremis*. The testimony offered by Band concerning his own boyhood as well as his reflections on the rise of Jewish studies within the American university indicate that the struggle involved in the creation of an integrated human personality often occurs within the confines of an orderly social life. For Band, as for Weinberg, meaning was sought and identity constructed in the face of multiple and at times discordant cultural worlds. In this instance, as in so many others, Band has provided a framework that allows a text to be explored in novel ways. In so doing, he alerts those whose lives he has informed to the diverse ways that human beings go about the task of constructing individual and social meanings. The tensions among the circles that constitute and inform a life can frequently find no clear resolution. Parallel worlds are at times confluent and fluid. At the same time, they are often discordant and no real equilibrium can be achieved between them.[48]

48 This perspective illuminates some of the dynamics at play here in this part of the Weinberg responsum. For this understanding, as for so much else, I thank Arnold Band. His scholarship and his person enrich my world immeasurably. It is an honor to pay tribute to him in this way.

17

A Jewish Legal Authority Addresses Jewish-Christian Dialogue

Two Responsa of Rabbi Moshe Feinstein

October 28, 1965 will stand as a milestone moment in the history of Catholic-Jewish relations. On that date, the Second Vatican Council, in response to a call first put forth by Pope John XXIII in 1960, issued a statement on the Jews, *Nostra Aetate*. This document provided a positive assessment of the role played by the Jewish people throughout history and sought to repudiate antisemitism. In many Jewish circles, *Nostra Aetate* was received with enthusiastic, albeit cautious, optimism. After all, the spirit of openness found in its pages contained a promise of hope. Its proponents heralded it as marking the advent of a new era in which almost two millennia of an often-tragic history between Jews and Christians might be coming to an end. The document charted new directions for Catholic-Jewish relations throughout the world, and the spirit of religious ecumenicism and tolerance contained in its pages opened the floodgates for Jewish-Catholic dialogue and debate.

The Orthodox Jewish world was not impervious to these developments. Indeed, foremost among those who paid careful attention to them was Rabbi Moshe Feinstein (1895–1986). Born to a prominent rabbinical family in Uzda, Belorussia, Feinstein came to the United States in 1937. He served from 1937 until his death as head of Metivta Tiferet Jerusalem in New York, and his multivolumed collection of responsa, published under the title *Iggerot Moshe*, gained him worldwide recognition as a decisor (*posek*) and interpreter of Jewish law.[1] In the United States, no Orthodox *posek* was more authoritative than Rabbi Feinstein was during his lifetime.[2] A leader of what is commonly labeled "sectarian"

---

1   For a brief biography of Rabbi Moshe Feinstein, see Rod Glogower, "Feinstein, Moshe," in *The Encyclopedia of Religion*.

2   Numerous articles exist on the role that Feinstein occupied as the leading Orthodox decisor of his era. Several of the most significant English-language publications that give insight into his legal corpus are Emanuel Rackman, "Halakhic Progress: Rabbi Moshe Feinstein's *Iggrot Moshe* on *Even ha-Ezer*," *Judaism* 13 (1964), pp. 365–73; Aaron

or "traditionalist" Orthodoxy,[3] his was a brand of Orthodox Judaism that has been described as "committed to resistance . . . to the surrounding culture."[4] Feinstein served as president of the *Agudat ha-Rabbanim* (Union of Orthodox Rabbis of the United States and Canada), an organization first established in 1902 by sixty Yiddish-speaking Orthodox rabbis. This group, in the words of Jeffrey Gurock, was from the outset "strident" in its "nonrecognition of the Americanized Orthodox rabbinate."[5] Feinstein also came to occupy the post of chairman of the American branch of *Mo'etzet Gedolei ha-Torah* (Council of Torah Sages) of the sectarian Orthodox Agudat Israel, a European-born organization that was initially planted in the United States in 1938. This group, to cite Gurock once more, was critical of what it regarded as "the old-time American rabbis' non-adherence to uncompromising principles."[6] Feinstein gave expression to these principles in 1956 when he, with a number of other authorities in the world of the American *yeshivot*, issued a joint *herem* (ban). This ban stated that Orthodox rabbis were "forbidden by the law of our sacred Torah" to be members of organizations such as the Synagogue Council of America (an interdenominational Jewish organization) or local boards of rabbis where these

---

Kirschenbaum, "Rabbi Moshe Feinstein's Responsa: A Major Halakhic Event," *Judaism* 15 (1966), pp. 364–73; Ira Robinson, "Because of Our Many Sins," *Judaism* 35 (1986), pp. 35–46; and Norma Baumel Joseph, "The Traditional Denial of Change: Women's Place in the World of Rabbi Moshe Feinstein," *Journal of Religion and Culture* 2 (1987), pp. 190–201; idem. "*Meḥitzah*: Halakhic Decisions and Political Consequences," in Susan Grossman and Rivka Haut, *Daughters of the King: Women and the Synagogue* (Philadelphia: Jewish Publication Society, 1992), pp. 117–34; and idem. "Jewish Education for Women: Rabbi Moshe Feinstein's Map of America," *American Jewish History* (1995), pp. 205–22.

3   For the use of these terms, see, among others, Lynn Davidman, *Tradition in a Rootless World: Women Turn to Orthodox Judaism* (Berkeley and Los Angeles: University of California Press, 1991), pp. 37ff.; Jeffrey Gurock, "Resisters and Accommodators: Varieties of Orthodox Rabbis in America, 1886–1983," *American Jewish Archives* (1983), pp. 100–187; Samuel Heilman, "Inner and Outer Identities: Sociological Ambivalence Among Orthodox Jews," *Jewish Social Studies* 39 (1977), pp. 227–40; and Charles Liebman, "Orthodoxy in American Jewish Life," *American Jewish Year Book* (1965), pp. 21–97.

4   Davidman, *Tradition in a Rootless World*, p. 38.

5   This description of *Agudat ha-Rabbanim* is taken from Jeffrey S. Gurock, *American Jewish Orthodoxy in Historical Perspective* (Hoboken, NJ: Ktav, 1996), p. 7.

6   Ibid.

Orthodox men would cooperate "with their Reform and Conservative counterparts."[7] In view of all this, it is hardly surprising that the ecumenical developments surrounding Vatican II concerned him. Indeed, his concern was such that he issued two responsa in 1967 on the issue of interreligious Jewish-Christian dialogue that mirrored the attitude he had adopted a decade earlier regarding intrareligious discussions. They are presented here in English translation, and reflect a consistent sectarian stance on his part.

The first responsum, dated 19 Adar I, 5727 (March 1, 1967), was addressed to Rabbi Bernard Lander, then a young Orthodox rabbi, today president of Touro College, who was scheduled to attend a Protestant-Catholic-Jewish dialogue four days later. Lander had apparently promised to attend this meeting and wanted to know from Feinstein whether such attendance was permissible from the standpoint of Jewish law. The alarm Feinstein felt over such matters is palpable in this document and his refusal to sanction Jewish attendance at such meetings was absolute.

Clearly agitated by the issue, Feinstein wrote less than three weeks later (9 Adar II, 5727 (March 21, 1967) to Rabbi Joseph Soloveitchik (1903–1993), expressing his uncompromising determination to prohibit such dialogue. In writing to Soloveitchik, Feinstein was not only addressing a man who was his relative;[8] he was communicating with the foremost leader of modern Orthodox Judaism in America.[9] Soloveitchik himself stemmed from the same sectarian Orthodox Jewish world as Feinstein. Indeed, his family was famed in his native Lithuania for its genius in the study of Talmud, and Soloveitchik brought that tradition with him to America. In 1941, he became *rosh yeshiva* at

7   Ibid. p. 56.

8   Rabbi Feinstein's grandfather, Rabbi Yeḥiel Yitzḥak Davidovich of Karelitz, was the great-grandfather of Rabbi Joseph Soloveitchik. Davidovich's daughter, Faya Gitel, was the mother of Feinstein, while her sister Guta Chisa, was the mother of Rabbi Soloveitchik's mother, Pesia. Pesia, the first cousin of Feinstein, married Moses Soloveitchik, and that union produced Joseph Baer. For the family tree, see Aaron Rakkefet-Rothkoff, *The Rav: The World of Rabbi Joseph B. Soloveitchik* (Hoboken, NJ: Ktav, 1999), vol. 1, p. xli.

9   For a fine description and analysis of the preeminent role Rabbi Soloveitchik played in Orthodox communal life at this time, see Charles Liebman, "Orthodoxy in American Jewish Life," in Marshall Sklare, ed., *The Jewish Community in America* (New York: Behrman House, 1974), pp. 144ff.

the Rabbi Isaac Elchanan Theological Seminary (RIETS) of Yeshiva University, succeeding his father, Rabbi Moses Soloveitchik, in that post. His presence linked RIETS to the realm of the Lithuanian yeshiva, and his ascribed and earned status in the Orthodox world can hardly be exaggerated. However, despite his ties to the world of sectarian Orthodoxy, Soloveitchik also affirmed the worth of secular culture. He received a Ph.D. in philosophy from the University of Berlin for a dissertation on the work of Hermann Cohen, and he championed the universe of "modern" Orthodox Judaism. This universe, in contrast to the realm of sectarian Orthodox Judaism, "explicitly advocates accommodation to the surrounding culture."[10]

Soloveitchik had already publicly expressed his views on the issue of ecumenical dialogue with Christians three years before Feinstein approached him on this matter. As Aaron Rakkefet-Rothkoff explains:

> With the advent of the ecumenical thrust of the Catholic Church in the 1960s, the Rav [Soloveitchik] was consulted regarding Orthodox participation in the dialogue initiated by the Vatican with Jewish leaders. Rabbi Soloveitchik opposed many aspects of this dialogue. He held that there could be no discussion concerning the uniqueness of the respective religious communities. Each, he held, was an individual entity which could not be merged or equated with the other, since each was committed to a different faith. The Rav presented a paper entitled "Confrontation" on this topic at the 1964 midwinter conference of the Rabbinical Council.[11]

Soloveitchik published this paper in expanded form later that year in *Tradition: A Journal of Orthodox Jewish Thought*, under the same title as his address, "Confrontation."[12] While Rakkefet-Rothkoff is certainly correct in asserting that Soloveitchik opposed dimensions of the dialogue, an examination of the Soloveitchik essay indicates that there were also elements in the Jewish-Christian dialogue that Soloveitchik strongly endorsed. At the outset, he maintained that there was value in having formal relations between Jews and non-Jews. In addition, he

10 Davidman, *Tradition in a Rootless World*, p. 38.
11 Rakkefet-Rothkoff, *The Rav*, vol. 1, p. 49.
12 Joseph B. Soloveitchik, "Confrontation," *Tradition* 6 (1964), pp. 5–28.

viewed Christianity as more than a source of hatred towards Jews, and he recognized that the modern world had witnessed significant transformations in the attitudes that gentiles adopted towards Jews. This meant that there were areas in which Jewish-Christian cooperation was surely desirable. His open, yet cautionary attitude is best captured in the following statement:

> We cooperate with the members of other faith communities in all fields of constructive human endeavor, but, simultaneously with our integration into the general social framework, we engage in a movement of recoil and retrace our steps. In a word, we belong to the human society and, at the same time, we feel as strangers and outsiders.[13]

As spiritual head of the modern Orthodox Rabbinical Council of America (RCA), Soloveitchik's stance led the RCA to adopt a policy statement on ecumenicism and interreligious dialogue at its 1964 convention. As a statement of Soloveitchik's opinion on the subject, the resolution is worth citing in full precisely because its tone, as well as parts of its nuanced content, stand in such sharp contrast to the position put forth by Feinstein. The RCA statement reads:

> We are pleased to note that in recent years there has evolved in our country as well as throughout the world a desire to seek better understanding and a mutual respect among the world's major faiths. The current threat of secularism and materialism and the modern atheistic negation of religion and religious values makes even more imperative a harmonious relationship among the faiths. This relationship, however, can only be of value if it will not be in conflict with the uniqueness of each religious community, since each religious community is an individual entity which cannot be merged or equated with a community which is committed to a different faith. Each religious community is endowed with intrinsic dignity and metaphysical worth. Its historical experience, its present dynamics, its hopes and aspirations for the future can only be

13   Ibid. p. 26.

interpreted in terms of full spiritual independence of and freedom from any relatedness to another faith community. Any suggestion that the historical and meta-historical worth of a faith community be viewed against the backdrop of another faith, and the mere hint that a revision of basic historic attitudes is anticipated, are incongruous with the fundamentals of religious liberty and freedom of conscience and can only breed discord and suspicion. Such an approach is unacceptable to any self-respecting faith community that is proud of its past, vibrant and active in the present and determined to live on in the future and serve God in its own individual way. Only full appreciation on the part of all of the singular role, inherent worth, and basic prerogatives of each community will help promote the spirit of cooperation among the faiths.[14]

In practical terms, this meant that Soloveitchik and members of the RCA endorsed Jewish-Christian dialogue on social and political issues of general human concern. At the same time, they were opposed to such dialogue on matters of faith. Each religious community is singular and its theological postures are axiological. They cannot be the subjects of joint discussion. Of course, precisely how this line can be drawn in *praxis* is unclear. After all, the social concerns and political commitments that religious persons adopt are presumably extensions of the faith affirmations they possess. Nevertheless, this was the policy position Soloveitchik and his followers advanced, and it has informed and guided the stance numerous Orthodox rabbis and Jewish lay people have taken towards Jewish-Christian dialogue for over three decades.[15]

14 Ibid. pp.27–28.
15 Lawrence Kaplan, "Revisionism and the Rav: The Struggle for the Soul of Modern Jewish Orthodoxy," *Judaism* 48 (1999), p.299, summarizes the Soloveitchik position well when he writes, "The Rav, with his delicate balance between universalism and singularism, never opposed interfaith dialogue. What he opposed, as he states in 'Confrontation,' was interfaith *theological* dialogue. He always, however, approved of interfaith dialogue about matters of general ethical and social concern." Kaplan also points out that Soloveitchik issued a second statement on this matter two years later that reconfirmed the policy position Soloveitchik had advanced earlier in "Confrontation." This statement has been published as an appendix to "Confrontation" in Norman Lamm and Walter Wurzburger, eds., *A Treasury of Tradition* (New York: 1967), pp.78–80.

In looking at the Feinstein letter to Soloveitchik on the topic, no element of Jewish-Christian dialogue is endorsed. Feinstein, in contrast to Soloveitchik, expressed the view that ecumenicism and the Jewish-Christian dialogue such ecumenicism fostered were nothing more than a thinly-veiled plot designed by the Catholic Church to convince Jews to abandon their faith and convert to Christianity. Only two types of Jews would participate in such efforts. The first were individuals like Reform and Conservative rabbis, people who advocated positions that could only lead to the assimilation of the Jewish people. The second were well intentioned but naïve people, like the young Orthodox rabbi who had approached him earlier on this matter. Their participation in such dialogue could lead to no positive end. Feinstein was particularly concerned that this latter group could inadvertently create an atmosphere that would allow the Church to entice Jews into abandoning their faith. However pure their motives, these Jewish leaders would be responsible for the apostasy of these Jews and Jewish law would therefore hold them culpable. It was this group Feinstein particularly sought to address, and he saw Soloveitchik as his natural confederate in this matter, as together the influential authority the two men could exercise together in the Orthodox world was considerable.

In reading the Feinstein responsa, it seems clear that Feinstein viewed the relationship between Jews and Christians as unaltered by modern developments such as Vatican II. From his perspective, only isolation from Christians and their representatives could ensure the survival of the Jews as a minority community. He could perceive no Christian motive for initiating joint religious dialogue other than conversion of the Jews. Furthermore, his responsa — inasmuch as they advanced a completely negative position regarding such dialogue — implicitly reveal that he had theological-legal grounds for rejecting such discussions, for Feinstein clearly maintained a classical Jewish posture that viewed Christianity in negative terms as a form of idolatry.

Jewish law, as recorded in *Sanhedrin* 56a, recognizes that God has a universal relationship with all humanity. This relationship, known in Jewish tradition as the Noahide Covenant, caused the rabbis to assert that God issued seven commandments through Noah to all humankind. Among these seven commandments is one that prohibits idolatry.

The relevance of this Covenant for understanding the positions of Rabbis Feinstein and Soloveitchik on the question of Jewish-Christian dialogue is vital. This passage led rabbinic authorities to ask whether Christian beliefs violated the Noahide stricture against idolatry. If so, then relations with Christians had to be circumscribed not only because Jews should distance themselves from such false beliefs, but also because interactions with Christians might lead Christians to swear by an "idolatrous deity," an act condemned as sinful by the Talmud in *Sanhedrin* 63b. Indeed, in such instances, the Jew would be held culpable for this transgression by Jewish law, for the Jew would be the proximate cause for the Christian having committed this sinful act.

Of course, Christians insisted that their doctrines regarding God adhered to monotheistic standards. However, a number of talmudic sages disagreed, and they explicitly condemned early Christian expressions concerning the doctrines of Trinity and the incarnate man-god, Jesus, as untrue and in opposition to genuine monotheism.[16] Most importantly, these attitudes caused no less an authority than Moses Maimonides to affirm that these doctrinal differences were of such import that Christians could be assigned to the talmudic category of "*ovdei kokhavim u-mazalot* — worshipers of idols."[17] These legal sources reflect the doctrinal emphases that have classically distinguished the Jewish from the Christian faith and possess normative implications that limit Jewish-

---

16 For example, see *Exodus Rabbah* 29:5. On this passage, see Samuel Tobias Lachs, "Rabbi Abbahu and the Minim," *The Jewish Quarterly Review* 60, no. 3 (January, 1970), p. 200; and Lieve Tugels, "The Background of the Anti-Christian Polemics in Aggadat Bereshit," *Journal for the Study of Judaism* 30, no. 2 (1999), p. 196.

17 For example, see his *Commentary on the Mishnah, Avodah Zarah* 1:3, and *Hilkhot Akum* 9:4. Of course, in fairness to the Rambam, his stance is a complex one. For instance, in his legal rulings of Responsum #364, Maimonides writes, "It is permissible to teach the commandments to Christians — *mutar l'lamed ha-mitzvot l'notzrim.*" This surely indicates that dialogue with them is permitted in certain instances, and implies that Christians do not fall under the category of "*ovdei avodah zarah* — idol-worshipers." I therefore want to be clear that I am not offering a complete exposition of Maimonides' perceptions concerning the legal status Christianity enjoys in Jewish law. That would be far beyond the limits of this paper. Rather, it should simply be noted that his stance on Christianity is not simple and it surely cannot be summarized in only a few sentences. At the same time, there are sources that serve as warrants for the contention that Christianity can be assigned to the category of "idol worship" in Maimonidean jurisprudence, and the trajectory that marks these sources appears to have informed Feinstein's views regarding Christianity. Indeed, I would unhappily even observe that this is probably the majority position in halakhic jurisprudence.

Christian interactions on religious grounds. Feinstein obviously stood upon these legal sources in issuing his views. He not only feared that such discussions would lead to Jewish apostasy, he also never modified his view of Christianity here as idolatry.

Other voices in Jewish tradition, however, took a different stance on these matters. They would not consign Christianity to the category of idolatry, nor, by extension, would they accept a definition of Christians as idol worshipers. In a comment upon *Sanhedrin* 63b, Rabbi Isaac (of late twelfth-century France, the nephew of Rabbenu Tam),[18] spoke of Christians and Christianity in the following terms:

> . . . Although they [Christians] mention the name of Heaven, meaning thereby Jesus of Nazareth, they do not at all events mention a strange deity, and moreover, they mean thereby the Maker of Heaven and Earth too; and despite the fact that they associate the name of Heaven with an alien deity, we do not find that it is forbidden to cause Gentiles to make such an association, . . . *since such an association (shituf) is not forbidden to the sons of Noah.*[19]

In taking this stance, Rabbi Isaac offered a distinction that was unknown in talmudic Judaism. While Trinitarianism constituted idolatry for Jews, it did not for Christians. Indeed, historian Jacob Katz has characterized its significance in the following way: "The assertion that the Gentiles are not bound to uphold the strict unity of the Godhead opens up the possibility of condoning Christian adherence to the doctrine of the Trinity so far as the Gentiles, though not the Jews, are concerned."[20] Katz further notes that this view was taken up and expanded upon by Rabbi Menaḥem Ha-Me'iri of Provence who, writing in the

18 This commentary is often wrongly attributed to Rabbenu Tam, Rabbi Jacob Ben Meir Tam (1100–1171), a grandson of Rashi and a leading French *tosafist* (medieval rabbinic commentator upon the Talmud) and twelfth-century scholar; however, Shalom Albeck's article, "The Relationship of Rabbenu Tam to the Problems of His Era" (Hebrew), *Tziyon* 18 (1954), p. 109, convincingly demonstrates that his nephew, Rabbi Isaac, another *tosafist*, was the author of this commentary upon *Sanhedrin* 63b.

19 The translation here is taken from Jacob Katz, *Exclusiveness and Tolerance: Jewish-Gentile Relations in Medieval and Modern Times* (New York: Oxford University Press, 1961; paperback ed., New York: Schocken, 1962), p. 35. (Emphasis mine.)

20 Ibid. p. 36.

early 1300s, stated that Christians "recognize the Godhead" and "believe in God's existence, His unity and power, although they misconceive some points according to our belief." In fact, Ha-Me'iri explicitly refused to place contemporaneous Christians in the Talmudic category of "idol-worshipers," declaring, "Now idolatry has disappeared from most places."[21] Commenting upon these writings of Ha-Me'iri, Katz has noted "that the exclusion of Christians . . . from the category of the idolatrous — an exclusion that had been suggested purely casuistically by earlier halakhists — was to be acknowledged as a firm and comprehensive principle."[22]

The trajectory that marked these rulings came to dominate among later generations of Jewish legal writers. The eighteenth-century Rabbi Yehuda Ashkenazi, writing on the *Shulḥan Arukh, Yoreh De'ah*, 151:2, in his authoritative *Ba'er Heitev*, echoed both Rabbi Isaac and Ha-Me'iri and granted their position normative Jewish legal status. His commentary there on Christians and their faith states, "In our era, when the gentiles in whose midst we dwell . . . [speak of God], their intention is directed towards the One Who made Heaven and Earth, albeit that they associate another personality with God. However, this does not constitute a violation of Leviticus 19:14, 'You shall not place a stumbling block before the blind,' for non-Jews are not warned against such association (*shituf*)."

Soloveitchik obviously stood upon this latter position in Jewish law. Had he not, he would simply have been compelled, as was Feinstein, to consign contemporary Christians to the talmudic category of "*ovdei avodah zarah* — idol-worshipers," in which case all dialogue with them would have been forbidden. The fact that Soloveitchik did not prohibit, but, in fact, allowed for Jewish-Christian dialogue on matters of common human concern, indicates that he felt that Christian faith was an acceptable form of monotheism for gentiles. It also reflects his conviction that Christians, not just Jews, were capable, on account of their religious beliefs, of performing beneficent acts that would contribute to the repair of the world and that their sole motive for participating in such dialogue was not conversion.

---

21 Ibid. pp.121 and 136.

22 Ibid. p.115. For an extensive recent discussion of Ha-Me'iri and medieval and modern scholarship on his position, see Israel Ta-Shema, *Exegetical Literature on the Talmud in Europe and North Africa* (Hebrew) (Jerusalem: Magnes Press, 2000), 167–70.

As a result, Soloveitchik did not respond to Feinstein's overture and refused to condemn Jewish-Christian dialogue in the harsh and overarching terms that Feinstein had. Nor would he reverse the position he expressed on this matter in "Confrontation." There is no indication that Soloveitchik signed the declaration that Feinstein appended to his letter; nor is there any record that Soloveitchik offered an alternative formulation. If he had agreed to do either of these two things, a document condemning dialogue of all types between Jews and Christians would have been issued by the two foremost leaders of late-twentieth-century American Jewish Orthodoxy. Instead, the Feinstein documents (translation below), considered in concert with the position put forth by Soloveitchik and the RCA, reflect the diverse sensibilities and differences in policy that emerged among the two camps of American Orthodoxy on this issue. They also reflect the commitments and principles that informed and guided each of these men. Feinstein did not hesitate to publish these documents as expressions of his views on the matter, nor did Soloveitchik — in view of his own writings on this issue — feel constrained to respond in any way.

These responsa are therefore significant sources for understanding the diversity that then marked Orthodox Judaism in the United States and for illuminating the ethos that then separated the ethos of sectarian Orthodox Judaism from the greater openness that characterized the more modernist camp. Those differences remain current. These documents thus not only shed historical light on Orthodox Judaism in America; they remain important sources for comprehending the diverse precincts that obtain in American Orthodoxy today.

1. Moshe Feinstein, Iggerot Moshe, Yoreh De'ah 3, no. 43
19 Adar I, 5727 – March 1, 1967

Two Responsa Concerning the Prohibition against Attending a Meeting with Christians on Matters of Rapprochement in Faith and Association with Them.

In regard to the matter wherein you promised to attend a gathering on 23 Adar I, 5727 (March 5, 1967) where Catholics and Protestants will assemble together with Jews who are members of the Synagogue Council of America as well as rabbinical colleagues from the Rabbinical Council of America: Even though what you will discuss there will be non-theological in nature,[23] it is clear and simple that such participation constitutes a grave violation of the prohibition against appurtenances to idolatry. For a plague has now broken out in many locales on account of the initiative of the new pope, whose only intent is to cause all the Jews to abandon their pure and holy faith so that they will accept Christianity. Indeed, it is much more convenient to convert them in this manner than to employ the methods of hatred and murder that popes prior to him utilized.[24] Consequently, all contact and discussion with them, even on worldly matters, is forbidden, for the act of "drawing near" is in and of

23 The precise Hebrew here is "*divrei be-alma*," literally, "mere words." In employing this phrase, Feinstein is referring to a position undoubtedly put forth by his interlocutor. This position, commonly advanced in modern Orthodox circles, holds that interreligious dialogue between Jews and adherents of other faiths on non-theological matters is permissible. Hence, discussion on matters of common social and human import between Jews and Christians can be held, as such discussions reflect a common task advanced by both religions and do not touch upon the unique religious posture that informs and characterizes each community. The foremost advocate of this stance in the Orthodox world, as explained in the introduction to these translations, was Rabbi Joseph Soloveitchik. For this reason, I have here elected to translate this phrase as "non-theological in nature." Elsewhere, I have translated these words as "social-political matters." Such translations capture the sense, if not the literal meaning, of these words.

24 Throughout history there have been Christian proponents of outreach to the Jews who felt that a kind missionary approach marked by love might well lead significant numbers of Jews to abandon Judaism and convert to Christianity. Perhaps the most prominent among them was Martin Luther who, in his 1523 pamphlet, "That Jesus Christ Was Born a Jew," stated, "I hope that if the Jews are treated friendly and are instructed kindly through the Bible, many of them will become real Christians. . . ." Of course, when virtually no Jews responded to this approach, Luther's fury against the Jews knew no bounds. In 1543, Luther, in his "Concerning the Jews and Their Lies," queries, "What then shall we do with this damned, rejected race of Jews?" These documents are found in Jacob R. Marcus, *The Jew in the Medieval World* (New York: Atheneum, 1938), pp. 165–69. Professor Marcus, commenting upon these passages on p. 165 of his introduction, observes: "In a work written as early as 1523 . . . Luther was very sympathetic to the Jews because he hoped that he might induce them to Protestantism. . . . Later in life Luther turned bitter against the Jews . . . the Jews did not flock to his new Christianity."

itself forbidden, as it falls under the category of the grave prohibition against "rapprochement with idolatry — *hitkarvut im avodah zarah.*"

And one should also consider this [drawing near] as falling under the category of prohibition against the "the one who entices (*ha-meisit*) and the one who leads astray (*ha-madiaḥ*)."[25] For even though you and

---

In light of the suspicions Feinstein expressed concerning Catholic motives for Christian dialogue with Jews, it is fascinating to note an entry recorded by Theodor Herzl, *The Diaries of Theodor Herzl* (New York: Dial Press, 1956), pp. 420–31, concerning audiences he held with Pope Pius X and Cardinal Merry del Val, the Vatican secretary of state, in January, 1904. In these pages, Herzl states that he asked the Holy See for assistance in creating a Jewish state. The Cardinal, according to Herzl, turned down the request. He also said, "So long as the Jews deny the divinity of Christ, we certainly cannot side with them. . . . A Jew who accepts baptism out of conviction is for me the ideal person. . . . In order that we should come out for the Jewish people in the way that you desire, they would first have to accept conversion." To this, Pope Pius X added, "If you come to Palestine and settle your people there, we will be ready with priests and churches to baptize all of you."

While there is no reason to believe that Feinstein had actually read either these statements or those of Martin Luther, the attitudes expressed by all these men are surely emblematic of positions long held by many Christian leaders regarding the Jews, and Feinstein clearly knew that. He also obviously regarded such postures as reflecting the true position the Church adopted towards the Jews on these matters. He disregarded the pronouncements of Vatican II that ran contrary to this position. Obviously, he could not conceive the modern Catholic position on ecumenicism that emanated from Vatican II as anything other than a ploy on the part of the church. The classical evangelical stance the Church had adopted towards the Jews was the only one Feinstein could imagine the church would ever take.

25 These Jewish legal categories stem from Deuteronomy 13. Verse 7 reads, "If your brother, your own mother's son, or your son or daughter, or the wife of your bosom, or your closest friend, entices you (*ye-si'tekha*) in secret, saying, 'Come, let us worship other gods . . .'" This is followed in verse 11 by the admonition, "You shall stone him so that he dies, for he sought to lead you away (*le-hadihakha*) from the Lord your God. . . ." One should also consult verse 14 in the same chapter, where the warning concerning those who "have led the inhabitants of their city astray" is repeated. Hence, the terms, "*meisit,*" the one who entices, and "*madiaḥ,*" the one who leads astray, are the noun forms of the Hebrew that appears in verbal formulation in the biblical text. As the penalty of stoning that the biblical text prescribes for such people suggests, the Jews to whom these categories apply are guilty of a most severe infraction of Jewish law. Feinstein's application of these categories in his responsa indicates the gravity he attached to this issue.

the other Orthodox rabbis (*rabbanim*)[26] who will go there will surely be cautious about what you say, and will also not behave obsequiously towards the priests and their faith, as is the wont of the Reform and Conservative rabbis (*rabbis*),[27] who by definition fall under the category of "those who entice and lead astray," nevertheless, many people will learn from your example and they will attend the sermons of missionaries and the like. Similarly, you should not even send a letter there expressing what you might be prepared to discuss, for all contact with them assists them in their most evil plot.

Similarly, it is forbidden to participate in any way in meetings like the ones I heard that they propose to hold in Boston and Rome. Anyone who participates with them, whoever they may be, will be considered among those who entice and lead the community of Israel (*klal yisrael*) astray." Catholic missionaries have labored for years to convert the Jews. Nevertheless, they succeeded only in rare instances. God forbid that it would be possible that many more Jews would convert to Christianity on account of such joint ventures and because of rabbis like these, rabbis who lack good sense and who desire to engage in such joint meetings with them. And one cannot put forward a claim on behalf of the "one who entices" that this was not his intent, for their souls will be culpable, God forbid, in this world and in the world-to-come.

You should pay no attention to the fact that you will not have fulfilled your promise to go there and speak. On the contrary, perhaps through your decision not to attend on account of the prohibition, others too will not go. In this way, you will be among those who gain merit for the public.

II. Letter from Moshe Feinstein to Joseph Soloveitchik
9 Adar II, 5727 – March 21, 1967

I am writing because of my concern over those young rabbis who are trapped in the snare laid by the Head of the Priests in the Vatican in the name of the Ecumenical Council, whose intent is to cause all the

---

26 Here, as in other legal writings of Feinstein, Orthodox rabbis are referred to by the Hebrew term, "*rabbanim*," while, when speaking of Reform and Conservative rabbis, Feinstein simply transliterates the English term "rabbis" into Hebrew letters.

27 Ibid.

Jews to convert to their faith, God forbid. The cardinals and the bishops are commanded by him to establish connections between priests and rabbis through committees and conventions in every locale. This deed of Satan has succeeded as a number of rabbis have engaged in such associations on the basis of a *heter* (permission) that allows for interreligious dialogue on social-political, albeit not religious matters. For, aside from the fact that nearly every matter is one of religion, as the priests have another way of viewing such matters, and aside from the fact that their only intention is to exploit these meetings to arrive at matters of faith, it is obvious that there is an *issur* (prohibition) against any connections with them, even on ostensibly social-political matters, at all times during every era. It is all the more so now as regards this evil design that emanates from the Head of the Priests. For we have seen that the newspapers take pride in the fact that this has already led to a leveling among faith and opinions, to joint worship and the like. I was recently asked by one of the young rabbis being sent by the RCA to speak at some type of joint meeting in New York on 23 Adar I, between priests and, *le-havdil*,[28] rabbis, whether it was permissible (*mutar*) to go there, since they will not discuss matters of faith.[29] I told him it was forbidden, as the grave prohibited category (*issur ḥamur*) of "*meisit* — one who entices" applies, even if this was not his intent. Thank God, he listened to me.

And now, there will soon be another larger convention like this one in Boston. Therefore, to overturn the conspiracy of the evil ones and the success of the deeds of Satan, as well as to rescue the Jewish people from apostasy (*shemad*), God forbid, it is my desire that Your Excellency sign the document I have included in this letter. It declares that there is an absolute prohibition (*issur gamur*) against associating with priests in any way. One can neither speak with them on social-political matters (*devarim be-alma*), nor attend the convention that will be held in Boston. This applies to any such convention with them in any place, either in this country or in Europe. One cannot in any way aid the conspiracy that the Head of the Priests has concocted through his ecumenicism. And I hope that the legal ruling issued by both of us will prevent any rabbi from joining in this, and the conspiracy that the wicked ones have

---

28 "*Le-havdil*" is an idiom that can perhaps best be rendered as, "not to be mentioned in the same breath."

29 See the first responsum translated in this article.

hatched with the ecumenical policy they pursue will thus be thwarted.

Or perhaps Your Excellency wants to write a document himself. If so, please send me a copy of your formulation. And I know of the trouble Your Excellency is experiencing during these days, May God have mercy.[30] But it is for the honor of God to stand in this great breach. Therefore, I am certain you will repress your distress and sorrow and immediately sign the document stating that it is prohibited to attend such gatherings and send it back to me.

Formula of the Prohibition

Concerning the matter of ecumenism that has been spread through the conspiracy concocted by the leaders of the Christian faith, whose only intent is to cause Jews to apostatize, God forbid. This act of Satan has succeeded in enticing a number of rabbis to join with priests in joint fellowship on permanent committees established in every locale as well as in conventions held here in this country and in Europe. Behold, we declare that there is an absolute and clear prohibition against joint meetings of rabbis and priests. One should not participate in the convention to be held in Boston, nor anywhere, either in this country or any countries. Just as it is forbidden to hold dialogues on matters of faith and religion, so there should be no joint discussion on matters of social-political concern, and there should be no excuses or rationalizations offered [by any rabbis for participating]. Indeed, it is prohibited to aid the project of ecumenism in any manner, as the participants in such conversation fall under the *issur* (prohibited category) of "one who entices — *meisit*," even though those who participate in such joint Jewish-Christian endeavors have no intention at all of engaging in this. On account of this, we have come to sign this document so as to proclaim the *issur* (prohibition) against this to all rabbis who preserve the religion of our holy Torah and we stand up against the breach on this day of the Fast of Esther, 5727.

---

30 Soloveitchik's wife, Dr. Tonya Lewitt Soloveitchik, was sick at this time and in fact died on the Fast of Esther, 5727 (1967), the date mentioned at the conclusion of the document Feinstein appended to the letter. (For the date that Mrs. Soloveitchik died, see Rakkefet-Rothkoff, *The Rav,* vol. 2, p. 8.) Feinstein was surely referring to Soloveitchik's anguish over his wife's illness.

18

Jewish Legal Interpretation and Moral Values

*Two Responsa by Rabbi Ḥayim David Halevi
on the Obligations of the Israeli Government
towards Its Minority Population*

The texts of a specific legal system provide a bedrock of authority and identity for the community that dwells within its precincts, and the community itself evidences its ideals and self-understanding through the ongoing way that its judges apply the rules and principles of that system to a contemporary case. The legal decisions that emerge from these writings mark a crossroads where traditional texts and current contexts meet in an ongoing process of legal hermeneutics. As the famed legal philosopher Ronald Dworkin has pointed out, a legal judgment is, therefore, an act of both fidelity and imagination.

Legal pronouncements constitute acts of imagination in the sense that the judge, "in the interpretive spirit," strives creatively through the use of analogy to apply inherited legal rules and principles to a current situation in order "to show" the community "the best route to a better future." At the same time, such judgments establish themselves as acts of fidelity, for by "keeping right faith with the past," the decisor sustains a universe of meaning that allows for the preservation of a communal identity that is expressed through citation of legal precedent.[1]

Dworkin maintains that this dialectical approach to the legal system means that judicial decisions must not be narrowly construed as always

---

1 Ronald Dworkin, *Law's Empire* (Cambridge, Massachusetts: The Belknap Press of Harvard University Press, 1986), p.413.

comprising nothing more than a simple application of relevant rules and principles drawn from analogous precedents to an instant case. Instead, Dworkin urges the legal analyst to recognize that such judgments are often better understood more generally as policy pronouncements.[2] In these instances, the judge rules broadly, assuming responsibility "for imagining what his society's public commitments to principles are, and what these commitments require in new circumstances."[3] In the final analysis, particular applications of the law in individual instances are thus reflective of the standards and values that inform and guide the community as its juridical leaders creatively attempt to address the demands of the present in light of the teachings of the past.

Dworkin's observations about the nature of the legal process, and the holdings that emerge from such a process, provide an illuminating framework for approaching several responsa issued by Rabbi Ḥayim David Halevi (1924–1998) of Tel Aviv. As a youth, the author of these responsa studied at the famed Jerusalem yeshiva *Porat Yosef*, where he became the *talmid muvhak* of Rabbi Ben Zion Meir Ḥai Ouziel, the first Chief Sephardic Rabbi of the State of Israel. He later competed unsuccessfully with Rabbi Ovadiah Yosef for the post of his teacher, and ultimately was selected instead for the position of Chief Sephardic Rabbi of Tel Aviv-Jaffa, where he served until his death. A prolific author, Halevi published nine volumes of responsa under the title *Aseh Lekha Rav*, as well as over a dozen more volumes on various religious topics — all of which gained him acclaim as one of the foremost exponents of traditional Jewish law and lore in Israel.[4]

In the responsa discussed below, Halevi seized the opportunity

---

2 See Dworkin, "Is Law a System of Rules?" in R. M. Dworkin, *The Philosophy of Law* (Oxford and New York: Oxford University Press, 1977), p. 45, for a discussion of how law frequently operates as "policy." To be sure, Dworkin also points out that when legal judgments are issued as "policy," "bad law" sometimes results.

3 Dworkin, *Law's Empire*, p. 413.

4 Two significant English language articles on R. Halevi are: Marc Angel, "Rabbi Ḥayyim David Halevy: A Leading Contemporary Rabbinic Thinker," *Jewish Book Annual* 52 (1994), pp. 99–109; and Zvi Zohar, "Sephardic Religious Thought in Israel: Aspects of the Theology of Rabbi Haim David HaLevi," in Kevin Avruch and Walter Zenner, eds., *Critical Essays on Israeli Society, Religion, and Government* (Albany: SUNY Press, 1997), pp. 115–36.

presented him by a questioner concerning selected points found in *Yebamot* 78b–79a. It led him to issue a policy pronouncement that demonstrates that even seemingly morally problematic texts can be mined by a skillful interpreter for humanistic strains. In so doing, he hoped to make his Israeli constituency aware that the authentic Judaism as presented in the Talmud contained a moral vision that required the Israeli government to adopt a policy that would accord respect and support even to its minority citizens. The rulings he offered here are of contemporary import inasmuch as Israeli Jewish treatment of its minority populations remains a matter of vital consequence today.

Halevi was, of course, aware that even in Israel his opinion as a rabbi on an issue such as this did not have the force of law and that it would not necessarily be enforced by the state. Nevertheless, he recognized that his reputation and moral stature as an outstanding *posek* was considerable among vast sectors of the Israeli public. Halevi clearly hoped that by couching his legal exegesis of this passage in the form of responsa that he could exercise an influential religious authority among an audience of traditional Israeli Jews — and that they would then be moved to act in an expansive way on the question of human rights.

It is in this spirit that I will analyze and present these responsa by Rabbi Halevi. In the first section of the paper, I will indicate how he addresses a series of textual and moral problems addressed in *Yebamot* 78b–79a in light of key Jewish values embedded in the text. After showing how he analyzes the talmudic solution to these difficulties in each instance, I will explore the political and moral entailments Halevi derives from these interpretations for Israeli life today. At the conclusion of my exposition of these major points, I will offer a few brief comments on what this genre of Jewish legal literature might mean to liberal religious Jews. Finally, I will attach relevant portions of the texts in complete translation so that others can use them as objects of study. My own identification of issues in these texts, as presented in this article, is hardly meant to be an exhaustive description of the matters raised by these writings. It is my hope that these sources can serve as stimuli for ongoing communal discussions of the significant issues contained in these texts and promote a Jewish tradition that seeks to provide meaning and identity in a world marked by complex moral dilemmas and challenges.

Halevi on Jewish Values and Selected Moral Dilemmas in Yebamot 78b–79a

An Ethic of Majority Responsibility

In *Aseh Lekha Rav* 7:70, dated 4 Tammuz, 5745 (June 23, 1985), Halevi noted that a questioner had expressed "astonishment" at a series of interpretations the Sages of the Talmud had offered in *Yebamot* 78b–79a. The individual who posed this query to Halevi was greatly disturbed by what he felt was an undue rabbinic concern for non-Jewish opinions about Jews. It troubled him that this concern seemed to be a major factor influencing the rulings of the ancient rabbis in the *Yebamot* texts.

Halevi responded to the query by focusing, at the outset of his first responsum, on an exposition of a passage found in II Samuel 21:1, a text with which *Yebamot* 78b was concerned. The first part of the verse states, "And there was a famine in the days of David three years, year after year; and David sought the face of the Lord," looking for an explanation from God as to why this disaster had befallen the people Israel. And the last part of this passage supplies the answer in the following words — "And the Lord said, 'It is for Saul, and for his bloody house, because he put to death the Gibeonites.'" Rabbi Halevi noted that the Talmud was puzzled by this explanation inasmuch as the Bible nowhere indicates that Saul performed such a deed. In light of this, the rabbis naturally queried, "Where do we find that Saul 'put to death the Gibeonites?'" And the Talmud, Halevi reported, answers this question by asserting, "The truth is that as he killed the inhabitants of Nob, the city of priests whom [the Gibeonites] were supplying with food and water, *Scripture regards it as if he himself had killed them*" (*Yebamot* 78b). (Emphasis mine).

In order to comprehend this cryptic talmudic justification for the biblical condemnation of Saul as the man who had slain the Gibeonites, it is necessary to turn to accounts of several episodes recorded in I Samuel 21 and 22 as well as in Joshua 9. In I Samuel 22, it is related that Doeg the Edomite killed the priests of God at Nob at the directive of Saul. As the Bible states, Saul said to Doeg:

You, Doeg, go and strike down the priests. And Doeg the Edomite went and struck down the priests himself; that day he killed eighty-five men who wore the linen ephod. He put Nob, the town of the priests to the sword: men and women, children and infants, oxen, asses, and sheep — all to the sword (I Samuel 22: 18–19).

Saul had issued this order because he was furious that the priest Ahimelech at Nob had provided refuge and arms to the fugitive David as he fled from the wrath of Saul. This story is related in I Samuel 21, where the Bible states that after David, fearing for his life, departed from his friend Jonathan, the unarmed David sought and received for himself provisions — as well as the sword with which he had slain Goliath — from Ahimelech. Saul had the priests as well as the inhabitants of Nob murdered by Doeg precisely because he regarded these acts by Ahimelech as treasonous.

Although it is clear that this act of murderous vengeance committed against the inhabitants of Nob was performed at the behest of Saul, it still remains unclear as to why Saul should, therefore, be held culpable for the deaths of the Gibeonites. After all, as Halevi himself observes, "According to the words of our Sages there in *Yebamot*, Saul did not actually kill even a single Gibeonite." In order to understand why the charge was leveled, it is necessary to look at Joshua 9, which reports that the inhabitants of Gibeon, fearful that Joshua would destroy them as he had other indigenous peoples of Canaan during his conquest, "resorted to cunning" (Joshua 9:4). These Gibeonites posed as non-natives, and told Joshua that they came "from a distant land." They then persuaded Joshua to "make a pact" with them in which they agreed to be his "subjects" (Joshua 9: 6–8). Joshua assented to their request and, as the Bible states, Joshua "made a pact with them [the Gibeonites] to spare their lives and the chieftains of the community gave them [the Gibeonites] their oath" (Joshua 9:15).

When Joshua and the entire community soon learned that the Gibeonite claim that they had come "from a distant land" was fraudulent, the people of Israel were furious. Despite this fury, Israel could not now destroy the Gibeonites, since Joshua and the chieftains had sworn an oath before God to spare them. Although the chieftains declared, "They shall live!" nevertheless, they consigned the Gibeonites to menial labor, and assigned them and their descendants roles as "hewers of wood and drawers of water for the House of God" (Joshua 9:21 and 23); that is, that they would perform subservient tasks for the priests.

The tale in Joshua is surely troubling to modern ethical sensibilities on several counts. Not only does the Book of Joshua seem to bespeak here, as it does elsewhere, an ethic of genocide against native peoples; here the Gibeonites are reduced to a permanent state of low-castestatus. In his responsa, Halevi did not address issues such as these, as such concerns were not dealt with in the legal tradition he had inherited. While in a broader study of these texts, these and other considerations would surely demand attention, here it was the line of reasoning put forth by the Talmud alone that was pertinent to the legal exegesis Halevi was to advance. As a result, he focused only on that which he had received from the tradition, and he vindicated the talmudic pronouncement that declared Saul responsible for the death of the Gibeonites. As Halevi explained:

> His entire punishment was meted out on account of the fact that through his slaughter of the priests of God in Nob, the Gibeonites lost their livelihood. We will now proceed with an explanation of the matter. As the Gibeonites had no part or inheritance in the land, they could not support themselves through farming. Their livelihood depended entirely upon their work as "hewers of wood and drawers of water" for the house of the Lord. And there is no doubt that as a result of the murder of the priests of the Lord in Nob, they suffered the indignity of famine, and many of them died as a result of famine. Therefore, they [the Gibeonites] said of Saul, "The man that consumed us" (II Samuel 21:5).

Halevi was not content to simply explain why Saul could legitimately be deemed responsible for the Gibeonites' deaths. He also offered an expansive interpretation of the episode and delineated what he regarded as the resultant legal obligations of those responsible for the administration of state. Joshua and the chieftains of the community had assumed responsibility for the Gibeonites inasmuch as they had sworn that they would allow this indigenous Canaanite people to live. They could discharge this obligation only by supplying the Gibeonites with work whereby they could earn a livelihood. Halevi therefore firmly maintained that Saul was "obligated to be concerned" and to find the Gibeonites work, "as this was his obligation as King of Israel."

Most importantly, Halevi felt that only one present-day legal conclusion could properly be drawn from this reading: subsequent generations of leaders were likewise bound by this oath. Halevi proclaimed this principle distinctively and succinctly. "It is therefore the obligation of every government to be concerned for the subsistence of its citizens, whether they are permanent residents or strangers." Obviously, it was the matter of how a majority Jewish government ought to act in regard to its minority populations that was of exclusive concern to Halevi in this responsum, and not any other ethical issue that could plausibly be raised in connection with these texts.

The Values of Ḥillul Ha-shem *and* Tzedakah *and the Imposition of Divine Punishment*

Halevi reinforced his argument concerning governmental responsibility for all citizens in a Jewish-dominated state by raising the notion of *ḥillul ha-shem*, the profanation of God's Name, as one of the utmost import in guiding his ruling in this matter. He maintained that the slightest failure on the part of a Jewish ruler to protect a dispossessed minority brought shame upon the Jewish people and thereby discredited the God of Israel before the nations of the world — a completely unacceptable outcome.

Halevi implicitly acknowledged that in this case one might argue that Saul had valid reasons for slaughtering the priests and Jewish residents of Nob. After all, Saul viewed their harboring David as an act of disloyalty. However, even if a hypothetical argument could be advanced that would justify the punishment Saul meted out at Nob, it would in no way be germane to the matter under discussion. Halevi insisted that it was Saul's responsibility towards the Gibeonites that was at issue here, and any feelings of fury that Saul, justifiably or unjustifiably, directed against the priests at Nob could under no condition touch upon or obviate the commitment he was required to fulfill concerning the Gibeonites. Indeed, by depriving those people of their meager livelihood through the murder of the priests at Nob, Halevi charged Saul with the additional sin of "*hillul ha-shem* — profaning the Name of God in public." Saul was guilty of that sin precisely because his determination to exact punishment from the priests at Nob made him impervious to his duty as king of Israel to care for the disenfranchised. His deed had, in effect, condemned the Gibeonites to death by famine. His responsibility to supply labor for the Gibeonites so that they could support their community could brook no compromise.

Halevi was also quick to note that Saul was not the only culpable party in this incident: the sin against the Gibeonites extended to the entire people of Israel. Halevi emphasized that "the entire people Israel saw and knew" of this wrong that Saul had perpetrated. Yet, "not one person protested," nor did a single Jew "demand justice for the Gibeonites." Halevi explained why this silence on the part of the Jewish people constituted a particularly egregious sin: "I do not know how every government in the ancient world conducted itself concerning its obligation for the support of all its citizens. However, even if this obligation was not accepted in the ancient world, there was surely such an obligation concerning the Gibeonites as a result of the sworn oath that had been made [by the leadership of the people Israel to the Gibeonites]." By neglecting their obligation to the Gibeonites, the entire people as well as their ruler were responsible for the death of this Canaanite people by famine, as neither had fulfilled the oath sworn by Joshua and the chieftains "to sustain them." All Israel had violated the oath their ancestors had sworn. The Jewish people, no less than Saul, had in effect committed the sin of *hillul ha-shem*.

In addition, Halevi maintained that the obligation to fulfill their oath to a hapless minority was incumbent upon the people Israel because a general ethic of *tzedakah* animated and informed the very core of Jewish religious tradition. As Halevi put it, "The people Israel have always acted so as to express concern for the poor." Indeed, he quoted Maimonides, who wrote, "We have never seen or heard of a community in Israel that does not have a *tzedakah* fund," as a warrant for the position that Jews are required to extend care to those in need. Halevi saw the duty to be concerned for those in dire straits as constituting the essence of the *mitzvah* of *tzedakah*, which, he contended, was the most central of Torah commandments.

As a result of their refusal to stand up and protest what Saul had done, the entire people of Israel were also guilty, then, of not fulfilling the commandment to provide *tzedakah* for those less fortunate than themselves. Thus God justly meted out divine punishment against them. As Halevi wrote, "The Holy One imposed the punishment of famine upon Israel on account of such sin, as they thereby publicly profaned the Name of God. It is noteworthy to emphasize that the decrees of God are meted out measure for measure — the sin against the Gibeonites resulted in death by famine, so here the punishment was famine." The iniquity of Israel was so great that only such divine retribution could atone for the wrongs they had committed against this people.

Kiddush Ha-shem *and the Problem of Retributive Justice*

The primacy that Halevi accorded *ḥillul ha-shem* and *tzedakah* as value concepts worthy of application in situations where Israel was responsible for the welfare of an impoverished and impotent minority was supplemented by the emphasis he now placed upon the ancillary commandment of *kiddush ha-shem*. He noted that the Sages, in the *Yebamot* text, commenting upon II Samuel 21: 2–6 and 8–9, had made special mention of the fact that seven of the male descendants of Saul were delivered unto the Gibeonites and "hung in the mountain before the Lord." In this way, the Gibeonite demand for strict retributive justice was served.

Although David was disturbed by their request and, according to the Talmud, regarded this action as unspeakably cruel, he had acceded to their petition and these sons and grandsons of Saul were put to death. Only then were the Gibeonites pacified. The rabbis in *Yebamot* 79a objected to this deed on other grounds: "But surely it is written, 'The fathers shall not be put to death for the children, and the children shall not be put to death for the fathers'" (Deuteronomy 24:16).

In other words, the Sages took note of an additional moral problem posed by the biblical story and its tale of the deaths of the seven sons and grandsons of King Saul — that of retributive justice. Even if it were acknowledged that responsibility for the deaths of the Gibeonites was rightfully assigned to Saul, he alone should have been punished for this crime. In light of the rule enunciated in Deuteronomy 24:16, his chil-

dren surely should not have been put to death on account of his sin. To
exact retribution against the descendants of Saul was morally reprehen-
sible. Rabbi Yoḥanan recognized this moral quandary. Nevertheless, he
boldly asserted, "It is better that a letter be rooted out of the Torah than
that the Divine Name shall be publicly profaned." In other words, on this
occasion, the directive from Deuteronomy should be ignored despite
the fact that it condemned the notion of retributive justice as a moral
violation of Torah law. In this case, Rabbi Yoḥanan insisted that the commandment to avoid the profanation of God's Name received priority over
the Deuteronomic injunction, and he therefore felt the punishment of
death imposed upon the descendants of Saul — however horrific — was
the proper course to pursue in this situation.

In short, two sets of Jewish values were in conflict in this element
of the story. On the one hand, the value concept of *hillul ha-shem* demanded that justice be done for minority populations under Jewish
rule, and the Gibeonites were within their rights to demand this morally problematic expiatory act. On the other hand, the Deuteronomic
commandment indicated that even though retributive justice was a
legitimate course of action for a court to pursue, such justice should be
meted out only against those persons who had actually performed the
transgression. The Bible here completely opposed any attempt to justify
such retributive justice: surely, the iniquity of the parents should not
be visited upon their descendants. However, Halevi accorded, as had
Rabbi Yoḥanan, primacy in this matter to the former value over the latter. He approvingly cited Rashi, who had stated in his gloss on Rabbi
Yoḥanan's statement, "Lest the nations [of the world] state, 'It is not fit
to cling to this nation [the Jewish people]. For they harmed strangers
[the Gibeonites] by taking away their livelihood, and they would not
exact revenge for them [the Gibeonites].'"

Indeed, it was precisely this line of reasoning that had disturbed
the man who had initially posed the question to Halevi. After all, the
man had observed, the Gibeonite demand was in and of itself unjust.
They were a malicious and fraudulent people. He therefore asked why
the people of Israel should be concerned "about what the gentiles
would say."

To this, Halevi responded, "The matter pained them [the Gibeonites]
greatly and justifiably so, and they were not able to forgive the injustice

that was thereby perpetrated against them. Therefore [this famine persisted] until they (the Gibeonites) exacted the cruelest revenge [i.e., the capital execution of Saul's sons]." This demand for justice on the part of the Gibeonites was morally troublesome to the Sages. Indeed, it was so horrific that the Talmud states that they thereby "demonstrated that they were not worthy of taking refuge in the inheritance of the Lord. David therefore issued an eternal prohibition barring them [the Gibeonites] from entering into the community of the Lord [i.e., from converting to Judaism] as is explained there in the *sugya* [*Yebamot* 78b]." Yet, Halevi continued, there was no way to avoid their demand, as "through this cruel deed itself [i.e., the execution of seven of Saul's sons], the Name of Heaven was sanctified" by Israel "among the nations." For, as Halevi pointed out, *Yebamot* 79a states, "For passers-by were enquiring, 'What kind of men are these (that are being hanged)?'" These passers-by were then told that these men were "the sons of a king," and that the men were being hung as a result of the crime their ancestor had committed against a disenfranchised minority. These passers-by then exclaimed, "There is no nation in existence that one ought to join as much as this one (Israel)." Indeed, this concern that justice be executed on behalf of such a minority at such a high cost constituted an act of *kiddush ha-shem*, and the Talmud reports that as a result of this "150,000 men immediately joined Israel" on that day.

Halevi believed that the mandate to be derived from Jewish tradition on the treatment that Israel ought to accord disenfranchised minorities as a result of these teachings was absolutely incontestable. Jewish law and ethics required Jews to display utmost care and concern for these people — even though their lack of moral sensibility and kindness in no way abrogated the duty of the Jewish people to behave properly in these matters. At the end of the previous responsum, Halevi had stated that the practical application to be derived from this obligation was that the Israeli government was required to provide "any person who lacks work" with "national insurance" as this would assure a minimal standard of living for such people. In this responsum he expressed a similar sentiment. Therefore, concluded Halevi, "The great moral to be derived by every government among the people Israel is that it possesses an obligation to conduct itself towards its minorities and those who are strangers in its midst with integrity and fairness. In so doing, it will sanctify the Name of Heaven and the name of Israel in the world."

Concluding Thoughts

The search for divine justice and religious meaning in the midst of the complex and oft-times nasty world that humans inhabit is hardly easy. Indeed, precisely how one attains perfect justice in the human setting may well always remain beyond our grasp. Yet, the struggles Halevi displayed in these writings remind us that enduring values of real worth are embedded in our tradition and a vital interpretive process remains at work in our religious heritage.

Ours is an age where the coercive power that formerly characterized the political structure of the medieval Jewish community has dissolved, and the religious certainty that formerly informed so many in prior ages now appears to be elusive. In such an age, Jews may or may not assign responsa literature the authority that it once possessed and such literature may or may not be considered definitive or binding. Nevertheless, it remains a crucial resource for the expression of Jewish teachings and a fundamental part of our patrimony as Jews. Acknowledging the importance of this literature brings us closer to the spiritual resources and truths found in our tradition. Responsa such as the ones presented here aid us in our search for a renewal of contemporary Jewish life rooted in the resources provided by a common Jewish heritage in an authentic Jewish idiom.

Portions of Aseh Lekha Rav *7:70–71*
The Obligation of the Government to Support Its Citizens

Behold, I received your letter dated 4 Tammuz, 5745 (1985), in which you expressed your astonishment at the words of our Sages, may their memory be for a blessing, regarding an interpretation they offered in *Yebamot* 78b on the passage in the Prophets, "And there was a famine in the days of David three years, year after year; and David sought the face of the Lord. And the Lord said, 'It is for Saul, and for his bloody house, because he put to death the Gibeonites'" (II Samuel 21:1). And our Sages there commented on the phrase, "'And for his bloody house, because he put to death the Gibeonites.' Where, however, do we find that Saul 'put to death the Gibeonites?' The truth is that as he killed the inhabitants of Nob, the city of priests who were supplying them with water and food, Scripture regards it as if he himself had killed them." [*See* I Samuel 21:2–7; I Samuel 22:6–18; and Joshua 9:23 and 27]. The Sages also stated there that in response to the demand of the Gibeonites, seven of the sons of Saul were delivered unto them [the Gibeonites] and they [the sons of Saul] were put to death and hanged in the mountain before the Lord, and they [the Gibeonites] were thereby pacified [*See* II Samuel 21:2–6 and 8–9]. And concerning this, our rabbis wrote (*Yebamot* 79a), "But surely it is written, 'The fathers shall not be put to death for the children, etc.' (And the thrust of their comment is directed to the continuation of that verse, 'And the children shall not be put to death for the fathers' [Deuteronomy 24:16]). And Rabbi Yohanan explained, 'It is a better that a letter be rooted out of the Torah than that the Divine Name shall be publicly profaned.'" And the commentary of Rashi, [on this passage in the *Gemara*, states], "Lest the nations [of the world] state, 'It is not fit to cling to this nation [the Jewish people], for they harmed strangers [the Gibeonites] by taking away their livelihood, and they would not exact revenge for them [the Gibeonites]."

This means, according to the words of our Sages, may their memory be for a blessing, there in *Yebamot*, that Saul did not actually kill even a single Gibeonite. Rather, his entire punishment was meted out on account of the fact that through his slaughter of the priests of God in Nob, the Gibeonites lost their livelihood. We will now proceed with an explanation of the matter. As the Gibeonites had no part or inheritance in the land, they could not support themselves through farming. Their livelihood depended entirely upon their work as "hewers of wood and drawers of water" for the house of the Lord. And there is no doubt that as a result of the murder of the priests of the Lord in Nob, they suffered the indignity of famine, and many of them died as a result of famine. Therefore, they [the Gibeonites] said of Saul, "The man that consumed us" (II Samuel 21:5). And according to the explanation of our Sages concerning "famine," it is known that those who perish by the sword are better off than those who die by famine.

And it is most obvious that, inasmuch as Joshua and the chieftains of the community had sworn to them [the Gibeonites] that they [the leadership of the people Israel] would sustain them (Joshua 9:20–21) — that is, that they [the leadership of the people Israel] would accomplish this by supplying them work whereby they could earn a livelihood — it is, therefore, the obligation of every government to be concerned for the subsistence of its citizens, whether they are permanent residents or strangers. And this is all the more so [in an instance such as this] where they [the leadership of the people Israel] had sworn [such concern]. Through this [act of destroying the priests of God in Nob, Saul thereby committed] the great [sin] of profaning the Name of God in public. For if Saul, for reasons of his own, slaughtered the priests of the Lord, then he was obligated to be concerned and find them [the Gibeonites] other work, as this was his obligation as king of Israel.

I do not know how every government in the ancient world conducted itself concerning its obligation for the support of all its citizens. However, even if this obligation was not accepted in the ancient world, there was surely such an obligation concerning the Gibeonites as a result of the sworn oath that had been made [by the leadership of the people Israel to the Gibeonites].

Moreover, the people Israel have always acted so as to express concern for the poor, according to the words of our Rabbi, Rabbi Moses ben Maimon (in the *Mishneh Torah*, Laws of Gifts to the Poor, Chapter 9, and cited by our Master [Joseph Karo] in the *Shulḥan Arukh*, *Yoreh De'ah* 256), and this is his language. [He writes], "Every city that has a Jew in it, is obligated to appoint prominent persons as collectors of *tzedakah* funds from among them . . . to collect from each Jew that which each one is able to give. And they divide the funds . . . and disperse them to all the poor. And we have never seen or heard of a community in Israel that does not have a *tzedakah* fund." And all this is widely known and recognized [as among the most important] of Torah commandments — to be concerned for the support of those in need. And today, this obligation is widespread among every advanced nation, and each person who lacks work is deemed worthy of national insurance [that will assure] a minimal [standard necessary] for subsistence.

Saul sinned against the Gibeonites when he caused their death through famine and neglected [not only] his governmental obligation,

[but] at the very least, the oath that the princes of the community had made [to the Gibeonites] "to sustain them." And this is the first thing we have to learn from the words of our Sages.

The Governmental Obligation to Act with National Integrity

And this we are also given to learn from their words: The Gibeonites were abandoned to die by famine, [whose ravages] we cannot grasp in all their dimensions and parameters, on account of the sin of Saul. And the entire people Israel saw and knew this, and not one person protested, and not one demanded justice for the Gibeonites. However, the matter pained them [the Gibeonites] greatly and justifiably so, and they were not able to forgive the injustice that was thereby perpetrated against them. Therefore, the Holy One imposed the punishment of famine upon Israel on account of this sin whereby they publicly profaned the Name of God. It is noteworthy to emphasize that the decrees of God are meted out measure for measure — the sin against the Gibeonites resulted in death by famine, so here the punishment was famine. [And this famine persisted] until they (the Gibeonites) exacted the cruelest revenge [i.e., the capital execution of Saul's sons]. Indeed, for this reason, they demonstrated that they were not worthy of taking refuge in the inheritance of the Lord, and David therefore issued an eternal prohibition barring them (the Gibeonites) from entering into the community of the Lord as is explained there in the *sugya* (*Yebamot* 78b).

Through this cruel deed itself (the execution of seven of Saul's sons) done at the demand of the Gibeonites, the Name of Heaven was sanctified among the nations [by Israel]. As it states there in the Talmud (*Yebamot* 79a), "For passers-by were enquiring, 'What kind of men are these (that are being hanged)?' Then they exclaimed, 'There is no nation in existence which one ought to join as much as this one (Israel),'... and 150,000 men immediately joined Israel."

From this, the great moral to be derived by every government among the people Israel is that it possesses an obligation to conduct itself with integrity and fairness towards its minorities and those who are strangers in its midst. In so doing, it will sanctify the Name of Heaven and the name of Israel in the world.

19

Interpretive Fluidity and *Psak* in a Case of *Pidyon Shevuyim*

An Analysis of a Modern Israeli Responsum as Illuminated by the Thought of David Hartman

A spirit of Jewish religious humanism animates the texts of Rabbi David Hartman, and two primary themes seem to find expression over and over again in his thought. On the one hand, Hartman displays the passionate conviction that Judaism is marked by an ongoing Jewish hermeneutical enterprise, a supple rabbinic ethos that remains capable, in multiple voices that are simultaneously authentic and measured, of guiding Jews through the shoals of a challenging modern world. He contends that Jews must recover and uncover that ethos, for the integrity of Jewish religious and national identity in both the Diaspora and Israel is contingent upon the manifestation of the values and spirit inherent in this interpretive tradition of Jewish law.

On the other hand, Hartman complements this emphasis upon the Jewish legal enterprise with a celebration that is both joyous and sober of the opportunity that the establishment of the State of Israel has provided for a fully mature revitalization of Jewish life in our time. Having been restored to political sovereignty in its own land, the Jewish people are now responsible for the ongoing drama of Jewish life in a way that was not possible during two thousand years of exile. Hartman fully appreciates the blessing the existence of the Jewish State provides as well as the challenge Israel presents to contemporary Judaism. The attempt to provide religious language for understanding what the State of Israel means for contemporary Jewish life and thought, as well as the role that the Jewish interpretive process might play in Zion today, has been central to his work as a Jewish philosopher.

This essay intends to employ the writings of David Hartman on the nature of Jewish law and the religious import of the State of Israel for the presentation and examination of a responsum the late Rabbi Ḥayim

David Halevi (1924–1998) issued on the question of *pidyon shevuyim*, the redemption of captives. In this 1985 responsum, Halevi specifically addressed the matter of whether the *Halakhah* permitted the redemption of three captive Israeli soldiers in exchange for the release of 1,150 Palestinian terrorists from Israeli prisons. By employing Hartman's work as a framework for the illumination and analysis of the responsum, this essay hopes to pay tribute to Hartman and the seminal role his writings have played in modern Jewish considerations of these topics.

The first part of this essay will present a synopsis of what Hartman has written on the nature of the Jewish legal process and the role it should play in the unfolding of the Jewish spirit in the State of Israel. The second part will move from the realm of theoretical discussion to that of the actual phenomenological analysis of *psak*, Jewish legal adjudication. We will indicate how the theoretical insights and descriptions Hartman provides on the nature of Jewish legal adjudication in both Israel and the Diaspora cast light upon the dynamics that are operative in the Halevi responsum. At the same time, the application of this Hartmanian framework to the Halevi responsum should also clarify the nature of *psak* in a general way as well as provide insight into the Jewish legal process as it unfolds in its Israeli milieu. By utilizing Hartman in this manner, we hope to engage him as a conversation partner in matters that lie at the very heart of his concerns and that through his efforts have become central points of discussion in modern Jewish thought.

Judaism as an Interpretive Tradition and the Israeli Venue
A Synopsis of the Hartman Position

A recurrent theme in the works of David Hartman is his ongoing insistence that Judaism centers upon a "method of interpretation that emphasizes the open-ended possibilities of learning from the received word. The covenant as reflected in the creative talmudic style of interpretation enables Jews to feel free to apply their own human reason to the understanding and application of Torah."[1]

From a Hartmanian perspective, such affirmation of the role that

---

1 David Hartman, *A Living Covenant* (Woodstock, Vt.: Jewish Lights, 1992), p.9.

humans play through their use of reason in "the understanding and application of Torah" in the Jewish legal process is not an expression of ḥutzpah klapei shamayim, of human hubris towards God. Rather, it is compatible with and integral to the ongoing rabbinic ethos that characterizes traditional Judaism. Unlike the Bible, which focuses upon moments of immediate encounter with God, the Talmud and the tradition that flows from it assert that "the living word of God can be mediated through the application of human reason." The Talmud portrays the rabbi as "competent to introduce new legislation defining how the community is to behave," Hartman maintains. "The intellectual mastery of the word of God . . . is all the scholar requires to understand and define how the community of Israel . . . [is] to behave."[2] He sees this claim as consonant with and reflective of the deepest currents contained in Judaism itself, for there is a "covenantal principle that encourages the human moral sense to play a creative role in the covenantal relationship."[3]

Since Hartman contends that the tradition itself affirms that God grants this warrant of autonomy to the human reader of Jewish sacred texts, it follows that the subjectivity inherent in the human condition guarantees that the texts themselves always remain open to a number of meanings. An empirical analysis demonstrates that the pluralism that marks Jewish law is not an accidental by-product of the system. For, as Hartman states, in Judaism "Revelation is not always 'pure and simple,' but may be rough and complex." He continues, "The religious personality this system tries to produce is able to interpret situations in multiple ways" and "offers cogent arguments for opposite positions and points of view."[4] In the language of Edmund Husserl, it can thus be said that for Hartman there is an "endless horizon" of halakhic possibility when committed students labor over the writings of Jewish tradition. A multiplicity of views has quite naturally characterized Jewish legal writings and teachings from the era of the Talmud and later Maimonides up through the present.[5]

---

2 Ibid. p.51.
3 Ibid. p.59.
4 David Hartman, *A Heart of Many Rooms: Celebrating the Many Voices Within Judaism* (Woodstock, Vt.: Jewish Lights, 1999), p.22.
5 See an interesting and nuanced explication of this point in David Hartman,

In a crucial paragraph in his writings on the topic of Jewish legal adjudication, Hartman, on the basis of these observations, characterizes the halakhic process and the factors that shape and inform those who frame its decisions.

> A serious study of the epistemology of halakhic argumentation may help the student realize that halakhic reasons never provide the cognitive certainty of a deductive syllogism. Legal decisions are not necessarily inferences drawn from true premises. In other words, decision-making in a legal system is not a mechanical process. The relative weights granted to principles and values and the appreciation of the particularity of different situations and historical contexts, all participate in halakhic decision-making.[6]

In offering this description of the mechanics of Jewish law, Hartman has not been without his detractors. Among them, Professor Haym Soloveitchik has put forth the most telling critique. In an article entitled "Criteria for the Designation of 'Halakhic Rulings,'" the Yeshiva University professor commented on an analysis Hartman had offered of Maimonides' *Iggeret ha-Shemad*.[7] While the critique was directed at a particular writing and a particular text, the criticism Soloveitchik offered in this case could well be applied in an overarching manner to the general view Hartman provides of the halakhic system and its decisors. It is worth pondering precisely because it illuminates the distinctive approach Hartman adopts on the issue of Jewish legal adjudication, and it indicates exactly where those who dissent from his position find fault with his stance.[8]

Maimonides: Torah and Philosophic Quest (Philadelphia: Jewish Publication Society, 1976), pp. 99–101.

6 *A Heart of Many Rooms*, p. 99.

7 In his "Criteria for the Designation of 'Halakhic Rulings,'" *Jerusalem Studies in Jewish Thought* 3:2 (1983–84), pp. 683–87, Ḥaym Soloveitchik responds to David Hartman's essay, "Maimonides' Epistle on Martyrdom," *Jerusalem Studies in Jewish Thought* 2:3 (1982–83), pp. 362–403.

8 In citing this article by Prof. Ḥaym Soloveitchik in *Jerusalem Studies in Jewish Thought*, I in no way mean to suggest that the criticism he issues in this instance of Hartman exhausts the corpus of his writings on the nature of Jewish law. His work on this topic has been extensive and worthy of treatment in its own right. However,

In his essay, Soloveitchik contends politely but firmly that Hartman is incorrect in his characterization of the halakhic process. In his view, Hartman is guilty of confusing archetypes. He claims that Hartman does not distinguish between what Soloveitchik identifies as the realm where a *posek* exercises "religious leadership," on the one hand, and the domain of *Halakhah* itself, on the other. In Soloveitchik's opinion, Hartman collapses the former into the latter. As a result, his schema is not sufficiently refined to provide the conceptual clarity necessary for distinguishing between public policy pronouncements that a rabbinic authority often makes and the act of genuine halakhic decision-making itself.

> Dr. Hartman identifies religious leadership with *Halakhah*. However, not every determination . . . from the standpoint of religious policy is *ipso facto* a halakhic determination. The truth of the matter is that the fundamental assumption of Hartman is identical with what is called "*da'at Torah*" — namely, that it is sufficient for the determination of a religious leader to be formulated in the language of the sources to render it a *halakhic* determination. It is not coincidental that in Hartman's article, as in many of the proclamations posted in B'nei Brak, the terms "Halakhah" and "Judaism" are used interchangeably.[9]

The Soloveitchik critique in this instance rests upon an essentialist posture that reifies the notion of *Halakhah*. Social and psychological factors undoubtedly impinge from time to time upon the halakhic system. The formal process of Jewish legal adjudication, however, rests upon the exact application of normative hermeneutical rules and principles to the body of Jewish legal texts. Rabbinic opinion issued outside these exegetical parameters, no matter how insightful, does not constitute authentic *psak*, reasoned juridical ruling.

The critique that Soloveitchik offers of Hartman is a powerful one, precisely because it is so incisive and clear. Yet, Hartman would surely

---

for purposes of this paper, the treatment Soloveitchik accords Hartman in this piece identifies the fault that critics find with Hartman's position.

9 Ibid. p.684. This translation is taken from Aryeh A. Frimer and Dov I. Frimer, "Women's Prayer Services," *Tradition* 33:3 (1999), pp.111–12.

not regard it as decisive: he would deny the "either-or" nature of how Soloveitchik here frames the issue. Simply put, Hartman would not accept the qualitatively theoretical distinction that Soloveitchik proposes between the "legalism" of *Halakhah*, on the one hand, and the "non-legalism" of other types of Jewish policy "determinations . . . formulated in the language of the sources," on the other. After all, courts routinely issue legitimate legal judgments that the philosopher of law Ronald Dworkin has identified as policy declarations. In rendering such judgments, judges aim imaginatively to express the community's highest principles and ideals in light of the constraints imposed by both legal precedent and contemporary context. The fact that they function as policy statements in no way reduces their status as legal pronouncements. In fact, as Dworkin points out, decisions issued by appellate courts routinely fall under this category.[10]

Nor would Hartman accept the contention that determinations "formulated in the language of the sources" can be labeled as "*da'at Torah*" as opposed to expressions of *psak*. The phrase "*da'at Torah*" is of course employed in modern ultra-Orthodoxy to designate "the authority of leading scholars to decide in all areas of policy . . . with no reasons provided."[11] To apply the term "*da'at Torah*" to the position Hartman advances in analyzing how rabbinic authorities formulate their policy pronouncements when issuing their decisions seems patently unfair. Indeed, he has nowhere described authentic Jewish decision-making in this way. To be sure, Hartman has stated, "A careful study of rabbinic interpretations and responsa would reveal that it is a near-impossible task to define the limits of interpretive freedom found in the tradition."[12] Yet, he has been equally careful to point out that despite the elasticity this provides, Jewish legal adjudication nevertheless always demands the construction of "a framework of rational moral argumentation" where reasons are put forth and texts cited. While such a system may be "without absolutes," it is surely "not equivalent to relativism" nor can it be reduced to "*da'at Torah*." As Hartman states, "not every point of

10 Ronald Dworkin, "Is Law a System of Rules?" in R. M. Dworkin, ed., *The Philosophy of Law* (Oxford and New York: Oxford University Press, 1977), p. 45.

11 This definition of *da'at Torah* is taken from Michael Walzer, Menachem Loberbaum, Noam J. Zohar, and Yair Loberbaum, eds., *The Jewish Political Tradition, Vol. 1: Authority* (New Haven: Yale University Press, 2000), "Glossary of Terms," s.v., "*da'at Torah*."

12 *A Living Covenant*, p. 8.

view is equally legitimate simply because it is someone's point of view. A point of view must always be subject to and vulnerable to counterargument and evaluation."[13] Such a description acknowledges that *psak*, juridical decision, and the process of *shakla ve-tarya*, the legal argumentation that justifies it, are always marked by a high degree of fluidity and subjectivity. It is a process where the *posek* has the right, indeed the duty, "to bring broader social and moral considerations to bear on the issue at hand."[14] Hartman asserts that this is so because "the rabbinic tradition" is animated by the belief that "God is revealed through the empowerment of human beings to uncover and expand the meaning of Torah through rational reflection and legal argumentation."[15] This belief bespeaks a legal process whereby rabbis and others "gain authority by virtue of the 'law which they teach,' that is, intellectual competence to reason and argue cogently about the law."[16] Such claims are far removed from a concept of *da'at Torah*, where "no reasons are provided."

Hartman's balanced description of the dynamics and methods that mark the Jewish legal process are paralleled by what the British philosopher David Hume wrote over two centuries ago about the nature of legal adjudication in his *Enquiry Concerning the Principles of Morals*. In treating this topic, Hume maintained that juridical reasoning is most strikingly characterized by its dependence on "imagination."[17] As Hume understood it, this means that the judge must employ the capacity of imagination to determine how and whether present cases are actually analogous to past precedents. The rationale that determines whether and how the rule contained in the precedent can be applied does not automatically lie in the merits of the rule or the case itself. Rather, the question is whether the rule and its logical entailments are germane to the case at hand and whether they provide an apt solution for the fact patterns the present case presents — and this determination depends upon a host of logical, contextual, and personal factors. Case law

---

13 *A Heart of Many Rooms*, p.35.

14 Ibid. p.16.

15 David Hartman, *Israelis and the Jewish Tradition: An Ancient People Debating Its Future* (New Haven: Yale University Press, 2000), p.110.

16 Ibid. p.112.

17 David Hume, *Enquiry Concerning the Principles of Morals*, ed. by L.A. Selby-Bigge (Oxford: Oxford University Press, 1975), pp.195–96, 210, and 308–9.

over time therefore proves to be open-ended and flexible, for answers to these questions can seldom be answered without recourse to subjective factors and individual proclivities that are by their nature highly personal on the part of judges.

All this does not mean that a rule stipulated in the law does not have a *pshat*, an intrinsic meaning, nor does this view suggest that precedent can be ignored in a legal system. After all, *stare decisis*, the use of precedent, remains at the heart of legal hermeneutics. However, as stated above, none of this indicates that the meaning contained in a particular standard can be judged as pertaining in a transcendent or *a priori* way to an instant case. The specific factors that mark each particular context and situation must be considered in detail before any judgment can be rendered concerning the application of past precedent to a contemporary case. Furthermore, how this is done often depends as much upon the inclinations of the judge as it does upon the substance of the precedent itself. Consequently, case law is supple. Legal decision-making and the rationales and causes that support the holdings that emerge from this adjudicatory process are therefore best treated as more or less highly persuasive rather than absolutely incontestable.

Hume's description of legal decision-making is consonant with Hartman's general approach concerning the fluid yet reasoned character of Jewish legal adjudication. Hartman is therefore on solid philosophical ground when he offers his textured description of the Jewish legal process. He consistently maintains that the elements of reason, precedent, and individual judgment that are vital to the holdings rendered within other legal systems are essential to Jewish *psak* as well. As Hartman sees it, all these factors constitute integral components of Jewish law, and they are part of the "accepted mechanisms of decision-making" that mark the Jewish legal system. The legal reasoning that supports and characterizes *psak* always "recognizes the need for and validity of decision-making procedures to resolve disagreements."[18] For this reason, "the intellectual experience" of the *posek* "is not an isolated lonely one. There is a community to which [the decisor is] responsible and with which [the rabbinic judge is] engaged in an ongoing conversation."[19] As Hartman sees it, the issuance of *psak* is therefore not arbitrary. There

18 *A Heart of Many Rooms*, p.22.
19 Ibid. p.36.

is a panorama common to the landscape of rabbinic adjudication, one wherein competent *poskim* appeal to an identical canon and affirm a shared method of rational discourse. Nevertheless, pluralism remains a vital feature of the Jewish legal process for the *posek* is careful not to present his "views as evident and necessary, i.e., as the only valid truths."[20] There is an awareness that colleagues may and often do advance contrary claims in virtually every case.

In phrases reminiscent of Hume, Hartman emphasizes and reaffirms this point. He concludes his discussion of the Jewish legal process at one point by asserting that despite the uniformity that characterizes the sources and marks the procedures of Jewish law, there remains a "rich variety of opinions" in the Jewish legal system. This is because the system insists upon the right and "the creativity of the moral *imagination* to make sense of alternative positions."[21] For all the cohesion that marks the processes of Jewish legal adjudication on any issue, an identity of outcomes rarely emerges as capable students of the law read and mine the resources of Jewish tradition in variegated ways. The Hartman characterization of the process that marks Jewish legal adjudication is designed to avoid the aporias of those who would reduce *Halakhah* to a simple reflection of social reality and individual proclivity, on the one hand, and those who would claim that decisions are arrived at solely on the basis of internally consistent, ahistorical readings of Jewish legal sources, on the other. Hartman adopts a middle ground between these two poles. Halakhic interpretation is neither a simple objective uncovering of what has already been revealed by God, nor is it an objective interpretation of what has been written in the texts of the tradition. Rather, the endeavor is a dialectical one, a "rational human enterprise of learning and understanding" that, by design, involves an act of creative and moral decision on the part of the *posek*.[22]

In providing this description and analysis, Hartman candidly admits that his interests are not just theoretical. He believes that the covenantal tradition embodied in rabbinic Judaism "reflects the divine decision to share responsibility for history with human beings."[23] His philosophical and practical concerns are "to locate specific tendencies

---

20   Ibid. p. 22.
21   Ibid. (Emphasis mine).
22   *Israelis and the Jewish Tradition*, p. 121.
23   *A Heart of Many Rooms*, p. 30.

or possibilities within the rabbinic tradition that could be supportive of a covenantal religious anthropology capable of participating adequately in the challenges of modernity."[24] In short, his goal is to apply halakhic inventiveness to the dilemmas of the modern situation so that the Jewish people can address these problems in an authentic Jewish idiom that binds them to the past as it simultaneously directs them in the present and guides them towards the future.

Nowhere are the trials modernity places before the covenantal tradition and the system of law that accompanies it felt with greater urgency than in the State of Israel. Israel not only offers Jews an unprecedented opportunity to regenerate the primary roots of Judaism; it also requires Jews "to assume responsibility for a total Jewish society."[25] The rebirth of Jewish nationhood brought about by the Zionist revolution is significant because of the fact that Israeli Jews, "in reestablishing the Jewish nation in its ancient homeland," unlike Jews in the Diaspora "have taken responsibility for all aspects of . . . life."[26]

For Hartman, the religious import of this responsibility is staggering. His Judaism is corporeal, embedded in the community and land of Israel, and he is mindful that Israel challenges Jews to be aware that Judaism is "shaped by what we do in the present. What we do as a community defines who we are. Neither memory nor prayerful hope counts, only present action."[27] Israel represents a healthy assertion of vitality and moral responsibility on the part of the Jewish people because it is only by assuming such "total responsibility for society" that Jews can "demonstrate the moral and spiritual power of the Torah to respond to the challenges of daily life."[28] The State of Israel provides the one genuine crucible where the values of Judaism can truly be tested and applied, for only in Israel do Jews possess a political sovereignty that entails full accountability. Hartman therefore unflinchingly proclaims, "True spirituality must be related to national-political frameworks."[29]

For these reasons, Hartman condemns a deracinated secular Zionism,

24　*A Living Covenant*, p.13.
25　*A Heart of Many Rooms*, p.xvii.
26　*Israelis and the Jewish Tradition*, p.147.
27　*A Heart of Many Rooms*, p.296.
28　*Israelis and the Jewish Tradition*, p.147.
29　*A Heart of Many Rooms*, p.232.

one that seeks to excise or caricature almost two millennia of Jewish history in the Diaspora while simultaneously ignoring or consigning the religious dimensions of Judaism to oblivion. In opposition to a secular ethos that would attenuate Israeli attachments to the Jewish past, Hartman maintains the State of Israel has a duty to serve as a conduit for Jews' "sense of memory and connection to Jewish history." There are "strong national and communal notions that underlie the Jewish heritage," and the State must meet the "needs of the present" while "carrying the weight of the past."[30] Hartman believes that Jewish law constitutes the "authentic content" of Judaism and that the renewal of *Halakhah* as a framework for the communal discussion of issues within the Jewish state is imperative.[31] Jews might otherwise lose "their covenantal identity by becoming a secular people with no more than a shallow attachment to Torah and to the tradition of a Torah, text-centered community."[32] Should that be the case, "the disappearance of the Jewish people as traditionally understood is possible."[33] For Hartman, such an outcome would be tragic. He remains confident that there is a "tradition waiting to be addressed and waiting to speak to us. The question is how to speak and listen to that tradition.... The crucial issue of our age is how ... to revive the Jewish discussion" in an authentically compelling moral and spiritual direction that will restore "the vitality of Jewish peoplehood and historical memory" in a way that will cause "Israelis and Jews throughout the world to engage with their tradition."[34]

Hartman insists that such an halakhic renaissance can and must take place in Israel. It will occur, however, only if those who are guardians of the tradition and participants in its discourse properly appreciate the Jewish past and respond to the revolutionary implications and opportunities of the present moment. Furthermore, these persons must possess the courage to present and apply the tradition in novel ways that are in keeping with the broad humanistic spirit and language that lies at the heart of Jewish tradition. According to Hartman:

30 *Israelis and the Jewish Tradition*, p.151.
31 *A Heart of Many Rooms*, p.280.
32 *Israelis and the Jewish Tradition*, p.155.
33 Ibid. p.156.
34 Ibid. pp.158–59.

When one enters a totally new frame of reference, such as the State of Israel, no adequate solutions for the development of *Halakhah* can be found without regaining an awareness of the wide range of values that inspired the development of this legal tradition. . . . What we need to learn from the past is not so much how previous generations solved particular problems, or the particular forms of their halakhic frameworks, but rather the underlying spirit and teleology that infuses *Halakhah*.[35]

Jews must ask how "the dignity and sanctity of human life taught in the halakhic tradition" apply to issues of state. "Modern religious leadership," he writes, "must learn from the innovative spirit of the talmudic tradition." In so doing, a moral "sense of covenantal holiness reflecting Judaism as the total way of life of a politically independent nation" will develop.[36] A Jewish national spiritual and moral renaissance must accompany the rebirth of Jewish sovereignty, and this spiritual and moral regeneration must emphasize the renewal of the innovative and ethically creative spirit inherent in the *Halakhah*. This requires the courage "to be bold in our halakhic decisions." As the Jewish people have properly decided, "to accept political independence," they must not evade "the bold halakhic changes" that such a decision entails.[37]

Such a goal is not easily achieved, Hartman acknowledges, but he is profoundly grateful for the opportunity to strive for its realization. He summarizes precisely what is at stake in these efforts and why they are so crucial as he reflects upon the factors and forces that have motivated a lifetime of intellectual-spiritual concerns.

The process began while I was still a rabbi in North America. The questions and concerns of a community that experienced modernity in all its forms yet sought anchorage in the Jewish halakhic tradition were a challenge I could not ignore, and served as an important catalyst for my earliest thinking about Judaism. Nor could the work have been completed had I not had the privilege of participating in the rebirth of the Jewish people in Israel,

---

35 *A Heart of Many Rooms*, pp. 242–43.
36 Ibid. pp. 244–45.
37 Ibid. pp. 274–77.

with its joys and sufferings, its hopes and disappointments. The knowledge that I can no longer speak of Judaism from the framework of a pulpit, but must enter into the total living experience of a nation and attempt to make sense of how Judaic spirituality can live in this new society, has been central to my work as a Jewish philosopher. *In the Israeli context, Jewish ideas may touch on life and death issues. The way one does Jewish theology and religious anthropology may decide the future existence of one's own children and grandchildren.* To philosophize in this context is both a privilege and an awesome responsibility.[38]

The Halevi Responsum

Nowhere do the issues and directions Hartman has addressed in his work concerning Israel and Jewish law converge with greater poignancy and urgency than they do in a responsum written by the late Rabbi Hayim David Halevi, former chief Sephardic Rabbi of Tel Aviv-Jaffa. Writing in 1985, Halevi confronted the issue of whether Jewish law would sanction a discharge by the State of over one thousand Arab terrorists held as prisoners in Israeli jails in exchange for the release of three Israeli soldiers held captive by Arab enemies of Israel. In addressing this matter, Halevi was not responding to a theoretical question. Three Israeli soldiers had disappeared on June 11, 1982, when their tank had fallen into Syrian hands during the battle of Sultan Yakub, and the Israeli government hoped to gain the release of these Israeli soldiers through an exchange for Arab prisoners held in Israeli jails.[39]

Rabbi Shlomo Goren responded to this governmental initiative by publishing an essay on the matter. Appearing in *Ha-Tzofeh*, the organ of the National Religious Party on 11 Sivan 5645 (May 31, 1985), the article, "The Ransoming of Captives in Exchange for the Release of Terrorists According to the *Halakhah*," stated that Jewish law absolutely forbade the Israeli government from redeeming "our captive soldiers in ex-

---

38 *A Living Covenant,* pp. ix–x. (Emphasis mine.)
39 The events leading to and surrounding this proposed exchange are reported in an article entitled, "Israel Would Swap Prisoners for Missing Soldiers," published by Reuters News Service (December 14, 1986). Ultimately, the prisoner exchange did not take place and the fates of the three Israeli POWs — Zachary Baumel, Zvi Feldman, and Yehuda Katz — are still unknown.

change for 1150 terrorists." Goren based this ruling on a *mishnah* found in *Gittin* 45a, "Captives should not be redeemed for more than their value, to prevent abuses (*mipnei tikkun olam*)."[40]

Halevi did not feel he could allow the ruling of Goren to remain uncontested. He offered an immediate response to the position that Goren had advanced, and offered a detailed analysis and exposition of Jewish law on the matter. At the very beginning of his remarks, Halevi maintained — *contra* Goren — that the governmental willingness to release these Arab terrorists from Israeli prisons in exchange for the return of three Israeli soldiers was not necessarily in opposition to Jewish law. In fact, Halevi held that it was possible to provide an innovative reading of Jewish law in this instance that would countenance such a decision.[41]

Halevi noted that the *gemara*, in explicating the *Gittin* passage, offered two possible justifications for the stricture. One explanation maintained that the aim of this judgment was to prevent captors from extorting the public for exorbitant sums of money. In this way, no undue burden that would financially imperil the community could be imposed. The other ground suggested by the rabbis for this decree was that a communal policy that refused to redeem these prisoners would ward off "the possibility that the activities [of the bandits] would be stimulated." It would

40 It is noteworthy that the issue addressed in this paper remains of contemporary import. In the *Jerusalem Report* (November 20, 2000), p. 104, there is an exchange of letters between Tel Aviv lawyer Amnon Zichroni and Yonah Baumel, father of one of the Israeli soldiers captured in Sultan Yakub in 1982, concerning the question, "Is Israel's approach to retrieving POWs and hostages flawed?" In one of his letters, Mr. Baumel, echoing the stance adopted by Goren, states, "Maimonides wrote that a hostage should not be redeemed for a price beyond his worth, so as not to make hostage-taking lucrative." In the course of this paper, the legal reasoning involved here and cited by Mr. Baumel will be discussed at great length. The article supports Hartman's claim that debates over matters of Jewish law and thought in Israel can be of "life and death importance."

41 The Halevi responsum cited here is found in his responsa collection, *Aseh Lekha Rav* 7:52. Two significant English language articles on Rabbi Ḥayim David Halevi are: Marc Angel, "Rabbi Hayyim David Halevy: A Leading Contemporary Rabbinic Thinker," *Jewish Book Annual* 52 (1994), pp. 99–109; and Zvi Zohar, "Sephardic Religious Thought in Israel: Aspects of the Theology of Rabbi Haim David HaLevi," in Kevin Avruch and Walter Zenner, eds., *Critical Essays on Israeli Society, Religion, and Government* (Albany: SUNY Press, 1997) pp. 115–36.

likely deter these gentiles from seizing even more Jews, for such seizure would be pointless inasmuch as these gentiles could not now extort excessive amounts of money from the Jewish people. As the Talmud states (*Gittin* 45a), the rule, "Captives should not be redeemed for more than their value," was advanced so "that robbers should not be tempted to kidnap persons and then offer them for ransom."

Halevi noted that while these rationales for the rule were not completely disparate, it was also true that these arguments were not identical. Nor was the Talmud concerned to resolve the question as to which argument was decisive. However, Halevi pointed out that several later rabbinic authorities concluded that the second explanation provided the foundation for this ruling, as this would prevent gentiles "from risking their own lives in order to capture more Jews." Thus, Maimonides, in *Hilkhot Matanot Aniyim* 8:12, wrote, "'Captives should not be redeemed for more than their value, to prevent abuses (*mipnei tikkun olam*),' for then enemies will not pursue [Jews] to capture them."

Halevi then observed that Rabbi Goren had amassed a significant number of sources that demonstrated that a majority of rabbinic authorities held the opinion that even if captives were in mortal danger, the community should still not redeem these captives for more than their value. Maimonides, speaking as the foremost of these interpreters, recognized that a captive might well be among "the hungry, the thirsty, the naked, and in mortal danger." Still, the Rambam concluded that the community should still "not redeem him for more than his value." The fact that Maimonides reached this conclusion despite his concern for and recognition of the personal plight of the captive only reinforced the explanation Goren had put forth concerning this ruling. Halevi acknowledged that Goren was undoubtedly correct when he claimed that the rationale for the Maimonidean ruling in the *Mishneh Torah* was a legitimate fear for the well-being of the community. These gentile kidnappers would surely seize and pursue other Jews should the community pay an excessive ransom to redeem a single Jewish captive.

In conclusion, Halevi observed that Rabbi Goren had reinforced his position by arguing that the principle of *pikuʾaḥ nefesh*, saving a life, could be adduced as an additional support for the notion that the community should not redeem such captives. Goren had contended that should the community in this instance apply the principle of *pikuʾaḥ nefesh* as a warrant for saving the life of these captives, the community would likely place all its members in a potential situation of mortal danger (*safeik sakanat piku'ah nefesh*). In his view, this would be wrong, as the principle of *piku'ah nefesh* would certainly obligate the community to engage in a utilitarian calculus that would lead to a maximal preservation of life. Therefore, the reasoning that supported the *psak halakhah* of Rabbi Goren, based as it was on the *sugya* in *Gittin* 45a and the decrees and interpretations of both early and later rabbinic authorities, was, as Halevi put it, "clear and correct." In other words, it was a legally cogent opinion. However, Halevi did not agree that the fact pattern in the current situation confronting the government of the State of Israel was identical to that confronted by the former authorities Goren had adduced. Therefore, asserted Halevi, "With all due respect, it seems, in my humble opinion, that no proof discussed above is decisive in our case," and he felt constrained to present a contrasting opinion.

In issuing an opposing responsum, Halevi had to demonstrate that his ruling was consistent with established and binding elements of the law and that it instantiated some accepted legal principle or rule. After all, judicial opinions can only attain normative status if they have recourse to some sort of legal argumentation. A *posek* must justify his conclusion as a conclusion of law. Goren had done so by citing the passage in *Gittin* as well as a host of later legal authorities to legitimate the position he advanced in this instance as an halakhic one. For Goren, the salience of the precedents provided by the *Gittin* passage and decisors such as Maimonides to the contemporaneous question was obvious. Their holdings could be applied as a sure guide for the decision to be arrived at in this case.

At the same time, Halevi contested this claim. In order to resist the Goren holding from a Jewish legal standpoint, Halevi had to deny the legal relevance of the *Gittin* precedent on the basis of reasoned discourse that could demonstrate that his rejection of the precedent Goren had put forth was not arbitrary. This he could do either by claiming that the fact patterns in the instant case were distinct from those at work in the precedent, or by offering an alternative interpretation and application of the precedent itself. As we shall see, Halevi employed both these options in rejecting the *psak* of Goren in favor of his own. In addition, as is the wont of many jurists, he would also employ a "consequentialist argument," one that would show that his ruling, in light of its consequences, was preferable to the likely results that would emerge from the alternative that Goren had proposed.

Indeed, Halevi proceeded to do this by marshalling several extensive legal arguments designed to demonstrate that Goren's decision was in his view problematic and faulty. Initially, Halevi argued that use of precedent in the Goren ruling was not germane to the present case, for the entire discussion advanced by Goren on the basis of the *Gittin* passage and other legal sources was based on a non-extant political reality. After all, the rabbinic authorities Goren cited as warrants for his position all spoke of a fact pattern where bands of robbers were motivated by the desire for financial gain. These robbers would kidnap Jews in order to receive significant sums of money for their release. They could do this by either extorting exorbitant amounts of capital from a Jewish community that had no recourse to military might, or by selling these captives into slavery and profiting thereby. In sum, monetary gain motivated these bands of robbers to kidnap Jews during countless epochs when the Jewish people did not enjoy political hegemony. In such situations, it made eminently good sense to conclude that any submission to such extortion would only increase the kidnappers' appetite "to pursue and seize Jews." The leaders of every Jewish community that confronted such circumstances correctly reasoned that the ransoming of captives for "more than their value" would only lead to the seizure of more Jews and financial ruin for the community. As a result, the rule, as stated in *Gittin* 45a and applied and affirmed by countless authorities including Maimonides over the centuries, made eminently good sense for the political contexts out of which the ruling emerged and for which the statute was designed.

Yet, it was for precisely this reason that Halevi held that the precedents adduced by Goren were no longer relevant, for the situations that obtained when these precedents were first issued no longer existed. As Hartman has stated, Israel has changed Jewish history by providing a national-political framework, and this insight illuminates the intellectual posture that informed Halevi's reasoning in this instance. Indeed, Halevi faulted Goren for his failure to take this distinction into account. As Halevi observed, a contemporary Israeli political situation where Jews enjoyed political sovereignty transformed the question here confronting the contemporary Israeli decisor of Jewish law from what it had been in the past. The Israeli *posek* did not contend with a situation where robbers were exclusively or primarily intent on financial gain. The issue of whether one can release over a thousand terrorists bent on the destruction of Israel from Israeli prisons in exchange for the release of Israeli hostages takes place against a political backdrop whose circumstances diverge completely from those that confronted earlier Jewish authorities.

Halevi then detailed precisely what was novel about the present situation and why he believed that the rule as stated in *Gittin* could not simply be applied, as Goren had suggested, to the present case. He argued that the bands of Palestinian fighters who performed cruel and wanton acts of destruction against the Jewish people in Israel were not motivated by financial considerations. Rather, their aims were "political-national." As Halevi stated, these groups of terrorists would continue to do all that was in their power "to wreak havoc among the Jewish people — *lifgo'a kashot be-am yehudi*," regardless of whether these prisoners were exchanged for Jewish soldiers. He claimed that there was "no doubt that if they were able to risk their lives and capture Jewish prisoners they would do so daily if this would permit them to free their captives and prisoners who are in the hands of Israel. And perhaps they would do so even to attain other political aims."

This analysis only strengthened Halevi's conviction that an exchange of prisoners would not fuel an Arab desire to capture more Jews. These Arab foes would seek to do this whether prisoners were exchanged or not. Indeed, they would only cease attempting such seizures when a political solution was found to the current conflict. Hence, he reasoned that a decision to return Palestinian terrorists in exchange for Israeli soldiers could not be regarded as an enticement that would lead to the abduction of more Jews.

Furthermore, in this changed setting Jews were no longer a hapless politically impotent minority. Jews living in the State of Israel, unlike past generations of Jews in the Diaspora, enjoyed political and military power, and, "due to the kindnesses of God upon us," the kidnapping of Jews by Palestinians seldom occurred. Several recent attempts to kidnap "soldiers and others Jewish citizens have not succeeded," for the Israel Defense Forces have proven able to defend and protect the citizens of Israel. "In my humble opinion," Halevi wrote, "this is a crucial factor that must inform our discussion concerning the matter of ransoming our captive soldiers." Halevi therefore disagreed with Goren as to the applicability of the *Gittin* precedent in the present case, maintaining that the rule it contained was unrelated to the present situation, as the current circumstances for all the reasons cited above were unprecedented. The original considerations that gave rise to the rule no longer obtained.

The current situation therefore demanded halakhic boldness and creativity. As Halevi phrased it, "At the outset, we must acknowledge that there are difficult problems that arise in our lives for which there is no clear and decisive halakhic precedent and solution." He continued by asserting, in words virtually identical to those of Hartman, that there was no real parallel "to the situation that we find ourselves in today. We therefore need halakhic innovation (*hidush hilkhati*) in this instance, one that is consistent with the spirit of earlier halakhic sources and suitable to them — i.e., a new halakhic decision (*hakhra'ah hilkhatit hadashah*)." In staking out this position, Halevi felt that he was only highlighting that quality of innovation that stood at the heart of the Jewish legal system. For, in summarizing this point, he wrote, "This was the power of our Sages," for whenever a novel situation arose, "they were not satisfied with those *halakhot* that had been transmitted to them up to that point. Rather, they struggled to offer innovative halakhic rulings."[42]

Indeed, a clear example of how they did this can be found in rabbinic

---

42 In making this point, Halevi was not unaware that there were opponents of this position. In *Aseh Lekha Rav* 7:54, he responded to one such critic, when he stated, "I do not agree that . . . innovations in the spirit of the *Halakhah,* as written and received and in utter faithfulness to it, constitute deviation — even if these innovations change, in a particular instance, the *Halakhah* as written. . . ." This is so because "permission was granted to the sages of Israel in every generation to introduce halakhic innovations in accordance with changes of time and circumstance. Only thus was it made possible for Torah to persist in Israel. . . ." Indeed, "such innovation is part of the *Halakhah* given to Moses, our Master. Whoever thinks that the *Halakhah* is frozen, and that we may not deviate from it right or left, errs greatly. On the contrary, there is no flexibility like that inherent in the *Halakhah.* . . . If the sages of our own generation will have the courage to introduce halakhic innovations true to Torah, with utter faithfulness to the body of Torah as written and received, then the *Halakhah* will continue to be the path of the Jewish people until the last generation." This translation of the Halevi responsum is taken from Michael Walzer, Menachem Loberbaum, Noam J. Zohar, and Yair Loberbaum, eds., *The Jewish Political Tradition,* pp. 295–97.

discussions concerning the *sugya* in *Gittin* 45a itself. For example, the *Tosafot*, commenting upon the phrase, "in order that activities of the robbers not be stimulated," offered the following thoughts. They noted that in *Gittin* 58a the Talmud related a story concerning Rabbi Joshua ben Ḥaninah. This tannaitic authority, in seeming opposition to the rule that it is forbidden to redeem a captive for more than his worth, had in fact redeemed a child from his captors in Rome for an excessive sum of money. These *tosafists* reasoned that Rabbi Joshua did this because this child possessed exceptional intellectual talents. According to the talmudic narrative, Rabbi Joshua, in explaining his decision, said, "I feel sure that this one will be a teacher in Israel." He was correct, and this boy grew up to be Rabbi Ishmael ben Elisha, a great tannaitic authority. Therefore, it appears obvious that there can be coherent and reasoned exceptions to the rule, and that when "good reasons" are put forth, the "absoluteness" of the rule can be circumvented.

In Halevi's opinion, Rabbi Joshua was to be praised, for he possessed the courage and confidence to offer "a great halakhic innovation for which there was no precedent in any prior legal source." He felt empowered to rule that when it is likely that the captive would one day be "distinguished in wisdom, the law, 'one does not redeem captives for more than their worth,' does not apply to him."

Halevi then observed that the Rosh (Rabbi Asher ben Yeḥiel) saw this precedent as legally applicable. In his commentary on *Gittin* 45a, the fourteenth-century Spanish sage stated that Joshua ransomed the boy for an exorbitant sum because he realized that this boy was "sharp and acute, and he foresaw that it was possible that one day he would become a great man." On the basis of this reasoning, the Rosh further expanded the category of those who would be excluded from the rule, "One does not redeem captives for more than their worth." For, he reasoned, if it was permitted to ransom a young man who showed great intellectual talent and promise for "more than his worth," it was surely permitted to ransom a captive who was already a great man for an exorbitant sum.

Furthermore, the son of Asher ben Yeḥiel, Rabbi Jacob ben Asher (1270–1340), in the *Tur, Yoreh De'ah* 252:4 and 5, as well as Joseph Karo, in the *Shulḥan Arukh, Yoreh De'ah* 252: 4 and 5, codified these exceptions into law. As Halevi saw it, there was no authentic precedent for these innovations. Rabbi Joshua had the confidence to issue these rulings simply on the basis of "the greatness of his authority and wisdom," and these other sages simply confirmed and extended his insights on the basis of what they regarded as their authority to expand the logical entailments of his position.

At the same time, Halevi did not insist that the halakhic tradition was univocal. Indeed, he regarded pluralism as an inherent feature of the Jewish legal system. Halevi hypothesized that it was therefore understandable that Maimonides did not follow Rabbi Joshua's lead and what could be regarded as his school of thought on this question. In this instance, he infers, the Rambam felt uncomfortable with the lack of precedent and he therefore refused to accept either the reasoning or affirm the novella of Rabbi Joshua as decisive. Consequently, in the *Mishneh Torah*, *Hilkhot Matanot Aniyim* 8, these exceptions do not appear. However, the failure of Maimonides to confirm the stance of Joshua and his school on this matter obviously did not obviate the right of either Joshua or his successors in their times to offer these exceptions to the rule. It simply meant that the halakhic system was a pluralistic one, and that Sages have a right to disagree.

Rabbi Halevi then turned to another factor cited by the *Tosafot* concerning the deed of Rabbi Joshua. It served as a second warrant for his position that the halakhic process is one that demands human involvement by allowing for criticism and debate. In further commentary, the *Tosafot* noted approvingly that Rabbi Joshua had circumscribed the applicability of the statute in *Gittin* 45a on additional grounds as well. They pointed out that he had ruled that "during the time of the destruction of the Temple," the basis for the law "that the activities of robbers should not be stimulated" did not apply. Halevi here engaged in purposive interpretation and stated that Joshua correctly realized that the aim of this rule was to preclude the possibility that enemies of the Jewish people would risk their lives to capture "more and more prisoners" for monetary gain. However, the period when the Temple was destroyed was a time when the curse contained in Deuteronomy 28:62, "There you shall offer yourselves for sale to your enemies, but none will buy," had come to fruition. The military might of the Jewish people in Jerusalem had then completely collapsed, and "precious sons of Zion worth their weight in the finest gold" were taken *en masse* by their Roman captors.

Under such circumstances, the reason for the law, "that the activities of robbers should not be stimulated," had been rendered immaterial, as the Jewish people had neither the financial nor the military means at their disposal to prevent such kidnappings. Rabbi Joshua therefore proclaimed the law itself inoperative "on the strength of his own logic and authority — *s'varato v'samḥuto*." He boldly adopted a novel halakhic posture and held that the law in *Gittin* 45a was not legally actionable when analogous political-financial circumstances made it unlikely that more Jews would be captured if captives were ransomed for "more than their value." Here the analogical imagination of the jurist and his right to exercise that imagination through reasoned interpretation were clearly displayed.

In this instance, as before, Halevi praised Rabbi Joshua for his courage and held him up as a model decisor. He observed, "This was the might and courage of the early Sages, who would innovate *halakhot* in response to contemporaneous events in the national life of the Jewish people." They refused to confine their applications of the law "to well-known and familiar sources of the law." In so doing, these rabbis, like Joshua, served as exemplars for all *poskim*. Halevi declared that the right to exercise such halakhic creativity and courage was not limited to the sages of the Talmud alone. The greatest rabbinic authorities throughout the ages had consistently followed the lead of these talmudic masters. These later authorities, like the *tannaim* and *amoraim* of old, "offered novel legal rulings by relying upon their own logic and wisdom."

Foremost among such authorities was the Radbaz, the sixteenth-century *posek* Rabbi David ben Zimri, who consciously extended the logic inherent in the second warrant put forth by Rabbi Joshua to limit the contemporary use of the *Gittin* ruling.[43] In looking at the social-political context of his own era, Rabbi Zimri observed that robbers no longer specifically went out to kidnap Jews and charge excessive ransoms for them. Instead, they randomly seized anyone they could succeed in capturing, Jew or gentile. They did not charge any greater sum for the redemption of Jewish captives than they did gentile ones. As a result, the decision to redeem a Jewish captive for an excessive sum of money did not entice these kidnappers to seize more Jews. In such circum-

---

43 This responsum of R. David ben Zimri is cited in *Pitḥei Teshuvah* on the *Tur, Yoreh De'ah* 252:4–5.

stances, there was no justification for not ransoming Jewish captives "for more than their worth." As the conditions of his era led him to arrive at the same conclusion that Joshua reached during the time when the Temple stood, the Radbaz felt at liberty to abrogate the actionability of *Gittin* 45a. He quoted the talmudic dictum, "*Hinah la-hem le-yisrael . . .* be lenient with Israel by allowing them to practice the attribute of mercy," as a concluding warrant for this stance.

Halevi opined that the reasoned interpretation (*sevara*) of the Radbaz was another example of halakhic daring (*ḥidush hilkhati*) "for which there was no precedent." Radbaz had acted upon his own sense of logic precisely because he recognized that when there are "new and changing situations, one cannot construct a legal ruling on the authority of the sources alone." Halevi, in a tone once more reminiscent of Hartman, stated, "There is a clear need to search for [new or novel] solutions that are consistent with the spirit of the sources and absolutely faithful to them in constructing novel rulings."

In making this claim, Halevi presaged the teachings of Hartman. As has been shown, Hartman, on the basis of talmudic narratives, consistently maintains that the tradition teaches that the rabbi is "competent to introduce new legislation defining how the community is to behave . . . . The intellectual mastery of the word of God . . . is all the scholar requires to understand and define how the community of Israel . . . [is] to behave."[44] In light of this dynamic, Halevi reasoned that the Jewish legal tradition granted him as much right as any past rabbinic authority to determine how or whether a precedent should be applied. His prerogatives as a *posek* were no less than theirs were. He could judge whether conditions had sufficiently changed to warrant the setting aside of the rule in this instance. Unlike Goren, Halevi therefore concluded that the rule was not actionable. He reiterated his earlier observation that the terrorists "are unable to kidnap Israeli captives. Those prisoners who fell into their hands were at war in Lebanon." The rule enunciated in *Gittin* ought not be employed as a precedent that would prohibit the government from engaging in the proposed exchange as the purpose for which the rule was originally designed had been rendered mute and obsolete by contemporary conditions. In offering this assertion, Halevi did so by employing the readings offered by one

44 See n.2 above.

school of Jewish legal exegesis on this passage as well as by relying upon his own authority as legal decisor. In his able hands, the halakhic process can be seen as "a rational human enterprise" marked by "learning and understanding."

Halevi ended his responsum with one final observation. He noted that the Israeli Minister of Defense had made an important point concerning the morale of the IDF soldiers that a *posek* had to take into account when rendering a judgment on this issue. The minister had stated that if an IDF soldier knew that the State of Israel would spare no effort or expense to liberate a captured soldier, then that soldier would be more likely to risk his life fearlessly during a moment of battle. However, if that same soldier thought that the *Gittin* rule as interpreted by Goren applied to his situation, then the soldier might be more likely to retreat during battle for he would not risk capture as a prisoner of war. Therefore, queried Halevi, "Who is now able to measure which poses the greater potential damage" for the defense of the State — "strengthening the power of the terrorists through the release of their comrades, or sustaining the morale of the IDF soldiers in future wars should they occur?"

Halevi felt that even to pose the question in this way was to engage in "halakhic innovation." Israel embodied a novel reality for the Jewish people. He felt that nothing in the vast halakhic literature on this passage was directly analogous to the issue at hand. The rule had to be applied and a decision had to be made against a novel backdrop where changed political conditions demanded a fresh response. In his view, the genius of the halakhic system was that it allowed for and encouraged such innovation. Consequently, Halevi was able to conclude his responsum with the following overarching observation. Of the halakhic process in such cases, he wrote:

> I am certain that if a question of this type had stood before our early Sages, they would have found a solution for it through their efforts to discover a novel halakhic application consistent with the spirit of the previous halakhic sources. Therefore, it cannot be said that the government of Israel acted here in opposition to Jewish law. Indeed, its seems that her deliberations in this matter were consistent with the type of halakhic innovation that Torah Sages might have introduced in such an event.

In offering these final thoughts, Halevi revealed a view akin to that of Hartman on both the meaning and import of the State of Israel for contemporary Judaism as well as a Hartmanian sensibility that regards the Jewish legal system as open and supple. Halevi had no doubt that the State represented a novum in Jewish history that demanded "novel halakhic applications." Yet, he was certain that Jewish law in the hands of competent and courageous decisors possessed the resources and spirit to meet such demands.

The capacity of the Jewish legal system to respond to novel challenges in authentic Jewish voices had been evidenced in the past. Halevi was therefore certain that confident and capable *poskim* could mine the resources of Jewish law in ways that would prove worthy in the present as the people Israel responded to the "life and death issues" presented by the Israeli situation in ways that would prove creative and life-affirming.

Final Thoughts

In his *A Heart of Many Rooms*, Hartman states: "The interpretive tradition, which defined Judaism in the past, was ambiguity and controversy. In fact, rabbinic Judaism can best be described as a bold interpretive culture amidst disagreement."[45] This paper, in looking at the divergent rulings of Goren and Halevi on the question of *pidyon shevuyim*, has demonstrated the accuracy of this observation. It is clear that two rabbis need not, and in difficult cases likely will not, agree that precedent be interpreted and applied in only one uniform way. Legal hermeneutics are "imaginative," and judicial discretion allows for a variety of outcomes in Jewish law just as it does in other legal systems.

For Hartman, the diversity that marks the Jewish legal process is not an accidental by-product of rabbinic culture. As he phrases it, "The legacy of the interpretive community requires its contemporary heirs to be fully awake to the possibility that the interpretive strategies they adopt may not be shared by all, and that diversity and disagreement are not signs of inauthenticity."[46] Halevi can disagree with Goren and argue with conviction on the basis of precedent and reason that his decision in the case is the preferred one. Nevertheless, this disagreement

---

45 *A Heart of Many Rooms*, p.5.
46 Ibid. p.36.

does not require him to label Goren judicially incompetent. By taking a stance in opposition to Goren, Halevi demonstrates the accuracy of Hartman's contention that the analogical mode of reasoning that is operative in the Jewish jurisprudential process allows for a multiplicity of legitimate legal opinions to emerge. Such variety is consonant with the deepest and most abiding currents of the rabbinic ethos. As Hartman points out, "In *Sotah* 7:12 it states, 'Make yourself a heart of many rooms and bring into it the words of the House of Shammai and the House of Hillel.'" A religious Jew "can live with ambiguity" and can "feel religious conviction and passion without the need for simplicity and absolute certainty."[47]

Hartman has by any standard been a constructive Jewish thinker of immense import. His aim has been "to provide an approach to Torah that can retrieve the vitality of the Jewish interpretive tradition" for our day so that Jewish authenticity can be maintained as Jews struggle with the demands of the hour.[48] Yet, he has also been the first to acknowledge that such retrieval is not easily achievable, for most modern Jews exhibit "tone-deafness to the music of Jewish tradition." Hartman is convinced that this situation will not change "unless we first rehabilitate the meaning of being a Torah-covenantal community." He is equally convinced, however, that such rehabilitation will not "come about" unless "we develop a compelling, intellectual, and moral vision of what it means to be an interpretive, text-centered community."[49]

Nevertheless, Hartman does not see the realization of such a vision as unattainable. This is because, as he puts it, "there are resources within the tradition for its own self-correction."[50] Large elements of the interpretive tradition bespeak a broad humanistic spirit that finds expression in a wide variety of ways that are ever responsive to the demands of the hour. The "ethical and legal implications" of these elements and manifestations indicate that the attitudes and processes that mark the Jewish legal system are dynamic and constructive, and the precedents and principles that constitute its core are not restricted to how they

47 Ibid. p.21.
48 *Israelis and the Jewish Tradition*, p.161.
49 Ibid. p.165.
50 Ibid. p.143.

were "employed in the past." They can attain renewed relevance in the future if competent and engaged students of the Law display the requisite determination to have these elements speak in innovative and sensitive ways to Jews in the present. If these persons succeed in doing so and proceed with the courage and boldness of Rabbi Halevi, the covenantal tradition will once more speak in authentic and compelling ways and will guide Jews towards the future. As Hartman puts it, "If we can rid ourselves of the obsession with certainty and finality — if we can internalize the spirit of the covenantal idea — then the uncertainties of the modern world will not deter us from renewing the vital interpretive processes that define our religious heritage."[51]

Hartman has argued that the texts and canon of the Jewish legal system grant the Jewish community its identity and that the ideals of our community are reflected in the reasoned judgments our decisors render. He has emphasized that the State of Israel has provided the Jewish people with an opportunity to exercise the power and spirit of the Jewish tradition in an unprecedented way. Our discussion of his thought has explicated his judgments and insights on these matters, and the analysis this essay has provided of Halevi's responsum has hopefully demonstrated that other practitioners of the Jewish legal tradition within Israel itself have shared Hartman's views. Halevi's *psak* indicates that Hartman's vision finds actual expression in Jewish law as jurists apply the holdings and insights of Jewish tradition in humane ways to existential questions of life and death in Israel. In turn, the writings of David Hartman illuminate the processes at play in the work of rabbis like Halevi and highlight the overarching dynamics at play in Jewish jurisprudence.

---

51 *A Heart of Many Rooms*, p.36.

20

Artificial Fertilization and Procreative Autonomy

Two Contemporary Responsa

Modern medicine has developed new reproductive technologies that have allowed the genetic, gestational, and social components of parenting to be separated in unprecedented and astonishing ways. As Professor Arthur Caplan of the University of Pennsylvania has observed, "[If] Leonardo da Vinci were suddenly transported to the United States in 1994," he would find "a reproductive clinic [where] we make babies in this dish and give them to other women to give birth . . . more surprising than seeing an airplane or even the space shuttle."[1] A cartoon on the editorial pages of the *Los Angeles Times* on January 21, 1994, makes a similar point. The cartoon depicts a man and woman modestly clad in their night clothes lying side-by-side in bed. The woman turns to the man and says, "Honey, I went to the sperm bank for semen. Then I picked up a donated egg and had it fertilized at a lab and implanted it in a 60-year-old surrogate mother. . . . Was it good for you?"

Astonishment and irony aside, artificial modes of reproduction have surely raised a whole host of questions that contemporary ethicists and religious leaders must confront. How do these new forms of non-coital and donor-assisted reproduction alter the nature of conception, the nature of the family, and our views of social existence? Should artificial reproduction be allowed to become a commercial venture? Should any boundaries be placed on the ability of adults to employ these technologies? These dilemmas and more have been created by recent medical advances in reproductive therapies.[2] They are not always easily resolved and have given rise to considerable controversies among diverse commentators and thinkers. Unanimity of opinion among ethicists has hardly been forthcoming, and no consensus on the questions posed

---

1 *The New York Times*, January 11, 1994, p. A1.
2 During the last decade leading journalists of medical ethics such as *Second Opinion*, *The Hastings Center Report*, and *The Kennedy Institute of Ethics Journal* have been replete with articles devoted to the variegated nuances and issues of this topic.

by these technologies is in sight. As medical ethicist George Annas of Boston University has pointed out: "Artificial reproduction is defended as life-affirming and loving by its proponents and denounced as unnatural by its detractors."[3]

These reproductive technologies and the quandaries they present have not escaped the attention of halakhic authorities. Leading halakhists in every denomination of Jewish life have begun to address many of these issues. One need only consult the writings of Reform rabbis such as Walter Jacob and Moshe Zemer, Conservative authorities such as Elliot Dorff and Daniel Gordis, or Orthodox rabbis and physicians such as J. David Bleich and Moshe Tendler, for evidence of the interest these technologies have evoked and the variety of responses they have elicited. This paper will deal with one circumscribed topic — artificial fertilization — in the vast field of artificial reproduction. Two responsa on the topic (*hafrayah melakhutit*) issued by two different Israeli Orthodox rabbinical leaders, will provide the central focus of discussion. The first was issued in 1981 by Rabbi Eliezer Waldenberg of Jerusalem, the Tzitz Eliezer, well-known as the world's leading Orthodox halakhic authority on issues of medical ethics, while the second was written in 1988 by Rabbi Ḥayim David Halevi, the Chief Rabbi of Tel Aviv-Jaffa, one of the most prolific authors of responsa on the modern Israeli scene.[4] Following the presentation of these responsa and the halakhic concerns and cautions that these Orthodox rabbis raise, we will consider issues of genetic, biological, familial, feminist, and social concern occasioned by these writings, as well as the manner in which such considerations ought to inform Liberal Jewish deliberations on this and related matters.

The Responsum of Rabbi Eliezer Waldenberg

In 1981, three years after the world's first child conceived by means of in vitro fertilization was born in England, and after such a procedure was replicated with success in a half-dozen other cases in various parts

---

3   George J. Annas, "Redefining Parenthood and Protecting Embryos," in *Judging Medicine* (Clifton, N.J., 1988), p. 59.

4   Waldenberg's responsum can be found in *Tzitz Eliezer*, 15:45. Halevi's responsum is located in *Mayim Ḥayim*, no 61.

of the world, Dr. David M. Meier, Director of Shaarei Tzedek Hospital in Jerusalem, asked Rabbi Waldenberg to provide an halakhic opinion about this "new medical technique — artificial fertilization in a petri dish," whereby children could be conceived non-coitally. Meier began his query to Waldenberg with a straightforward explanation of the medical procedure involved in employing this therapy for an infertile married couple. Ova, he wrote, are removed from the woman by laparoscopy and then placed in a petri dish (a laboratory medium) with sperm ejaculated by the woman's husband for fertilization. After undergoing a number of cell divisions, the developing zygote is inserted into the uterus of the woman from whom the ovum was removed, and from then on the pregnancy continues until the child is born. In this instance, where the genetic, gestational, and birth mother were one and the same, and where the semen to fertilize the ovum was donated by the husband, was there any halakhic objection to employing this procedure as a way to alleviate infertility?

Waldenberg answered Meier in a responsum dated 8 Elul, 5741 (September 7, 1981). He stated in the prologue that there were, in his opinion, both implicit and explicit "halakhic stumbling blocks" to the procedure. Artificial *insemination* (*hazra'ah melakhutit*), he noted, had already been the subject of a great deal of halakhic literature.[5] In that procedure, all the husband's sperm could be deposited into the wife's uterus, where it would remain as it would "in natural intercourse." Nor are the wife's ova removed surgically. Waldenberg himself countenanced artificial insemination, but only when every effort to conceive "naturally — *ke-derekh kol ha-aretz*" had been exhausted. If after ten years had passed, the woman was not pregnant, or if an Orthodox doctor indicated prior to the passage of this ten-year period that the woman could not become pregnant "in a natural manner," such insemination could be permitted if the donor was the husband of the woman. Waldenberg also voiced total opposition to this procedure when the donor of the semen was a male other than the husband. Indeed, in such an event the woman "was obligated to receive a divorce from her husband."[6] In other words,

---

5 Waldenberg's review of this literature is found in *Tzitz Eliezer*, 9:51 ch. 4, sec. 17–18 and 20–21.

6 Ibid. 13:93.

he restricted his *heter* (permission) only to instances of AIH (artificial insemination when the husband is the sperm donor). It did not extend to AID (artificial insemination when the sperm donor is not the husband).

Waldenberg's ruling on the matter of artificial insemination and the limited scope of his permission casts light on his holding in the case of artificial fertilization described above. Due to the number of steps involved in artificial fertilization, the possibility of fraud and abuse — apart from simple error — was great, and there was no way, in Waldenberg's opinion, to guarantee that the donor would be the husband. He dismissed the assurances of the medical community's reliability in this matter as "a total lie — *shav va-sheker havtaḥatam zot*," designed to assuage public outcry against this medical innovation. Thus his opposition was based upon his fear that family lineage would be confused and that the traditional understanding of the family could be blurred by a technology that so easily allowed for distinction between genetic, gestational, and child-rearing parenthood. "Heaven forfend," he exclaimed, "against anarchy (*hefkeirut*) such as this which is likely to erupt into serious breaches against the wall [that protects] the purity (*be-ḥomat ha-taharah*) and lineage of the family (*ve-ha-yiḥus ha-mishpaḥti*)." With this, Waldenberg's prologue to the responsum came to an end. His aversion to the possibility of collaborative conception between donors and gestators other than husband and wife in this mode of artificial reproduction led him to condemn artificial fertilization. It could not serve as a Jewishly-sanctioned solution to the problem of infertility — even for a married couple!

The remaining sections of Waldenberg's responsum only reinforced the substance of his ruling on this matter. In the course of elaborating upon his decision, Waldenberg made a great effort to distinguish halakhically between artificial insemination and artificial fertilization as non-coital modes of assisting infertile couples in their quest and desire for progeny. The former therapy, as stated above, could be permitted in certain instances. The latter, he felt, was always to be condemned. There was no symmetry between the laws governing artificial insemination and those addressing artificial fertilization. In the former procedure, the husband's sperm was inserted directly into the womb of his wife, and she either became pregnant or she did not "in a natural manner" (*be-ofen tiv'i*). Since all of the husband's sperm could be deposited into the wife's uterus, artificial insemination need not involve "a wasting of seed."

In the case of artificial fertilization, such was not the case. The remaining sperm not used in the artificial fertilization of the ova in the petri dish were either "wasted" or, echoing a theme voiced earlier in his responsum, used to fertilize the eggs of another woman! The husband, in cases of artificial fertilization, was therefore guilty of violating the halakhic ban against "the spilling of seed."

The distinction between artificial insemination and artificial fertilization as permissible and impermissible modes of non-coital reproduction was made by Waldenberg in other ways as well. In the case of artificial insemination, it was possible to argue that the man fulfilled his obligation to "be fruitful and multiply." This was because his semen was directly injected into the womb of his wife as it would be in an instance of "natural insemination." The process of gestation would be the same whether the sperm was inserted artificially or naturally. Thus, many authorities, like Waldenberg himself, relied upon this understanding during "a time of emergency" so as to permit AIH as a halakhically-sanctioned mode of non-coital reproduction.

Artificial fertilization, Waldenberg wrote, was different. He stated, "They (the couple) alter the order of creation through [this] (*heim meshanim ba-zeh sidrei bereishit*), and the sperm of the husband does not enter the uterus of the mother but is placed into a petri dish." So, too, with the woman. A surgical technique is employed to remove her ova and place them in the petri dish, outside of her body. There is thus "no relationship — *ein bo inyan klal shel hityahasut*" between the fertilized ovum and the couple, as the process of fertilization in the petri dish takes place outside the body for a period of a week or longer[7] until the doctors are certain that fertilization has taken place. Only then is one fertilized ovum implanted in the womb of the mother. Waldenberg therefore condemned artificial fertilization as an "unnatural process both from the standpoint of the man and the standpoint of the woman —

---

7 Waldenberg uses the terminology of "a week or longer." This is a bit of an exaggeration. Common practice is for the fertilization to take place for only several days. It may be that Waldenberg's contention reflects the state of this therapy at that time. It may also be that he simply wanted to emphasize that there was an extensive duration of time in which the ovum was removed from the mother's body. However, from Waldenberg's standpoint, the actual time outside of the mother's body would only be a technicality and would have had no bearing on the point he was making.

ein hazra'ah ke-darkah, lo mi-tzad ha-ish ve-lo mi-tzad ha-ishah." It is a "third power (*ko'aḥ shelishi*)," i.e., the petri dish, "that causes [the conception to occur]."

Waldenberg's observations here, as Rabbi J. David Bleich has noted, "are not based upon cited precedents or analogy to other halakhic provisions."[8] However, Waldenberg's sentiments on in vitro fertilization (IVF) do parallel a position that Rabbi Michael Gold has associated with some of the teachings of the Catholic Church. As Gold states:

> Many religious leaders in the Catholic Church . . . have objected to these procedures as 'unnatural'. . . . In vitro fertilization . . . has been attacked by the Catholic Church as contrary to natural law. To quote a recent Catholic legal document: 'Advances in technology have now made it possible to procreate apart from sexual relations through the meeting in vitro of the germ cells previously taken from the man and the woman. But what is technically possible is not for that very reason morally admissible. Marriage does not confer upon the spouses the right to have a child, but only the right to perform those natural acts which are per se ordered to procreation.'[9]

Waldenberg's position and the concerns he advanced in this section of his responsum demand commentary. I will reserve my own for later. For the time being, it is sufficient to note that Waldenberg would undoubtedly both be stung by Bleich's critique and possibly surprised to see how closely his own views parallel those of certain Catholic teachers. Nevertheless, it should not obscure the fact that this reasoning allowed

8   J. David Bleich, "In Vitro Fertilization: Questions of Maternal Identity and Conversion," *Tradition*, vol. 25, no. 4 (1991), p. 82. As my aims in this article are broader than determining the halakhic identity of the fetus' "mother," i.e., who has the Jewish legal right to claim maternity in cases of in vitro fertilization, my goal is distinct from Bleich's. I will not comment upon his article except to note that an interesting and dissenting response to many of the points Bleich makes in his piece can be found in Ezra Bick, "Ovum Donations: A Rabbinic Conceptual Model of Maternity," *Tradition*, vol. 28, no. 1 (1993), pp. 28–45.

9   Michael Gold, *And Hannah Wept: Infertility, Adoption, and the Jewish Couple* (Philadelphia, 1982), p. 104.

him to assert that the commandment to "be fruitful and multiply" was not fulfilled through an "unnatural mode of non-coital reproduction" such as artificial fertilization. The Torah, Waldenberg averred, teaches that no commandment is fulfilled when it is performed "in an unnatural manner." IVF was no exception. Nor, Waldenberg wrote, was the corollary *mitzvah* of "*lashevet yatzrah*" (derived from Isaiah 45:18: "Not for void did God create the world, but for habitation [*lashevet*] did God form it [*yatzrah*]") fulfilled by this operation, "which is performed in an unnatural and abnormal manner."

In the penultimate section of his responsum, Waldenberg displayed an almost Luddite aversion to this particular type of advancing medical technology and expressed his fear that an acceptance of in vitro fertilization as a legitimate form of non-coital reproduction technology would lead humanity onto a "slippery slope" from which there would be no escape. Medical technology would soon be able to produce "biological creatures" from single cells conceived and nurtured solely within the laboratory. Such "creatures" would have been produced with no recourse to "natural modes of reproduction" and would bear no relationship to humanity. They would have neither father nor mother. The technology involved with in vitro fertilization must therefore be resisted, as it would lead to untoward consequences for humanity.

Finally, in concluding his responsum, Waldenberg returned to several themes he had outlined at the beginning of his opinion. Since no procedure, he wrote, could guarantee with absolute certainty that the sperm donor would not be mixed up or confused, grave genetic and familial problems could arise in connection with this therapy. In apocalyptic tones he wrote, "The earth will be full of incest and a father may well marry his daughter and a brother might marry his sister," since the identity of a sperm donor might well remain unknown and his anonymous identity might well be protected by law. Indeed, it would not be unthinkable, in light of this, that a single man's sperm might well impregnate thousands of women over the course of a year. The potential consequences of this procedure were, Waldenberg stated, "shocking and alarming! . . . Is the fear associated with the prospect of a father marrying his daughter or a brother marrying his sister not one based on a real and immediate possibility? Therefore, no leniency can be permitted in this matter. . . . In my humble opinion, the *Halakhah* absolutely does not countenance or permit artificial fertilization in a petri dish." With this final statement, Waldenberg concluded his responsum.

Rabbi Ḥayim David Halevi — A Different Sensibility

Eight years later, on 15 Kislev, 5749 (November 24, 1989), a related, but different, set of questions from those posed to Waldenberg concerning the halakhic attitude toward artificial fertilization were addressed to Rabbi Ḥayim David Halevi of Tel Aviv-Jaffa by an anonymous doctor. The physician, apparently an American, wrote that his questions dealt with artificial fertilization in a petri dish:

> Nearly every medical laboratory in the United States which deals with fertilization customarily gathers a number of ova from the mother at one time and mixes them with the ejaculate of the father in the petri dish. [The doctors] examine the ova after they have been fertilized for several days, and then they decide which of them they will inject in the womb of the mother. My question is, 'What is the halakhic standing of the ova that were fertilized during the time that they were still in the dish? . . . Is it permitted to dispose of the ova that were not selected for transplantation?

Halevi began his responsum by dealing with the issue of Jewish law's attitudes toward artificial fertilization in general. Only then could he address the specific question of the pre-embryo's moral status. He noted that the previous decade had witnessed a contrariety of halakhic opinion on this matter. No consensus had emerged among the "sages of this generation" on the issue. Some authorities permitted it if great care was taken to assure that only the ova of the mother and the semen of the father [i.e., husband and wife] were used, and if there was no shred of suspicion that the ova or semen were donated by any other person. Rabbis in this group maintained that the father did fulfill the commandment to "be fruitful and multiply" through IVF, and they gladly permitted employment of this non-coital method of reproduction for a couple that was otherwise unable to conceive. In opposition to them, other rabbis asserted that the child produced by such a procedure had no relation to his parents at all, and the father did not thereby fulfill the commandment to "be fruitful and multiply," though he did, in their opinion, fulfill the *mitzvah* of "*lashevet yatzrah*." Yet others in this latter group, like Waldenberg, were even more stringent. They insisted that the father did not even fulfill this latter commandment thereby, and they attacked the permission to sanction this technology ferociously, claiming that one could never depend upon the veracity of the doctors in this matter. Halevi, up to this point in his responsum, simply listed these various positions. There was clearly no agreement among Orthodox authorities on this matter. As Halevi presented these opinions, it appeared that a variety of opposing halakhic positions were equally valid and that an Orthodox Jew could select among them with a clear conscience that he or she was electing an halakhically-legitimate option.

Halevi himself failed to offer an explicit judgment as to which viewpoint he favored. However, he proceeded by observing that many Orthodox Jewish couples availed themselves of this technology and that these Jews who did so undoubtedly depended upon those authorities who were lenient on this issue. Inasmuch as Halevi himself neither protested this practice nor castigated those rabbis who offered such permission, one can only assume that he felt IVF was an halakhically-sanctioned method for resolving the problem of infertility for married couples. For those Jews who followed the lenient authorities on this issue, it was permissible, Halevi ruled, to dispose of those ova that were not selected for transplantation since the law forbidding abortion applied only to a fetus in the womb of a woman. He did not explain fully why a judgment that embraced artificial fertilization as a permissible halakhic solution to the problem of infertility for married couples necessarily led to the position he sanctioned concerning the disposal of pre-embryos. Indeed, his decision to permit the disposal of the preembryo was reached independently of any considerations regarding artificial fertilization. Instead, his reasoning about the status of the preembryo stemmed from a judgment that abortion did not constitute murder in Jewish law. Therefore, the disposal of the pre-embryo was not absolutely forbidden.

Halevi did not feel, however, that such judgment justified destroying such ova cavalierly. After all, the pre-embryo, as well as the fetus, deserved profound respect as each possessed the potential to develop into human life. Yet, as they had not yet attained that status, discard of the former or abortion of the latter was permissible when good reasons for such actions could be put forth. The inclination to decide in this manner was further revealed in the second part of his responsum. Here he took note of a previously infertile woman who had taken medication to reverse her condition. As a result of the medication, it was not uncommon, Halevi noted, for a multiple pregnancy to result. Indeed, sometimes as many as eight or nine ova were fertilized. Even though each ovum may initially be healthy, Halevi reasoned as follows:

> . . . if the pregnancy continues, it is a virtual statistical certainty that all of [the ova] will be born prematurely (around 26 weeks into the gestational period) and, in light of this, they will be very weak, with physical defects or serious brain damage. The absolute majority of these premature infants will either die in a few weeks after their birth or will suffer greatly all the days of their lives. The situation of the premature infant is aggravated even more if the moment of birth is even earlier and the moment of birth is influenced by the number of fertilized eggs.

Halevi concluded this section of the responsum by observing. "One should also consider the danger to the pregnant mother who is carrying so many fetuses."

The question to be addressed here concerned the procedure of "reducing the number of fetuses — *dilul ha-ubarim*." In the first trimester of pregnancy common practice is for a needle to be inserted into the womb in order to destroy several of the fertilized ova. The purpose of this procedure is to assure that one or two of the fetuses remain alive, are born, and grow up "whole and healthy — *beri'im u-sheleimim*." Statistics indicated that there was little risk of danger to either the mother or the remaining fetuses if only one or two were carried to term, and that there was significant risk if there were four or more. Statistical evidence concerning three was inconclusive. Halevi had to determine whether it was permissible to engage in this procedure and, if so, until what point in the pregnancy was destruction of the fetuses allowed? Finally, an ancillary query asked Halevi to determine how one would decide how many fertilized ova to remove?

Halevi noted that on these questions, as with the set of questions posed to him in the first part of the responsum, there was much disagreement among the rabbis. Here, as in the initial section of his reply, he contended that an answer to the question was contingent upon determining the Jewish view on abortion. Some authorities, Halevi reported, maintained that aborting a fetus fell under the category of "destroying a soul — *ibud nefesh*." These rabbis ruled stringently on such questions and were inclined to discourage the use of fertility drugs to stimulate ovulation precisely because of questions Halevi now faced. However, these authorities were in the minority. Most rabbis ruled leniently on such questions because they did not view the destruction of an ovum or even a fetus as "murder."

In view of this majority position, Halevi wrote, "Inasmuch as it has already been established that if these ova remain alive they will be born with serious physical birth defects or brain damage, we may certainly rule leniently and destroy several of the fetuses on the condition that one or two remain who will be born whole and healthy." It would be best to perform this procedure as early as possible in the pregnancy. However, if the procedure were not done in an early stage for any reason, "there is no impediment to perform the operation at any moment that is possible." The exact number of ova that should be destroyed depended upon the judgment of the doctor. However, as the statistical probability was that two could be carried to full term and emerge as healthy and intact babies, Halevi felt that there was an obligation to leave two fertilized ova intact. Therefore, even here he observed that if there was any reason to assume that two fetuses would endanger either the mother or the other fetus, or if there was any other consideration (e.g., the health and strength of the mother) guiding the decision of the doctor, then it was permitted to destroy one of the two remaining ova.

While Halevi may have possessed personal reservations or misgivings about this technology and the allied questions it raised, he did not allude to them. He clearly believed that it was halakhically permitted to authorize medical interventions that would aid a married couple in overcoming their problems with infertility. In vitro fertilization or the use of fertility drugs to stimulate ovulation, far from being halakhically proscribed, were regarded by Halevi as praiseworthy means for assisting married couples in their attempts to "be fruitful and multiply" and "inhabit the world." It is clear that the issues that so provoked Waldenberg did not disturb Halevi. His sensibilities as reflected in his responsum were clearly distinct from those of his Jerusalem colleague.

Reflections and Commentary

The modes of reproduction that constitute the subject matter of the responsa considered in this paper have presented severe challenges to those who would seek guidance from *Halakhah* on the issue of artificial fertilization. Collaborative techniques that enable persons to routinely separate genetic, gestational, and social aspects of parenting have virtually no precedent in Jewish law. The sparseness, if not the total absence, of traditional sources that directly address the issues involved in arriving at a Jewish position on artificial fertilization is reflected in the inability of either Waldenberg or Halevi to cite direct precedents that would inform a Jewish position on this matter. Indeed, this paucity of sources in their responsa is quite striking. However, in light of the novel problems produced by contemporary advances in medical technology, it is not surprising.

Rabbi Herschel Schachter of Yeshiva University has observed that when halakhic decisors confront a particular issue, they do what *poskim* have done for centuries. They juxtapose "the particulars of [their] own case and various halakhic precedents and principles, thereby deciding into which category [their] own case falls. Then they must apply these precedents and principles to the situation at hand." The problem, Schachter asserts, is that situations presented to rabbis by advances in medical technology are "unique to our generation." There simply may be no precedent to offer guidance.[10]

Rabbi Ezra Bick of Yeshivat Har Etzion in Israel echoes Schachter's observation and maintains that certain questions related to IVF are simply "not susceptible to the classic halakhic approach of analogy with an existent halakhic ruling." There exists "no clear indisputable halakhic source" for determining "motherhood" in a case of IVF where the genetic donor of the ovum and the woman who carried the fetus

---

10   Herschel Schachter, "Determining the Time of Death," *Journal of Halacha and Contemporary Society,* vol. 27 (1989), p. 32.

to term and gave birth to it are distinct. "Is there any halakhic source sufficient to resolve [this question]?" Bick queries. "The answer," he responds, "is no."[11]

What then is one to do in an instance such as this when no biblical or talmudic source speaks directly to the welter of issues under consideration? Furthermore, how are we, as liberal Jews, to evaluate responsa such as the ones under discussion in this paper when the ethos and proclivities that inform their decisors are so removed from the sensibilities and concerns that inform so many liberal Jews? After all, the irony that no woman's voice is heard in this entire discussion concerning procreation cannot avoid capturing the attention of many a liberal Jew![12] Indeed, in reading these responsa, one hears the echoes of a warning issued by Professor Norma Juliet Wikler of the University of California at Santa Cruz when she writes of these new procedures, "Feminists fear that the application of the new reproductive technologies will be manipulated so as to limit women's autonomy . . . [as well as] a woman's right to control her body." While Professor Wikler applauds and endorses many of the new reproductive options, including artificial fertilization, she fears "the consequences of these technologies if they are not controlled by women for women."[13] One need not affirm all of Professor Wikler's sentiments to acknowledge that all decisions made in this area must be fully informed by women's diverse views as well as by a feminist ethos that would consider these questions in the context of society and interpersonal relationships. Rules alone will not be sufficient to guide us through the thorny ethical thicket this or any other area of bioethics presents.

Nor is the notion that a single parent or a gay or lesbian couple

11 Bick, "Ovum Donations," pp. 28, 32, and 38.

12 I am mindful that Halevi considers the health of the mother in rendering his decision. However, the personal, direct voice of the woman — or men for that matter — is never heard in either his or Waldenberg's responsa. In light of my own sensibilities and beliefs, I find this a glaring omission and weakness in the process of Jewish legal decision-making on this and other issues. For a powerful and insightful article on this point, see Dena Davis, "Beyond Rabbi Hiyya's Wife: Women's Voices in Jewish Bioethics," *Second Opinion*, vol. 17 (1991), pp. 10–30.

13 Norma Juliet Wikler. "Society's Response to the New Reproductive Technologies: The Feminist Perspectives." *Southern California Law Review*, vol. 59 (1986), pp. 1044 and 1050.

might desire to employ this technology to fulfill their own reproductive urges even considered in the responsa analyzed in this paper. The "ideal" of the "procreative, heterosexual" family surely is privileged in this discussion. Yet, as many could undoubtedly attest, significant numbers of single, homosexual, and lesbian people have availed or desire to avail themselves of these technologies in order to achieve the same reproductive goals as infertile heterosexual married couples. A liberal Jewish approach to this question must consider all these persons, as well as the individual voices of men and women, when speaking about ethical issues associated with the techniques and therapies of artificial procreation. A liberal *halakhah* must orient itself in a manner that is more inclusive than is reflected in these responsa.

What then can traditional *Halakhah* and traditional halakhists offer liberal Jews to guide us as we confront the issues of artificial fertilization raised in this paper? The answer, despite all the misgivings and reservations I have expressed, is that these and other responsa can teach us a great deal. They and the tradition embody elements of truth and we will be impoverished if we ignore many of the sentiments and views expressed in them as we attempt to construct a liberal Jewish approach in this area. Indeed, these responsa indicate that the ethical issues involved in this field are rather complex. For most liberal Jews, and, as Halevi testified, for most halakhic authorities as well, advances in non-coital reproductive technologies are to be applauded and welcomed. They allow otherwise infertile persons to experience the blessing of conception. As Rabbi Moshe Zemer has phrased it, "Sages throughout the generations ... were lenient and encouraged infertile couples to be helped by such medical treatment and by other new medical discoveries so that the first commandment in the Torah, 'Be fruitful and multiply, and fill the earth,' could be established."[14]

The procreative bias of the tradition surely provides all Jews with a powerful conceptual apparatus with which to approach these reproductive options. It can lead, Waldenberg notwithstanding, to a celebration of these discoveries for they permit previously infertile persons to experience some, if not all, of the genetic, biological, and social components of parenting. Furthermore, Halevi's concerns about the

14   Moshe Zemer, *Halakhah Shefuyah* (Tel Aviv, 1993), p.288.

viability and health of the fetus suggest that technologically-assisted forms of conception should be heralded because they possess the potential to avoid the transmission of certain genetic diseases. As Gold states, "Using the techniques of in vitro fertilization, an egg can be fertilized outside the womb and then can be genetically manipulated before it is implanted in a woman's uterus. There are obvious advantages to genetic engineering. Someday it may be possible to cure such genetically-based diseases as hemophilia, diabetes, sickle cell anemia, and Tay-Sachs."[15]

For this reason, Waldenberg's view that techniques such as IVF represent an unjustified tampering with the "natural processes" of creation is unacceptable. To accept his argument on this point would be to condemn all technological intrusions into the natural order. All medical treatment objectifies and attempts to manipulate the natural order for human ends. Judaism applauds the active efforts of medical science to ameliorate the physical ills of humanity.[16] Extracorporeal conception no more tampers with the body than any other medical procedure. Reproductive interventions are no different in kind or degree from other interventions in the natural order.

On the other hand, one need not fully embrace the apocalyptic vision of a mutant race of "biological creatures" conjured up by Waldenberg to recognize that these techniques can easily be abused. Programs of government-sponsored eugenics have not been confined in this century to the literary imagination of a Huxley in his *Brave New World*. One need only consider how Adolf Hitler and Dr. Mengele attempted to transform such fantasies into practice to recognize how dangerous and open to abuse such visions can be. On a more prosaic level, Waldenberg's fears indicate that people might try genetically to engineer such "desirable traits" as strength, intelligence, beauty, and gender. There is no reason to assume that the manipulation of genes will be confined to the cure of serious diseases. Nor should the possibility be overlooked that these technologies could transform lower class women into reproductive machines who could be exploited by members of the upper classes. Jewish law would presumably look askance upon such developments.

15 Gold, *And Hannah Wept*. p.147.
16 Ibid. p.82.

Waldenberg's responsum has the virtue of reminding its readers that non-coital reproductive technologies are in and of themselves morally neutral. Depending upon the context, these technologies may be employed for either desirable or abhorrent ends. They can be used to demean human dignity. At the same time, they increase reproductive choice. They allow women to control the time of their pregnancy and permit infertile couples to raise children of their own genes and gestation. Women without ovarian or uterine function can be genetic and gestational as well as rearing parents. Waldenberg's writings indicate that these non-coital reproductive technologies must be approached cautiously. While these cautions do not justify denial of safe and effective infertility treatments for both individuals and couples who desire them, they do indicate that procreative autonomy ought not to be regarded as an absolute good — even by liberal Jews. These reproductive technologies cannot be viewed abstractly, apart from the people and goals they are serving. Social and familial concerns that seek to minimize harm and maximize benefits for donors, recipients, offspring, and society occupy a legitimate role in Jewish reflections on established and developing reproductive procedures.

Such a perspective parallels considerations voiced by Maura A. Ryan, a Yale-educated feminist ethicist, when she contends, "A feminist perspective [on these technologies] includes commitments to human relationality as well as autonomy, and attention to the social context of personal choices. Questions of individual freedom, even in matters of reproduction, must be raised in conjunction with other equally compelling considerations about what is needed for human flourishing and what is required for a just society."[17] Ryan argues, quite cogently, that "persons ought to be protected in their right to determine when and in what manner they will reproduce, and they should be free to shape familial life in a way meaningful for them. But such a right should not be understood as unlimited, as extending as far as the acquisition of a concrete human being."[18]

Ryan insists that one of the problems surrounding much current discussion of these technologies is that too often only "the procreative

17   Maura A. Ryan. "The Argument for Unlimited Procreative Liberty: A Feminist Critique," *Hasting Center Report,* vol. 20, no. 4 (1990), p. 6.
18   Ibid. p. 7.

initiator's interests" are considered, while a concern for the persons who collaborate with such parties and the interests of the offspring of such unions tend to be ignored. "The question of how such treatment may affect that child's quality of life, sense of identity, or development is hardly raised . . . Interest in a genetically-related child cannot be seen as an independent end, the value of which automatically discounts concern for the future state of the offspring, [or] for the physical and emotional safety of the collaborators." This means, as Ryan sees it, that "particular techniques used in collaborative reproduction need separate evaluation."[19]

Surrogacy, in Ryan's opinion, is morally problematic: the potential for psychosocial conflict among donor, gestator, and offspring would be great. Given the complexities of human relationship, Ryan doubts whether an *a priori* contract between donor and gestator could ever account for the myriad emotional bonds and conflicts that might well develop among these parties. The actions and feelings of Mary Beth Whitehead and the Sterns in the famous case of "Baby M" only indicates how well-founded Ryan's strictures are in this matter. AID or IVF, in contrast, would be acceptable "as the risks to the donor are small and the benefit great."[20] Yet, even here a cautionary note must be sounded. One need not adopt the alarmist tone of a Rabbi Waldenberg to acknowledge that artificial conception raises the hypothetical possibility that a single donor might sire genetic siblings living in the same community. The right of children conceived through such means, regardless of the collaborators' desires, to learn of their genetic origins therefore seems reasonable. Furthermore, children, in their quest for identity, often seek knowledge of their biological origins. One need only think of adopted children who wish to discover their birth parents' identity. The same psychological forces that drive such children may inform these children as well. At the very least, such matters ought to be placed on the agenda of the Jewish community as it discusses these issues.

Ryan's article and the concerns she voices in it resonate loudly to a Reform Jewish community whose theological anthropology is steeped in

19   Ibid. p.11
20   Ibid.

Martin Buber's teachings on the reality of relationship among persons as the irreducible datum of human experience, as well as Eugene Borowitz's notions of the "Covenantal Self" as the foundation for Jewish thought and action.[21] The individual self, living in splendid isolation, can never be the Archimedian point from which liberal Jews begin their theological and ethical reflections. Jewish commitments rather demand that persons be viewed as embodied and relational, as well as autonomous.

Non-Orthodox *poskim* on questions of artificial conception have already implicitly recognized these concerns in their writings. Conservative Rabbi David Golinkin, head of the Rabbinical Assembly's Israeli Law Committee, has treated the question of AID in the context of Jewish family concerns.[22] Similarly, Reform Rabbi Walter Jacob, in a case dealing with IVF with ova donated by the wife's first cousin, wrote, "We would give reluctant permission to use IVF in the manner you have described. The potential problems are numerous and should lead to great caution."[23]

In this instance, Jacob obviously decided that the parents' desire to produce an offspring, as well as the benefit to the child of existence as opposed to non-existence, outweighed the potential psychological problems that might arise. However, his last cautionary remarks reflect his own awareness of the complexity of the issues involved in therapies

---

21   For Borowitz's notion of the "Covenantal Self" see his *magnum opus, Renewing the Covenant* (Philadelphia, 1991), as well as an explication of his thought on this subject in David Ellenson and Lori Krafte-Jacobs, "Eugene B. Borowitz," in Steven T. Katz, ed., *Interpreters of Judaism in the Late Twentieth Century* (Washington, D.C., 1993), pp. 21–26. One should also note that this covenantal approach to Jewish theology and the application of this approach to questions of ethical import are not confined to Eugene Borowitz or other liberal Jewish thinkers. Irving Greenberg and David Hartman are Orthodox rabbis who also use this approach. For an insightful discussion of their religious thought and its "covenantal" dimensions, see David Singer, "The New Orthodox Theology," *Modern Judaism,* vol. 9, no. 1 (1989), pp. 35–54. In my own piece, "How to Draw Guidance from a Heritage," in Barry S. Kogan, ed., *A Time to be Born and a Time to Die* (New York, 1991), pp. 219–32, there is an analysis of these thinkers and an exposition of how they have applied this covenantal approach to Jewish ethics.

22   *Responsa of the Va'ad Halakhah of the Rabbinical Assembly of Israel* (5748–5749), vol. 3, pp. 83–92.

23   Walter Jacob, *Contemporary American Reform Responsa* (New York: CCAR, 1987), p. 32.

such as in vitro fertilization. Knowledge that a therapy is effective does not obviate the question of whether there is a moral need for a discussion of its application. Liberal halakhists must continue that discussion and spell out its ramifications in light of the concerns voiced above.

This paper has not sought to provide anything approaching a broad survey of the many responsa written on matters of artificial reproduction in general and artificial fertilization in particular. Nor has it attempted to provide definitive answers to the many questions advances in this field present. It has rather sought, in a modest way, to present two Hebrew language responsa on this subject to supplement previously published work in English on this area. Most importantly, it has employed these responsa as vehicles to alert its readers to the complex nature of the moral and Jewish concerns that surround this technology. Hopefully, it will serve as a springboard for advancing liberal as well as traditional Jewish discussions on these and related issues.

New Initiatives, New Directions

21

A New Rite from Israel

Reflections on Siddur Va'ani Tefillati *of the*
Masorti (Conservative) Movement

The *siddur* and the ritual performance that has accompanied its communal recitation have long occupied a central role in Jewish life. As the classical repository of Jewish memory and faith, the *siddur* is in a profound sense a conservative document. For nearly two millennia, the basic form and content of Jewish prayer has remained remarkably consistent.

At the same time, the Jewish prayer book has hardly remained static. Flexibility and freedom have always marked its texts. Throughout the centuries, the variegated nuances and emphases of ongoing Jewish life and faith have found diverse expression in the liturgy. Different customs (*minhagim*) and countless textual variants (*nushaòt*) have recorded the broad range of beliefs and teachings, hopes and aspirations, tragedies and triumphs that have informed and forged the people Israel. Thus the authorship of new Jewish prayer texts has not been limited to the modern era.

Nevertheless, with the advent of modern Jewish religious denominationalism in nineteenth-century Germany, the production of new *siddurim* increased markedly. Reform Judaism bounded onto the stage of history with the composition of the Hamburg Temple *Gebetbuch* in 1819, and Jews in subsequent decades encountered a constant stream of new prayer books as rabbis of every denominational stripe on both sides of the Atlantic employed the *siddur* as a major vehicle for making their own doctrinal statements. The impulse to utilize the *siddur* for such programmatic expression has continued unabated throughout the twentieth century, and Hebrew liturgical creativity has flourished until the present moment.

The Orthodox, Reform, Conservative, and Reconstructionist movements have all produced new *siddurim* in recent decades. In the United States alone, the *Art Scroll Prayer Book*, *Gates of Prayer*, *Siddur Sim Shalom*, and *Kol Haneshamah* have all been published since 1975. In addition, the Jewish Renewal movement has written its own text, *Or Chadash*, and the noted Jewish feminist Marcia Falk published her celebrated liturgy, *The Book of Blessings*, in 1996. Each prayer book bears the impress of those who authored it, and each projects a distinct approach to Judaism — its history and beliefs.

Nor has such modern prayer book authorship been limited to North America. Non-Orthodox movements in Great Britain and on the continent have published their own *siddurim* in recent years, and the Israeli Progressive (Reform) movement produced its own liturgy, *Ha-Avodah Shebalev*, in 1982. Now the Masorti movement has followed suit with the 1998 publication of its long-awaited prayer book, *Va'ani Tefillati*, the first Conservative *siddur* written in Israel.

The sensibility that marks the pages of *Va'ani Tefillati* is unmistakably Conservative. Like *Siddur Sim Shalom* and other Conservative prayer books written earlier in the century, *Va'ani Tefillati* decisively affirms tradition. At the same time, it countenances change in a manner that has marked other Conservative *siddurim*. Thus, an analysis of its contents and form grants insight into the nature of Conservative Judaism as a distinct Jewish denomination.

Nevertheless, even among Conservative prayer books, the *Va'ani Tefillati* liturgy is singular, for its Israeli context informs its substance and shapes its message in a manner that distinguishes it from rites produced in the Diaspora. Indeed, this liturgy reflects the particularistic commitments and aspirations of a community located in Zion and presents a unique statement of group identity and belief. Hence, this essay documents many of the specific directions and commitments that mark the still nascent Masorti movement and charts one path on which Judaism has embarked as it seeks old-new expressions in its ancient home.

Foundational Considerations

The principles and considerations that guide *Va'ani Tefillati* are articulated at the very outset of the volume. Rabbi Michael Graetz, chair of the *siddur* commission that produced the work, as well as Rabbi Simcha Roth, its editor and principal architect, provide complementary introductory statements that capture the book's defining characteristics.

In his introduction, Graetz displays an appreciation for the continuity that marks Jewish prayer. There is, he states, a template (*matbe'a tefillah*) that constitutes the compulsory framework for Jewish worship. This framework authenticates the communal formulation of Jewish identity, and it sustains the religious meanings that have been at the heart of Jewish faith for two thousand years. *Va'ani Tefillati* strives to display fidelity to this framework.

At the same time, Graetz acknowledges that Jewish liturgy has never been frozen. Throughout history, the liturgy of *am yisrael* has been altered as Jews have responded to ever-changing environments. Moreover, *Ḥazal*, the talmudic Sages who established the earliest canons of Jewish prayer, claimed that *kavanah*, intentionality, as well as *keva*, fixed prayers, were hallmark features of *tefillah*. The Sages wanted Jews to be fully present at the moment they prayed. Therefore, the Jerusalem Talmud, on the subject of prayer, asserted, "It is necessary that something novel mark it every day" (T.Y. *Berakhot* 4:3). Jewish prayer must always contain an element of flexibility, for every age bears witness to an inescapable tension — the need, on the one hand, to speak to God out of a tradition, and the obligation, on the other, to address God out of a felt truth. Conscious of this ongoing challenge, Graetz contends that while the requirement to address God out of the tradition is absolute, the obligation for prayer to express the promptings of the mind and heart cannot be voided. Therefore, writes Graetz, "Our sages said that one should not express in prayer anything which one does not take to be a truth."[1]

The warrant for this position, as Graetz views it, is found in *Yoma* 69b, which states that both Jeremiah and Daniel changed an element in the *Gevurot* benediction of the *Amidah*. The original wording extolling God's powers is attributed by the tradition to Moses. Nevertheless, each man — because of personal doubts — refused to praise God with the precise words that Moses had prescribed. For the talmudic Sages, this posed a major problem. After all, Moses was assigned an unsurpassed position of authority in Jewish tradition. Some argued that Jeremiah and Daniel had no right to alter the prayer that Moses had composed.

---

1   *Va'ani Tefillati* (New York, 1998), p. vi.

However, the Talmud emphatically asserts that such is not the case. Jeremiah and Daniel "knew that the Holy One, blessed be He, is truthful. Thus, they did not lie to Him." Graetz, basing himself on this text, therefore concludes, "God does not tolerate false statements by people. We must express the true beliefs of our hearts."[2]

Simcha Roth echoes this conclusion. At the very beginning of his preface, he cites *Midrash Mishlei* 12, which, quoting the words of Proverbs 12:21 ("But the wicked are filled with evil") asserts: "This refers to one who says one thing, but means another." Jewish prayer must display integrity," writes Roth. "When the prayer that we utter does not conform to the truth that is in our heart, it is considered an 'abomination' and the worshipers are considered as 'wicked' — according to the midrash."[3]

Va'ani Tefillati seeks to prevent this breach. The very name of the *siddur*, taken from Psalms 69:14, expresses the hope, as Roth puts it, that "my prayer and I are one. I do not say one thing while meaning another. What my heart prompts is what determines the prayer that I utter."[4] With this title, the Israeli rite proclaims its warrant to alter the manifest content of traditional Jewish prayer. The demands of the past are not absolute, nor is Jewish liturgical tradition frozen. The claims and sensibilities of the present are vital as well.

Roth delineates four characteristics of the new prayer book he has edited: Masorti (Conservative), Israeli-Zionist, pluralistic, and innovative.[5] Though the demands posited by each of these elements are at times divergent, Roth devotes considerable attention to an explanation of how *Va'ani Tefillati* goes about balancing the claims of the past against those of the present. Furthermore, he will not concede that adaptations, when they are made, constitute deviations from Jewish tradition. This is because, as Roth phrases it, "The text of the prayers offered in this *siddur* is that which we have inherited from our forebears." *Va'ani Tefillati* does not countenance deviation from the classical template for Jewish worship, nor does it depart "from the accepted order and contents of the benedictions and the prayers."[6] Having said this, he is equally aware that textual variants have always been present

2 Ibid. p.vi.
3 Ibid. p.ix.
4 Ibid.
5 Ibid. pp.ix–xiii
6 Ibid. p.x.

in Jewish worship. Indeed, Roth cites a responsum of Ovadiah Yosef, former Chief Sephardic Rabbi of Israel and a leading halakhic authority, from *Yab'ia Omer* 6, *Orah Hayim* 10, to maintain that Jewish law itself sanctions Jewish liturgical variety. In this responsum, Yosef asserts that each one of Israel's tribes had its own unique liturgy. This was so, he wrote, "for the order of service of each tribe must be appropriate to the ethos of its soul."[7] Roth draws the conclusion from this responsum that pluralism characterizes Jewish worship, and that Jewish prayer, as Yosef suggests, must be tailored so that it expresses the specific ethos of the group that employs it.[8] The Jewish prayer book tradition seeks unity. At the same time, it promotes diversity. All liturgists must negotiate between these two poles as they compose their services.

Va'ani Tefillati, as Roth views it, is therefore consonant with Jewish tradition. The elements that mark it transcend denominational boundaries: they are features of Judaism itself. Indeed, these elements allow him to contend that *Va'ani Tefillati* is both an authentic book of Jewish prayer and the *siddur* of a movement. The new Israeli rite strives to articulate an ethos for Masorti Judaism. As such, it constitutes a new and important chapter in the ongoing history of Jewish liturgy. An examination of these elements will grant insight into the nature of the Conservative movement in Israel.

Continuity with Tradition

As mentioned above, *Va'ani Tefillati* maintains the traditional order and affirms most of the content of classical Jewish prayer. As a glance at the contents indicates, all the classical Jewish services — *Shaharit, Musaf, Minhah,* and *Ma'ariv* — for weekday, Sabbath, New Moon, and holiday prayer are preserved, and the forms prescribed for Jewish prayer by

7 Ovadiah Yosef, *Yabi'a Omer* 6, *Orah Hayim* 10, quoted in n. 6 above.
8 Of course, from the standpoint of logic, one can observe that the Yosef responsum, in speaking of "each tribe," refers to a community of descent. The Masorti movement, in contrast, constitutes a *voluntaristic community* created by individuals who confirm the principles and practices of Conservative Judaism. Consequently, a critic might contend that the Yosef responsum does not provide an apt justification for alterations in modern Jewish prayer books produced by specific religious denominations. This point notwithstanding, it is clear that Roth employs the responsum in order to legitimate his claim that Jewish tradition countenances liturgical variety.

Ḥazal are maintained (e.g., two blessings before, and one blessing after, *Kriat Shema*). Traditional additions to the service — such as the reciting of the *Hallel* psalms for the New Moon and holidays; the prayer for rain (*geshem*) on Simhat Torah and the prayer for dew (*tal*) on Passover are included, as are Torah readings for Mondays, Thursdays, and holidays.

Other features of the classical *siddur* find expression in *Va'ani Tefillati*. Like most traditional Jewish prayer books, it offers home prayers and rites — notably the blessings for the lighting of candles on Sabbaths and holidays (and Hanukkah); *Kiddush* and songs for the Sabbath and holiday table; and the concluding *Havdalah* prayer. *Birkat ha-Mazon* (Grace after Meals) is included, as are *birkhot ha-nehanim* (blessings for various occasions). Ceremonial texts are also to be found — for instance, that of *brit milah* (covenant of circumcision), *pidyon ha-ben* (priestly redemption of the first-born son), *kiddushin* and *nisu'in* (betrothal and wedding); and *ushpizin* (symbolically welcoming guests such as the patriarch Abraham, the lawgiver Moses, and the great King David into the *sukkah*).[9] *Va'ani Tefillati* also contains the prayer for creating an *eruv tavshilin*[10] and a service for *bedikat u-vi'ur ḥametz* (searching for and destroying leaven before Passover). As a Conservative liturgical work, the traditional character of *Va'ani Tefillati* is consistent with the movement that produced it.

Its Conservative Character

Conservative prayer books have been marked by a strong tendency to preserve the manifest content of the Hebrew texts of the classical Ashkenazic *siddur*. Even when elements of the received texts have offended modern sensibilities, Conservative authors have been most reluctant to alter the Hebrew versions of Jewish prayer. In such instances, they have often employed translation as a tool to mute the meanings of the Hebrew. This practice stands in sharp contrast to *siddurim* produced by

9   The *ushpizin* text, however, contains an addition, as will be described below.
10   An *eruv tavshilin* is a legal fiction that permits food to be cooked for the Sabbath on a holiday, whenever one of the days of Sukkot, Passover, Shavuot or Rosh Hashanah falls on a Friday. Normally on a festival, one is not allowed to perform any labor in preparation for the following day.

Reform and Reconstructionist liturgists, who have felt a greater liberty to transform the Hebrew text itself.[11]

For example, as Jakob Petuchowski pointed out, Liberal Jews for the last two centuries have often found the notion of *tehiyat ha-meitim*, bodily resurrection, disturbing, and they have typically not affirmed this classical Jewish dogma. Having had little difficulty with the idea that the soul is immortal, however, many have stressed "the idea of Immortality... at the expense of the belief in Resurrection."[12] Reform and Reconstructionist prayer books have therefore commonly removed such passages as "*mehayei meitim be-rahamim rabim* — who in great mercy resurrects the dead," and "*mehayei ha-meitim* — who resurrects the dead," from the *Gevurot* benediction of the *Amidah*, and substituted phrases such as "*mehayei kol hai*," translated liberally as "who gives and renews life," in their stead.[13] In contrast, all American Conservative prayer books have retained the classical Hebrew wording in this benediction. However, Conservative liturgists have sometimes displayed the same theological objection to this doctrine as their more liberal colleagues. Thus, the Conservative *Sabbath and Festival Prayer Book* (1946) maintained the Hebrew conclusion of the *Gevurot* benediction, but through its translation, "Who callest the dead to life everlasting," it affirmed the doctrine of spiritual immortality rather than the dogma of bodily resurrection.

Va'ani Tefillati displays this Conservative penchant for maintaining the classical Hebrew versions of most prayers while expressing certain modernist sensibilities regarding the manifest content of selected texts. However, *Va'ani Tefillati* cannot resolve these issues in the same manner as its North American counterparts. Translation is not an available

11 On this point, see David Ellenson, "How the Modern Prayer Book Evolved," in Lawrence A. Hoffman, ed., *Minhag Ami: Traditional Prayers, Modern Commentaries*, 2 vols. (Woodstock, Vt: Jewish Lights Publishing, 1997 and 1998).

12 Jakob J. Petuchowski, "Modern Misunderstandings of an Ancient Benediction," in Jakob J. Petuchowski and Ezra Fleisher, eds., *Studies in Aggadah, Targum, and Jewish Liturgy in Memory of Joseph Heinemann* (Jerusalem: Magnes Press, The Hebrew University and Hebrew Union College Press, 1981), pp. 45–46.

13 This example is taken from *Kol Haneshamah: Shabbat Vehagim* (Wyncote, Pa: Reconstructionist Press, 1995).

option for a populace whose native tongue is Hebrew. Instead, *Va'ani Tefillati* selects another alternative — commentary. Two examples will suffice as illustrations of how this *siddur* utilizes commentary to address textual areas deemed problematic.

In the *Gevurot* benediction of the *Amidah*, the classical Hebrew text remains untouched, yet the commentary indicates that *Va'ani Tefillati*, no less than other non-Orthodox *siddurim*, distances itself from the notion of *tehiyat ha-meitim*. Stating that this benediction contains two ideas — that of eternal life (*hayei netzah*) and that of bodily resurrection (*tehiyat ha-meitim*), it observes that Maimonides considered it difficult to accept the latter doctrine literally. He taught instead that bodily resurrection was at best a temporary state, and that only the soul, not the body, would ultimately enjoy eternal life. Immediately after citing this warrant from the tradition, *Va'ani Tefillati* quotes a paragraph penned by Milton Steinberg, the American Conservative-Reconstructionist rabbi, who, in his own commentary on this benediction, emphasized that this prayer actually teaches that life is of infinite worth, and that it must therefore be embraced with open arms. "With the help of these thoughts," concludes the commentary in *Va'ani Tefillati*, "we are able to recite the second benediction much more easily."[14] Thus the Hebrew text of the benediction is preserved while the commentary, at the very least, attenuates its classical meaning.

An identical use of this approach can be seen in the treatment that *Va'ani Tefillati* accords Deuteronomy 11:13–21, the biblical passage that constitutes the second paragraph of the *Shema*. Again, Liberal liturgies have often found this paragraph problematic. As the Reconstructionist *Kol Haneshamah* puts it, "Its detailed description of the devastating consequences of Israel's collective relationship to the *mitzvot* . . . offers a supernatural theology that many contemporary Jews find difficult."[15] Simply put, this passage presents a doctrine of reward and punishment that many Liberal Jews cannot accept. It is absent altogether in certain Reform *siddurim* such as *Gates of Prayer* (1975), while others such as *Kol Haneshamah* and the Israeli Progressive (Reform) *Ha-Avodah Shebalev* (1982), have provided alternate readings.

14 *Va'ani Tefillati*, p.67.
15 *Kol Haneshamah*, p.279.

As a Conservative prayer book, *Va'ani Tefillati* has not followed suit. It has retained the Hebrew text in its entirety. Nevertheless, it has voiced in its commentary a similar objection to the contents and points out that one central idea contained in this paragraph is that of "free will — *beḥirah ḥofshit*." "Contemporary Jewish thought has no problem with the notion of 'free will,'" it states. "However, it does have difficulty with the notion of 'reward and punishment' as it finds expression in the second paragraph of the *Shema*."[16] The editors go on to suggest that the sentence contained in the second passage be redivided so that a new meaning emerges, one in which an emphasis is placed upon the idea that even should God "bless you with economic abundance and all that is good, you must still be exceedingly careful to avoid idolatry. . . . Especially in an abundant society, idolatry poses a danger."[17] What this commentary essentially does is detach the text from reward and punishment. Obviating this meaning of the text, it stresses instead its moral warning. In this way, it resolves the theological difficulties embedded in a text deemed offensive to *modern* sensibilities.

The examples cited thus far demonstrate a Conservative reluctance to alter the received Hebrew texts of Jewish worship even where there are perceived difficulties in the manifest content of those prayers. However, the movement's opposition to such change is not absolute. Indeed, in certain instances, Conservative prayer is characterized by the same impulse towards textual emendation that marks the Reform and Reconstructionist movements. Chief among the texts prone to be changed are those dealing with *korbanot* (sacrifices), and petitions for the restoration of the sacrificial cult in a rebuilt Temple in Jerusalem.

Discomfort with the sacrificial cult has found expression in varying ways in North American Conservative *siddurim*. For example, biblical and talmudic passages in the *Birkhot ha-Shaḥar* section of the daily service relating to sacrifice, as well as comparable passages in various holiday and Sabbath rites, are absent from Conservative prayer books such as *Siddur Sim Shalom*, and replaced either with passages such as Leviticus 19 or paragraphs from rabbinic literature that convey the ethical teachings of Judaism. In addition, *Sim Shalom* as well other

16 *Va'ani Tefillati*, p. 331.
17 Ibid. p. 331.

predecessor Conservative prayer books have excised the passage at the end of the *Amidah* that calls for the Temple to be rebuilt so that "the *minḥah* offering of Judah and Jerusalem will reach God as in the ancient days and the earliest of years."

Even more prominently, the Conservative *Festival Prayer Book* of 1927, and all subsequent Conservative liturgies, including the 1946 *Sabbath and Festival Prayer Book* and *Sim Shalom*, have transformed the passage in the *Musaf* service that calls for the restoration of animal sacrifice in a rebuilt Temple in Jerusalem into a prayer of "recollection." In the traditional Ashkenazic rite, the text reads as follows:

> Thou hast commanded *us*, O Lord, our God to bring thereon the additional offering of the Sabbath in due form. . . . May It be Thy will, O Lord, our God, . . . to lead us in joy Into our land, . . . where *we* will prepare unto thee *our* sacrifices of obligations . . . and the additional offering of this Sabbath day *we will* prepare and offer up unto You in love . . .[18]

In the 1946 *Sabbath and Festival Prayer Book*, it appears in this form:

> Thou didst ordain, O Lord our God, that *they* [our forefathers] bring the additional Sabbath offering as set forth in the Torah. . . . May it be Thy will, O Lord our God, . . . to lead us joyfully back to our land, . . . where our *forefathers prepared* the daily offerings and the additional Sabbath offerings.

In Conservative liturgy, mention of the sacrificial cult no longer possesses a petitionary character. Rather than as "petition" (*bakashah*), as Orthodox prayer would have it, it is presented as "remembrance" (*zekhirah*). As Rabbi Jules Harlow, editor of the *Siddur Sim Shalom* explains, "Conservative liturgy continues to pray for the restoration of the Jewish people to the Land of Israel and for the experience of worship there, particularly in Jerusalem, but the liturgy merely recalls with reverence the sacrificial ritual of our ancestors; it does not petition for its restoration."[19]

---

18   See Joseph H. Hertz, ed., *The Authorized Daily Prayer Book* (New York, 1948), p. 533.
19   Jules Harlow, "Revising the Liturgy for Conservative Jews," in Paul F. Bradshaw and Lawrence A. Hoffman, eds., *The Changing Face of Jewish and Christian Worship in North America* (Notre Dame, Ind.: Notre Dame University Press, 1991), p. 126.

This attitude toward sacrifice, and the manner in which this approach has found practical expression in North American Conservative *siddurim*, is echoed in *Va'ani Tefillati*. In two lengthy sections of commentary, the Israeli rite articulates the Masorti position on the matter of the sacrificial cult and the Temple, stating forthrightly, "Few members of the Masorti movement hope for the restoration of sacrificial worship."[20] As a result, in *Birkhot ha-Shaḥar* as well as at the end of *Kabbalat Shabbat*, the biblical and talmudic passages relating to sacrifice have been removed, and they have been replaced by readings from biblical and rabbinic sources that express Judaism's religious concerns and moral commitments. The final paragraph of the *Amidah* calling for the restoration of sacrificial worship in the Temple has likewise been excised.

In *Ein Keloheinu*, sung near the completion of the Sabbath and holiday services, the final line of the traditional Ashkenazic text speaks of the incense offerings that our ancestors offered in the Temple ("You are He before whose countenance our fathers burned the spices of incense"). According to the commentary in *Va'ani Tefillati*, a description of worship as it took place in the Temple was introduced at this concluding point in the service because "prayers were a type of substitute for the Temple worship itself." Indeed, additional readings concerning sacrificial worship in the ancient Temple are added at this point in Orthodox services and they are linked logically to the preceding prayers through the insertion of this line. However, since these readings are removed from *Va'ani Tefillati* because of its opposition to the sacrifices that took place in the Temple, the final line of *Ein Keloheinu* is also omitted. Instead, following Sephardic tradition, the verse from Psalms 102:14 — "You will surely arise and take pity on Zion, for it is time to be gracious to her; the appointed time has come" — is substituted.[21]

Similarly, in the first of the final three benedictions of the *Amidah*, the classical *siddur* states, "Restore the *sacrificial* worship (*ha-avodah*) to Your sanctuary, and accept Israel's fire-offerings. . . ." This prayer has troubled non-Orthodox liturgists for over 150 years, and Conservative *siddurim* like *Siddur Sim Shalom* have routinely omitted the phrase "*ve-eishei yisrael* — Israel's fire-offerings."[22] *Va'ani Tefillati* follows suit,

---

20 *Va'ani Tefillati*, p. 382.
21 Ibid. p. 397.
22 On this particular passage and the manner in which non-Orthodox liturgies have

but it omits the definite article prior to the word, "worship" (changing *ha-avodah* to *avodah*). With the omission of this article, the entire meaning of the sentence is changed. *Ha-avodah* is a specific reference to sacrificial worship, whereas *avodah* refers more generally to worship. Hence, the altered prayer, while asking that God rebuild the Temple, does not request that the sacrificial cult be restored.

This last alteration in the classical liturgy of the synagogue can be understood in light of the explicit position *Va'ani Tefillati* has adopted toward the manifest content of the *Musaf* prayer for Sabbaths and holidays. In its commentaries upon this prayer, *Va'ani Tefillati* indicates that the Conservative movement has adopted two approaches to the issues of a rebuilt Temple and a restored sacrificial rite. One approach asserts that Masorti Judaism looks favorably upon those prayers that call for the rebuilding of the Temple while at the same time rejecting the notion that sacrificial worship should be restored. After all, the desire for a Third Temple simply "symbolizes the yearning for the renewed unity of the Jewish people and the realization of the values of peace and universal human tolerance contained in the vision of the prophets for the end of days."[23] However, this desire in no way bespeaks the hope that animal sacrifices will once again be offered. While the exact nature of future prayer is yet unknown, it will be completely different from that of the ancient cult and will surely not be that of animal sacrifice. This view, as *Va'ani Tefillati* sees it, has precedent in the visions that informed the ancient prophets as well as the teachings put forth by Maimonides in his *Guide for the Perplexed* (3:32).

The second approach, identified as the dominant one for Masorti Jews, does not oppose the first; in fact, it complements it. It states that sacrificial worship represents an historical stage in the development of the people Israel. Thus, there is no need to deny it. It constitutes an important historical memory, and it cannot simply be excised from Jewish consciousness. However, sacrificial worship must not be the object of future hope; rather, it is defined as an historical memory alone.

---

regarded it, see the relevant sections of David Ellenson, "How the Modern Prayer Book Evolved," as well as chap. 9, "The *Israelitische Gebetbücher* of Abraham Geiger and Manuel Joël," in the present volume.

23 *Va'ani Tefillati*, p. 383.

Therefore, *Va'ani Tefillati* only employs the past tense when referring to this mode of worship.[24]

This second approach finds practical liturgical application in the treatment *Va'ani Tefillati* accords the *Musaf* services on the Sabbath, New Moon, and holidays. For each of these services, the Israeli Masorti prayer book essentially adopts the formula employed in the *siddurim* of the American Conservative movement. Hence, on Rosh Hodesh, the New Moon, *Va'ani Tefillati* speaks of the place "where our ancestors offered their obligatory sacrifices before You," and it indicates, just several lines later, that they did so "in love." The Sabbath *Musaf* service repeats precisely the same phrases, as does the holiday rite.[25] Conservative prayer books display an absolute consistency on this point and *Va'ani Tefillati* here explicitly reveals its identity as a Conservative liturgy.

In highlighting the Conservative character of this Israeli *siddur*, one further quality must be emphasized. As is well known, Conservative Judaism is the ideological offspring of the nineteenth-century German Historical School of Zacharias Frankel. From the moment of its inception, Conservative Judaism has avowed the developmental character of Judaism and embraced critical-historical methods as a means to arrive at truth. Indeed, this approach is such an integral part of Conservative thought that it is incorporated into the Conservative movement stance towards matters of Jewish law.[26] Thus, it is hardly surprising that historical explanations concerning the origins and development of Jewish prayer abound in *Va'ani Tefillati*, and that academic research regarding specific prayers is cited. Commentaries accompany texts such as *Avinu Malkeinu*, Kaddish, Torah readings and the blessing for the New Moon.[27] In a particularly telling note on the hymn *Ana be-Koaḥ*, *Va'ani Tefillati* asserts that while the authorship of this poem is ascribed by Jewish mystical tradition to a first-century sage, "such attribution is not accepted by modern academic scholars."[28] As a Conservative prayer book, the Israeli rite embraces such critical scholarship.

24 Ibid. p.518.
25 See *Va'ani Tefillati*, pp.119, 387, and 523.
26 On this issue, see David Ellenson, "Conservative Halakhah in Israel," *Modern Judaism* (1993), pp.191–204.
27 *Va'ani Tefillati*, pp.84, 114, 359, and 374.
28 Ibid. p.286.

Textual Diversity and Theological Affirmations

As both Roth and Graetz have pointed out, *Va'ani Tefillati* is also marked by an affirmation of textual pluralism. One section of the prayer book is entitled, "*Eilu ve-Eilu*" ("These and These"). This phrase, drawn from the Talmud, champions pluralism as a basic principle of Judaism; hence, in this section of the prayer book, alternative formulations for various prayers are given. In the case of *Kaddish* and *Kiddushat ha-Shem*, texts principally derived from the Sephardic tradition are offered. These options are hardly controversial, especially in a Jewish world as ethnically diverse as the contemporary State of Israel. While such choices may be novel from the standpoint of Ashkenazic liturgical traditions, they are quite familiar to Jews from other backgrounds. If anything, they bespeak the efforts being made by the Masorti movement to attract Jews of non-Ashkenazic origins to their synagogues.

In addition, in the last of the middle benedictions of the daily *Shemoneh Esreh*, the *siddur*, like its Reform Israeli counterpart, *Ha-Avodah Shebalev*, has substituted the Sephardic phrase "*tefillat kol peh* — the prayer of every mouth," for the Ashkenazic "*tefillat amha yisrael*" — the prayer of Your People Israel," as the penultimate words of this blessing. In so doing, *Va'ani Tefillati* has adopted a precedent well embedded in Jewish liturgical tradition as a warrant for its own text. At the same time, it should be noted that the Israeli Conservative *siddur* selected this substitution precisely because it allowed the authors to shape a liturgy whose content is more in keeping with the universalistic sentiments that mark Masorti Judaism than the particularistic formula found in the received Ashkenazic liturgical version of this prayer. This alternative formulation, like those described in the previous paragraph, has venerable Jewish sanction. However, other alternatives possess no such precedents, and bespeak the distinct ideological affirmations that mark the distinctly modernist ethos of *Va'ani Tefillati* and the Masorti movement.

The *Aleinu* prayer, which marks the end of all daily services, also comes under scrutiny. As Jakob Petuchowski declared, "While the prayer, as a whole, kept the balance between 'particularism' and 'universalism,' the form in which 'particularism' was expressed has generally been found to be disturbing by the liturgists of Liberal and Reform Judaism." For the past two centuries, non-Orthodox liturgists have struggled with this prayer, seeking a textual solution to those phrases that promote what Petuchowski termed an "invidious comparison" between Israel and the nations.[29] On this score, *Va'ani Tefillati* once more reveals itself to be a Liberal prayer book. While the traditional *Aleinu* text is placed in the main body of the prayer book, a substitute formulation is provided in the *Eilu ve-Eilu* section. In this section, for example, the phrase, "He did not let our portion be like theirs, nor our lot like that of all their multitude," is purged from this text and replaced by a sentence adopted from the Reconstructionist rite, "Who gave us teachings of truth and planted eternal life within us."[30]

Textual variant also manifests itself in the choice of blessings *Va'ani Tefillati* provides for the parents to recite on the occasion of the *bar/bat mitzvah* of their sons and daughters. Classically, the father alone recited the words, "Blessed is the One who has released me from the punishment of this one," after his son is called up to the Torah.[31] *Va'ani Tefillati* retains this classical text as one option for parents on this occasion. However, for those who might consider the sentiments expressed in this line inappropriate at such a joyous moment, three alternatives are provided. One is the traditional *Sheheheyanu* blessing recited on happy occasions. Another text reads, "Blessed is the One who has made my son/daughter worthy of *mitzvot*," while the third makes use of the traditional blessing made on the occasion of glad tidings, "Blessed are You, O Lord our God, who is good and grants goodness." Here, as with the *Aleinu*, the traditional text is provided, and the traditionalists in the community can select it; for worshipers with more modernist sensibilities, other prayer options are provided. In this way, the editors of *Va'ani Tefillati* celebrate liturgical pluralism, expanding the choices placed before their congregants beyond those contained in the tradition.

In other instances, *Va'ani Tefillati*'s modernist ideological proclivity

29 Jakob J. Petuchowski, *Prayerbook Reform in Europe* (New York: World Union for Progressive Judaism, 1968), pp. 298ff.

30 For the Reconstructionist formulation, see *Kol Haneshamah*, p. 445.

31 The traditional notion is that a father is responsible for the sins of his son while the son remains a minor. At the age of *bar mitzvah*, the son assumes responsibility for his own actions.

results in the rejection of a traditional prayer text even when multiple options can be provided. For example, by the Middle Ages, Jewish liturgical tradition (as evidenced in the writings of several *ge'onim*)[32] had determined that the Jewish male was obligated to recite three daily blessings that praised God, "Who did not make me a gentile, . . . a slave, . . . [or] a woman." The Israeli rite will not even countenance the possibility of such wording. In taking this stance, *Va'ani Tefillati* contends that there are traditional grounds for such objections.[33] However, in making such claims, it is equally obvious that the Masorti rite has aligned itself with a modern Liberal prayer book tradition that has condemned such wording as negative, xenophobic, and sexist.

Numerous Liberal *siddurim* have struggled to reformulate these blessings in a variety of ways. *Siddur Sim Shalom*, as well as the Israeli Reform prayer book *Ha-Avodah Shebalev*, have done so by transforming the blessings into positive statements. In each of these *siddurim*, "Who has not made me a gentile," has been changed to "Who has made me a Jew," while "Who has not made me a woman," has been reworded as "Who has made me in His image," and "Who has not made me a slave," has been reformulated as "Who has made me free." Other non-Orthodox *siddurim*, such as Isaac Mayer Wise's *Minhag America* (1857), omitted these three blessings altogether and placed in their stead the single benediction, "*She-asani yisrael* — Who has made me a Jew."

Va'ani Tefillati has sanctioned both these options, though it prefers the latter. Thus, the editors place the positively worded variants of these blessings as a prayer option for Masorti Jews in the *Eilu ve-Eilu* section. In the *Birkhot ha-Shahar* section, however, *Va'ani Tefillati* includes only one blessing, "Who has made me a Jew," in lieu of three. As the editors state, they have selected this as the preferred option because they do not wish to write new blessings; moreover, this single blessing, in their opinion, includes the meanings found in the other two.[34]

32 These responsa are delineated and discussed in Yoel H. Kahn's "The Three Morning Blessings, '. . . Who Did Not Make Me . . .': An Historical Study of a Jewish Liturgical Text" (Ph.D. thesis, The Graduate Theological Union, 1999).

33 *Va'ani Tefillati*, pp. 16–17.

34 Ibid. p. 17. While the writers of *Va'ani Tefillati* do not say so, it may also be, given their penchant for talmudic precedent, that they favor this particular formulation because it is found, in the name of Rabbi Meir, in *Menahot* 43b. Moreover, Rabbi Abraham Gombiner, in his authoritative and influential commentary *Magen Avra-*

Gender-Based Pluralism

The approach *Va'ani Tefillati* adopts towards women and their status is a critical element in the movement's broad commitment towards pluralism. In their introductions to *Va'ani Tefillati*, both Graetz and Roth contend that this *siddur* will affirm the central role that women have played in transmitting Jewish faith throughout the generations.[35] This commitment is given liturgical expression at numerous points throughout the *siddur*.

The Masorti rite does not permit "*avoteinu* — our patriarchs" to stand alone. Virtually everywhere the term appears, the word "*imoteinu* — our matriarchs" is placed alongside it in brackets. While Roth acknowledges that *avoteinu* is an inclusive term in Hebrew, he recognizes that many people desire to give clear expression to the presence of women in Jewish prayer. By placing the word *imoteinu* in brackets, all Conservative Jews are able to choose for themselves how they will approach this issue.[36]

Va'ani Tefillati displays this penchant for choice, and allows for both gender-inclusive and male-only imagery in a number of other places as well. At the end of the *Pesukei de-Zimra* section of the morning service, the Sephardic rite is offered as a prayer option, and Masorti congregants are thus able to recall that Miriam as well as Moses led the people in song and celebration after the crossing of the Red Sea. Similarly, in *Birkat ha-Mazon*, *Va'ani Tefillati* follows the path adopted by other gender-sensitive modern liturgies and permits the recitation of "*al britkha she-natata be-libeinu* — for the covenant that You have planted in our hearts," in place of the gender-exclusive "*she-ḥatamta bi-vesareinu* — that You have sealed in our flesh."[37]

More noticeably, *Va'ani Tefillati*, like *Ha-Avodah Shebalev*, provides two options for the *Avot* benediction of the *Amidah*. Every time this blessing appears, the page is divided, and two textual variants appear.

---

ham, *Oraḥ Ḥayim* 46:4, notes explicitly, as does the Masorti commentary, that this single blessing contains the meanings of the other two. Undoubtedly, the Masorti rite depends upon this ruling as the basis for its preferred liturgical practice at this point in the service.

35 Ibid. pp. vi, xii

36 Ibid. p. xii.

37 Ibid. p. 231. See *Siddur Lev Chadash* (London: Union of Liberal and Progressive Congregations, 1995), p. 554.

One text maintains the traditional wording of the prayer and speaks only of the patriarchs of the Jewish people. In contrast, the second includes "our mothers" as well as "our fathers," and names the matriarchs Sarah, Rebecca, Rachel, and Leah, along with Abraham, Isaac, and Jacob, in the prayer's formula. Most noteworthy is that this textual variant concludes, "Blessed are You, Shield of Abraham and Sarah."

Roth is aware that these changes in such a well-known prayer text are hardly uncontroversial. In his introduction, he indicates that the gender-inclusive text of this benediction was the subject of heated debate among members of the *Va'ad ha-Halakhah* (halakhah committee) of the Israeli Rabbinical Assembly. However, he claims that it was only the issue of the paragraph's "eulogy" or conclusion (*ḥatimah*) that elicited controversy, as alterations in the conclusion of a prayer present a greater halakhic difficulty than changes elsewhere in the text.[38] Aware that some congregants might feel uneasy about a change in the *ḥatimah*, Roth suggests that they opt to use the body of the prayer, which includes the matriarchs, but to conclude the section in the traditional manner.[39]

While *Va'ani Tefillati*, here as in other examples, provides both a tra-

---

38   As this article has consistently pointed out, Jewish prayers have long been marked by diverse wordings. Notwithstanding, by the Middle Ages, a number of principles had been developed. Two of the principles regarding alterations or additions in the traditional text are that such changes should be 1) placed in the body of a benediction, not at its conclusion; and 2) in thematic harmony with the content of the benediction. As Ruth Langer points out (see her *To Worship God Properly: Tensions Between Liturgical Custom and Halakhah in Judaism* [Cincinnati: 1998], p.27), in both the Babylonian and Jerusalem Talmuds, rabbinic authorities held that "the concluding blessing (eulogy) of the prayer must be correct." This view was reinforced by medieval halakhic authorities. My point here is not to enter into discussion of this complex matter, which extends far beyond the parameters of this article, but simply to note the particularly thorny nature of the problem faced by Roth and members of the Israeli halakhah committee when they debated whether to alter the conclusion of a benediction.

39   *Va'ani Tefillati*, p.xii. Rabbi David Golinkin, chair of the *Va'ad ha-Halakhah* of the Masorti movement, has told me that the Israeli committee has actually issued no decision on this benediction and that the change in the word, "*go'el* — redeemer," to "*ge'ulah* — redemption," in the text of the gender-inclusive version, also elicited heated debate. Be that as it may, the Conservative *heter* (permission) that permits these gender changes to the prayer was written by Rabbi Joel Rembaum of Temple Beth Am in Los Angeles. The Rembaum responsum was adopted by the Committee on

ditional as well as an egalitarian option, the commentary that precedes the benediction bespeaks the strong sympathy for the gender-inclusive choice. Thus, the commentary notes that the concept of *zekhut avot* (Merit of the Fathers), which finds expression in this benediction, refers to the "deeds of lovingkindness performed by our father Abraham *and our mother Sarah.*" Furthermore, the commentary continues, "The first patriarchs *and matriarchs* bequeathed their faith in Judaism to subsequent generations, . . . and thus it is in every generation."[40] The feminist ethos and egalitarian sensibility that inform *Va'ani Tefillati* are here obvious, and an unmistakable tone of gender equality marks the prayer book as a whole.

As mentioned earlier, naming ceremonies for baby girls (*zeved bat*) as well as the *bat mitzvah* for adolescent young women are presented as normative in *Va'ani Tefillati*, and the mother, not only the father, offers her blessing to her child on the occasion of a *bar/bat mitzvah*. Similarly, in the *Ushpizin* text, matriarchs are welcomed along with patriarchs each day into the *sukkah*. In the *Birkat ha-Mazon*, the text of *Va'ani Tefillati* makes the request — not in brackets — that divine blessing descend upon the company that has just dined together, "*just as our matriarchs, Sarah, Rebecca, Rachel, and Leah*, and our patriarchs, Abraham, Isaac, and Jacob, were blessed."[41]

Va'ani Tefillati also manifests its commitment to gender inclusion in the *brit milah* ceremony. As Rabbi Lawrence Hoffman has pointed out, the two figures who have traditionally played the central role in this ceremony, beyond the baby boy himself, are "the *mohel* and the father, the two men who share the ritual responsibility." While women did participate in this ritual during early medieval times, *brit milah* was ultimately "transformed from a family event with father, mother, and child at the center into a male-only ritual. . . . That mothers had once brought their children, held them during the rite, . . . would soon be forgotten." Most

---

Law and Standards of the Rabbinical Assembly in the U.S. by a vote of 9–6, with several abstentions. Interestingly, this responsum does not address the halakhically thorny question of the *hatimah* itself, but only the notion of textual variation in Jewish prayer. I am grateful to Rabbi Golinkin for sharing this responsum with me.

40 Ibid. p.303.
41 Ibid. p.259ff (*zeved bat*); pp.364 and 368 (*bat mitzvah*); pp.220–21 (*Ushpizin*); 237 (*Birkat-ha-Mazon*).

significantly, at the key moment in the ceremony when the blessing is recited that confirms the entry of the baby into the covenant of Abraham, only the father has been charged with the responsibility and given the privilege of uttering this benediction.[42]

The Masorti *siddur* reverses a near-millennium of such Jewish practice. Thus, in its instructions for this rite, *Va'ani Tefillati* asserts, "In the *brit milah* ceremony, the mother, father, and *mohel* play an active role." The baby is to be given to the mother, and, at the beginning of the ceremony, both parents, or either father or mother, thank God "for this most precious gift of new life." Immediately prior to the circumcision itself, the blessing affirming that God has commanded that this boy be entered "into the covenant of Abraham our father," is called *"Birkat ha-Horeh (ah)* — the Parents' Blessing," and not, as Jewish law has termed it, *"Birkat ha-Av* — the Father's Blessing."[43] In this rite of social birth, the responsibility shared by both mother and father for raising the child is acknowledged ritually.

This move towards gender-inclusivity is most fully and obviously expressed in a picture printed at the front of the book. In a section devoted to instructions on how to put on *tefillin*, prominently featured among the photographs is one that shows a woman with a *kippah* also wearing the head *tefillin*.[44]

This picture delivers a powerful statement: it indicates that the Masorti movement has internalized a feminist critique contending that patriarchal cultures posit the male as normative and consign the female to the status of "other." Rather than the prayer book's presenting a lengthy verbal statement arguing these positions, it features an icon that clearly refutes that notion. From the standpoint of semiotics, this is the single most powerful example of innovation contained in the *siddur*. It presents a new, even radical, representation of reality. The icon presents the gestalt of the prayer book as egalitarian. The overarching message of the Israeli rite, affirmations of pluralism notwithstanding, is remarkably unambivalent on the issue of gender equality.

42 See Lawrence A. Hoffman, *Covenant of Blood: Circumcision and Gender in Rabbinic Judaism* (Chicago: University of Chicago Press, 1996), pp. 74, 193 ff., 204, and 180.

43 *Va'ani Tefillati*, pp. 254–56.

44 Ibid. p. 10.

The Israeli Context

As mentioned at the outset of this article, an Israeli-Zionist character is one of the most outstanding features distinguishing *Va'ani Tefillati*. Quite naturally, this Israel-based work views *Medinat Yisrael* as a *bonum* and takes cognizance of the Jewish state in sundry ways. Old prayers are reworded to reflect the reality of renewed Jewish independence, and new prayers have been composed that affirm the blessings wrought by the creation of the State of Israel. Nor does *Va'ani Tefillati* shrink from confronting the trials created and the obligations imposed by a reborn Jewish commonwealth.

In taking this stance, *Va'ani Tefillati* once more reveals its lineage as a Conservative rite. Conservative Judaism has always been linked strongly to Zionism,[45] and since the 1950s, liturgical renewal in the Conservative movement has been marked by a conscious effort to affirm the significance of *Medinat Yisrael* in Conservative prayer. As Jules Harlow puts it, "For centuries Jews have prayed for the restoration of Jerusalem and for the re-establishment of a Jewish state in the Land of Israel. Those prayers have been answered, thank God, and the liturgy should not remain unaltered, as if nothing has changed in this regard."[46]

North American Conservative prayer has insisted that Israel is of the utmost religious importance, and it has given liturgical expression to that importance in several ways.[47] At the same time, in characteristic American fashion, this liturgy refuses to concede that Jewish life outside

45 The literature on this linkage is voluminous. For representative and comprehensive articles on this relationship, see Naomi G. Cohen, "'Diaspora Plus Palestine, Religion Plus Nationalism': The Seminary and Zionism, 1902–1948," in Jack Wertheimer, ed., *Tradition Renewed: A History of the Jewish Theological Seminary,* 2 vols. (New York: Jewish Theological Seminary, 1997), vol. 2, pp. 115–76; Eli Lederhendler, "The Ongoing Dialogue: The Seminary and the Challenge of Israel," ibid. pp. 179–270; and Arthur A. Goren, "Spiritual Zionists and Jewish Sovereignty," in Norman Cohen and Robert Seltzer, eds., *The Americanization of the Jews* (New York: New York University Press, 1995), pp. 165–92.

46 Harlow, "Revising the Liturgy for Conservative Jews," p. 131.

47 For a full description of how American Conservative Jewish liturgy has dealt with the State of Israel, see David Ellenson, "Envisioning Israel in the Liturgies of North American Liberal Judaism," in Allon Gal, ed., *Envisioning Israel* (Jerusalem and Detroit: Magnes Press and Wayne State University Press, 1996), pp. 127–38.

of Israel ought to be regarded as *Galut* (Exile). For example, *Siddur Sim Shalom* bestows religious meaning upon the State of Israel. However, it will not affirm territorial centralization as the precondition for the existence of the Jewish nation, and it rejects a Zionist vision that would affirm Israel as the exclusive center of Jewish life.

This approach to *Medinat Yisrael* in American Conservative prayer is found most clearly in the alterations *Siddur Sim Shalom* has introduced in the traditional text of the *Musaf* service for Sabbaths and holidays. While Orthodox *siddurim* make no mention of the State of Israel in this prayer, asking only that God replant the Jewish people at some future date in the land so that the sacrificial order can once again be renewed, *Sim Shalom* gives thanks to God, "*Hameishiv banim li-gevulam* — who restores His children to their land." Inclusion of this phrase in the *Musaf* service reflects the Conservative conviction that "the re-establishment of the Jewish State in the Land of Israel" represents a divine answer to the millennial-old prayers of the Jewish people. The State of Israel bears metaphysical import, and that import demands acknowledgment and recognition in the prayers of the Jewish people.

At the same time, however, each of these *Musaf* services includes the sentence, "*U-tekabel be-raḥamim et tefillat amkha yisrael be-khol mekomot moshvoteihem* — Accept with compassion the prayer of your people Israel, *wherever they dwell.*" These last three words have ample biblical precedent. However, their inclusion represents a noticeable departure from the traditional manifest content of the liturgy. The text is no longer exclusively centered on Israel. The Jewish people dwell in the Diaspora as well, and their presence in the lands of dispersion is not an evil from which the Jewish people must seek release. Whereas the State of Israel has sanctified status, this status does not obviate the Diaspora as an equally fit venue for Jewish life.[48]

Just as *Siddur Sim Shalom* reflects an American Zionist sensibility, so *Va'ani Tefillati* manifests a distinctive Israeli character. Thus, in the same

---

48 It is significant to note that the 1998 edition of *Siddur Sim Shalom* has removed the sentence "Accept with compassion the prayer of your people Israel, wherever they dwell" from its rite. In so doing, the authors of the contemporary North American Conservative prayer book expressed their discomfort with the ideological stance of the 1985 prayer book and their willingness to restore the "Israelocentrism" of the classical prayer.

Musaf services discussed above, the Israeli Conservative *siddur* adopts a different stance than its 1985 American Conservative counterpart. The text in one part of the service reads: "May they willingly come up to the land which is the beloved of our dispersed" (*she-le-yisrael ḥemdat nefuzoteinu mi-ratzon ya'alu*), while, in another paragraph, it boldly prays, "May our dispersed come up in joy to our land, and may You plant them within our border" (*she-ta'aleh nefuzoteinu be-simḥah le-artzeinu ve-tita'em bi-gevuleinu*).[49] In either case, the centrality of *Eretz Yisrael* in Jewish prayer is affirmed. Not surprisingly, the approach *Va'ani Tefillati* adopts towards this concept of *kibbutz galuyot* ("Ingathering of the Exiles") reflects a position closer to that contained in the Israeli Progressive *Ha-Avodah Shebalev* than with that evidenced in *Siddur Sim Shalom*. The power of place in shaping thought is herein apparent, and a common sensibility shaped by a shared Israeli context manifests itself in these two Israeli works.[50]

Va'ani Tefillati also reveals its Israeli roots in other ways. In the paragraph before the *Shema*, the traditional phrase "and cause us to walk upright into our Land" is reworded so as to read "in our land." Likewise, the word *le-artzeinu* ("to our land"), is added to the tenth benediction of the daily *Amidah*, so that when the petition for *kibbutz galuyot* is recited, there is a recognition that Masorti Jews are offering this prayer in the land where they dwell.[51]

Prayers that contain references to the destruction of Jerusalem have been changed to reflect the contemporary reality of Jerusalem restored. Thus, in the afternoon service for Tisha be-Av, *Va'ani Tefillati* refuses, as Orthodox liturgy has it, to simply mourn an ancient Jerusalem destroyed. Instead, it also recognizes that there exists a contemporary Jerusalem, one that "has been rebuilt from her destruction" and "restored from her desolation," and a hope is expressed that God will grant peace to Israel.[52] Similarly, *Va'ani Tefillati* accords canonical status to Yom ha-Atzma'ut (Israeli

49 *Va'ani Tefillati*, pp.387–88.
50 For example, in the prayer prior to the *Shema*, *Ha-Avodah Shebalev* asserts, "Gather our Exiles from the four corners of the earth, and cause *them* to walk upright into our land" (p.36). For the treatment *Ha-Avodah Shebalev* accords the notion of *kibbutz galuyot*, see Eric L. Friedland, *"Were Our Mouths Filled with Song": Studies in Liberal Jewish Liturgy* (Cincinnati: Hebrew Union College Press, 1997), p.260.
51 *Va'ani Tefillati* pp.61, 137; also see p.xi.
52 Ibid. p.139.

Independence Day), and it contains a prayer of gratitude, introduced by the *Al ha-Nissim* benediction, which is based on the traditional formula employed on Purim and Hanukkah.[53] Like *Sim Shalom*, it "follows the text of Rav Amram Gaon's *Al ha-Nissim*, amending the introductory formula which expresses gratitude for miracles 'in other times at this season' to read 'in other times and in our day.'"[54]

The State of Israel is celebrated in *Va'ani Tefillati*. However, the wars that have ravaged the State since its inception, and the ongoing need for defense, are deeply etched in its pages and find expression in many ways as well. In the *Birkat ha-Mazon*, the "All-Merciful One" is asked to bless the soldiers of the Israel Defense Forces as well as all those who labor on behalf of the state's defense. *Hazkarat Neshamot*, the Memorial Service, recites a separate *El Malei Rahamim* prayer on behalf of those who have fallen in defense of Israel, and a special *Misheberakh* is devoted to the state and the IDF forces.[55]

An entire section of the prayer book, "*Eretz, Eretz, Eretz,*" contains services that reflect the rationales for and rhythm of Jewish life in Israel. Here the pain of the Holocaust is recalled. A lengthy service is devoted to Yom ha-Shoah, and a special paragraph is inserted in the daily *Amidah* that reflects the pain and concerns of the Holocaust memorial day. In both these liturgical expressions, the horror of those years and the annihilation of so many are appropriately mentioned. At the same time, there is a reminder that the Jewish people still live and that *Medinat Yisrael* reverses the situation of powerlessness that marked Jewish life in *Galut* (Exile).[56] There are also moving services combining traditional

53 Ibid. pp.169, 170–71. Of course, in granting such status to Israel Independence Day, the Masorti rite echoes the approach adopted by Israeli Orthodox and Progressive *siddurim*. For example *Siddur Rinat Yisrael, Nusaḥ Sepharad* (Jerusalem: 1995), pp.441–47, has a special service that marks Israel Independence Day, as well as prayers for the welfare of the state and for the memory of soldiers who have fallen in its defense (pp.281, 395). Similarly, *Ha-Avodah Shebalev* has a service for Israel Independence Day (pp.220–25) and prayers for the welfare of the state and in memory of its fallen soldiers (pp.129, 218).

54 This quotation, taken from Jules Harlow, is cited in Ellenson, "Envisioning Israel in the Liturgies on North American Liberal Judaism," p.136.

55 *Va'ani Tefillati*, p.236 (*Birkat ha-Mazon*); p.510 (*Yizkor* service); p.373 (*Mi she-berakh* for IDF soldiers).

56 Ibid. pp.547–84 ("*Eretz, eretz, eretz*"); pp.559–70 (Holocaust Memorial Day).

and modern elements for Yom ha-Atzma'ut (Israel Independence Day), Yom ha-Zikaron (Memorial Day), and Yom Yerushalayim (Jerusalem Day),[57] as well as a service whose title, *Lo ira ra* ("I will fear no evil"), is taken from Psalm 23. This last service is reserved for *"sha'ot kashot"* (difficult hours) — presumably including times of war, the aftermath of terrorist attacks, and accidents. Prayers for rain during times of drought, and the Counting of the *Omer* take on new meaning now that the Jewish people have been returned to their land.[58] Finally, for all those familiar with the carnage and destruction that so often mark the Israeli highway, a special prayer composed for this *siddur*, *"Tefillat ha-Nehag"* — ("The Driver's Prayer") merits particular attention.[59]

Aware of how ignorant many secular Israelis are of Jewish religious praxis, *Va'ani Tefillati* also provides detailed explanations on Jewish ritual prayer practice. For example, there are explicit instructions on proper ritual conduct when one is called to recite the blessings over the Torah, on how to place *tefillin*, and the correct procedure for the waving of the *lulav* on Sukkot.[60] Graphically, the text of the siddur is divided and printed in a way that makes the liturgical Hebrew more accessible to the average Israeli.

Manifest in *Va'ani Tefillati* is a sense of gratitude for what is regarded as the miracle of Israel's existence. *Medinat Yisrael* embodies a religious hope. At the same time, it is embedded in sometimes mundane, sometimes daunting, sometimes inspiring realities. *Va'ani Tefillati* seeks to do justice to all these elements, and its pages reflect the attempts of its authors to give religious voice to the rhythms of Jewish life as it has been experienced and, it is hoped, will one day be lived in the reborn Jewish state.

57 Ibid., pp.576–84 (Israel Independence Day); pp.571–75 (Israel's Memorial Day); pp.556–59 (Jerusalem Day).
58 Ibid. pp.554–55 (*"sha'ot kashot"*); pp.551–53 (prayer for rain); 178ff. (counting the *omer*). The counting of the *omer* is recited during the seven weeks between the second day of Passover and Sukkot. This period marks the time between the planting and the harvesting of the season's first grains (an *omer* is a measure of grain); in talmudic times, it also became a period of semi-mourning, commemorating the death of thousands of students in a plague during the time of Rabbi Akiva.
59 Ibid. pp.275–76.
60 Ibid. pp.362–63 (blessing for the Torah); pp.8–11 (*tefillin*); pp.499, 502–3 (Sukkot).

Final Thoughts

As the study of their liturgy shows, Jews, for more than a millennium, have felt the need to give ever more precise expression to their yearning for the divine. They have done so while being rooted in the narratives and memories found in a received liturgical tradition. At the same time, they have lived in a present that makes novel demands. Consequently, every *siddur* can be seen as reflecting an effort to navigate between the pull of tradition and the push of its own time and place. *Va'ani Tefillati* is part of this prayer book tradition.

As a Masorti rite, *Va'ani Tefillati* evinces a keen awareness of the struggle this tradition demands. The Israeli Conservative rite strives for fidelity to the past while acknowledging the urgency of the present. Like other modern Liberal prayer books, it self-consciously attempts to adjust the language and experience of Jewish prayer to the realities and rhythms of its contemporary milieu.

Va'ani Tefillati will undoubtedly have its critics, for no prayer book can calibrate the claims of the past and the demands of the present in a fashion that will be pleasing to everyone. Some will therefore surely see it as too far-reaching in its changes, while others will criticize it for not being bold enough. Such claims can seldom be adjudicated objectively. Nevertheless, by self-consciously insisting upon its right to give expression to its own voice, *Va'ani Tefillati* affirms that a present generation, like past ones, possesses the privilege of participating in an ongoing Jewish liturgical conversation. For that affirmation, the Israeli Conservative *siddur* does not apologize. Its voice is a creative one, and in its pages, we see the character of the Masorti movement as it has developed in *Medinat Yisrael*.

In a famous statement, Abraham Isaac Kook, the late Chief Ashkenazic rabbi, once observed that in the Jewish state, "the old should be renewed, and the new should be made holy." Through its prayers, the Masorti rite has sought to give expression to this directive. Mindful of the past, attentive to the present, concerned for the future, *Va'ani Tefillati* bears witness to the aspirations that direct Israeli Conservative Judaism as it seeks a legitimate place in Israeli society.

22

David Hartman on Judaism and the Modern Condition

A Review Essay of A Heart of Many Rooms *and* Israelis and the Jewish Tradition

As discussed above, Rabbi David Hartman of Jerusalem is surely renowned in the English-language Diaspora as the preeminent Israeli philosopher and representative of traditional Jewish thought. A week rarely passes in which Hartman does not appear on CNN or speak in the pages of publications such as *The New York Times*, *The Jerusalem Report*, *The Jerusalem Post*, or *Ha'aretz* as an authoritative Jewish voice on the issues of the day. For over three decades, scores of rabbis and lay people of all stripes from both Israel and the Diaspora have justifiably flocked to study with him at both the Hebrew University and at the Shalom Hartman Institute. He has nurtured a generation of Israeli scholars, and their writings bear the unmistakable impress of his approach and influence. His Jewish knowledge and passion are palpable to all who hear him, and he bears himself with a charismatic authority that mesmerizes audiences and spreads his fame both in Israel and abroad.

However, Hartman has not confined himself to oral presentations in the classroom or to the media. His many essays and books on the enduring importance and relevance of traditional Jewish values and thought for a contemporary world represent engaged scholarship at its best. He has been one of the foremost contemporary authorities on the works of Maimonides and the significance of the Sage of Fostat for present-day Judaism. Indeed, the writings of Hartman and of those who constitute his circle have captured the attention of elite intellectuals both within and outside Israel, and his influence on religious and political thinkers of all types has been considerable.[1] David Hartman is therefore part of

---

1 On the increasing influence that Hartman and his circle have begun to exert in Israel, see Charles Liebman, "Modern Orthodoxy in Israel," *Judaism* (Fall, 1998),

of a rare breed we have hardly seen since the days of Abraham Joshua Heschel — a serious student of Jewish religious thought who is engaged at the same time as a public intellectual.

His two most recent books, *A Heart of Many Rooms: Celebrating the Many Voices within Judaism* and *Israelis and the Jewish People: An Ancient People Debating Its Future*, build upon themes he has addressed in the past and constitute vital additions to his literary-philosophical corpus. Since the themes he expressed earlier in *A Living Covenant* are developed and provide the foundation for the subjects he addressed in his two most recent publications, we will therefore begin with a synopsis of the ideas and themes contained in that earlier work. We will then turn to *A Heart of Many Rooms* and focus most prominently — though not exclusively — on the sense of Jewish history Hartman displays in its opening pages and in the first chapter, "Judaism as an Interpretive Tradition." From the outset, he anchors his positions within the panorama of Jewish intellectual and political history, and the first chapter embodies the systematic reflections of a mature Hartman on the nature of Jewish legal hermeneutics. These topics stand at the center of much of his writing, and they comprise an original and valuable contribution for comprehending the nature of modern Jewish thought. They also provide for a Jewish legal process that has potential significance for the modern world. In *A Heart of Many Rooms*, Hartman goes on to create

---

pp. 405–10. There Liebman discusses the intellectual ferment that marks large sectors of Orthodox Judaism in Israel, and a large number of the names he mentions — among them Avi Sagi, Menachem Fisch, and Moshe Halbertal — have long been associated with the Shalom Hartman Institute. The impact of Hartman on leading Jewish philosophers of a secular bent can be seen in the writings of such world-class intellectual figures as Michael Walzer, Hilary Putnam, Michael Sandel, and Joseph Raz in Michael Walzer, Menachem Loberbaum, Noam J. Zohar, and Yair Loberbaum, eds., *The Jewish Political Tradition: Vol. 1: Authority* (New Haven: Yale University Press, 2000). This book, labeled by Arnold Eisen as "an event of major cultural importance," bespeaks the direct influence of Hartman as well as the Shalom Hartman Institute. Hartman himself provides the "Foreword" to this work, and contributes a "Commentary" to it. In addition, virtually all its contributors are within the ambit of the Hartman Institute. It is doubtful that any person other than Hartman could have inspired such a diverse body of secular Jewish intellectuals, in addition to religious ones, to engage so seriously in a dialogue with Jewish tradition. Finally, the work of Christian theologians such as Krister Stendahl and Paul Van Buren has been refined and honed through conferences and study sessions at the Hartman Institute as well.

a holistic Jewish theology — one in which his thoughts on Jewish law are connected to the importance and centrality he assigns the modern State of Israel as the most appropriate locus for the manifestation of that law. Through these stances, Hartman emerges as the engaged academic he is. In "Judaism as an Interpretive Tradition," he roots modern Jewish religious thought firmly in the soil of Jewish tradition. He demonstrates that modern Judaism remains capable of speaking in an authentic Jewish voice that draws idiomatically upon a flexible past for guidance to meet the challenges of the present.

Having explicated Hartman in these ways, this review essay will culminate with an exposition of his most recent work, *Israelis and the Jewish Tradition*, where the themes and intellectual trajectory of a lifetime have converged in a single volume. In this latest book, Hartman continues his ongoing efforts to revitalize Jewish tradition and apply Jewish law and teachings in ways that allow them to speak in meaningful cadences to modern Jews and Gentiles. Hartman struggles to articulate the religious-cultural meaning Jews and others can attach to the present-day State of Israel. First delivered as the prestigious Terry Lectures at Yale in 1998, the essays in this book represent the climax of a lifetime of theological and academic reflections. As before, Hartman reveals himself to be a constructive Jewish theologian of the first rank whose written efforts merit careful scrutiny and consideration by all who would comprehend the course and direction of Judaism in the modern world.

A Living Covenant *and the Intellectual-Religious Foundations of* A Heart of Many Rooms *and* Israelis and the Jewish Tradition

First published by the Free Press in 1985, *A Living Covenant* was reissued by Jewish Lights in 1997 and must be regarded as a vital prelude to both *A Heart of Many Rooms* and *Israelis and the Jewish Tradition*. Indeed, the three works constitute something of a trilogy, and the careful reader will be rewarded by noting the points of continuity as well as the elements of development among them.

At the very outset of *A Living Covenant*, Hartman indicates that his is what can be described as a corporeal Judaism, one that is embedded not only in tradition but also in the living reality of people and land.

Hartman states, "How does one express gratitude to a people that had the courage to expose their religion to the severe test of a total Jewish society? Without that courage, I doubt I would have felt the urgency to provide new directions for Judaism as a living covenant" (pp. ix–x).

In offering this declaration, Hartman reveals the twin passions that have occupied his theological attention. On the one hand, he attempts to grapple with and revivify a covenantal tradition anchored in a *Halakhah* forged primarily in the Diaspora. He insists that a legal tradition resides at the heart of Judaism, and he contends that Jewish law is capable of engagement with the modern world in a manner that is both faithful to the past and germane to the present. On the other hand, he is urgently aware that the State of Israel represents a *novum* for both the Jewish people and the Jewish religion. For the first time in almost two millennia both Judaism and *am yisrael* are responsible for the governance of a nation and the application of Jewish ethics in a situation where Jews enjoy political sovereignty. Turning his attention to the State of Israel, Hartman strives to articulate how the Jewish law and political theory might be approached so that a selective application of its resources can provide appropriate and authentic guidance for the novel venue created by the establishment of the third Jewish commonwealth.[2]

In order to do this, Hartman turns to the thoughtful and deliberate sobriety that marks the processes of the rabbinic tradition, particularly as that tradition finds expression in the writings of the great medieval philosopher Maimonides and other rabbinic teachers. From this rabbinic tradition, Hartman learns that God is not primarily discovered — as the Bible alone would have it — in the immediacy of personal encounter and experience. Instead, he asserts, "From my many years of Talmud study, I learned that one can sense the living God of revelation . . . in the writings of any committed and learned covenantal teacher" (p. 9). Hartman calls upon modern Jewish teachers to master

---

2 In this sense, the series of already published and three forthcoming volumes on *The Jewish Political Tradition* mentioned in n. 1 above can hardly be seen as an accidental by-product of Hartman and his circle. Such works reflect the very essence of Hartman's concerns and these volumes will help committed Jewish intellectuals and others to mine the tradition for direction in the present political situation that confronts the State of Israel in particular and the Jewish people in general.

the texts written by these past savants. He also challenges contemporary students of the Law to have the courage to assert their own authority and display the confidence past generations of rabbis did when they applied such textual mastery in novel ways to meet the challenges of ever-changing situations. Hartman emphasizes the authenticity and creativity he believes inherent in this process:

> The Talmud contradicts the idea that "later" means "spiritually inferior" when it insists that the rabbinic sage is superior to the prophet. To accord the Talmud equal status with the Bible is to augment revelation not merely with a particular body of literature or school of teachers but with a method of interpretation that emphasizes the open-ended possibilities of learning from the received word. The covenant as reflected in the creative talmudic style of interpretation enables Jews to feel free to apply their own human reason to the understanding and application of the Torah (p. 9).

Maimonides, Hartman contends, properly understood all this, and Hartman asserts "that the covenant with the Jewish tradition was made for the sake of the oral tradition." The epistemological posture subsumed in this stance grants Hartman the license to maintain confidently that Judaism accords a rabbinic tradition of interpretation "the central place" in Judaism, and that such tradition is mediated through human understandings and discussions. On this basis, Hartman is able to state, "I philosophize within a tradition in which human teachers mediate my covenantal relationship with the God of Israel" (p. 10).

By making this declaration, Hartman reveals his preference for what he has long argued is a Maimonidean naturalistic approach to Jewish tradition, an approach that focuses upon the role that human agents play in establishing the parameters and demands of the covenant through the processes of rational legal interpretation. Some Orthodox colleagues have been sharply critical of what they regard as the anthropocentrism of this stance.[3] However, Hartman himself defends this

---

3 For example, see Daniel Landes, "A Vision of Finitude: David Hartman's 'A Living Covenant,'" *Tikkun* 1:2, pp. 106–11, for a representative Orthodox critique of this type.

position as true to the tradition and even contends that his own posture on this question is true to elements of the legacy that his teacher, Rabbi Joseph Soloveitchik, bequeathed him.[4]

Nevertheless, Hartman recognizes that this attitude stands in sharp contrast to another trajectory in Jewish tradition, one that Hartman identifies with the Bible and the teachings of Judah Halevi. Both the Bible and Halevi, as Hartman views them, eschew a focus on the legal tradition. Instead, they contend that an emphasis upon an unmediated sense of God's immediacy resides at the heart of Judaism. In reflecting his preference in *A Living Covenant* for the mediation present in rabbinic tradition, Hartman not only builds upon his previous work as expressed in books such as *Maimonides and the Philosophic Quest;* he also foreshadows a linchpin in the larger argument he will ultimately advance in both *A Heart of Many Rooms* and *Israelis and the Jewish Tradition.* There, as we shall see, Hartman will contrast the approaches Judah Halevi and Maimonides take to Jewish tradition, and he will advance his own arguments to explain why he prefers the posture of Maimonides to that of Halevi.

The identification of these two poles of Jewish tradition as represented by these two twelfth-century sages facilitates and supports Hartman's contention that Judaism is not monolithic. This polyvocality allows Hartman to acknowledge that his own approach to Jewish tradition, no less than theirs, is a conceptual one, and that Jewish intellectual-religious history provides a warrant that legitimates pluralism. Hartman is thus completely comfortable in candidly admitting that his own approach to Jewish tradition is selective. Indeed, he states that his rendering of the tradition is totally "related to my philosophical concern to locate specific tendencies or possibilities within the rabbinic tradition that could be supportive of a covenantal religious anthropology capable of participating in the challenge of modernity" (p. 13). He makes a persuasive case that Jewish tradition itself extends its blessing to this type of self-conscious and selective approach to Jewish law.

In arriving at this conclusion, Hartman underscores one of the major themes that, as we have already seen, have long characterized his work.

---

4 See Hartman's response to Daniel Landes in David Hartman and Daniel Landes, "Current Debate: Human Autonomy and Divine Providence," *Tikkun* 2:1, pp. 121–26.

For over thirty years, he has attempted to interpret and renew the Jewish legal tradition and to demonstrate its vitality in a modern setting, even though most Jews are so distant from this tradition that they no longer relate to its language nor find its holdings compelling. As a result, it is hardly surprising to find this theme articulated so intensely in the pages of *A Living Covenant*. Indeed, Hartman eloquently and passionately summarizes his position when he writes, "The living word of God can be mediated through the application of human reason . . . to the revealed norms of Torah. This is the essence of the dialectical vitality of talmudic Judaism" (p. 40). From narratives contained in the Talmud itself, Hartman finds support for this posture. He maintains that the tradition itself teaches that the rabbi "is competent to introduce new legislation defining how the community is to behave. . . . The intellectual mastery of the word of God . . . is all the scholar requires to understand and define how the community of Israel . . . [is] to behave" (p. 51).

For Hartman, halakhic interpretation is an act of creative decision, not simply an uncovering of what is already there, for the text is always open to a number of meanings. Hartman will develop this point at greater length in *A Heart of Many Rooms*. For now it is enough to note that this argument stands at the center of his concerns. He does not apologize for maintaining that rabbinic Judaism countenances the notion that an autonomous human moral sense can play a legitimate and seminal role in covenantal Judaism. This insight from the pen of an Orthodox rabbi constitutes a signal contribution to a philosophy of Jewish law as well as a significant gift to modern Jewish thought.

However, it is by wedding this concern to an emphasis upon the State of Israel as the major venue for the expression of this ethos that Hartman marks himself as unique among modern Jewish thinkers. By lavishing his attention on the State of Israel in *A Living Covenant*, Hartman developed a theme that was present but more muted in his earlier writings.[5] In linking his emphasis upon Jewish law to the theological significance of the Jewish State in his 1985 book, Hartman heralded a new emphasis in his thought. He contended that the State of

---

5   Moshe Sokol, "David Hartman," in Steven T. Katz, ed., *Interpreters of Judaism in the Late Twentieth Century* (Washington, D.C.: B'nai B'rith Books, 1993), pp. 91–112, has pointed this out in this fine essay.

Israel now constituted the necessary precondition for the full realization of the covenant: for the first time, Israeli Jews were fully responsible for the homes they would build and the institutions they would construct.

This focus on the connection between a covenantal life grounded in *Halakhah* and the primary import accorded the Jewish State as the major though hardly sole locus for its expression surely distinguished Hartman even at this juncture in his career from other Jewish thinkers with whom he was then identified.[6] While elements of his thought surely overlap with ideals put forth by prominent Jewish thinkers such as Eugene B. Borowitz and Irving Greenberg, the differences between Hartman and these thinkers were surely pronounced as well. His is not a theology that looks to the Holocaust for direction, like Greenberg, nor does he, like Borowitz, fail to accord preeminence to the richness of a living Jewish legal tradition or the centrality of an ever-responsive and evolving Jewish state. Indeed, his dual emphasis upon both a vital Jewish law and a vibrant Jewish state grant Hartman a unique position among the pantheon of contemporary Jewish thinkers. This singular posture has characterized Hartman since the publication of *A Living Covenant*, and an awareness of this position sensitizes his readers to the propositions he has developed in his two most recent books. Indeed, describing and analyzing how Hartman engages in developing these views in a passionate yet nuanced form will constitute the substance of the remainder of this essay.

A Heart of Many Rooms
Celebrating the Many Voices within Judaism

A Heart of Many Rooms is divided into four parts — "Family and Mitzvah within An Interpretive Tradition"; "Educating Toward Inclusiveness"; "Celebrating Religious Diversity"; and "Religious Perspectives On the Future of Israel." The book is divided into sixteen chapters and exhibits the lively and lucid writing style for which Hartman is known. More importantly, it indicates that Hartman continues to engage the themes that have animated a lifetime of concerns.

In his preface, Hartman celebrates the genuine pluralism he defines as an integral part of the Jewish legal system. He writes, "I cherish the

---

6 For such connections between Hartman and other prominent Jewish thinkers, see David Singer, "The New Orthodox Theology," *Modern Judaism* 9:1, pp. 35–54.

conviction that a committed halakhic Jew need not feel threatened by different halakhic understandings and interpretations of normative Judaism" (p. xiv). In adopting this stance, Hartman makes it clear that he stands in sharp contrast to a long line of Ashkenazic Orthodox thinkers such as Samson Raphael Hirsch and Moshe Feinstein and their absolutist postures concerning an unchanging Jewish law. After all, Hirsch, the nineteenth-century German rabbi, had stated in his classic *Horeb* that "the Law, both Written and Oral, was closed with Moses."[7] Feinstein, the famed twentieth-century Eastern European and American *posek*, in his *Iggerot Moshe*, had written, "The entire Torah, whether Written or Oral, was revealed by God Himself through Moses at Mount Sinai. It is impossible to change even a single jot, whether for purposes of stringency or leniency."[8] Such dogmatic visions of Jewish revelation and the halakhic process are completely alien to Hartman and his vision. Instead, he desires to align his own position on this question with the thought of men such as Rabbi Ḥayim David Halevi (1924–1998), former Chief Sephardic Rabbi of Tel Aviv. In his own responsa, the prolific Tel Aviv *ḥakham* had asserted, "Whoever thinks that the *Halakhah* is frozen, and that we may not deviate from it right or left, errs greatly. On the contrary, there is no flexibility like that of the *Halakhah*."[9] Hartman takes up and expands upon this theme at length with great passion and insight.

However, at this juncture, Hartman returns to the other great motif that informs his work — the importance that the State of Israel occupies in modern Jewish life and thought. In timbres reminiscent of *A Living Covenant*, he reminds the reader, "The rebirth of the Jewish people in its homeland challenges us to articulate a sober and responsible religious anthropology capable of energizing Jews to assume total responsibility for a total Jewish society" (p. xvii). Indeed, in this single sentence, he once again weds the chief foci of his work — a Jewish legal system that stands at the heart of covenantal Judaism and a love and concern for the Jewish people and the Jewish State.

In advancing this argument, Hartman accentuates his conviction that Judaism must be principally concerned with the present, and that it must resist an inappropriate addiction to a mythic past. He notes that

---

7 Samson Raphael Hirsch, *Horeb: A Philosophy of Jewish Laws and Observances*, trans. by Dayan Dr. I Grunfeld (London: Soncino, 1962), p. 20.

8 Moshe Feinstein, *Iggerot Moshe, Oraḥ Ḥayim* (Bnai Brak: 5741), 4:49.

9 Hayim David Halevi, *Aseh Lekha Rav* (Tel-Aviv: 5746), 7:54.

there are historical precedents for this position within the tradition. Rabbi Yoḥanan ben Zakkai and the Pharisees successfully and courageously confronted the challenge of a contemporaneous moment, and they forged Yavneh and made possible the survival of Judaism. However, Hartman contends, the first-century model they established can only be of limited utility to Jews today. Since these tannaitic masters could not fully tolerate the destruction of the present, they focused almost obsessively on a glorious national past, lamenting the destruction of the Temple and praying for its restoration.

For this reason, Hartman insists that ours is a different epoch. The Jewish people live and a Jewish state has been born. *Medinat Yisrael* means that a new memory must be forged. A healthy Judaism cannot emerge from an obsessive fixation upon martyrdom and persecution. Present-day Jews should not approach their tradition through a liturgical yearning for a past that speaks as if nothing had changed. The epiphany that led Hartman to this realization came in the summer of 1967. He relates a tale of his return to his Montreal synagogue shortly after the Six-Day War. During the observance of Tisha b'Av in his Diaspora *beit kenesset*, he was struck by the incongruity of Jews in the Diaspora mourning for the destruction of an ancient Jewish state while present-day Jews in Israel were rejoicing over the current reality of Jerusalem restored. The dissonance between the manifest content of his congregants' traditional lamentations and the existence of a modern Jewish state could not be ignored. As Hartman phrases it, "Mourning after the liberation of Jerusalem seemed to me to be like the case of a parent who continues praying for a child to get well even after the child's recovery because he or she fell in love with the prayer" (pp. xxii–xxiii).

Devising a language to articulate how past Jewish memory can be appropriately reconfigured in light of the events of history as well as the ongoing claims of authentic tradition has been the task Hartman has assigned himself as a Jewish theologian ever since. His courage in facing this challenge, as well as the solutions he has suggested as resolutions for this conundrum, have placed him at the center of Jewish religious and philosophical discourse. His statement of the quandary and his vital efforts to resolve it resonate in the minds and souls of countless modern Jews.

In his attempt to respond to the novel state of affairs in which contemporary Jewry finds itself, Hartman obviously does not reject the past. Elements of that past — particularly as expressed in the interpretive tradition of Jewish law — can and must guide present-day Jews if modern Judaism is to arrive at a legitimate mature identity. At the same time, Jews cannot submit themselves to the tyranny of a lachrymose memory of suffering. In an attempt to balance all these concerns, Hartman himself avers, "I live in Israel as a Jew in the spirit of the talmudic tradition who nevertheless is open to the events of history as potential organizing moments in mediating the living presence of God" (p. xxiv).

In order to comprehend what this means for his thought as a religious Jew committed both to Zion and *Halakhah* as the most enduring features of Jewish civilization, Hartman has to stipulate his own understandings of these notions. He therefore immediately indicates how his sense of Zionism is distinct from that of major schools of thought in Israeli society. He of course completely rejects the notion put forth by the *ḥaredi* community that the State of Israel constitutes "a spiritual danger." Nor does he find Rav Kook's ideal — that Israel represents the ongoing fulfillment of a messianic vision — an acceptable alternative. The dangers such a posture presents to reasoned political discourse are all too apparent in an epoch where this ideology has spawned a dogmatically explosive settlers' movement and Gush Emunim. Finally, Hartman cannot celebrate the "normalization" that secular Israelis strive for (pp. xxv–xxvi). The threat this approach poses to authentic Jewish continuity is a theme Hartman will address at length in *Israelis and the Jewish Tradition*. The preferred course is a balanced one that "attempts to be in history and to accept the responsibility for building a total society, while retaining the sobriety of certain features of the talmudic sensibility" (p. xxvi).

> My picture of a genuinely religious person is . . . one who does not await divine intervention but who experiences God's presence in efforts to discharge the responsibilities he or she feels for the welfare of a total society. . . . We allow the rhythms of modern history to enter into our normative relationship with God (p. xxvii).

Such a relationship has the virtue of conferring religious significance upon the Jewish state within the framework of covenantal Judaism. However, the type of religious Zionism that Hartman advocates does more than reject the quietism of *ḥaredi* Judaism; it refuses to affirm the fanaticism implicit in a messianic Zionism as well. Hartman demands that Jews rejoice in the "public domain" that Israel embodies, and that Israeli and Diaspora Jews acknowledge that the "responsibility" such a domain entails comprises a blessing for the Jewish people. As he writes, "Israel offers Jews an unprecedented opportunity to regenerate the primary roots of Judaism. As a traditional Jew I am grateful to Zionism and to Israel for renewing the significance of the beginning, not necessarily for bringing about the end" (p. xxviii).

In his attempt to maintain this stance, Hartman must of course offer a compelling description of *Halakhah* and the halakhic process in order to indicate how this task of regeneration can be achieved in an authentic Jewish religious manner in the modern situation. As is his wont, he does not shrink from a candid recognition of how immense this challenge is. After all, "Today the daily life of most Jews is not organized by the principles of *Halakhah*" (p. xxix), nor do most Jews feel bound by the *praxis Halakhah* mandates. The task remains one of making the Jewish ethos as it is embedded in the Talmud "a living . . . compelling option" (p. xxxiii).

Hartman is confident this challenge can be met, for he believes that "the practices and conceptual frameworks of *Halakhah*" can be presented as a system that can positively "influence a person's character and perspective on life" (p. xxx). This is because rabbinic Judaism "takes into account the lived reality of a people when formulating norms and directives" (p. xxx), and thus asserts that "love for God must lead to a love for real people" (p. xxxi). Jewish law holds that "fragile human beings are deemed capable of becoming responsible and mature" (p. xxxii).

It is here with these thoughts and sentiments that the ethos of Zionism and the spirit of rabbinic Judaism converge in the Hartmanian system, and an explication of how and why these two parts of Jewish tradition must be joined becomes the overwhelming focus of his efforts. Hartman recognizes that such exposition is crucial for defining the course of Judaism must take in the present as well as for mapping out the directions the Jewish people and Jewish religion ought to follow in the future. In this sense, *A Heart of Many Rooms* takes up the tasks and themes Hartman has outlined in previous works, but addresses them here with an unprecedented intensity and sophistication.

Hartman approaches this assignment he has set for himself in *A Heart of Many Rooms* by turning initially to a description and analysis of the rabbinic tradition. He is, of course, aware that his critics can argue that there are significant differences between the secular outlook that informs the ethos of classical political Zionism and the religious spirit that marks the posture of rabbinic tradition. After all, the Jewish legal system can surely be portrayed as championing a heteronomous ethic of submission to God rather than an autonomous ethic of responsibility that is required for the governance of a modern nation. Indeed, Hartman freely admits that this can be the case, and he must respond to the challenge this poses if he is to maintain his stance concerning the affinity between the ethos of the Jewish state and the ethic of rabbinic tradition. If he does not produce a portrait of rabbinic tradition that is both meaningful for modern Jews and compatible with an ethic of accountability that is necessary for the administration of modern Israel, then his entire overarching project fails. This is why his essay on "Judaism as an Interpretive Tradition" is both the most crucial as well as most seminal chapter in *A Heart of Many Rooms*. The entire Hartman project depends upon his ability to draw a convincing portrait of the rabbinic tradition of interpretation as one that embodies a teaching of human responsibility sufficiently strong and lithe to meet the rigors and strains imposed by the need to direct a modern nation-state.

Hartman meets this challenge by turning to the figure of Abraham. He observes that "the biblical narrative of Abraham is . . . a source for two different organizing images of God" (p. 12). One is the Abraham of the *akedah*, a figure who submits to God even when God commands the death of his son Isaac. His own teacher, Rabbi Joseph Soloveitchik, as well as his dialogical partner, Yeshayahu Leibowitz, insist that this Abraham is the "dominant paradigm of religious life and thought" for the religiously faithful Jew. As Hartman puts it:

> For them, the survival and continuity of the tradition require the unconditional surrender and loyalty that the *akedah* represents.

> To be claimed by God, I must be willing to sacrifice my intellect
> and intuition, to give up everything I know and cherish as a human
> being, in deference and obedience to the word of God (p. 14).

Hartman has already argued at length that Judaism is characterized by
a multiplicity of viewpoints. He therefore betrays no hesitancy when he
declares that there is another vision of Abraham contained in the Torah. This is the Abraham who boldly protests "the divine decision to destroy the city of Sodom" — and Hartman prefers this Abraham as the
exemplar for the modern Jew. This Abraham, no less than the "*akedah*
Abraham," is a "deeply religious and ethical personality." He embodies an
"integrity and consistency" that "is actually necessary for recognizing the
validity and applicability of the divine command" (pp. 12–14). Hartman
has no doubt that the patriarch who has the courage to confront God
on the basis of his own moral scruples is a more appropriate model for
the contemporary Jew than the patriarch who is prepared to murder
his own child at the behest of a commanding God. Indeed, Hartman
believes that the Jewish interpretive tradition can be a meaningful one
deserving of application in the modern setting only if it is approached
in the spirit of a devoutly religious Abraham who recognizes that the
God of the covenant has endowed the human interpreter with moral
integrity. In stating this preference, Hartman moves beyond Soloveitchik and Leibowitz and has the boldness to reject their opinions secure in his knowledge that this Abraham is fully embraced by Jewish
religious tradition.

By opting for this Abraham as his exemplar, Hartman is able to construct an important foundation for his general theological project. He
demonstrates that Jewish religious tradition can be regarded as empow-
ering its adherents, and that Judaism grants Jews authority through the
aegis of its legal system. The Jew who understands this, no less than
the Abraham who confronted God when Sodom was to be destroyed,
is "a deeply religious and ethical personality." His words "are not those
of a Promethean challenger to God but of a lover to God, a humble and
reverent religious personality with a strong sense of moral autonomy."
The God who established the covenant with Israel "invites independent
moral judgment" and is not beyond "moral argument and persuasion"
(p. 14). From this perspective, "moral autonomy is not an expression

of hubris," but a divinely sanctioned prerequisite for the application of "religious consciousness" (p. 13).

As we noted in chapter nineteen, since Hartman contends that the tradition itself affirms that God grants this warrant of autonomy to the human reader of Jewish sacred texts, it follows that the subjectivity inherent in the human condition guarantees that the texts themselves always remain open to a number of meanings. A phenomenological analysis of Jewish law indicates that pluralism is not an accidental by-product of the system. For, as Hartman states, in Judaism "revelation is not always 'pure and simple,' but may be rough and complex." He continues, "The religious personality this system tries to produce is able to interpret situations in multiple ways" and "offers cogent arguments for opposite positions and points of view" (p. 22). In the language of Edmund Husserl, it can thus be said that for Hartman there is an "endless horizon" of halakhic possibility when committed students labor over the writings of Jewish tradition. In a crucial paragraph in a later essay in *A Heart of Many Rooms*, Hartman provides a classical description that summarizes his views on the topic of Jewish legal adjudication, and characterizes the halakhic process and the factors that shape and inform those who frame its decisions. He writes:

> A serious study of the epistemology of halakhic argumentation may help the student realize that halakhic reasons never provide the cognitive certainty of a deductive syllogism. Legal decisions are not necessarily inferences drawn from true premises. In other words, decision-making in a legal system is not a mechanical process. The relative weights granted to principles and values and the appreciation of the particularity of different situations and historical contexts, all participate in halakhic decision-making (p. 99).

As a result, Hartman is proud to proclaim that "ambiguity and controversy" have always characterized the rabbinic interpretive tradition. Indeed, he states that "rabbinic Judaism can best be described as a bold interpretive culture amidst disagreement" (p. 5).[10]

10 Hartman has made and demonstrated this point often in his scholarship. In *A Living Covenant* (p. 8), Hartman writes, "A careful study of rabbinic interpretations

Hartman argues that such a claim concerning Jewish religious culture does not "undermine divine authority." On the contrary, this portrait reinforces that authority for it reveals the nature of the covenantal partnership that obtains between God and humanity. Hartman selects the words of *Sotah* 7:12, where it states, "Make yourself a heart of many rooms and bring into it the words of the house of Shammai *and* the House of Hillel, . . ." for the title of his book because it provides the warrant that legitimates his conviction that rabbinic Judaism is marked by a religious ethos of pluralism. He argues that God calls upon each Jew in light of his / her existential situation to confront the tradition in ongoing ways and to struggle with others through the application of reason and conscience to uncover divine teachings and truths. As a result, Judaism demands that humans respect truths that are expressed by others. A committed Jew, Hartman writes, can and must "live with ambiguity," for one can never "eliminate the rich variety of opinions or diminish the creativity of the moral imagination that is able to make sense of alternative positions" (pp. 21–22).

On the other hand, Hartman does not surrender to a relaxed pluralism that knows no boundaries. He asserts that there are established procedures that do impose certain constraints upon Jewish legal adjudication. Jewish law demands the construction of "a framework of rational moral argumentation," and reasons must be put forth and texts cited. While such a system may be "without absolutes," it is surely "not equivalent to relativism." As Hartman states, "Not every point of view is equally legitimate simply because it is someone's point of view. A point of view must always be subject to and vulnerable to counterargument and evaluation" (p. 35). Such a description acknowledges that a juridical decision and the process of legal argumentation that justifies it are always marked by a high degree of fluidity and subjectivity. It is a process where the decisor has the right — indeed the duty — "to bring broader social and moral considerations to bear on the issue at hand" (p. 16). The ideal of covenant that underscores this process constitutes

---

and responsa would reveal that it is a near-impossible task to define the limits of interpretative freedom found in the tradition." As the historian Jacob Katz once remarked to me, the limits are simply what the community is in fact prepared to accept as Torah."

the most defining element in the Jewish religion. It is an ideal that "reflects the divine decision to share responsibility for history with human beings" (p. 30), and it calls upon contemporary Jews not to shirk their obligations as "an *interpretive community.*" Jews are called by God to serve as "shapers of revelation" (pp. 32–33).

In issuing this call, Hartman does not betray Jewish tradition. Instead, he fulfills its deepest and most abiding impulse, one that calls upon Jews to combine a "loyalty to the tradition . . . with a corrective process of reinterpretation" (p. 34). Jews should recognize that the Jewish legal spirit is one that asserts "love can grow out of partial understanding," as well as "an appreciation of the knowledge that our convictions and beliefs are inherently limited and incomplete" (p. 35). Hartman therefore concludes that diversity is an enduring characteristic of the Jewish legal process. The arguably unprecedented uncertainties of the modern world should not prevent Jews "from renewing the vital interpretive processes that define" the Jewish "religious heritage" (p. 36). The interpreter of the Law must reinterpret and renew that Law in view of the conditions of the day. If the interpreter of Jewish law is not bold enough to do this, then Jewish law will fail to express a vital religiosity. *Halakhah* will retreat into a sterile legalism or focus only upon an empty ritualism that recoils from the demands of life.

By taking this stance, Hartman calls upon Jews to meet the challenge of the present. In so doing, he interestingly echoes elements of a position Martin Buber adopted at the turn of the century when the famed philosopher of dialogue called for the renewal of the Jewish spirit in a trope that parallels the call for Jewish religious and national renewal that Hartman issues today. Indeed, a glance at select passages in Buber's writings highlights the thrust of Hartman's project and places its distinctiveness in sharp relief; Hartman is disturbed by those who today would straitjacket Jewish law and deny its vitality, just as Buber was troubled by what he regarded as the barrenness that dominated the Jewish landscape during the early decades of the 1900s. In his famous essay on "Jewish Religiosity," Buber called upon Jews to engage in a revitalization of the Jewish spirit, for he believed that Jews could once more recapture and display a sense of genuine "religiosity" that lay at the heart of Judaism. Inherent in this Judaism was the "human urge to establish a living communion with the unconditioned." For Buber, such an urge could only authentically be realized by "deed." The Jewish religion requires "a leap of action." As Buber phrased it:

> Genuine religiosity has nothing in common with the fancies of romantic hearts, or with the self-pleasure of aestheticizing souls, or with the clever mental exercises of a practiced intellectuality. Genuine religiosity is *doing*.[11]

However, for Buber, *Halakhah* had no role to play in acquiring this active Jewish religious impulse.

> Ever since the destruction of the Temple, tradition has been at the center of Judaism's religious life. A fence was thrown around the law in order to keep at a distance everything alien or dangerous; but very often it kept at a distance living religiosity as well. . . . When . . . religion keeps men tied to an immutable law and damns their demand for freedom; when, instead of viewing its forms as an obligation upon whose foundation genuine freedom can build, it views them as an obligation to exclude all freedom; when, instead of keeping its elemental sweep inviolate, it transforms the law into a heap of petty formulas and allows man's decision for right or wrong action to degenerate into hairsplitting casuistry — then religion no longer shapes but enslaves religiosity.[12]

Such a description of Jewish law and the process that marks it is a caricature of the interpretive tradition Hartman describes. Indeed, Buber's portrayal of *Halakhah* reflects an assessment of the Jewish legal tradition that Hartman the constructive theologian inveighs against in his own analysis of the procedures and spirit that often have and always ought to mark the Jewish legal system. However, this dissimilarity in their approaches to Jewish law should not obscure a fundamental harmony in the thought of the two religious philosophers, both of whom emphasize that the renewal of Judaism in the modern world is dependent upon the adoption of a genuine Jewish religiosity that is open and responsive to the current moment. One must prove one's convictions

11 Martin Buber, *On Judaism* (New York: Schocken Books, 1967), p. 93.
12 Ibid. pp. 91–92.

in daily deeds, and not in theoretical pronouncements. As Hartman states towards the end of *A Heart of Many Rooms*, "We understand ourselves through our doing" (p. 262).

However, Hartman and Buber obviously do depart from one another over the issue of law. Indeed, this is why the proposed linkage between the two thinkers seems so incongruous on one level. As we have seen in his antinomian tirade, Buber decries Jewish law as barren. As he sees it, law is antithetical to the spirit of immediacy and openness required by genuine religiosity. From a Buberian perspective, the law shackles the creative spirit of spontaneity that defines true religiosity.

Hartman dissents strongly from this stance. No less than his own teacher Joseph Soloveitchik did in his book *Halakhic Man*, he proclaims that authentic Judaism has at its core a halakhic tradition that he has demonstrated is infused with an authentic and active religious ethic, one that demands mature responsibility from those who would be its adherents. The task that confronts the contemporary interpreter of the tradition is to mine the *Halakhah* so that the values and spirit of immediacy and human accountability that mark the Jewish legal tradition will be made manifest in the world. Hartman therefore states that ultimately what Jews "need to learn from the past is not so much how previous generations solved particular problems, or the particular forms of their halakhic frameworks, but rather the underlying spirit and teleology that infuses *Halakhah*" (pp. 242–43).

It is precisely for this reason that the State of Israel assumes such paramount importance in Hartman's thought. Only *Medinat Yisrael* offers a holistic venue where the interpretive culture of religious Judaism can find full and mature expression. Israel becomes the ultimate testing ground for the power and flexibility of the Jewish interpretive tradition that Hartman has so eloquently outlined, for only in Israel do Jews possess a political sovereignty that entails full accountability. Hartman therefore unflinchingly proclaims, "True spirituality must be related to national-political frameworks" (p. 232).

The rebirth of Jewish political sovereignty provides an opportunity to demonstrate that "a sense of covenantal holiness" can be actualized as a "total way of life" for "a politically independent nation" (pp. 244–45). A Jewish national spiritual and moral renaissance must accompany and ought to guide the revival of Jewish political rule. However, such spiritual and moral regeneration can occur only if the Jewish people display the courage to emphasize the renewal of the innovative and ethically creative spirit in the *Halakhah*. This requires, as Hartman phrases it, the daring "to be bold in our halakhic decisions." As the Jewish people have properly decided "to accept political independence," their teachers must not evade "the bold halakhic changes such a decision properly" entails (pp. 274–77).

In concluding *A Heart of Many Rooms*, Hartman therefore asserts that Israel challenges Jews to be mindful that Judaism is "shaped by what we do in the present. What we do as a community defines who we are. Neither memory nor prayerful hope counts, only present action" (p. 296). The State of Israel is not simply an addendum in the Hartman system. In the Jewish theology that Hartman has created, Israel becomes the logical lodestar that complements and completes his portrait of Judaism as an interpretive tradition. How he grants full and mature expression to this position becomes the subject of *Israelis and the Jewish Tradition*, where he articulates this stance within the context of a holistic Jewish theology.

Israelis and the Jewish Tradition
The Culmination of a Modern Jewish Theology

Israelis and the Jewish Tradition represents a climactic crossroads where the intellectual-religious concerns that have occupied Hartman for a lifetime come together. This book is a natural outcome of a philosophical trajectory that was first established with the publication of his *Maimonides and the Philosophic Quest* as well as *Joy and Responsibility*. In *Israelis and the Jewish Tradition*, Hartman brings together the concerns of a career. He not only reflects upon the meaning the State of Israel holds for modern Jews, but explains why the ever-developing Jewish character of the state is of the utmost theological importance for the future of both Judaism and the Jewish people. *Israelis and the Jewish Tradition* is of vital significance because it does not confine itself to abstract speculation and theory. As in all his work, Hartman addresses and seeks to guide the course of modern Jewish existence. This book is a work of applied theology.

While *Israelis and the Jewish Tradition* bears the impress of the concerns and directions of a career, Hartman concentrates here, with exceptional intellectual intensity and passion, upon Israel and its meaning The title of his first chapter, "Crisis and Tradition," recounts a familiar motif in modern Jewish thought and history — and Hartman himself has addressed this theme on many occasions. However, here that crisis is not explicated in a manner that commonly marks discussions of this type. Hartman does not center his concerns on the predicament that European Enlightenment and Emancipation presented to the continuity of Occidental Jewish life and thought. Instead, this crisis is set against the backdrop of variegated Zionist responses that led to the creation of the State of Israel as a proposed comprehensive solution to this crisis.

Hartman points out that both secular and religious Zionism turned to the Bible for inspiration and guidance in the establishment of a present-day Jewish commonwealth. For the secular Zionists, the Bible presented a vision rooted in the *urtext* of Judaism that could inspire and legitimate a modern Jewish revolution against two thousand years of perceived Jewish political passivity that consigned the Jewish people to exile. This school of Zionist thought mined the Bible for heroic models of political activism and sovereignty that would provide for a radically new anthropology of the Jew while still anchoring that Jew in a non-theistic narrative of Jewish history. For the religious Zionists, the immediacy of God in the Bible captured their yearning for the presence of God in history and served as the *locus classicus* for their ascribing religious significance to the Jewish national renaissance. For these Jews, the rebirth of the Jewish state constituted a new chapter in an ongoing biblical drama of messianic redemption.

Hartman points out that these two forms of Zionism do more than possess a shared disdain for an ultra-Orthodox Judaism that ascribes no worth to the Zionist enterprise. More importantly, each eschews an emphasis upon rabbinic culture. Indeed, this observation provides a decisive insight that will connect *Israelis and the Jewish Tradition* to the total literary corpus that Hartman has produced as well as provide the framework for the argument that Hartman will construct in this book. He notes that secular Zionism condemns rabbinic Judaism because the rabbinic tradition is seen as politically quiescent. Its culture of disembodied intellectualism as well as its perceived ethic of overdependence upon God promoted an ethos of political complacency that is regarded as antithetical to the modernist recognition that Israel must become responsible for its own destiny. On the other hand, the certainty and zeal of religious Zionism has unambiguously affirmed that God has been an active presence in modern Jewish history. This position thus reviles an interpretive rabbinic culture that has been much more hesitant to define how God manifests such presence in the events of history. Religious Zionism has had little use for the spirit of judicious consideration as well as human judgment and mediation that characterize the rabbinic ethos.

Hartman argues that this disengagement from the interpretive tradition of rabbinic culture on the part of these two Zionist camps has been unfortunate for two principal reasons. He correctly observes that the secular Zionists — by arguing that the primacy of the nation is a sufficient end in itself — have been unable to provide adequate secular grounds for sustaining Jewish character in a meaningful way. One cannot truncate two thousand years of memory and construct a mature modern Jewish identity. On the other hand, by opting for the immediacy of a biblical consciousness, the religious Zionists have created a messianic Zionism so single-minded and fanatical that it is unresponsive to the actual tasks required of a government in a real world where *realpolitik* demands reasoned and subtle judgment. Hartman's book is a crucial attempt to explain how rabbinic Judaism and the interpretive culture that informs it can ultimately produce a meaningful sense of Zionist identity — one that allows for a mature Jewish character that draws fully upon historical roots while rejecting the fanaticism inherent in a messianic religious Zionism. *Israelis and the Jewish Tradition* attempts to navigate a positive middle course between these two extremes. It displays fidelity to the categories and languages provided by a covenantal religious tradition while guiding the Jewish community towards full participation in a modern future.

In order to root this discussion more deeply in the soil of Jewish tradition, Hartman returns to themes he has addressed in previous works and reformulates them in light of his concerns in this book. He therefore revisits the medieval Jewish philosophical tradition, and devotes the next two chapters to an explication of the thought of Judah Halevi and Moses Maimonides. In so doing, he commits the richness of his knowledge to the enterprise addressed in this book and indicates how the ethos that marks the writings of these medieval savants is of contemporary import for the modern Jewish state.

At the outset of the second chapter, Hartman acknowledges that Halevi and Maimonides had a great deal in common. Both were totally committed to halakhic practice and to the talmudic tradition that explicated and legislated that practice, as well as to the notion that God had revealed the Torah. However, these shared commitments should not obscure the fact that "their understandings of Jewish spirituality as mediated and structured by *Halakhah* were very different" (p. 26). He entitles this chapter "The God of History in Yehudah Halevi" and aptly observes that Halevi believed that God established a singular ontological status for the Jewish people. The ultimate redemptive moment for all humanity, inherent in the act of creation itself, will unfold only when the people Israel fulfills its divinely appointed destiny by returning to *Eretz Yisrael* and living their national life in accord with the commandments God revealed to Moses at Sinai. Divine reality becomes accessible for all humanity only through the history of Israel.

Hartman convincingly demonstrates that for contemporary Judaism the most extraordinary element of the argument that the *Kuzari* advances is not that of a chosen people. Rather, the key implications of Halevi's thought for modern Zionism are twofold. As mentioned above, the first is the metaphysical linkage the Spanish Jewish thinker made between the people Israel and *Eretz Yisrael*. However, the second point is of even greater import for the position that Hartman is constructing: Halevi, as Hartman presents him, also maintained that "communion with God cannot be achieved through human reasoning" (p. 39). Israel has been blessed by God with a "unique religious capacity." However, Halevi argues that this capacity "cannot be nurtured by the intellect but only by following the way of life prescribed by revelation" (p. 40). The "essence of revelation" for Halevi is not the social and ethical laws that are accessible to all humankind through reason, but the ceremonial practices and rituals "that are binding only because they were given by God" (p. 41). Meticulous observance of each detail surrounding all of these commandments is required of every Jew, and no person should attempt to approach God through an application of human wisdom independent of a revelation that provides absolute access to communion with God.

Hartman offers a succinct summary of these two parts of the Halevi position when he writes, "The people Israel in the Land of Israel alone are capable of achieving prophecy. Without the revelatory grace of God and the trustworthiness of the transmitters of God's revelation one cannot approach and understand the God of Israel" (p. 49). Nor does Hartman shrink from what such a posture entails for present-day Jewish proponents of this view, and he concludes his chapter on a sobering note when he states:

> Those who live by and practice Judaism in the spirit of Yehudah Halevi find security and comfort in believing that they alone possess the one true way to worship God. They can allow themselves the luxury of observing the *mitzvot* with complacency because of their certainty that their way of worship is pleasing to God. Those who must rely on human rational arguments to order their religious lives are exposed to uncertainty, doubt, and confusion. (pp. 50–51).

This observation provides a perfect segue for Hartman to turn to a consideration of Maimonides, for Hartman now presents a Maimonidean attitude towards Judaism and revelation that is diametrically opposed to that advanced by Halevi. Maimonides believed that the notion of "irrational divine legislation" was "absurd," and he affirmed that all God's laws had to be "comprehended in terms of what human beings would consider rational and useful" (pp. 56–57). Divine revelation and election are, for Maimonides, not "incompatible with universality and intelligibility." On the contrary, they are the sources of "a cultural imperative to translate particularity into universally intelligible terms" (p. 58). Maimonides advances a posture that asserts that Judaism recognizes an ethical framework independent of revelation, as well as a foundation that allows for human understanding to animate and determine normative conduct.

Hartman argues that Maimonides looks to the figure of Abraham as a warrant for this position. In contrast to Moses, who spoke "in the language of legislative authority," the biblical patriarch established "a community based on a shared intellectual understanding of God achieved through the persuasive power of rational argument" (p. 68). Maimonides thereby makes Judaism available to all, for he views Jewish religious existence and doctrine within the naturalistic categories of history and reason and not as manifestations of inexorable cosmic processes implanted by God at the moment of creation. This means that Maimonides believes that "God becomes accessible to humanity... through observation and rational speculation" (p. 95). This view maintains that insecurity and perplexity are necessary concomitants of religious faith, and "that we can move from a naïve to a mature love of God and the Torah only through struggle with religious uncertainty and confusion" (p. 86).

Hartman believes that this Maimonidean position is supported by the rabbinic tradition of interpretation itself, and that this tradition is one that Jews have always regarded as "a much greater determinant of their religious consciousness than the Bible" (p. 95). The Talmud contains a rational religious sensibility that affirms that "God allows the natural world to pursue orderly patterns," and that God "does not interfere and disrupt the inherent patterns of nature" (p. 100). This naturalistic *tendenz* allowed rabbinic Judaism to put forth the notion that the Torah, "as the word of God, became a substitute for events as carriers of the living God." This represented a crucial shift in Jewish religious tradition, for Judaism was no longer "an event-based" but rather "a text-centered theology" (p. 104). As a result, an interpretive tradition of legal hermeneutics came to be the preeminent characteristic of Jewish religious civilization. In the rabbinic tradition, the paramount belief became the idea that God was "revealed through the empowerment of human beings to uncover and expand the meaning of Torah through rational reflection and legal argumentation" (p. 110). Authority was vested in the rabbis by virtue of their "intellectual competence to reason and argue cogently about the law" (p. 112). Israel was perceived as enjoying a covenantal partnership with God, and this created a religious paradigm that taught that God granted persons "dignity, freedom, and control" (p. 114). As a result, Hartman maintains that halakhic Judaism puts forth values that are congruent with the "ethic of responsibility" that Zionism has championed. As Hartman phrases it, "In the Talmud, as Maimonides understood it, divine revelation is collapsed into the strictures and categories of human reasoning and analysis" (p. 121).

Having drawn these portraits of both Maimonides and Halevi, Hartman concludes in characteristic pluralistic fashion that both approaches represent significant strands in the tradition. However, he does not hesitate to assert, "I am drawn to the intellectual sobriety of

Maimonides and of the talmudic tradition as ways of moderating the event-driven passions of traumatic historical events" (p. 125). Hartman does not believe that Jewish "religious passion must be fueled by the nonrational, numinous features of Judaism" (p. 126), for a notion of a revealed law mediated through human understanding and reason can better serve "a social and political function in building a healthy Jewish community" (p. 129).

The halakhic tradition does not allow for a simple-minded application of rules or an overly zealous single-minded understanding of historical events to reveal how it is that God is present in history. Life is always too complex for that, and events as well as texts can and should always be understood in diverse ways. In demanding clear-headedness, pluralism, salience, and open-mindedness, the covenantal system affirms "the fullness of the human person" (p. 141). As Hartman sees it, *Halakhah* demands that people neither "repress their intellectual curiosity" nor suppress their "sense of honesty" (p. 142).

With a self-confidence that typifies his thought, Hartman declares that "the scope" of the "ethical and legal implications" inherent in the tradition are "not restricted to how" they were "used in the past." The authors of the tradition do not "have control over the implications or applications of their rich and suggestive teachings" (p. 143), and Hartman asserts his own right to draw out what these "implications or applications" might mean for Jews today. Inasmuch as he wishes to focus on the "religious and moral vitality of our own society," (p. 145) Hartman applauds the Jewish legal tradition for redirecting "religious passion from the external arena of history to the internal domain of character, and individual and communal behavior" (p. 146). In a clarion call that summarizes the focus of his thought and efforts, Hartman reiterates an oft-cited challenge once again. He asserts, "Through the establishment of the State of Israel, we are called upon to demonstrate the moral and spiritual power of the Torah to respond to the challenges of daily life" (p. 147). Hartman remains convinced that Israeli society will not shrink from this challenge, and he is certain that the rabbinic tradition of interpretation he has described is sufficiently supple to direct Jews in the modern situation no less than it has guided generations past.

For these reasons, Hartman condemns a deracinated secular Zionism, one that seeks to excise almost two millennia of Jewish history in the

Diaspora while simultaneously ignoring or consigning the religious dimensions of Judaism to oblivion. Instead, he maintains that the State of Israel has a duty to serve as a conduit for Jews' "sense of memory and connection to Jewish history." There are "strong national and communal notions that underlie the Jewish heritage," and the state must meet the "needs of the present" while "carrying the weight of the past" (p. 151). Jews might otherwise lose "their covenantal identity by becoming a secular people with no more than a shallow attachment to Torah and to the tradition of a Torah, text-centered community" (p. 155). Should that be the case, "the disappearance of the Jewish people as traditionally understood is possible" (p. 156). Hartman here gives voice to countless numbers of Jews, for whom such an outcome would surely be tragic. Indeed, he speaks here for many Jews who are unprepared to jettison their attachments to Jewish tradition.

Hartman has always confronted modernity and its challenges with the utmost seriousness, and here he tackles the trials it imposes with characteristic straightforwardness and intellectual honesty. He realizes that the concept that a community can set standards, adopt values, and become authoritative in the life of human beings is not obvious in our culture. Yet, he also recognizes that culture and identity fall apart without such standards and values. Jews, no less than others, are in vital need of community. At the same time, no less than others, they experience more intense degrees of alienation from their heritage today than ever before. The need has therefore never been greater "to interpret Judaism in a way that would empower Israelis and Jews throughout the world to reengage with their tradition" (p. 158). Indeed, Hartman remains confident that this task can be accomplished despite such unprecedented and ever growing alienation, for there is a talmudic "tradition waiting to be addressed and waiting to speak to us. The question is how to speak and listen to that tradition. . . . The crucial issue of our age is how . . . to revive the Jewish discussion" in a moral and spiritual direction that is authentic and compelling. Only if this is done will "the vitality of Jewish peoplehood and historical memory" be restored in a manner that will cause "Israelis and Jews throughout the world to engage with their tradition" (pp. 158–59).

That revival can be done only if Jews "feel intellectually empowered to participate in Judaism's ongoing interpretive tradition." Jews must be taught "a new orientation to the classical texts of our tradition and to the meaning of participation in an interpretive community." The leaders of the community must comprehend that "presenting Judaism as a closed system with a fixed menu prepared exactly according to divine requirements can stifle and inhibit genuine engagement with the tradition" (pp. 160–61). Such an approach does nothing more than confirm the indictment Buber hurled against the tradition a century earlier and consign it to a dustbin of irrelevance. Here, as elsewhere in his work, Hartman has attempted to show that the Jewish interpretive tradition is a vital one, congenial with the modernist notion of a rich multidimensional interpretive culture. The Torah allows for differing religious sensibilities. "The directions and paths a Torah discussion can take" are enormous, and the "traditional texts" themselves "can make room for new possibilities" (p. 162).

In what must be regarded as a radical but coherent conclusion to the argument he has put forth in *Israelis and Jewish Tradition*, Hartman offers a truly democratic and appealing vision of the *Halakhah*. The interpretive tradition of Jewish law ought to be explored in diverse ways that "suggest rather than dictate the forms of Jewish spiritual living. *Halakhah* would thus be understood as a more inviting and flexible mode of discourse" (p. 164). If such "a compelling intellectual and moral vision of what it means to be a text-centered community" can be achieved, then Jewish tradition can serve in the future as it has in the past "as the natural context in which" Jews would "express their concerns" (p. 165).

Concluding Reflections

In both *A Heart of Many Rooms* and *Israelis and the Jewish Tradition*, David Hartman provides an existential and phenomenological description of the meaning structures contained in a *Halakhah* that he demonstrates is responsive to the ever-protean vicissitudes and demands of life. He makes rabbinic Judaism an ally of a modern Zionist ethos that highlights human dignity and responsibility, and in so doing, conjoins the seemingly divergent sensibilities that inform the realm of traditional Jewish law on the one hand, and the life and death demands of governance imposed upon a contemporary Jewish state on the other. In this sense, Hartman rehabilitates the spirit of traditional Judaism for a modern-day, western Jewish audience, and indicates that the interpretive tradition of Judaism possesses the capacity to address present-day human and political concerns in a compelling and authentic Jewish manner.

Hartman understands that no worthwhile spiritual legacy can be mechanistically transmitted from one generation to another. Each generation of Jews has the freedom as well as the obligation to appropriate and employ an inherited Jewish tradition in accord with its own capacities and comprehensions — which can only be done when each current generation recognizes that any attempt to evade responsibility and fit history into a fixed pattern constitutes a delusion. People do not receive community as if by fate. Instead, Judaism impresses upon *am yisroel* that the notion of covenant provides for an interpretive tradition that asserts that God empowers the Jewish people to forge such community in freedom.

Hartman accepts this awesome and in our day unprecedented opportunity in joy and responsibility. He does all this in an unapologetic way, and his unqualified love for and devotion to the people, land, nation, and religion that constitute the vital components of an authentic Jewish life are palpable and absolute. He never wavers from these commitments, and his passion and his thought ignite the pages of his writings. His struggles and his wrestlings provoke and move the hearts of his readers. His genius displays the humanism — the *vox humana* — inherent in a primordial tradition of Jewish interpretation. For Jews who are unprepared to abandon either their humanistic proclivities or Jewish attachments, *A Heart of Many Rooms* and *Israelis and the Jewish Tradition* are unique gifts of sense and sensibility that can and must be applied to the predicaments that mark the modern Jewish condition. They are sources of reflection and inspiration, and they combine to provide an articulate and compelling description and program that are worthy of reawakening and redirecting an ancient faith.

23

Marcia Falk's *The Book of Blessings*
The Issue is Theological

Poet and translator Marcia Falk has long been known for her English renderings of Hebrew poetry and prayer. The publication of her new prayer book, *The Book of Blessings: New Jewish Prayers for Daily Life, the Sabbath, and the New Moon Festival* (1996), has elicited both praise and criticism, and above all, careful attention on the part of many commentators.

Simone Lotven Sofian's review in the *CCAR Journal*, "Pushing the Envelope: Reflections on *The Book of Blessings* by Marcia Falk,"[1] focuses on the issue of gender in an appreciative, yet critical review essay. Her detailed, knowledgeable, as well as passionate appraisal of the Falk liturgy taught me a great deal, and it caused me to reflect more deeply on the issues that Marcia Falk raises in her prayer book compositions. For this, I am in her debt. However, I find that my own assessment of *The Book of Blessings* is distinct from that of Sofian. In this response to her review, I will indicate why I feel the basic thrust of her remarks on Falk's approach to gender are misdirected, and I will explain why I think the theological posture that informs and directs Falk's work must stand at the center of any discussion of her liturgy. In the course of this discussion, I will also offer a few judgments of my own on the nature of *The Book of Blessings*.

At the very outset of her article, Sofian reveals her chief concerns about the volume. In speaking of how Falk names God, Sofian asserts, "When the Divine is specified, it is only in feminine-gendered terms." This perceived exclusivity disturbs her, and she continues by stating, "Because, for Falk, terms for the Divine in the masculine immediately bring to mind a male, patriarchal hierarchy, she never uses them." Sofian therefore concludes, "I find this a replacement of one hierarchy by another in which the feminine is superior to the masculine, thus resulting in a constriction and qualification of the Divine. Although Falk

---

1 Sofian's review essay is in the Spring, 1999 issue of the *CCAR Journal* pp.84–95.

sees God in all of us and in every element of the universe (for me, a problematic pantheism), by using only the feminine-gendered words to evoke the Divine, she excludes that half of creation that is male or at least named in masculine-gendered terms."[2]

I would maintain that this depiction of the *Book of Blessings* is simply unfounded. As I read Falk, I do not believe she has any objection to using nouns of either grammatical gender in composing her blessings. After all, *ma'ayan*, one of the nouns cited by Sofian that Falk employs in her *Sheheḥeyanu* blessing, is, in fact, masculine, not feminine. In addition, a phrase such as *nitzotzot ha-nefesh*, again masculine, appears in the Falk *Havdalah* ceremony. Thus she does create images for divinity that are, in terms of grammar, both masculine and feminine. Sofian fails to take note of this and, consequently, blurs the distinction between grammatical gender and semantic gender. Yet I believe that an appreciation of this distinction is crucial for an assessment of Falk's approach to Jewish prayer. Sofian, it appears, does not, and this leads her to claim that Falk defines "only feminine God-imagery" as "acceptable" and that, in a classic reversal of gender roles, she consigns the male to the role of "Other."[3]

Falk, as we have seen, often does employ images for Divinity that are, from the standpoint of grammar, masculine. However, precisely because of her own theology, Falk employs images that, from a semantic standpoint, are exclusively gender-neutral. As Sofian correctly notes, Falk consciously "rejects any anthropomorphic words for the Divine," as Falk herself never creates an "image of God as Person."[4] To the best of my knowledge, Falk nowhere mentions the "transgendered" term *av ha-raḥamim*, for example. Her failure to employ this term, as others, I would maintain, does not stem from the fact that "all maleness must be banished," as Sofian contends.[5] Rather, I believe her decision emerges from her judgment that *personal* images of God, whether masculine or feminine, are limiting and stand in opposition to her emphasis upon divine immanence. Sofian's desire not to "go into a discussion of theology" is therefore misplaced, and her emphasis upon gender obscures

2 Sofian, pp. 86–87.
3 Ibid. p. 88
4 Ibid. p. 87.
5 Ibid. p. 87.

the crucial theological issues that lie at the heart of this work. Her discussion of Falk would have been more valuable, in my opinion, had she engaged in a more lengthy consideration of what she labels Falk's "misplaced pantheism." While Sofian never indicates precisely what she means by this term, I can easily imagine two major possible explanations — one essentially philosophical-ethical, the other principally theological-anthropological — of her stance. An outline of each of these postures will shed needed light on the nature of what is at the center of the debate over Falk's prayer book in many liberal Jewish precincts.

A philosophical-ethical critique of Falk would undoubtedly follow the path hewn almost a century ago by Hermann Cohen in his severe attack on pantheism. Informed by the same Kantian legacy that caused the famed British ethicist G. E. Moore to distinguish between the natural realm of "is" and the ethical kingdom of "ought" in Moore's celebrated 1903 essay, "The Naturalistic Fallacy," Cohen, in his writings, pointed out that the moral realm was marked by freedom and choice. The natural world, in contrast, operated according to set laws and patterns. Pantheism, by defining humanity as one with nature, collapsed these realms together. Consequently, Cohen emphasized that there was an ethical imperative that humans be seen as distinct from nature, for pantheism rendered morality philosophically incoherent. Guided by the messianic conviction that humans could choose to improve and perfect the world, Cohen taught that this belief made sense only if it could be affirmed that humanity possessed free will, a quality that could not be claimed if the human sphere was collapsed into the mechanistic domain of nature. Humanity, Cohen concluded, stood in a special correlative relationship with an ideal of God. Consequently, Cohen advocated a philosophical monotheism in which this transcendent ideal of divinity functioned in a regulative manner. An advocate of a nonpersonal vision of God, Cohen nonetheless maintained an idealistic commitment to hierarchy, and he therefore had no objections to the traditional way in which Jewish liturgy spoke of God. Hence, it may be that an opposition to the religious vision that guides Falk and her application of that vision in her prayers might be established on the basis of these philosophical claims.[6]

---

6   For a fine English summary of Cohen's position on this matter, see Jehuda Melber, *Hermann Cohen's Philosophy of Judaism* (New York: Jonathan David Publishers, 1968),

On the other hand, a theological-anthropological critique might also be offered, and it is here that the argument with Falk has classically been joined. Indeed, it is this stance that I suspect Sofian shares. Over a decade ago, biblical scholar Edward Greenstein was the first to criticize Falk for not naming God in personal terms. He charged that her decision to affirm "an impersonal pantheism" led to prayer book compositions that were, at best, "preludes to prayer." According to Greenstein, for "prayer to be prayer," it "must relate to God personally, in direct address. To pray in any meaningful sense one must say 'You.'"[7]

In more recent years, sympathetic critics such as Rachel Adler, Lawrence Hoffman, and Arnold Jacob Wolf, while expressing their appreciation for Falk's prayers, nevertheless challenged what they see as her complete rejection of a personal God. Hoffman, in an oft-cited response to Falk, stated that he favored a model of "covenantal relationship" with God as opposed to one of absolute immanence. "God," he wrote, "can be known only in relationship and can never adequately be described outside of relationship." In his article, Hoffman, like Falk, rejected a notion of God that would "deteriorate into hierarchical opposition." Nonetheless, he maintained that the images and metaphors used in Jewish liturgy ought to "denote a being that exists independently and enters into relationship with us."[8] And Wolf, writing on Falk's approach in the pages of *Judaism*, contends that only a personal vision of God "can inspire or mandate religious commitment."[9]

Adler, in a respectful and thoughtful consideration of the theology that animates *The Book of Blessings*, observes that "Falk's unique innovation is to incorporate this theology of immanence into the primary forms of Jewish liturgy. She has coined a *b'rakhah* formula that counters traditional theologies of transcendence by collapsing God into nature and community." The notion of divine immanence that Falk advocates therefore demands that God not be "imaged as an Other at all." Yet, Adler takes issue with this stance, echoing Hoffman's criticism, when she con-

---

pp.77–79 and 247. The Cohen primary text is found in E. Jospe, ed., *Reason and Hope* (Cincinnati: Hebrew Union College Press, 1993), a collection of Cohen's writings.

7   Edward L. Greenstein, "A Critique of Impersonal Prayer," *Reconstructionist* 53:7 (1988), p.14.

8   Lawrence A. Hoffman, "A Response to Marcia Falk," *Tikkun* 4:4 (1989), p.57.

9   Arnold Jacob Wolf, "The New Liturgies," *Judaism* 46 (Spring, 1997), p.239.

tends that "eradicating otherness, breaking down all boundaries between self and other, self and God, God and world simultaneously eradicates relatedeness." Covenant, Adler affirms, demands "an Other." Adler concludes, "Opposite Falk's unitive spirituality, I would set a spirituality of otherness."[10]

Falk herself has taken specific note of Adler and Hoffman in her Commentary, and she contends that she, like them, has an appreciation for the theological importance of relationship. However, she asserts that they maintain a sense of God as "transcendent Other," which she rejects. Writing in *The Book of Blessings*, she phrases the points of agreement and disagreement she has with Adler and Hoffman in the following way: "While I would agree that relationship is an important element in theology, I do not see why it is necessary to envision God as transcendent Other in order to affirm relationship. This view certainly fails to account for the deep sense of connectedness I personally feel when I am in touch with my participation in the greater whole of creation."[11]

In staking out her posture on this matter, Falk has noted that she is not alone. Arthur Green has also emphasized divine immanence in his *Seek My Face, Speak My Name: A Contemporary Jewish Theology*. Green writes, "We seek a religious language that goes beyond the separation of 'God,' 'world,' and 'self' that seems so ultimate in most of Western theology. . . . We refer rather to a deity that embraces all of being, a single One that contains within it all the variety and richness of life, yet is also the Oneness that transcends and surpasses all. . . . But where do we allow room for the truth that all is One if our religious language is that of 'Self' and 'Other?'"[12]

Although this position does not lead Green to abandon personal language in prayer, Falk departs from Green on this score and main-

---

10   Rachel Adler, *Engendering Judaism* (Philadelphia: Jewish Publication Society, 1998), pp. 90–92.

11   Marcia Falk, *The Book of Blessings New Jewish Prayers for Daily Life, the Sabbath, and the New Moon Festival* (San Francisco: Harper Collins San Francisco, 1996; paperback ed., Boston, Mass.: Beacon Press, 1999), p. 420.

12   Arthur Green, *Seek My Face, Speak My Name: A Contemporary Jewish Theology* (Northvale, N. J.: Jason Aronson , 1992), p. 9.

tains that prayers ought to be composed that are in keeping with a faith posture that affirms divine immanence. Falk long ago staked out her position on this matter. Writing in *Tikkun* in 1989, she explained, "I create and use new images — images such as *eyn ha-ḥayim*, 'wellspring of life,' *nishmat kol ḥai*, 'breath of all living things,' and *nitzotzot ha-nefesh*, 'sparks of the inner, unseen self' — to serve as fresh metaphors for Divinity. With these images, and still others, composed of all the basic elements of creation — earth, water, wind, and fire — I hope to construct a theology of immanence that will both affirm the sanctity of the world and shatter the idolatrous reign of the lord/God/king."[13] *The Book of Blessings* and the non-personal images for Divinity found in it testifies to the consistency Falk has displayed on this matter for over a decade.

My purpose in offering this summary of the positions put forth by Falk and her dialogue partners on issues of theology and prayer is to indicate that disagreement with Falk is surely legitimate. Indeed, as I have tried to show, there are both philosophical and theological postures that allow for legitimate differences with her. Persons have every right to articulate their own theological preferences, to feel passionately about them, and to employ them as a basis for a critique of the beliefs that mark *The Book of Blessings* and the images of Divinity that appear in its pages. Falk, in turn, has every right to respond. However, it is only fair that such dissent be based on an accurate understanding of the posture Falk adopts. In my reading of her, Falk simply does not imply that "all maleness must be banished." Consequently, a critique of Falk ought not to center upon specific gender issues that Falk never raises.

In the end, I personally applaud *The Book of Blessings* for the dialogue, multiple opinions, and passionate voices it has fostered and encouraged. This is apparent when, for example, one considers that none of Falk's English blessings represent literal renderings of the Hebrew. Instead, she consistently authors Hebrew and English blessings that reflect her own struggles with prayer. These blessings are meant to complement one another, and English-language-only readers are

13 Marcia Falk, "Toward a Feminist Jewish Reconstruction of Monotheism," *Tikkun* 4:4 (1989), p.55.

invited to share in Falk's grappling by not only reading her English prayers, but by consulting the literal translations of the Hebrew that are found in her extensive commentary. This emphasis upon multilingualism is emblematic of her desire not to provide dogmatic answers to the questions her liturgy raises. Instead, Falk consistently seeks to provide options and provoke thought.

This also helps to explain why no personal images of God are found in her prayer book. Such imagery is already ample in Jewish prayer, and, given her own theological proclivities, she undoubtedly sees no need to add such personal metaphors and images. However, this hardly indicates that Falk would deny others the possibility of employing them should they so choose.

In the end, I do not think Falk is the ideologue that Sofian believes she is. Hers is neither a work of "absolutism" nor "insistence." Poetic ambiguities abound. Her work, as I see it, is not about setting new rules. It is about opening new doors. It is about the heart and the spirit, as well as the mind, and it is certainly not about excluding men, or anyone else. For these reasons, her influence upon contemporary Reconstructionist liturgy has been extensive, and it might well be instructive for persons in other precincts of the liberal Jewish religious world to consider her postures as well as they debate the legitimacy of diverse theological views in their own denominations. *The Book of Blessings* broadens our horizons as to possible ways of finding expression for divinity in the on-going experience of Jewish tradition.

Permission Acknowledgments

Grateful acknowledgement is made to the following for permission to reprint previously published material in revised form:

Behrman House, West Orange, N.J. Portions of the Preface were previously published as "A Separate Life" in Rabbi Lawrence A. Hoffman and Arnold Jacob Wolf, eds., *Jewish Spiritual Journeys: Twenty Essays Written to Honor the Occasion of the 70th Birthday of Eugene B. Borowitz*, 1997, pp. 93–101.

Oxford University Press for the Avraham Harman Institute of Contemporary Jewry at the Hebrew University of Jerusalem. "Judaism Resurgent? American Jews and the Evolving Expression of Jewish Values and Jewish Identity in Modern American Life" was originally published in Eli Lederhendler, ed., *Studies in Contemporary Jewry* 17, 2001, pp. 156–71.

Harvard University Center for Jewish Studies. "Jacob Katz on the Origins and Dimensions of Jewish Modernity: The Centrality of the German Experience" was originally published in Jay M. Harris, ed., *The Pride of Jacob: Essays on Jacob Katz and His Work*, 2002, pp. 97–123.

The College of William and Mary: Department of Religion. "Max Weber on Judaism and the Jews: A Reflection on the Position of Jews in the Modern World" was originally published in Marc Lee Raphael, ed., *What Is Modern About The Modern Jewish Experience?*, 1997, pp. 78–88.

Bibliotheca Rosenthaliana, Amsterdam University Library. "Emancipation and the Directions of Modern Judaism: The Lessons of *Melitz Yosher*" was originally published in Emile Schrijver, ed., *Studia Rosenthaliana*, Assen, The Netherlands: Van Gorcum, 1996, pp. 118–36.

Secker & Warburg, London. "A Disputed Precedent: The Prague Organ in Nineteenth-Century Central European Legal Literature and Polemics" was originally published in *Leo Baeck Institute Year Book* XL, 1995, pp. 251–64.

Rodef Shalom Press, Pittsburgh. The Solomon B. Freehof Institute of Progressive Halakhah. "Samuel Holdheim on the Legal Character of Jewish Marriage: A Contemporary Comment on His Position" was originally published in Walter Jacob and Moshe Zemer, eds., *Marriage and Its Obstacles in Jewish Law: Essays and Responsa*, pp. 1–26.

Routledge, New York. "Traditional Reactions to Modern Jewish Reform: The Paradigm of German Orthodoxy" was originally published in Daniel H. Frank and Oliver Leaman, eds., *History of Jewish Philosophy: Routledge History of World Philosophies*, vol. 2, 1997, pp. 732–58.

United Jewish Center, Danbury, Connecticut. "The Rabbiner-Seminar Codicil: An Instrument of Boundary Maintenance" was originally published in Aron Hirt-Manheimer, ed., *Through Those Near To Me: Essays in Honor of Jerome R. Malino*, 1998, pp. 200–207.

Secker & Warburg, London. "The *Israelitische Gebetbücher* of Abraham Geiger and Manuel Joël: A Study in Nineteenth-Century German-Jewish Communal Liturgy and Religion" was originally published in *The Leo Baeck Institute Year Book* vol. 44, 1999, pp. 143–64.

The CCAR Journal: "The Prayers for Rain in the *Siddurim* of Abraham Geiger and Isaac Mayer Wise: An Exploration into a Dimension of the Relationship Between Reform Jewish Thought and Liturgical Practice" was originally published in the *CCAR Journal*, Summer 2004, pp. 1–15.

The Jewish Theological Seminary of America. "German Jewish Orthodoxy: Tradition in the Context of Culture" was originally published in Jack Wertheimer, ed., *The Uses of Tradition: Jewish Continuity in the Modern Era*, 1993, pp. 5–22.

Indiana University Press. "*Gemeindeorthodoxie* in Weimar Germany: The Approaches of Nehemiah Anton Nobel and Isak Unna" was originally published in Michael Brenner and Derek J. Penslar, eds., *In Search of Jewish Community: Jewish Identities in Germany and Austria, 1918–1933*, 1998, pp. 36–55.

Jewish Theological Seminary of America. "A Seminary of Sacred Learning: The JTS Rabbinical Curriculum in Historical Perspective" was originally published in Jack Wertheimer, ed., *Tradition Renewed: A History of the Jewish Theological Seminary*, vol. 2: *Beyond the Academy*, 1997, pp. 527–91. Co-authored with Lee Bycel.

The Schechter Institute of Jewish Studies, the Hadassah-Brandeis Institute, and Indiana University Press. "Women and the Study of Torah: A Responsum by Rabbi Zalman Sorotzkin of Jerusalem" was originally published in *Nashim: A Journal of Jewish Women's Studies and Gender Issues* no. 4, 2000, pp. 119–39. Co-authored with Elissa Ben-Naim.

Rodef Shalom Press for the Solomon B. Freehof Institute of Progressive Halakhah. "Gender, Halakhah, and Women's Suffrage: Responsa of the First Three Chief Rabbis on the Public Role of Women in the Jewish State" was originally published in Walter Jacob and Moshe Zemer, eds., *Gender Issues in Jewish Law,* 2001, pp. 58–81. Co-authored with Michael Rosen.

Brown Judaic Studies. "Parallel Worlds: *Wissenschaft* and *Pesaq* in the *Seridei Eish*" was originally published in William Cutter and David Jacobson, eds., *History and Literature: New Readings of Jewish Texts in Honor of Arnold J. Band,* 2002, pp. 55–74.

The Jacob Rader Marcus Center of the American Jewish Archives, Cincinnati. "A Jewish Legal Authority Addresses Jewish-Christian Dialogue: Two Responsa of Rabbi Moshe Feinstein" was originally published in *The American Jewish Archives Journal* 52:1 and 2, 2000, pp. 113–28.

The Central Conference of American Rabbis. "Jewish Legal Interpretation and Moral Values: Two Responsa by Rabbi Hayyim David Halevi on the Obligations of the Israeli Government toward Its Minority Population" was originally published in *The CCAR Journal: A Reform Jewish Quarterly* 48:3, Summer 2001, pp. 5–20.

Ashgate, Burlington, Vermont. "Interpretive Fluidity and *Psak* in a Case of *Pidyon Shevuyim*: An Analysis of a Modern Israeli Responsum as Illuminated by the Thought of David Hartman" was originally published in Jonathan W. Malino, ed., *Judaism and Modernity: The Religious Philosophy of David Hartman,* 2001, pp. 341–67.

Solomon B. Freehof Institute of Progessive Halakhah. "Artificial Fertilization and Procreative Autonomy: In Light of Two Contemporary Israeli Responsa" was originally published in Walter Jacob and Moshe Zemer, eds., *The Fetus and Fertility: Essays and Responsa,* 1995, pp. 19–38.

Oxford University Press for the Avraham Harman Institute of Contemporary Jewry at The Hebrew University of Jerusalem. "A New Rite from Israel: Reflections on *Siddur Va'ani Tefillati* of the Masorti (Conservative) Movement" was originally published in Ezra Mendelsohn, ed., *Studies in Contemporary Jewry*, no. 15, 1999, pp. 151–68.

Oxford University Press. "David Hartman on Judaism and the Modern Condition: A Review Essay" was originally published in *Modern Judaism* 21, 2001, pp. 256–81.

The Central Conference of American Rabbis. "Marcia Falk's *The Book of Blessings*: The Issue Is Theological" was originally published in *The CCAR Journal: A Reform Jewish Quarterly,* Spring 2000, pp. 18–23.

Index